AT WAR ★ AT HOME
WORLD W

FROM THE PAGES OF THE Omah

AT WAR ★ AT HOME
WORLD WAR II

EDITOR
DAN SULLIVAN

DESIGNER
CHRISTINE ZUECK

PHOTO IMAGING
JOLENE MCHUGH

EXECUTIVE EDITOR
MIKE REILLY

PRESIDENT
AND PUBLISHER
TERRY KROEGER

ON THE COVER:
"THE HOMECOMING": The World-Herald's Pulitzer Prize-winning photo of Lt. Col. Robert Moore's reunion with his family at the Villisca, Iowa, train depot in 1943.

ON THE PREVIOUS PAGE:
CLARENCE CHRISTENSEN of Valparaiso, Neb., and other Midlands veterans salute during the playing of taps at the National World War II Memorial. They were in Washington as part of the Honor Flights program in 2008.

Omaha World-Herald Co.
1314 Douglas St.
Omaha, NE 68102

First paperback edition, second printing
ISBN: 978-0-615-55822-6
Printed by
Walsworth Publishing Co.
Marceline, MO

WE HAVE FAITH that future generations will know that here, in the middle of the twentieth century, there came a time when men of good will found a way to unite, and produce, and fight to destroy the forces of ignorance, and intolerance, and slavery, and war.

— PRESIDENT FRANKLIN D. ROOSEVELT
FROM AN ADDRESS TO WHITE HOUSE CORRESPONDENTS' ASSOCIATION, WASHINGTON, D.C., FEB. 12, 1943

MIKE REILLY
Executive Editor of the
Omaha World-Herald

WHEN AMERICA WOKE UP to Pearl Harbor and went to work defending freedom, The World-Herald went to work, too.

Throughout World War II and for six-plus decades afterward, generations of World-Herald journalists have chronicled the service and sacrifice of those who fought the Axis abroad and aided the war effort at home.

World War II was an important period in the newspaper's history. It won two war-related Pulitzer Prizes, including a public service award for starting scrap metal drives to combat a dangerous shortage of metal for armaments.

During the war, the newspaper sent correspondents to both Europe and the Pacific to find Nebraskans and Iowans and tell their stories, to show how they fought and lived. Those assignments began a tradition of overseas war coverage that has endured through Vietnam, Iraq and Afghanistan.

In the decades since World War II, The World-Herald has interviewed thousands of veterans and civilians from that momentous era. Some told their stories willingly, some haltingly and some only after decades had passed. Those who talked of their war experiences spoke for the many who could not, so future generations would not forget.

The very best of 70 years of coverage follows in these pages, edited and presented together for the first time.

The book is a treasure trove of beautifully restored World-Herald photographs — some poignant, some heartwarming, some disturbing.

The book is a thousand stories of ordinary people — men and women of good will — united to accomplish extraordinary feats under difficult circumstances.

The book is one story of one remarkable generation.

A NEW B-17 BOMBER drew a crowd to Omaha's Municipal Airport, now Eppley Airfield, in July 1941.

Table of contents

At war and at home, everyone played a part

BY DAVID HENDEE

BYRON M. JOHNSON

WHEN BYRON M. JOHNSON and his Nebraska Wesleyan University fraternity brothers sat down for Sunday dinner on Dec. 7, 1941, their housemother came out of the kitchen carrying a little United States flag.

"I'm afraid all you boys won't be around this table very long," Johnson recalled her saying.

Everyone in the old frame Delta Omega Phi fraternity house at the Lincoln school had just heard a radio broadcast that the Japanese had attacked the U.S. Pacific Fleet at Pearl Harbor.

Johnson, who went on to become the Scotts Bluff County public defender, was a 21-year-old senior from Potter, Neb., majoring in political science.

But within two months of hearing the news of Pearl Harbor, he had enlisted in the Navy and started learning to fly a Piper Cub on a grass strip near Waverly, Neb. Within two years, he was a combat ace in the South Pacific.

Much of the world was already at war when Johnson and his fraternity brothers heard about the attack on Pearl Harbor.

The war didn't come to America's shores, but Japan's attack unleashed events that dramatically changed the lives of Americans — and the role of their country in global affairs.

THE WORLD-HERALD WON a Pulitzer Prize for launching a drive that led Nebraskans to collect nearly 300 million pounds of scrap metal.

The dinner table at Johnson's fraternity house — and those at countless homes across the nation — soon had vacant chairs as men and women rallied behind their country. Many joined the armed services. Others worked in war industries.

The war knocked America out of the Great Depression. Families were uprooted and scattered around the world. War industries turned rural communities into boomtowns.

War-bond drives, rationing and the draft were universal experiences to those living when the United States fought wars against the Japanese in the Pacific and Nazi Germany in Europe from 1941 to 1945.

Bombs and the aircraft to drop them were wartime products of Nebraska, but one of the state's greatest contributions to the war, other than its sons and daughters, was the production of food.

"Grain and meat to feed our troops, their allies and our people was so important to the war effort," Frederick Luebke, a history professor at the University of Nebraska-Lincoln and a board member of the Nebraska State Historical Society, said in a 1991 interview.

"Farming was an essential industry, and this had a spin-off effect on the draft. Lots of young men could get draft deferments because they were working on the farm."

MORE THAN 14,000 worked at the Martin Bomber Plant at Fort Crook, south of Omaha.

Many young rural Nebraskans did trade their overalls for khakis. The state's most celebrated military unit was the National Guard's 134th Infantry Regiment, which played a key role in the early battles in Normandy.

The Midlands felt the war in many ways.

The Union Pacific Railroad, headquartered in Omaha, and other railroads played a big role in the war, moving millions of military men and women and tons of war munitions across the nation.

In Nebraska alone, 10,578 military trains carried 3.6 million military personnel and 12,138 cars loaded with war munitions and equipment from 1942 to 1945.

A memorable stop for servicemen was North Platte. Every day throughout the war, as many as 8,000 military personnel were served each day at the North Platte Canteen.

War industries such as the Martin Bomber Plant at Fort Crook near Bellevue employed thousands. The government also built 12 Army air bases, four ordnance plants and 26 prisoner of war camps in the state.

"Nebraska's midcontinent location had a lot to do with locating these facilities here," Luebke said. "The military wanted them in lightly populated areas a long way from the coasts. And the Army had the idea that Nebraska's weather was good for training."

The war-production facilities turned many communities into overnight boomtowns.

Bellevue's population in 1940 was 1,184. During peak production of the B-29 bomber at the Martin plant, more than 14,000 people were on the payroll.

By 1950, Bellevue's population had increased 226 percent, to 3,858. Other towns, such as Alliance and Mead, echoed Bellevue's boom. Housing, schools and police and fire services were strained as itinerant construction workers, many from the South, poured into dozens of small Nebraska towns.

"A lot of these towns had more yeast than they had experienced since the early days of their frontier beginnings," Luebke said. "These people brought with them different values, speaking patterns and accents, and that creates tension."

In Sidney, where the Army was building the Sioux Ordnance Depot to store ammunition, the population swelled to 10,000 in 1942 from 3,388 two years earlier.

On paydays, a line of workers with paychecks would stretch for a block outside the city's only bank, according to Jack Lowe, the longtime editor of the Sidney newspaper.

"People were renting out sleeping rooms on an eight-hour shift to accommodate the round-the-clock workers," Lowe said. "One would leave the room and another would come in to get his eight hours. It was incredible for a community this size."

Blacks who followed the jobs into the Midlands gained economic opportunity, and that later led to gains in civil rights, Luebke said.

"It's not immediate or direct but the climate is there for it," he said.

The war also opened the door for women in the workforce. They were hired in great numbers to fill vital production jobs as men left for military service. At one point, 42 percent of the Martin plant's workers were women.

The women proved to be excellent workers. One woman at the Martin plant took apart a B-26 machine gun, named each part and function and reassembled it in 24 minutes. She did it blindfolded.

"In the '30s, the tendency was not to hire women because there weren't enough jobs to go around," Luebke said. "A family had one breadwinner. After the war, some women didn't want to give up their jobs and incomes, and although the 1950s were famous for the stay-at-home mom with her station wagon, women were being hired at unprecedented levels that continue today."

Whether on the homefront or the battlefront, the war eventually touched all who lived during that time.

First Lt. Elmer Trentman of Grand Island looks for enemy planes while serving with an anti-aircraft unit in the Philippines.

16TH AND FARNAM STREETS in Omaha was bustling with shoppers and workers in 1941. A rousing military parade would pass the corner in April 1942, rallying the spirits of war-shocked Nebraskans and Iowans. Thousands would gather around the intersection in August 1945 to celebrate the war's end.

THE MORNING HEADLINES OF DEC. 7, 1941

Pearl Harbor

"AIR RAID, PEARL HARBOR! THIS IS NO DRILL!"
Loudspeakers all over the Hawaiian island of Oahu blared similar messages
that sleepy Sunday morning of Dec. 7, 1941. By then most people on the island
knew it was not a drill. The bombs were real, the torpedoes were real,
and soon, America would really be at war.

THE CREW OF A SMALL BOAT rescues a sailor from the USS West Virginia.
The U.S. Navy photograph was color-tinted.

THIS AERIAL VIEW OF THE ATTACK on Pearl Harbor was taken from a Japanese plane during the torpedo attack on ships moored on both sides of Ford Island. The caption on the captured photo read: "This distant view of Ford Island immediately after the attack of our assault force shows the enemy capital ships (battleships) lined up on the opposite side of the island. In the foreground is the cruiser fleet, including the battleship Utah. The enemy ships around the island have all become tempting targets."

Time has not softened the memories

MORE THAN 90 SHIPS WERE AT ANCHOR in Pearl Harbor when the Japanese attacked on Dec. 7, 1941.

The surprise assault struck a blow to the U.S. Pacific Fleet in Hawaii and launched the United States into World War II.

The primary targets were eight battleships. Seven were moored on Battleship Row along the southeast shore of Ford Island Naval Air Station, while the USS Pennsylvania lay in dry dock across the channel.

Within minutes, all the battleships adjacent to Ford Island sustained bomb or torpedo hits.

The USS West Virginia sank quickly, and the USS Oklahoma capsized. About 15 minutes into the 110-minute attack, the USS Arizona was hit by an armor-piercing bomb that ignited the ship's forward ammunition magazine. The explosion and fire killed 1,177 crewmen, the greatest loss of life on any ship that day.

In all, the American dead numbered 2,403.

Time never softened the memories of frustration and helplessness for those who were at Pearl Harbor that morning. The American soldiers, sailors and aviators were part of a peacetime military presence on the island, ill-prepared for war and skeptical of the possibility it might erupt.

The survivors of the sneak attack by 183 Japanese planes formed a unique group. They saw the first sparks of an inferno that changed the world.

'The wounded were carrying the dead'

BY JOHN TAYLOR

SEAMAN FRANK THURTELL was an eyewitness to the Japanese attack on Pearl Harbor. He retired from the Omaha Public Power District in 1986.

ORDINARILY, THE MEDUSA, A REPAIR VESSEL for battleships and cruisers, would have been moored off Ford Island, in the middle of Pearl Harbor, tending to the U.S. Pacific Fleet's big ships. On the morning of Dec. 7, 1941, however, the target-training ship Utah was tied up in the Medusa's spot, its port side exposed to the open water.

Frank Thurtell, who was an 18-year-old seaman aboard the Medusa, recalled in 1986:

"Two aircraft carriers had come in previously, but they left on Friday (Dec. 5), and we hadn't moved back there yet. The Utah came in and tied up at that spot."

The Medusa was across the channel to the west, just off the southern tip of Pearl City. It was from that vantage point, through a porthole, that Thurtell was a witness to the beginning of the Japanese surprise attack that thrust the United States into World War II.

Thurtell was a farm boy in Akron, Colo., on Feb. 8, 1941, when he and a friend made a spur-of-the-moment decision to enlist in the Navy. After training in San Diego, he was sent to Hawaii, arriving in early August for what was considered a choice assignment. His workdays were taken up by routine machinist chores. On Saturday, Dec. 6, he kept busy making angle iron supports for gun decks. The next morning, about 8 a.m., he was taking his breakfast tray to the kitchen. He passed an open porthole. "There was a loud noise from airplanes," he said. He thought to himself, "Those things are coming in awful low."

He looked out. "There were two Japanese torpedo planes coming right over the ship, heading right for the Utah. On their sides you could see the Rising Sun," he said. "All of a sudden they dropped their torpedoes and hit the Utah. It started rolling over immediately. People were scrambling and running over the side."

Images of the next 16 hours ran together for Thurtell. He became more than just a witness; he was a participant in America's first battle of a then-undeclared war. It took the

THE BATTLESHIP USS CALIFORNIA is ablaze after being hit with torpedoes and a bomb. She later sank to the bottom of Pearl Harbor.

Medusa's crew a while to man the vessel's four anti-aircraft weapons, guns that fired 3-inch diameter shells. "There was a lot of confusion," he said.

Thurtell's job was to set the sights on one of the weapons, to make adjustments for the speed and altitude of the target.

"The first plane we shot down we shot the tail right off of it," he said. The aircraft crashed into a dredging vessel and set it afire. Ship crews knocked down another Japanese aircraft, this one landing on top of the Curtiss, a submarine tender tied to the Medusa's starboard side.

At one point the attention of the crews was diverted from the sky to the channel, where the conning tower of a small submarine could be seen. "We lowered the gun to shoot at the submarine," Thurtell said. "But I hadn't adjusted the sight back to zero from shooting at the airplanes. Our first shot knocked a hole in a smokestack on the side of a sugar factory. I set the sight down to zero, and we shot between the lower life ring and the deck. It sank."

The two men aboard the sub, one of two mini-subs that made it into the harbor, were killed. The sub later was raised and sent to the U.S. mainland, where it was put on display.

At 10 a.m. Thurtell was assigned to a 50-foot motor launch to recover the wounded and the dead. There were 3,700 of them. "You saw all these fires," he said. "In times of peril like that you see a lot of brave actions going on. The wounded were carrying the dead."

The launch concentrated on the battleship Nevada, which had been hit but which had begun to make its way past the burning battleships Arizona, West Virginia, Oklahoma and California, four of eight battleships lost that day.

In its attempt to escape, the Nevada was hit again, perhaps by one of the mini-subs, and officers, fearing it would block the channel, ran the ship aground. At 4 p.m. Thurtell was called back to the Medusa. "I was one of four qualified divers at Pearl Harbor," he said. "We started diving on all these ships that were hit. The purpose was to determine how much damage was done and the location of the damage."

The divers in heavy helmets and bulky suits were able to stay underwater only an hour at a time. They couldn't get close to some of the burning ships. "Around the Arizona we saw a mess of metal where it was split right in two," Thurtell said.

The divers weren't aware that more than 1,000 men were trapped in the Arizona. It became their resting place. "We couldn't get to it because it was burning so fiercely," Thurtell said. "But we picked three guys off the Oklahoma four days later. They were trapped in an air pocket and were tapping on the hull when we were diving."

He said they dove until midnight on that Sunday. "We were completely worn out. We went to sleep on the deck of one of the battleship tenders, the Argonne. We slept there till the next morning. Then we got up and started diving again. We dove all day Monday, Tuesday, Wednesday and Thursday."

During the attack there was no time to measure feelings. "You didn't have time to think about what happened," Thurtell said. "You didn't even get time to get scared."

In the days that followed, however, nerve ends were exposed and people would shoot at phantoms.

"There was constant gunfire," he said. "Somebody would get an itchy trigger finger and would shoot, and as soon as one shot was fired everything went off. People were edgy."

THE USS ARIZONA SANK in Pearl Harbor, and 1,177 lives were lost.

'A hard thing to come to grips with'

DEC. 7, 1941, IN THE TERRITORY OF HAWAII dawned like any other for Seaman 2nd Class Maurice "Mauri" Hall, except for one thing. He was in sick bay aboard the destroyer tender USS Dobbin with the mumps.

Nearly two years after enlisting in the Navy and six months after arriving at Pearl Harbor, the 19-year-old Omahan was minutes from being tossed into the United States' opening battle of World War II and spending the rest of his six-year enlistment at war in the Pacific.

Hall was up at 5:30 the morning of the Japanese attack and had chow in sick bay on the main deck of the Dobbin as it sat moored alongside a nest of five destroyers. The USS Phelps,

for instance, was receiving steam, electricity and fresh and flushing water from the Dobbin. One of the destroyer's rear guns was inoperative because its breech mechanisms were being overhauled.

Across Ford Island Naval Air Station sat the fleet's battleships.

About 8 a.m., while milling around on the deck, Hall heard a noise.

"I looked over the island to the battleships and saw the Arizona go up in a sheet of flames 100 feet in the air," he recalled in 2001. "They dropped a bomb down the smokestack, and almost 1,200 men died in a second."

The Dobbin and the destroyers came under at least one direct attack. Three enemy planes with the Japanese Rising Sun red disks on their wings came in low from the starboard quarter. Heavy fire from the Dobbin and the destroyers caused the planes to swerve and cross just astern.

Three bombs — appearing to be 300-pounders — barely missed the Dobbin, but fragments sprayed across the deck, killing three and wounding two others at an anti-aircraft gun near the rear of the deck.

Hall said one of the men killed was a sailor who had taken his place at the gun.

The destroyers started clearing out of the mooring within 10 minutes of the attack. Hall and other personnel from the Dobbin scrambled to assist the big ships in getting under way in the chaos, including passing over replacement ammunition and manning spare machine guns.

Hall later served aboard the destroyer USS Helm and the small seaplane tender USS Bering Strait, receiving six battle stars from campaigns throughout the Pacific. He was in Okinawa when the war ended in 1945.

Hall, a 1939 graduate of Creighton Prep, was discharged in April 1946 as a signalman 1st class. The next month he married Ann Monaco of Omaha in Washington, D.C. They eventually returned to Omaha, where Hall worked in the insurance business for more than 30 years. He retired from Mutual of Omaha in 1984.

"We did a pretty good job," Hall said of the Pearl Harbor battle. "But it's a hard thing to come to grips with."

MAURICE "MAURI" HALL in 2001

WARREN E. MILLER in 2004

The ship 'jumped up'

SEAMAN APPRENTICE WARREN E. MILLER sat in the brig — the prison — of the USS Utah.

A week earlier, Miller had been to the Black Cat, a popular bar among the military men stationed at Pearl Harbor. He was 17 and skinny, and he held his liquor about as well as you'd expect, which wasn't very well.

The group spotted a Japanese man riding a motorcycle. Miller bragged that he could take the bike out for a ride. Yeah, right, his shipmates responded.

A short time later, after trying to ride the bike up some courthouse steps, Miller found himself flat on the ground.

Somebody picked him up, Miller recalled in a 2004 interview, hauled him back to the ship and ordered him to the brig. It was there, three decks below, that Miller and two other sailors felt three torpedoes hit the Utah during Japan's attack on Pearl Harbor.

The ship "jumped up," Miller said.

Then the call went out: "Release all prisoners and abandon ship."

Miller didn't recall the thoughts that went through his head as the ship turned over.

"Survival, I guess," the Omahan said with a shrug.

The ship had a crew of about 450, roughly 150 of whom escaped death at Pearl Harbor.

"I'm sure there's a lot I have forgotten," he said. "A lot that I don't want to remember. I lost a lot of good friends, a lot of good buddies."

Survival depended on crawling to port side, then swimming 50 or so yards to land. Some never made it off the ship. Others were killed as they tried to abandon ship, Miller said.

Once on land, Miller looked skyward. Japanese pilots were flying so low, Miller said, he could see their smiles as they whizzed over his head.

7

MEMORIES OF A GENERATION ★

ROBERT ZUKOWSKI

Town: Bellevue

In the war: Was a machinist mate 2nd class on the U.S. Taney, a Coast Guard cutter.

In his words: "We had just come into the harbor the night before, coming in from Samoa. So we were still under light steam at the time.

"The first thing I remember is getting awakened by general quarters. Then a few minutes later our 5-inch and 3-inch guns started firing. Then we started steaming out of the harbor.

"We went out toward Sand Island, which is out in the channel, about halfway to the sub nets. On the way out, we took a Japanese fishing boat out of commission. It had a bunch of radio gear on it.

"We made it outside the sub nets and went on patrol, looking for Japanese submarines. We went back into the harbor about an hour later. We escorted the USS Detroit out of the harbor. It was on fire. Other ships were sinking all over the place. It was a mess.

"I was confused. Everybody was confused. People were just running around like chickens with their heads cut off.

"Today, when I think about it, it still doesn't seem real. It doesn't make much sense that something like that could have ever happened."

A SERVICEMAN AT HICKAM FIELD, *adjacent to Pearl Harbor, watches as the USS Shaw goes up in flames.*

BERNARD SEDLACEK

Town: Bellevue

In the war: Was in the Army Air Forces stationed at Hickam Field.

In his words: "I was a ground radio guy at the time. I was in the barracks that morning, up on the third floor. I think I was probably one of the few who got up and went to chow that morning.

"I was sitting there in the chow hall addressing Christmas cards to send back home. I heard that first bomb drop over at Pearl Harbor. Some other guys came up and asked what it was, and I said those Navy boys are playing it a little close today.

"About that time, we watched a plane come right over the mess hall and drop a bomb. It blew up everything, killed a bunch of the cooks. He was so low that we couldn't see a red ball on the plane or anything, but everybody right away started yelling, 'Japs!' It was total chaos after that.

"A bunch of people ran over to the armory, trying to get at some guns so we could shoot back, but it was all locked up. There was a lot of confusion and arguing. I just headed back to the barracks.

"Every time you stuck your head outside or tried to go to another building, the Jap planes would strafe you and bomb you. We were completely helpless."

BERNARD SEDLACEK IN 1991

BURTON AMGWERT

Town: Lincoln

In the war: Was a corpsman at the hospital in the Navy yard.

In his words: "I was on liberty. I heard the first bomb go off, of course. And then I saw a plane coming toward the hospital with smoke coming out of it. It crashed right there on the lawn of the hospital. It crashed into a corner of the hospital and destroyed our guinea-pig and rabbit hutch. I still have a valve cover from that plane, and I plan on handing it down after I'm gone.

"It was the first plane shot down that day. It was 8:05 in the morning on Dec. 7. A little later I saw a Japanese submarine coming right into the harbor. You could see it under the water and its periscope sticking out of the water.

"We were within 100 yards of the Shaw when it exploded after getting hit. The blast blew all the windowpanes out of the hospital. It blew our hair and clothes like a good old Nebraska tornado.

"We started taking in a lot of casualties by that afternoon. I think, if memory serves me, that the hospital had about 350 beds. A patient census taken that night showed that we had 960 patients. We had wall-to-wall patients. And outside the hospital, there were 313 bodies stacked like cordwood. They were some of the ones who had been killed that day. They were under armed guard.

"We certainly weren't expecting it. And I can't say that I was really scared at the time. To me, it seems just like yesterday. I can remember every single detail, at least where I was.

"To many, Pearl Harbor was a devastating defeat. History records it as a devastating defeat. But I think of it as a victory, strange as that may sound. I say that because never before and maybe never again have people come together instantaneously in a common bond: destroy the evil Japanese Empire.

"I can forgive the Japanese, but I can't forget what happened. Nobody who was there will ever forget it."

BURTON AMGWERT IN 1991

THE USS OKLAHOMA capsized after being hit by Japanese torpedoes.

DONALD HAAS

Town: Lincoln

In the war: Was stationed on the USS Oklahoma at Pearl Harbor. He spent the rest of the war on the USS Helena and the USS Jenkins. Haas was a washer and dryer repairman in Lincoln until his retirement in 1994.

In his words: "I got up at 7 a.m., had breakfast and was done eating by 7:30. Then I went up topside and was going to clean my gun, which was a 5"/25. We were going to have a ship inspection Monday.

"At 7:55 a.m., the first wave of Japanese planes entered Pearl Harbor. I thought they were American aircraft just making practice runs through the harbor. I remember thinking, 'What in the world are they doing on Sunday?' Almost immediately these planes dropped bombs on Ford Island, the naval base at Pearl Harbor, and the bombs blew up on the hangars. I saw the planes coming toward the USS Oklahoma. I could see the yellow-and-orange Rising Sun insignia on the bottom of the wings of the Japanese aircraft. They came so close I could see the pilots sitting in the cockpits.

"They dropped six or seven torpedoes on the USS Oklahoma, and almost immediately the ship started listing to port side. In 10 minutes, it had completely capsized. I just followed it over and then climbed onto the bottom of the ship. I never had time to be scared. You just kind of go on instinct in situations like that. From there, I saw the USS Arizona explode. It was a huge explosion. The Arizona dropped like a rock.

"Then the Japanese started strafing the Oklahoma, so I jumped overboard. I swam about 15 to 20 yards through burning oil and fire to get to the USS Maryland. Once on board, I just ran to the nearest anti-aircraft gun and began passing ammunition. That's all I could think to do. The battle lasted about two hours. A lot of my friends went down with the ship. There was a kid named West from Council Bluffs that died. I heard about it right away from another friend.

"I've always had a soft heart, but I didn't cry that day. We were supposed to be grown men and all. I think a lot of it was just plain shock, too. You just can't believe what's happening. So you kind of walk through it in a daze and just keep working. I just kept busy until I got on another ship. That's the other thing. I never really knew where a lot of my shipmates were. Everybody who survived got on with other ships in a few days. So you never really knew who was dead or alive.

"I do remember, though, all the bodies and all the wounded. All the men lined up in beds in the barracks and the mess halls. Bomb flashes really burn the skin, so there were a lot of guys with terrible burns. There was lots of moaning, lots of blood. I guess I hate more than anything to see people hurting. There was so much suffering that day — guys just totally broken apart. I think that's what upset me the most about the whole deal. But I guess the main reaction from everyone was anger. Everybody wanted a piece of the Japanese after that. Everybody wanted to get on a ship and get a piece of them for what they did."

MEMORIES OF A GENERATION ★

ED GUTHRIE

Town: Omaha

In the war: Was a 23-year-old Navy electrician's mate 2nd class on the USS Whitney, a destroyer tender. He enlisted in 1940 and had been in Hawaii about a year. After Pearl Harbor, he was assigned to the USS Banner, an attack transport. After his discharge in 1946, he returned to Omaha and eventually worked for the Omaha Public Power District until retiring.

In his words: "We were anchored in the harbor and had destroyers on both sides of us. We had three or four on one side and about eight more on the other side, all tied up in little nests.

"We had an old ship, the USS Utah, that they often dropped sandbags on for target practice. Most people thought it was just another one of those tests — except it was Sunday, and they never did those tests on Sunday.

"I had free time and was getting ready for church. I was up on deck and saw the whole show. They were flying so low you could see the smiles on their faces and their white scarves.

"You could feel the explosion from the Arizona all over the harbor. It was a very lucky hit for a bomb to go down the stack and into the explosives section. It was something you couldn't believe. The water was black with diesel fuel. People in the water came out like they were coated in tar.

"It was chaos. Nobody knew what to do. Afterward I was assigned to a boat, and we spent four days picking wounded, dead and whatever out of the water. It was a mess, but we came out of it."

GRADY QUINN

Town: Omaha

In the war: Was a 21-year-old Navy seaman 1st class aboard the USS Ramapo, an oiler. A native of North Carolina, he enlisted Dec. 7, 1940, and arrived in Hawaii from the Philippines about 10 days before the attack. In 1944, he was reassigned to Peru, Neb., to help manage the Navy's officer candidate program at area colleges. After the war, he worked for a trucking company and a sheet-metal business.

In his words: "The first planes came through the fork in the mountain as close to ground as they could get. I was on deck just mucking around. Then all hell broke loose. Everybody started screaming that (the Japanese) were attacking. They were after the battleships right by us. Ships never came into Pearl Harbor with loaded guns, so on most every ship people had to go down into the ship to get the ammo.

"We had a couple of 5-inch guns and different machine guns. Everybody went to the guns and stayed with the guns. They had everything going. In general quarters my place was on the bridge as the stand-by helmsman.

"We got the motors running but felt it was safer sitting there than out at sea. We were a rusty old tanker. It took a few days to realize that this actually happened."

LUDWIG "LOU" RADIL

Town: Omaha

In the war: Was a 22-year-old Navy seaman 2nd class in charge of the library aboard the battleship USS California. After working in a packinghouse and at a soft-drink bottler, he enlisted and landed at Pearl Harbor in August 1941. After the attack, he was transferred to Pearl Harbor's submarine base and went to yeoman's school. He was discharged in 1947 and returned to Omaha, working for a packinghouse and then becoming a federal food inspector.

In his words: "We were moored alone on Battleship Row. Most of the others were moored in pairs.

"Three of us were rigging for church, setting chairs on the deck, when the first planes flew over us. All at once, bombs were dropping on Ford Island, and we were ordered to battle stations.

"We got a torpedo hit, and then another, and then a bomb hit. We started listing to one side. We got word that the ship was sinking and could capsize. So the captain ordered a call to abandon ship.

"We opened the hatches and hurried down about seven ladders to the deck. That's when I saw the ships on fire and thought, 'My God, what happened?' Some people were trying to get into boats. Others were jumping overboard. I jumped with them and swam to Ford Island about 200 yards away.

"Oil was burning in the water around the bow. I had oil on me, but I wasn't burned. Somebody gave me some civilian clothes to wear. That night we were on duty watching for an invasion force. They could have taken the islands lock, stock and barrel. It was a mess.

"The next day we got called back to the ship to help carry out bodies of those who died trapped, like on ladders trying to get out. There were lots of them. I was still a punk kid and had never seen anything like it. Even thinking about it gets tears in my eyes."

HOWARD LINN

Town: Omaha

In the war: Was a 1st class petty officer on the battleship Nevada when Pearl Harbor was bombed. The Arizona was 200 or 300 feet away at the time, and pieces of it came through the portholes of the Nevada. No one around Linn on the lower decks was hit, but every man topside was killed. After the attack, his commanding officer asked how everyone was doing.

In his words: "I said I was doing fine but was concerned about my dad, as he was working in the fire room on a carrier. He had enlisted in the Navy after serving in World War I in the Army. In the meantime, the officer made arrangements for my dad to come back to my ship and bunk with me until five or six weeks later. He then got him a job driving a car for an admiral. For the rest of the war he said at 42 he should never have been able to enlist again."

JACOB "JAKE" GEHLSEN

Town: Lynch, Neb.

In the war: Originally from Gross, Neb., he was part of a detachment of Marines at Pearl Harbor when the Japanese attacked. He later served on Johnson Island in the Pacific, helping lay the concrete for a runway. For two years, he was part of a secret mission in San Diego (with a team from the California Institute of Technology) to test then-new rockets captured from the Germans. Later, the unit tested rockets developed for the Americans. He was en route to Quantico, Va., for training — to prepare him to be part of an invasion force to land in Japan, he presumed — when he learned of the atomic bomb attacks.

In his words: "On Dec. 7, 1941, I was washing dishes after breakfast in the mess hall in Pearl Harbor when there was some noise in the harbor. Some thought it was a drill. I saw the Japanese plane fly by with the Rising Sun on it and said, 'That's no practice.' I could have thrown a rock and hit that pilot.

"I and others ran to the barracks and grabbed our .30-caliber rifles to shoot at the planes. I said they couldn't do much but distract them. But that's all we had. When you're in battle, you're a different man. One plane was shot down and there was a question if it was our group or not. One plane was really smoking (after it flew by). I really think our guys shot one down, and I think I was responsible for that.

"This is the sad part of it. Here comes 10 o'clock and they're still bringing men into our mess hall all shot up and covered in oil (spilled into the harbor)."

WAYNE HAGERBAUMER

Town: Genoa, Neb.

In the war: Was a 19-year-old Navy seaman 2nd class, working as a radio operator on the USS Argonne, a repair ship. He enlisted in January 1941. After Pearl Harbor, he served aboard the USS Blue Ridge, a communications ship. After the war, he inseminated cows and before retiring operated a drive-in restaurant in Genoa.

In his words: "Another guy and I were on deck because we were supposed to go on watch at 8 o'clock. At first we thought it was our own planes practicing. We saw the planes come diving down, the bombs falling and the torpedo planes coming at us. They were so close you could see the goggles on the pilots' faces.

"We never got hit. We were between a couple of docks and the torpedo planes couldn't get at us. The Helena was across the dock, and the Arizona was north of us. You could see it plain from our ship.

"I never saw more (of the attack) after that. I was in the radio shack the rest of the time. There were about 15 of us on different frequencies. Everything came over in Morse code, and we typed out everything. The radio shack was above deck and had no windows. All I could do was hear the guns going off.

"We were receiving reports that the Japanese were landing paratroops. We were pretty confused. Of course, they never tried. They probably could have if they had known how successful they were going to be. They were probably more successful than they figured."

THEODORE CZERWINSKI

Town: Omaha

In the war: Was a 20-year-old Navy seaman 1st class aboard the battleship USS Pennsylvania, the fleet flagship. He enlisted in 1939 and had been at Pearl Harbor for 17 months before the attack. He served the duration of the war aboard the ship, supporting 13 amphibious landings. The vessel spent 22 straight months at sea at one point. After the war, Czerwinski returned to Omaha and ran a bar with his brother.

In his words: "We were lounging around talking. We had a football team on our ship, and they were going to play another ship's team that day. One of the players and I were shooting the breeze as he was putting on his equipment to go play.

"Then we heard an explosion outside the port hole over at Ford Island. We wondered, 'Gee, what happened there?' Then there was another. And another. We ran out on the quarterdeck and saw the airplanes with the Rising Sun buzzing around.

"Everybody got to their battle stations. We were in dry dock, and the first thing we did was flood the dry dock. They couldn't get us with torpedoes, but we got a direct (bomb) hit that killed about 27 Marines at an anti-aircraft gun.

"I was the firing point. I elevated the guns and fired them. I used a periscope to look through, and all I could see was smoke and fire. Everything was on fire, including the water. We didn't know what danger the other ships were in. After the attack, the bodies started coming in. They'd lay them out on the hospital lawn in mattress covers. They didn't have body bags."

"We were one of the first ships to get hit at the start of the war and one of the last. We were at Okinawa just before the war ended, and a Japanese plane torpedoed us, knocking our screws off. It would have sunk us if we'd been at sea. You could see the goggles on the pilots' faces."

THE MORNING HEADLINES OF DEC. 8, 1941

SCARCELY HAD THE FIRST BULLETINS of the bombing of Hawaii and
the Philippines gone out over the radio than The World-Herald was flooded with calls
from people with relatives in the two bombed areas or elsewhere in the Pacific.
"Have you heard how many were killed?"
"Do you have any word on whether the Oklahoma was hit?"
"Were any killed at Wheeler Field?"
Some of those who called were sobbing. Most were reserved.

— FROM A PAGE 1 WORLD-HERALD STORY ON DEC. 8, 1941

OMAHANS GATHER on Dec. 7, 1941, to listen to radio broadcasts at a storefront along the north side of Farnam Street between 17th and 18th Streets.

MEMORIES OF A GENERATION ★

FRANCES JOHNSTON GRANT

Town: Sidney, Neb.

In the war: Was a high school student at St. Patrick Academy in Sidney.

In her words: "My family lived on a farm east of Dalton, Neb., and I remember the day we heard about the attack on Pearl Harbor. We were listening to the radio with family friends on the Sunday of the attack. One of the visitors had served in the Navy at Pearl Harbor, and he explained the seriousness of the attack and its implications."

MARY JANE MASTERS

Town: Omaha

In the war: Was 12-year-old Mary Jane Mullen at the outbreak of war. She went on to teach at St. Cecilia Catholic Elementary School for 12 years and was principal of Mary Our Queen Catholic Elementary School for 14 years.

In her words: "When growing up in Omaha in the 1930s and early 1940s, how I spent Sundays was quite predictable. The routine began with Mass at St. Cecilia Cathedral, followed by breakfast, reading the Sunday funny papers and an early afternoon dinner. The afternoons varied slightly. Often aunts and uncles and cousins would drop in, or we would go for an auto ride. In the evening, after we had a light supper, we'd turn on the radio for comedian Jack Benny, and Charlie McCarthy with Edgar Bergen the ventriloquist.

"As a child, I was restricted to family activities on Sundays and rarely played with the children in the neighborhood or school chums. As I got older, I was allowed to go to the matinees at the neighborhood theater on occasion and to sporting events held on our parish school field, providing the weather was good and no family visits were planned.

"Dec. 7, 1941, was such a day. The eighth-grade boys on St. Margaret Mary's football team were coming to our field to play our eighth-grade team. I walked over to watch them. It was a nice day for December. It was not too cold to stand outdoors and watch the boys running up and down the field. I don't remember how the game went. I was more interested in laughing and talking with the other girls, so I couldn't tell you who won.

"When the game ended, some of us were still visiting with each other, and one of the younger priests came out of the rectory's back door. He told us that Japan had attacked our naval base at Pearl Harbor and that we should go home. I didn't have any idea where Pearl Harbor was. Was it nearby? Would I make it home? I ran.

"When I reached home, the grown-ups were all gathered around the radio listening to the newscasts and talking quietly among themselves. President Roosevelt was going to ask Congress to declare war the next day.

"After that, Sundays were never the same. At Mass, we prayed for the safety of those in the armed forces and for a speedy end of the war. At home we had to decide how to use our sugar ration when planning desserts. Gasoline rationing made Sunday car rides seem unpatriotic. The neighborhood theater fare changed from Western cowboy movies to shows with war stories. The newsreels showed actual shots of warships, tanks and airplanes. The adults' dinner conversation had never been of interest to me when they discussed politics and economic things such as Roosevelt's NRA and CCC camps, but now that changed.

"Oh, yes, I remember what I was doing on Pearl Harbor Day. I don't remember what I did three days later on my 13th birthday or what I got for Christmas that year. But I do remember Dec. 7, 1941, because my life was never the same after that."

WILLIAM COOPER

Town: Omaha

In the war: Served in the Army as a technical corporal in the Pacific Theater. The longtime member of Salem Baptist Church worked for Eastman Kodak for 45 years.

In his words: "In 1941, I was working for Eastman Kodak in Omaha and was an active member in Salem Baptist Church. The week before the bombing, I attended a national Baptist convention in Houston with three others from our church. It was a weeklong convention that ended Saturday night. Sunday morning, the four of us left on the drive back to Omaha. We wanted to make it to Dallas the first evening. As we were driving, the news of the bombing came over the radio.

"We all were silent for a few minutes, just sitting on pins, listening to the report in shock and trying to figure out what it all meant. The first thing we did, really, was pray. We couldn't do anything else but drive and pray. We prayed to God to protect our families and protect the United States from the Japanese. We prayed for God to give us the strength and the initiative to overcome the Japanese attack.

"At the time, we had no idea where Pearl Harbor was or whether this meant the Japanese would soon be bombing the United States. We were driving along not knowing if bombers would soon be flying overhead. We were terribly worried about Omaha being hit because of the bomber factory in Bellevue. We kept the radio on the whole way, waiting for reports of more bombings. It may seem strange to people now, but we really had no concept of how far the Japanese could go, how quickly, or the range of the bombers, or our ability to stop them, or anything like that. We prayed a lot that day. It was one of the darkest days of my life.

"Once we reached Omaha, things were still in turmoil. Everybody feared that Omaha would be bombed. A lot of people I knew worked at the bomber factory. They were scared. After a while, though, those fears began to subside. There were so many special prayers. Give us the strength, Lord. See our people home safely. Protect us in this time of darkness. And He did spare us, and He has spared us even to this day."

BILL SCHOCK

Town: Falls City

In the war: Was a B-17 bomber pilot in Europe during the war. After being shot down over northern Germany, he was a prisoner of war for more than a year. After the war, he returned to Nebraska to work for the Falls City Journal, becoming the publisher in 1973.

In his words: "I was stationed at Camp Joseph T. Robinson outside Little Rock, Ark., on Dec. 7, 1941. Four of us GIs from Company B, 134th Infantry, were in town watching the movie "Sergeant York," which depicts the life and World War I heroics of that famed soldier. Midway through the show, the action on the screen was halted, the theater lights came on and an announcement was made for all men stationed at Camp Robinson to return to camp immediately. We left the theater along with many other soldiers. On the street, excited people were loudly passing the word: Pearl Harbor has been attacked by the Japanese! No one in my group had ever heard of Pearl Harbor, but we were quickly enlightened. The news, while startling, really should not have been. All furloughs had been canceled two weeks earlier, and latrine rumors had run rampant about our immediate future. We were aware that negotiations with the Japanese had been going on in Washington, but we couldn't imagine that the Japanese had a war with the United States up their sleeves.

"Cars and military vehicles with public address systems were covering Little Rock, blaring out the order for all 35th Division men (of which Nebraska's 134th Infantry was a part) to return immediately to camp. We decided we weren't going back to Robinson without a Sunday evening meal, and we dodged into a favorite diner away from the city's business district and its excited crowds. We ordered our meal but never got to eat it. Military police entered the diner and ordered us out of the building and back to camp. They meant business. We went.

"At Camp Robinson, things were in an uproar, and the Company B area was right in the middle of it. We quickly were clued in. When the news bulletin of the Pearl Harbor attack had come over the radio, Sgt. George Smedley, a World War I veteran, had rushed out into the company street yelling loudly: 'Men, get your uniforms on! We're at war!' The old 1st sergeant was one to demand attention, and he sure alerted the troops in a dickens of a hurry.

"We weren't quite ready to move out that night to who knows where, but we found out the next morning it wouldn't be long before we were on our way. I was a company clerk, and my job put me in the 134th regimental headquarters building, where on Monday morning excited chatter about our future came to a quick stop. President Roosevelt was on the radio, declaring war against Japan in his historic 'Day of Infamy' speech.

"Rumors 'spreading like wildfire' is an overworked cliché, but that was what Camp Robinson was all about as orders came to prepare for moving out. Where were we going? What would we do without cars? Could we call home? And what could we tell our families when we did? Our years of training and the famous Louisiana maneuvers had exposed us to pseudo-warfare, but it was difficult to comprehend that war was really here. And we were destined to be in it."

LOUIS L. MILLER

Town: Denison

Service: U.S. Army Signal Corps

In the war: He served from August 1942 to November 1945 in the southwest Pacific. He trained as a high-speed radio operator (Morse code) in Kansas City, Mo., and was deployed to Milne Bay, New Guinea. He was detached to the U.S. Navy as a blinker-tower operator. Then he was detached to Sixth Army Gen. Walter Krueger's boat as a radio signalman. The boat was used for conferences and area tours. He also was detached for a few months to a quartermaster boat to deliver orders to convoy ships. He participated in a beach landing on Noemfoor Island, Indonesia, in a radio truck in July 1944, and in two other beach landings in the Philippines. He also once helped a liberty ship captain bring the vessel to its berth at Kure Naval Base in Japan. The captain had asked Miller to handle the visible signals and operate the "big light on the bridge wing."

In his words: "All in all, my tour of 31 months — 16 of which were on the ocean in small boats — was not always pleasant, but there are many remembrances that I recall with nostalgia. Morning coffee mixed with the smell of the sea air; quiet nights at anchor with the ripple of water against the hull of the boat; the tug of the anchor rope. Then there's, among other things, the unforgettable sound of white-hot shells screaming overhead, fired from the ships offshore at the beach. And the devastation."

RITA SULLIVAN

Town: Omaha

In the war: Was a child in Superior, Wis., during the war. Three of her brothers served during the war, and one was taken as a prisoner of war on the island of Corregidor in the Philippines.

In her words: "I was horrified when I came in the house from sledding on that icy cold December day and my mother announced, with tears, 'Pearl Harbor has been bombed!' Horrified, because my brother, Navy Seaman Hank Zielinski, was stationed at Pearl Harbor and was assigned to the Shark submarine. Horrified, because twice we learned that he had been killed in action, when the first Shark was sunk and again, when the second Shark was sunk, only later to learn that he had been transferred each time."

The darkest days

AFTER 24 HOURS OF SAVAGE HAND-TO-HAND COMBAT, about 11,600 U.S. and Filipino soldiers were forced to surrender in 1942 to overwhelming Japanese forces on the Philippine island of Corregidor. ★ Edward Hoffman of Omaha, an Army corporal at the time, recalled seeing Lt. Gen. Jonathan M. Wainwright raise the white flag of surrender that night, about a month after the Japanese had captured the Bataan Peninsula. ★ Like those captured on the peninsula, the Corregidor prisoners were forced to march to a prison camp. "It was hell," Hoffman said. "They beat us up along the way, they didn't feed us much to eat, and they threatened to kill us."

AMERICAN LEGION MEMBERS IN TAYLOR, NEB.,
salute the flag-draped casket of Pvt. Clive John Raish,
who was killed in 1942 during training to head overseas. Raish, 20,
had enlisted after the attack on Pearl Harbor. Hundreds stood outside
the Evangelical Church to hear the sermon through loudspeakers.

MARJORIE 'WINNIE' DANIELS

Town: Alliance

In the war: Born in England, she was just starting school there when war was declared. Schoolchildren were issued gas masks (the younger children had ones with Mickey Mouse on them) and had to file into underground shelters when daylight raids occurred. She even had to put on the mask and go into a gas chamber to see if the mask leaked.

In her words: "(One time) the air raid siren went off, but my friends and I were having fun and took our time heading home. The next thing we knew this German plane was overhead. It was shot and hit . . . the pilot parachuted out. Boy, did we all run for cover. The pilot was captured in a plantation adjoining the field we had been playing in."

The Pacific

WAKE ISLAND, THE PHILIPPINES AND OTHER U.S. POSSESSIONS IN THE PACIFIC WERE ATTACKED AT THE SAME TIME AS PEARL HARBOR.

DEC. 23, 1941
U.S. forces surrender Wake Island to the Japanese, and Gen. Douglas MacArthur withdraws his headquarters from Manila.

MARCH 1942
Under orders from President Franklin D. Roosevelt, MacArthur leaves the island fortress of Corregidor and moves his headquarters to Australia.

APRIL 1942
U.S. forces at Bataan surrender.

MAY 1942
The U.S. garrison on the island fortress of Corregidor surrenders.

Major Gen. Frederick E. Uhl, commander of the Army's 7th Service Command, warned the public of the danger from enemy bombs in 1942. The country was divided into nine service commands during the war, with each directing training, supply and other military functions within its boundaries. Fort Crook near Bellevue was the headquarters of the 7th Service Command, which included Nebraska and Iowa. Omahans' fear of bombing had subsided by 1945, when a Japanese balloon bomb exploded over Dundee. It caused no damage.

'Every drop in that canteen was your life'

BY JOSEPH MORTON

WHEN ALBERT BROWN RETURNED home after years in Japanese camps for prisoners of war, a doctor told him to get out and enjoy life while he still could.

The native of North Platte, Neb., was unlikely to see 50, the doctor told him, given the illnesses, extreme malnutrition and physical abuse he suffered as a POW.

Brown not only survived the Bataan Death March, he lived to see his 105th birthday.

In the late 1930s, Brown — who had been in ROTC in high school and college — got the call from Uncle Sam. He was to leave his Council Bluffs dental practice and report to the Army in two weeks.

In 1941, when he was 35, Brown was shipped off to the Philippines, not long before the Japanese attacked there. Out of supplies and with no reinforcements in sight, American forces and their Filipino allies surrendered after months of fighting in 1942.

The exact numbers vary somewhat from account to account, but more than 70,000 American and Filipino soldiers were captured. Overwhelmed with the task of transporting so many prisoners, the Japanese forced them to march north. Disease, thirst, hunger and killings marked the brutal ordeal, which lasted for days.

Brown in 2007 recalled being lined up and forced to march with no food and no water. He said local civilians would approach and try to throw food to the marchers.

"The Japanese would beat the hell out of them," he said. "They'd go over there and take the butt of their rifle and just beat the hell out of those people, girls and boys, that threw stuff in there."

Brown also witnessed the beheading of a 17-year-old Marine, who was forced to the ground "on his hands and knees, and then they took the samurai sword out and severed his head."

Brown himself was stabbed.

"I started faltering and got to the back of the pack, and then the Japanese (soldier) came up and stuck a bayonet in my fanny and he yelled 'Speed-o!,' and I knew what 'speed-o' meant. I never was at the back of the pack after that."

At the prison camps in the Philippines, the violence and the shortages of food, medicine and water continued. Brown recalled how the temperature soared while the tens of thousands of men in camp relied on a single brass faucet for water.

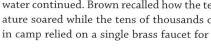

ALBERT BROWN had been the oldest survivor of the Bataan Death March when he died at 105 in 2011.

Fights would break out over places in line for that spigot, he said.

"Every drop in that canteen was your life."

Later, Brown was one of the soldiers packed into a "hell ship" bound for camps in Japan and China. He remained a prisoner until the end of the war.

He suffered numerous health problems as a result of his captivity, even losing his eyesight for a time.

Brown's memories also wind their way back to his childhood in North Platte. His father, an engineer with Union Pacific Railroad, was killed when a locomotive exploded in 1910.

The family lived a couple of blocks from William F. "Buffalo Bill" Cody. Brown said his family became friends with the former Wild West hero, whom he described as a quiet man who liked to sit on their porch. As a child, Brown recalled, he would sit on Cody's lap and run a hand through his beard.

"I don't know whether he liked that or not. Anyway, I kept doing it."

The family later moved to Council Bluffs, where Brown attended high school.

At Creighton University, he played quarterback on the football team and was a forward on the basketball team. Brown later graduated from the CU dental school. He received a medallion during Creighton's centennial celebration in 2005.

LARRY DOYLE

Town: Bellevue

In the war: He was 4 years old when Pearl Harbor was attacked, 8 when Japan surrendered.

In his words: "At the time, my family was living a couple of blocks from the ocean in Long Beach, Calif. I remember anti-aircraft gun and coastal artillery gun emplacements along the beach (and) camouflage nets over key industrial plants. ... One night in early 1942, I woke up frightened by the sound of explosions and flashes of light.

"My mother came and comforted me, telling me it was just a thunderstorm. Years later, I learned it was anti-aircraft guns firing at an unidentified plane. A woman who lived down the street went to her roof to watch the fireworks and was killed by the shrapnel from the exploding shells.

"My birthday is on Aug. 14. In 1945, about a week before my birthday, my mother asked me what I wanted for my birthday. I replied I wanted the war to end. On my birthday, I was playing on the front porch of my grandmother's house when she came to the door and said the Japanese had surrendered. A short while after that, the town fire whistle started blowing. A few minutes later, a firetruck came down the street, siren wailing, while the crew sprayed everyone with water. It was the best birthday present I ever had."

MARIAN GOODENKAUF

Town: Table Rock, Neb.

In the war: Was in high school during the war. Her future husband, Arley Goodenkauf, was a paratrooper who jumped into Normandy on D-Day, was captured and later escaped from a POW camp.

In her words: "We lost our male teachers who were called to serve by the draft or enlistment. Many of the trips to away sports, musical and drama events were things of the past, torpedoed by Japan and Germany. We were able to compete in some close meetings by riding in a farm parent's stock truck. …

"In my senior year, I was pulled from high school to fill in as the teacher in a country school for a month to replace a male teacher who was called to serve. Lady Luck was with me, because I returned in April to finish school and graduate with what was left of my class."

ROBERT PARADISE RETURNED *from the war and met in 1946 with Father Edward Flanagan at Boys Town.*

'If they fell, they were dead'

BY ROBERT MCMORRIS

ON THE DAY THE JAPANESE BOMBED the American naval base at Pearl Harbor, Hawaii, 1938 Boys Town graduate Robert Paradise was in the Philippines. He was a sergeant, a surgical technician in the Medical Corps.

ROBERT PARADISE
IN 1995

Several hours after the attack on Pearl Harbor, other Japanese squadrons bombed the Philippines' Clark Field, destroying nearly 100 American bombers and fighters, many of them on the ground.

Paradise was with the forces that took to the jungles of the Bataan Peninsula, fighting a valiant delaying action that finally ended with the fall of the peninsula on April 9, 1942.

"I had a medical supply tent next to the general's tent," said Paradise, referring to Maj. Gen. Edward King, commander of the Bataan defenders. King's superior officer was Gen. Jonathan "Skinny" Wainwright, who was at Corregidor, the fortress island at the foot of Bataan.

"I heard General King talking by phone to Wainwright," Paradise recalled. "King said, 'Skinny, at noon today, I'm going to surrender Bataan.'

"King had been ordered to keep on fighting no matter what. But there was no way those men could fight any longer, they were so weak — either from their bad diet or disease.

"General King said, 'I don't care if they court-martial me. People are dying like flies of malaria, dysentery, beriberi and dengue fever.' "

The infamous Bataan Death March followed. Forced by the victorious Japanese to march to Camp O'Donnell at the northern end of the Bataan Peninsula, thousands of American prisoners of war died. Many were shot or bayoneted to death. Paradise, who retired in Camarillo, Calif., witnessed some of the atrocities.

"I was ordered to go ahead by truck to make preparations for medical services at O'Donnell," he said. "I was standing on a knoll, looking down a slope when the first of our men showed up, making their way toward the camp.

"I saw at least seven men killed within 500 feet of their destination. The march had taken six days. But even when they were in sight of their goal, if they fell, they were dead. The ones I saw die were killed by bayonets or swords.

"There were (thousands of) men who didn't show up at O'Donnell. They had been alive at the time of the surrender."

Later, as Paradise was helping tend the sick and wounded, it was learned that a Japanese general was on his way to inspect the prisoners.

"A Japanese lieutenant, a kind of advance man, announced that everybody was expected to stand at attention when the general arrived," Paradise said. "Those too sick or wounded to stand were supposed to lie at attention on their stretchers.

"One poor guy had a broken collarbone, so naturally he couldn't lie straight. But the lieutenant didn't take that as an excuse. He kicked the guy in the face.

"I couldn't take any more. I hit the lieutenant and knocked him cold. It was a good hit. I could feel it down to my toes.

"Then about six Japanese soldiers grabbed me and beat me unconscious. I expected that. I knew it would be sure death for me for striking an officer. But I thought I was a dead man anyway."

In fact, the Japanese left the blood-covered Paradise for dead. "But two American doctors dragged me to their tent," he said. "I had a skull fracture, a broken arm, a broken shoulder and what you call a twisted trunk. But I recovered."

He said the Japanese had not yet taken inventory of the prisoners, so they did not discover that their lieutenant's attacker had survived.

In the next two-plus years, Paradise was transferred to two other POW camps, one of which was on Formosa, now called Taiwan. "The Japanese commander on Taiwan was a pretty nice guy," Paradise said. "He told me that he and his wife used to go to a place in Tokyo called the Paradise Club. He said anybody with a name like Paradise couldn't be all bad."

At another camp, Paradise said, his captors learned he had lived at Boys Town. He recalled: "They called me in and said, 'Is this Father Flanagan a famous man?'

"I said yes, he was, he was a very great man, and I thought of him as my real father. The first thing I knew, they were making up letters that were supposed to be from me to Father Flanagan. They were full of propaganda about how great the food was and how I was being paid for work I was doing at the camp. All lies.

"They broadcast the phony letters, knowing they would be picked up by the Americans."

Despite the "good" food he was served as a POW, Paradise weighed just 97 pounds upon his release at war's end. He weighed 160 when he played football at Boys Town.

Paradise found himself in temporary trouble when he returned to the States. "It was those propaganda letters," he said. "Some people in the Army took them seriously. Father Flanagan convinced them that I wasn't the kind of guy who would write something like that."

The Boys Town director, in fact, arranged a hero's welcome for him. "When I stepped off the train in Omaha, a band started playing, and I rode with Father Flanagan in a parade through downtown Omaha," he said. "It was amazing."

Paradise was born in Valentine, Neb. When he was 4 his parents deserted him and his two brothers, 2 and 7.

"Our parents just took off," he said. "I was adopted by Fred and Nell Paradise of Long Pine, Neb. My older brother was brought up by our grandmother, and my younger brother was adopted by another couple.

"I lived with my adoptive father after he and his wife were divorced," Paradise said. "I was pretty happy until my dad — my adoptive father — died. A priest talked to Father Flanagan about me, and that's how I came to Boys Town."

In 1946 Paradise re-enlisted in the Army as a staff sergeant assigned to escort soldiers charged with desertion. "I signed up for four years and stayed 15," he said.

He retired on a disability pension because of recurring problems associated with the beating he suffered at the hands of the Japanese. He had two cranial operations. "I can't stand exactly right because of my twisted trunk," he said.

In his post-Army years, he pursued his old ambition to make it in show business. In Hollywood, screenwriter Dore Schary helped him qualify for membership in the Screen Actors Guild. The two met during the filming of the movie "Boys Town."

"I'm in two scenes in that picture, but I don't have speaking lines," Paradise said. "In one scene you couldn't recognize me. I'm in the choir."

The Bataan Death March

THE FORCED MARCH involved about 70,000 U.S. and Filipino World War II prisoners captured by the Japanese in the Philippines. From the southern end of the Bataan Peninsula, the starving and ill-treated prisoners were sent 63 miles to a prison camp. Only 54,000 prisoners lived to reach the camp; as many as 10,000 died on the way and others escaped into the jungle. In 1946, the Japanese commander of the march was convicted by a U.S. military commission and executed.

'Hitting the bamboo'

DR. FRED G. NASR GRADUATED from the Creighton University School of Dentistry in 1938 and joined the Army in 1940.

Nasr, a dental surgeon, was stationed in the Philippines when the war started and was taken prisoner in 1942.

"At times, we buried 400 to 500 men a day," he said. "Some gave up. They would just lie down on their bamboo cots and die. 'Hitting the bamboo,' we called it.

"But I never lost faith that I would get home.

That's how I made it. Faith."

While a prisoner, Nasr learned to speak Japanese in an effort to curb the brutality against American soldiers. He also helped smuggle food, medicine and money into the camps.

Upon his release in February 1945, Nasr weighed 80 pounds, down from the 200 pounds he weighed at the time of his capture. Nasr earned three battle stars in the Bataan and Corregidor campaigns. He also was awarded the Bronze Star and the Purple Heart.

FRED G. NASR in 1970

NANCY LEE REISSIG

Town: Weeping Water, Neb.

In the war: Fifth-grader at Central Valley School in Cass County

In her words: "Being very young did not diminish the impact the war had on me. ... The most vivid memory I have had was that of going to a movie called 'Hitler's Children' and being so frightened that I was sick all night. The tone of the movie and the harshness of the Nazi voices was more than I could understand.

"My mother had been concerned about the movie and called a friend who thought it would be OK that her daughter and I could go. My friend fell asleep, and I was left to absorb the frightening scenes. The war was a mixed blessing, as my father got a job at the Martin Bomber Plant and, for the first time, we had money to enjoy life the best we could. ...

"The general dismal atmosphere caused many parents to wait anxiously for thin patriotic letters to arrive in the mail, and pray often for their sons."

'Scoring victories at a time when no one else was'

THE JAPANESE WERE PILING UP battle victories so readily after bombing Pearl Harbor that they appeared invincible. Then they felt the bite of a band of daredevil American mercenaries flying planes painted to look like grinning sharks.

The unit that called itself the "Flying Tigers" overcame monumental logistical hurdles and pioneered revolutionary air combat tactics to stop, or at least slow, the Japanese early in World War II.

"Their symbolic value can't be overemphasized," said Bernard Nalty, an Omaha native and former Air Force historian who wrote a book about the Flying Tigers. "They were scoring victories at a time when no one else was. It certainly did help sustain morale at a very important time."

A Nebraska veteran of the Flying Tigers, Norman Brown of Stromsburg, said that when he traveled to China in 1994 he encountered Chinese citizens who had been paying tribute to five Flying Tigers pilots who were killed trying to stop Japanese air attacks.

The Chinese citizens had been caring for the fliers' graves for the past 50 years and conducted regular memorial services at the burial site near the city of Lijiang, which was close to a Tigers base during the war, Brown recalled in 1995.

"The Flying Tigers were one of the most respected groups of soldiers to ever serve in this part of China," Brown said.

A history professor in Kunming, China, helped in the effort to return the remains of the five pilots to the United States.

"You can rest assured that the people here always remember those 'Flying Tigers' who fought for them," Wang Zhusheng wrote in a letter to Brown.

The first Flying Tigers were volunteers recruited by Claire Chennault, a retired Army Air Corps officer who helped Chinese leader Chiang Kai-shek bolster his country's air defenses in 1941.

The unit started out with 100 Curtiss P-40 fighter planes flown by soldiers of fortune hungry for adventure and the bonus money promised for aerial dogfight victories or successful strafing runs against Japanese planes.

Chennault developed an innovative system for detecting enemy bombers so his fighters could intercept them before the bombs were unleashed on Chinese cities. He also personally trained them to fight as teams instead of in the traditional one-on-one dogfights.

In 1943, the unit became an official part of the U.S. military when it was transformed into the 14th Air Force. Chennault, who had been recalled to active duty and named a brigadier general in 1942, commanded the 14th.

In addition to the P-40 fighter planes, the 14th Air Force also flew bombers and transport aircraft.

The 14th Air Force Association says the unit had an impressive wartime tally.

By May 1945, it had destroyed 2,135 enemy aircraft, 445 ships, 817 bridges and 1,225 locomotives.

The wartime accomplishments of the Flying Tigers are all the more remarkable considering how difficult it was to maintain a steady flow of ammunition, aircraft parts and other supplies to the unit's bases in China. Because Japan controlled the east Asian coast, the Allied forces had to use either the 700-mile Burma Road to get their military supplies into China or fly over the mountainous region pilots called "the Hump."

Dallas Nelson of Bayard, Neb., said he dreaded going to China when he received orders to join the Flying Tigers unit. He had seen fierce fighting during the early days of the war in North Africa and Italy. He served on a ground crew that maintained the aircraft to keep the Flying Tigers in the air.

"We had a pretty tough time over in Europe," Nelson said. "We used to say, 'At least we don't have to fly the Hump.'"

Fenton Isaacson of Omaha flew C-47 cargo planes for the Flying Tigers in the months before the war ended. He often had to dodge ground fire while ferrying 100-gallon drums of aircraft fuel and ammunition for 50-caliber machine guns. Before the Japanese surrendered, Isaacson was told that his unit would be carrying troops and pulling gliders involved in the invasion of Japan.

"We were realizing we were going to get involved in some pretty heavy stuff," he said.

Following the bombing of Pearl Harbor, the Japanese made quick work of conquering Hong Kong, Malaya, the Philippines and Burma.

Herb Carter of Omaha said he was proud to have served with the Tigers during World War II.

"They were the only thing in China, especially during the early part of the war," Carter said. "If it were not for them, the Japanese would have had a free hand over there. They probably saved China."

FENTON ISAACSON in 1995. He flew C-47 cargo planes for the Flying Tigers.

THE FLYING TIGERS, featuring distinctively painted P-40 fighter planes, were credited with destroying more than 2,000 enemy aircraft.

'We shouldn't have been there'

WHEN THE JAPANESE ATTACKED Pearl Harbor, Dec. 7, 1941, Pfc. Kenneth Davis, serving in the U.S. Marines and stationed in Beijing, had problems of his own. While Japanese bombers devastated the naval base in the Hawaiian Islands, Davis and about 180 other Marines stationed at the U.S. Embassy in Beijing were surrounded by Japanese troops and ordered to surrender.

The Marines didn't dare fight because they were so outnumbered, he said. Japan already was at war with China and had 40,000 troops in Beijing, he said.

While Americans remember "the day of infamy" on each anniversary of the Pearl Harbor attack, Davis said he always did his best to forget.

"I don't think about it much," the Franklin, Neb., resident said in 1987. "I don't care to."

Davis said he didn't mind that U.S. history has largely focused on Pearl Harbor and overlooked others who were attacked that day. Captured alive on a day when 3,700 people died in the Pearl Harbor attack, Davis could be considered lucky. He would spend the next 45½ months in prisoner-of-war camps in China and Japan.

Military officers told the enlisted men at the embassy in Beijing about the Pearl Harbor attack shortly after they were ordered to surrender.

The Marines were to have left China by then, Davis said, but the Japanese prevented them from shipping out.

"We shouldn't have even been there," he said.

The 180 men were to spend almost four years in Japanese prison camps in China, shuttled by train from one to another. Later, Davis and others would be taken to a camp in Japan.

Seventeen did not survive.

The men spent most of their POW camp time working, Davis said. Their captors set work quotas that the men had to meet in order to be fed. Prisoners ate rice, fish heads and watery millet soup. Davis said he lost about 70 pounds and weighed slightly more than 100 pounds when he was released. After being freed, he was promoted to corporal.

JAPANESE PROCLAMATION after U.S. surrender of Wake Island.

'It was either work or die'

NOT ALL PRISONERS were military men.

Ben Comstock of Bellevue and his father, civilian carpenters working for a defense contractor on Wake Island, were captured by the Japanese two weeks after Pearl Harbor.

During the next four years, he worked 10- to 12-hour days in a steel mill in Japan. "It was either work or die — one of the two," Comstock said.

"We got one day off a month, supposedly, so we could clean our clothes and, hopefully, get a bath. Sometimes we did, and sometimes we didn't."

BEN COMSTOCK in 1999

Food was scarce, and many men died of malnutrition.

"We got a handful of cooked rice a day, if we were lucky," said Comstock, who served as national director of the American Ex-Prisoners of War.

During nearly four years in captivity, he lost about 100 pounds and weighed 97 pounds when he was liberated.

The Japanese, he said, "tried to break the human spirit. Starvation and things like that, typical things with prisoners, degrading them as much as possible."

SANDY WIEBOLD

Town: Hooper, Neb.

In the war: Turned 5 years old on Aug. 2, 1941, and started first grade in a country school northeast of Arlington, Neb., that September. Pearl Harbor was attacked a few months later, on Dec. 7.

In her words: "My brother and I were allowed to go to the movies on Friday night, and the newsreels were full of war news. Unfortunately, the names of young men and women from our area who were dead or missing grew quite long. The nightly blackouts where no one could show any light became a way of life. I had just seen 'Mrs. Miniver' at the movies, and I remember hiding beside those dark drapes and trembling with fear that we would be bombed like those families in England.

"Thankfully, that never happened. We received news that an uncle was killed in the Philippines, but shortly thereafter, the news of the war gradually became more encouraging. … Then in August of 1945, on a hot summer afternoon that I will never forget, we received news that the Japanese had surrendered unconditionally, and the war was over. My dad and I were driving in the car toward the west and there was this fabulous setting red sun — of course, the symbol on the Japanese flag. My dad said, 'Even the sun knows that Japan's day is over.' "

MEMORIES OF A GENERATION ★

JANE E. MARTIN

Town: She lived in Papillion for nearly 10 years as an Air Force wife, later in Manchester, Tenn.

In the war: She was a young child living on a farm in central England.

In her words: "The memories I have were seen through the eyes of a child who was 3½ at the onset of the war. … My father managed an estate, or large farming area, near Coventry, a coal and steel city they thought was well-defended with one large anti-aircraft gun and a large number of barrage balloons, or 'blimps,' to impede aircraft. The gun was blown out the first week, and for Coventry it was all downhill from there. This city was famous for its beautiful cathedral. It was burned and mostly destroyed, but a huge wooden cross in the sanctuary stood charred but remained in position for the entire war in an almost defiant gesture. After the war, a new building was erected around the ruins, and the cross still stands and draws many visitors each year.

"As the bombs continued to rain terror and destruction, people poured out of the city each night to sleep at friends' or even in the open, no longer waiting for the air-raid sirens. Those who were brave made shelters under their stairwells. My father decided that running for the air-raid shelter in the middle of the night was too dangerous. So he cleared a closet under the stairs and put in a mattress, lantern and games for me to play. Strangely enough, when the siren went, the first thing in the shelter was my Yorkshire terrier, without being told to go. I can remember seeing fewer homes standing each week on trips to cattle market with my parents. Life still continued as much as possible in routine; people refused to give up and became more determined not to be victims.

"We shared our home with many people all through this part of the war. My parents, like many others, shared all they had in the way of food and supplies. Cards and darts (with Hitler on the dartboard) became regular evening entertainment, and a great sense of fellowship prevailed. I was often afraid of the noise of air-raid warnings and planes, but often felt warmth, love and a sense of protection from everyone around me. …

"It is well known that Jewish people suffered greatly at the hands of the German SS. My parents were in touch with an organization that smuggled people out of Germany, and they took in a Jewish girl who had managed to hide during a house raid in Germany but had watched her entire family slaughtered. Her name was Nora, and she lived with us and helped my mother in the house and took care of me. She was always afraid of loud noises and was very nervous. I was told to be very quiet around her so as to not upset her. … There were a few German sympathizers that were English. My father discovered a secretary on temporary hire making notes from ordnance maps in his office and called the police. She was arrested and taken away."

EARLE M. SCHAD

Town: Mount Ayr, Iowa

Service: U.S. Navy, chief gunner's mate

In the war: He joined the Navy in January 1941 and took his training at Great Lakes Naval Station in Illinois. He left there by troop train in April 1941 for San Diego, where he boarded the USS Bridge. The Bridge, based out of San Francisco, was a fleet store ship with a cargo that consisted of fresh, frozen and dry foods. The crew's job was to keep the battle fleet and shore stations supplied with food. He later spent nine months on occupation duty after his ship was damaged by a mine. The ship was repaired but then was decommissioned, and Schad was honorably discharged in January 1947. He had served most of his Navy career on the USS Bridge.

In his words: "We loaded stores from Pier 56 at the foot of Third Street, had a lighter (transport vessel) loaded with construction equipment as a tow and left for Honolulu where we parted with the lighter and then proceeded to Pearl Harbor, loaded some more construction equipment and proceeded to get under way for Midway Island. Unloaded some cargo, then to Wake Island, where we unloaded more stores and construction equipment, and from there to Guam. On this trip, I was treated to an encounter with the first of several typhoons that we went through. Also on this trip, we had our first experience of the coming war with Japan. We were advised to shoot to sink any vessel that did not properly identify itself. After several more trips to Pearl Harbor, we went into major overhaul at Mare Island in October 1941. On Feb. 4, 1942, we were loaded with provisions and proceeded to Pearl Harbor in a convoy, and from Pearl we left in convoy for Pago Pago, Tutuila, American Samoa. Encountered our first sub attack, and our destroyer escort fired depth charges and reported the sub as sunk. This trip was the forerunner of many trips to the many Pacific islands."

GEORGE SEDLAK

Town: Omaha

Service: Army

In the war: Native of Garland, Neb., drafted in California in February 1942. Assigned to machine-gun platoon, A Company, 1st Battalion, 35th Regiment, 25th Division at Schofield Barracks, Hawaii. Relieved Marines on Guadalcanal in December 1942. There, the 25th won the nickname Tropic Lightning Division. Next, made a beachhead landing on Vella LaVella in the Solomon Islands, capturing an airfield from Japanese. Landed unopposed on Luzon in Philippines in January 1945 but then saw 165 straight days of combat; relieved in June 1945 to train for invasion of Japan, which never came. Ended war as staff sergeant in charge of machine-gun platoon.

In his words: "I was proud to have served with the 25th Division. It saddens me to remember the many good friends and brave men who were wounded or killed by the enemy. I was just lucky. I lost my best friend in the Philippines. We were in a shell hole with a lot of big boulders in it. He got shot in the chest and died later in an aid station. Another time a good friend was digging a foxhole on a hillside, and I told him I'd dig for a while and he sat on a log behind me and was shot in the shoulder. It crippled him up, and he was shipped stateside. I was never shot but the jungle living got to me, and I was sick with yellow fever and later cholera."

KATHLEEN MANAHAN MCEVOY

Town: Omaha

In the war: She was 10 when World War II began and living in Plymouth, England, a naval town with a dockyard and British naval, marine and army barracks.

In her words: "It was in late spring of 1940 that the blitz on Plymouth began. My mother and I were on our way home from an afternoon service when the sirens sounded. We weren't too alarmed as there had not been any air raids up till then — only testing of the sirens. Then the 'take cover' sounded and we started to run, arriving home just a few minutes before the bombs started to fall. We took shelter in a large room under the front steps of the house, along with two other families who shared the house.

"The raids continued almost every night for a few weeks. Later that year we moved, along with another family, to a house that had a bathroom, which the other hadn't had. When the raids began, we took shelter in a large cupboard under the stairs in the basement. When the gasworks was bombed, my mother was hard-put to prepare a warm breakfast for us. School was never canceled, and we had to walk past the bombed-out houses on our way to school then, and the local shopping center. Of course, the dockyard was the main target, as was the naval and marine barracks.

"My father worked at an army office establishment — he was ex-army himself. At night he and our downstairs neighbor and his two older daughters were air raid wardens. He never spoke of his experiences of those nights on patrol, but some of them must have been quite harrowing."

FRANK HEDGES

Town: Lyons, Neb.

Service: Army

In the war: Native of Walthill, Neb. Enlisted March 1941. Basic training in Manila, where he was when the Japanese attacked Pearl Harbor and, shortly afterward, the Philippines. Captured on the Bataan Peninsula, he was a POW in the Philippines and in Japanese-held Manchuria. Discharged as a buck sergeant in 1946.

In his words: "We woke up Monday morning and the (Pearl Harbor) news was coming in. ... We headed for Bataan. Japanese were landing troops. ... They drove us back. They practically wiped out one of our companies in the first battles. We were short of ammunition. We were short of everything. We had World War I guns." Hedges was taken prisoner after U.S. forces in the Philippines surrendered.

"If you were able, you'd have to be on work detail cutting wood for cooking. Or you were on a burial detail. They loaded 2,000 of us on a ship (in the fall of 1942), and they had about 2,000 of their own troops on there. Our pastime was picking seam squirrels (lice) out of our clothes. We got up to Manchuria in December. It was cold as could be, and all of us had light clothes on, like you wear in the Philippines. We had shoes on without any socks. I went down to 77 pounds. I had weighed about 165 all the time. I volunteered to go into the machine-tool factory and work. I got three meals a day that way. I rose to 130 pounds."

Back in the United States in October 1945, he was hospitalized in San Francisco. "They took our clothes away from us. The first night four or five of us snuck out of the hospital. We hailed a taxicab and went downtown and went into a bar in our pajamas. We got a bunch of sailors around us, and they escorted us in."

Answering the call

MORE GRIM NEWS FOLLOWED the attack on Pearl Harbor, from Japan's string of victories in the Pacific to Germany's tightening stranglehold on Europe. ★ A 1945 World-Herald editorial looked back at the uncertainty of the war's early days and observed, "Many of us thought the blackness of doom was closing over our civilization." Fear was accompanied by a dread of the hardships lying ahead. ★ Nan Viergutz Rickey, a 1942 Benson High graduate, recalled a New Year's Eve dance that she and some classmates attended as 1941 gave way to 1942. With the attack on Pearl Harbor only weeks behind them, it was certain that many of the young men would head for war. "We knew they were leaving," she said. ★ Were Americans ready to answer their nation's call to serve and to sacrifice? Sixty-thousand Nebraskans and Iowans gave their answer at the April 1942 Army Day parade in downtown Omaha.

COLUMNS OF THE 4TH CAVALRY ride down Farnam Street during the Army Day parade of 1942. The view is west from near 17th Street.

SHIRLEY KENEALY

Town: Neola, Iowa

In the war: Was in eighth grade when the war started. Her late husband, Vince, served in the Air Force and flew 50 missions into Austria.

In her words: "I remember the National Guard unit marching out of our town to the depot and off to war. The signs 'Slip of the lip sinks ships' and 'Uncle Sam needs you.' . . . I would look up into the sky and wonder where the guy was that I would marry. He was up in the sky all right, in a B-24."

No hesitation to serve

ROBERT F. MILLER in 2010

HIS FIRST REACTION TO THE NEWS of Pearl Harbor was, "Where's that?" His second was to enlist.

Robert F. Miller of Omaha responded as a lot of Americans did. The only reason Bob didn't enlist sooner was that the attack came on a Sunday. He volunteered first thing Monday.

He stayed in for the duration, celebrated victory with lots of French wine, wept at the welcome-home to U.S. soil, returned to active duty in Korea, became a lieutenant colonel in the Air Force Reserve and raised a family in Omaha.

He had arrived in Europe as a second lieutenant in the Quartermaster Corps, attached to the Army Air Forces in the 56th Fighter Group. He recalls days when so many planes flew so close together that "they blocked out the sun."

He worked mainly in supply lines, but was shot at by Germans from churches as the Allies marched toward victory. "Some of those towns were so beat up, it was pathetic."

As the war in Europe ended, GIs came across a canal with a ship that Germans had loaded down with stolen French wine. "We took so many cases out," he recalled in 2010 with a hearty laugh, "that the ship came up out of the water."

His WWII service, which started with news of Pearl Harbor, came full circle with his arrival in Boston Harbor. Bands played, and people cheered. "There wasn't a dry eye on our ship, mine included."

ROBERT F. MILLER

AN ARMY RECRUIT, suitcase in hand, receives a bag of sweets from the American Legion in Grand Island, Neb., before boarding a train for training just three weeks after Pearl Harbor.

"THE MECHANIZED UNITS were impressive, but the prancing sleek horse troop caught the crowd's fancy," The World-Herald reported.

GERALD GUDE

Town: Hamburg, Iowa

Service: Navy

In the war: Served on oil tanker USS Merrimack and headquarters ship USS Ancon.

In his words: "There were times things could have gone the other way. It wasn't a lead-pipe cinch we would come out on top."

THE CHILLED CROWD was 10 deep in spots, with people eager to cheer on the military men.

'The 4th rode into Omaha to play its final role'

MORE THAN 60,000 PEOPLE lined the streets of downtown Omaha on April 6, 1942, ready to show that America was up to the challenge of fighting a formidable enemy.

The Army Day parade provided a welcome break after a winter darkened by grim daily headlines from the war. Charles Wood of Cedar Rapids, Iowa, a corporal who served with the Army's 4th Cavalry during World War II, said his unit came to Omaha from Fort Meade, near Sturgis, S.D., to participate in the parade. It was a solemn occasion.

CHARLES WOOD in 1989

"Many of the men, like me," he said, "had been drafted in 1941, expecting to serve one year and then be discharged. The declaration of war against Germany and Japan the previous December changed our lives, and we soon were in combat in Europe."

Ak-Sar-Ben racetrack's grounds, used as the staging area for the parade, were transformed into an army camp with 1,500 officers and men.

JAMES PATTERSON

Town: Oshkosh, Neb.

Service: Army,
475th Infantry

In the war: Rifleman,
served in Burma, where
he helped keep open
the Burma Road supply
line into China and later
trained Chinese troops.

In his words: "It would
rain 20 or 30 inches,
and then the sun would
come out and the steam
would roll. ... They
parachuted all of our
rations to us. The Japa-
nese were getting about
as much of it as we
were. ... It's funny now.
There's two ways of
doing it: the right way
and the Army way."

Two days before the parade, 4th Cavalry officers received orders from Washington that the unit, after the parade, was to turn in its horses to the Quartermaster Corps at Fort Robinson in northwest Nebraska.

"This was the official announcement that we were changing from horse soldiers to become fully mechanized," Wood said. "This was sad for many of the men, like myself, who had come to appreciate the horses that we rode."

In 1942, the unit had 1,500 men and 487 horses in Omaha for Army Day, which was first celebrated in 1928 on the anniversary date of the U.S. entry into World War I and last observed in 1949.

"I told our veterans," Wood said, "that the 4th rode into Omaha to play its final role as a mounted cavalry unit, passing in review for the last time, in a parade before a large crowd. We then exchanged our beloved horses and equipment for light tanks and mechanized armor."

In addition to the spectacle of the cavalry, it was also the first glimpse of mechanized armor for many of those who turned out.

World-Herald reporter Lawrence Youngman watched the cavalry line during the chilly march of April 6 and wrote:

"It was the 4th Cavalry's horse platoon that really stole the show. Pulses quickened as the matched animals, in columns of squads, eight horses in a line, clattered along. There was a poignant realization that it might be the last time Omaha streets would ever echo to the hooves of the horse cavalry, mechanized warfare being what it is today."

Youngman added:

"The horses covered the entire parade route at a brisk trot. Many of the riders had never mounted a horse until a few months ago, but the formations were excellent, and the crowds were impressed by the perfect alignment as the squads rounded the corners."

Dignitaries in the reviewing stand included Army generals,

Omaha Mayor Dan Butler and Rep. Charles McLaughlin, D-Neb.

Youngman recalled later that it was the cavalry that brought people out for the parade.

"We (the World-Herald staff) considered it quite an event because here you had 487 horses marching in line through the business district," he said. "We all knew that it wouldn't be long and the horse would no longer be a part of the war that was just getting under way."

Both en route to Omaha from Fort Meade and from Omaha to Fort Robinson, the horses were carried in trucks. Overnight stops were made on both trips in Kearney and Alliance, Neb.

The mechanized caravan included Jeeps and other vehicles that brought the soldiers. In Omaha, the cavalry camped at Ak-Sar-Ben Field.

During their stay, the troopers attracted between 20,000 and 25,000 visitors to Ak-Sar-Ben, where the soldiers demonstrated such things as drills involving mounted machine gun crews.

The 4th Cavalry was organized in 1855 and served in the Civil War, an Indian campaign and in the Philippines during and after the Spanish-American War. Wood said most soldiers were from Iowa, Minnesota, North Dakota and Nebraska.

Tom Buecker, curator of history for the Nebraska State Historical Society at Fort Robinson State Park, said the 4th reached the fort on April 9 after leaving Omaha.

"An official review was held in a field between Crawford and the fort," Buecker said. "The horses then were officially turned over to Fort Robinson. The men from the 4th then continued their return trip to Fort Meade."

Buecker said the 4th eventually was sent to the Southwest and was assigned to light tanks. The 4th saw combat during the Normandy invasion, landing on Utah Beach.

As for the horses, Buecker said, they were put on the auction block.

BETTY EDWARDS
Town: Omaha

In the war: Her new husband was drafted in March 1942 and was sent to a base near Seattle. She stayed with her parents on the sheep ranch she grew up on in southeast Montana and helped with the spring work. By the end of May, she traveled to Seattle and lived with in-laws, getting a job at Boeing Aircraft as a rivet-bucker in the tail section of B-25s.

In her words: "You can imagine how frightening it was for a young girl from ranch country to arrive in Seattle, to see huge blimps with long steel cables hanging from them covering the sky. This was to provide protection to the city from enemy planes. Later that fall, I moved to Kansas to be with my husband. There was no work to be had in this town for me. Our next move was to Fort Custer, Mich. While there, I worked at Kellogg filling K rations for our soldiers overseas. There were three lines (breakfast, lunch, dinner) running 24 hours a day. Each spring, I took a four-week leave from my job to go home to Montana to help my parents with the lambing operation. It was impossible to hire help during the war years."

BOYS PUSHED THEIR WAY to the front to catch a glimpse of the horses and soldiers.

THE PARADE OFFERED the chance for many to get their first look at mechanized armor.

'We do not intend to be caught napping'

PAUL ANDREAS STAMPED THROUGH the dark streets of the Lincoln neighborhood, with only the moonlight illuminating his patrol path.

Air-raid sirens screamed in the distance. Residents peered through drawn shades, straining to see the young man wearing the armband of an air-raid warden.

It was 10 p.m. on a crisp night in 1942, and southeast Nebraska was pitch black.

The blackout lasted about 20 minutes. Finally, the sirens' wail faded and lights were slowly switched on.

Andreas recalled clearly the wartime blackout drills he experienced as a teenager.

"It was my responsibility to walk down the middle of the street — about four blocks — and tell everyone to turn their lights out," Andreas said in 1994. "It was eerie, but I was young, emotional and patriotic then. It was an honor, in fact."

Two years before he stormed Omaha Beach as an infantryman, Andreas began his wartime service with the Civilian Defense Corps.

Like the soldiers on the front lines of World War II, thousands of civil defense volunteers feared and prepared for the worst.

They memorized silhouettes of enemy aircraft in order to plot the planes' locations on area maps. They attended Red Cross nursing and nutrition classes. They listened to recordings of London bombing raids and watched movies on British war activities to get used to "the real thing."

They would not be caught off guard, Omaha Mayor Dan Butler vowed at the time.

"We do not intend to be caught napping, and we haven't been loafing," Butler said.

By 1944, the ranks of the Omaha Citizens' Defense Corps had swelled to almost 9,000. The Citizens' Service Corps totaled about 15,200 volunteers.

The city was one of nine regional headquarters for the nationwide civilian defense program directed by New York Mayor Fiorello La Guardia. The center for the Seventh Defense Region was on the eighth floor of the First National Bank Building at 16th and Farnam Streets. Looking back on the intense practice and preparation for a possible attack, some Nebraskans wonder whether the state ever faced any real danger.

"I mean, here we are in Lincoln, Nebraska, and we're talking about air raids," said Andreas.

"Deep down, everyone had to see that there was really nothing we should be worried about," he said. "But, oh boy, you didn't dare say that."

Instead, volunteers on the homefront took their own wartime protocol just as seriously as the soldiers on the front lines did.

Corinne Daly of Omaha was in her early 20s when she volunteered as a member of the ground observer corps. She and about five other people met regularly at night in the basement of the Scoular-Bishop Grain Building at 20th and Dodge Streets to take phone calls from area "spotters."

Watchful farmers, housewives, businessmen and children would call in reports of suspicious activity, including possible enemy aircraft. Daly was one of the call-takers responsible for placing aircraft silhouettes matching the callers' descriptions on a large, glass map.

PAUL ANDREAS, *above on the right and at left in 1994, was in the Civilian Defense Corps and later took part in D-Day.*

"We would plot them using coordinates, so you would know exactly where the planes supposedly were," she said.

Edward A. Becker Jr. of Omaha was also a member of the volunteer ground corps. He said the operation had direct communications with commanders at Fort Crook (now Offutt Air Force Base), and the two agencies worked together to verify reports.

"I don't know how realistic the threat really was, but because Offutt was here, we didn't want to take any chances," he said.

The downfall for Omahans, city leaders repeatedly warned, would be adopting a false sense of security. No one, they said, should be unprepared for an attack.

Children, often in the roles of Junior Commandos, joined in the effort. They collected scrap metal and rubber, contributed pennies for war stamps and received armbands for their participation. Schools adopted guidelines on what to do in case of an attack, and air-raid drills were held regularly. Classes were held to familiarize children with enemy aircraft, and during recess children would often look to the sky to put what they had learned into practice.

"Children definitely picked up the feeling," Becker said. "They couldn't help it. No one could."

But as the Allied victories increased, the need for a large civil defense corps diminished.

Officials of the Seventh Defense Region locked their office doors for the last time in the summer of 1944.

State defense councils and local civil defense units continued to operate, but the glory days of volunteerism dwindled.

Becker said they would always be remembered.

"People were all gung-ho about it," he said. "I mean, when you see posters of Uncle Sam pointing his finger at you, it really got you down deep. I'll never forget it."

THEODORE WICKARD

Town: McCook

Service: Navy, signalman on destroyer USS Welles

In the war: Saw action in Pacific campaigns, including the Philippines, where he engaged in a conversation with an Army officer with "lots of gold on his uniform." Turned out to be Gen. Douglas MacArthur.

In his words: "He introduced himself as Doug and asked me how much I liked the Navy. I told him I was Ted and we stood there and talked a bit. . . . Someone asked me (later) if I knew who I was talking to, and I said all I know is he was Army."

'YOU'RE IN THE ARMY NOW …'

OMAHA MUNICIPAL JUDGE LESTER PALMER administers the oath to four nurses who enlisted in the Army Nurse Corps in 1942. From left, Palmer, Army Capt. Anna Montgomery, Helen Wochek, Agnes Ritter, Isabelle Mefferd and Mae Fisher.

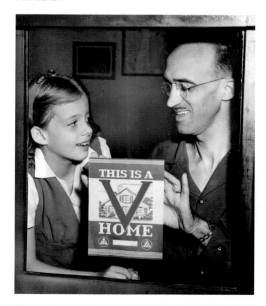

ROBERT PAGE OF OMAHA and daughter Janet display their V-Home sticker, which announces that they are following the recommendations of the civil defense program for safety, security and conservation of resources.

THE AMERICAN FIGHTING SPIRIT at home was symbolized by the "V for victory" campaign. Fifteen-year-old Gene Albanese of Omaha put his patriotism to work at the barbershop, to the enjoyment of his buddy, 14-year-old Bob Ackerman.

FORREST HALVORSEN

Town: Syracuse, Neb.

Service: Army, coast artillery

In the war: Was a communications technician for an artillery unit serving at Pearl Harbor, Canton Island and Saipan.

In his words: "The thing I really missed over there was a drink of cold water. They didn't have ice. I said over there if I ever got home and got thirsty working in the field, I would shut the tractor down, go downtown and get me a malt. And I did, too."

MEMORIES OF A GENERATION ★

CHESTER B. CRAIL

Town: Papillion

Service: U.S. Naval Reserve (Fire Controlman 2nd Class)

In the war: He enlisted in the Naval Reserve in April 1942, four months after the attack on Pearl Harbor. He and three of his buddies wanted revenge for the Japanese sinking of the USS Arizona, because his best buddy's older brother had been aboard the doomed battleship. He had his boot training at Great Lakes Naval Training Station in Illinois. He was then sent to Fire Control School. He later was sent to Miami for three months to help train new officers in the use of large and small naval guns.

In his words: "After all this training, I was finally sent to help commission a ship at Mare Island, Calif., up the bay from San Francisco. I, along with a crew of 200, was going to sail under the flag of the USS Wileman, a destroyer escort. This ship had been used by the British navy. It had been heavily damaged in waters around New Guinea and had limped to Mare Island for major repairs. On arriving to board the ship, I noticed a seaman on a scaffold painting out the letter 'B' on the name of the ship. It had been named BDE-22, but since it was now part of the U.S. Navy, the name was changed to read DE-22, without the 'B' for Britain. As I took my gear to store it below decks, I saw another seaman removing a nameplate near a large storage locker. The nameplate read 'Rum Locker.' I later saw the replacement nameplate, which read '3-inch shells.' This meant that the Brits had enjoyed their rum, but such was not to be for American seamen.

"In fact, in all my two years at sea, I had only one warm beer after playing sandlot baseball on a dinky island called Tarawa, which our Marines had just captured. Our ship helped protect our troops and supply ships throughout the battle areas. These included Wake Island, American Samoa, Pago Pago, New Zealand, Kwajalein, Iwo Jima, Guam and other islands. I was honorably discharged in October 1945 and was shipped back to San Francisco. A friend met us there and offered to buy dinner to celebrate at the Top of the Mark. This was a ritzy restaurant/lounge at the top of the Mark Hopkins Hotel, from whose windows one could look out in all directions and see the whole city, the bay and waterfront. But after ordering our beverages, we looked out the windows in dismay because all we could see was a San Francisco fog as thick as pea soup. I am proud of my service to the good old USA, a country that I dearly love."

LEE GEIER

Town: Omaha

Service: 551st Air Engineering Squad 24th Service Group

In the war: Geier enlisted in September 1940 and was stationed in Puerto Rico for 23 months in the 25th Air Depot, repairing and testing planes. He also spent nine months in Guam in the 247th Maintenance Group. Geier enjoyed the Puerto Rican weather but said he was lonely, missed his then-fiancee (future wife, Monica) and found himself drinking rum during his time off.

In his words: Geier and his crew worked 32 hours straight on a C-47/DC3, changing both the engines, taking the starters, generators and exhaust mechanisms off the old engines and putting them on the new before testing them for four hours. The next morning Geier and his buddies were going to fly the plane to San Juan for some fun. "Something told me, 'Don't goof off, get off and wait for the afternoon airplanes because they would need to be worked on.' So we (he and a buddy) got off while the plane was taxiing down the runway." About an hour and a half later, Geier learned the pilot got off course, went into the wrong valley and could not clear a mountain on the other side. All 23 men onboard died. "I think the normal instinct is you get the chance to goof off a little, you goof off. Somebody was looking out for me."

PHYLLIS SCHUPBACH

Hometown: Lincoln

Service: Navy WAVES

In the war: She volunteered for the Navy's all-female service while a University of Nebraska student. She first served in New York as a mail clerk, then in San Francisco as a clerk in the Fleet Post Office.

In her words: "Everyone was contributing to the war effort, and I thought this was something I could do. . . . We were sent to New York City to boot camp in the Bronx, where we were for six weeks. . . . We worked as mail clerks until Christmastime, another six or eight weeks, and then I was sent with maybe 15 or 20 other girls to San Francisco. . . . It took a week in a Pullman. The men in the Fleet Post Office were not very happy to see us, because we were replacing them so they could go off to fight in the Pacific. The war there was getting pretty bad. . . . Overall, it was a great experience. I hurt my back lifting big mailbags in the post office, though. They would bring the bags up the elevators, through these big doors, and Marines would bang them down. We'd pick them up and put them on the conveyor belt and sort the mail."

MARY MCLENDON

Town: Omaha

Service: Army Nurse Corps

In the war: When Pearl Harbor was bombed on Dec. 7, 1941, McLendon was a student nurse at Immanuel School of Nursing in Omaha. Student nurses filled many vacancies on the staff when many nurses went to war. Upon graduation, she enlisted in the Army Nurse Corps as a second lieutenant-reserve. She began her Army career at Camp Carson, Colo., where nurses were trained. From there, she was sent to Camp Crowder in Neosho, Mo., where she was assigned to the 57th Field Hospital unit. The 57th served in Scotland, England, France and Germany. Her tour of duty lasted two years. She became a first lieutenant before leaving the service.

In her words: "The war ended and we were sent home. It was then that I learned of the shortages that existed during the war. . . . The war's end was a great time, but also a sad time because of the many who gave their lives, the many requiring hospitalization because of war injuries. . . . Many marriages and elopements occurred during the war. Sailors, soldiers home on leave or waiting for assignments overseas married and then left for their duty. At my sister's wedding, the attendants and ushers were female because of the shortage of men. The only men in the wedding party were her husband, his best man and the minister. . . . Rehabilitation of the wounded veterans and handicapped people opened up new fields in medicine. Physical, occupational and speech therapists used their skills to restore returning veterans to an active life."

TOM SELZLE

Town: Omaha

Service: Staff sergeant, 8th Air Force, 401st Bomber Group, B-17 tail gunner

In the war: Selzle enlisted in the Army Air Forces in June 1942. His mother was less than pleased, as she had already lost two other sons to illness. He started out flying PT-19's in pilot training in San Antonio. Because of depth perception problems, he was eventually transferred to B-17 aerial gunnery school in Pyote, Texas. There he set a base record for gunnery accuracy. In March 1944, Selzle and his crew were shipped to Deenethorpe, England. He flew 30 missions over Germany, dodging fighters and intense flak. His B-17 once was shot up badly and lost power in two of the four engines. Thanks to an American P-51 fighter escort, though, he and the crew were able to return to England safely. By the time he finished his tour in June 1945, Selzle had earned three Bronze Stars, four Oak Leaf Clusters and an Air Medal.

In his words: "We were young then, and we felt invincible. If anything bad was to happen, it would be to some other guy. Overall, though, I felt I had it good compared to other soldiers. Between missions, most of the time was my own. I had three meals a day and a warm place to sleep. Everyone contributed to the war effort back then. My dad was an air raid warden. My mom and sister Catherine worked at the bomber plant at Fort Crook, and my other sister Betty was an Army nurse."

RICHARD D. EARL

Town: Lincoln

Service: U.S. Army

In the war: Served with the 24th Division Field Artillery, S1-S4.

In his words: "On Jan. 4, 1942, Col. Fred Gardner, professor of military science and tactics at the University of Nebraska, inducted all junior and senior ROTC cadets into the U.S. Army. We bunked in four-high beds in Love Library and ate in the Student Union. Got Pfc. (private first class) pay after a trip to Omaha for physicals and uniforms. Next it was renovating Camp Funston at Fort Riley, Kan., then on to OCS (officer candidate school) at Fort Sill, Okla. After being commissioned, spent time at Fort Sill as an instructor, then on to Fort Bragg, N.C., where we taught motor mechanics and refurbished all the vehicles for the units going overseas. I was selected to go to Camp Gordon at Augusta, Ga., to build infiltration courses using live Japanese weapons, at the request of Gen. 'Vinegar Joe' Stilwell, commander of the China-Burma-India Theater. We later went to a replacement center in Hollandia, New Guinea, where I was detailed as assistant S1-S4 to the 24th Division Field Artillery. Months of island hopping landed us in the Manila area preparing to invade Japan . . . when the bombs were dropped. The 24th was slated to be first onshore on the island of Shikoku, so this was where we first touched Japanese soil. On the big island of Honshu, we were responsible for about an 80-mile area from Kobe to Okinawa. In addition to war materiel destruction, we also repatriated Koreans and provided some air traffic to corporate headquarters in Kyoto. My last move was again to Fukuoka on the South Island. I then came home to my wife, Helen (Preditt) Earl, and family, arriving on the Burlington on Aug. 26, 1946."

Fighting back

PRESIDENT ROOSEVELT BELIEVED IT WAS CRUCIAL to strike Japan, which Japanese warlords had said was protected by a "divine wind." ★ On Feb. 1, 1942, Lt. Col. James H. Doolittle went to an airfield near Columbia, S.C., looking for volunteers for a secret and perilous mission. Two-and-a-half months later, 80 men took on the challenge. ★ Their bold raid on Tokyo didn't do all that much physical damage, but it was a boost to U.S. morale. ★ "People talk about sacrifice and commitment," said Bob Joyce, son of Doolittle Raider Richard O. Joyce. "For people in my generation, life has been pretty comfortable. I've never been in the situation where I've had to make the kind of sacrifices and commitment those guys made."

Lt. Col. James H. Doolittle (in dark cap at far left) gathers his raiders together in 1942. 1st Lt. Richard O. Joyce of Lincoln is highlighted to the right of Doolittle.

AUDREY WOLFE

Town: Lincoln

Service: Army, medic with 40th Division, 185th Infantry

In the war: Went into Guadalcanal for mop-up duty before making three beach landings in the Philippines.

In his words: "The worst fighting was on Luzon. We went in under a lot of fire. I was a medic, so I was pretty busy. … Our own planes bombed us one night, and that was the only wound I got. Shrapnel in the arm. I didn't even report it. I treated myself."

'One of the most daring air missions of all times'

DOOLITTLE'S RAID TOUCHED OFF a wave of confidence across an America that had barely recovered from the shock of Pearl Harbor.

The U.S. planes materialized out of the blue Pacific to strike at Tokyo and other large cities of Japan with their bombs. In so doing, the United States made clear that despite the crushing blow at Pearl Harbor and the relatively easy conquests of Wake Island, the Philippines and southeast Asia, Japan was vulnerable.

It was on April 18, 1942, that the Tokyo raiders took off in heavy seas from the flight deck of the USS Hornet, a Navy aircraft carrier, and struck military targets for the first time in the heart of Japan. Eighty officers and enlisted men flying in 16 B-25 medium-size bombers participated in the raid.

RICHARD O. JOYCE

Richard O. Joyce, a first lieutenant at the time, was pilot of one of the planes. Another Lincoln man, Sgt. Donald E. Fitzmaurice, gunner on another B-25, lost his life when he was believed to have drowned after crash-landing in a lake in China. Six other crewmen were killed in the raid and 12 others died in crashes and other combat action after returning from the mission.

Joyce said he had first encountered James H. Doolittle, then a lieutenant colonel, as Doolittle was seeking volunteers from B-25 crewmen flying anti-submarine patrols off the East Coast.

"I was stationed in Columbia. S.C.," said Joyce. "Colonel Doolittle came through on February 1 and asked for volunteers. I figured, 'What the hell, why not?' "

Preparations for the mission required not only the skill and daring of the best military planners, but also the utmost care in working out every detail of the flight. It was the first time medium-size bombers in numbers had taken off from the deck of a Navy carrier. The B-25 was selected as the most practical plane for the job.

The reliable two-engine plane had a range of 1,950 miles for a bomb load of 2,000 pounds. A 500-pound demolition bomb and a cluster of 128 incendiary bombs were selected for the payload. Other armament consisted of from 700 to 900 rounds of .50 caliber ammunition and about the same amount of .30 caliber. Several weeks were spent in preparation, during which time the crews, the ground maintenance men, armorers and other technicians were trained together. The Navy sent a carrier pilot to Eglin Field, Fla., site of training, to advise the B-25 crew on carrier operations and help in takeoff instruction.

A number of modifications were required to make the B-25 useful for the mission.

Those included:

- Removal of the lower gun turret and installation of a plate over the hole to avert possible mechanical troubles with the turret.

- Installation of two metal gasoline tanks and one collapsible rubber tank.

- Increasing capacity of one tank by 10 to 15 gallons through air pressure, and storing 10 five-gallon tanks in a rear compartment, giving a total gasoline capacity of 1,141 gallons.

- Installation of anti-icers and de-icers on each plane (a requirement that proved useless when the Soviet Union refused to let the planes land in Russia).

- Replacing Norden bombsights with simplified sights for low-level bombing.

- Removal of liaison radio sets.

- Equipping each flight leader with small, automatic, electrically operated cameras.

Using white lines on a runway at Eglin Field to measure the takeoff distance aboard a carrier, the fliers concentrated on takeoffs in a minimum distance. Joyce said crew members (five to a plane) pored over maps, pictures and silhouettes, learning to recognize instantaneously the features of the routes they were to travel over Japan and the objectives they were to bomb. After negotiations had been completed with Nationalist China to permit the planes to land on a makeshift, crushed-rock runway in the Chinese interior, final plans were made.

The planes were flown to Sacramento, Calif., where new propellers were installed. Joyce and his crew flew their B-25 from Sacramento to San Francisco, where it was placed on the Hornet.

By 1945, James H. Doolittle was a general.

"En route I flew under the Golden Gate Bridge," said Joyce, who later was president of Henkle & Joyce, a Lincoln wholesale hardware company. "I just thought to myself, 'Let 'em call us now for violating air regulations.' "

A large task force guided the Hornet out of San Francisco Bay and into the open waters of the Pacific Ocean. "I couldn't help but wonder that we must have attracted attention," Joyce said. "It must have been a strange sight, seeing 16 B-25s sitting on the deck of a Navy carrier."

The bombers occupied 400 of the 800 feet of take-off space on the carrier. Original plans were to proceed through hazardous Japanese coastal waters to a point within 400 miles of Tokyo. There the planes were to be launched at about 5 p.m. on April 18. But when the Hornet was still 800 miles from Tokyo, an enemy patrol spotted the vessel. The enemy was sunk, but it was feared that the Japanese sailors might have warned their homeland defense forces by radio.

Joyce said that after the war, American military officials learned that the patrol ship had radioed a warning. "But the warning was not heeded by air defense crews in Tokyo," he said. "So what we had was a Pearl Harbor in reverse."

Instead of waiting until 5 p.m., the B-25s took off 10 hours ahead of schedule. The distance to be flown added to the hazards of the mission. At the time of the takeoff, each pilot was told to fly to the target and ditch his plane in the water and take to a rubber boat if he could not fly to the Chinese coast.

The sea was rough on the morning of April 18, Joyce recalled. "One by one, the bombers roared down the pitching, rolling deck and off into the sky," he said. "My B-25 was the ninth to take off, Colonel Doolittle's the first."

Joyce said no effort was made to fly the planes in a group. It was each plane for itself. The Lincoln pilot's target was the Japanese Special Steel Company in south Tokyo.

"We had a two-mile bomb run and by the time we reached Tokyo, there were plenty of anti-aircraft fire and fighter squadrons to welcome our entrance over the city."

After dumping his bombs, Joyce headed southwest, twice flying under fighter planes. "I finally found a cloud and lost them," he said. "It was then 'China, here we come.' "

The fliers were aided by unusual wind conditions. In pre-raid briefings, the pilots had been told to expect a 20 mph headwind all the way to the targets and on to the Chinese coast. This headwind did exist all the way to Tokyo for Dick Joyce and his crew, but after dropping their bombs and setting a course for China, they suddenly had the assist of a 30 mph tailwind. The difference in wind conditions meant an additional 50 miles for every hour they winged toward Chinese-held territory. Most of the B-25s, during the eight hours they were helped by this unexpected tailwind, covered 400 miles more than Doolittle had anticipated, making a total flown of nearly 2,400 miles.

Unable to reach Chinese airfields, crews of 12 of the planes, including Joyce's crew, bailed out over China from altitudes of 6,000 to 10,000 feet. Three others made crash landings on the Chinese coast and one plane landed in Russia, where the crew was interned. Joyce had his greatest scare of the flight when he, the last of his crew, bailed out.

"It was pitch dark," he said. "And as I came down I kept hearing the plane. It sounded as though it was coming right at me and that I would be chopped to bits."

Joyce became separated from the other crewmen and was forced to live on candy bars most of the next seven days. "I had one bite per meal," he said.

His destination was Heng Yang, where the crewmen were to assemble and be flown to Chungking. Joyce had difficulty finding his way, because he couldn't communicate with the Chinese mountain inhabitants. Mostly through sign language, he found trails that led to freedom.

"I never knew whether the Japs were nearby, but I've always had a feeling they were," Joyce said. "I was befriended by an English-speaking physician who had a hospital in the countryside near Heng Yang. He probably did more than anyone in seeing that I reached my destination."

After the raid, Joyce "flew the Hump" in the China-Burma-India Theater. He returned to the United States near the end of 1942 following the death of his father. He was reassigned to an air base in the United States and was discharged a lieutenant colonel. He and all members of the Tokyo mission received the Distinguished Flying Cross.

Recalling the experience, Joyce said, "It probably was one of the most daring air missions of all times. It took a man like Doolittle to make it a success."

ROBERT CHATT

Town: Tekamah

Service: B-25 bomber pilot with the 90th Squadron, 3rd Group, 5th Air Force; 1941 to 1946

In the war: He received his wings from James H. Doolittle at Kelly Field in San Antonio. He flew 64 missions in the South Pacific before returning to the United States. He was sent to Command and General Staff School and the Air Force Staff School before going to the Pentagon. He retired as a major and returned to Tekamah in 1946.

In his words: "The biggest battle I took part in was the Battle of the Bismarck Sea. On March 3, 1943, I took off at 8:40 a.m. and got into formation with 12 B-25 bombers. We hadn't been flying very long when we went over a cloud bank. … We started to dive and as we came down we could see more of the sea, and as far as we could see, there were ships of all kinds. We were probably seven to 10 miles from them at the time. We went into echelon and kept diving at about 2,000 feet. We began to peel off, and the battle was on.

"Each bomber started after a ship. I had decided that if I could fight my way to a warship, I could sink it. I doubted that I could get in, and I knew if I did, I'd never get out so I thought I might as well make it worthwhile. I picked a large destroyer and started my run. We were doing about 300 mph and low on the water. The big ships couldn't depress their guns down low enough to hit us. We had our 50-caliber guns red hot. … We dropped our bombs and pulled the plane up over the masts and slapped it right down over the water again. Two of our bombs skipped right into the bow of the boat and two others landed on the deck. The two on the deck completely cleaned it of all superstructure, the bridge masts and the guns. The two that hit the water lifted it out of the water and turned it 90 degrees from its original course, and it came to a complete stop, and the bow was almost all underwater. The ship sank 22 minutes later."

'I didn't have time to worry'

B-25 CREW (from left): pilot Ted Lawson, co-pilot Dean Davenport, navigator Charles McClure, bombardier Robert Clever and flight engineer David Thatcher. Lawson's book, "Thirty Seconds Over Tokyo," told of the crew's involvement in Doolittle's Raid.

DAVID THATCHER in 2011

FOR DAVID THATCHER, the 2011 reunion of Doolittle's Raiders in Nebraska was a homecoming.

An Army enlistee, he completed a five-month airplane and engine mechanic course in Lincoln shortly after the Pearl Harbor attack. He and others from the 17th Bomb Group squadrons bunked at the downtown YMCA and walked to mechanics school.

Thatcher, along with the four other surviving co-pilots and crewmen from the raid, gathered at the Strategic Air & Space Museum near Ashland. Raider Richard O. Joyce's sons, Bob of Omaha and Todd of Louisville, Neb., organized the 2011 reunion. The survivors have met almost every year since the late 1940s and had last gathered in Nebraska in 1976 at Offutt Air Force Base.

Thatcher said he has fond memories of his Nebraska training.

"I could go out in the country and hear the corn growing," the Montana native said. "I enjoyed the State Capitol lit up at night. That was really something."

The soldiers marched to Memorial Stadium one Saturday in October 1941 and watched coach Biff Jones' Nebraska Cornhuskers beat Kansas 32-0. (Jones, a former Army major, gave up coaching the Huskers after the season when recalled to service.)

Thatcher's pilot on Doolittle's Raid was Lt. Ted Lawson. He wrote the first account of the raid, "Thirty Seconds Over Tokyo," which was adapted into an Academy Award-winning movie in 1944. Their plane, nicknamed the Ruptured Duck, flew southwest along Japan's east coast before turning west toward China. After about 13 hours in the air, Lawson attempted a landing during a rainstorm in the dark on a Chinese island beach. The bomber flipped tail over nose and came to rest upside down in shallow water.

Thatcher was briefly knocked unconscious in the back of the aircraft. The four others were tossed out of the bomber and badly injured. Lawson and the co-pilot still were strapped to their armor-plated seats. Thatcher opened the escape hatch in the bomber's floor — now above his head — and scrambled out.

Chinese villagers helped the crew that night and the next day rigged bamboo pallets to carry the injured Americans. Most of the crews that came down in China made it to safety with the help of Chinese civilians and soldiers.

"It took us two days to cross the islands and get to free territory and a hospital in Lenhai on the mainland," Thatcher said. "We found out later that the Japanese landed 65 soldiers on the island to find us, but we had a head start. They never found us. If not for the Chinese, we would have been taken prisoner, I'm sure."

Nearly seven decades after his first combat mission, Thatcher recalled his lack of anxiety swooping in over Japan.

"I didn't have time to worry about it."

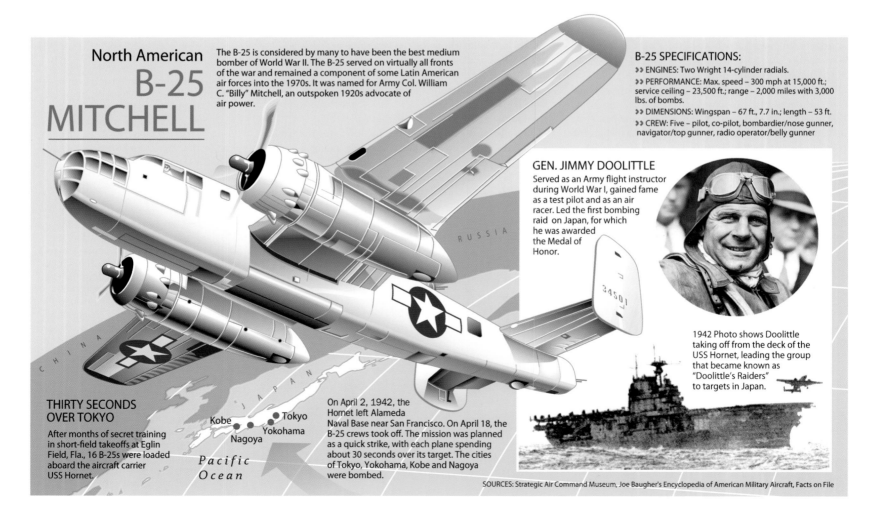

North American
B-25
MITCHELL

The B-25 is considered by many to have been the best medium bomber of World War II. The B-25 served on virtually all fronts of the war and remained a component of some Latin American air forces into the 1970s. It was named for Army Col. William C. "Billy" Mitchell, an outspoken 1920s advocate of air power.

B-25 SPECIFICATIONS:
›› ENGINES: Two Wright 14-cylinder radials.
›› PERFORMANCE: Max. speed – 300 mph at 15,000 ft.; service ceiling – 23,500 ft.; range – 2,000 miles with 3,000 lbs. of bombs.
›› DIMENSIONS: Wingspan – 67 ft., 7.7 in.; length – 53 ft.
›› CREW: Five – pilot, co-pilot, bombardier/nose gunner, navigator/top gunner, radio operator/belly gunner

GEN. JIMMY DOOLITTLE
Served as an Army flight instructor during World War I, gained fame as a test pilot and as an air racer. Led the first bombing raid on Japan, for which he was awarded the Medal of Honor.

1942 Photo shows Doolittle taking off from the deck of the USS Hornet, leading the group that became known as "Doolittle's Raiders" to targets in Japan.

RUSSIA

CHINA

JAPAN

THIRTY SECONDS OVER TOKYO
After months of secret training in short-field takeoffs at Eglin Field, Fla., 16 B-25s were loaded aboard the aircraft carrier USS Hornet.

Kobe
Tokyo
Nagoya
Yokohama

Pacific Ocean

On April 2, 1942, the Hornet left Alameda Naval Base near San Francisco. On April 18, the B-25 crews took off. The mission was planned as a quick strike, with each plane spending about 30 seconds over its target. The cities of Tokyo, Yokohama, Kobe and Nagoya were bombed.

SOURCES: Strategic Air Command Museum, Joe Baugher's Encyclopedia of American Military Aircraft, Facts on File

Battle of Midway a turning point

BILL BROOKS WAS A 23-year-old Marine Corps pilot on June 4, 1942, the day he spent 80 minutes in a fierce air battle over Midway Island in the Pacific Ocean.

He piloted a Brewster F2A-3, also known as a "Brewster Buffalo," a plane that was no match for the speed and agility of Japanese Zeros. Four cannon holes the size of volleyballs scarred his plane. Bullet holes — 72 in all — pocked it. Bul-

BILL BROOKS in 2010

lets flew into his cockpit and over his shoulders before lodging in the instrument panel.

They also blew out the tires because the plane's wheels had failed to retract fully after takeoff, according to the pilots' logs filed after the battle. Brooks took shrapnel in his leg and was awarded the Purple Heart.

The Allied victory at Midway Island marked an important turning point in the Pacific campaign, but the toll was grim.

Only eight of the 25 pilots in Brooks' squadron survived. Just two of the 25 Brewster Buffaloes that took off in the morning could be flown afterward.

Brooks also flew in the historic Battle of Guadalcanal a few months later.

Asked if he was scared either time, he would respond, "I was too busy to be scared."

"He was so humble about it," Bruce Belgum of Omaha, his son-in-law, said in 2010 of Brooks' military accomplishments.

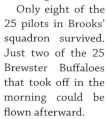

BROOKS FLEW A "Brewster Buffalo," pictured with him, at the Battle of Midway.

Brooks, who grew up in Falls City, Neb., worked in the Civilian Conservation Corps during the Great Depression. He quit his studies at Peru State Teachers College to enlist during World War II. Later, he returned to college to finish his bachelor's degree, and he earned a master's degree from the University of Oklahoma.

After the war, he and his family moved to Bellevue, where he helped found Bellevue's Chamber of Commerce, Bellevue College (now Bellevue University) and Midlands Hospital.

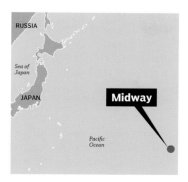

Midway

'Somebody has to go first ...'

IT WAS A HARROWING STORY, but one that Robert R. Sheehan liked to repeat.

He was a petty officer aboard the U.S. aircraft carrier Yorktown in June 1942. The Yorktown was engaged against the Japanese in the Battle of Midway during World War II.

Enemy airplanes bombed the Yorktown, crippling it. The crew got the ship going, only to see it hit again an hour later. With the ship listing badly, the order went out: Abandon ship.

Recalling his stories in 2004, Peg Gallagher said her brother always had been a strong swimmer.

"When we realized the ship was sinking," Gallagher said, repeating Sheehan's tale, "one of the officers said somebody has to go first. So I went first."

Sheehan attended Omaha's Creighton Prep and Central High but enlisted in the Navy in the mid-1930s before receiving a diploma.

In early June 1942, the Yorktown and other U.S. ships were near Midway Island expecting to engage the Japanese fleet. And they did.

"As the torpedoes hit, three terrific explosions occurred, and the ship listed at almost a 45-degree angle," Sheehan wrote to his mother in a letter published in The World-Herald three months after the battle. "Word was passed to abandon ship. ... Swam toward the nearest ship, but it seemed ages before I was picked up."

After the war, Sheehan, a Navy meteorologist, was sent to a Naval weather station in Norman, Okla. He retired from the Navy in the 1950s, after 20 years in the service.

CHARLES F. PATTON

Town: Bellevue

Service: Navy

In the war: Joined the Navy at age 18. Was assigned to aircraft carriers and flew in fighter planes as a radioman/gunner. Assigned to the CV-7 Wasp aircraft carrier and was in the air when it was torpedoed and sank in the Battle of the Coral Sea. He then was sent to Guadalcanal. After the war, he flew as a radioman on transports and later as a radioman/radar operator on surveillance missions out of the Philippines, Iceland and Newfoundland.

In his words: (As told to his wife, Mary) "When I was on the Wasp aircraft carrier, my pilots and I were on a mission looking for Japanese planes and ships. When we returned to the Wasp, we could see that it was on fire. It had been torpedoed. We flew on. There was another carrier, the Hornet, in the area. We landed on that carrier, and from there we flew into Guadalcanal."

'It was all I could do to remain sane'

THERE WAS MORE THAN WIND rustling the palms that New Year's Eve in 1942. The steamy Guadalcanal air also carried the mournful strains of a bugle.

Among the listeners was Peter H. McDonald, the lanky, likable carrot-top who ran the mail operation for the Army's 164th Infantry Regiment.

"At the cemetery here today, we had a most impressive service for those boys laying there & those in the hills who gave their lives in the battle of Guadalcanal," the sergeant from Devils Lake, N.D., wrote in his diary.

"I shall always remember today when I hear taps. It was beautifully played in final tribute today."

It had been 11 cavity-loosening weeks since the North Dakota National Guard unit had landed on Guadalcanal, welcomed by the Marines, who had established a toehold on the island.

Guadalcanal

The men of the 164th had experienced death from the beginning, losing their first comrade in a bombing raid just hours after their dawn landing on Oct. 13.

McDonald came close to getting killed that first day. A 16-inch naval shell hit 8 feet behind his hole, throwing him 20 feet and covering him with dirt. Bloodied and bruised, he scampered back to the hole.

"Next morning I looked at the hole," he wrote, and "it scared the hell out of me."

On that New Year's Eve, McDonald was thankful his number had not yet been called.

"To God — who has seen me through this hell," he wrote in his flowing cursive, "I shall try to live up to you, & repay that which I can for giving me my life as yet."

To his parents, a plea for them not to worry.

And to a girl back home who had hold of his heart at the time, he wished nothing but happiness. "Guess I am just extremely unfortunate in being still so much in love with you that all others will forever be meaningless."

McDonald would spend 2½ more years in the South Pacific, finally rotating out in June 1945.

He would not go on to become a writer. He would, in fact, go on to become a hotelier in the small town of Rolla, N.D., operating the T.M. Hotel with his wife, Patricia, for nearly four decades until his death in June 1992.

But in three sturdy, hard-cover diaries, whose age is betrayed only by slightly yellowing pages and creased covers, the bespectacled sergeant turned his green eyes inward and produced a wartime account so vivid that the bombs can practically still be heard whistling to earth.

"One can feel every single one driving right into his own back: The ground heaves with each burst & it was all I could do to remain sane that 1st raid," he wrote on Oct. 13.

"We hug the ground & feel like we are floating 10 ft. in the air, you just know you are."

Such was the confusion and terror that day that some members of the 164th sought cover in an old Japanese latrine, finding themselves in dung up to their knees.

Upon his death, Patricia gave the diaries to the couple's son, Mike McDonald of Omaha.

Peter McDonald, who was awarded two Bronze Stars for valor, was one of those veterans who didn't talk much about the ugliness of combat. He, like many others, took the awful World War II recollections to his grave. History books can recount the battles, which ended more than 65 years ago. And Hollywood can bring the war to the big screen with pictures like "Saving Private Ryan" and "The Thin Red Line," a movie about Guadalcanal.

But it's through the words of the veterans that the war, in all its unvarnished horror, can truly be understood.

For Mike McDonald, his dad's service was something of a mystery.

"If you asked him, 'Did you ever kill anybody?' — which is a natural question a kid is going to ask his father, you know — right away, he would always say, 'Not to my knowledge,' whatever that means," he said in 1999.

"That was always his answer, it was never any different. So whatever he had there, he just kept to himself.

"And I know he must have lost a lot of friends during that period of time — he would have had to — and he never talked about that, either. But I'm sure he missed a lot of people, because that kind of friendship is hard for us to imagine. ... I know there had to have been missing pieces in his life."

Guadalcanal was 2,500 square miles of purgatory.

Malarial mosquitoes swarmed the place. Rats ran around soggy, stinking jungles. Prickly grass as tall as a man grew where there was no jungle.

PETER MCDONALD passed on his wartime diary and other memorabilia to his son.

SAM ITALIA

Town: Omaha

Service: Army Air Forces, 13th Air Force, 29th Air Service Group

In the war: Personnel sergeant major for three years, inspecting all clerical work, such as payroll records and promotions paperwork. Stationed in Guadalcanal, other islands, then the Philippines.

In his words: "We had air raids every day. We had foxholes deep enough to stand up in, and we'd sit in there and wait for the all-clear. The Japanese would drop bombs on us and they'd strafe us, too."

"I hardly remember the trip back — only watching out so as not to step on dead (Japanese) laying all over. They look horrible in the half moonlight sprawled in all sorts of shapes — eyes open seeing nothing."

— A PASSAGE FROM
PETER H. MCDONALD'S
WARTIME DIARY

DON STELLA
Town: Ralston
Service: Marines,
2nd Division

In the war: Rifleman fought during mop-up on Guadalcanal and was part of the invasion of the Solomon Islands.

In his words: "It was scary. We hit the beach and dug in. ... We were young and it was the war. The mood was just different then. When they attacked us, it just stopped everything. Everyone wanted to be in the service."

And there was the heat, always the heat. It was in this environment that some of the most bitter fighting of World War II took place.

Marines landed on Guadalcanal in August 1942, seizing a Japanese airfield. Through seven months of hard fighting, American forces drove the enemy from the island, knocking Tokyo back on its heels.

On Guadalcanal, the Japanese lost nearly 25,000 men through fighting, illness or capture. American casualties, borne largely by the Marines, numbered 1,600 killed and 4,245 wounded.

Hundreds of men from the 164th, which won the lasting admiration of the Marines for its tough fighting, were among the dead and wounded.

McDonald had two days on Guadalcanal where a grave seemed an almost welcome escape.

Usually stationed behind the front lines, McDonald was part of a team ordered to resupply troops on Matanikau Ridge, a devil of a place where the Japanese and Americans were eyeball to eyeball.

Lugging mortar shells, machine-gun rounds and 5-gallon water cans in jungle heat, the unit made two trips up and back the night of Nov. 21, 1942. Their route took them into the no man's land between American and Japanese lines.

"You get so tired you walk by habit uphill & down — stumble — get up & walk some more," he wrote.

"So tired you don't give a damn whether they kill you or not — almost wish they would to end the misery. I passed out cold once — thought my heart would burst my chest — can't breathe. ..."

"I hardly remember the trip back — only watching out so as not to step on dead (Japanese) laying all over," he continued. "They look horrible in the half moonlight sprawled in all sorts of shapes — eyes open seeing nothing."

When Mike got the diaries in 1992, he used them as bedtime stories for his son Dan, who was 12 at the time. Together, they filled in the blanks that Peter McDonald never did while he was living.

Coming of age in the 1960s, Mike didn't always see eye to eye with his pop, the man who saw no shades of gray — just black and white. Later in life, father and son became close.

The war, Mike said, molded his father. It made him courageous and patriotic. It defined him.

"He was just an ordinary person from a small town . . . who got caught in the whirlwinds of war, and it changed him and made him who he was."

MEMORIES OF A GENERATION ★

RALPH SMITH

Town: Omaha

Service: Navy, 107th Construction Battalion (Seabees)

In the war: Built bases and airstrips on islands that had been recaptured from the Japanese.

In his words: "We worked night and day to build bases for the B-29s. We built the largest air base in the world on Tinian. That's where the atomic bomb took off from, if you know your history. . . . I can say we were pretty proud of what we did. We ended the war and accomplished a lot of things."

FRANK L. MARKS

Town: Ralston

Service: F Company, 2nd Battalion, 35th Infantry Regiment, 25th Infantry Division

In the war: He was an infantry soldier who fought in the Pacific. At Guadalcanal, his division was sent to relieve Marines who had been fighting the Japanese for months. His division was then nicknamed Tropic Lightning for its quick success in taking the island from the Japanese. He also participated in the invasions of Vella Lavella in the Solomon Islands and Luzon in the Philippines.

In his words: "For the combat on Guadalcanal, I got a Bronze Star. I was wounded twice (by shrapnel). After the war, I went and located 567 men out of 700 that went through our company, and we formed an association and had reunions. We made friendships in the Army, and the boys we were with, we were closer to each other than blood relatives. When we talk about the movie 'Band of Brothers,' that's what we were."

CLAUDIO ORSI

Town: Omaha

Service: Army Air Forces, 13th Air Force, 5th Bomb Group, 394th Bomb Squadron

In the war: Served as a radio operator and tail gunner on a B-24. Flew 43 missions, including a 16-hour mission to bomb oilfields in Borneo.

In his words: "After we dropped our bombs, we threw everything out of the airplane: machine guns, flak suits, everything. Then we all moved up front. We got back. When we did, we had about 15 minutes of gasoline left. ... I'd say half of the planes didn't make it back."

JEROME KUDRON

Town: Columbus

Service: Navy, escort carrier USS Shamrock Bay

In the war: Served as machinist in many Pacific campaigns, including Philippines, Iwo Jima and Okinawa.

In his words: "Our planes did a lot of strafing and bombing in the South Pacific. I didn't even know half the time, because I was working below decks. ... We were young, and we didn't care. We wanted to get this war over with, so we could head home. I'm thankful we all went in and got the job done."

JOHN P. KAISER

Town: Omaha

Service: U.S. Navy; boiler tender, second class. He joined the Navy in February 1942. He had boot training at San Diego and was sent to Pearl Harbor, where he went aboard his first ship. He spent all his service time in the Pacific and was in the Battle of Midway, served at Guadalcanal and in other engagements. He served on three destroyers: the USS Benham, the USS Hoel and the USS Albert W. Grant. He also served on the cruiser USS Helena. He was discharged in St. Louis in October 1945. He returned home and went to work for the Metropolitan Utilities District at the Florence Pumping Station, retiring after 41 years.

In his words: "I went aboard my first ship, the Benham DD-397, the first of May (1942). It was operating with Task Force No. 16, the Enterprise and Hornet aircraft carriers. The first engagement was the Battle of Midway, June 4-7, 1942. The next action was the Guadalcanal campaign, Aug. 7, 1942. Was in the Solomon area and took part in a battle on the night of Nov. 15, 1942, in which the Benham was sunk and survivors were rescued by the destroyer Gwin and taken to New Caledonia. At that time, I was sent to the cruiser Helena. Was on it from end of November to April 1943. Was sent back to the States in April, came home on leave, and after leave was assigned to the destroyer Hoel being built at Hunters Point in San Francisco. It was commissioned July 1943. I was part of her crew when it was sunk in the Philippines.

"When I went into the Navy, I had dropped out of school. I had gone to Tech High. I decided I could go into the war and get some sort of education. I don't think at 17 you really know what war is all about until you get there."

HELEN BETTE W. WALLACE

Town: Kentfield, Calif. She grew up in the Elmwood Park area of Omaha.

Service: Women's Army Corps (WAC)

In the war: To avoid being drafted, her husband, Joseph B. Wallace, started taking flight training, and she took a job as receptionist and stenographer in the president's office at the University of California, Berkeley. There she had the opportunity to meet Eleanor Roosevelt and WAC Director Oveta Culp Hobby, who had come to visit the university's president. When the Battle of Midway began and things were looking bad, she decided to join the WAC without even telling her husband or family. She arrived in Fort Des Moines by train the day before Thanksgiving 1942 and spent three months learning to be a soldier. She was in a staging area with her company waiting to be sent to Washington, D.C., but before she left, she was invited to go through officers training. She accepted and spent three more months in training at Fort Des Moines. She became a second lieutenant and was assigned to the service command based in Omaha.

In her words: "The commander sent me to Cedar Rapids, Iowa, to be a recruiter — no easy assignment since Iowa was 'isolationist.' Those who volunteered wanted to join the Navy and see the world, not fight in the trenches. I finally got leave and went to see my husband, who was still in training. Guess what? I got pregnant! The service command asked me to report to Omaha once the pregnancy tests were positive. They didn't know what to do with me. I was their first pregnant WAC in the area, I think. No mommas allowed in the Army then. After six weeks of waiting in a hotel in Omaha, I was given an honorable discharge and I went back to California in 1944 — half sorry, half glad. My husband had graduated and was assigned to train pilots in King City, Calif. Because he was 26½ years old, he was considered too old to fly in combat. While waiting for my child to be born in King City, I climbed the tower stairs of the local hotel to watch for enemy planes every day. I already knew the insignia of various planes."

HOMER SARGENT

Town: Scottsbluff

Service: U.S. Navy Seabees, November 1942 to January 1946

In the war: He was in a transportation area with 1,100 men in the 71st Battalion of the Navy Seabees. He joined as a truck driver with the rank of fireman 1st class. By the time of his discharge, he was promoted to the rank of machinist's mate 3rd class. His battalion moved in detachments of 100 men with the advancing Marines to build and repair roads and equipment. "The Marines couldn't move without us," he said. His battalion also ran a tire shop, where in peak periods the men worked 12-hour shifts to survey truck, Jeep and road-grader tires for shrapnel and other damage. He served in Guadalcanal, Bougainville, the Admiralty Islands and Okinawa.

In his words: "My favorite experience was an appendectomy in a foxhole on Bougainville. The surgery was in a constructed area with coconut trees for the roof and sides. Light was provided by Coleman lanterns. The doctor gave me a spinal and told me to hold the top from a C ration box so I could not watch him. It took longer, and a corpsman gave needle shots for the pain as the spinal wore down. I laid on a cot two days before joining my buddies. A lot of shots were given to me. To this day, I shake when a needle is in sight. I call it the Bougainville shakes."

The common cause

GUNS, GENERALS AND GIs fought the battles, but World War II was won on the homefront. The shooting and bombing were thousands of miles away, yet American civilians — Nebraskans and Iowans among them — were on the front lines producing arms and food that tipped the balance on the battlefield. It was the common cause. ★ Midlanders combed the corners of their counties for anything that could be turned into armaments — old flatirons and pianos, discarded overshoes and historic relics of previous wars. Families planted "victory gardens" to produce their own vegetables. Shoppers learned to decipher the alphabet of gasoline stamps and the red and blue ration stamps. ★ The slogan of the time was, "Use it up, wear it out, make it do, or do without."

NEARLY 5,000 PEOPLE lined the streets of Plattsmouth in 1942 for a "Skrap Karnival" parade.

Scrap metal in Sidney, Neb., waits to be shipped out on the Union Pacific Railroad.

'Get in the scrap!'

The World-Herald received a Pulitzer Prize for public service in 1943 for organizing the scrap-metal drive.

THE MILLIONS OF AMERICANS with no direct memories of World War II may not appreciate just how precarious the United States' situation was at the beginning of the war.

Adolf Hitler's regime had constructed a military machine of extraordinary strength and nimbleness. Japan was extending its military might across Asia with frightening speed and boldness.

Nebraska's most dramatic and boisterous demonstration of unity and love of country was the remarkable scrap-metal drive during the summer of 1942.

The scrap drive was the brainchild of World-Herald Publisher Henry Doorly. In the first months of the war, Doorly was exasperated at the repeated failure of efforts around the country to provide the nation's foundries and factories with the metal for desperately needed munitions, artillery pieces, tanks and ships. In developing his idea for a scrap drive, Doorly added a vital new element: a spirit of competition.

WORLD-HERALD PUBLISHER Henry Doorly

THE WORLD-HERALD removed the metal ornaments from its building at 15th and Farnam Streets to add to the scrap pile.

The scrap drive wouldn't merely be a public service endeavor. It would be a contest — spread over a three-week period and on a statewide basis.

"In this contest," Doorly said in announcing the drive on July 11, 1942, "county will be pitted against county on a per capita basis, firm against firm, individual against individual and junior groups against junior groups. And The World-Herald will pay $2,000 in war bonds to the winners."

From every corner of Nebraska, people stepped forward to participate, spurred by a determination to make their county the No. 1 collector.

Community pride shone brightly, and hometown leaders cheered for an all-out effort, historian James J. Kimble of Seton Hall University wrote in an extensive study of The World-Herald's scrap drive.

"Let's go, McCook and Red Willow County! Get in the scrap!" read an advertisement in the McCook Daily Gazette early in the contest. From Washington County came the boast that "there won't be a needle left in a Washington County haystack when the Nebraska salvage contest is over."

SCRAP CONTRIBUTED by business owners Sam Epstein, left, and G.R. McGargill brought Omaha's donated total to a value of $25,000.

BELOW: ANGELO DiGIACOMO, LEFT, AND SAM GULIZIA contribute a metal lamp.

COUNCIL BLUFFS PITCHES IN, with donations from Mrs. James Hickey, left, Mrs. C.V. Edward and Mrs. Raymond G. Peterson.

One week's collection of scrap metal during July of 1942 was enough to fill a lot at 11th and Jackson Streets in Omaha.

Elsie McLain drops off an old license plate for use in the war effort.

Life magazine reported that the frenzy across Nebraska was so great that the race "took on all the enthusiasm of a (football) conference championship."

Five days before the contest even officially began, several thousand people had shown up in Omaha with their scrap at the first major rally of the contest. Soon, Omaha became home to a gigantic "Scrap Mountain" that covered the entirety of the block at 11th and Jackson Streets.

Because the contest was judged on a per capita basis, small counties had ample opportunity to compete. Hooker County took the early lead, then was passed by Red Willow County, and on the competition went.

With the encouragement of Gov. Dwight Griswold, at the very end Nebraskans dropped their normal routine and devoted themselves entirely to the great collection crusade. A report by Editor and Publisher magazine described the final weekend as tumultuous:

The last two days "found Nebraska working at fever pitch, with volunteer men and women scouring for scrap throughout the day and far into the night." Such searches turned up "tons of dormant scrap, long-forgotten caches of metal, unsightly city water tanks, steel rail buried under flooded riverbanks, bridges abandoned and forgotten, debris left after fires (and) ancient tractors in farm gulleys."

Lakes were dragged for iron. Veterans of World War I contributed their old helmets, and the town of Fairbury donated its cannon from the Spanish-American War.

It all adds up, as the World-Herald pointed out:

- One radiator would provide enough scrap steel to make 17 .30-caliber rifles.
- One lawn mower would help make six 3-inch shells.
- One tire would yield enough rubber to make 12 gas masks.
- One shovel would provide the required amount of metal for four hand grenades.

It's no wonder that Doorly later summed up the spirit of the event by describing it as "a Billy Sunday revival combined with a horse race."

By the time The World-Herald's contest officially concluded on Aug. 8, 1942, Nebraskans had collected more than 67,000 tons of scrap — more than 102 pounds a person.

Small counties won particular commendation. The contest's winner was Grant County (population: 1,327), with a staggering 638 pounds per person.

Other lightly populated areas also earned a salute, including Hooker, Phelps, Red Willow, Thayer, Dundy and Thomas Counties.

In Washington, D.C., federal officials hailed what was soon dubbed the "Nebraska plan." The Roosevelt administration brought Doorly and his assistant, J.M. Harding, to the nation's capital to brief a gathering of 150 U.S. newspaper publishers on what Editor and Publisher called "the magnificent record already made by the citizens of Nebraska."

THE LOOMIS COMMERCIAL CLUB AND HOLDREGE CHAMBER OF COMMERCE paid $10 a ton for scrap to assist the Phelps County drive.

BETTY ZACHARIAE

Town: Omaha

In the war: Her father, a widower with two young girls, moved the family to Longmont, Colo., in September 1941 to take over the Continental Oil Bulk Plant.

In her words: "(My dad's) job was deemed to be exceptionally important, making sure the farming community was well taken care of with the needed fuel products. He had no help and many times we ate supper at 9 p.m. or later, waiting for Dad to come home. We bought war bonds, war stamps, collected newspapers, smashed tin cans and helped our stepmom make soap. (Ugh!) One big memory I have: I heard the breaking news that President Roosevelt had died suddenly and ran to tell my parents and they couldn't believe it. Everyone was elated as the war ended, of course. Friends came home and no more rationing! My sister and I sneaked cans of condensed milk, divided and drank all of it, and could never stand the taste again."

Marshall C. Bitney, Joy Vance and Charles Kelly pull apart an automobile at an Omaha salvage yard.

Omaha movie theaters collected 30,000 pounds of scrap by offering a free show to children who brought in 2 pounds or more of copper or brass. At right, H.M. Corning checks out the contribution of 12-year-old Bill Hall.

The result was a national scrap drive in 1943, organized (of course) on a competitive basis. The campaign brought in a staggering total of nearly 5 million tons, and Nebraskans collected another 123 pounds of scrap per person. Nebraska finished sixth in the national competition, which was won by Kansas.

For its work in this cause, The World-Herald in May 1943 received a Pulitzer Prize for public service. The lack of metal for civilian use meant, however, that the actual Pulitzer medal did not arrive in Omaha until October 1944.

Historian Kimble summed up Nebraska's scrap drive of 1942 by writing that it "could, with only some hyperbole, be described as the horseshoe nail without which the war could have been lost."

The demise of 'Bosco'

OMAHA'S AMATEUR BASEBALL ASSOCIATION received a less than enthusiastic response when it installed a bronze statue in Elmwood Park in 1927.

With a granite pedestal topped by a bronze batter swinging his bat, "Bosco" became the subject of neighborhood complaints. One of the criticisms was that Bosco appeared to be striking out. So when The World-Herald ran a story with the headline "Last Half of the Ninth for Scrap" on the final day of the scrap metal drive in 1942, some Central High School students stepped forward with crowbars and wrenches. Bosco was ejected from the park and delivered to the scrap pile downtown.

Bill Kizer Sr., one of the students who hauled away the 315-pound statue, recalled that it was not an act of mischief.

"It was like we had permission," Kizer said. "Everybody was putting everything they had into the war effort. Things like that were fair game."

The World-Herald reported the next day that Bosco had "finally made a hit (with everyone)."

ABOVE: NORTH SIDE CLUB MEMBERS Mrs. R.M. Sutton, Mrs. David Northup, Mrs. John C. Hardy and Mrs. Edwin N. Soloman added their contributions from a cleanup drive.

LEFT: BEALS SCHOOL pupil Delores Cochran, 10, was saluted for her efforts.

BELOW: SCRAP RALLY SPONSOR S. Edward Gilbert weighs a contribution from the Rev. L.A. Story (back) and Richard Stanley.

DONNA KIRK

Town: Omaha

In the war: Was a teen during the war years. Her parents farmed and kept a large garden, so most rationing didn't bother them — except for sugar and coffee.

In her words: "A sticker on the car windshield said, 'Is this trip necessary?' About the only time the car was driven was to town for groceries. We did a lot of walking. ... We had a large map on the front room wall. We'd follow the fighting from the radio news. It was a sad time for everyone, lots of tears as the young, strapping country boys were classified 1A and drafted. Too many never came home."

BUSINESS WAS BRISK at the ration board office at the Faidley building at 16th and Douglas Streets in 1943.

'Even if you had money, you couldn't buy anything'

ELIZABETH CALLAWAY OF LINCOLN remembered how hard it was to shop. "The ration points for meat and sugar were difficult to stretch during the war," she said. "All buying was done in three steps. First, does the store have meat, sugar or soap? Second, do I have ration points? Third, do I have money? My husband was in the Army, and I was on a $57-a-month allotment — with a baby."

Ration stamps were each worth 10 points. Red stamps were used for meat, cheese and fats; blue for processed foods. Small round tokens, about the size of a dime, were given as change for points.

Rationing was an attempt by the U.S. Office of Price Administration, in combination with price controls, to equally distribute scarce goods and to control inflation.

I.E. ROBERTS pulls off 11 points for a jar of canned corn for clerk Bessmarie Gless.

GROCER FRED JEPSEN posts a point-value chart on the shelves next to the canned goods.

Sometimes a sympathetic butcher could chop through the ration rules, said Callaway, who grew up on a farm near Fairbury, Neb.

Living on the outskirts of Oak Park, Ill., a Chicago suburb, while her husband was in training or overseas, Callaway took her infant son for a stroll in his secondhand buggy. They stopped at a grocery store outside their usual walking area.

"The soap shelves — I needed Ivory flakes for washing diapers — had two boxes of Lux, one box of Ivory and 6 feet of empty space," she recalled in 1993. "As I put the box into the buggy I heard a well-dressed woman wearing a fur coat quarreling with the butcher. I needed bacon for the baby's diet, so I moved that way and asked politely, embarrassed by the overheard quarrel, if he had any bacon that day.

"The butcher put his finger across his lips to hush me, and whispered, 'Come back,' and then said out loud, 'No, ma'am. No bacon.'"

The white enamel trays of the meat case were nearly empty.

"The fur-coat woman came storming back, almost screaming, 'Are you selling bacon to her after you told me no?' I drifted on, looking at the mostly empty shelves until she stomped out. Back at the meat case, the butcher wrapped a pound of bacon he had brought out from somewhere, and we pretended Mrs. Fur Coat had not been there."

Callaway said her doctor told her that he would give her a prescription for red meat if she couldn't buy it in stores.

Rationing was a nuisance that all learned to endure, said Anna May Cullison of Harlan, Iowa.

Cullison said she used her home economics background in providing balanced meals for her lawyer husband, three children, mother-in-law and a maid.

"The maid, Anna, was German and very dependent on her coffee," she said. "We had ration tickets for only so much coffee. All the adults cut back on their coffee so Anna could have hers. Rationing really cut us down on coffee and sugar."

WITHIN A MONTH AFTER JAPAN BOMBED PEARL HARBOR on Dec. 7, 1941, the first War Production Board order to the nation instituted rationing. Americans had to learn to handle a maze of books and coupons that limited the food or gas they could buy. The rationing was based on a point system in which each person in a family was allotted a certain number of points per week. The amounts varied as each coupon book was issued, depending on supplies. Following are comparisons from wartime shopping guides: A pound of porterhouse steak was worth 11 points, and a pound of hamburger 6 points. A pound of butter 8 points, and a pound of cottage cheese 3 points. A 16-ounce can of peaches 6 points, and a 14-ounce bottle of tomato catsup 15 points.

FRAN MAZIUK CASSITY

Town: Omaha

In the war: Had two brothers and many cousins in the service. Was too young to join then, but served from 1948 to 1953 when the Navy started accepting women again.

In her words: "My hometown, Stamford, Conn., is on Long Island Sound, so we were darkened at night. Window shades had to be black on the outside, storefronts were darkened, all neon lights were off, car headlights were painted black halfway (the upper part), streetlights were dimmed. We also had air raid drills every few weeks."

Ration stamps had to be sorted and counted at the home of Jerry Douda and his family, who operated Tom & Jerry Grocery & Meats, 2702 S. 10th St. A news story called the sorting bee "the grocer's headache." Douda and his wife, Agnes, are on the right. The others, from left, are Rose Mertz, Agnes' sister; Sidney Douda, Jerry's brother and the store's butcher; and Charles Mertz, Rose's son.

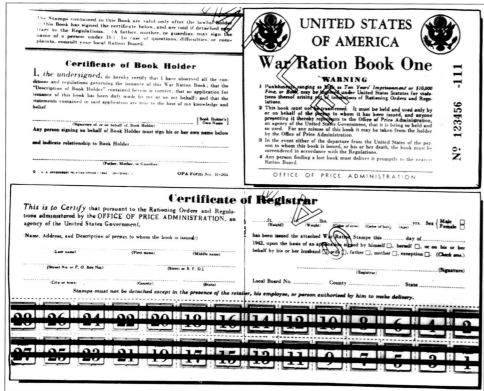

Included in ration books from the U.S. Office of Price Administration: "Never buy rationed goods without ration stamps. Never pay more than the legal price. In accepting this book, I recognize that it remains the property of the United States Government. I will use it only in the manner and for the purposes authorized by the Office of Price Administration. It is a criminal offense to violate rationing regulations. IMPORTANT: When you have used your ration, salvage the tin cans and waste fats. They are needed to make munitions for our fighting men. Cooperate with your local Salvage Committee."

It was left to the grocers to sort the stamps for redemption at banks.

Agnes Douda of Omaha, whose husband, Jerry, was proprietor of a grocery store at 10th and Bancroft Streets, recalled the tedious task of sorting the stamps at home in the evening.

Family members would gather around the kitchen table and sort stamps into at least six bowls.

"It was a headache," Agnes Douda said.

Gasoline was rationed in an effort to save tires. The war with Japan had cut off the supply of rubber from the Far East. A stamp affixed to the windshield allowed the owner three gallons of gas a week.

"We were in Wichita on the first day of strict gas rationing in 1942," Callaway said. "I stepped outside to walk to the store — we didn't have a car — and there wasn't a single vehicle on the street. It was like a deserted town. Everybody was afraid to use any gas because they had no idea how far two or three gallons would take them."

Marie Merriman's late husband, Fred, supervised many local rationing offices in Nebraska while living in Loup City during the war.

"When you tell your neighbor he can't have a tire or can't have gas, you could make enemies, but people accepted it," said Merriman, who later lived in Lincoln. "A lot of Loup City boys were in the service and people realized that the kids were out there with their lives on the line. Everybody helped."

Patriotism was widespread, said Jerry Wittenberger of Cozad, Neb., who as a teenager worked in his father's drugstore in Carleton, Neb.

"The black market appeared, but paying extra for anything in short supply was very unpatriotic and, probably, the most criticized thing I can remember," Wittenberger said.

MUTUAL BENEFIT HEALTH AND ACCIDENT ASSOCIATION and the United Benefit Life Insurance Company, which later became Mutual of Omaha, donated the services of their workers to file and distribute more than 1 million ration books to Nebraskans.

MARY JEANNE (LARKIN) ADAMS

Town: Bellevue

In the war: When the war started, she was about 12 years old, in the eighth grade at Adams School in the Keystone area. She graduated from Benson High School.

In her words: "I remember listening to the radio on Dec. 7, 1941, and how upset my parents were. My dad was a printing salesman so he needed his car and was able to get ration stamps for gas and tires. My mom had to figure out how to buy a lot of food like butter, meat, flour, sugar and everything else that was rationed. Luckily, we lived on the edge of town (74th and Bedford) so we had a half-acre of garden, and she had always canned a lot of vegetables. ... When VJ Day came in August of 1945, I was home. My mother was working out of town and Dad was in downtown Omaha. He called me and said he was coming out to get me because he wanted to make sure I could be a part of history by being in the celebration in downtown Omaha. It seemed like the whole city was on 16th Street between Douglas and Farnam. I think we stayed there almost all night. He was right. I've never forgotten it."

Clothing went to war, too.

"Even if you had money you couldn't buy anything," Merriman said. "The boys grew out of shoes pretty fast. They had homemade pants made out of Fred's old corduroys until I was able to buy overall material."

Women used liquid leg makeup when stocking materials — silk, rayon and the new synthetic, nylon — were diverted for powder bags and parachutes. Some even painted seams down the back of their legs to make it look as if they were wearing hosiery.

Betty Busboom Kohl of Ogallala, Neb., lived in her hometown of Hastings, Neb., while her husband, Guy, was in Europe with an Army tank corps.

"You had to get on a list at the store to get a pair of nylons," Kohl said. "Some people made a living repairing runs in nylons with a little latch-hook type of tool. The repair showed, but it was better than going without hose."

Kohl wasn't among those who shaded their legs with makeup. "I never messed with it because I couldn't do it properly," she said. "I just shaved my legs and said heck with it."

Cullison recalled the thrill of receiving a pair of nylon hose in the mail from the Younkers store in Des Moines.

"I had a charge account at the store and they apparently got some nylons in and just sent each of their customers a pair," she said. "Of course, we had to pay for them, but what a thrill."

For some, the routines of war didn't fade over the years.

At Christmas, Callaway said, her friends were amazed at how early she completed her shopping for gifts.

"When my husband was in the Pacific, I had to get the packages in the mail by Nov. 1 for him to get them in time," she said.

The Cullisons kept their ration books and coupons in a drawer in their dining room buffet.

"We called that the ration drawer for years afterward," Cullison said.

JEAN WRIGHT helps package ration books for distribution.

CHILDREN JOINED in the effort when they went to the grocery store.

BURLINGTON EMPLOYEES Meredith Wurtz, left, and Phyllis Knutsen tend to a victory garden on land at Second Street and Poppleton Avenue that was donated by the railroad.

Memories of making do

COOKING IN THE MIDLANDS during the war was a waste-not, make-do effort by families who seemed willing to do whatever was necessary to help the nation win World War II. Shortages and rationing of everyday commodities encouraged ingenuity as families worked to feed themselves with home gardens, orchards, home-raised livestock and wild game and berries. Victory gardens, home canning, rationing, sugar shortages and margarine were common memories for those who lived through the war years. Government rationing of such commodities as sugar, bread, meat, gasoline and leather shoes also were prominent memories. Here are some 1993 recollections of World-Herald readers:

Raymond C. Matson of Omaha: "We had opened the Hilltop House restaurant at 49th and Dodge Streets on Jan. 28, 1941, and were just getting started when war was declared (on Dec. 8, 1941). Within a short time we were allocated red stamps for meat, blue stamps for sugar, oils, butter, coffee and other foods that soon were unavailable. Because of these shortages we were compelled to stop serving lunches and only serve dinners. At that time we owned the ground at 75th and Dodge Streets. This was virgin ground so we brought in water, had it plowed and made ready for the victory garden. By 1943, we were in full swing, raising potatoes, carrots, onions, beets, corn, radishes, green peppers, tomatoes, sweet potatoes: everything we could use in the restaurant. We canned hundreds of quarts. It was a lot of work, but we did enjoy the results and saved some money. We had the time and felt we were helping the cause."

Edith Berg Frerichs of Alliance, Neb., recalled having butter at home until the war arrived: "One day I came home from school to find my mother mixing something in a bowl that smelled terrible. It was margarine that came in a white, 1-pound brick with a yellow tablet that was dissolved and mixed in. It tasted as bad as it smelled, so I ate my bread dry after that."

Shirley Benash of Bellevue said coloring the margarine was a pleasant childhood memory: "How soothing a job to squeeze the plastic bag until the food color capsule inside burst and made the oleo look like butter."

Jerry Ryan of Omaha recalled the window-box victory gardens at his Chicago apartment: "There were no garden or lawn areas, but this did not stop my mother. She took several fruit crates, lined them with paper and filled them with dirt. She made a space on her windowsill, between buildings, and placed each crate outside a window. She planted radishes, carrots, onions, etc., and waited for the two or three hours each day when the sun would shine between the buildings. Her crops were harvested periodically and she would reseed and replant."

Doris Artz of Elwood, Neb., was in high school during the war and remembered the rationing: "We always had a large vegetable garden and peach trees, which provided food for canning, storing and sharing with others," she wrote. "It was sometimes difficult to purchase enough canning lids, and they weren't of the best quality, which caused spoilage of the canned goods. Syrup and honey sometimes substituted for sugar in canning fruits. With the shortage of meat, main dishes were made from chicken, eggs and cheese. We ate lots of vegetables, fruits and homemade bread. A pretty healthy diet at that!"

Marianna Smith of Omaha: "I still remember a victory garden that my parents and I cared for. The problem was that it was over eight miles away. We did have a car and we would load the tools and take clothes for gardening and better shoes in case it was muddy. Mom had been a farmer's daughter, so she knew something about gardening. She even bought a machine so we could can in tins. We canned tomatoes, green beans and sauerkraut."

Rita Sullivan of Omaha: "As an 8-year-old in 1941, I spent lots of time with my mother and dad helping with the gardening and

canning. I have vivid memories of sitting on the side porch with Mother and my sisters and brothers (there were 12 of us) shelling peas, snipping beans, washing cukes (cucumbers) and carrots and assisting Mother with the canning in the kitchen. I remember how proud we all were of Dad, a blacksmith and an artisan with iron, who made our victory garden flagpole. I remember how not a morsel was wasted; any leftover mashed potatoes were used for patties for the next meal. Mother baked all our bread using white and rye flours. The cloth 50-pound (flour) sacks were made into dish towels."

Janet Conrad Dumdei of Manilla, Iowa, said the war years intensified her family's interest in gardening and home canning: "Even though we had always had a big garden and fruit trees, rhubarb, strawberries, etc., my brother and I now had a victory garden of our own to take care of. We were happy to do anything that would help the war effort. Everyone tried to do what they could."

The World-Herald sponsored two demonstration victory gardens, the one above at 13th Street and Deer Park Boulevard and another at Fontenelle Park. Visitors could receive advice about planting, watering and garden pests.

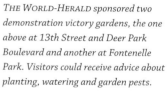

Nebraskans joined in the purchase of war bonds during World War II. Americans were encouraged to spend at least 10 percent of each paycheck on bonds, which were used to help finance the war effort. For example, the purchase of an $18.75 bond would buy two gas masks. In May and June 1943, Union Pacific Railroad's 65,000 employees increased their bond purchases by $379,000. In appreciation, the U.S. War Department christened a B-17 Flying Fortress "The Spirit of the Union Pacific."

Don Chattfield, left, and Mickey Dalton pull a plow operated by Dwight MacAfferty at a garden that covered four city blocks in Holdrege, Neb.

GROCER RAY G. EGGEN explains to Mrs. J.W. Balenti that from a ration-point standpoint, it's better to buy the two small cans of vegetable juice rather than the larger can.

Erma E. Blakely of Harlan, Iowa, was a minister's wife, with children, during the war years: "Children were encouraged not to take more on their plates than they planned to eat and to clean their plates, 'victory plates.' We fished, and hunted squirrels and rabbits, and added nuts, bread and cracker crumbs to meat loaves. We rarely dined out. But we did lead lots of picnics, potlucks, pitch-in dinners and covered-dish get-togethers in our homes. It brought us closer. We grew very innovative seeing how much and how good we could make something from nothing." She also recalled the impact of gasoline rationing on her life as the wife of a minister during the war years. In those days, she said, clergymen and their wives called on every parishioner in his or her home. Often they took their children. "We would take our lunch and call all day and plan our route up one road and down another in order not to retrace routes and use extra gasoline. We walked all over town making calls and ministering. We survived those days with heads and spirits held high."

Irene Glaubius of Wisner, Neb.: "The thought of canning fruit without adding a cup of sugar to each quart jar was unheard of. We found out it could be done, and for years I have canned sugarless fruit."

BUTCHER RAY WRIGHT TAKES stock of what he'll have to ration in 1943.

Nick Miller of Herman, Neb., remembered the contrast between sugar conservation at home and sugar-syrup waste by servicemen overseas: "While the cooks at home were severely rationed, our mess-hall cooks at the air base in England were punching two holes in the tops of gallons of peaches, pineapple, etc. and turning the cans upside down in the sink to drain. Our mess-hall plates had no provision for the juice. I tried to get to the mess hall early enough to drink a canteen of juice on the spot and catch another cup to drink with my meal."

Dorothy Vaclavek of Grand Island, Neb.: "Even with ration stamps, it was almost impossible to get much meat. The only ones who really ate well were farmers who raised their own livestock. We could get chickens, whole and scrawny, and we cooked them every way we could. We ate lots of spaghetti. I also had a recipe, long since lost, that was shredded cabbage, shredded carrots and English walnuts with some sort of sauce over it and baked. I guess we didn't eat like we do now, but we all survived and maybe we didn't gain so much weight."

Mrs. Robert Schenkel of Bennington: "I remember well the ration stamps you needed to purchase sugar, oils, etc., and how frustrated my mother would become when she couldn't bake when she wanted due to lack of ingredients and how she would substitute in recipes. You had to save all grease from meats. Some you used in cooking and the rest you sold to the grocer for Uncle Sam, who used it in explosives. My special job was to wash out tin cans, cut both ends off and flatten them out with lids in them."

Jean Powers, formerly of Venango, Neb., and now of Silver Creek, recalled the shortage of tires: "My sister drove me to Silver Creek, Neb., to teach on her way to her job in Omaha," she wrote. "At Silver Creek, we had a blowout that ruined a tire and found the spare worthless. We couldn't find a replacement anywhere. In desperation we called a relative who ran a country filling station at Phillips. He told us he could help us out but had no way to get the tire to us. So we rode a Greyhound bus to Grand Island (and) caught another one to Phillips, where we had to wait several hours for another bus back to Grand Island. The bus was packed and the driver wasn't going to let us put the tire on the bus: no room in the luggage compartment. Finally, he felt sorry for us and allowed us to stand in the aisle with the tire propped between us to Grand Island. There we again transferred to another bus where we stood with the tire until we got to Silver Creek. Believe me, tires were hard to come by in those days."

Mildred R. Galus of Omaha recalled standing in line to buy nylon hose: "Ugh! (Rayon stockings were) not flattering. Also, the stockings had lines or seams in the back. The nylon ones didn't and if you had one pair you washed them out, dried them in a towel and put them back on. I remember when I had my wedding shower you could not get any appliances. I was lucky and got a toaster from someone who bought it on the black market. I remember when I opened that gift, the oohs and aahs and how lucky I felt to be able to get something so hard to come by."

Grace Henry of Cozad, Neb., remembered shortages of shoes and stockings: "I was a waitress during World War II and worked a split shift in a small cafe in our little town (Beaver City). Since leather shoes were bought only if you had a shoe stamp, I wore my leather shoes during the breakfast and lunch hours. Upon coming back for the evening work I wore red low-heeled pumps with a bow on each cloth pump. I wasn't used to wearing nylon stockings. They had silk ones then if you could find them. We gals either 'painted' stockings on our legs or just plain went without. I was delighted when I was able to purchase a pair of silk stockings, which I saved for my wedding day — June 14, 1946. They were not a matching pair but near enough. My (wedding) dress was a silk print that came above my knees, as that was the style then. We went to the courthouse and were married by the judge."

Servicemen added to the crowd at Omaha's Union Station in 1943.

Guelda Shirley Jensen of Norfolk, Neb., remembered her wedding on June 30, 1943: "Because of rationing there were not many formal church weddings among civilians on the homefront. I had my dress made by a seamstress. It was the last yardage of white dress material in the entire city of Norfolk. I borrowed the pattern from a high school girl and had it made street length, instead of formal. I could not buy new shoes since I had more than two pairs. Fortunately, I had a pair of white sandal pumps. I could not buy a shoulder-length veil. For gifts … most metal cookware of any kind could not be bought unless it was secondhand. It had to be either enamelware or glass. The wedding cake was a three-tier, all-white cake from the bakery. The shortening was a wartime substitute for what the bakery had always used and (the cake had) less sugar."

Joel Boucher of Council Bluffs remembered two months in 1943 when sliced bread was prohibited as a way of conserving paper. Sliced bread, he wrote, required thicker waxed paper to keep it fresh while whole loaves could be wrapped in thinner paper. "Consumer demand called for a return of sliced bread."

Dorothy Arp of Manning, Iowa: "(The war) was a low mark in all our lives. We were fighting on two fronts: Europe and the Far East. My husband was serving Uncle Sam, and I felt I was doing my part saving all fats and aluminum foil and flattening cans to turn in for use in the war effort. Our gasoline, coffee and sugar, as well as car tires, were rationed. Every so often, stamps could be turned in for the purchase of these precious items. I remember standing in long lines to purchase nylon hosiery. We were all pulling together making do or doing without for the war effort."

'Vacation close to home'

THE WORLD-HERALD, JULY 3, 1943

FEAR IS FELT by officials that this wartime Fourth of July may bring a crush to the already overburdened transportation lines.

In this connection they urge that if you deserve a vacation and intend to have one, take it close to home.

If you must travel either for vacation or business, you are urged to give as much thought and planning for the trip as you do in scheduling rationed mileage for your automobile or in shopping for food under the points systems.

"Transportation is perhaps the most important phase of war," said one official. "The public must realize that overburdening transportation facilities is one way to help Hitler and Tojo."

THINK BEFORE YOU TRAVEL:
1. First decide if your trip is necessary and essential.
2. Use railroads only when necessary.
3. Plan exactly when you are going.
4. Use direct routes — eliminate side trips.
5. Transact your travel briefly — give the other fellow a chance, too.
6. Buy your tickets in advance — don't crowd stations.
7. Cancel reservations immediately when your plans change.
8. Leave your pets at home.
9. Travel light — baggage cars are needed, too.

Nearly all 1943 pennies were struck in zinc-coated steel, because copper and nickel were needed for the war effort. Only a handful were mistakenly made of copper that year, according to the U.S. Mint.

MEMORIES OF A GENERATION ★

BARBARA 'BETTY' (BECKER) SIREK

Town: Pierce

Service: Taught first- and second-grade children at Fort Hood, Texas, in 1945, while husband Winferd Sirek was stationed there. Winferd was a staff sergeant. He died in 1984.

In the war: The trailer homes on the base did not have running water — in the center of the trailer village was a washroom with toilets, showers and laundry facilities. Sirek said it was hard to develop close relationships with the children she taught because they would often be pulled out of school when their fathers would be on furlough.

In her words: "In the mornings when I would open my desk drawer (in the schoolroom), huge crickets would jump out. … I put phosphorous paste on the edge of the sink and other cracks in our trailer home to keep the cockroaches out. It would smoke when you put it down, but we didn't have children then. … One of the couples we chummed with had an armadillo they kept as a pet. One day we were going shopping and went over to their house and my friend had the little armadillo in the bed with her. It made sounds like a pig. … I was lucky I never saw a rattlesnake. … Quite an interesting life for a little Nebraska farm girl."

MARY SUE (GOLDING) OFFERJOST

Town: Papillion

Service: Dad, Robert A. Golding Jr., was a "Frog Man" in the Navy. Listed in the book "Frog Men of WWII."

In the war: Little girl during the war; Dad served in the Navy; Mother cared for three children; lived in the Florence neighborhood; remembers collecting scrap metal, paper and fat.

In her words: "Growing up with a dad in the war, we (the children) were more aware of it. At the movie theater there was a newsreel and you got to see the actual pictures. It was very sad because they'd show you the men being killed. … (Even so) we looked forward to the newsreels. … You always looked to see if there would be somebody you knew. You always had the hope maybe you'd see your dad. … We stayed by ourselves when I was 5 or 6 and my mother went to work. The neighbors really watched out for us. Everybody watched out for us in those days." (Mary Sue is pictured below, on the left).

SHIRLEY HARRIS

Town: Omaha

In the war: Harris was a young Australian woman when she met her future husband, John "Jack" Harris, an Omaha native who served six years in the Navy. Shirley Harris traveled from Australia on a ship filled with 245 war brides and 200 babies called the "diaper run."

In her words: "He had a 30-day leave, and instead of going to the U.S. he came down to marry me. We had a 30-day honeymoon right there on the Indian Ocean. We were married almost 54 years. During the war, Australia was rationing, like other countries around the world. We had air raid shelters out on the streets. All the stores, the windows were covered up with boards. I was on a train one time going home from work and the siren went off and the train stopped because a Japanese plane was coming down the coast. The northwest coast of Australia was bombed, but citizens didn't find out about it until the war was over."

GENEVIEVE L. (JENS) HUNT

Town: Glenwood

During the war: In May 1944, husband Charles was drafted and went to Texas to train. Genevieve was left in Glenwood with a 3-year-old boy and a 2-year-old girl. She was in a small rental house and took in boarders.

In her words: "Charlie was married, had two kids, worked at the bomber plant, and was nearly 26 years old. I didn't think he would be drafted, but he was. I had friends and boarders stay with me the whole time he was gone. They also helped out with my two little ones. We used ration stamps and walked where we needed to go. Charles was in the Philippines and then later in Japan. I would be so happy when a letter came from him. He wasn't allowed to say where he was, and the letters were censored anyway. In his letters to me he would put a tiny little dot under certain letters of the alphabet, and that would tell me where he was — Leyte, Manila, on a transport ship, or Tokyo. The day he came walking up the street in February 1946 was the happiest day of my life. … Charles died in June 2007 at age 88."

★ MEMORIES OF A GENERATION

LOIS WOOLDRIDGE

Town: Cozad

In the war: She was a girl growing up in Chappell, Neb.

In her words: "I was 13 years old when Pearl Harbor was attacked, so I remember that very well. So many of my schoolmates and relatives were called to the service or enlisted. I grew up in the small town of Chappell, and there were quite a few of the young men that didn't make it back. My brother was in the Navy, and thank God, he returned to us. I had two brothers-in-law in the service, and my first husband was in the Navy. He passed away in 1968, and I later married an ex-soldier, Spike Wooldridge. I remember selling war savings stamps at the school I worked at and lots of rationing of different things at that time. I graduated from high school the year the war ended, 1945."

FAYE (TANNER) COOL

Town: Broken Bow

In the war: I was a sophomore in high school in Sterling, Colo., when Pearl Harbor was bombed.

In her words: "Because nylon thread was used in the production of parachute material, women's nylon stockings were often a scarce item. Whenever a local store was heard to have a shipment of nylons, there was quite a crowd of us hoping to be lucky enough to get a pair. In May 1944, when I graduated, most of the boys in my class went immediately into service. On Aug. 6, 1945, as I walked home from my job, I heard sirens sounding. At first I thought there was a fire, but a woman came out of her house and called out 'THE WAR IS OVER!' That is my most vivid memory of all."

ILA MAE KUNC

Town: Ralston

In the war: Eighth-grader in Wilber, Neb.

In her words: "My father, Henry Otte, operated a small truck line. His work was considered essential to the war effort so he was able to get gasoline and tires for his trucks. He picked up milk from area farms, taking it to the big dairy in Lincoln. Tons of Vise-Grip wrenches were hauled from the manufacturing plant in DeWitt to shippers in Lincoln and Omaha. His drivers brought meat and groceries and other merchandise back to Wilber and other nearby communities. ... Because he could get unlimited gas and tires, a sideline developed. The superintendent of the high school soon asked Dad to take the athletic teams to their out-of-town games. Dad fitted the closed milk truck with some used church pews and a single light bulb. ... Not only did the teams use this mode of transportation, but often other students got to go along to be a cheering section. ... The women's garden club even hired this truck to take them over then-gravel roads to the famous gardens in Shenandoah, Iowa. ... Whenever we return to Wilber for a class reunion, people still come up and tell us about their memories of being hauled around in Otte's truck."

MARJORIE RECEK

Town: Omaha

In the war: She gave birth to a set of twins in 1943 — while her husband, Felix, was at boot camp in Oregon — and to a daughter less than a month after he was discharged. (They eventually had four children.)

In her words: "I was pregnant both times he was gone. It was no good for me when he was away. ... All I could do was take care of those kids — it was worse than a handful." She said she and Felix wrote many letters, and she saved all of hers.

MARY ELLEN BLATCHFORD

Town: York

During the war: In May 1942, Blatchford started working in the Cedar County rationing office in Hartington, Neb. She worked there until June 1946. As a clerk, she distributed war ration books. The books contained stamps that allowed people to purchase such items as sugar and tires, gas and shoes, heating oil and canned goods.

In her words: "After the war ended, the fellas came home, and they hadn't had dates for years. This one boy asked me for a date on Halloween (in 1946)." That first date with Howard Blatchford led to 53 years of marriage. "You meet the right person, it's fine. Just be choosy ahead of time." They raised two children and had five grandchildren and three great-grandchildren. The late Howard Blatchford fought at Normandy and elsewhere.

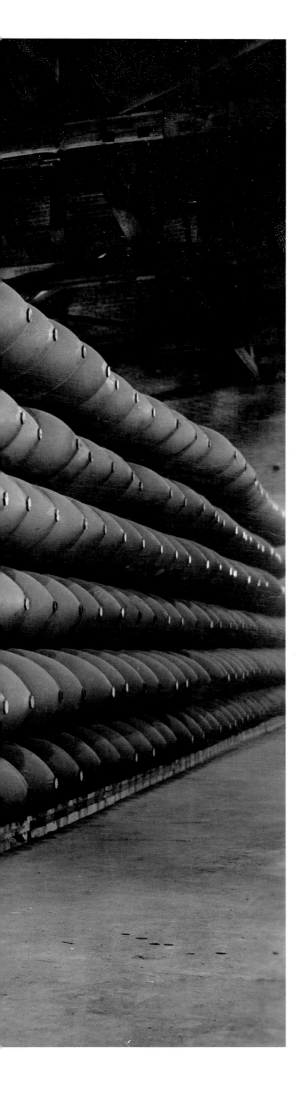

Starting a new job

HILDRETH MADSEN SAID SHE USED TO think a lot about her brothers as she punched rivets into the bellies of the B-29 bombers made at a plant south of Bellevue. ★ Madsen's brothers were both serving in the U.S. Navy, one on a submarine and the other on the aircraft carrier USS Saratoga. The lives of servicemen, possibly one of her brothers, were going to depend on some of the planes Madsen helped build at the Martin Bomber Plant. ★ "I felt like every rivet I put in had better be done right," she said. "I felt very patriotic to do my job."

STACKS OF 500-POUND BOMBS await shipment from the Nebraska Ordnance Plant at Mead.

BOMBS ARE STENCILED and prepared for shipment from the Cornhusker Ordnance Plant in Grand Island.

'Everyone was working together to help those who were fighting for us'

BY DAVID HENDEE

NEBRASKA MANUFACTURERS, who made everything from air conditioners to windmills before the war, retooled to turn out anti-aircraft shells and amphibious landing craft.

"Omaha and Nebraska were very aggressive in trying to bring in military activity," said Janet Daly Bednarek, who has written books about aviation and the history of Omaha.

"As early as 1940, John Latenser, the architect, went to Washington, D.C., to lobby on behalf of the Omaha Chamber of Commerce for a defense project. The biggest thing they landed was the Martin Bomber Plant."

Ground was broken for the plant near Bellevue in March 1941 — nine months before Japan's attack on the U.S. naval base at Pearl Harbor brought America into the war. By the next year, the huge facility was making 125 B-26s a month, and by 1943 was building B-29 Superfortresses. Peak employ-

ment topped 14,500. The plant closed at the end of the war and became part of Offutt Air Force Base. Nebraska had what military planners sought: a location in the center of the country, mostly level terrain and a sparse population.

War industries in the state would be protected from coastal invasions, and flight crews could train safely in remote areas without obstacles such as hills.

"The government was already in Nebraska in the summer of '41 surveying probable sites (for military installations)," aviation historian Robert Hurst of Lincoln said in 1994. "They found it ideal. We were pretty much well prepared for war. Pearl Harbor was the catalyst."

The creation of tens of thousands of construction and war-industry jobs, the influx of thousands of military personnel and the rallying against a common foe — the Axis powers of Germany, Italy and Japan — jolted Nebraska out of the Depression.

TNT FLAKES ARE DUMPED *from their boxes and raked into a duct that leads to an explosives production line at the Nebraska Ordnance Plant at Mead.*

Viola Grote of Council Bluffs was paid $65 a month as the secretary to the president of an Omaha business college when she left to go to work as a secretary at the Martin plant.

It was December 1941, and she was 18 years old.

Grote, then Viola Lee, soon was making $124 every two weeks. Her job included crawling into wings of B-29 Superfortress bombers and taking notes as her engineer boss inspected fuel tanks. The B-29s were the largest combat planes flying in the war. A B-29 from the Martin plant — the Enola Gay — dropped the atomic bomb on Hiroshima, Japan, that helped end the war in the Pacific.

"I was never sorry I went down there," Grote said. "It was like a family. Everyone was working together to help those who were fighting for us."

It was impressive, she said, to walk through the Martin plant near Bellevue where the giant bombers were being put together and see women involved in all phases of the production.

"People drove a long way to work there," she said. "It was good-paying and gave people a chance to do their part," she said.

Grote's parents and two brothers also worked at the plant.

At one point, production demands required her to work 16-hour days without a day off for two months.

Vi Starr was 11 years old and living in the all-black town of Taft, Okla., when the United States entered the war.

Those who didn't join the service soon left Taft for jobs in war industries across the country. Among them were Starr's parents, who moved to Hastings, Neb., to work at the new Naval Ammunition Depot.

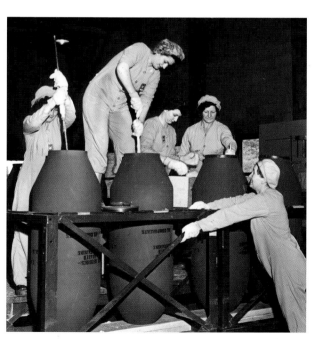

WORKERS FINISH WORK *on bombs after filling the tail with liquid TNT.*

★ MEMORIES ★
OF A GENERATION

GWEN (BEEBE) PORTER

Town: Modale, Iowa

In the war: When she was 17, she and five other young women from Modale went to Burbank, Calif., to work at the Lockheed "A" factory as "Rosie the Riveters." The six friends were Gwen, her sister Loretta Beebe, sisters Marietta Vittitoe and Jerry Vittitoe, Betty Jean Thomas and Lucille John. The Beebe sisters and Vittitoe sisters were cousins. Together, the six girls lived in a little house that Gwen described as a made-over cabin of a motel. They shared household chores and "furnished the place very well." Gwen first worked as a riveter at Lockheed, then later installed windshields and heat units on planes. A wartime newspaper clipping from the Council Bluffs Nonpareil, saved in her scrapbook, reads, "They are a wholesome example of the finest type of young American womanhood, this sixsome from Iowa."

In her words: "I had worked for the superintendent of schools in Modale. There, we worked for $25 a month. Not even a dollar a day. When we got 75 cents an hour in California and could go up to 90 cents an hour, boy, we thought we were rich. We helped build airplanes. It turned out to be quite an adventure. We felt like we helped win the war."

67

EMPLOYEES WORK INSIDE B-29 engine housings at the Martin Bomber Plant.

"People came from all over to work there," Starr said. "There was no place to live. People were staying in private houses and doubling up."

Starr stayed in Oklahoma until graduating from high school in 1948, but she spent summers and holidays with her parents in Hastings.

Starr, who later moved from Hastings to Omaha, said it was a shock to many Hastings area residents when black families arrived. The communities, however, generally responded positively, she said.

"There wasn't overt prejudice. Most of the blacks lived in one area of town in little cracker-box houses. But everyone took pride in it. It gave us a good foundation."

Black workers in Hastings were not automatically relegated to backroom jobs such as stock clerks and elevator operators, she said. The opportunity to live and work in a rural city during and after the war helped shape many of Starr's civil rights beliefs.

"I'm me. I'm not black or white. I've paid enough taxes to be called an American. I could express myself (at PTA meetings) and be respected for it. I wouldn't trade it for the world."

Hastings also had black sailors and civilian personnel among its 10,000 workers.

"I know the Navy had a challenge in how to provide entertainment to those kids in a town of 15,000 (white) people," said LaVon Crosby of Lincoln, who sold newspaper advertising and worked as a USO hostess in Hastings, her hometown, during the war.

"Some of them stayed after the war," she said. "I think the people tried to reach out and work with everybody."

The Hastings depot was the world's largest naval depot, covering 78 square miles. It produced 40 percent of the Navy's ammunition during the war. One day in the summer of 1945, the depot shipped out an 81-car train of ammunition to the Pacific Fleet.

Four explosions at the depot in 1944 killed 21 workers, including nine who died in a Sept. 15 blast that left a crater 550 feet wide and 50 feet deep. The concussion caused extensive damage in nearby towns and injured 10 children in Harvard when the roof of their school collapsed.

Labor shortages were common during the war.

The need for 350 extra workers at the Nebraska Ordnance Plant in Mead in May 1944 led officials to offer free daily bus transportation from 15th and Farnam Streets in downtown Omaha to the plant 30 miles away. The bomb-loading plant also was hiring wounded war veterans returning home.

Sidney's Sioux Ordnance Depot, an Army ammunition storage site, was erected almost overnight following the attack on Pearl Harbor in 1941. It stored and shipped everything from small-arms ammunition to hand grenades and howitzer shells to 10,000-pound bombs.

Like other Nebraska ammunition factories and depots, the depot in Sidney provided thousands of jobs and put millions of dollars into the local economy. When the plants closed a generation later, workers scattered to other assignments around the world or found local jobs and blended into the community.

Many Midlands manufacturers also retooled to produce war materiel and earned Army-Navy "E" awards for excellence in quality and for meeting production goals. Omaha — more than 1,000 miles from either coast — had two operations that were involved in ship-building.

The homefront was dedicated to winning and ending the war, Crosby said.

"It was a romantic time, in the sense there was drama every day," she said. "We all felt we were sharing the experience. It was very close to us. We lost classmates. We knew where the young men we served doughnuts to were going. Most of us never knew what happened to them."

DOROTHY BLOMQUIST OF OMAHA, formerly of Albert City, Iowa, operates a drill press at the Martin Bomber Plant. She got her job after completing a four-week course at one of Omaha's technical schools, followed by two weeks of training at the plant.

ALTHEA NISPEL MOHAR

Town: Papillion; grew up on a farm in Jefferson County, Neb.

Service: Worked at Rocky Mountain Arsenal in Denver testing incendiary bombs (firebombs) and white phosphorous bombs from 1943 to 1945

In the war: Mohar monitored a machine that tested the viscosity of the napalm and gasoline. She was responsible for accepting or rejecting the mix. She eventually moved to California in 1946 with her husband.

In her words: "Every time you had a day's work done, you knew that many bombs were going to do some good for our 'livability' for the United States." Mohar said she was not scared working in the lab with dangerous chemicals. "You didn't run around helter-skelter. You used good judgment and it turned out fine."

A WORKER MOVES PARTS of anti-submarine depth charges at the Naval Ammunition Depot in Hastings.

ARMED GUARDS were on patrol outside the Hastings Naval Ammunition Depot.

A FARM FAMILY removes furniture from its home, which was ordered vacated because of its proximity to the explosives plant in Mead.

Nebraska's munitions facilities

Naval Ammunition Depot at Hastings:
Construction started in July 1942. Produced 40 percent of the ammunition (bombs, mines, rockets and 40 mm and 6-inch shells) used by the Navy during the war. Employment ranged from 6,000 to 8,000.

Nebraska Ordnance Plant at Mead:
Between September 1942 and Aug. 15, 1945, the plant's 3,000 workers produced more than 3 million bombs. Site covered more than 26 square miles.

Cornhusker Ordnance Plant at Grand Island:
Workers loaded bombs with 800,000 pounds of TNT every 24 hours. Peak employment was 4,229 workers, 40 percent of them women.

Sioux Ordnance Depot at Sidney:
Received, stored and issued Army ammunition. Peak employment was 2,161 workers.

SOME FORMER FARM-HOUSES in the Grand Island area were used as storage and field offices. This one was nicknamed "the White House" because of its color and the porch columns.

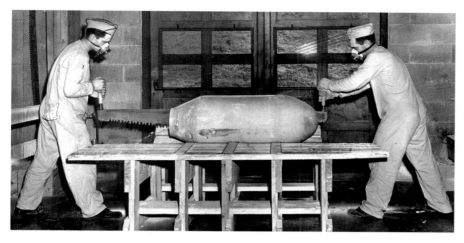

A NUMBER OF BOMBS were sawed through each day as part of inspection at the Cornhusker Ordnance Plant in Grand Island.

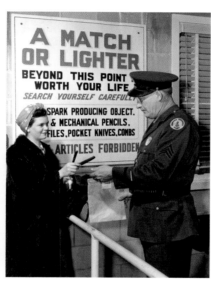

WORKERS AT THE NEBRASKA ORDNANCE PLANT in Mead, in addition to surrendering matches, wore special uniforms and removed jewelry that might produce a spark. Wedding rings were allowed, however.

THE FINAL PROCESS of filling the bomb was the tail pour, at far left. One worker breaks down air bubbles, while another pours liquid TNT.

WORKERS AT THE CORNHUSKER ORDNANCE PLANT were required to wear safety visors when pouring hot liquid TNT.

EDITH FOY GIFT

Town: Born and raised in Omaha, later lived in Laurel, Mont.

In the war: After graduating from high school in 1940, she went to college to become a nurse and worked at a nursing home in Omaha. But on Dec. 7, 1941, the day Pearl Harbor was attacked, everything changed. Her college plans were put on hold. She soon began working at the Martin Bomber Plant near Bellevue. She got the job primarily because she knew how to read blueprints, from helping her two younger brothers with their college studies.

In her words (as told to her daughter Jan Naylor): "I started working in the bomber plant at the age of 19. I believe it was shortly after the plant began making the B-29 bombers. I worked the 4-to-midnight shift, or the 'swing' shift as we called it. I remember getting to take a break about every two hours or so. In other words, if you were seeing double from reading blueprints, you would take a break for a cup of tea or coffee, then go back to work, maybe doing something else. We worked hard and got plenty dirty every day, so we had to wear a type of bib overall with a string that tied around the neck to hold them up. I remember the days being long and tiring, but I also felt a real sense of pride doing something valuable for our country at war. As a blueprint reader, I typically ran from one end of the plant to the other, but I also learned other jobs as well. I learned to work a drill press. My partner next to me would measure and mark the holes, and I would drill them. The holes were drilled where the rivets would go to assemble the aircraft. I also met my husband working at the plant. He was a section manager and went from area to area, checking to see that everything was done correctly. The most memorable part about working at the plant was knowing that at one time or another we worked on the Enola Gay. "

MARTIN BOMBER PLANT workers applaud President Franklin D. Roosevelt during a visit in 1943.

'I knew what I had to do'

DURING ITS PEAK OF PRODUCTION, 14,500 workers were employed at the Martin Bomber Plant on what is now Offutt Air Force Base south of Bellevue.

The bomber plant, with 56 buildings and hangars that covered more than 63 acres, produced 1,585 B-26 Marauder bombers and 531 B-29 Superfortress bombers from 1942 to 1945. It also modified more than 3,000 other aircraft.

Two of the plant's B-29s, named the Enola Gay and Bockscar, dropped the atomic bombs on Hiroshima and Nagasaki, Japan, that led to the end of the war in 1945.

Hildreth Madsen, who commuted each day from Nebraska City during the three years she worked at the plant, said she did not learn until after the war that she had helped build a plane with such historical significance as the Enola Gay.

"It was very secretive at the time," said Madsen, who later moved to Omaha.

Glenn Smith of Council Bluffs said people at the plant felt as if they were participating in the war even though they never crossed the ocean.

ROSIE THE RIVETER symbolized the attitude of women lending their labor to the war effort.

THE B-29 ASSEMBLY LINE put out more than 500 Superfortress bombers.

Martin Bomber Plant

- The Army Air Corps chose Fort Crook as the site for a new bomber plant in late 1940.

- The construction included two mile-long concrete runways, six large hangars and a 1.2 million-square-foot aircraft assembly building.

- The plant produced more than 1,500 B-26 Martin Marauders in two years of production.

- In the summer of 1943, the plant started production of more than 500 B-29 Superfortress bombers, including the Enola Gay and Bockscar, the aircraft used to drop atomic bombs on Japan.

- Peak employment was 14,500 in November 1943.

- About 40 percent of the workforce was women.

"It was contributing," Smith recalled in 1993. "Somebody had to stay home to do the work."

Ethric Brown of Red Oak, Iowa, remembered the frequent 12-hour shifts and the one time he worked 36 hours straight. Workers struggled to fill the orders for planes that the war effort demanded, he said.

One time, plant workers were given only hours to modify B-26 bombers by installing torpedo racks. Some of the modified planes were rushed to the decisive Battle of Midway in 1942, and one of them helped sink a Japanese aircraft carrier.

Carmen Grasso of Omaha, who worked on the final inspection assembly line, said that having a loved one fighting in the war gave her the determination to do her job — and do it well.

Grasso started working at the plant for 60 cents an hour when she was 23. She said she felt some trepidation when waiting at 4:30 a.m. for a streetcar on a corner populated by drunks and derelicts.

"But I had so much guts at the time," Grasso said. "I knew what I had to do."

She said she often worked 16 hours a day, because "when work had to be done, it couldn't wait."

Mary Rocha of Council Bluffs assembled machine guns on the planes just before they were sent off to war.

She recalled a time when a bolt accidentally had been dropped inside a wing. Other workers at the plant were unable to reach inside to remove it.

At 4-foot-6, Rocha was the smallest person at the plant.

"They lowered me down and sent me into the wing," she said. "Nobody else could get into it. That's what we were there for, to do what we can."

CARMEN GRASSO OF OMAHA recalled in 1993 that she often worked 16 hours a day at the Martin Bomber Plant, because "when work had to be done, it couldn't wait."

MARY DUNCAN, who had worked as a waitress in Falls City, Neb., runs a turret lathe.

DOROTHY BURKLAND OF OMAHA welds parts at the Martin Bomber Plant.

'It was patriotic for women to work'

BEHIND THE MEN WHO FIRED THE GUNS, who dropped the bombs, who sailed the ships, who planned the battles that won the war — were women.

They ran streetcars and corner bars. They loaded bombs at the factory and comforted the dying at the front.

World War II brought hundreds of thousands of women into America's factories, farms and armed forces.

The U.S. military took 15 million men from the labor force, and America suddenly faced a shortage of workers at a time of all-out mobilization, after a Depression decade when at least a fifth of the workforce was unemployed.

There was subtle social pressure for women to not seek jobs in the 1930s because they would be competing with men who needed work to support their families.

"But when men went to war, it was patriotic for women to work," said William Pratt, who taught history at the University of Nebraska at Omaha. "Jobs that were traditionally men's work were open to women and minorities."

In the four years beginning in 1942, 6.5 million women went to work for wages across the country.

The symbol of the new working woman was Rosie the Riveter, the composite image of the women who wore coveralls,

NORMA WOODKA LYKINS of West Point, Neb., in a 1994 photo, worked six days a week at the Nebraska Ordnance Plant at Mead.

tied their hair up in bandanas and built weapons to defeat the enemy. "We Can Do It!" Rosie declared, flexing her muscle, in a poster of the time.

"It was essential work," said Norma Woodka Lykins of West Point, Neb. "We were saving American lives."

In 1942, Lykins went from frosting cinnamon rolls in a West Point bakery to painting yellow stripes on 500-pound bombs at the Nebraska Ordnance Plant at Mead.

Single and restless, Lykins moved to Omaha and worked eight-hour shifts, six days a week, at the Mead plant. She lived with a family near 38th and California Streets, exchanging housework and child care for room and board. She joined a car pool to make the 70-mile round-trip journey to Mead each day.

Chick Hastert of Wahoo, Neb., who was an inspector and civilian manager of the 3,000-worker plant, said women made up 75 percent of the workforce at one time.

"They did everything," Hastert recalled in 1994. "They drove trucks and forklifts and loaded bombs with TNT."

The liquid TNT explosive was poured into bombs during an assembly-line procedure that involved 4-mile-long buildings.

"It was like filling beer bottles," Hastert said.

At least half of the women had never worked outside the home before taking jobs at Mead, Hastert said.

"Most were young, and a lot had husbands in the military," he said. "They adjusted right away and were reliable. The biggest problem I had was hearing their complaints about the uniforms — and they couldn't smoke anywhere."

All production workers were required to wear drab tan coveralls. The starting wage for explosives workers was 65 cents an hour. Inspectors were paid 75 cents and supervisors about 95 cents.

Lykins worked at the plant for more than a year, then finished the war with a higher-paying job cutting sheet-metal wing pieces for P-51 Mustang fighter planes at Grand Prairie, Texas.

After the war, she married and held a variety of jobs before ending her working years with a 23-year stint on the production line at Wimmer's Meat Products in West Point.

By October 1944, more than 18,000 women were estimated to be at work in Omaha-area war plants. About 40 percent of the 14,000 workers at the Martin plant were women. Women also filled jobs at Omaha Steel Works, which had war contracts, and at local awning companies, making silk parachutes for fragmentation bombs.

In addition to defense jobs, women replaced men at local breweries, railroads, taxicab and construction companies and the streetcar line. They also broke race and gender barriers at local meatpacking companies, where livestock was slaughtered and prepared for wholesale distribution.

One of the black pioneers of the packinghouses was Rowena Moore of Omaha.

Few, if any, black women had been hired by some Omaha packers when Moore and a few others took up the issue with the union local for Armour & Co., said history professor Pratt. The union took the issue to Armour and then sought federal intervention.

"In some communities," President Franklin Roosevelt said in 1942, "employers dislike to hire women. In others, they are reluctant to hire Negroes. We can no longer afford to indulge such prejudices."

MARY GROTE OF BELLEVUE enjoyed the unveiling of a "Rosie the Riveter" statue at Heartland of America Park in Omaha in 1996. She said she quit high school to work at the Martin Bomber Plant during the war. "Patriotism was very high," she said. "Everyone wanted to do something."

Roosevelt issued an executive order intended to eliminate racial discrimination in hiring in defense plants.

As a result of Moore's initiative, Armour changed its hiring practices, and other uncooperative packers also started hiring black women, Pratt said. Moore got a job at Armour and became a union official.

"There was plenty of work in those days, and I was available," said Moore. "Most women felt they were helping the war, but they also needed work and jobs. We didn't think of it as making history. We were working and enjoying it."

Other trailblazers on the homefront included Elizabeth Taylor, one of Omaha's first female streetcar operators, and Lorna Hoar, the city's first woman to be assigned a mail route.

Women were hit hardest by the massive layoffs that followed the end of the war as defense contracts were canceled. Sixty percent of those fired in the months after the war with Japan ended were women.

"Women were laid off disproportionately," Pratt said. "In some cases, they were glad to give up their jobs and be homemakers. But in many situations women weren't happy to leave, because their jobs had been the best times of their lives."

HELEN (HOUSKA) SEDLAK

Town: Omaha

Service: Civil Service, War Department

In the war: Native of David City, Neb., hired in November 1941 as a clerk-stenographer at the Mead, Neb., ordnance plant. Moved to Omaha after U.S. entered war and worked for Army at Fort Crook. Because of manpower shortage, she was made post sergeant major with a rank equivalent to master sergeant.

In her words: "I know it was unusual as a young civilian woman to be assigned as the post sergeant major, but the general and the colonel had faith in me and thought I would do a good job. They kept me in that job for nearly three years. The men in the headquarters unit were all wonderful to me. They treated me with the greatest respect and did whatever they could to help me. I hated to quit work, but when George (whom she had met before the war) finally came home, I got married and love prevailed."

ROWENA MOORE was one of the first black women to work for an Omaha meatpacker. "We didn't think of it as making history," she said in 1993. "We were working and enjoying it."

OMAHA RED CROSS WORKERS prepare surgical dressings for the U.S. Army.

ED FLYNN, who farmed 2,000 acres north of Valley with L.S. Hunt, operates what The World-Herald described as "the first self-propelled corn-picking machine in Nebraska" in 1944. Implement dealer George A. Reed went along for the ride. The nation's agricultural productivity increased about 25 percent during the war, despite a 17 percent decline in farm population.

'They needed this food'

BY DAVID HENDEE

BEFORE ANNA TIEDJE'S BROTHERS LEFT THE FARM to go to war, they taught her two things: how to start the tractor and how to stop it. Then they were gone.

"I had to learn the rest from scratch," said Tiedje. "It wasn't easy."

But she traded her dresses for overalls and went to work in the fields.

During World War II, farm work was war work, said Michael Schuyler, who taught history at the University of Nebraska at Kearney.

"The people of the Great Plains contributed to the war effort in many ways, but there's no question that the major contribution was the production of food," Schuyler said in 1994.

Farmers felt they were a part of the war effort, said Barbara Marcy of Chadron, Neb., who was a teenager on her parents' farm near Amherst, Neb., during the war.

"It wasn't something we talked about," Marcy said. "We just knew it had to be. . . . They needed this food."

U.S. farmers produced enough to feed half a world and its armies. It wasn't easy. So many young men — like the Tiedje brothers, George and Ernest — left the farm for the military or higher-paying jobs in war industries that rural areas suffered an acute labor shortage. As a result, the draft law was amended in 1942 to allow the deferment of essential agriculture workers until satisfactory replacements could be found.

"The decision to defer farmers was something of a controversial issue because the same thing was not initially available for industrial workers," Schuyler said.

Migrant workers, prisoners of war, townspeople and women eased the shortage.

Anna Tiedje helped out on her family's farm near Bennington after her brothers went off to war.

Charles Miller of Lincoln said Mennonite farmers who refused to join the military and were assigned to a camp for conscientious objectors near Syracuse helped out on many farms.

"The terraces they built for us in the '40s are still there," he said. "They did good work."

Miller, who farmed 11 80-acre parcels of land with his father and another man, was told by his draft board a few days before his scheduled induction at Fort Crook that he was needed more on the farm than in the military.

Charles Marcy of Chadron, who ranched near Hay Springs with wife Barbara, said migrant workers from Mexico would help cut hay on Sand Hills ranches during the summer before moving on to help with the fall sugar beet harvest in the North Platte River Valley around Scottsbluff.

Marcy, who was a crewman on C-47 transport planes supplying ground troops in the north Burma war zone, said shopkeepers in Hay Springs would shut their stores and help ranchers shock grain and stack hay.

Similar twilight crews — named because of the time of day they would arrive on farms — operated in eastern Nebraska. Ed Janike of Lincoln, a retired extension dean at the University of Nebraska-Lincoln, said some of the crews were organized by service clubs.

"We'd find out who needed help, and we'd get a crew together," Janike said. "Many of us had farm experience, and we knew what the farmers were up against."

The help was appreciated, Janike said. "The farm wives were pretty generous with snacks and lunches to keep us going and to keep us interested," he said. "The farmers wanted to pay us, but we were doing it as a service. It was part of the war effort."

Farmers often toiled from dawn to dark to keep up with the work.

"We also patched a lot of machinery," Miller said. "Things we used with horses we'd put behind a tractor we bought in '37. That tractor saved us."

Farm machinery was so scarce that when dealers would

receive a corn picker, for instance, they would hold a drawing to determine who would get to buy it. "Sometimes there'd be 50 people wanting the same machine," Miller said.

Following years of drought and depression, the 1940s brought rain and wartime prosperity to the farm. "The war years were good years," Schuyler said. "Prices were high and the weather was good. That meant more income."

Miller said his father's experience between 1937 and 1943 is a good example of the new prosperity.

"We had a good wheat crop in '37, but we were so hard up," he said. "When Dad got the check (for selling the wheat) it was made out to the banker and the land bank. He didn't get any of it. But by '43 he had paid off the entire debt on his land."

The nation's agricultural productivity increased about 25 percent during the war, despite a 17 percent decline in farm population, Schuyler said.

Wheat production in Nebraska increased by 146 percent from 1940 to 1945. Corn production was up 144 percent. The average sale price per acre rose from $14.33 in 1940 to $44.52 in 1945. Rain increased, too. The statewide average in 1945 was 22.7 inches, compared with 17.4 inches five years earlier. Part of the reason for the production increases was mechanization. Most Midwestern farmers still used horses to work in fields through the early 1940s. The government added a million tractors to the country's farms during the war, showing its commitment to the farm front, Schuyler said.

That was barely enough, Miller said. "There were only 12 (one- and two-row) corn pickers allotted to Otoe County," he said.

Tiedje learned to live with the shortages — and she learned to drive the tractor. "I didn't mind farming after a while," she said. "I liked farming better than working in the house."

She and a third brother, Fred, ran their elderly parents' 200-acre farm. Their parents, who had immigrated separately from Germany, started the farm after their marriage in 1900. Fred had a deferment from military service because his father was ailing.

Anna Tiedje drove the tractor, and her brother ran a team of horses. Before and after field work, Anna helped with chores, such as milking 12 cows morning and night.

Her brother Ernest, who served in the Army in North Africa and Italy, worked briefly at the farm after returning from the war. George was wounded in Normandy during the battle for St. Lo, a bloody victory in which Nebraska's 134th Infantry Regiment played a key role. He died in England and is buried in the German cemetery near Bennington.

Wearing overalls, a shirt, heavy gloves and a broad-brimmed hat tied to her head, Anna Tiedje said in an April 1942 interview that she accepted her job.

"I can't say that I like it," she said. "It's just a matter of having to do it."

War's Effect on Ag Production

A comparison of agricultural production in Nebraska for 1940 and 1945. Grain production in millions of bushels, sugar beets and potatoes in millions of tons and livestock in millions of animals. Value is in millions of dollars.

	YEAR	PRODUCTION	VALUE
WHEAT	1940	34.6	$ 23.5
	1945	85.2	125.3
CORN	1940	105.6	61.2
	1945	258.32	68.6
OATS	1940	34.2	10.2
	1945	74.1	43.7
BARLEY	1940	21.1	8.2
	1945	13.4	12.6
RYE	1940	2.7	1.1
	1945	4.5	5.4
SUGAR BEETS	1940	0.93	4.6
	1945	0.63	5.8
POTATOES	1940	11.3	5.2
	1945	12.1	13.9
CATTLE	1940	2.2	67.5
	1945	3.2	161.2
HOGS	1940	0.8	94.7
	1945	1.02	18.3

Source: 1945 Nebraska Blue Book

"The war years were good years. Prices were high and the weather was good. That meant more income."

— MICHAEL SCHUYLER

MEMORIES OF A GENERATION ★

MARIE (SWIRCINSKI) MADSEN

Town: Omaha

Service: Hired when she was 17 as a part-time statistical draftsman for the Army 7th Service Command in the Federal Building at 15th and Dodge Streets. Drafted scale drawings of bridges and other structures slated for demolition by the resistance movement in Europe prior to the Allied invasion. Collected and recorded data on all soldiers in the 7th Service Command who were killed or wounded in action.

In her words: "I remember V-E Day and V-J Day and the happy crowds celebrating the end of the war around the Walgreens drugstore and Orpheum Theater downtown. I went home the night of V-J Day, and a neighborhood boy who had been a POW in Europe came to our house with several other neighbors. And we stayed up late singing, while my younger sister Virginia played the piano. It was quite a time — the war was finally over."

ESTHER HAYNES

Town: Omaha

Service: Worked as a seamstress at Standard Tent and Awning and later at a factory that made waterproof bags to ship war supplies.

In the war: Married Roy on Feb. 22, 1942; Roy left for Fort Leavenworth, Kan., on March 6, 1942. Esther lived with her parents while Roy was in the Army.

In her words: While working as a seamstress, Esther made 40 cents an hour. She said the company employed about 70 seamstresses and "more than one-half had a personal stake in the war effort: brothers, sons, husbands in the armed services. ... I wrote a lot of letters (to Roy) and got a lot back. I still have a lot of letters that I haven't thrown away. God watched over us, and we were very thankful."

JANET "JAN" BLUE

Town: Lincoln

In the war: She worked in the Nebraska Department of Insurance at the State Capitol in Lincoln after completing one year of college at Peru State. She married Wayne Blue in March 1944 and was a homemaker for 18 years, then a license administrator for nearly 27 years with Bankers Life Nebraska.

In her words: "I was working in the Insurance Department at the State Capitol when Pearl Harbor was bombed. I had met Wayne at Bob's Coffee Shop (14th and O Streets) when he worked as a host during the noon hours. He was on a football scholarship, playing fullback, and I frequented the coffee shop more than a couple times a week. While stationed at Colorado Springs, he flew the P-38 into Lincoln a number of times, and he always managed to buzz the Capitol. My friend was secretary to the governor at the time, and she told me that on one occasion when (Wayne) buzzed, the governor was dictating to her and he stopped to look out the window to see what was happening. Ours was strictly a platonic relationship, with many letters while he went through flight training and then overseas to join the Northwest African Strategic Air Force.

"After 10 months and 50 missions, he returned to the States. He sent me a Western Union telegram to say he would be in Lincoln on Friday night, Feb. 25. I had a date, but I broke it and went to the Cornhusker to welcome my pilot home. He went to his home near Tecumseh on Saturday, and on Tuesday, Feb. 29, 1944 (Leap Year Day), while we were having lunch at the Capital Hotel coffee shop, he said to me, 'Are you going to California with me?' I looked at him and said, 'I can't go to California with you.' Then he said, 'We'll get married.' That was not the formal proposal I had always dreamed about. I told him, 'I can't get married because I'm not 21 and my folks have never met you. I'd need permission from my parents.' He told me to ask my folks and if I didn't, then he'd ask them.

"As it all turned out, we were married at the Methodist Student House on the university campus at 3 o'clock in the afternoon, and at 5 o'clock we were watching the Nebraska Boys High School Basketball Tournament in the Old Coliseum. Yes, we did go to California together on a cattle train — we really only had one seat because he hadn't asked for two, not knowing for sure if all would work out."

CHARLOTTE REES SCHULTZ

Town: Omaha

In the war: She was head nurse at Nebraska Methodist Hospital in Omaha. In September 1940, she married Frederick Schultz, who was in the Nebraska National Guard. In December 1940, the Guard was mobilized and sent to Camp Robinson in Little Rock, Ark.

In her words: "We were naive enough to believe at the end of a year the Guard would return home and Fred could then start medical school. In December 1941, war was declared, and in January 1942 the Guard was ordered to California. I had kept my job at Methodist, and Fred called that they had orders and were being sent out of the country. Although my work was declared essential, I took a leave of absence and left for Monterey, where Fred was stationed in a country club, living in tents on the grounds. During the next eight months we lived in suspense each week of his being shipped out of the country.

"In August 1942, the 35th Division was all together in Ojai, Calif., to be sent overseas. Most were moved to the European Theater, and many lost their lives in the Battle of the Bulge and on Omaha Beach. Fred's unit was sent to the Aleutian Islands in Alaska. The island of Kiska was occupied by the Japanese. He landed on Adak. They lived in tents in zero and below temperatures, built the airstrip, and felt fortunate to miss several Japanese bombs. One bomb missed the troop ship he was on when heading for the battle for Kiska. When they landed on Kiska, the Japanese had hastily deserted the island, leaving hot rice on the stove. He spent 26 months on Adak without a furlough, came home in 1944 and was sent to Fort Hood, Texas, to train troops. He was discharged September 1945. ... He retired from the Nebraska National Guard after 31 years of service, a chief warrant officer.

"When Fred went to the Aleutians I returned to my work at Methodist Hospital. Many nurses had joined the Army or the war industries for better pay. The few of us remaining in hospitals did anything that needed to be done. Red Cross Gray Ladies were very helpful, and they and the student nurses did most of the patient care, while we were responsible for nursing service and nursing education. The National Nurse Corps had been introduced, and enrollment in nursing schools soared. ... In addition to working long hours, several of us attended night school at the University of Omaha, working for a bachelor's degree in nursing. I received my degree in 1952, my master's in education in 1956, and established one of the first counseling programs in the nation at Methodist School of Nursing. I retired as director of student services in 1979. The war really changed our lives, but we felt we were very fortunate."

MARJORIE SLIZESKI

Town: Omaha

Service: Worked as a secretary for the Navy base on Treasure Island in San Francisco Bay

In the war: Her job was updating sailors' records.

In her words: "George Slizeski was a student in the gunnery and electric hydraulic school. I met him when he brought the muster lists to my counter. He was top man in his class, so was kept on as an instructor. We started dating and were soon engaged. Of course, there came a day when I had to type his orders to go aboard a sea plane tender. We were married when he returned home after the war. We were together over 62 years."

EULA WICKERSHAM CAMPBELL

Town: Scottsdale, Ariz.; born and raised on a ranch 15 miles northeast of Harrison, Neb.

In the war: She graduated from Sioux County High School in 1939 and then attended Grand Island Business College. When she turned 18, she went to Washington, D.C., to be a "government girl," working as a secretary at the Army War College. Later, she worked at Hill Field near Ogden, Utah, as a secretary for the Army Air Forces. After the war, she went to San Francisco to continue her secretarial career.

In her words: "My cousin, Billie Pepper, was married to Freeman (Pep) Pepper, who was a guard on Alcatraz. They lived on the 'Rock' in an apartment house along with other senior guard families. It was from their balcony that I watched our victorious Pacific Fleet sail under the Golden Gate Bridge. This was the most magnificent sight — all our great ships, fireboats shooting water, bands playing 'Sentimental Journey,' and the decks crowded with our brave, happy sailors! And there I was, a little Nebraska ranch girl, with tears of joy, waving, screaming and jumping up and down. Since then, I have watched an early space shuttle land at Edwards Air Base in California, our gymnastics team win the gold in Los Angeles, met and talked to many significant people, but watching our fleet come home remains the most memorable patriotic moment of my life."

Lifting spirits

TEN DAYS AFTER THE BOMBING OF PEARL HARBOR in 1941, North Platte residents heard that their own Company D of the Nebraska National Guard would pass through the city by train en route to the West Coast. ★ About 500 residents rushed to the Union Pacific Railroad station with cookies, candy, cake and cigarettes. This Company D turned out to be from Kansas, but the unit was still welcomed with gifts. ★ The experience gave one woman in the crowd an idea. Rae Wilson arranged for people in the city to start meeting all of the trains, beginning on Christmas Day 1941. ★ Terry Terranova of Brecksville, Ohio, recalled stopping at the canteen as an Army infantryman. "After spending a night in the Chicago stockyards on the troop train, stranded between a train of cattle and another one of pigs, we were in pretty sad shape. When the train pulled into North Platte it was a real blessing ... because we got off, and there was this whole troop of beautiful women dressed in prairie skirts and whatnot, and they were carrying these baskets loaded with candy, cigarettes and chewing gum. I was just so impressed with that whole experience I never forgot it."

COLUMBIAN ELEMENTARY SCHOOL STUDENTS pass out food to servicemen at Union Station in Omaha in 1943. The children brought 372 hard-boiled eggs and 1,112 homemade cookies after reading in The World-Herald that donations had dropped.

'They made us feel like heroes'

"When those trains would come in and when they'd leave, you would have a big lump in your throat, because you just knew that some of them wouldn't come back."

— WYLMA CANTRAL, WHO HANDED OUT COOKIES AND CAKE AT THE NORTH PLATTE CANTEEN

IT WAS ONLY A FEW MINUTES out of a long train ride across America. But as the years and decades passed in a blur — like the 1940s Nebraska countryside that rolled by to the clickety-clack rhythm of the rails — the memories never faded.

Nineteen-year-old Ray Merrell, on his way to Marine Corps boot camp, thought it was a USO club.

Jean Cashier, traveling to a new Coast Guard assignment in San Francisco, was surprised with an angel food birthday cake.

Vincent Anderson, a veteran of Marine campaigns in the South Pacific and an earlier visit to the remote stop, went straight for the deviled eggs.

For 6 million troops who passed through Nebraska on Union Pacific Railroad trains during World War II, the North Platte Depot's canteen was a fleeting moment of home.

For five years, the residents of North Platte and about 125 Nebraska, Colorado and Kansas communities — sharing rationed food and fuel — served endless platters of sandwiches, cakes, cookies, hard-boiled eggs, doughnuts, popcorn balls, beverages, cigarettes and magazines. Not once did the canteen run out of food.

No other town in America matched North Platte's volunteer venture during the war.

THE VOLUNTEER EFFORT in North Platte served up to 8,000 troops a day.

FORMER NORTH PLATTE CANTEEN VOLUNTEER LORENE HUEBNER greeted ex-Marine Vincent Anderson at a canteen reunion in 2004.
"It was shoulder-to-shoulder servicemen, and we sure smiled at them a lot," she said of the canteen. "But we also knew we were a nation at war."

The canteen operated daily from Dec. 25, 1941, through April 1, 1946. Canteen workers served up to 8,000 troops from as many as 23 trains a day.

Lorene Huebner of North Platte was a high school student when she accompanied her mother to peel eggs, make sandwiches and wash tea towels.

"It was shoulder-to-shoulder servicemen, and we sure smiled at them a lot," she said. "But we also knew we were a nation at war. Our friends were going off to war, and we knew we'd never see some of them again."

Cashier, of Fayetteville, N.Y., said the dedication of those who devoted much of what they had to strangers was overwhelming.

"Nobody forgets North Platte," she said.

The war in Europe was winding down when Cashier stopped at the canteen. When somebody asked if there were any birthdays, she piped up that she would be turning 22 in a few days.

"We had a birthday party on the train," she said. "It was such a good time."

Merrell, of Liberty, Mo., was in civilian clothes with other Marine recruits when their train stopped in November 1942.

He wrote in his diary of all the sandwiches, cookies and drinks they were offered. "We didn't know it was a canteen," he said. "We just knew that ladies were there and they were happy to see us."

Merrell fought at Bougainville, Guam and Okinawa as a Marine Raider. His 10 minutes at North Platte rank among his best wartime memories.

"It's unbelievable that those ladies met all those troops," he said.

Anderson, of Palm Desert, Calif., was a survivor of an attack on the aircraft carrier USS Lexington in the Coral Sea and anti-aircraft battery combat in the South Pacific when he stopped at the canteen in April 1945.

He was a platoon sergeant in charge of 10 other Marines en route from San Francisco to Camp Lejeune, N.C., for Officer Candidate School.

"We were in the sleeper car, and the military police on the train told me that we're going to be stopping at North Platte, the best stop you'll make in crossing the United States," Anderson said. "I asked what they meant. They said, 'Wait until you see.'"

Like Cashier, Anderson was greeted by a woman with a big birthday cake. "It was close to my birthday, so she said, 'We'll make it your birthday in North Platte.' I didn't know what to do with it. I got coffee and divided it with the guys with me."

A few months later, when Anderson returned to the West Coast, he knew what to expect. "I made sure I was good and hungry by the time I got to North Platte," he said.

Anderson squeezed into the crowded canteen and headed for the far end of a table. "I got four or five stuffed eggs."

When the train pulled away a few minutes later, the canteen women were on the platform, waving.

"They made us feel like heroes."

DORIS DOTSON (in a 1990 photo) decorated a wall of her North Platte tavern with pictures of servicemen who had stopped at the canteen.

Daily shopping list

DORIS DOTSON, who started working at the canteen when she was 10, was too young to be a "platform girl" — canteen workers age 16 and up who took supplies out to trains that carried wounded men or those whose duties were considered top secret. But she made up for her youth.

"In the corner there was a jukebox and piano," Dotson said in 1990. "Some of the girls my age would jitterbug with the men. Many a time they'd dance and then on the way out to the train they'd grab the food and then eat it on the train. They'd rather dance than eat."

She kept records on canteen activities. One daily shopping list reads:

160 to 175	loaves of bread
100	pounds of meat
15	pounds of cheese
2	quarts of peanut butter and other spreads
18	pounds of butter
45	pounds of coffee
40	quarts of cream
500	half-pint bottles of milk
35	dozen rolls
18 to 20	birthday cakes were handed out each day

KEEPING THE TROOPS IN THEIR THOUGHTS

HELEN HARVEY (LEFT) AND ADRIENNE HARMS arranged the Benson High Victory Corps display in the school's lobby. The nationwide program promoted physical fitness and community service.

MANY BUSINESSES SALUTED EMPLOYEES who had joined the military. The World-Herald's "Roll of Honor" hung in the newspaper's lobby.

JANET J. ZUCHOWSKI OF THE WOMEN AIRFORCE SERVICE PILOTS AND ARMY LT. B.J. WHITE added their signatures to the 3,000 on the walls at the Red Cross canteen at the Omaha airport.

MARY LOIS (HARMON) RADFORD

Town: Grew up in Pacific Junction, Iowa; lived in Glenwood

Service: Navy WAVES Nurse

In the war: While in boot camp, joined the singing platoon and sang for President Harry Truman. After boot camp, served as a nurse at Camp Moffett in Great Lakes, Ill., and then at a hospital in Corvallis, Ore.

In her words: "One of the reasons I went to the Navy was because my brother was in the Navy. . . . I enjoyed working with people my own age. They all needed our help and they liked us. I liked to joke around with them. If they had to have shots, I'd say 'OK, let's line up and stand at attention. Now drop your drawers and bend over!' They liked to be joked with. . . . I feel like joining the service was one of the best things I've ever done, serving the country and helping my people."

USO VOLUNTEERS IN OMAHA served refreshments to servicemen on Christmas Day 1942.

Community spirit funded the USO

USO (UNITED SERVICE ORGANIZATIONS) CENTERS were established throughout the Omaha area, including Union Station, north Omaha, South Omaha and Bellevue.

The community efforts to greet, feed and entertain the men and women in uniform ranged from a network of 21 community organizations that took turns staffing the Union Station Service Men's Center to a club of four South Omaha girls who called themselves "Uncle Sam's Little Helpers."

The girls raised $5 by selling lemonade and telling neighborhood kids' fortunes.

The USOs served both homefront soldiers stationed at such places as the Bruning, Neb., Army Air Field and those passing through Omaha by train.

The volunteer efforts sometimes reached massive proportions. During the summer of 1942, as many as 115 women packed rooms in the Union Pacific headquarters building to meet a daily quota of 2,000 rolled bandages for the Red Cross.

The Junior Red Cross of the Edward Rosewater School donated 250 kolaches, 200 dozen cookies and rolls and 40 cakes to the Union Station center in April 1944.

SOUTH OMAHA USO DIRECTOR KATHLEEN O'GRADY accepts $5 raised by "Uncle Sam's Little Helpers," from left, Bonnie Jean Hancock, Elaine Hess, Shirley Bernard and Barbara Bernard. The girls made money by selling lemonade and telling fortunes.

STUDENTS FROM HOWARD KENNEDY ELEMENTARY SCHOOL brought gifts for the USO at 2717 N. 24th St. to replace losses from a fire at the building.

TOBACCO MERCHANT J.J. EARLY receives a check from Mrs. E.C. Williams, Mrs. Sarah Salleng and Mrs. Harry Jensen of the MacArthur Mother's Club for 1,500 packs of cigarettes to be sent overseas to servicemen. The club had placed containers in local businesses for donations to "Cigarettes for Soldiers."

BEVERLY M. (WOODRING) GEYZA

Town: Omaha

Service: Women's Army Auxiliary Corps, U.S. Navy

In the war: Clerical worker until 1945

In her words: "Lots of us were in both the Women's Army Auxiliary Corps and the Navy. I did office work in south Florida and the Washington, D.C., area. We were relieving the men. They didn't like it (office work), and they had to go out and fight."

Thanksgiving dinner in 1944 was served to 3,000 at Union Station. The menu included 22 turkeys, 20 pounds of Canadian bacon, two chickens, 150 pies, 1,400 buttered rolls and 600 sandwiches.

In commemoration of Mother's Day in 1943, the MacArthur Mother's Club raised money to have 1,500 packages of cigarettes sent to service personnel in Australia.

The Benson West Elementary School Junior Red Cross in 1943 collected fresh fruit for distribution at the Union Station canteen. The tally: 922 apples and 877 oranges.

But the USO didn't have a monopoly on hospitality during the war.

As fleets of transcontinental troop trains pulled into Omaha's Union Pacific and Burlington Railroad passenger depots daily, the terminals exploded with action.

"The trains would pull in, and it wouldn't be one minute before you'd see a sea of service people come running up the street to the string of taverns across the street," said Bill Kratville, who often watched the race at Union Station with his mother, a USO volunteer.

When trains such as the Los Angeles Challenger and the Portland Rose steamed into Omaha each evening during the war, troops poured from the passenger cars, raced up stairs into the terminal, dashed through the lobby and ... made a choice.

RALPH TURKEL

Town: Omaha

Service: Navy, Navy Dental Corps

In the war: The dentist examined troops in California, some leaving for war and some returning.

In his words: "The guys that came back needed a lot of dental care. They were fighting a war, after all. They didn't have time for things like fillings."

SEAMAN 2ND CLASS BOB WALTMIER OF OMAHA entertains a USO crowd with his original dance moves.

They could either climb another set of stairs to the Servicemen's Center and its free mountains of sandwiches and rivers of coffee, or continue their sprint through the west doors and across the trolley car tracks to one of the nearby taverns.

Many chose the taverns.

"Now and then, some of the soldiers and sailors would learn of a shortcut from the train crews," Kratville recalled in 1994. "They'd take the elevated causeway (connecting the U.P. and Burlington stations) and go through the Burlington depot. They only had about 30 minutes in town until their train moved on. It was quite a sight."

Joe and Georgia Herdzina, who owned Joe's Parkway bar and restaurant near 32nd Avenue and Frederick Streets, displayed a German saber on a wall. It was given to Herdzina by a soldier who appreciated his friendship as the serviceman was preparing to go overseas.

"They were a nice bunch of guys," Georgia Herdzina said of the servicemen and locals who patronized their business around the clock during the war.

Joe Herdzina said, "We were always packed. The stockyard fellows would come after their shifts. Bomber plant workers and military men would be there, too."

He gave his business cards to servicemen to distribute when they were overseas. The back of the cards listed the rank of poker hands to help novice players. The cards could be redeemed at Joe's Parkway for a free drink after the war.

"I had those cards all over Europe and in the South Pacific," Joe Herdzina said. "Those were the days."

THE WORLD-HERALD REPORTED that the female-to-male ratio was 4-to-1 at a USO dance in 1942. Pvt. Ray Johnson of Sergeant, Iowa, was a popular fellow, gaining the attention of, clockwise from left, Margery O'Neill, Maxine McIntyre, Margaret Bastin, Mary Piper, Shirley Spar and Betty Welsh (on Johnson's lap).

'WE'LL MEET AGAIN, DON'T KNOW WHERE, DON'T KNOW WHEN …'

A 1943 EVENT HOSTED by the Jewish Community Center allowed an opportunity for dancing cheek to cheek.

EVELYN (MCBRIDE) CARTER (left)
Town: Gretna

In the war: She was in second grade, just one month shy of her seventh birthday, when Pearl Harbor was bombed. Her family lived in Springfield.

In her words: "The boys went into the service as soon as they graduated from high school. They looked so handsome in their uniforms. When they came home on furlough, they came by bus or train or once in a while hitchhiked. I had two uncles in the service, and we met them at Union Station in Omaha. As big and tall as Union Station is, it was way too small for the amount of people in it. I was 8 years old and too big to be held by an adult, so I was packed in tighter than a sardine in a can. All I could see was the ceiling, the tops of windows and the ticket booths, the one tile under my foot, and the butt or belly of the person in front of me. The noise was such that you couldn't hear yourself think, people talking, trains coming and going all the time, and they were announced by the PA system, which added to the din. I could not understand a word they said and didn't know how anyone else could. My uncle Wayne McBride was killed Feb. 3, 1944, in a plane crash over or near Barksdale, La., while practicing for the invasion of Normandy. The young man who accompanied his body home was killed at the invasion."

'An arsenal of powerful visual symbols'

JOHN FALTER PRODUCED MORE THAN 300
World War II posters that encouraged the
romantic ideal of patriotism and reminded
the public of what was at risk.

IN THE WORLD WAR II BATTLEGROUND of public opinion, Nebraska-born artist John Falter was one of America's chief combatants.

Falter, best known for his cover illustrations for the Saturday Evening Post, produced more than 300 recruiting and incentive posters while on active duty as a lieutenant with the U.S. Naval Reserve.

Wartime posters were designed to sway public opinion and behavior with a careful combination of symbols, pictures and slogans, said Stacey Bredhoff at the National Archives in Washington.

"Posters appeared everywhere on the American homefront — constant reminders of the many ways citizens should support the war through bond drives, scrap drives, ration plans and war work," Bredhoff said in 1994.

"Poster designers drew from an arsenal of powerful visual symbols, which were strategically combined with words to evoke . . . confidence, optimism and patriotism . . . guilt, grief and fear."

Motivational posters sought to instill patriotism by using the colors red, white and blue. Pictures of muscles and weapons conveyed American strength.

"Some of the posters were so effective in their designs, they remain as powerful today as they were years ago," Bredhoff said.

Among Falter's major wartime works were portraits of Gen. Mark Clark, Adm. William Halsey and Lt. Clark Gable for Look magazine. He also did a series of 12 paintings of American war heroes — including Pacific air ace Joe Foss of South Dakota — for Esquire magazine.

The Esquire paintings of 1943 and 1944, although not widely known, could be Falter's greatest legacy, said Gail Potter, curator of the Museum of Nebraska History.

The Esquire stories were devoted mainly to winners of the nation's highest award for bravery, the Medal of Honor. Their deeds were recounted in stirring, impassioned prose. Falter's illustrations were cut out and pinned on thousands of kids' bedroom walls and in high school homerooms.

Falter was born in Plattsmouth and grew up in Falls City. He painted 185 cover illustrations for the Saturday Evening Post from 1943 to 1969. Only Norman Rockwell painted more.

A park in Falls City features a 15-foot replica of the 75-foot water tower that Falter often climbed as a boy to look down on the town. The elevated perspective is seen in several of his illustrations of small-town America.

Falter also produced many oil paintings depicting the westward migration from the Missouri River to the Rocky Mountains in the 1800s. He also did sketches of jazz musicians.

He died in Philadelphia in 1982 at age 71.

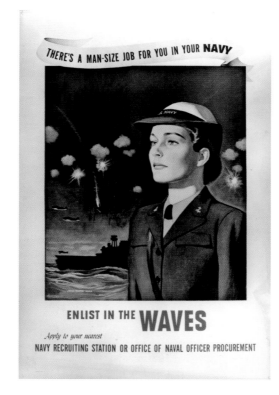

WAR POSTERS PRODUCED by Nebraska-born artist John Falter.

GERALDINE "GERRY" KILLION NELSON

Town: Omaha; moved to Arizona in 1972

Service: Served in the Navy WAVES, was discharged in 1945 as a yeoman 1st class. She did general office work in Recruit Records at the Great Lakes Training Center in Chicago. She became secretary to the lieutenant in charge of the unit. She remained friends with several of her bunkmates from that time and was active in WAVES National Unit 114 in Mesa, Ariz.

In her words: "Service-women at that time were accepted reluc-tantly and needed to prove themselves, which we did. Many used the benefits earned — GI Bill for education, home ownership, civil service opportunities — all the benefits were the same as our servicemen."

MEMORIES OF A GENERATION ★

ESTELLE LEINEN

Town: Dow City, Iowa; grew up in Chicago.

Service: U.S. Navy WAVES, from 1942 to 1945, reaching the rank of storekeeper 1st class.

In the war: After 11 weeks of boot camp in the Bronx, N.Y., Leinen worked in storekeeping at Great Lakes Naval Station near Waukegan, Ill., for the duration of the war. She maintained supplies for the cooks and bakers in the station's 11 galleys. There she met a sailor from Iowa, Lavern Leinen, who was a cook on an aircraft carrier. They married after the war, and he took her back to Dow City, where they raised six children.

In her words: "My job as a storekeeper wasn't a very strategic one, but I thought that I would try to do my part. Some of the guys didn't appreciate us women coming in, however, because then they got put on ships and sent off to war."

BETTY VANDEVEER RADOSTI

Town: Creighton, Neb.

Service: Yeoman 3rd class, Navy WAVES

In the war: Boot camp at Hunter College in New York City, then yeoman training at Cedar Falls, Iowa. Worked in the Armed Guard Center at Treasure Island in San Francisco, in the receiving and transfer department. The Armed Guard Center put gunners on tankers and transport and supply ships. Her job was to see that sailors' records were sent with them wherever they were transferred, and to keep track of the records for those who were sent to Treasure Island.

In her words (as told to daughter Susan Radosti): "When I was sent to Treasure Island in San Francisco Bay, there were no places for the women to stay on the island, so they stayed in private homes in San Francisco until quarters were established on the base. Some time later my mother came out to visit me and I found some rooms in a home where my mother could stay. I got permission from the base to stay at the home while my mother was in town, but when she left, I never told the Navy and continued to stay in that home until I got married. The owner of the house and her husband were separated, but the husband arrived there every morning and worked down in the basement. I went to the basement one day and found a bank of telephones. The husband was a bookie!"

JOSEPHINE J. (DELAHUNTY) SEMERENA

Town: Lincoln

During the war: Semerena graduated from Creighton University in 1942 with a degree as a registered nurse and was sworn in at old Fort Omaha that same year. She served in several military hospitals around the United States before the end of the war.

In her words: "My first station was in Colorado at Lowry Base in Denver. I was there until June of that year, and then I was transferred to Kansas City, Mo. There were several radio schools around Kansas City, and those soldiers came to our hospital, along with those from the big train depot. … I was transferred to Jefferson Barracks in St. Louis for a time, and ended up at Yuma Air Force Base in Arizona in 1944, back before the Air Force was called the Air Force. … We helped all stateside soldiers, anyone who was feeling sick, and worked the maternity ward for wives of soldiers who were pregnant. … I got married in Yuma, and about six months later got pregnant. Back in those days, they discharged women when they got pregnant. I was discharged on April 5, 1945. … It was a wonderful experience, being a nurse in that time. I enjoyed every minute of it."

JUNE SPORLEDER

Town: Bancroft, Neb., formerly Carroll, Iowa

Service: Women's Army Corps

In the war: She was in the Women's Army Corps from January 1945 to May 1948. She took basic training at Fort Des Moines, Iowa, and medical training at Fitzsimmons General Hospital in Denver. She then was sent to a field hospital at Fort Francis E. Warren in Cheyenne, Wyo., where she worked as a circulating technician in surgery. Her orders next took her to Winter General Hospital at Topeka, Kan., where she was made orthopedic ward mistress and worked under the charge doctor and head nurse. Her next assignment took her to Halloran General Hospital at Staten Island, N.Y.

In her words: "The orders were to report to Halloran General Hospital on Staten Island. This ended up being quite an experience for me. Mable Mummey (a friend from Allentown, Pa.) promised to wait for me at Penn Station on her way home. Somehow, she forgot our plans and she was nowhere around! I went directly to traveler's aid … (and) the lady there was very helpful. She gave me a map of the boroughs and Manhattan Island. I have this map in my scrapbook. She explained the subway systems and showed me where Halloran was located. She called the WAC quarters to tell them I was that far. Then a miracle happened! A Red Cross van stopped to come in and get warm. A bunch of ladies were going out to the hospital to entertain the patients. The aid lady said, 'Please take this WAC with you, only take her to the WAC area office so that she gets there on time.' Again, I feel that the Lord was guiding me. I had to be there by 11, and I arrived at the WAC area at 9. Mabel begged my forgiveness that she had forgotten to wait for my train to come in to Penn Station."

PAUL ARAUJO

Town: He grew up in Lexington, Neb., and retired in Omaha

Service: 383rd Regiment, 96th Division, 10th Army

In the war: He turned 19 on a troop ship en route to the South Pacific island of Saipan to prepare for the invasion of Okinawa, which began April 1, 1945. Awards he received include the Bronze Star with Valor device and Combat Infantry Badge. He also received two Purple Hearts, the first on May 15, 1945, and the second on May 19, 1945. He spent two to three months recovering from shrapnel wounds at Naval Fleet Hospital 115 in Guam and then another two months hospitalized in Hawaii.

In his words: "I was called up for pre-induction before graduating from Lexington High School. Every time I go by the Durham Museum it takes me back to that fateful day we loaded on the troop train on that very site to make the trip to Camp Wolters, Texas, for basic training to go to war. After basic training, I came home on leave and then left a short time later for Fort Lawton, Wash., for final preparations prior to shipping overseas. The train stopped in North Platte, Neb., at the canteen, and I discovered I had left with the keys to our family car. A hostess in the canteen was gracious enough to agree to make arrangements for getting my parents those keys they needed back in Lexington. Whoever you are that helped me, if you read this, the keys made it back, and thank you again."

JEANNE C. HOUSTON

Town: La Vista

Service: United Service Organization

During the war: Before joining the USO, Houston used to go to the Music Box in Omaha. She and her friends, 18 at the time, fixed their IDs to get into the 21-and-up hall to dance with servicemen. A friend convinced her to join the USO in 1942, when she was 19, and she spent that year as a USO Junior Hostess to servicemen in Omaha.

In her words: "The bus would take us to Fort Omaha, and we danced with the boys, they'd just bring them in. There were always more men than ladies, so we weren't allowed to dance with one all night. They made sure to let the men meet as many of the girls as possible. … It was so much fun, I just loved to dance. I remember one boy from New York came in, he had red, curly hair. We danced and he'd swing me all around, up over his shoulders and in the air. I must've been crazy. … One time a group of French sailors came in. They didn't speak a word of English, and we didn't speak a word of French, but we still got along just fine. … It was strange, the war was going on, but we didn't even think about the fact that most of these boys, some of these boys, were going to go off and die in the war. So it was a sad time, but it was a fun time. … They say you shouldn't live in the past, but that was a good time for me. Those were my best years."

LORRAINE L. HEDMAN

Town: Omaha

Service: Army Nurse Corps

In the war: She graduated from a basic nursing program in the fall of 1944 and joined the Army Nurse Corps in January 1945 in Kansas City, Mo. She was sent to Camp Carson in Colorado Springs, Colo., for basic training. From there, she was sent to Fitzsimons Army Hospital in Denver. Fitzsimons was a large hospital caring for servicemen and women who, because of their injuries, were unable to return to the front lines. Most of the patients came from combat or POW camps in the Pacific Theater. Nurses were being prepared to go to the South Pacific for the invasion of Japan. But then the bomb was dropped, the war ended, and she and the other nurses did not have to go.

In her words: "My duty was as head nurse on two psychiatric wards. We cared for those patients suffering emotionally from effects of the war or having been confined in prisoner-of-war camps in the Pacific. Many were diagnosed as 'shell-shocked.' Today, we'd say post-traumatic syndrome. Our first duty on their arrival from the train was to clean them up, provide clean clothes, give them plenty of good food and a bed to sleep on. What a change in the first few days. As they recovered, many VIP groups would visit the wards, greeting the men. One of my duties was to tour the VIPs and introduce them to patients. One particular day stands out in my memory for two reasons. It was April 12, 1945. I was touring a group that included Mr. Ty Cobb, a baseball legend. I couldn't believe it. Here he was in person. A very nice person. Shook my hand and talked with all the GIs. As the tour continued, I was called to the office for a message. I was to tell the group that President Roosevelt had passed away in Warm Springs, Ga. This I did, and the group left immediately."

The war comes home

THE ARMY AIR BASE IN ALLIANCE, NEB., trained between 12,000 and 15,000 troops at a time from 1943 through the end of the war in 1945. "In that century, it was about the biggest thing that happened to Alliance," said Gloria Clark, a former Alliance resident who researched the base history. At the time, the population of Alliance was about 6,600 people, Clark said, so the influx of 5,000 construction workers and then the trainees had a huge influence. ★ When the base was dedicated, an estimated 66,000 people attended a program that included a re-enactment of the recent invasion of Sicily. One witness said the drop of dozens of paratroopers during the event looked like "popcorn falling from the sky." ★ Such dedication ceremonies were rare during wartime, according to Clark, for fear of providing information to the enemy. But military officials apparently thought that Nebraska's Panhandle was far enough from either coast and invited Life and Time photographers to document the event.

CREIGHTON UNIVERSITY ENDED ITS FOOTBALL PROGRAM during the war, one of countless disruptions of everyday life. The 1942 Army War Show at the stadium featured a display of the latest military equipment.

A SOLDIER STANDS GUARD
at the airfield in Kearney.

'Most people in town were involved'

PARATROOPERS FROM THE
ALLIANCE AIR BASE jump near 42nd
and Bancroft Streets in Omaha.
About 25,000 people gathered to
watch the demonstration.

DURING WORLD WAR II, scores of B-24 bombers and P-47 fighter planes, their engines at full throttle, arced into the Nebraska sky.

Nebraska was the site of 12 Army airfields, all but one of them constructed soon after America's entry into the war.

Glider pilots and paratroopers practiced for the D-Day invasion in the grassy Sand Hills and in the wooded Pine Ridge at nearby Fort Robinson.

In one exercise, the paratroopers "captured" the Denver airport.

As in other towns with new air bases and ammunition plants, the airfield at Kearney provided hundreds of jobs for civilians and strained city services and resources.

"Most people in town were involved in some way with the base," said Jean Lynch of Kearney, who was a USO hostess and later married a soldier from Georgia she met at a dance. "Some local carpenters went in there on the first day and were still there when it closed."

Housing was provided on the base for about 4,000 military personnel. Kearney's population was about 9,600. Rents soared until federal controls were imposed in 1943.

"People lived in unfinished basements, any place they could find," Lynch recalled in 1994.

School enrollment swelled. Some classrooms had more than 50 pupils. Five brothels were tolerated by local officials, and venereal disease was usually within the midrange of rates experienced by other bases in the country, said Todd Petersen of Minden, who has studied the base history.

B-24 Liberator bombers used for training are lined up at the Fairmont Army Air Field.

The Kearney airfield was a processing center for tens of thousands of bomber crews on their way to the battlefront. The most widely known soldier to pass through Kearney was actor Clark Gable, who served as a gunnery instructor in England.

During the three- to seven-day processing routine, airplanes were given final inspections and men were issued gear, inoculated and provided final instructions. They also wrote wills.

Kearney residents also faced another change in their community when a squadron of black soldiers — who primarily worked in the airfield mess halls — was stationed at the base.

"Kearney only had one black family at that time," Lynch said. "I remember that an old hotel downtown was designated for black people."

America's armed forces were segregated during World War II, and a separate recreation center and swimming pool had to be provided for the black troops. The opening of a canteen in Kearney for blacks caused an uproar, unlike the canteen for white servicemen, Petersen said.

The issue was resolved after the Army said the city would be declared out of bounds for all officers and enlisted men unless some provision was made to provide a place for black troops to drink beer and relax, Petersen said.

Maj. Robert Storz of Omaha, operations officer at Lincoln Army Air Field, explains the mysteries of the belly turret guns of a B-17 Flying Fortress to members of the Boys Town choir, which toured the field before performing.

Army airfields

Fort Crook in Bellevue was already a strong presence in the Omaha area before the war began. The base was established in 1894, with its airfield created in 1921. The Army Air Corps chose Fort Crook as the site for a new bomber plant in late 1940. The Martin Bomber Plant produced more than 1,500 B-26 Martin Marauders in two years of production. In the summer of 1943, the plant started production of more than 500 B-29 Superfortress bombers, including the Enola Gay and Bockscar, the aircraft used to drop atomic bombs on Japan. Employment peaked in November 1943 at 14,527, about 40 percent women. The plant had two mile-long concrete runways, six large hangars and a 1.2 million-square-foot aircraft assembly building. Other bases:

	YEAR BUILT	NUMBER OF ACRES	NUMBER OF BUILDINGS	PRIMARY FUNCTION
AINSWORTH	1942	2,400	64	Trained crews of B-17 bombers and P-39 and P-47 fighters. Conducted camouflage experiments. Barracks for 544 enlisted men and 112 officers.
ALLIANCE	1942	4,200	775	Trained C-46 and C-47 troop transport crews, glider pilots, 14,000 paratroopers and B-29 crews.
BRUNING	1942	1,720	234	Trained B-24 and P-47 crews.
FAIRMONT	1942	1,844	275	Trained B-24 and B-29 crews. Engine and air-frame repairs. Barracks for 3,700 officers and enlisted men; 350-bed hospital.
GRAND ISLAND	1942	2,100	173	Trained bomber crews; major staging area for crews bound for Guam and Tinian in South Pacific; engine and air-frame facility for B-17s and B-29s.
HARVARD	1942	1,700	277	Trained B-17, B-24 and B-29 crews.
KEARNEY	1942	2,700	485	Training and processing center for B-17 and B-29 crews.
LINCOLN	1942	3,000	1,016	Trained military aircraft mechanics; basic training for Army aviation cadets; staging area for bomber and P-38 and P-51 fighter squadrons.
McCOOK	1943	2,100	110	Trained B-17, B-24 and B-29 crews.
SCOTTSBLUFF	1942	1,755	108	Trained B-17, B-24, C-47 and glider crews.
SCRIBNER	1942	2,060	87	Trained B-17, B-24 and P-47 crews. Tested airfield camouflage techniques.

Source: 1945 Nebraska Blue Book

THE WRECKAGE OF A B-24 Liberator bomber rests on railroad tracks near the Fairmont Army Air Field.

'It was sad, but that's the way it was'

BY PAUL HAMMEL

RAY DREES in 2007

ON A WARM JULY MORNING IN 1944, a B-17 bomber crashed near Daykin, Neb., after a P-47 fighter from nearby Bruning Army Air Field collided with the bomber's right wing. Seven of the 10 bomber crew members died, along with the pilot of the fighter.

Hazel Schmidt recalled hearing the loud noise as she was baking a mulberry pie. She emerged from her farmhouse and saw pieces of the bomber falling from the sky.

"For a moment, it looked like planes doing maneuvers. When it started falling, I knew it was a plane crash," she said.

Her husband, Lawrence, and son Mark were among the first on the scene. They saw a dead airman in a ditch, encountered a dazed survivor walking on the road, and peered into the tail section and fuselage, which landed on opposite sides of the road.

Ray Drees remembered hurrying back to his family's farm a couple of miles away. A crater marked where the P-47 barreled to Earth. Army personnel carried a black bag holding the pilot's remains.

"You hear a lot about guys getting Purple Hearts, even posthumously, and Medals of Honor. But these guys got nothing, as far as I know. Yet they really contributed to saving lives of others later."

— JERRY PENRY OF MILFORD

A B-24 LIBERATOR NARROWLY MISSED a house when it came down near Fairmont Army Air Field.

★ MEMORIES ★
OF A GENERATION

DELTA MEYER VOSTEEN
Town: Pender, Neb.
In the war: Graduated from high school in Wakefield, Neb., in 1939 and was staying at home to help her dad on the farm.
In her words: "One summer afternoon we were cutting oats. We looked to the northwest and saw a squadron of bombers from the Sioux City Air Base. There was a cloud of black smoke. Two bombers had collided and plunged to the ground. The crew was killed. Another time I was staying overnight with a friend and we were awakened by the roar of a low-flying bomber. It crashed over the hills and the crew was killed. ... I was dating a young man, Alvin Vosteen, from Pender. He was drafted February 1942 and we exchanged letters through the war. He was sent to the 636th Tank Destroyer Battalion, 36th Division. He was in two invasions (Italy and southern France), five major battles and over 500 days in combat. He was awarded the Purple Heart with oak leaf cluster and two Bronze Stars. He was discharged Aug. 14, 1945. We were married Jan. 9, 1946. We farmed in the Pender area for 37 years. Alvin died Aug. 27, 2001."

The Army sent a $15 check for damage to their cornfield and a livestock tank, Drees recalled in 2007. For years, they plowed up shards of metal when tilling that field.

"It was sad, but that's the way it was back then," he said.

A total of 229 men perished in the Nebraska crashes, part of the 15,530 deaths related to training flights in the United States during World War II.

"You hear a lot about guys getting Purple Hearts, even posthumously, and Medals of Honor. But these guys got nothing, as far as I know," said Jerry Penry, a Milford surveyor who chases history in his spare time. "Yet they really contributed to saving lives of others later."

The airmen were the forgotten casualties of World War II, said Anthony J. Mireles, author of "Fatal Army Air Forces Aviation Accidents in the United States, 1941-1945." Medals were reserved for combat casualties, not those killed in training accidents, he said.

About 7,100 aircraft were lost in such crashes in the United States, compared with 4,500 lost in battles with Japan during World War II, Mireles said. That prompted Gen. Curtis LeMay to say it was safer to fly a B-29 over Japan toward the end of the war than to fly a training mission at home, the author said.

The crashes didn't get much publicity. Battles overseas grabbed headlines, and the Army wasn't always forthcoming about details of such accidents. The accident reports weren't declassified until 1996, he said.

Mireles attributed the high number of training crashes to the rush to prepare fliers for war and the age of the young pilots, many of whom were fresh out of high school.

"Kids can be a little reckless," he said, adding that pilot error was the most common cause of the crashes.

The most publicized crash in the United States occurred when a B-25, in foggy conditions, slammed into the Empire State Building in New York City in July 1945. But Nebraska saw its share.

One of the earliest occurred in May 1942, during the test flight of a B-26A bomber from the Martin aircraft plant near Bellevue. During a steep climbing maneuver just west of Offutt Air Field, the canopy flew off. It struck the bomber's tail, causing the plane to plummet nearly straight down.

The two pilots died, but Penry said the crash identified a design flaw that probably saved lives.

Three B-17 Flying Fortresses collided over Nebraska's Harvard Army Air Base on Aug. 28, 1944, with 14 fatalities.

Earlier that month, near Naper, Neb., 28 pilots en route to South Dakota from the Bruning Air Field perished when their C-47 transport crashed in bad weather.

Naper residents have dedicated a monument to the deadliest training crash of the war in Nebraska. A site near Chappell has a monument, and state historical markers denote crash sites near Milligan, Wood River and Laurel. But Penry said other crash sites have no markers.

In the 1944 midair collision near Daykin, the bomber's tail gunner, Leo Rizzuti, then a 20-year-old farm boy, was one of three crew members able to parachute to safety.

In the Army's report, Rizzuti described a bright flash and a violent rocking of the plane before it began spinning wildly to the ground, 16,000 feet below.

"I had trouble getting (to the escape hatch) because the plane was in a spin and it kept forcing me further to the rear," Rizzuti said in his statement.

The plane split in two at about 8,000 feet. Rizzuti bailed out moments before the bomber plowed into pastures about four miles southeast of Daykin.

"Probably another couple of seconds and I wouldn't be around," he said.

Neighbors gathered around the home of Mr. and Mrs. Joe Ciecior in Tarnov, Neb., to examine the damage from a test bomb filled with sand and a small charge.

'Not too many towns get bombed in the U.S.'

ON AUG. 16, 1943, Army Technician Isidore Kwapnioski was protecting America from Japanese forces in the Pacific. He later would help invade the Philippines and witness Gen. Douglas MacArthur's historic return there.

But from his station on the island of New Guinea, he couldn't protect his small hometown, Tarnov, Neb., from the U.S. Army Air Forces.

Bombs rained on the Platte County village early that morning, pummeling through a roof and passing just inches from two sleeping young sisters. Although no one was hurt, Tarnov became perhaps the only town in the continental United States ever to be bombed — and by its own troops.

Kwapnioski's mother immediately mailed him a letter describing the event.

Isidore Kwapnioski of Tarnov, Neb., in 1999.

The Army Air Forces, in an era of military secrecy, never explained why it dropped several 100-pound test bombs filled with sand and small charges. Had they been the 500-pound bombs the Germans dropped on Tarnov, Poland, the town would have been wiped off the map.

After the bombing, the civil defense squadron and military officials rushed to Tarnov, removed the bombs, evacuated residents and sealed off the town during the investigation. The military released little information on the incident.

At the time, there was speculation that one or two B-17 bombers, possibly taking off from Harvard, Neb., or Kansas, dropped six or seven bombs between 4 and 4:30 a.m.

Kwapnioski and fellow Tarnov resident Tim Sliva in 1999 recalled hearing that the town's three streetlights resembled lights marking a bombing range near Stanton, which is about 25 miles from Tarnov.

A report in The World-Herald from Wednesday, Aug. 18, 1943, read: "The good people of this little Polish village (population 70), who were bombed accidentally by an army plane early Monday, went to bed early Monday night. It had been a tremendous day — the biggest day for continuous excitement they had ever known."

No villagers were injured. Newspaper reports describe residents scurrying outside in nightgowns, waving gas lanterns. Even a man who had a bomb land just feet from the car he was sleeping in avoided injury, Sliva said. The sheriff roused the man, who had fallen into an alcohol-induced slumber after a Sunday night harvest festival.

"There's bombs in town," Sliva said the sheriff told the man in the panic that followed. The man looked around and said, "Then run 'em out," mistaking "bombs" for "bums."

One woman who grew up in Tarnov later married a crew member involved in the bombing, Sliva said. Among the visitors at the 50th anniversary commemoration in 1993 were representatives of Offutt Air Force Base.

"They just came to say that after 50 years, they're sorry," Sliva said with a laugh. "Not too many towns get bombed in the United States."

The apology was the closest thing to an official comment that Sliva or anyone has heard about the incident. Some years later, the Norfolk Daily News talked to a Norfolk businessman for a story about the bombing. The man, who flew bombing missions over Europe, said that when he reported for training at the Harvard base, crew members mentioned the Tarnov incident.

James Howard, an archivist at the Air Force Historical Research Agency in Alabama, found little information on the bombing. The Army used central Nebraska for many training missions, he said, "so there were a lot of really green people."

If crews erred while calibrating their navigation systems before takeoff, planes could fly as much as 10 or 15 degrees off course, he said.

Despite their claim to fame, most Tarnov residents talked little of the bombing over the years, although a local bar used to sell "Get Bombed in Tarnov" T-shirts. No potholes or markings exist to show how the military attacked the civilians it was supposed to defend.

But Kwapnioski kept copies of yellowing newspapers that detailed the event. And Sliva said he got a kick out of discussing it.

"It's just something that's unique about the town," he said.

"Nobody got hurt, and there's not much else to celebrate."

THE BOMB HIT just outside the window where 8-year-old Lucy Ann Ciecior (left) and 5-year-old Davida Rose Ciecior slept.

THE CIECIORS POINTED OUT the damage from a 100-pound bomb, in case it wasn't evident to a World-Herald photographer. The bombs dropped in Tarnov, Neb., were filled with sand and had only small charges.

DALLAS ANDERS

Town: Stanton, Neb.

In the war: Anders was a teenager attending Stanton High School.

In his words: "There was a practice bombing range about four miles from my family's farm. B-17 planes would drop 100-pound bags of sand with shotgun shells in them toward targets made out of wood. That set off the smoke so they knew where it landed. (The shotgun shells exploded the sand.) A lot of times they'd miss them. We even found a few around our farm. As teenagers we'd sneak out to the range to watch if they were hitting their targets. ... Young men were drafted for military service monthly. Everything was by bus at that time, so Stanton's high school band would play for the draftees as they left to camp from the bus depot. ... Those guys were the real heroes. I was drafted myself in 1952 for the Korean War, and ended up in Europe in '54. When we were in Germany, there was still heavy damage from bombings during the war."

GERMAN PRISONERS POSE OUTSIDE a building used as a theater at Fort Robinson in 1944. The marquee, in German, reads, "Enjoy Life."

'They were people just like the rest of us'

BILL KESSLER ALWAYS REMEMBERED the wonder he felt when he arrived in Holdrege, Neb., to begin, as he calls it, a "little adventure" as a German prisoner of war on the plains of Nebraska.

While traveling by train from New York in 1944, Kessler said, he and other captured Germans spent days pressing their faces against the window to see the passing landscape.

"Everything was 'ooh' and 'aah,'" Kessler, who retired in Mesa, Ariz., said in a 1993 interview. "We had no idea how large this country was. It was unbelievable."

A member of a German tank corps, Kessler was captured and sent to Camp Atlanta, a POW camp about six miles south of Holdrege along U.S. Highway 6. He was among more than 12,000 prisoners from Germany, Italy and Japan who were kept in the four main camps and nearly two dozen temporary work camps in Nebraska from 1943 to 1945, said Tom Buecker, a historian and curator of the Fort Robinson Museum near Crawford.

Nebraska had 22 other camps, while Iowa had at least two. Nationwide, there were more than 120 housing about 426,000 military prisoners, Buecker said.

Nebraska is about as far north as the camps were situated. Most were established farther south, where the climate is milder. Because nearly all the young and able-bodied men were sent to war, local farmers and business owners were glad to see prison camps established in Nebraska.

"They were a lifesaver for many farmers," said Marge Richards of Holdrege. "We could not find help anywhere else."

In Phelps County, for example, about 1,440 young Americans — nearly 20 percent of the local population and the heart of the local labor force — left for military service, said Glenn Thompson of Holdrege, author of a book about the prison camps in Nebraska.

Farms, flour mills, seed companies, other agricultural processing firms, bakeries and factories all struggled because of the labor shortage, Thompson said.

With prison camps in Scotland and England filled, U.S. military officials turned to American communities, he said.

Seeking workers, the Holdrege Industrial Committee, irrigators and farmers asked for a conscientious-objectors camp, Thompson said.

"What they got was some Army men who were jumping up and down, saying, 'Oh, my gosh. Here is a little town asking for labor and have we got something for them,' " Thompson said. "They were looking for a place they could put a newly built POW camp. They were out here in just a matter of days."

As crucial as the prisoners were for the work they performed, the Germans at Camp Atlanta were not viewed by local residents and camp workers solely as a source of labor.

"A lot of them were close to my age," said Byron Nelson of Holdrege, who worked for the fire department at Camp Atlanta. "People started to realize they were people just like the rest of us."

When Nelson and his wife, Lois, were married, one of the prisoners presented them with a gift: a handmade letter opener engraved with their names and fashioned from the broken windshield of a B-17 bomber that had crashed near Kearney.

The owner of a Hastings factory where Kessler worked as a prisoner exchanged letters and cards with Kessler after he returned to Germany. The owner of the factory, the Western Land Roller Co., eventually invited Kessler to return to America and agreed to serve as his sponsor for immigration purposes.

Kessler returned to the United States in 1953 and eventually became a U.S. citizen.

As warm and friendly as the relationships eventually grew between prisoners and townspeople, that is not how they began.

Newspaper accounts and other information of the time had led many Nebraskans to think of nearly all Germans as vicious Nazi monsters. Daily contact gradually led them to other conclusions.

"The people we worked with — I have to say it — at first treated us like at any minute we would be attacking them," Kessler said.

Richards admitted that it was some time before she was comfortable having enemy prisoners working on her land and eating in her home.

"I was very nervous at first, especially the first few times they came into our home," she said.

Much of the wariness began to melt away at the kitchen table. Richards recalled one prisoner telling her husband, "Democracy begins in the stomach."

"We got to where we realized that if we expected hard labor out of them on the farm, we had to feed them well," said Richards, who often baked cherry pies and other treats for the Germans.

Kessler said the meals he and other prisoners received on farms made them want to work much harder.

"The farmer and the family treated us so nice," Kessler said. "We came from camp with a brown bag and an apple. Then here we are sitting at a table with a nice warm meal and coffee."

Food eased the prisoners' apprehension in another way. The prisoners heard that Richards cooked delicious pheasant, so they asked guards to shoot some birds that they could take to the ranch.

"The guards shot and missed every one," Richards said. "The prisoners said they were much more relaxed after that."

'I planned to get captured'

WHEN THE WAR BEGAN, Werner Prautzsch was a German paratrooper. When it ended, he was a Nebraska farmer.

Prautzsch was a prisoner of war in a camp near Mitchell, Neb., after he surrendered to American troops in France in June 1944.

Prisoners from the camp helped local farmers thin and harvest sugar beets, stack hay, paint buildings and do other chores.

Drafted in 1939 as he prepared to enter a university to study medicine, Prautzsch saw his first combat when German soldiers occupied Crete in the Mediterranean. He served in the Afrika Korps and sometimes worked as an interpreter for captured British soldiers.

When American troops defeated the Germans in North Africa, Prautzsch's unit fled to Naples, Italy. He later suffered a head wound in fighting in Italy that left him in a coma for several months.

After the Allies invaded France, Prautzsch, his head still bandaged, was ordered to the front.

"That is when I decided that if I saw any Americans, I was going to surrender and go to America," Prautzsch said in a 1991 interview. "I planned to get captured."

During fighting in Brittany, Prautzsch got his chance when a U.S. Army lieutenant and a driver approached Prautzsch's position in a Jeep.

He and his comrades stopped the Americans and told them they wanted to surrender.

"The lieutenant actually didn't know if he was captured or we were. He said he wasn't in a position to take us and then he left."

A short while later, after an artillery barrage on the German position, the Americans returned with five tanks to take control of the Germans, some of whom Prautzsch had to talk into surrendering with him. Two weeks later, Prautzsch was in England and on his way to America.

Repatriated after the war, Prautzsch married and prepared to return to the United States. His family's land in East Germany had been nationalized by the communist government. In 1951 Prautzsch and his wife, Erika, arrived in Mitchell.

"Nobody at the start of war is more excited than youth," Prautzsch said. "Their thoughts can be molded. The best example of this was the German army. Hitler led an army he didn't deserve. They should have got rid of him years earlier."

POW camps in Nebraska

About 12,000 Germans, Japanese and Italians were held during various times at 26 camps. Number of prisoners and type of work at 23 of those camps as of July 1, 1945:

	NUMBER OF PRISONERS	TYPE OF WORK
ALMA	106	Farm
ATLANTA	946	Farm
BAYARD	182	Farm
BERTRAND	87	Farm
BRIDGEPORT	180	Farm
ELWOOD	N/A	Not available
FORT CROOK	747	Military
FORT ROBINSON	1,247	Military
FRANKLIN	84	Farm
GRAND ISLAND	98	Farm
HASTINGS	90	Other
HEBRON	76	Farm
INDIANOLA	482	Military, farm
KEARNEY	300	Farm
LEXINGTON	73	Farm
LYMAN	302	Farm
MITCHELL	213	Farm
MORRILL	N/A	Not available
OGALLALA	230	Other
PALISADE	111	Farm
SCOTTSBLUFF	3,294	Military, farm
SIDNEY	613	Military, farm*
WEEPING WATER	153	Farm, other

Sources: Nebraska State Historic Preservation Board; Offutt Air Force Base; Nebraska State Historical Society; The World-Herald

*As of spring 1944

WOMEN'S ARMY CORPS ROLLED OUT OF AK-SAR-BEN

Lt. Amelia Smith of the Women's Army Corps gives the starting signal in 1944 for what The World-Herald billed as "the first all-WAC Army truck convoy" featuring women driving and in command. The unit was based in Omaha on the grounds of Ak-Sar-Ben. The convoy was bound for Fort Des Moines.

Viola Atobee, left, and Lucille White prepare the finish on an auto bound for military service. They are working inside the Ak-Sar-Ben Coliseum.

Cpl. Pearl Tretter, left, and Staff Sgt. Thelma Roush check under the hood of an Army vehicle.

Horse racing at Ak-Sar-Ben was suspended during the war, and the Coliseum and grounds served as an Army vehicle depot. In the foreground, from left, are Cpl. Geraldine Denham, 1st Lt. Amelia Smith and Pvt. Ruth Blackstone.

AMERICA'S DOGS WERE READY TO DO THEIR PART

SOLDIERS AT FORT ROBINSON trained dogs of various breeds for guard duty to help free up men for combat. Below, the dogs and their Navy trainers spelled out K-9 with the Pine Ridge as a backdrop.

PATRICIA (HOTCHKISS) JAMES

Town: Omaha; grew up in Stromsburg

In the war: Was in elementary school during the war. Sisters were older and their husbands were in the Army, Navy and Merchant Marine.

In her words: "I remember the frequent brownouts when the sirens blew. Every home pulled its shades down to blacken the windows at night. Bomber planes regularly flew over our town. It seemed like they were just above the treetops. The Fairmont Air Base was pretty close, and when our family would travel to York to shop, my dad would always pick up a soldier who was hitchhiking on Highway 81. It was fun to hear all about them and where they were from."

MILITARY SHOWED ITS STUFF AT THE ARMY WAR SHOW

THIRTEEN-YEAR-OLD JAMES GUFFEY of Omaha brought his BB gun to a display of vehicles at Ak-Sar-Ben.

SIDNEY, IOWA, GIRLS PLEDGE THEIR SUPPORT for the 1942 Army War Show at Ak-Sar-Ben and Creighton University in Omaha. Back row, from left, Mary Butts, Marylu Carter, Lucille Jones, Claire Nelson, Marjorie Broughton and June Hill. In front, Mickey Stiles and Donna Reade.

THE CROWD ENTHUSIASTICALLY WAVED handkerchiefs, as planes flew over Creighton University's stadium during the show. "It looked like a snowstorm," The World-Herald reported.

GIVING TROOPS THE MESSAGE: 'WE'RE BEHIND YOU'

THE WORLD-HERALD'S "WAR CENTER" in its building at 15th and Farnam Streets featured stations for enlisting in branches of women's services.

MEMBERS OF THE WOMEN'S ARMY AIR CORPS attended flag dedication services at Clair Chapel in Omaha. Taking part were, from left, Lt. Glendora Moore, George Bivens, Lt. Charline May, the Rev. C.C. Reynolds, Lt. Myrtle Anderson, stewardess Estelle Titus and Lt. Mary Miller.

DOROTHY SUBJECT GOT A LIFT from meeting Pvt. Frank S. Komasinski when he arrived on furlough at Omaha's Union Station in 1942.

BLANCHE B. BICKEL

Town: Omaha

Service: Army lieutenant

In the war: Bickel served with the 2nd General Hospital in England for two years. During this time, she was invited to Buckingham Palace, where she met the future Queen Elizabeth. She later transferred to a field hospital, where she was head nurse. She served with the 46th Field Hospital until the end of the war. The field hospital was prepared to handle 500 patients, but at one time during the Battle of the Bulge, it took in more than 1,500 patients. It operated just over enemy lines. Bickel received many of her patients just 15 minutes from the time of injury.

In her words: "I had been in the military for a couple of years when someone went through the military records and discovered that Margaret (a fellow nurse and friend) and I had not had our military training. We went through Lord knows what, but not basic training. Margaret and I were both head nurses at heavy surgical areas. We were pulled out of those jobs and put up in the hills with a bunch of freshmen who had just come from the USA. We did all of the things you do in basic training. They taught us how to carry patients on a litter, how to move them, and how to take care of the wounded."

'It has been righted'

A LETTER FROM THE PRESIDENT arrived in 1990, a formal apology to Em and Bob Nakadoi of Omaha.

It was an apology for herding them from their California homes, stripping them of their belongings — except what they could carry in two suitcases — and forcing them to live for a year in a camp hemmed in by barbed wire and armed guards.

"That's the negative part," said Em Nakadoi, who also received one of the $20,000 checks mailed out to thousands of Japanese-Americans interned on the West Coast during World War II.

The Omaha woman chose not to dwell on the Tule Lake Camp, the cot she once slept on, the chilling cold and an elderly fellow prisoner who she said was shot to death because he dared to go through the fence to retrieve his dog.

Instead, she treasured a color photograph of 64 members of her family — brothers, sisters, children, grandchildren, nieces and nephews.

And she pointed at the faces of nearly a dozen non-Japanese people who had married into her family and their nearly dozen children.

The discrimination of the war years seemed like a very long-ago thing.

> "These are the nicest, most understanding and most helpful people. There is no comparison to the East or West Coast."
>
> — EM NAKADOI,
>   SPEAKING OF OMAHANS

"It has been righted," she said quietly.

One reason, she said, was Omaha. She said it had been an extraordinarily tolerant city since she and her husband arrived in 1945.

"These are the nicest, most understanding and most helpful people," Em Nakadoi said. "There is no comparison to the East or West Coast."

Bob Nakadoi said, "We went through a lot of suffering on account of Japan. But now, so many moons have passed over."

He was 28 and his wife was 25 when U.S. authorities ordered their families to leave their homes near Sacramento, Calif., and go to the Tule Lake Camp in northern California.

The camp housed about 18,000 prisoners. There were 48 blocks and each block had 20 barracks. The barracks had no ceilings, no insulation and no partitions between rooms.

It was 1942.

Em Nakadoi — Masako Matsunami was her maiden name — was the daughter of a truck farmer. Bob Nakadoi was the son of an orchard farmer. They both had been born in California, children of Japanese who had immigrated there years earlier.

They met at the camp, although their romance didn't flourish until after he had left to go to Chicago and take a job as a cook. Prisoners could leave the camp if they didn't return to their original homes in excluded areas near the coasts.

Nakadoi began a correspondence that captivated his bride-to-be, who worked in the adult education program at the camp.

One day, the principal of the adult education program told Em that she was wasting her life in the camp.

"Go to Omaha. I have friends there," the principal said.

In October 1943, she came and lived with the friends, getting a job at the old Aquila women's apparel store.

In July 1944, she left Omaha to go to Chicago and marry Bob, but they returned to Omaha for good in 1945.

Bob Nakadoi worked for 13 years as a body-and-fender man for the old Lied Motor Co. at 27th and Harney Streets. Later, he worked as an appraiser for the one-time Rosen-Novak auto dealership. He retired in 1979.

The money they received in 1990 wasn't as important as the apology, Em said at the time.

"We didn't want the money. We wanted this (apology) so it is understood that the wrong is righted."

EM AND BOB NAKADOI look at the letter from President George H.W. Bush in 1990 offering a formal apology for internment of American citizens of Japanese descent.

NU 'restored faith in people again'

THE UNIVERSITY OF NEBRASKA welcomed Japanese-American students during World War II, while many other universities rejected them.

Nora Maehara Mitsumori remembered sending letters seeking acceptance to numerous universities. Only the University of Nebraska (now the University of Nebraska-Lincoln) and the University of Arkansas accepted her, she said.

The university's kindness "restored (our) faith in people again because we had been hurt so much because we were Japanese," Mitsumori said in a 1994 interview.

Tom Miya in 1994

University officials estimate that the school admitted 50 Japanese-American students who had been forced into internment camps by the U.S. government in 1942. The officials say 3,500 students were placed in schools around the country by the National Japanese Student Relocation Council, an organization that was sympathetic to their plight.

About 120,000 Japanese-Americans, both citizens and resident immigrants, were ordered into internment camps several months after Japan bombed Pearl Harbor. The U.S. government in 1988 formally apologized and began paying some compensation to internment camp survivors.

Tom Miya said numerous universities turned down his applications. The University of Nebraska was the only school that accepted him.

He met his wife, Midori, while at Lincoln. One college had sent her a rejection letter that referred to her as a "Jap."

Miya, who went on to become a faculty member in pharmacology and toxicology at Purdue University and the University of North Carolina, said he did not know why the university was open to Japanese-American students.

"It's just the character of the people," he said. "It's something that you sense, you know? And it's very difficult to describe that."

The alumni frequently mentioned three people who were important to their stay at the university: Chancellor Chauncey Boucher; George Rosenlof, the registrar; and the Rev. Robert Drew, a Methodist campus minister.

Rosenlof and Drew welcomed the new students at the bus stop or train depot and helped them find housing when they arrived in 1942.

William Drew of Beverly, Mass., said his father steered some of the students to part-time jobs and found one a winter coat. Drew said the man never threw away the coat.

Mitsumori said Rosenlof told her and her friends — Shizue Murashige, now of Honolulu, and Jeanne Namba Stanwood of Lihue, Hawaii — that Lincoln would be receptive to them. They appreciated the reassurance, she said, "because we were scared."

Miya reflected on his bewildering relationship with this nation in the 1940s. He said he graduated second in his Hanford, Calif., high school class in 1941 and received praise from a state bankers' association for an essay he wrote on the value of American citizenship.

The next year, the U.S. government ordered his family out of its home and into an internment camp.

In 1944, the U.S. Army drafted him while he studied in Lincoln. He did basic training in Arkansas, not far from the internment camp where his family had been relocated.

"There's really no time for bitterness," he said. "And you play the cards that you get, and you play the cards full tilt, the best way you know how."

'Fear of invasion in the early days'

IN 1941, MITS KAWAMOTO'S Japanese immigrant father had lived in California for 39 years. His mother was born in Hawaii, an American territory. And Mits was a 20-year-old Californian preparing to enroll at the University of Southern California with the goal of becoming a doctor.

Mits Kawamoto in 1991

But in May 1942, the Kawamoto family was among thousands of Japanese-Americans on the West Coast who were rounded up by the U.S. government and confined to inland camps.

"There was real fear and anxiety of war and fear of invasion in the early days of the war," Kawamoto said in a 1991 interview. "Ack-ack guns would fire into the night sky at imagined targets.

"My father was concerned that with the tremendous losses suffered by American troops that our government would hold us as pawns to be used in exchange for prisoners."

Kawamoto said he joined the Home Guard, defending local water and power facilities with empty rifles, but was told after six weeks that he wasn't needed. The unspoken reason was his Japanese ancestry.

"For a young man being wronged without the opportunity to prove his innocence and loyalty to his country, this greatly concerned me," he said.

The family was initially housed with others in tar-paper shacks and stables at the Fresno County Fairgrounds before being moved to a camp with 9,000 detainees in Arkansas.

Kawamoto and a brother, Haruo, eventually were allowed to join the Army. They were assigned to the 442nd Infantry Battalion, a unit of Japanese-Americans that served with distinction in Italy during the war. Haruo was killed in Italy. He was 18.

The U.S. government's treatment of its own citizens of Japanese ancestry and black and white racial tensions during the war years deeply affected Kawamoto.

"I noticed there seemed to be differences in how employers handled black labor. I noticed there were no blacks in management and supervision," said Kawamoto, who with wife Eunice came to the Omaha area in 1951. "I wondered if this could happen to me."

BETTY J. (PORTER) HIGGINS

Town: Omaha

In the war: Attended high school in Denver and worked after school at the Greyhound bus station to earn money to buy savings bonds to help finance the war. She lived with her sister in a south Denver apartment after her sister's husband went to serve in the war. She and her sister would invite airmen from Lowry Field in Denver over for Thanksgiving dinner. Those airmen were based in London and had flown missions over Germany. They were at Lowry on leave.

In her words: "I met my husband (Billy M. Higgins) in Denver. He was a tailgunner and had flown 25 missions over Germany. When I brought him home to meet my parents for Christmas, my dad took him pheasant hunting. He told my fiance not to feel bad if he couldn't hit one right away. But he had experience as a tailgunner shooting ahead of the planes. He fired and shot one pheasant, fired again and shot another. My dad said, 'Gracious, you're a good shot.'"

MEMORIES OF A GENERATION ★

ROBERT G. CUNNINGHAM

Town: Omaha

Service: U.S. Marine Corps

In the war: He grew up in South Omaha and graduated from South High School in 1941. He attended Omaha University (now the University of Nebraska at Omaha) and studied aeronautics. From the age of 5, he had yearned to be a pilot. His first flying lessons were at the Omaha airport. He joined the Naval Cadets in 1942 and continued flying instruction at a base in Pascal, Wash., and later trained in twin-engine aircraft and PBY seaplanes in Corpus Christi, Texas. He transferred to the Marine Corps in 1943 and was an instructor at the Marine base at Cherry Point, N.C. He also learned to fly the B-25, or Billy Mitchell bomber. His unit shipped overseas in 1944 to a small Pacific island called Emirau. His squadron (413) flew bombing missions over its main target, the major Japanese base at Rabaul, New Guinea. His next duty station was at Mindanao in the Philippines, where his unit and many others were preparing for the invasion of the Japanese mainland. But the dropping of the atomic bomb on Japan ended the war. In the Philippines, he received orders to deliver a top secret satchel to a Russian officer in China. On that mission he had an unscheduled landing on Iwo Jima. Low on fuel and battling high winds, he had no choice but to land the plane there with zero visibility. He remained in the service until his discharge in July 1946. Cunningham later served as interim mayor of Omaha from November 1976 to June 1977.

In his words: "I always loved to fly, and the Marine Corps gave me plenty of opportunities. I even trained for a time on a biplane. That's where you experienced the excitement of flying. Our aircraft was never hit in combat, but we had many close calls. My closest brush with death was at Cherry Point during a training flight. I was instructing a young pilot for his two-engine qualification. On the takeoff, the student made an error. I desperately tried to gain control but our plane flipped, tearing off a wing and crashing into some trees. I ordered the crew to get away from the plane as quickly as possible. As we were running for cover, the fuel tanks exploded, showering debris around us. Thank God there were no serious injuries. I have always been grateful to Omaha University and the U.S. Marine Corps for launching my flying career, which allowed me to serve my country in time of war."

EDWARD DOWNING

Town: Omaha

Service: Sergeant with the 8th Air Force

In the war: He spent a year training in the States, including several months of radio operator school in downtown Omaha. He spent two years overseas as a switchboard operator.

In his words: "Having participated in WWII, the thing that sticks to me most is the enormity of it all. ... And in this country, you heard a lot about North Platte, Neb., serving the GIs at the railroad station, which was on a volunteer basis. I get a lump in my throat every time I hear about them. What a huge effort! They worked around the clock. Omaha had its own North Platte, in a way. Everyone did his or her part in WWII. Everybody volunteered. For instance, there was the Fred and Gladys Hartman story. Fred worked at the bomber plant helping to turn out B-26 light bombers. That is where I came in. They had two lovely daughters who were just out of high school and were both working for the phone company. ... The oldest Hartman girl and I began to date, and after the war we married. Through different churches, Fred and Gladys began to invite (into their home) some of the guys, and it became known by the GIs that they could stop by for a visit. There were guys from California, New Jersey and wherever else. Later on, Gladys showed me letters from parents thanking the Hartmans for taking such good care of their sons. 'A home away from home,' you might say."

CAROLYN KAY ORR

Town: Omaha

In the war: She was born in September 1937. A training air base in Sergeant Bluff, Iowa, was situated about four miles northeast of her family's farm in Dakota County, Neb.

In her words: "One winter night, on the 26th of January, 1944, about 9 p.m., I was on the second floor of our family home. I heard some very terrible, horrifying and indescribably loud sounds coming from the outdoor sky. I ran to our north bedroom window to see what appeared to be the sun — an extremely huge glowing ball of orange and yellow-gold light — which was very close to the ground. My 6-year-old mind thought that the fiery sun was going to destroy the Earth! Sadly, it was one of the planes from the base that had caught fire while on a training mission. The plane crashed approximately 1½ miles south of our home. All five crew members on board (around the ages of 19 to 24) lost their lives. I shall never forget the brightly colored light and the sounds of the terrifying event!

"During the war, my uncle, Sgt. Donovan M. 'Bing' Quimby, originally from Wakefield, Neb., and currently from South Sioux City, Neb., was stationed in Iran. As a diesel locomotive engineer, he drove a supply train near the Russian border. He wrote letters to me and talked about the young kids my age who ran to his train and asked for 'chum gum' — chewing gum. They also shouted 'buckshee' — begging for anything. Uncle Bing sent me a very small coral-colored silk handkerchief, which had 'Bethlehem' embroidered diagonally across one corner. It is a wonderful keepsake, which is framed and currently displayed in my home."

VIRGINIA R. (BAKER) HUETTELMAIER

Town: Omaha

Service: Women's Army Corps

In the war: She enlisted in the Women's Army Corps in December 1942, and in January 1943 entered basic training at Fort Des Moines, Iowa. One highlight during basic training was when first lady Eleanor Roosevelt came to review the troops. After basic training, she was sent to Nacogdoches, Texas, for administrative schooling. She then was dispatched overseas to Swansea, Wales. The trip aboard an old British ship took 14 days. Men and women troops were aboard as they traveled in a large convoy. Food was barely palatable, so she ate a lot of candy bars. She did not experience the seasickness many others suffered. Her next assignment was to the 172nd Company at Stone England Army Base near London. The duty station where she did stenography work for the Allies was located in an old castle. She often joined others in the bomb shelters during German bombing raids. In her off-duty hours, she visited wounded soldiers in the hospitals and wrote letters for those who wanted to correspond with loved ones back in the States. She returned to the U.S. in May 1945 and was discharged from service July 28, 1945.

In her words: "We were a lucky bunch. We were on a ship going over where we got to mix with the GIs. They'd play the guitar, and we'd have a good time on the ship. (In London), we used to go — they'd have dances for servicemen and women. We'd get in these big trucks, all of us, and go to wherever they were having the dance."

(On the visit by Eleanor Roosevelt) "As it turned out, we were all waiting for her. Our sheets were so straight you could flip a quarter on them, but she didn't end up coming to our barracks."

WALTER J. BOTSCH

Town: Norfolk, Neb.

Service: Combat engineer, infantry for a little over one year; Air Forces for 3½ years

In the war: He was assigned to the 88th Infantry Division of the 313th Engineers at Camp Gruber, Okla. He transferred to the Air Forces in December 1943, based in Texas, as a navigator. He was then assigned to Memphis to fly to many destinations in the Atlantic. He landed in England just prior to the invasion of France.

In his words: "I met my future wife, Doris Jane Henderson from Cedar Bluffs, Neb., at Midland Lutheran College and decided that she was the one for me! When I was flying and taking (navigation) training, I purchased Doris Jane's engagement ring in Bloomington, Del. I thought I would be able to go home and give her the ring when I got leave in 1945. Instead, I was assigned a flight to Calcutta. I wore the ring for safekeeping around my neck with my dog tags. The ring traveled to South America; Ascension Island in the south Atlantic; across Africa; Khartoum; Cairo; Abadan, Iran; Pakistan; New Delhi; and on to Calcutta. I returned via Memphis and met (Boston Red Sox left-fielder) Ted Williams, which made my day as a true baseball fan! I returned to Omaha, where I met Doris Jane and gave her the ring."

JIM JIRSAK

Town: Omaha

Service: 12th Air Force under the Mediterranean Allied Air Force from Feb. 13, 1943, to Dec. 2, 1945

In the war: Had basic training at Sheppard Airfield in Wichita Falls, Texas. Served in Oran, North Africa, Sicily and Italy.

In his words: "After graduating from South High School in June 1941, I took an aircraft sheet metal course offered free by the U.S. National Defense Training Department. … (Then) I worked at the Martin Bomber Plant at Fort Crook (now Offutt Air Force Base) as an apprentice second-class engine mechanic. The starting pay was 60 cents an hour. While working there, I received my draft papers. The Glenn Martin Co. offered me a deferment to stay working there, but I declined. … Before completing my basic training, the government issued a directive that they needed a lot of glider mechanics to work on C.G. 4A gliders. If you know how the government sometimes operates (guess what), I was one of many that was selected to be a glider mechanic with most of my experience with aircraft engines. … Our gliders took part in the invasion of southern France."

ROBERT EARL CONNELL

Town: Chadron

Service: Army, 5th Armored, and later Army Air Forces

In the war: Went through tank training when drafted in 1942 before he was shifted to the Air Forces. After graduating from flight school in Waco, Texas, he trained other bomber air crews. He then trained in B-17s and was preparing to fly to the Pacific for the planned invasion of Japan when the war ended.

In his words: "I liked flying very much. I had one scary moment. We were coming into the field one evening, and there was a big thunderstorm moving over the field. The tower told us to circle awhile. But this wise owl (on the mission) had a date that night, and he had us go on in. There was a terrible downdraft, and we lost 15,000 feet in 10 seconds. That was the only time I was scared."

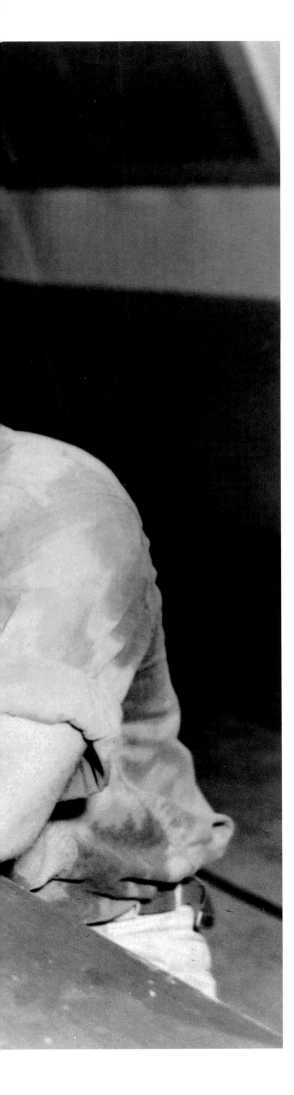

Letters

KATHRYN BROTT WAS 3½ YEARS OLD when a letter from her father, a young surgeon serving on the front lines of World War II, arrived in the family mailbox in Beatrice. She was too young to comprehend its meaning, too young to even read the words. Her mother read them. ★ "March 4, 1943. Dear Kathryn, at this time your father is many miles away, yes even a thousand or more away and I believe you might appreciate a few lines for future reference in case I should not return." Capt. Clarence Brott told his daughter to obey her mother, Viola, and above all else, believe in God in the event he became a casualty of war. "It has been impossible for your father to provide you and your mother with ample financial means as he desired, but by you cooperating with your mother and being thrifty, I believe you shall not suffer." ★ Years later, Kathryn Brott Higgins of Lincoln could still hear the voice of her father, who died in 1988, when she read his letter. ★ "He was just a very special person. And there were just so many others," she said.

FIREMAN 2ND CLASS LYMAN HEWITT OF OMAHA,
stationed in the Philippines in 1945, writes a letter to his wife.

Letters home still tell a vivid story

BY MICHAEL KELLY

KENNETH PLUMMER NEVER WANTED to be a hero. He wasn't eager for combat. He just wanted World War II to end so he could go home to Council Bluffs. He was a prolific letter writer, and his words made his feelings clear.

Plummer never got to come home. His remains lie in the Henri Chapelle Cemetery in Belgium, marked by a simple white cross. On Christmas Day 1944, a shell from a German tank tore off his left leg at the hip.

He died three days later at age 20.

His parents, sister and brother mourned his death, just as thousands of other families have mourned the losses of loved ones in America's wars. The years passed and the Plummer family's pain lessened. They were left with their memories, especially on Memorial Day.

But more than four decades after the war ended, nephew Joel Fritz discovered a suitcase full of letters in an attic — Kenneth's letters home.

"The family hadn't talked about him a lot," Fritz said in a 1993 interview. "All I knew was that he had died in the Battle of the Bulge. I had the idea right away to do something with the letters, but I put it on the back burner.

"Then I was reading a Louis L'Amour book, and it hit me — here I have all these letters, like a gold mine, and I could

get to know Kenneth personally. And I wanted to do something special as a gift to my grandparents."

L'Amour, the novelist, had written: "Without the written word, a man knows nothing beyond what occurs during his own brief years and, perhaps, in a few tales his parents tell him. How much do you know of your own family, who they were, how they lived, and what they thought?"

Fritz spent a year assembling the 161 letters chronologically, gathering photographs and researching the Battle of the Bulge, the Nazis' last-ditch attempt to avoid defeat. He typed the letters and arranged them in a loose-leaf binder.

He made only four copies. The cover of each is embossed with the words, "Letters Home."

Along with the letters, Fritz made another discovery. While his uncle was stateside training in the Army, he had made a "wax," a primitive recording that allowed him to send his voice home. On that decades-old scratchy record, a minute and 25 seconds long, Kenneth Plummer speaks.

"Hi, folks," the young soldier said in the spring of '44 from Camp Roberts, Calif. "You're surprised to hear my voice, I know.

"I can't hardly think of much to say. I haven't been doing much here today. I went out and had some scouting and patrolling."

On the wax, Kenneth asks about his brother Bernard's new skates and tells the family he has gained 30 muscular pounds, to 158, in his months since joining the Army.

"You ought to see me," the 6-footer said. "I'm feeling great, and I'm filling out my clothes like I was poured into 'em."

He closed with a reminder that the family should keep writing letters.

"I need 'em a lot," he said, signing off as if ending a letter. "They really help. . . . All my love, Kenneth."

As a boy, Kenneth had missed a year of school because of scarlet fever. He was still a student at Thomas Jefferson High when he was drafted in the fall of 1943 after his 18th birthday.

He had hoped for an early discharge so he could join his father in driving a truck for Watson Brothers, on the grounds that the job was essential to the stateside war effort.

"Well," he wrote on Oct. 24, 1943, "I've been in the Army a week and a day, and it seems like a year and a month. . . . Just finished peeling potatoes. Two sacks full."

On Nov. 29, he wrote to Bernard: "How are you getting along in school? That's where I wish I was."

And after getting some shots Nov. 30: "The needles have 1½-inch points on them. The heavenly doctors stand and run at you with them. It feels like they're pinning your arms to your lungs."

In December, he wrote about a friend from home who was in combat: "I hope I never have to see that kind of action, or I should say action of any kind."

He wrote regularly about the humdrum of camp life — but the skinny kid from the Bluffs could feel himself getting stronger. He asked again about the possibility of the discharge. On Jan. 11, though, the first notion of going overseas appeared in a letter to his mother.

December 20, 1943

From: Cpl. Henry Doncheski

To: His wife, Dorothy Doncheski

Dorothy was living in Craig, Neb., when she received this letter from her husband. The letter was sent from "European Theater, 9th Army Air Force, 409 Service Group." The couple later lived in Tekamah, Neb.

My Darling Wife
and Sweet Baby Cheryl,

IT'S SO CLOSE TO CHRISTMAS and I feel so alone. I can't tell you just where I am, it would be censored anyway. All I can say I'm writing, down in a trench and it's so cold, hard to see, and all the noise of planes and other warfare all around me is deafening. I love the outline from paper of our baby you sent so I can see how she has grown. She was just two weeks old when I had to leave you both. I carry it and your beautiful pictures in my shirt, close to my heart. I can't get all the love I feel for you both in this V-mail letter, it is too small. I'm praying soon I can hold you both in my arms.

All my love and kisses,
Your Loving Husband

PFC. KENNETH PLUMMER'S *letters home during the war were preserved by nephew Joel Fritz, left. The soldier is in the framed photo. Also pictured in 1993 were the soldier's brother, Bernard; his mother, Hazel; his father, Frank; and Kenneth's sister, Vernelle Fritz, Joel's mother.*

"You're pretty sure I'm going across, aren't you?" he wrote. "From the looks of all the papers, and by the time I get through with my training, it may be over. Let's hope."

On a day when he was emotionally down, the teenager wrote of his desire for a civilian truck-driving job: "I'd take any run anywhere on the Watson system if he (the company owner) could get me out of this hole."

But his confidence grew, and in March he wrote: "Well, your son is a hell of a lot better man than you or he probably ever thought he would be."

Two weeks later, doctors discovered that Plummer's left foot was fractured. The foot and a case of poison oak that wouldn't go away gave him hope — as did the progress of the Allied effort in the war — that he wouldn't be sent overseas.

> *"From the looks of all the papers, and by the time I get through with my training, it may be over. Let's hope."*
>
> — KENNETH PLUMMER,
> IN A LETTER SENT HOME
> JAN. 11, 1944

He looked forward to his first furlough and a trip home and wrote a teasing note about his little brother, who had taken up horn-playing: "If B.J. gets me up by playing 'You Gotta Get Up,' I'll throw that horn in the street and run over it."

Kenneth began drawing cartoons about Army life and sending them home. As he got better at it, other soldiers asked him to draw their likenesses. He made a trip to Hollywood on a weekend pass and got pulled on stage at a show with three other GIs.

After delays because of his poison oak, he got a furlough and went home in late May. It was his final visit.

On his return to California, his letters indicated he thought he'd be sent to the South Pacific. In sad irony, given the day he was mortally wounded six months later, Plummer wrote: "The war may be over by Christmas, I hope."

He moved to Fort Ord, Calif., and in July took a six-day train ride to Camp Butner, N.C., to join the ill-fated 106th Division. He wrote that his feet hurt but that "it sounds like the war with Germany will be over before long."

The young man speculated that he might be part of an army of occupation. On Aug. 29, the battalion commander announced that the 106th would be sent overseas in two months.

In September, Kenneth was sent to Camp Atterbury, Ind. His parents drove there to visit him. Afterward, he wrote: "I sure did hate to see you leave last night."

By mid-October, he could write only that he was in the eastern United States and that an Army censor was checking all letters.

"I'd be much happier working for Watson," the newly promoted private first class wrote, "than for Uncle Sam."

On Oct. 27, from farther away: "I've seen all the saltwater I care to."

From England in early November, Plummer apparently knew he was headed for tough times and discouraged the sending of presents: "You can tell everybody to forget me this Christmas."

The poison oak finally had almost disappeared. Later he wrote from France and then Belgium, where snow was 6 to 8 inches deep.

On Dec. 15, he wrote the final letter that made it home: "Everything is all right here in Germany. ... The lighting is awfully poor, and my eyes are beginning to hurt, so will close for now. Love, Kenneth."

At the moment Kenneth wrote, things appeared to be "all right in Germany." But nephew Joel Fritz noted in an epilogue that at 5:30 the next morning, more than 250,000 Germans attacked 83,000 American troops thinly deployed along an 85-mile front in the Ardennes Mountains.

Historian John Toland wrote that the hard-hit 106th Division "was not only the newest division in the Ardennes; it was also the newest Allied division on any front."

Back home in Council Bluffs, his mother, Hazel Plummer, had followed newspaper reports tracking the movements of American forces.

"I knew exactly where Kenneth was," she recalled. "So we weren't surprised. We followed him."

The 106th, meanwhile, suffered terrible losses. But a turning point in the miserably cold Battle of the Bulge came on Dec. 25, the day Pfc. Kenneth Plummer was wounded. The Allies mustered reinforcements, Fritz explained in the epilogue, and a 10-day layer of clouds and fog cleared, enabling U.S. fighter-bombers to play a significant role.

On Jan. 28, 1945, exactly a month after Kenneth died, the Battle of the Bulge was over. The Germans had about 100,000 casualties. The Americans had nearly 81,000, including more than 10,000 killed.

Hazel Plummer answered the door at her home in early January and saw a man with a telegram. He suggested that she sit down. As many other mothers had when confronted with this knock on the door, she knew why he was there.

She told the stranger: "I'll take it standing up."

The Germans surrendered May 7. Harold Paddock of Kansas City, Kan., who said he was 15 feet from Kenneth when he was wounded on Christmas Day, visited the Plummers in Council Bluffs and told them what had happened.

Kenneth Plummer didn't have a long and glorious war record, but in his short time overseas he honorably did what he had to do. Joel Fritz said that after reading the letters, the words of historian Toland seemed to apply.

The GI, Toland wrote in "Battle: The Story of the Bulge," was always only as good as he had to be.

"In the Bulge," he wrote, "he had to be very good. His love of luxury made him a poor soldier in his first moments of battle. But in the Bulge, he soon learned that there was only one way to survive: He had to fight. And he fought, not for political or ideological reasons, but for his life."

Fritz, whose discovery in the attic had opened a window of opportunity to learn about his family's past and to preserve it, said he felt as though he had gotten to know Kenneth Plummer.

"He was gentle-hearted," Fritz said. "When he went into the Army, he was just a kid. But by the end, he was a man."

May 12, 1945

From: Capt. Margaret Gaule
To: Her husband, John Gaule

Omahan Margaret Gaule wrote to her husband when she was stationed in Okinawa.

My darling Husband,

HONEY, I'M WRITING on duty while we are having a lull in patients, which may not last for but a few minutes. My hours are from 10 a.m. to 10 p.m. so that doesn't give me much time to write.

I am really working hard doing just what I have always wanted to do. I wish I could just tell you half of what I have done today. You would really be so proud of me. I'm working with a shock team instead of being in the wards. It is really valuable experience. I don't have to wait for any orders from the doctors, but just go right ahead giving blood, plasma, penicillin, morphine, etc. Already I have received many compliments so I feel kind of proud today. These patients are brought right from the aid station, so I'm the first nurse they see. You should see the look on their faces when they see a nurse. Tonight one of the fellows was just coming out of the anesthetic and one of the fellows asked him how he would like a nurse to hold his hand, and he said, "Don't joke like that." The corpsman yelled for me to come, and I wish you could have seen his look of amazement when he saw me.

Well, my darling, I'm now off duty and dead tired, but it is a wonderful feeling of tiredness, because I know I have done a lot of very necessary nursing, and I feel so good inside.

All my love,
Midge

'She was real faithful about writing'

December 13, 1944

From: Capt. Lillard E. Pratt
To: His wife, now Pauline Spence, and children

Pauline Spence of Beatrice, Neb., received this letter from her husband, who was serving in the 343rd Field Artillery, 90th Division. Pratt was killed by an 88mm shell on Feb. 22, 1945.

My Loves: Pauline, Dave and John:

Your old fat Daddy sends his love again. Not again, but forever.

We are having a plenty tough time just now. The battle for Germany is much more savage than Normandy ever thought of being. Here we have a more dangerous enemy in the weather than actual bullets. Some soldiers have trench foot so bad they can barely get their bare feet into overshoes. These men will all lose their feet. War is terrible at its best, but at its worst it is a living and dying hell. Someday, however, the guns will stop booming and we can clear the battlefield and go home.

Don't think my spirits are low because I know such a condition is like death itself, so I force myself to keep my chin up. And it is possible to search hard enough to find a bright ray of hope. I know we are going to win, and that in itself must keep us going.

Love, it is time for chow so I will close with love for all.

All my Love,
Daddy

MARY NICKELS KEPT THE $5 engagement ring Bobby Nickels sent her as he shipped off to World War II service in France in 1944. Mary said yes — as long as Bobby promised to return.

"I opened it up and here was the most beautiful $5 ring I had ever seen in my whole life."

— MARY (REMPLE) NICKELS,
AFTER RECEIVING AN ENGAGEMENT
RING BY MAIL FROM BOBBY NICKELS

AROUND CHRISTMAS OF 1944, days before he boarded a ship and sailed to war, Bobby Nickels took a leap of faith.

Nineteen years old and hundreds of miles farther from home than he'd ever been — and fueled by mugs of free beer, courtesy of Baltimore's grateful dock workers and shipbuilders — Nickels stopped at a small jewelry shop after a night on the waterfront. He chose the only ring he could afford on his $21-a-month soldier's pay: a simple gold-plated ring with a tiny stone. He paid $5.

A few weeks later, in Henderson, Neb., Mary Remple's father handed her a worn envelope.

"My dad had scrutinized it very much before he gave it to me, because he knew who it was from," she recalled in 2008.

"I opened it up and here was the most beautiful $5 ring I had ever seen in my whole life. I was so happy — though very unhappy that I didn't get it right away."

In the bitter winter of early 1945, as Nickels marched over bomb-cratered roads through ruined French villages, Remple's reply reached him:

"Yes! But not until you get home."

For the next year, letters postmarked in Henderson — as much as clean socks, warm meals and dry tents — helped Bobby Nickels cross war-ravaged Europe. As an infantryman in the "Big Red One" — the Army's legendary 1st Division — Nickels began the long march through wintry Europe just after the Battle of the Bulge. Sometimes he wore nine layers of clothing — anything he could find to ward off the deadly cold. With the Big Red One, he helped chase the last German resistance across the countryside.

One day, a mortar hit a nearby building and sprayed hot shrapnel into Nickels' shoulder and neck. Another time, Nickels improvised a Molotov cocktail and threw the fiery bomb into the back of a German tank, destroying it — and later earning a Silver Star for the act.

All the while, he waited for Remple's latest letters.

"It was tough, but she was real faithful about writing to me," Nickels recalled. "More so than I was, probably."

Back in Nebraska, Remple worked in a Grand Island defense plant. She did whatever else she could to help the war effort: saving tires, conserving gasoline and coffee ... and writing letters to the soldier she hoped would come home to her.

"You did everything you could in those days. Everyone did," she said.

Nickels' unit was hiking up a large hill near the town of Halle, Germany, when word of the Germans' surrender reached them. He eventually found himself in Nuremberg, guarding a nearby prisoner of war camp and standing watch in town during the first motions of the famous Nuremberg war crimes trials.

In February 1946, Nickels headed for home. On Remple's birthday, March 31, Nickels was formally discharged in St. Louis. Nineteen days later, back in Nebraska, he and Remple were wed.

Sitting in his Columbus living room in 2008, with his wife's hands on his shoulders, Bobby Nickels smiled at the memory of the hastily mailed wedding ring — which Mary said had become worn and thin.

"After you get so much beer in you, back then, you'd get some crazy thoughts that seemed like good ideas," he said, patting his wife's hand. "But I guess it worked out OK."

'I would write you every hour'

IN THE MIDST OF THE HORRORS OF WAR, Army Pvt. Harold B. Galley found reason to be thankful.

"I've learned many things in this war. It never came to my mind before that people could endure so much and still live and be thankful just to be alive and thank God for being spared to live another day. I do realize it now."

Galley wrote those words to his daughter, Carolyn, during World War II.

Galley worked for the Metropolitan Life Insurance Co. in Omaha when he was drafted in March 1944. He went through basic training in Camp Fannin, Texas, and was sent overseas in September. Just a few months later, Carolyn, then 9, and her mother, Irene, would receive the terrible news.

PVT. HAROLD B. GALLEY is shown with his wife, Irene, and daughter, Carolyn, in August 1944. He was killed in action that year.

"In late 1944, there were so many American soldiers being killed in action that there were no military personnel to visit the family and give them the news," Carolyn recalled in 2008. "A telegram was sent and delivered to the home. I remember that day very well. My mother was at work and I was outside playing when the dreaded telegram arrived."

Carolyn Givan has many mementos of her father: a letter written to her and her mother by the secretary of state, a letter from President Franklin Roosevelt, her father's Purple Heart — and a touching, heartfelt letter he wrote her from Belgium:

My Dearest Daughter Carolyn:

IT HAS BEEN A FEW DAYS since I have written to either you or your mother. At times writing is out of the question. I hope the both of you will understand that if it were possible I would write you every hour of the day.

For the first time in several days I am at least dry again and the sun has come out of hiding. It seems to rain more here than anything else. I don't mind it in the least, I'm getting used to it now.

In the country that I am in, the people really know what war is. Their homes have been bombed and shelled until there just isn't much left to them. The windows are broken out and even sides of the houses are gone too, but they live in them just the same. Many of the children have very few clothes, let alone enough to eat. Wouldn't it seem very funny to you to have to beg soldiers of another land in order to get a little bit of sugar or candy or cookies or gum that you might have any at all. You see their stores don't have it to sell, there just isn't any to be had here. And how would you like to wear wooden shoes like the little Dutch children do, or even worse yet wear heavy high-top shoes that in many cases don't fit with wooden soles on them. I also saw little children that are crippled because they get hurt in the awful war.

I went to their church for services, this church had been bombed or shelled and was caved in, the windows broken and it was cold but they went anyway. I saw them pray and sing and give their money and be thankful that they could do so without being bombed or shelled while they were at church.

Yes, Carolyn, I've learned many things in this war. It never came to my mind before that people could endure so much and still live and be thankful just to be alive and thank God for being spared to live another day. I do realize it now. And I only hope that another war does not come again. I realize that you are young and it is hard for you to understand the evils of war and I also suppose you have many times wondered why your daddy had to go to war. At times I did too. It is only natural that to save the best country on earth, the best people. I have discovered that we are the best, the strongest, the bravest, the most ingenious, the brightest people in the world today. I know we have more of everything and better things than any other people in the world today. The way we live and think and do was not given to us, you or I but it was paid for by our forefathers, by fighting, bloodshed, prayer and the will to live as free people. And to achieve, and don't you ever let anyone tell you different. Your daddy is fighting to cause the rest of the world to be free and live like we do.

> "The way we live and think and do was not given to us, you or I but it was paid for by our forefathers, by fighting, bloodshed, prayer and the will to live as free people."
>
> — PVT. HAROLD GALLEY'S LETTER TO HIS DAUGHTER CAROLYN

I have been writing at this letter now for a couple of weeks or more and feel that I should end it soon, but before I do I imagine you would like to hear about how we travel around over here. One way, of course, is in trucks, but generally not very far at a time. Mostly, it has been in boxcars, such as your grandpa sends cattle or sheep to market in. On the outside of the car is a sign, worded like this, "40 Hommes or 8 Chevaux," which mean 40 men or 8 horses in one boxcar.

Well, that's how we ride — 40 men in a car plus our packs and rifles, to say the least, it is very crowded in the daytime, but at night it is even worse trying to sleep. Everyone tries to lay down on the floor. Some, of course, can't but if you do lay down, you soon wake up because of being cramped or someone has his foot in your face. You can imagine the groans and grunts all night long. Just as everyone is all settled again, someone decides that he must go to the toilet, so he gets up and starts to walk over the others. My, how everyone howls when you step on someone by mistake. At last you get to the door that is the toilet. If the train is stopped you can go to the toilet outside on the ground during the daytime. Just as soon as the train stops, the fellows climb out and run around the train to see what they can see.

One day a couple of fellows ran over into a pasture and tried to milk a cow. I guess he got some to drink, as least I hope he did, he tried hard enough to get some. The fellows are always trying to build a fire to make coffee or warm up some food. Generally, as soon as the fire gets going good the train starts to go again. The fellows will play with handcars that are along the tracks, push them around or play with some farmer's dog that is close by. Sometime when you are with mother down in South Omaha, have her stop in and you talk to Mr. Flynn. He will tell you all about the box cars and 40 & 8. He was over here last war.

I hope you and mother are both feeling well and that your mother's business is good. I nearly forgot to ask about how the cats are or do you still have them? I thought they were so cute. I suppose Mischief will have some more by the time I get home again. And how is your music teacher? Are you learning anything from her? And did Uncle Milton have to go to the Navy and stay?

Well, Carolyn, you can look at the map and find Belgium on it. That is where I am at now. So, Carolyn, with all my love to you and mother.

Your Daddy.

September 23, 1945

From: Keith B. Lynch

To: Folks at home

Lynch wrote this letter home to Crab Orchard, Neb., from the USS Ruticulus. He had just toured the bombed-out remains of Nagasaki, Japan. Following are excerpts of his impressions. The letter was sent from Nagasaki.

Dear Folks:

Now I know what they mean when they say "a dead city." You remember when I first described the place to you? About the city being in two valleys going at right angles to each other from the harbor, with a string of mountains between them? The smaller of the two, about the same size and five or six times the population of Tecumseh, was the first we visited. It was damaged of course by the concussion of the atomic blast and also by two previous bombings. But the main part of the place, in the other valley, about the size of Lincoln I would say, and five or six times the population, was completely inundated.

The sight I saw from the top of the hill, over which it was approximated the center of the blast, was a sight I hope my children, if I am so fortunate, will never have to see, hear of, or ever think of. It was horrible and when you get to thinking, unbelievable. To think that a thirty-pound bomb the size of a basketball, exploding a thousand feet in the air, could cause such a holocaust was simply unbelievable. I shudder to think what these people underwent when the blast occurred. A blast that literally dissolved their homes, family, friends and any other material thing in the vicinity. A blast that pushed over huge steel structures a mile and a half away as if they were made of blocks.

Now I can see what they mean when they say "Dead City." A city with no buildings, no trees, no facilities, and no people. All you see from the top of the hill is a ground covered with bricks, burned wood, twisted and pushed over steel frames of buildings for several miles in each direction. There is nothing for the people of this "Dead City" to do but walk around and think, "What manner of people would do such a thing to us, who are a peaceful, courteous, and civilized people?" I wondered what they thought when they looked at us as we were driving along. "Are these the barbarians who did such a thing to us? What can we expect now that we are at their mercy?"

I only wish they could be made to suffer a tenth of the atrocities that they performed on our men whom they held prisoner. People can say these people are simple, ignorant of the facts, or under a spell, but a nation cannot wage war as they have without the backing of the majority of their people.

Such a thing as I saw yesterday cannot be described in words. You have to see it and I hope no one ever has to see such a thing again.

Love,
Son

Lost in the mail — and found

WHEN FRANK DINOVO HEARD VOICES rise from the spinning records that had been lost since World War II, his lips curled into a smile and his mind drifted back in time.

If only for a few minutes, he was 25 again — and a sailor in the U.S. Navy.

A rare coincidence had his young bride's two brothers, stationed elsewhere, taking a military leave in the same spot as Dinovo.

FRANK DINOVO

The trio celebrated heartily near Pearl Harbor, knowing that in wartime the reunion could be their last. They wound up at a USO club, putting their voices onto discs that Dinovo would mail to his wife, Mary, in Council Bluffs.

"Don't laugh," a stammering Dinovo told his wife at one point during the 1945 recording. "I'm having a hard time thinking of something to say."

MARY DINOVO

If it were just the two of them together, he teased, he would not be at a loss for words.

"Beings we're not — and everybody's listening — I wouldn't want your face to get red or anything."

The playful passage was among the audible parts left on a pair of record discs that remarkably found their way to Dinovo in 2010 after being lost for more than 65 years.

With the help of Omaha North High School teacher Therese Laux and her Music and Media Technology class' special equipment and expertise, Dinovo was able to listen to the letters-on-records.

Dinovo actually had forgotten he had made them until a friend, Jack Larsen, surprised him with a package he came across and bought at an auction.

The parcel was postmarked June 11, 1945, and was addressed to Dinovo's wife.

Dinovo was in disbelief at the find. "Flabbergasted," he said.

The problem then, however, was that he didn't have handy an old-style phonograph that would play the discs at 78 rpm.

A friend provided hers, and some words were audible, but the new multimedia technology lab at North High had higher-tech equipment that could filter out background noise and, as a treat, convert the records into a CD form that Dinovo could listen to every day.

Laux and about 25 students gathered around Dinovo, who spoke about his wartime experiences before listening, with the class, to the recordings.

Laux called his visit a "priceless learning history moment" that contrasted the slow modes of communication used by the World War II generation to the rapid-fire text messages and email her teenage students are accustomed to.

"I'm so used to instantaneous responses," student Nick Brown said as he fidgeted with his cellphone. "It would be completely frustrating" to depend on snail mail to get word to your family during wartime.

Dinovo showed the class the piece of a worn dollar bill that was in his wallet when he swam for his life. Once a full dollar bill, he ripped it and gave half to the sailor who swam alongside him.

"It was inspiring," said Zenith Sharma, another student. "I could feel the emotions he had when we played the recordings."

Katelyn Forrest said Dinovo made her recall her grandpa telling stories about his wartime service. "I feel like I want to spend more time with him before he goes."

Laux's connection went deeper. Her own father served in WWII and died when she was a toddler. The first time Laux heard his voice was on a disc — similar to the one Dinovo had recorded — that she uncovered years after his death.

Despite differences in years and experiences, Laux told her class that they and Dinovo have the common goal of wanting to connect with loved ones. "We all share the same desire to connect and communicate."

Dinovo's long-lost discs also included voice messages from his two brothers-in-law, Sam and Jim Garafalo, Mary's only siblings.

Sam spoke as if addressing his parents and a whole group of family and friends.

"I suppose you're all over to the Cash family listening to the phonograph there because I know they got the kind you can play this record on."

He said that it took a long time for the three men to get together but that they were having a good old time. "Kind of reminds me of back home when we was in Council Bluffs," Sam said. "I hope it won't be long now, and we'll be all back there together."

Jim died while in the service; Sam died years later.

Mary passed away in 2003, having never listened to the recordings.

LT. COL. RICHARD CHADWICK of the 35th Division's rear echelon takes time to read a letter while in France.

Crafty troops evaded censors

WORLD WAR II VETERAN BUD HUGHES of the Elkhorn area recalled arriving in Seattle before heading overseas: "Our mail was censored, and we were warned not to divulge our whereabouts under threat of prosecution."

Some of the troops mailed postcards from downtown Seattle while on pass, Hughes said in 1991, "but we were intimidated enough to sign names only our families would recognize. Our destination was kept secret even from us."

The Army cunningly diverted attention from the ship's destination by issuing the men cold-weather gear.

"It was an obvious attempt to make us believe we were headed for the Aleutian Islands," Hughes said. "Actually, we went to Hawaii and then to the tropics."

Hughes said some of the World War II censors "took great pains to cut anything that might be construed as banned information, while others were quite liberal."

"Most of us soon found an officer who merely skimmed over our letters quickly. Some men went to great lengths to devise a code so they could tell their wives or girlfriends where they were. One way was to use the first letter in every other paragraph to spell the location."

Hughes said he believed that the total-secrecy exercise was largely "a game."

"Many of us felt this censorship was just another way to make everyone feel a part of the war," he said.

No loose lips, or anything else, sank his ship. "But the second day after we arrived," he said, "our outfit, the 389th Bombardment Group, was welcomed by name to Okinawa by Tokyo Rose in her daily radio broadcast."

Omahan Ed Schafer, an Army Air Forces pilot in World War II, for a time was a censor for the British.

"In Africa I crashed after the nose gear of my plane collapsed," he explained. "They took me to a British army hospital. While I was recuperating, the doctors thought it

THREE NEBRASKANS took a break for mail call aboard a Coast Guard vessel in the Pacific. From left, Don R. Hotz of Omaha, Francis Hughes of Lincoln and Melvin L. McClean of Lincoln.

would be good for me to have something to do, so they put me to work censoring the letters of British servicemen."

Schafer at first protested, saying he didn't know anything about the Brits' censorship rules, but he was told not to worry: "They said, 'Our rules are just like yours. No troop movements. No names, etc.'"

Schafer said the letters "were typical of the kind soldiers everywhere write home to girlfriends and family."

One letter was memorable. "The guy was writing to Florence, his girlfriend," Schafer recalled.

"He said, 'I know you're going to date some of those Yanks. Just be careful. They have ways of meeting their objective without aid of military procedures.'"

November 26, 1944

From: Sgt. Kenneth Munhall

To: His wife, Elizabeth Munhall, and new daughter "Baby Karen Jean," who later lived in Grand Island. Munhall wrote this letter from "Somewhere in England."

To My Baby Karen Jean,

THIS IS MY FIRST LETTER to you as a person. Today you are 28 days old and I haven't seen you or have so much as a picture to tell me what you look like. Your father left the United States before you were born, knowing your arrival was just a short time away and wanting very much to be there when you did arrive.

Your mother and I wanted a little girl like you. Fathers usually want a little boy but I wanted a little girl as much like her mother as possible. You see, I love your mother very much and I couldn't think of anything nicer than to have a little girl just like her. All I know about you right now is that you weighed five pounds, eight ounces when you were born, and that you have black hair (which your mother writes me was two inches long in back), and dark blue eyes. That sounds to me like an extremely nice baby girl. Your aunts, grandparents and uncles all think a lot of you. Your daddy does too and wants more than anything else in the world to come back home soon and take care of Karen Jean and her mama. Your job is to eat, sleep, play, develop a good disposition, and grow like a baby should.

Goodnight my darling, sleep well, and your daddy will come home to you soon.

Love from your father

MEMORIES OF A GENERATION ★ ═══════════════

RAYMOND W. STEHNO

Town: Stratton, Neb.

Service: Radar navigator, B-29 bomber, 20th Air Force

In the war: Left San Francisco Aug. 3, 1945, with 11-man crew on new B-29 Superfortress, with refueling stops at Hawaii, Johnson Island, Kwajalein and Guam, then on to Tinian Island. Two days later, was assigned to a crew that had lost its radar navigator, and on Aug. 5 and 6, flew first 15-hour bombing mission over Japan. Flew three more missions over Japan before the war ended. Flew 13 additional search-and-rescue missions looking for downed planes and dropping food and supplies to POW camps in Japan. Spent two weeks on Iwo Jima, then was transferred to the Philippines, and took part in the Philippine independence ceremonies on July 4, 1946. After 38 months of service, returned to San Francisco by troop carrier after 15 days on a rough sea.

In his words: "I wouldn't trade my experience in the service for anything in the world. It took some time to get readjusted to civilian life, but settled down to a happy marriage and a career in farming and government service. I remained in the Reserve for an additional nine years and reached the rank of first lieutenant. I still have all the daily letters received from and sent to my fiancee (future wife) during that 38 months, and occasionally refer back to them."

LENORE DEETHS

Town: Omaha

In the war: She was 2 years old when her father, the late Edward J. Baburek, shipped off to war. She was 5 when he returned. Baburek served with the 2nd Bombardment Group on the B-17 Flying Fortress as a radio communicator. He entered the war as a captain in the U.S. Army Air Forces. He eventually retired as a lieutenant colonel after serving in the Reserves, U.S. Air Force. Her uncles, the late Joseph and the late Robert Baburek, served in the Navy during the war.

In her words: "My uncle Joe Baburek was at Pearl Harbor when it was bombed by the Japanese. He wrote a letter dated Dec. 7, 1941, which he sent to my grandma. It shows the calm before the storm! … My father wrote very fine letters, which my mother always read to me. I was rather apprehensive when he came home. He wanted me to rush right into his arms, and I didn't really want to do that. It took some bonding. The big shock to me was all the ones born after the war. I got a new father, and nine months later I got a baby brother."

JAMES E. PRESLAR

Town: Omaha

Service: U.S. Army — 361st Regiment, Company G, 3rd Squad, 91st Division

In the war: In the spring of 1942, he was sent to Camp Roberts, Calif., for basic training, then on to Camp Adair, Ore. By May, he shipped out from Newport News, Va., Naval Ship Yard to Naples, Italy. Once in Italy, he became part of the invasion force that made its way to the Battle of Anzio. From there, the 91st Division continued into Rome, Leghorn and Pisa, and ultimately captured the Gothic Line. He was made sergeant, field commission. He was wounded twice, in Leghorn and again while fighting the Gothic Line. He received the Purple Heart and Oak Leaf Cluster.

In his words: "The hardest part of the war was being so far from home. The letters we got were sporadic and censored to protect our location. This made us appreciate the buddies we had and the Italian people. I was able to visit the Catacombs and the Vatican. My favorite memory would be celebrating my last New Year's Eve in Italy at the top of the Leaning Tower of Pisa, Dec. 31, 1944."

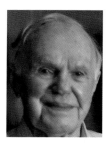

ROBERT G. LUEDER

Town: Omaha

Service: 2nd lieutenant, then promoted to 1st lieutenant, U.S. Army from April 1944 to March 1946

In the war: Served with Company B, 318 Infantry 80th Division in Luxembourg, Belgium, France and Germany, where he was wounded. Received Purple Heart and Bronze Star.

In his words: (From a letter to his parents after he was wounded in February 1945) "We had to cross a river (the border) by boat and then go up almost vertical cliffs. Jerry (the Germans) had our crossing zeroed in with everything he had, but after two successful attacks I found myself about two miles into Germany and most of my platoon still with me. … We were doing too well, I guess, because suddenly Jerry took the attitude to hell with his own troops and everyone and started dropping mortars all around us as we were only a few yards from the Germans. They got hit, too, and came running out to surrender. One fragment got me in the middle of the back. I rolled over and my D.U. Sgt. said it went through my clothes but only scratched my back. Just then wham! My thigh got hit. … Funny, it was all so quick it didn't even hurt."

MORRIS A. ODVARKA

Town: Clarkson

Service: U.S. Army, December 1941 to June 1946

In the war: A Reserve officer, he was called into duty shortly after Pearl Harbor was attacked. His duty lasted 54 months, with service in the 89th, 65th, 66th and 71st Divisions as an infantry company commander, a battalion S-3 and a troop convoy leader escorting troops to Africa and Italy. While with the 65th Division attached to Gen. George S. Patton's Third Army, his unit came across the first discovered concentration camp at Ohrdruf, Germany.

In his words: "At war's termination, I was given the job as commander of the 1513th Labor Supervision Company to repair and maintain a German airfield for U.S. occupation, which duty I maintained until my return to the U.S. With this new assignment, I was to supervise the loading of over 1,000 POWs, held in France, onto rail boxcars for shipment to the airfield at Fritzlar, Germany. I traveled by Jeep with a sergeant and my stray pet rat terrier dog for two days nonstop to take charge of the POWs at the airfield. This was the beginning of the 1513 LSC. During the first night at Fritzlar, I was awakened in my quarters, a fourth-mile from the stockade, by a guard informing me a POW wished to speak to me. The POW, a man in his sixties speaking perfect English, said the POW SS members in the group were planning a breakout. So I had a machine gun mounted on a Jeep to patrol around the stockade. Sure enough, a place was found where the POWs began to dig. From that night on, I could not let my informant, named Karl Gennert, remain in the stockade. They would have killed him. So now my 1513 LSC comprised 10 battle-hardened GIs and 10 hand-picked, screened POWs, an interpreter, orderly, cooks, mechanics and carpenters who lived unguarded in a building across the road from the stockade. I even secured a huge German aircraft searchlight generator for which the POW assistants kept running to provide floodlights for the stockade.

"Karl Gennert, the interpreter, was a great help for me. He told of many incidents about SS and Gestapo operations. Many weeks after our arrival at the airfield, he told me he was concerned about his wife, who was living in Bremerhaven. Somehow, he had learned that the Gestapo opened the floodgates to flood the subway in the city, where many people took refuge during an air raid. He wondered if I could get a letter to his wife into the German mail system. This was against my regulations, but as a favor to him for the favor he did me, I mailed his letter. He eventually learned she had survived. Many months after I returned home, I received a package containing a boy and girl doll in native Alpine dress made by his wife, in gratitude."

ROY C. MURPHY

Town: Council Bluffs

Service: Staff sergeant, 740th Railway Operating Battalion, Transportation Corps

In the war: After basic training in New Orleans and Clovis, N.M., he was shipped to the European Theater just one month after D-Day. His battalion was to rebuild the railroads in France, Belgium and Germany fast enough to keep up with the advancing troops. His job was to see that the trains were sent to the proper railheads for unloading heavy equipment or ammunition. The battalion's commanding officer kept the men on the railroad all the time, putting them into four battle areas, including the Battle of the Bulge.

In his words: "One occasion that is easy to remember is when buzz bombs landed about two blocks away from my station, hitting a day-care center. That was not a pretty picture. The buzz bombs in those days were the noisy kind. They had just enough fuel to reach our location in Bonn, Germany, and you could hear them coming. When they ran out of fuel, you knew they were going to land so you headed for cover. They were not the guided type so they landed at random. When our battalion would change locations, moving forward as the troops advanced, we would have to ride in boxcars. These were lovingly known as '40x8s.' I attempted to write home one time to let people know where I was. I mentioned getting 'an eye full' on our way through Paris. When I returned home, I was shown the letter with the phrase 'an eye full' neatly cut out by Army censors."

'We regret to inform…'

WHEREVER GAYHART GERLING WENT IN LIFE, his best friend Melvin Schmuecker was sure to be there. The two grew up on farms north of Emerson, Neb., and attended a one-room school together. In their late teen years, they drove into town together on Saturday nights in an old Model A Ford. In 1944, when both were drafted into World War II, they shared the rigors of boot camp together. After a Christmas furlough at home, they both shipped out for Europe. ★ A man at the train depot with the unenviable task of delivering War Department notices called on both the Schmuecker and Gerling families within a week of each other in February 1945. When he arrived at the Schmuecker home, he found only Melvin's mother and refused to leave the telegram. Melvin's father went later to the depot office to claim it. "When he came back, he was crying," Marge Cadwallader, Melvin's sister, recalled in 1995. "I think he knew what it was before he went there." ★ Days later, as planning was under way for Schmuecker's memorial service, the depot messenger paid a visit to the Gerlings. "It was a rainy, rainy day and it was milking time," said Gerling's sister, Helen Wentworth. "My parents just looked at him, and they knew what he was bringing."

COL. ROBERT MOORE, in uniform, returned to a hero's welcome in Villisca, Iowa, in 1943. But shortly after he arrived at the train station, he met with Montgomery County Sheriff Frank Miller, whose son Wes Miller was the first soldier from Moore's company to die in North Africa.

Two big brothers didn't come home

Jim Ziemba holds pictures of brothers Louie, left, and Eddie in 1998.

BY CHRISTOPHER BURBACH

FOR YOUNG JIMMY ZIEMBA, World War II was a war of waiting.

Waiting for his brother Louie to come home and answer Jimmy's questions about ships and the sea. Waiting for his brother Eddie to come home and take him to the Peanut Island tavern to drink orange pop and play pinball. Waiting for his brother Johnny to come home and take him horseback riding. Waiting for his brother Joe to come home and bring his own wife and children to Sunday dinner at the family house in South Omaha.

The waiting ended only when the war did. Jimmy had four big brothers when it started. He had two when it ended. The answers to his questions about the Navy sank with Louie's ship in 1942. The dreams of more brotherly outings to Peanut Island died with Eddie in Italy in 1943.

Jim's parents, John and Eva Ziemba, immigrated to Omaha from Poland as teenagers. They eventually had 12 children — six boys, six girls. Three died as infants.

The family, which lived in a small house on South 36th Street, quickly merged into American culture, with the children playing with Irish, German and Czech immigrant children from the neighborhood. But John and Eva usually spoke Polish to each other.

John Ziemba worked at the Wilson and Co. meatpacking plant. Eva ran "the ranch," as the family jokingly called their household.

Jim was the youngest child. He doesn't remember much of his brother Louis, who was 18 years older. Louis joined the Navy to see the world in the late 1930s, when World War II was on the far-off horizon. Jim's memories of him come from stories and pictures.

The three other Ziemba boys were drafted into the Army after the war was on. So Jim was old enough to hang out with them before Uncle Sam called them away from the ranch.

"Johnny loved horses," Jim recalled in 1998. "He would take me to go horseback riding at Bar None stables on South 36th Street, where you could rent horses."

Joe was occupied with his own family. The fun-loving Eddie often took his baby brother along on outings.

"He would say, 'C'mon, Jimmy, let's go for a ride,' and phhht, I'd be gone to the car," Jim said. The best trips ended at Peanut Island, a bar at 24th and Vinton Streets that also was known as Paramount Liquor Co. There, Eddie would drink draft beer and eat peanuts with his buddies, throwing the shells on the floor. But first they set Jimmy up at the pinball machine.

"They would get me a chair to stand on," Jim said. "They bought me an orange pop and gave me a handful of nickels. I was in heaven."

Jimmy was 8 in the early spring of 1942 when a telegram came while his father was at work. One of his sisters accepted the telegram. She read it. But she did not tell her mother what it said — that Louie was dead at 25, killed in the sinking of the USS Houston off the coast of Java.

"She waited until evening when my dad came home from work, and she told him," Jim said. "She didn't want my mother to be alone when she heard. My father was the one who told my mother, and he told it to her in Polish. I remember she said, 'No.' "

Eva refused to believe it, Jim said. And he was too young to understand that it meant Louie would never come home.

A letter arrived in the winter of 1943. Eddie wrote from Italy to his sister Mary. The letter, cheery in spots, tells between the lines of the toll the war was taking on the Ziembas. Eddie thanked Mary for the candy the family had sent. He acknowledged the news of a new nephew.

"I was glad to read that the addition at the ranch was a boy." He asked for help getting in touch with Joe, even though Joe was in the Pacific Theater and actually closer to Eddie than to home.

"Say, sis, if Joe comes home during the holidays, tell him that I would like to hear from him."

But Eddie's news about himself was brief.

"I have seen plenty of action and as I write this letter we are still on the line." The letter was written Dec. 7, 1943. Twelve days later, Eddie was killed near Anzio, Italy. He was 24.

This time, when the telegram came, Jimmy understood.

"I accepted the fact that Louie was not coming back," Jim said. "And then I had to accept that Eddie was not coming back, either."

But it was too much for his mother.

"It went the same way (as with the telegram about Louie)," Jim said. "My sister waited until my dad got home from work. He told my mother in Polish. She did the same thing. She just said 'No,' and she never accepted the fact that he wasn't coming back."

Eva died in 1950, officially of a stroke.

"But everybody said she died of a broken heart," Jim said.

Before she died, though, she was able to see Johnny and Joe again after the war.

Jim remembered clearly the thrill of Johnny's arrival.

"It was quite a thing," he said. "He brought his duffel bag, and he dumped it out on the kitchen floor. I thought everything was so neat. I wore his hat. He let me hold his medals. He brought me a harmonica."

★ MEMORIES ★
OF A GENERATION

MYRON ROKER

Town: Glenwood, Iowa

Service: Army, 44th Infantry Division, 324th Regiment

In the war: Served 204 days in combat with his unit during the fight across France and Germany. At one point, the unit saw 144 consecutive days of combat.

In his words: "This is hard for me to tell. ... (My friend), he always called me Rokes. He said, 'Rokes, what about a cup of coffee?' " As they drank the coffee, sharing a cup, his friend was called to go examine some tripwire mines. "They weren't gone five minutes and I heard explosions, and I figured right away it might be bad. ... He was supposed to be married. Sometimes there are things you don't understand in a war."

Southwest Iowa dealt a heavy blow

SOUTHWEST IOWA FAMILIES gloried in war reports of Feb. 21, 1943, which told how one of their own — Capt. Robert Moore of Villisca — had saved their husbands and sons from becoming a "lost battalion."

The Red Oak Express reprinted a dispatch telling how Moore led his unit in a daring night escape after they had been surrounded by the Germans at Faid Pass in Tunisia.

By March 6, however, the rejoicing turned to silence. At Red Oak, the mournful knocks on wooden doors echoed across the community like death knells: "We regret to inform you . . . "

Again and again the knocks came that day, first one house, then another and another.

Twenty-seven telegrams March 6, ". . . your son is missing in action."

". . . Your husband is missing . . ."

"Missing . . ."

". . . Missing in action."

As the news spread, families of the 168th Infantry Regiment's soldiers shuffled into the lobby of the Hotel Johnson, next to the Western Union office, to await the dreaded words. By March 11, the toll of missing in Company M reached 37. Two more names were added March 15.

After 10 days Red Oak listed 44 missing; 56 were missing from Montgomery County. Red Oak was not alone. Telegrams arrived in Glenwood, Atlantic, Council Bluffs and Clarinda.

"There have been other casualties," an officer was quoted as saying at the time. ". . . But there is no place, to my knowledge, where in this war there has been such a large group from such a comparatively small area."

"We were horrified," said Dorothy Reynolds of Villisca, whose husband, Ed, led his company to safety with Capt. Moore. "We didn't know what had happened."

Information from the African front was sporadic. Even letters from the men came weeks apart, in bunches.

The AP dispatch on Moore's escape was printed a week after the fact.

Two of the 168th Regiment's three battalions were overrun at Faid Pass. Spread too thinly on a five-mile front, the men could only watch helplessly as German Field Marshal Erwin Rommel's Afrika Korps chewed up their outnumbered and outgunned armored support, the 1st Armored Division.

At the battle's end, only four tanks of the 1st Armored were still operating and the 2nd and 3rd Battalions of the 168th Infantry were surrounded.

The southwest Iowa units held out through two days of shelling, strafing and infantry attacks. The night of Feb. 17 they were ordered to retreat, without cover, through 13 miles of desert crawling with German units.

By the time the 168th — which had been an Iowa National Guard unit — regrouped at Tebessa, Algeria, its losses numbered 2,242 men, including 59 killed and 176 wounded. Among them were 200 southwest Iowans held prisoner.

E.A. Alderman in the New York Herald-Tribune pointed to Red Oak, which then had a population of 5,600. By war's end, the community had lost 50 men. A comparable loss in New York City, Alderman wrote, would mean 70,000 men.

Life and Look magazines featured the community. Life printed an aerial photo of the community marking homes where men were missing. Popular singer Kate Smith mentioned the losses on her national radio program.

"We all hung together," Lois Bryson, whose husband, Fred, was wounded at Faid, recalled in 1993. "Everybody had somebody who had left."

Anxiety about the fate of those missing lasted several weeks. By April 29, all but 13 of the Red Oak guardsmen had been accounted for, most in prisoner-of-war camps in Germany and Poland. Most relatives received word through shortwave radio dispatches from the Vatican in Rome.

Lois Bryson, who had moved to Omaha to work in the Martin Bomber Plant, was one of those.

"I suppose it was the nuns at the hospital in Italy," where her husband was taken, she said.

Someone in Philadelphia monitored the radio broadcasts and notified Omaha Postmaster Harley Moorehead, who posted notices in The World-Herald for those he couldn't contact.

Bryson's notification came in a roundabout way. It came for her father-in-law, Everett, but the last name was spelled Bresson, and it was sent to South 32nd Street, when she had an apartment on South 25th Street.

"My landlady had seen the notice and told me, 'Here, I think this one is for you,' " Bryson said.

Some reports came directly from the prisoners, through Red Cross exchanges.

Most of the men ended up together again in Stalag III B at Furstenberg near Berlin. Letters from one prisoner would mention the names of others with requests to contact families.

Such military losses to a single area have been rare since. The sinking of the warship Juneau in 1942 brought home to the military a hard lesson.

The 500 sailors who died included five Sullivan brothers — Joseph, Francis, Albert, Madison and George — of Waterloo, Iowa. Units are now mixed with those from other parts of the country to prevent such debacles.

Those regulations were in place, an officer said at the time, but "the Iowa units of the old National Guard got out of the country before this plan went into effect."

Southwest Iowa families waited

Action in North Africa took a steep toll on some communities in southwest Iowa. Reports from the 168th Infantry in the spring of 1943:

	COMPANY	POWs	FATALITIES
ATLANTIC	K	46	3
COUNCIL BLUFFS	L	42	3
GLENWOOD	I	39	1
RED OAK	M	50	2
SHENANDOAH	E	23	-
VILLISCA	F	9	7

Source: U.S. Army
Note: An infantry company might typically have around 100 to 150 soldiers.

LOIS BRYSON OF RED OAK, IOWA, below in 1993, kept the World War II telegram that announced her husband, Fred, was missing in action in North Africa, along with the World-Herald clipping.

'Like attending one's own funeral'

JULIE CROFOOT NERVOUSLY WAITED for almost a month before the mail finally brought a scrawled note on a slip of pink paper that eased her fears. Her beloved husband, Michael, had survived D-Day. Then, two days later, on July 5, the government telegram arrived that she had dreaded. Lt. j.g. Michael Crofoot, her husband of four years and the father of three sons, was missing in action. But Crofoot survived his wartime ordeals and returned to Omaha, where he practiced for more than 30 years as a pediatrician. He died in 1982 at the age of 70.

WAYNE R. WINSLOW

Town: Blair, Neb.

Service: U.S. Army Air Forces

In the war: He had basic training at Buckley Field near Denver and, after waiting for top-secret security clearance, cryptographic school at Chanute Field in Rantoul, Ill. He was stationed at Northwest Field, Guam, with the 315th Bomb Wing.

In his words: "Gen. (Frank) Armstrong, 315 BW commander, asked me if I would help him by writing letters to the families of crew members we lost. He said he wrote a personal letter to each family, and he was way behind.

"They gave me six crews that were lost and the bombing missions they were on. I was able to write a lot of unclassified information to help families learn a little bit more about the loss of their loved one. I only knew the first name, rank and crew position. Gen. Armstrong signed the letters and sent them. I wrote about 60 letters."

The telegram Julie Crofoot received on July 5, 1944

THE NAVY DEPARTMENT DEEPLY REGRETS TO INFORM YOU THAT YOUR HUSBAND LIEUTENANT MICHAEL CROFOOT USNR IS MISSING FOLLOWING ACTION IN THE PERFORMANCE OF HIS DUTY AND IN THE SERVICE OF HIS COUNTRY. THE DEPARTMENT APPRECIATES YOUR GREAT ANXIETY BUT DETAILS NOT NOW AVAILABLE AND DELAY IN RECEIPT THEREOF MUST NECESSARILY BE EXPECTED. TO PREVENT POSSIBLE AID TO OUR ENEMIES PLEASE DO NOT DIVULGE THE NAME OF HIS SHIP OR STATION.

— VICE ADMIRAL RANDALL JACOBS
CHIEF OF NAVAL PERSONNEL

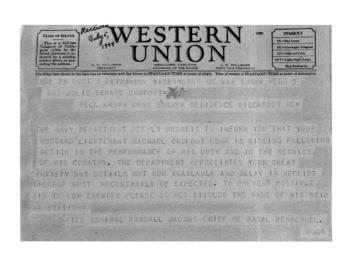

JULIE CROFOOT,
in 1994

She wrote her husband the next day:

Mickey darling,

WHAT AM I to do? Jo just telephoned from Omaha with information from Aunt Fran that you were reported "missing" on June 27th. How can it be? Now all my hope is gone. I had hoped the telegram referred to your D-Day experience, that it was all a mistake. You said you were in a relatively safe position. After escaping from one hazardous experience it doesn't seem possible that anything could happen to you so soon again. Oh darling, I don't know what to do or what to think. Come back to me sweetheart.

Your ever loving wife, Julie.

LT. MICHAEL CROFOOT

Several weeks later, her prayers were answered in a letter from her husband:

ONE LETTER FROM you today, Lass, written July 6th full of despair. Darling, you were warned not to believe any missing in action report. The one that caused all the trouble was sent in by our commanding officer on June 15th, I returned 16 June. Another report about my return went in June 16th, but evidently only the first one got forwarded. As for the 27th June date, that may be the day the report cleared Washington.

What a ghastly mistake! At any rate, you have your lost sleep back now. We were in no particular danger after June 13th except for the outside chance that one of the few bombs the Germans dropped nightly might land square on our fox hole. Coming across the Channel there was a remote chance of hitting a mine or being struck by a buzz bomb. But Lass, this was infinitesimal compared to the danger of machine gun fire of the first day.

If God got me safe out of such a pickle he has business for me at home (to be sure he does — three boys and a wife like you). From the last phrase in your letter I can see you have not abandoned hope — which is well. It was a beautiful letter you wrote — one I shall keep always. Lass, I shall come back to you before the year is out.

Damnation; to think you have had all that uneasiness; mother too. It is like attending one's own funeral, makes one feel ridiculous, annoyed and sorry. Do you remember in Huckleberry Finn — or possibly T. Sawyer — how the boys sneak into the church for their own funeral sermons?

I love you. Love, Michael.

THE LOSSES HIT HARD IN THE MIDLANDS

ORCHESTRA LEADER GLENN MILLER, who was born in Clarinda, Iowa, and lived 10 years in western Nebraska, joined the Army in 1942. He disbanded his orchestra at the height of his career and enlisted at age 38 despite having a wife and child. Miller said he intended to improve the morale of fellow soldiers through his music and assembled a military orchestra whose programs were broadcast to units around the world. He later was assigned to England, where his broadcasts became one of that nation's few forms of entertainment. Miller's plane disappeared in 1944 on a flight to Paris, where he was to arrange a Christmas Day concert for Allied troops. At right: Miller was stationed at the Lincoln Army Air Field in 1942 when he made an appearance in Omaha and signed autographs for Norma Young , left, and Rita Bartos.

HEISMAN TROPHY WINNER NILE KINNICK, below, joined the Navy on the eve of the U.S. entry into World War II. On June 2, 1943, the University of Iowa graduate was alone in his Grumman Wildcat fighter plane when it developed an oil leak on a training exercise off the coast of Venezuela. He made a water landing, normally a survivable accident, but was gone by the time rescuers from the USS Lexington got there. Ed Kiddoo, a football teammate of Kinnick at Benson High in Omaha in the 1930s and a World War II flier, knew him well and named his only son Nile. "I don't care about legends," Kiddoo said in 1991. "He was just a great person. I wouldn't have cared whether he was a legend or not. There are a lot of 'legends' I wouldn't name my boy after."

EVELYN REDMON AND BABY VICKIE received 1st Lt. Evan Redmon's Bronze Star from Lt. Col. D.K. Scruby at a ceremony in Omaha in 1945. The citation for Redmon, at left, who was killed in the Philippines, said he had "moved forward in the face of intense hostile fire and administered first aid to a wounded fellow soldier. In the performance of his heroic deed, 1st Lieut. Redmon was mortally wounded."

MARY FINN HANCOCK

Town: Grew up on a farm near Emmetsburg, Iowa; lived later in Sacramento, Calif.

Service: Lieutenant in the Navy Nurse Corps 1942 to 1945. She was stationed in San Diego, Pearl Harbor, Hawaii, and Quantico, Va.

In the war: Hancock met President Franklin D. Roosevelt when he visited the wounded men at a Pearl Harbor hospital. She met her future husband, Lt. Col. Edward "Tony" Hancock, while stationed in Hawaii. Her brother, Patrick, died aboard the USS Franklin. Hancock toured the ship after it was towed back to Pearl Harbor and saw a huge bomb crater in the radio compartment, where her brother had worked as a radio operator. She was sent back home to tell her parents about the death.

In her words: "All the friends and relatives had gathered at the house to celebrate what they thought was my return home. Instead, I had to inform them of Pat's death. I remember looking at my dad, and tears were pouring down his cheeks. He didn't say a word."

MEMORIES OF A GENERATION ★

VERNON HOOPS

Town: Byron, Neb.

Service: Army, 45th Infantry Division

In the war: Served as an infantryman and scout in France and Germany starting in January 1945.

In his words: "We crossed the Rhine River the day I got wounded. … As the first scout, they asked me to see if I could spot some enemy forces ahead. Before I could spot them, they spotted me. I had this book in my pocket, this Bible my pastor had given me. … I thought I was a goner. But (the bullet) went through my arm and just skinned the edge of my skin on my chest."

RAYMOND MEDUNA

Town: Wahoo

Service: Navy, USS Sanders

In the war: Served on a destroyer escort that accompanied the USS Indianapolis on a secret mission: delivering the atomic bomb to the air base on Tinian Island.

In his words: "Nobody knew. Even the people aboard. … A bunch of my buddies got put on the Indianapolis … and they were teasing me because it was the bigger ship. … Well, it turns out the Indianapolis sunk (after delivering the bomb) and those poor suckers hung on rafts for … days. Most of them didn't make it."

GILBERT HILL

Town: Omaha

Service: Navy, Pacific Fleet

In the war: Took basic training in Farragut, Idaho, in the summer of 1944 and then was assigned to an ammunition ship, the USS Manderson Victory, sailing from San Francisco with 8,000 tons of ammunition. The Manderson Victory, a converted U.S. Merchant Marine ship, pulled alongside warships and delivered ammo. After two years and 21 days of service, Hill retired as a yeoman second class.

In his words: "We sailed into Pearl Harbor on Christmas Day, 1944, and saw the terrible results of the Japanese attack. During 1945, we pulled alongside many of our warships to unload ammo. The warships were often beaten and battered but still afloat! … We participated in the invasion of Okinawa, where a kamikaze plane dove at our ship. Fortunately, the plane missed and crashed into the sea or I wouldn't be here to tell my story. … We were anchored in Leyte Gulf in the Philippines when the atomic bombs were dropped. I'll never forget the rejoicing on that ship when we heard the war was over."

HILLARD NERO

Town: Omaha

Service: Army, 1330th Engineer General Service Regiment

In the war: Served in both the European and Pacific Theaters. First repaired bombed airfields in England, then followed the front lines into Germany, repairing bridges and fighting in foxholes during the Battle of the Bulge; after the German surrender, sailed to Okinawa, encountering Japanese resistance in the Caroline Islands.

In his words: "They asked for volunteers to go fight on the Rhine, so I did that. … I just remember how cold it was. You had two guys in a foxhole, and you didn't mind hugging your buddy down there for warmth. … We sailed out of Nice, France, after the (German) surrender — I always remember that — and went through the Panama Canal and on to Okinawa. It took 58 days. … I can remember the bombs falling. We stopped at the Caroline Islands on the way to Japan. … Every night, we had to man the machine guns. I lost one of my buddies. He was feeding me shells and he just went down. I'll never forget, I told him, 'Come on, fellow! Come on!' But he was dead."

BEN PATTERSON

Town: Omaha

Service: Three years in the U.S. Navy

In the war: The Gretna native enlisted Jan. 4, 1943, and was sent to Great Lakes Naval Station in Illinois for training. He was assigned to quartermaster school, also at Great Lakes. Among ports of call were the Marshall Islands, Solomon Islands, the Philippines, Ulithi Atoll in the Caroline Islands and Buckner Bay in Okinawa. He was at Buckner Bay on April 1, 1945, the day the Japanese began sending in kamikaze planes.

In his words: "Our mother was a single parent with two sons serving in harm's way. My brother was a fighter pilot serving aboard various aircraft carriers, as his squadron was moved from one flattop to another in the Pacific. Three times we were in the same port together and were able to get together for a few hours. After the war, our neighbors told of the many nights they would see our mother walking up and down the street in front of our house reciting the rosary. Today when I occasionally see film of the great battles of Iwo Jima, Tarawa and others, I think of all the young men 17 and 18 years old who died on the beaches without ever having enjoyed the pleasures of growing old, marriage and children."

RICHARD LANG

Town: Omaha

Service: Marines, 3rd Division

In the war: Served in the invasion of Saipan and then was seriously wounded during the invasion of Guam.

In his words: During Lang's evacuation, medics accidentally switched his toe tag with that of a critically wounded Marine. "That's how I was reported killed in action. My folks were notified. ... When we got to Oakland, they told me I should call home right away. My dad answered. ... He said, 'Oh, I knew they couldn't kill you.' "

FRANCIS L. KIRK

Town: Omaha

Service: First Army, 4th Division, 22nd Infantry, Company C

In the war: Sailed on troop ship to Norway, then traveled by rail to France and then to Belgium, where he was injured in the fighting at Aachen and Duren, Germany. The year was 1944.

In his words: "From a foxhole I moved forward with my bazooka and fired three shots at a German machine gun, when the sergeant called me back into a bombed-out crater. A 31-caliber German machine gun opened fire several times, killing our sergeant, hitting the medic and me. The wounded medic put a tourniquet on my arm that was squirting blood from an injured artery. I then followed a telephone cable to the field hospital."

Kirk was sent to a hospital in France, where he learned that his brother had been killed a month earlier. He returned to the States, where he underwent several more surgeries on his arm.

JOE SKOFF

Town: Omaha

Service: Navy

During the war: Fired anti-aircraft batteries for troop carriers and supply ships in the Pacific. His two brothers also served in the Navy aboard aircraft carriers.

In his words: "I went in right after I graduated from South High. They gave us a diploma in one hand and welcome to the service with the other. I said I wanted to be a Marine but the guy said, 'Skoff, your brother's in the Navy, right? You ain't no Marine. You're a sailor.' ... Sometimes you couldn't see the sky it was so full of (enemy) planes. We all saw a lot of action. We were very, very lucky, all three of us brothers."

Turning the tide

MONTHS BEFORE A SINGLE ALLIED SOLDIER landed on France's Normandy coast during the D-Day invasion, communities throughout England were coping with an invasion of their own. ★ Thousands of American soldiers and their war-fighting equipment took towns and villages by storm, as they camped in nearby fields and moved in with local residents. ★ Nelly Ponting's cozy brick cottage in the village of Breamore in southern England served as home to her, her husband, her baby son and her mother-in-law and father-in-law. But when asked, she squeezed out additional room so that three Allied soldiers would have a place to sleep. ★ "It was our duty," Ponting said. "We had some fun, and we made the most of it. You should have seen my parlor at night."

SOLDIERS OF THE 134TH INFANTRY REGIMENT, originally a unit of the Nebraska National Guard, march through St. Ives in southwestern England in preparation for shipping out to France.

WILLIAM SCHWARTZ

Town: Omaha

Service: Army, 1st Armored Division, 6th Armored Infantry Battalion

In the war: Served as a machine gun platoon leader and staff sergeant during the invasions of North Africa and Italy.

In his words: "If a kid came up to me and told me he thought he was going to be killed, I'd send him (off the front line). ... We were battling for the last hill in Africa and this kid asked me to take over his machine gun. I didn't, and it was the best decision I ever made. ... A mortar dropped right beside him ... and that was it."

For his 90th birthday in 2008, William Schwartz was surprised with nine medals and campaign ribbons for his service. With him at the presentation was son Dale.

'When you got your mess kit out to eat, you ate sand'

VETERANS OF THE NORTH AFRICAN DESERT in World War II remembered their time fighting the elements as well as the enemy. Americans arrived in North Africa in 1942 to help British, Australian and French soldiers fight the Italian and German armies.

Some early battles went against the Allies. Then the course of the conflict changed and Allied armies pushed east, pinning the enemy in Tunisia. By May of 1943, the battle was done. The Allies had secured Africa.

For Stanley Kotlarz, a 1939 graduate of Omaha South High School, the heat and the sand were among the most striking memories of the months he spent in the Moroccan desert.

"The heat is fierce, and the sand is doggone hard to walk through," the retired mail carrier said in 1990.

"The sand and dirt blew around to beat hell," he said. "Every day at exactly 5 minutes to 1 o'clock a miniature tornado would come up. At lunchtime when you got your mess kit out to eat, you ate sand."

Drafted in the fall of 1942, Kotlarz volunteered in the 10th week of basic training for the still largely unproven business of paratrooping.

"Young, I guess," he said, explaining why he volunteered. "Adventure."

Kotlarz reported to jump school in Georgia. Less than a month after completing school, he and other members of the 82nd Airborne Division were taken to New York and placed on a ship for North Africa. After 12 days at sea, his convoy put in at Casablanca, Morocco, on the Atlantic Ocean on the northwest coast of Africa. By then it was late spring, and the battle to the east in Tunisia was well under way.

Casablanca was pretty, with pleasant coastal weather and palm trees, Kotlarz said. Then they were moved to a large tent encampment near Oujda, on the Moroccan side of the border with Algeria.

"When we got into Oujda, oh God, the weather was fierce. It was always over 100 degrees there," he said. "I think once it got up to 119 degrees."

The 82nd was sent to Oujda to prepare for the invasion of Italy starting in July 1943. The heat limited the training they could do, Kotlarz said. The paratroopers jumped both day and night, he said, but heavy physical activity such as digging had to be reserved for darkness. Even at night, digging was difficult, Kotlarz said, because of the sand.

"As soon as (the trench) got 10 feet deep it was as big as a swimming pool because that sand kept falling in," he said.

Water for the camp of thousands was drawn from a single well some distance away and was trucked back to the troops, he said. Because of the effort involved in obtaining water, showers were a rare treat.

"You had to drink a lot. That pump was going constantly day and night," Kotlarz said.

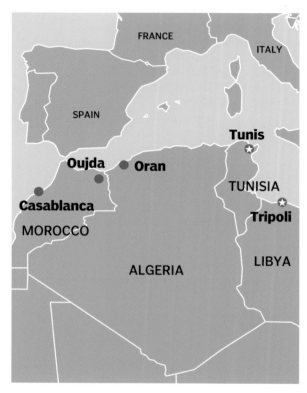

North Africa

Disease was a problem, too. Many soldiers came down with dysentery, Kotlarz said, himself included.

In July, the 82nd Airborne was dropped into Sicily ahead of Allied forces that stormed the beaches. After Sicily was secured, Kotlarz and other paratroopers returned to Oujda to await further orders.

"Pfff! I wouldn't want to go there for love or money," he said of the desert.

In September, he jumped into Italy near Salerno. Kotlarz said he later jumped ahead of landing forces on D-Day, and later still in Holland. He entered the war a private and left it a sergeant.

Another South High graduate, James Poulicek, said that after the war, he was wary of volunteering for anything.

In November 1940, 1½ years after graduating from South, he was jobless and couldn't scrape together the money for college. So he enlisted in the Army. The United States hadn't joined the war in Europe yet. And Poulicek was a clarinetist who auditioned for and won a spot in an Army band. The Army sent him to Fort Sill, Okla.

"All brains and dumb, I volunteered," said Poulicek.

Then he volunteered a second time, for a unit closer to home — the 168th Infantry Regiment in Council Bluffs, part of the 34th "Red Bull" Division. An Iowa National Guard unit, it had just been activated. He called his transfer to the Red Bull Division "my boo-boo."

"First ones overseas and the last ones back, the outfit longest in combat," he said.

In early 1942, after Pearl Harbor, the 168th shipped out to Northern Ireland for training. There, the band members of the divisions were told they would have to pull other duty: guarding the command post, carrying stretchers, hauling ammunition.

Next stop, North Africa.

"I went in on the third wave in Algiers, Nov. 8th of '42. It was about 6 o'clock in the morning," he said.

Other Allied forces landed at the same time in Casablanca and Oran, both farther west. Poulicek remembered a fair amount of rain in North Africa. For him, the heat was not especially trying.

"The African desert is a lot like western Nebraska — hot in the daytime, cold at night." he said. "You wore regular clothes. You know, a jacket. At night you put on an overcoat. It was cold. It was so cold."

The terrain was sandy, Poulicek said, but it was dotted with brush and crossed by depressions, called "wadis," that offered cover.

Poulicek said most of the fighting was done in the 200-mile belt along the Mediterranean coast. Farther inland, he said, the country grew more arid and desert-like. The sand gave troops some trouble, especially those who worked with machinery, he said: "The guys with tanks would talk about it. Some (tanks) wouldn't run."

> "The African desert is a lot like western Nebraska — hot in the daytime, cold at night"
>
> — JAMES POULICEK, WHO SERVED WITH THE 168TH INFANTRY REGIMENT

Poulicek was attached to a command post, which kept him off the combat line — "until the whole bottom fell out" on Feb. 14, 1943.

Members of the 168th Regiment were deployed forward of the Allies' main forces on hills in Tunisia. Poulicek was with the regiment's commanding officer on Hill Ksaira. The Germans attacked with infantry and Panzer tanks, surrounded Ksaira and, six days later, forced its surrender.

Poulicek was captured. He said the Germans took him and hundreds of other prisoners by "shoe-leather express" to the coast and then by plane to Germany. He said he spent the rest of the war sewing POW overalls.

"I tell you, I was down and lonely. I never expected this. I mean, I signed up to be a musician."

Robert Owen was another member of the 168th Regiment's band, a French horn player who wound up in North Africa playing anything but music.

ROBERT OWEN spent 10 days behind German lines in Tunisia while he was a member of the 34th "Red Bull" Division. (1990 photo)

A 1940 graduate of Abraham Lincoln High School in Council Bluffs, Owen enlisted that October in the 34th "Red Bull" Division. In February 1943, Pvt. Owen was among other Red Bull troops who were surrounded by German tanks and infantry in Tunisia.

As German tanks approached their hill from the American side of the lines, the commanding colonel decided to withdraw his troops. Owen said he was near the front of the column of walking soldiers when Germans intercepted them.

Hundreds of American troops were taken captive, but Owen and about two dozen others found each other a short distance from the column and set out for the safety of Allied territory. The fleeing Americans quickly ran into more Germans, however, and some went no farther.

"It was 12 guys left out of 25," Owen said.

The terrain was varied — rugged mountains laced through with open areas. Owen said the group, which included a few wounded who had to be carried over rough spots, moved mostly under cover of night.

"We didn't worry much about airplanes. But we did worry when we were on the plains and there was no place to hide."

Food and water were scarce, he said. For food, they sometimes raided Arab huts. Or they befriended Arabs, who made them "pancakes" cooked directly on an open fire.

"We ate some cactus, which wasn't a very good idea. It tasted like green beans with glue on it."

To slake their thirst, Owen said, each member of the group kept a pebble in his mouth to stimulate release of saliva.

There was the heat, too.

"When sand heats up it's just like a bake oven. You feel the heat coming up as much as down.

"But see, we weren't thinking much about heat at that time," he said. They mostly thought about "keeping alive."

On what they later calculated was their 10th day behind German lines, Owen said, the group came upon French troops. They had walked across about 125 miles of North Africa to avoid capture.

DOYLE MUNN

Town: Grand Island

Service: Army, 45th Infantry Division

In the war: Served as a mortar observer, directing artillery fire; first served in North Africa, then marched across Sicily, Italy, southern France and into Germany after the Battle of the Bulge; was one of five brothers in his family of 12 to serve overseas; all five made it home.

In his words: "I was hit twice with shrapnel. The first one hit me right in the face. I got a piece of shrapnel right in my nose, and I was out for four or five days."

JEAN STECKMYER

Town: Central City

Service: Army Air Forces, 464th Bomb Group, 779th Bomb Squadron

In the war: Flew 36 missions as a B-24 bomber pilot after 1944, based out of Italy.

In his words: "One mission was flying over Auschwitz, Poland, which is where the death camp was. We bombed right alongside it, but we didn't know at the time that's what it was. There was a hospital there marked with red crosses, and we weren't supposed to bomb that. But otherwise, we had no idea what was inside that camp."

Iowans part of 'forgotten outfit'

THE IOWA NATIONAL GUARD TROOPS in the "Red Bull" 34th Division were among the first Americans to fight in World War II and slugged it out in treacherous combat through the mountains of Italy.

The unit, nicknamed for the red bull on its patch, logged nearly 600 days in battle — far more than any other division — and captured prisoners by the thousands.

Yet obscurity largely has been the reward for the sacrifice and efforts of the division's soldiers.

"I think we were a forgotten outfit," said Charles Radford of Glenwood, Iowa, who served in the 34th's 133rd Infantry Regiment. "But we did what we had to do."

After a long, bloody and brutal campaign, the Germans surrendered unconditionally in Italy on May 2, 1945. It would be another week before German troops defending their homeland would end the fight.

The 34th Division was activated in February 1941. After training in Louisiana and in Ireland and Scotland, the division became the first American unit deployed in World War II's European Theater.

CHARLES RADFORD
in 2007

Many soldiers of the 34th were captured by German Field Marshal Erwin Rommel's Afrika Corps soon after landing in North Africa in November 1942.

The soldiers who made it out of North Africa or joined the unit later would face fierce fighting against Germans dug in throughout the mountains of Italy.

Radford said the mountainous terrain and the elements took almost as much of a toll as the enemy.

"The wintertime was the toughest," Radford said in 1995. "You were frozen and wet and cold in the snow. Then you were fighting all the time. It was miserable."

The Allied troops in Italy were not the focus of the war then or now, yet they played a vital role, said Paul Gauthiere, a World War II veteran from Corning, Iowa, who has written a book about the 34th Division.

"It tied down a lot of German forces early in the war," Gauthiere said.

German troops busy in Italy could not rush to join the fray once the Allied forces began their push from the beaches of France's Normandy Coast into the heart of Germany.

The soldiers who fought there said it was clear that Italy was a secondary battlefront.

"Because the main effort was not in Italy, we didn't receive quite as much supplies, support or reserve units as we needed," said Dennis Neal, a 34th Division veteran from Villisca, Iowa.

Allied troops were not the only forgotten soldiers in Italy, Gauthiere said.

Shortly before their surrender in Italy, German soldiers

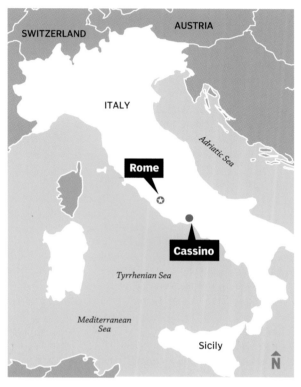

Sicily and Italy

began running desperately low on ammunition and other critical supplies.

"They were hurting, no question about that," Gauthiere said. "Toward the end, Hitler had forgotten about the Italian front. He was so desperate about what we were doing to him in Normandy and the rest of the European Theater."

Neal said not all the German soldiers in Italy just gave up, even when it was clear an Allied victory was just a matter of time.

"Their supplies were pretty much depleted, but there was still plenty of fight left in them," Neal said.

Before the 34th Division came home in November 1945, it served 550 days in actual battle. Some of its units had contact with the enemy on 650 days.

Members of the division received 10 Medals of Honor, 98 Distinguished Service Crosses, 1,052 Silver Stars, three Presidential Citations, 116 Legion of Merit Awards, 1,713 Bronze Stars and 15,000 Purple Heart medals for injury in combat.

Radford had been sent home after being wounded a year before the end of the war in Italy.

Radford said he did not feel like celebrating when he heard the Germans had finally surrendered. The combat had been brutal, and he had lost many friends in Italy.

"We were just glad it was over," he said.

'It was the worst, dirtiest kind of combat'

THE BATTLE OF CASSINO in 1944 was typical of the intense fighting that marked the Italian campaign.

The town of Cassino was surrounded by a series of ridges and valleys running east and west, said Tom Bolton, director of the Iowa National Guard Memorial Association. The 168th Infantry Regiment, formerly a unit from the Iowa National Guard, was part of the 34th Division that was among those that engaged German forces in a secondary front across the mountains of Italy.

"It was the worst, dirtiest kind of combat you could get into," Bolton said in 1994.

Allied forces were trying to move north.

"It became fighting from one hilltop to the next," Bolton said. "It was a terrible, grind-it-out kind of war."

Veterans who survived the experience remembered the territory near Cassino as a mountainous region that provided little place to hide from the almost constant torrent of rain, snow and wind and the exploding shells and bullets fired by the Germans.

The Germans had dug into positions on a hill that was home to a 400-year-old monastery known as Monte Cassino. The hill, the highest in the area, gave the Germans the perfect vantage point from which to fire upon the approaching Allied troops. Adolf Hitler had ordered his troops — some from an elite fighting force of paratroopers — to defend the hill at all costs.

The battle of Cassino started Jan. 17, 1944, and continued for four months. The Allied forces eventually took the monastery and the hill on which it stood, but not before the battle claimed about 175,000 casualties, 115,000 on the Allied side.

Veterans who were there said so many were killed and wounded because the Allied troops found few trees or other barriers to offer them shelter.

Herb Grote of Omaha remembered seeing little vegetation other than scattered, thorny bushes that grew about waist high. Allied troops improvised to find cover from enemy fire.

"All you had was rocks piled around you," said Grote, who served with the 135th Infantry Regiment.

The rain, snow and wind seemed to take as much of a toll as the barrage of fire unleashed by the Germans.

"I remember being wet most of the time," Grote said.

Glenn Carlson of Council Bluffs served with the 168th Regiment. He said the most bitter Nebraska or Iowa winter did not seem as bad as the weather in Italy 50 years ago.

"It was totally miserable," Carlson said. "The living conditions were pathetic."

Trench foot was common. Grote said: "If you took your boots off, you could not put them back on again. We had frostbite and cases of pneumonia. We had guys who were really shaking."

The troops probably were more susceptible to being worn down by the weather and the fighting at Cassino because most had just come from fierce battles in North Africa, Grote said.

"We were just pooped out to start with," Grote said. "Then there was all this miserable stuff."

Tragedy added to the misery. Allied generals initially tried to spare the historic monastery from attack. But as the battle progressed, Allied war planners became convinced that German troops had taken shelter inside the stone structure.

HERB GROTE with nephew Larry Grote in 1942.

HERB GROTE IN 1994. At the University of Nebraska in 1940, Grote set the all-time Big Six Conference record in the javelin throw. He also won Big Six titles in the javelin after the war, in 1946 and '47.

Orders were made in the middle of February to send in the bombers.

The bombers reduced the monastery to rubble, killing some of their own troops in the process.

"When the bombers came in, it was our guys that got hit," said Robert Owen of Council Bluffs, a member of the 168th Regiment. "We had a lot of casualties because of the bombing."

Owen said he was about 200 yards from the monastery, trying to rescue a soldier from a foxhole, when the bombing began. The soldier, who had a serious leg wound, took off running as the bombs began to explode all around them.

Carlson said he had a vantage point much farther away when the bombing began. He said he was mesmerized as he saw Allied bombs reduce the beautiful structure to rubble.

"I remember sitting there watching them bomb the monastery up on the hill," Carlson said. "That had been holding us back, but nobody wanted to bomb the monastery."

SEDGEFIELD D. HILL
Town: Plattsmouth
Service: 15th Army Air Force
In the war: "Sedge" was stationed in Italy, serviced B-24 Liberators. This involved making mechanical repairs, loading bombs, refueling and patching holes in the fuselage caused by exploding flak shells from that day's mission.
In his words: "We had a commanding officer who was a West Point grad who instilled in us the pride of organization, pride of job and pride of personality. There was unspoken pride in our organization, and people who were around us and connected to us found out that you don't mess with the men in the 451st Bomb Group or you are in trouble. If a plane wasn't ready, there would be a closed-door meeting as to the why that plane couldn't fly. There was no two ways about it, we were going to put planes in the air and put the best planes in the air. I was no hero, just one of the rookies who twisted wrenches and slapped masking tape on the bullet holes."

'They kept us out of the war'

PRESERVING THE STORY of the "Sweet 16" was a mission for Bill Melton of Omaha.

He was one of 16 black Omahans who served in the same World War II supply company. They provided ammunition, food and fuel to Allied troops as they marched through North Africa and Italy and into Germany. They guarded German prisoners of war.

"They kept us out of the war," Melton said in 2002. "They didn't want the blacks on the front lines, so they put us in the supply companies. Now nobody remembers what we did."

The 16 men were drafted in 1943 and sent to Camp Butner, N.C., for basic training.

North Carolina was the first encounter with racial segregation for these lifelong Midwesterners.

"I got real curious what the water tasted like in the white people's fountain," Richard Headley said, "so one day I just took a drink. I was disappointed. It tasted the same."

Another time, the driver of a city bus told them to sit in the back. They refused, and the driver threw them off. The next time a driver told them to move to the back, they threw the driver off, Headley said.

THREE MEMBERS OF THE SWEET 16 — Bill Melton, below on left, Rever McCloud and Richard Headley — met in 2002 with mementos from their days of service. Melton is on the left in the photo above, and Headley is on the right. Between them are two other members of the 530th Quartermasters, Joe Fountain and Clark Washington.

The military police were called. The MPs told the soldiers they had to abide by local laws.

"Fine," Melton said he told the MPs. " 'You take us away. Whatever you do to us, just remember we won't be going to the back of the bus.' After we threw that driver off, we never had that problem again."

"Rosa Parks wasn't the first," Melton said of the Alabama woman who refused to give up her seat to a white man in 1955. "She just got the recognition."

Fifteen of the Sweet 16 shipped out to Oran in North Africa in 1943 as part of the 530th Quartermasters. The 16th man, Cornelius Henderson, did not serve overseas.

The supply company's job was to keep the Fifth and Eighth Armies stocked with food, fuel and ammo. The men were tight. They were one another's link to home.

"When one of us got a letter from home, we all got a letter from home," Melton said.

The mail took four months to catch up with them in North Africa and southern Italy. When it did, Rever McCloud got what seemed like 100 letters.

McCloud was different from the other men, Melton remembers. He'd been married the longest, since 1937. A deeply spiritual man, he kept to himself when not on duty.

"All that man did was soldier. When he wasn't soldiering, he was writing his wife or reading the Bible."

The others, however, gathered to play cards and throw dice during off-duty hours.

"We had it going on back then," Melton said, pointing to a photo of some of the 16 seated shirtless on a hot North African day. "We've got the pictures to prove it."

In their late teens and early 20s, they were thick-chested, with big biceps and slim, tight waists.

"We used to sit on boxes of live ammunition and bombs to play cards," Headley said. "Lord, we were young. It's amazing we all survived."

While the Sweet 16 didn't march into combat, combat often came to them. The German bombings were so frequent the fellas nicknamed the planes "bed-check Charlie."

"BOOM, BANG, BOOM," Melton said. "They shot at us and bombed us from every angle. The Germans knew. We were the backbone of the Army. Without our food, they go hungry. Without our gas, those tanks are dead in the road. Without our ammo, they can't shoot. But that's the story that never gets told."

The men eventually got to see the Germans up close, as guards over the former Nazi soldiers during work details at the prison camp and supply company. The Germans surrendered in May 1945. Most of the Sweet 16 went home later that year. Melton and Headley were sent to Okinawa, Japan, where they worked for a supply company and POW camp. All 16 men moved back to Omaha after the war. A few moved away for work or warmer climates as they retired.

Prejudice eventually eased — President Harry Truman desegregated the armed forces in 1948 — and the nation changed. Melton said he could understand how people would forget the role black soldiers had in the war.

"Have you seen (the movie) 'Patton'?" Melton asked. "How many blacks did you see? I'll tell you. There was one. He was Patton's assistant. But when (General George) Patton's Third Army came through and got our food and our gas and our ammo, you know who was driving those Sherman tanks? Blacks."

The honor came at last

VERNON J. BAKER, a former Boys Town resident and high school quarterback from Clarinda, Iowa, in 1997 was among the first seven black soldiers from World War II to receive the Medal of Honor.

VERNON BAKER in 1997

His actions in 1945 at a German army mountain stronghold in Italy earned him the honor.

"I had suppressed the memory. It was something I didn't want to remember. There was a lot of killing and bloodshed that day. I lost a lot of good men," Baker said.

A platoon leader in the 92nd Division, 1st Lt. Baker put the muzzle of his M-1 into the slit of a bunker and killed two Germans. Then he killed two more who were in a camouflaged machine-gun nest.

He shot another enemy soldier fleeing, and then blasted open with a grenade the hidden entrance of another dugout. He broke in and killed two more Germans with a submachine gun he had picked up.

Thinking back, Baker said: "It was like someone was sitting on my shoulder, talking in my ear, telling me what to do. Everything I did was right. Going back and thinking about it, it's hard to realize all the things I really did."

Vernie Baker was born in Cheyenne, Wyo., but his parents were killed in an auto accident when he was 4. He was raised by his grandfather.

One day the Boys Town band came through town on a train. Baker said he spotted a boy playing a trumpet and later talked to him. Young Vernie spoke with his grandfather and was accepted at the home, where he lived for about three grade-school years in the 1930s.

Baker later attended a funeral in Clarinda with his grandfather and learned that he had relatives there. So he stayed there for high school, playing football at 5-foot-5, 139 pounds, and playing in the school band.

He graduated from high school in Clarinda in 1939.

After Clarinda, Baker worked as a railroad porter but volunteered for the Army before the Japanese attack on Pearl Harbor. He went through Officers Candidate School. Although he was wounded in October 1944, Baker spent 28 years in the Army.

Black veterans of World War II

- More than 2.5 million blacks registered for the draft.
- 1.2 million blacks served in the armed forces.
- Approximately 909,000 blacks served in the Army.
- Approximately 167,000 blacks served in the Navy.
- 19,168 blacks served in the Marines.
- More than 5,000 served in the Coast Guard.

JAMES T. CASPERSON

Town: Omaha

Service: 15th Army Air Force

In the war: Casperson was a co-pilot on a B-24 Liberator with the 451st Bomb Group based in Italy and flew 25 missions over heavily defended targets in Europe.

In his words: "We had the Germans shooting back at us, of course, and one time we had to bail out over Hvar (Yugoslavia). We landed in a farmer's field, and fortunately he was on the side of the Allies. Before we bailed out, one man picked up his parachute by the rip cord, and it opened in the plane. Our pilot said for the rest of us to jump, and took the plane down with the man without a parachute. They crash-landed in the water but survived, and the pilot was awarded the Silver Star for heroism. It was quite a brave thing to do."

THE AIR WAR A NEW WAY OF FIGHTING AND A NEW WAY OF WINNING

P-51 Mustang pilot 1st Lt. Kendall Anderson receives congratulations in 1945 for completing his 100th mission in the Philippines. Anderson, formerly of Lincoln, named his plane "Rolling Along" for the title of a column by uncle Guy Williams of The World-Herald.

Confirming the value of air power

THE CREATION OF THE AIR FORCE grew out of the successful projection of air power in World War II.

The Army took its first step into the infant field of powered flight in 1907, forming the aeronautics branch of its Signal Corps.

In addition to balloon operations, which dated to the Civil War, the obscure branch was placed in charge of planning for the possible future Army use of dirigibles, then emerging in Germany, and flying machines like those built by the Wright Brothers.

In 1909, the Signal Corps bought its first Wright Flyer and three years later, the Army had 17 "aeroplane" aviators.

While there was a big buildup of Army air resources in World War I, few American planes were built soon enough. The approximately 350 U.S. pilots had to fly European aircraft.

In 1922, Brig. Gen. Billy Mitchell showed the possibilities of air power by flying a World War I bomber off the U.S. East Coast and sinking several captured German ships stationed as targets. However, his criticism of top officers of the Army and Navy in speeches and magazine articles led to a demotion to colonel and an assignment in Texas.

He continued to speak out in favor of air power. His criticism of military decision-makers eventually led to his court-martial conviction for bringing discredit to the service.

The push for aviation in the military finally succeeded in 1935, when General Headquarters-Air Force was created within the Army.

The United States had begun arming itself before the Pearl Harbor disaster. The Battle of Britain convinced President Franklin D. Roosevelt that air power would be critical to victory if America entered World War II.

Roosevelt ordered the production of 50,000 warplanes and military transports a year, and the Army Air Corps grew into the Army Air Forces in mid-1941.

The changes weren't enough to avert the disaster of Pearl Harbor, but air power turned out to be an important factor in the Allied victory over Germany, Italy and Japan.

The Air Force became its own branch of the U.S. military in 1947.

Capt. John D. Ashford of Omaha, at right, and his crew with their B-26 Marauder bomber in Europe in 1944. Ashford had the Ak-Sar-Ben crest and "AK-SAR-BEN KNIGHT" painted on the aircraft.

'It got me home every time'

THE B-17 BOMBER will always hold a special place in Russell Minks' heart.

"It got me home every time," the Omahan said in 2005. "What more can you ask?"

Forty-five times during World War II, Minks took his post as a gunner aboard a B-17 and took off for perilous bombing runs over Germany. And 45 times, the "Flying Fortress" — although almost always battered — got Minks and his crewmates home safely.

Minks, a 1942 South High graduate, volunteered for the dangerous bomber duty. The 6-foot-1 Omahan had to stoop slightly during his physical to stay within height limits. But he said they probably would have taken him anyway. The 15th Air Force in Europe was losing 500 bombers a month to strafing fighters and the thick flak that darkened the skies.

At the time a fearless 20-year-old, Minks remembers the feeling of excitement before each mission aboard his B-17, dubbed "Naughty Narda."

"I never dreaded them," he said. "That's why I was there."

Naughty Narda almost always had holes in her when they returned to their base in Italy. An anti-aircraft burst once sent flak through the floor by Minks' foot. One time, the plane lost an engine and began shuddering, forcing it to leave formation because it posed a hazard to other planes. But the crew was able to ease her home. Three times Naughty Narda crash-landed. And they saw countless other U.S. planes go down.

But amazingly, all 10 crew members came through their six-month tour of duty without a scratch.

"At the time, I never thought much about it. But when I look back, man, oh, man, were we lucky," Minks said.

RUSSELL MINKS HAD A FEELING of excitement before each of his 45 missions aboard a B-17 bomber in Europe during World War II. At Eppley Airfield in 2005, Minks again pointed a .50-caliber machine gun out the waist-gunner window of a B-17, when the Experimental Aircraft Association offered rides on a classic Flying Fortress.

B-17 SPECIFICATIONS:

›› Engines: Four Wright Cyclone radials.
›› Performance: Max. speed – 299 mph at 25,000 ft.; service ceiling – 37,500 ft.; range – 1,300 miles with 6,000 lbs. of bombs.
›› Dimensions: Wingspan – 103 ft., 9 in.; length – 74 ft., 9 in.
›› Crew: Ten – pilot, co-pilot, bombardier, navigator, flight engineer, radio operator, tail gunner, belly gunner, two waist gunners.

Boeing B-17 FLYING FORTRESS

Perhaps the most well-known U.S. heavy bomber of World War II, the B-17 dropped more bombs during the war than any other aircraft. It developed a reputation for absorbing enormous amounts of damage and continuing to fly. That made it a favorite of its crews, although the daylight precision bombing campaign against Germany during 1943, '44 and '45 incurred heavy losses. About one-third of all B-17s built were lost on combat missions. When the B-17 prototype Model 299 made its maiden flight in 1935, legend has it that a reporter, struck by the guns bristling from various positions on the plane, remarked, "Why, it's a flying fortress!" and the name stuck.

"12 O'CLOCK HIGH"

As daylight bombing of Germany increased in the spring of 1943, German fighter attacks on Allied bombers became better coordinated. The Germans had discovered blind spots in the B-17's top and nose turrets' field of fire, and had begun attacking from the "12 o'clock high" (above and head-on) position. Additional guns were added to the B-17's nose.

DAYLIGHT PRECISION BOMBING

Daylight bombing of Germany began in earnest early in 1943. Losses mounted as 8th Air Force B-17 squadrons encountered increasing resistance. Loss rates of well over 10 percent were not uncommon. As bombing techniques and equipment improved, and with the arrival of long-range escort fighters such as the P-51 Mustang, the tide gradually turned. By 1944 groups of 1,000 planes at a time were hammering German aircraft factories, severely reducing German oil-refining capabilities and paving the way for the D-Day invasion.

Bombing runs to Germany were staged from bases in England.

Berlin

ENGLAND
London

GERMANY

Paris

FRANCE

SOURCES: Strategic Air Command Museum, Joe Baugher's Encyclopedia of American Military Aircraft

'Most Honorable Son'

DONALD SLAUGHTER

Town: Kearney

Service: Army Air Forces, pilot with 440th Troop Carrier Group

In the war: Co-pilot of a C-47 transport, he mostly flew shipments of gas to fuel Patton's drive into Germany.

In his words: "We hauled a few loads of displaced persons from different places in eastern Germany, where concentration camps were located. They were skin and bone. I have very little patience with modern people who say there wasn't any such thing."

BEN KUROKI FOUGHT THE GERMANS and the Japanese. But as a Japanese-American — who won an exemption to become the only "Nisei" to bomb mainland Japan — he also battled racial prejudice.

Cal Stewart, who met Kuroki while both served in Britain, said Kuroki's contributions toward quelling anti-Japanese attitudes in America — the "inner war" — might have been as important as his heroics on 58 bombing missions in Europe, North Africa and the Pacific.

BEN KUROKI in 1942

In 1944, Kuroki was asked to speak before San Francisco's exclusive Commonwealth Club.

He told that group he'd learned more about democracy in the war than in any book because, "I saw it in action. When you live with men under combat conditions … you begin to understand what brotherhood is all about, what equality and tolerance really mean."

His speech earned a standing ovation. Some have said it helped change attitudes in California, where Japanese-Americans were sent to internment camps during the war.

"This war hysteria in general was bad for anyone," Kuroki said in 2004.

A native of Hershey, Neb., he earned a journalism degree at the University of Nebraska and ran a weekly newspaper in York after the war before settling in California. He retired as news editor of the Ventura Daily Star-Free Press in 1984.

Stewart, a former Lincoln and O'Neill publisher, wrote a booklet about Kuroki. That and lobbying efforts by 93rd Bomb Group veterans led to Kuroki receiving the Army's Distinguished Service Medal in 2005.

"I was satisfied after the war that I'd survived. I'd never thought about getting additional honors," he said.

The son of Japanese immigrants, Kuroki grew up on a potato farm near Hershey, west of North Platte. He credits his rural Nebraska upbringing and his father, Shosuke, or "Sam," for his strong patriotic "foundation."

"The day after Pearl Harbor, he was the one who urged my brother, Fred, and I to volunteer," Kuroki said.

Throughout the war, Kuroki faced a constant battle to prove that loyalty.

His initial enlistment in the Marines was blocked by uncertainty on how to handle Japanese-American volunteers. After weeks of waiting, he heard a radio advertisement seeking volunteers for the Army Air Forces. He and his brother eagerly joined up.

Kuroki's brother soon was transferred to kitchen duty. Kuroki said he "walked on eggs" fearing he would be bounced for any misstep. "It was the loneliest year in my life. I had no friends."

But Kuroki endured. Colleagues helped reverse two transfer orders and a last-minute hitch in his shipping out with his unit for Europe.

BEN KUROKI acknowledges a standing ovation in Lincoln in 2005 after he received the Distinguished Service Medal.

His 30 combat missions as a B-24 tail gunner were five more than required — at his request — and included the daring daylight raid on Adolf Hitler's aviation fuel refineries in Ploesti, Romania. The average life span of a bomber crew was five to six flights.

His crewmates named him "Most Honorable Son" for his bravery. Later in the war, a bomber he flew was named "Most Honorable Sad Saki" in his honor.

Staff Sgt. Kuroki returned to the United States a hero, was the subject of stories in the New York Times and Time magazine, and was put to work by the War Department giving speeches. He went behind the barbed wire of internment camps to recruit other "Nisei," American-born Japanese.

But Kuroki said he tired of that duty. Inspired in part by the death of his boyhood friend Gordy Jorgenson at the hands of the Japanese, Kuroki sought reassignment to a bomber group in the Pacific.

Even while flying missions that included raids on Japan, he faced prejudice. One drunken soldier slashed him with a knife during a race-related fight. The wound required 20 stitches.

And when his crew received the Distinguished Flying Cross, Kuroki didn't get an invitation to the ceremony. Even though it was his third time receiving the honor, he sat alone in the barracks.

Kuroki's commendation was in line to be upgraded, but both Kuroki and Stewart said it didn't happen at that time because he was Japanese-American.

"It's an incredible story," Kuroki said of finally receiving the Distinguished Service Medal, "not so much what I did in the war, but how these good Nebraska people have gone to bat for me."

Nebraskans part of attack on 'Hitler's Gas Station'

Ploesti, Romania

Lt. Robert Storz receives the Distinguished Flying Cross from Gen. Lewis H. Brereton in North Africa in 1943. Storz, whose family owned a brewery in Omaha, flew his B-24 — the "Brewery Wagon" — in the raid on the Ploesti refineries.

JOE BRITTON

Town: Omaha

Service: Army Air Forces

In the war: Served in Trinidad and Natal, Brazil, before returning to the U.S. for gunnery school. Shipped to 8th Air Force in England in January 1945. As a tail gunner with the 384th Bombardment Group, achieved the rank of staff sergeant.

In his words: "On my 19th mission over Germany, our plane took several hits from flak. One engine lost, rudder controls cut and waist gunner wounded." On the way back to England, an engine caught fire over the North Sea. "The pilot reversed course and performed a wheels-up landing on a fairly level field with some young trees. With the craft still burning, all escaped, the only casualty being the waist gunner, who died before reaching a hospital."

GLENN BINDER, THEN 23, was only four months into World War II service when he and his Army Air Forces colleagues were asked to do the impossible. Fly B-24 bombers 2,400 miles, without fighter protection and many miles at tree-top level, to attack "Hitler's Gas Station," the refineries at Ploesti, Romania. Two hundred planes and 320 anti-aircraft guns protected the site.

"They told us if half of us got back it would be a success," Binder, of Pawnee City, said in 2003.

But Binder, a co-pilot, made it back alive. And his bomber group, the "Sky Scorpions" of the 389th Bombardment Group, so crippled the Steaua Romana refinery that it was knocked out for five months, never regaining full production during World War II.

Nebraska provided 31 of the 1,763 airmen who participated in the 1943 Ploesti Raid, including Robert Storz, a member of the Omaha brewing family. Of the participants, 310 died and 200 others were wounded or taken prisoner. Fifty-four of the 178 bombers that took off crashed or were shot down.

Cal Stewart, a former newspaper publisher in Lincoln who co-authored a 1962 book, "Ploesti," on the low-level raid, joined Binder in calling the operation a forgotten chapter of World War II. Because it happened early in the war and was launched from North Africa, it didn't gather the publicity of other battles or bombing campaigns, Stewart said. Yet it knocked out Hitler's prime supplier of aviation fuel, disrupting air operations and slowing the flow of fuel for months, he said.

"It was a good sock in the jaw in the second round," Stewart said.

The B-24s flew below 300 feet for some time, considerably lower than their normal bombing altitude of 18,000 to 24,000 feet, to avoid radar. Allied fighter planes had to stay behind — they didn't have the range of the bombers for the nearly 14-hour flights.

"We were the 14th ship over the target," said Binder. "You could look up and see the top of smokestacks and people jumping off the roofs of the buildings. They were surprised to see us."

Binder said he regretted that there were civilian casualties, but called it a necessary operation to slow down Hitler's war machine.

Binder said he didn't want to make a big deal about his role in the raid on Ploesti, saying the honor belongs to those who didn't make it back. "They paid the ultimate sacrifice."

Glenn Binder in 2003

LT. WALTER CHEWNING JR. scrambles aboard Byron M. Johnson's Hellcat to free the Nebraska pilot from the flaming wreckage on the carrier USS Enterprise.

A crash to remember

BYRON M. JOHNSON

NAVY PILOTS FOUGHT WORLD WAR II in relative luxury compared with soldiers and Marines on the ground, according to Byron M. Johnson of Gering, Neb.

During invasions of enemy-held South Pacific islands, Johnson and other pilots would strafe the beach and drop naphtha before U.S. troops landed.

"That's who I really admire," Johnson said in 1991 of the ground troops. "They're the ones who really fought the war. A lot of those men were lost and so badly injured."

While he was a combat ace in the war, it was his crash-landing of an F6F Hellcat fighter on the USS Enterprise for which he was best known. A photo of the crash was published nationwide.

The aircraft carrier was steaming for the Gilbert Islands when the accident occurred Nov. 10, 1943.

Lt. Johnson was flying combat air patrol around the convoy when his Hellcat's engine started fluctuating. He signaled an emergency and the carrier turned into the wind for Johnson to land.

The engine continued to surge as Johnson was making his approach, and at the last moment he was waved off to try again. But as Johnson gunned his engine and started to climb away, his aircraft's tail hook snagged a landing line.

In a flash, the Hellcat spun to the port side and crashed into defensive guns mounted on the edge of the carrier. The Hellcat's belly fuel tank exploded and Johnson's canopy jammed, trapping him inside the flaming wreckage.

Lt. Walter Chewning Jr., a catapult officer, sprinted across the flight deck, jumped atop the burning fuel tank and reached to pop open the canopy with an emergency release.

"It was just one of those things that happens," Johnson said. "I never thought much about it other than the bravery of the man who helped me get out of it.

"You really lose more planes and pilots in operations accidents than in combat."

Johnson went on to fly nearly 60 combat sorties, many during a campaign from March through September 1944 from the new carrier USS Hornet.

During the last year of the war, he trained fighter pilots in Atlantic City, N.J. In 1944 he married Ferne Evertson of Kimball, Neb. Her brother was an Army pilot who was shot down during a bombing raid on Berlin and spent the last years of the war in a German prison camp.

'We were first-class citizens in the air'

THE CADETS AT THE *Basic and Advanced Flying School for Negro Air Corps Cadets undergo inspection in 1942. The Tuskegee Institute in Tuskegee, Ala., was home to the training.*

CHARLES LANE LOVED AIRPLANES. As a boy growing up in St. Louis, Lane built models out of wood and paper. On weekends, he pedaled his bike 36 miles round-trip from his home to what was then Lambert Field, finally talking a pilot into letting him clean airplane wheels to earn a ride. In high school, he joined an aviator club, even though he knew he might never fly because of his skin color.

But everything changed when he turned 17. America was at war, blacks were flying fighter planes and a pilot who helped blow up an enemy destroyer visited Lane's junior college. He applied to the Army Air Forces pilot training program and was sent to the Tuskegee Institute in Alabama, where he excelled. He graduated and left for Italy, flying 26 missions helping to protect U.S. bombers.

Friends died and Lane almost did, too, when his plane took 14 bullets during a raid on a train depot in southern Germany. The white bomber crews, grateful for the Tuskegee Airmen's protection, bought them dinners and drinks.

But others didn't accept the black pilots. Lane once spent a night in a Nashville, Tenn., jail after the war, suspected of impersonating an officer. A military policeman intervened to confirm that Lane indeed was an officer.

Years later, on assignment in Germany, he felt more at home with the Germans and the French than his fellow Americans.

"The way we looked at it, we were first-class citizens in the air, second-class citizens at the base and third-class citizens in the community," Lane, an Omahan, recalled in 2002. "The salvation there was that we wanted to fly."

Paul Adams of Lincoln said he and other blacks were kept

FORMER TUSKEGEE AIRMEN *Charles Lane, left, of Omaha and Paul Adams of Lincoln in 2002.*

from flying because of their skin color until first lady Eleanor Roosevelt made a trip to Tuskegee, Ala., to see if blacks could indeed successfully fly planes. After flying with one of the pilots, she became an ardent supporter.

Adams recalled that black men did not have the option of moving onto an established military installation.

"The whites did not want blacks on their base," he said.

Lane, who also served in the Korean and Vietnam Wars, was assigned to the Strategic Air Command in 1963. After retiring from the Air Force as a lieutenant colonel in 1970, he headed Greater Omaha Community Action, the city's largest anti-poverty agency at the time, for 21 years.

Despite his poor treatment in World War II, Lane said he saw himself as American first and wanted to contribute.

"We were the best-kept secret of World War II."

Tuskegee Airmen

According to Tuskegee Airmen records, at least six other Omaha men attended the Tuskegee flying school during World War II.

- Alfonza W. Davis
- Ralph Orduna
- Edward W. Watkins
- Lawrence King Sr.
- John L. Harrison Jr.
- Woodrow F. Morgan (captured by the Germans and later released)

- Clarence A. Oliphant of Council Bluffs was one of a dozen Iowans who trained at Tuskegee.

FLOYD D. RASTEDE

Town: Papillion, originally from Thurston, Neb.

Service: Army Air Forces pilot

In the war: Lead pilot and instructor of a 10-man crew. Flew a B-24 over the Adriatic, bombing many locations in Vienna, Innsbruck and northern Italy.

In his words: "In the last nine months of the war, I was stationed in Lecce, Italy. From there I flew 22 missions. We bombed the train trestles in Innsbruck along with bombing several other locations. We wore electric suits because it was so cold. We also had to wear oxygen masks during all of the missions. One memory I have of a close call was during a routine flight. After releasing bombs from the aircraft, the co-pilot's window was knocked out from bullets being shot from below. There was shattered glass all over. I noticed the co-pilot had been hit in the arm and his air mask had fallen off. I quickly put his mask back on and flew them all to safety. I still hear from the radio communicator. He always told me I was the best pilot he had ever flown with. After my nine months in the war, I was sent back to the States. Soon after that I rejoined my wife and young son."

AMERICANS IN ENGLAND

Pfc. Harry H. Cuda, left, of Seward and Bob Fulton of Beatrice at St. Ives harbor in Cornwall, England, in 1944.

Training, watching and waiting

ARMED WITH RIFLES FROM WORLD WAR I and handles from hoes and rakes, Arthur Maidment and other Englishmen patrolled through the night in 1944, looking for German invaders.

"Lots of people were talking about what they would do if the Germans invaded," Maidment recalled in 1994.

While he and other members of the Home Guard patrolled the area around Salisbury in southern England, the Allies were planning the largest amphibious invasion ever undertaken.

Gen. Dwight D. Eisenhower, the Allied commander, was working at two country estates near Salisbury, waiting to execute the plan that he knew would cost thousands of lives.

Across southern England, Americans and Allied troops from other countries were training for the invasion of German-occupied France. And waiting.

Back home, the families of American troops read and listened to news accounts from Europe, waiting.

Ever since German forces conquered France in 1940, the question had been not "Will there be an Allied invasion across the English Channel?" The question was, "When?"

"We knew," said Angelena Mascarello, who was a student at Omaha Technical High School during the war. "They kept talking about it. They were going to invade."

British citizens, surrounded by an ever-increasing mass of troops and equipment, were even more certain that the invasion was imminent.

"It was so obvious it was going to happen," said Maidment, who wrote several books on the history of the Salisbury area after retiring as a printer. "We just didn't know when."

As Allied troops continued to mass in England and Josef Stalin, leader of the Soviet Union, became more vocal in his calls for an Allied landing in France, it was widely suspected through the late spring of 1944 that the invasion would come any day.

"The sun streamed down clear and bright on Dover Strait and a light northerly breeze rippled the sea," began a report that appeared in the June 3, 1944, edition of The World-Herald.

Similar reports of the weather in England and France were appearing almost daily on the front pages of newspapers in the United States, alongside the latest casualty reports and news about the progress of battles in Italy.

The weather reports were offered as clues to the arrival of the day that was anticipated, yet dreaded.

As a high school student in Table Rock, Neb., Marian Goodenkauf worried about the safety of the boys she knew who were fighting for their country in Italy — and those who would do the same in France and Germany after the invasion.

"I remember grabbing the paper every day," Goodenkauf said. "We knew all these people. Some of them were boys I had dated."

Writing to her husband when D-Day finally arrived, Julie Crofoot of Omaha tried to describe the gamut of emotions that she felt.

"First, breathless excitement, then fear for those we love; desire to pray, a daring to hope not only for a quick victory, but each one of us for the return of our particular loved one," Crofoot wrote to her husband, Michael, a medical officer in the Navy.

With bombs falling in London and sometimes in the countryside, the people of England clearly were fearful and apprehensive about the war. In Southampton, a key port city, many people would head for the forest at night and sleep in cars because they feared being hit by the bombs.

Yet, Maidment said, Prime Minister Winston Churchill's rallying rhetoric and a hearty English spirit left people optimistic and ready to make the sacrifices that came with severe rationing and the presence of war.

"Somehow we got through," Maidment said. "You had to. What else could you do?"

For many months before D-Day, as Eisenhower and his commanders drafted their invasion plans, American soldiers slowly made their way across the Atlantic Ocean. Roger McCarthy of Omaha was 19, cold, seasick and scared as he headed for the war in Europe on a converted Liberty Ship named for the American social reformer and journalist Dorothea L. Dix.

"I doubted I would ever come home," said McCarthy. "We knew what we were in for. I didn't give up hope, but you know it's a distinct possibility that you won't see your family again."

McCarthy, who left for Europe in late December 1943, would go ashore with the first wave of men to land at Omaha Beach on D-Day six months later.

During his 12-day journey across the Atlantic, Mort Sheffloe of Omaha often stood on the ship's fantail lost in thought, watching other ships in the convoy.

"Being 19-year-old kids, we were anxious to get over to the war," said Sheffloe. "You didn't openly admit to worrying about being killed."

Sheffloe survived, but he carried scars from a vicious wound left in his side by a sniper's bullet fired at him as he was fighting his way through France.

Crammed into the lower deck with hundreds of other soldiers on the transport ship, Phil Mascarello of Omaha was miserable as he left New York for Europe.

"The ocean was so rough," said Mascarello. "It was terrible. I couldn't stand it. I couldn't breathe."

Mascarello, who landed on Utah Beach on D-Day, would come home and marry Angelena.

Thoughts of food were rare among many of the seasick soldiers. For those who did feel like eating, menus filled with fare like mutton and kidney stew often extinguished what appetite was left.

"I lived on candy bars," Mascarello said.

Arrival in England would bring months of training.

"They would take us out in the morning, and we would walk and run 20 miles before lunch," said Arley Goodenkauf of Elm Creek, Neb., a paratrooper who later married Marian.

Goodenkauf's unit made a handful of practice jumps while he was stationed in England near the town of Newbury. His outfit once jumped as Eisenhower, King George and his daughter Princess Elizabeth watched from below.

"That's quite an episode in my life," Goodenkauf said.

Mascarello felt the tension grow during a personal encounter with the supreme commander of the Allied troops just weeks before the invasion.

While training with his anti-aircraft unit in Bridgwater, England, Mascarello stood in formation as Eisenhower walked up and down the rows of soldiers reviewing the troops.

"I thought, 'Not me,'" Mascarello said.

Eisenhower slowed as he neared Mascarello, turned and waited to receive the young soldier's rifle.

"He checked the barrel," Mascarello said. "Then he handed it back to me."

'We never paid for a drink'

ED BECKER OF OMAHA called the tiny village of Quorn in the Midlands of England his home for part of 1944.

"During our time here, the people were friendly," Becker recalled in 1994. "They did what they could for us."

Becker was stationed in England with the 505th Parachute Regiment of the 82nd Airborne Division, arriving in February 1944 after fighting in North Africa and Italy.

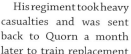

He jumped into Normandy early on D-Day, June 6, 1944, and was in a unit that captured Sainte Mere-Eglise, the first town liberated from the Germans.

His regiment took heavy casualties and was sent back to Quorn a month later to train replacement troops and rest for future battles.

ED BECKER in 1994

The training before and after D-Day involved a strenuous regimen of calisthenics, forced marches and practice parachute jumps.

"Our days were filled," Becker said. "They made training so tough that combat would be a relief."

When they found a moment to break away, Becker and his buddies frequently headed for one of their favorite pubs, usually the White Horse or the Bull's Head.

Arley Goodenkauf of Elm Creek, Neb., was stationed near Newbury, England, with his parachute regiment of the 101st Airborne Division during the war.

He too recalled days filled with tough training and weekend nights spent relaxing in a local pub.

Goodenkauf said he spent many hours playing the piano while his good friend Rudy Reeves sang with a voice that rivaled Frank Sinatra's.

"We never paid for a drink," Goodenkauf said.

ALVA SMITH

Town: Fairmont, Neb.

Service: Army Air Forces, 386th Bomb Group, 554th Squadron

In the war: Worked in England, France and Belgium as a mechanic on short-range bombers that provided close air support for troops.

In his words: "The first plane I had flew 139 missions. It would get so much battle damage, but I would fix it up and kept it flying. I got a Bronze Star for that. ... We tried to make things a little easier for the troops."

FAYE J. (MACMANNIS) NITZ

Town: West Point, Neb.

Service: Army

In the war: Enlisted in the Army in 1943 after graduating from nurse's training at Children's Hospital in Pittsburgh in 1941. In 1944, she served with the 120th Station Hospital, working with prisoners of war. She arrived in Le Havre, France, on May 29, 1945, and worked with injured servicemen. Her unit arrived in Bayreuth, Germany, in August 1945. Her husband, the late Edward C. Nitz, served with the 3rd Armored Division in England, France and Germany from August 1942 to December 1945.

In her words: "I met my husband, Ed, in 1943 while stationed at (Fort) Indiantown Gap, Pa., base hospital where he was recovering from knee surgery, shortly before shipping out. He claimed his first sight of me was my legs as I entered the mess hall. We became engaged in London, England, after Ed had his mother and sister pick out an engagement ring, which they shipped to him in a Band-Aid box. While in England I met Clark Gable, who was visiting our base, and we shared a few words."

TWINS ELEANOR, LEFT, AND ELOISE LETTE of Lincoln worked at the same Army hospital in England.

'I wanted adventure'

NOT ALL WOMEN who aided the war machine were on the homefront. Some served near the battlefront. Mary L. Smith of Sioux City, Iowa, went from nursing ailing ranchers in Colorado to wounded GIs in Normandy.

"I was at a little hospital in Sterling, and it was lonesome," Smith said in 1994. "I was 21. I wanted to be where other young people were. I wanted adventure."

Smith, a registered nurse who had trained in her native Sioux City, enlisted in the Army Nurse Corps in early 1943. Two years later, she and 41 other nurses in the 85th Evacuation Hospital were following closely behind Gen. George Patton's tanks as they raced across France and into Germany in the last months of the war. Smith remained friends over the years with two other nurses from her unit, Erna Maas McKeon of Prescott, Ariz., and Eleanor Hurley Morrisey of Holyoke, Mass.

The nurses' unit was based at Mitchell Field on Long Island in New York before moving to Europe in January 1945. Although they were across the ocean from the Allied invasion of German-occupied France on June 6, 1944, the three nurses were treating American soldiers wounded in the fighting within 24 hours.

"We knew something was going to happen because they changed our procedures — like how to mark bodies — because casualties would be coming in so fast," Morrisey said.

Seemingly endless flights of C-47 transport planes brought wounded troops to New York and the waiting team of Army doctors and nurses. Some soldiers were paralyzed. Others had severe sores from lying wounded and motionless for hours in the sand on the invasion beaches.

"We were on 12-hour duty," McKeon said.

Around Christmas, the unit sailed to France on a troop ship with 5,000 soldiers. The nurses' first stop was Camp Lucky Strike, a vast tent city near Le Havre used as a reception and recuperation site. Among the first wounded soldiers they treated were casualties of the Battle of the Bulge. After receiving first aid on the battlefield, wounded soldiers were taken to an evacuation hospital — such as the 85th — where their conditions were stabilized so the men could be transported to more permanent facilities behind the lines.

"If nothing else," Morrisey said, "you had the infantrymen's heartfelt thanks."

The three nurses — who were tentmates during the war — returned to America in December 1945 and January 1946.

The contributions of military nurses during the war are usually overlooked, said McKeon, who eventually left nursing and returned to college under the GI Bill to earn a degree in library science.

"We also served," she said.

Morrisey said she and others came home from the war and got on with their lives. She spent the rest of her nursing career at a veterans hospital.

"Those who weren't there couldn't relate to what we did," she said. "So we got busy living."

"We contributed," said Smith, who retired as a school nurse. "And we'd do it again, but it's made me a pacifist."

'LONG AGO AND FAR AWAY'

CPL. DELWYN WHITEHEAD of Mason City, Neb., takes Sgt. Edgar P. Fernhaber of Seward, Neb., for a ride in an English jaunting cart in Redruth, Cornwall.

'They were gone'

TO THE ENGLISH CHILDREN during the war, the soldiers marching and driving about in their trucks and tanks created a wonderland of activity.

"It was a child's heaven," said Michael Dodds, who grew up in Salisbury, England, and later moved to Omaha. "There was all this excitement."

Dodds, who was 7 years old on D-Day, recalled in 1994 that the American soldiers he met filled a gap in his life during the war. His father, like most of the men in Salisbury, had been away fighting for years.

"We became their children," Dodds said.

Traffic jams were common as trucks and tanks clogged the narrow roads during the buildup of the Allied forces, said Arthur Maidment, who wrote books on the history of Salisbury.

On the weekend of June 3, 1944, however, the city returned more or less to the way it was before the war, Maidment said. Soldiers had virtually disappeared, and there was a conspicuous absence of heavy traffic.

Dodds remembered waking on June 6, to the buzzing noise of swarms of planes flying over his house toward the beaches of Normandy.

"I opened my window and looked out to see the sky full of aircraft and gliders," Dodds said. "The very ground vibrated because they were flying quite low."

Dodds and his friends ran to the woods where once there were row upon row of canvas tents and throngs of American soldiers who had been their buddies for months.

"They were gone," Dodds said.

'For I knew what was coming'

This is an excerpt from a poem written by Mae Smale, who allowed Eugene Elder of Cherokee, Iowa, and another American soldier to live in her home near Cornwall, England, during World War II. Elder received the poem after he and his fellow soldier had left England to participate in the D-Day invasion and join the fighting in France and Germany.

*EUGENE ELDER
in 1994*

*I know they dreamed at the end of the day,
Of home, and the time they'd go back to stay.*

*They were aching to go, and get their job done;
Life seemed too slow, because they were young.*

*I knew I was old, I thought I was wise,
But I learned a lot more when I looked thro' their eyes.*

*They marched down the road with a laugh, and a wave,
Those two boys of mine, so young, and so brave.*

*Oh! How I missed them! And often I'd pray,
For I knew what was coming — the dreaded D-Day!*

MEMORIES OF A GENERATION ★

DELBERT L. OTTO

Town: Pierce

Service: U.S. Army, 339th Infantry, Service Company, 85th Division, May 21, 1942, to Dec. 6, 1945. Signal Corps Training Center, Camp Gordon, Ga., Sept. 30, 1950, to Aug. 29, 1951, during Korean War.

In the war: Trained at Camp Shelby, Miss., and had desert training in California. Sent to Fort Dix, N.J., December 1943. Arrived in Casablanca, Morocco, in January 1944. Landed in Italy in March 1944. Fought as part of the Fifth Army up the Italian west coast until VE Day on May 8, 1945. Finally received orders to go home Oct. 28, 1945. Came by slow boat and arrived home Dec. 7, 1945.

In his words: "We were trained in Gas School and each man had a drop of mustard gas placed on his arm. All had a blister the next day. It made me respect the danger of gas warfare. … From Casablanca, we rode in old World War I French boxcars, which carried 40 men or eight mules. On Jan. 17, we began six weeks of mountain training. We landed in Naples, Italy, on March 14, 1944. Here we became 'combat soldiers.' We drove by blackout. Once in a while, flashes of artillery fire broke the blackness. The battlefields were in the mountains. I was in charge of the motor pool, and sometimes we loaded the mules into trucks along with the men. … We had been in action for 60 of 62 days, and Rome was to be a rest and training area. It was more training than rest. Since I was part of the group I was awarded the Bronze Star and could wear a gold wreath on my left sleeve. We continued battling our way up the coast to Hitler's Last Ditch. Many of our outfit were injured, but fortunately I was not."

EVERETT L. "SLIM" VANNIER

Town: Council Bluffs

Service: U.S. Army

In the war: He left Hildreth, Neb., in 1941 for training and in 1942 shipped out. His vessel was the first to land at Safi, Morocco, in North Africa, and he was the first man over the side and down the ladder. He was on land about 12 hours, exchanging gunfire on the streets, before he was shot in the right lung. He was taken to a large warehouse in Safi that was serving as a dressing station. While there, Gen. George S. Patton came by and shook his hand. After surgery aboard ship, he went to Walter Reed Army Medical Center in Washington, D.C., where he was photographed with other wounded American soldiers from North Africa and featured in an article in Life magazine. He served out the rest of the war as a training instructor at Camp Shanks, N.Y.

In his words: "I always told the people at the hospital when they wanted to know how I got shot, I told them I got shot by a jealous husband. … I landed on a destroyer, and the destroyer ran up on the beach. We were supposed to land on a dock, but we landed on a beach, and when we went over the side, we landed on dry ground. I was the leading scout for the company."

HERMAN ROSENTHAL

Town: Omaha

Service: U.S. Army

In the war: He was drafted from Chicago in 1942 and assigned to L Company, 142nd Regiment of the 36th Division. While in North Africa, Gen. George S. Patton visited the group and watched it in training exercises. In September, the division sailed by convoy to Italy and landed with the second wave of troops on the beach in Salerno. Decorations he received include the Victory Medal, American Theater Ribbon, Good Conduct Medal, Combat Infantry Badge and Bronze Star.

In his words: "We were told the night before (landing at Salerno) that the Italians had surrendered. But we didn't know the Germans had taken over. We thought it was going to be easy. But the Germans were already looking down at us. They had already secured the beach and were waiting for us. When we did land, we had to take the little town of Altavilla, and we did take it. But the Germans counterattacked and took it back. It was three times between the Germans and us before we finally secured it. It was a bitter battle. I never prayed in my life, but I sure prayed then."

KENNETH P. TORPIN

Town: Doniphan

Service: U.S. Navy, Nov. 6, 1942, to Dec. 26, 1945. Attained the rank of pharmacist's mate, first class.

In the war: Participated in invasions at Sicily and Salerno in Italy, and made three routine voyages to Naples, Italy. Then later set sail to the Pacific, where he saw the devastation at Pearl Harbor. There he spotted his brother's ship, the USS Landsdown. The brothers had not seen each other in two years but had arrived at Pearl Harbor within hours of each other.

In his words: "On June 8, 1943, we left Portsmouth, Va., for Africa and reached Oran, Algeria, June 21. On July 5, my ship left Oran. I had no idea where we were going but on July 10 we started our initial invasion — Sicily. Of the 31 boats used in the operation, only 10 were usable after completion of the action. It was there that we experienced our first burial at sea. … In order to make room for the wounded, officers' quarters were turned into sick bay. We had approximately six doctors and 30 corpsman on our ship. We rotated responsibilities, bandaging wounds, assisting in surgery, caring for patients, and medical records, where because I could type, I spent a good deal of my time."

WAYNE "BIG BRUISER" BLUE

Town: Lincoln

Service: Lieutenant colonel, U.S. Air Force

In the war: As a pilot of Gen. James Doolittle's Northwest African Strategic Air Force, he completed 50 missions in the North African invasion, Tunisian campaign, bombing of Pantelleria and Sicilian campaign, and escort missions over Italy.

In his words: "I was in my fourth year at the University of Nebraska when the war broke out. Having a name near the beginning of the alphabet, I figured I would be pretty high on the list for the draft, so I signed up for pilot training with an Aviation Cadet Team that visited the campus in December 1941. I received my pilot's wings in August 1942. I flew 50 missions, was credited with one confirmed victory and was honored to receive the Distinguished Flying Cross, the Air Medal and 10 Oak Leaf Clusters. I had to always remember that our mission was to continue to escort the bombers in this North African campaign. As each mission was flown, I would get into my airplane, 'Big Bruiser,' and I would acknowledge the fact that there was someone greater than I who was with me, and I'd say, 'Here we go again.' "

FRANK ZAMBUTO SR.

Town: Omaha

Service: U.S. Army Air Forces; staff sergeant and crew chief on C-47s (Gooney Birds)

In the war: He was drafted at age 19 while living in Chicago. Half of the draftees went into the infantry, while the other half went into the Air Forces. After basic training in Gulfport, Miss., and Atlantic City, N.J., he was transferred to tech school in Detroit to learn about trouble-shooting C-47 engines. He eventually attained flight status and was sent to North Africa — Tunis, French Morocco — Italy and England to assist U.S. troops and Greek and Italian partisans. He evacuated many wounded U.S. servicemen, including downed pilots.

In his words: "We never stayed in one place for long — going from base to base, following the troops from North Africa to southern France. We delivered ammunition, took troops to the forward lines and helped the flight nurses with the wounded. While in the northeastern part of Italy, my uncle from Sicily found me by coincidence after eight days of searching. He had a picture of me and was asking every American soldier if they'd seen me. It was a joyous occasion. I was still flying in the C-47s when we were told that Germany surrendered. Everyone was ecstatic. ... The U.S. military placed us in six-man tents in Naples, Italy, before sending us stateside. We disembarked at Staten Island, N.Y., after which we were sent home by train. I was discharged in December of 1945. However, in 1948 I re-enlisted in the U.S. Air Force, was sent to Korea and earned the Bronze Star in 1953. Final discharge from the service was in February 1954."

WILLIAM A. "BILL" RACHOW

Town: Scottsbluff

Service: U.S. Army Air Forces

In the war: He enlisted in the Army Air Forces in June 1942 after his junior year at Peru State College. He had his basic training at Jefferson Barracks, Mo., and was selected for flight training as well as gunnery and bombardier school at Carlsbad, N.M. He was commissioned a second lieutenant and assigned to Tonopah, Nev., to the 781st Bomber Squadron of the 15th Air Force as a bombardier on a B-24 long-range bomber. He was assigned overseas to Italy's Pantanella Air Base. He completed 30 sorties, which is equal to 52 missions, and was discharged in September 1945. He returned to Peru State to finish his schooling and had a long career in education. He retired in 1984 as superintendent of the Gering, Neb., school district.

In his words: "On our fourth sortie, we were shot down over Vienna and landed in Yugoslavia. I was there eight days before I was rescued. We walked quite a ways — 20 or 40 miles, somewhere in there — and then we found a British encampment. A C-47 came in and took Allied airmen and wounded partisans back to Italy."

DE EMMETT B. ZERBE

Town: Omaha

Service: U.S. Army

In the war: He was drafted at age 18 into the Army in the fall of 1943. After basic training, he was assigned to the 1st Armored Division and shipped to Naples, Italy, where he entered into combat. He became a staff sergeant and squad leader.

In his words: "After the war, I was hospitalized in Milan, due to battle fatigue. While there, I heard a boisterous crowd below my window. I got out of my bed and observed a huge crowd below witnessing, I later learned, Mussolini and his mistress being hanged up by their heels. They had been shot by the Italian underground previously on the shore of Lake Como in northern Italy. In another example of 'timing is everything,' I was given a few days of leave in London, where I witnessed the changing of the guard at Buckingham Palace, with all its pomp and circumstance and huge crowds. While peering through the black wrought-iron fence surrounding the palace, all of us jammed together. I turned to leave after the ceremony and bumped into the person next to me, and I said, 'Excuse me.' It was my high school pal, Knox Kuppinger, who lived right behind our house in Omaha."

D-Day

MORE THAN 10,000 ALLIED SOLDIERS — including more than 6,600
Americans — were dead or wounded on France's Normandy coast by the end
of the day on June 6, 1944. ★ Roger McCarthy said he survived the landing
on Omaha Beach by the grace of God. "I was 20, on the beach, and I had no
idea what we were getting into," the Omahan recalled. "It was a shock to see
the death. You hear the term 'combat.' But what the heck is that?
You don't know. Even before the landing craft got to the beach, there was
complete confusion. The impression was that somebody screwed this up
— this isn't how it was supposed to be."

*AMERICAN SOLDIERS WADE ASHORE AT OMAHA BEACH
after disembarking from a Higgins boat under heavy
gunfire from German coastal defense forces.*

'We knew that this was it'

WAKING EARLY IN THE MORNING to the buzzing drone of a sky filled with airplanes, Larry Gaughran knew that D-Day had arrived.

"We knew that this was it," said Gaughran, a P-47 fighter pilot from Omaha. "We had all been anticipating it. It was a great relief because something was happening to finally bring this thing to an end."

As the largest naval armada ever assembled steamed toward the beaches of the Normandy coast, the 22-year-old pilot soared over the English Channel in his sleek fighter aircraft scouting for German submarines. By the end of the day, 10,000 Allied soldiers — about 6,600 of them Americans — lay wounded or dead on Omaha Beach and four other seashore sites scattered with the wreckage of bombed tanks, jeeps and boats. The price paid in casualties helped the Allied forces secure a toehold from which they would drive across Europe in the successful push to crush Hitler's Third Reich.

June 6, 1944, remains one of the most important days in the history of the United States.

D-DAY, JUNE 6, 1944: 'BLOODY OMAHA'

"It is an important turning point," Alan Wilt, an Iowa State professor who authored five books on World War II, said in 1994. "America came of age."

Aside from placing the United States in a leading role on the world stage, D-Day is awe-inspiring simply for its colossal size and complex logistics. Nearly 7,000 ships and landing craft and more than 12,000 planes helped get 155,000 troops ashore by the first day. The battle of Normandy — the campaign that followed D-Day — eventually would involve more than 2 million Allied troops.

Soldiers, seamen and pilots who were there recalled the experience as a time that they, too, came of age.

Pete Schuler of Omaha remembered his buddies who did not return. Schuler crossed Omaha Beach with the Army's 30th Division, which saw some of the fiercest fighting of the war.

The D-Day beach that shares a name with Nebraska's largest city claimed so many casualties that many who were there still remember the spot as "Bloody Omaha." For the bulk of the troops crossing the Channel that day, D-Day was their initiation into combat. Those who survived would see months of fighting that they considered more brutal than D-Day.

From the sky, it was easier to see D-Day as the monumental spectacle that it was. Piloting his lumbering B-17 to bomb German targets near the coast, Lee Seemann of Omaha saw ships of all sizes and description — from battleships to landing craft — covering the water six abreast, curling like a snake all the way from the coast of England to the beaches of France.

"The sight going over was one of the thrills of my lifetime. We were going shorter distances, which was much easier. It was like running the 100-yard dash versus the 440. They were milk runs to us after we had been to Frankfurt, Munich and Berlin," Seemann said.

Flying hundreds of miles through flak-filled skies on previous missions to hit cities in France and Germany had sometimes left the veteran pilot shaken. He was shot down once but survived to take a seat in the cockpit again. He flew one mission from which 26 of three dozen bombers didn't return.

In the weeks before D-Day, Seemann dropped bombs on Calais, a French town north of Normandy, in a move designed to confuse the Germans and convince Hitler that the Normandy coast was not targeted for the Allied invasion.

For most of the soldiers and airmen involved in the D-Day invasion, the historical magnitude of the moment was lost. Whether they arrived by parachute, glider or boat, all were struggling to survive in the chaos and confusion that hung over the battlefields like the lingering smoke from an exploded artillery shell.

Pvt. Glenn Pedersen boarded a landing craft on June 4 and bounced around on the choppy waves just off Dorchester, England, for two days before he and the other members of the 197th Anti-Aircraft Artillery Battalion headed across the Channel to France on D-Day.

As Pedersen's boat was heading for Omaha Beach about 8:30 a.m. — two hours after the first troops landed — it struck one of the mine-tipped poles placed among other underwater obstacles that lay in wait as deadly greetings to the invading soldiers.

"It seemed like everything was a mess," said Pedersen. "Nothing was going right. They landed us in the wrong spots."

Smoke from falling shells, machine-gun fire and splashing water filled Pedersen's view as his halftrack lumbered off the front of the landing craft. Medics ran about frantically. Pedersen scrambled onto the beach, looking for cover. He would spend much of that first day pinned down just under the seawall at the top of the beach by Germans firing from above.

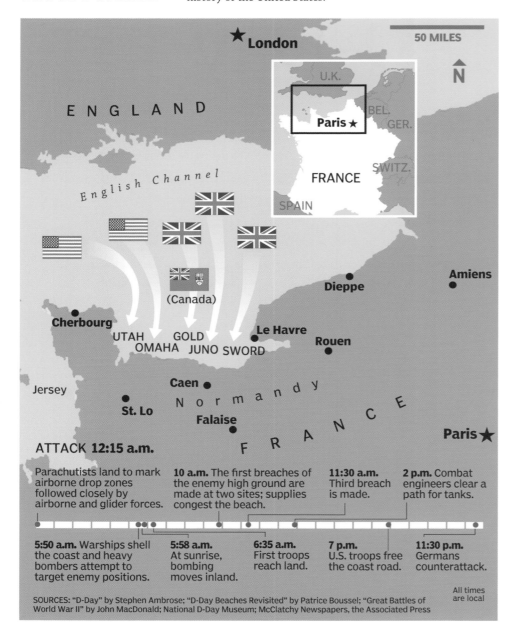

SOURCES: "D-Day" by Stephen Ambrose; "D-Day Beaches Revisited" by Patrice Boussel; "Great Battles of World War II" by John MacDonald; National D-Day Museum; McClatchy Newspapers, the Associated Press

P-47 FIGHTER PILOT LARRY GAUGHRAN, pictured above in 1994 and at right during the war, recalled feeling a sense of relief on D-Day.

Phil Mascarello of Omaha was a 22-year-old gunner for an anti-aircraft artillery battalion on a landing craft heading for Utah Beach, the other stretch of sand the Americans were responsible for wresting from German control.

British and Canadian forces were simultaneously moving toward three beaches to the east known by the code names of Sword, Juno and Gold. As dawn lighted the sky, Mascarello was treated to the view of ships filling the English Channel as far as he could see.

"I couldn't believe what I saw," Mascarello recalled in 1994. "I started getting a little queasy. I thought, 'This is it.' "

Mascarello watched as the first jeep off his boat foundered in the water, spilling the soldiers and equipment into the sea.

"We thought it was funny," Mascarello said. "We were laughing."

Then it happened to him. Mascarello managed to scramble ashore, but he lost his pack, his food and the shovel he needed to dig the trenches that would provide refuge from the falling artillery shells. His extra sock filled with $18.75 in pennies that he was saving to buy a war bond also was gone.

"It's all in the ocean," Mascarello said.

Roger McCarthy of Omaha tried to pray as he waited for dawn, bracing himself against the unceasing rocking of the storm-churned Channel. The boats had circled in the middle of the Channel for hours, waiting for dawn.

The seven-hour journey from England had been so rough that "even the Navy guys were seasick," he said.

McCarthy, then a 20-year-old member of the 149th Combat Engineer unit, was sent in the first wave of troops. His mission was to help clear a path among the underwater obstacles that Hitler's forces had placed to form the "Atlantic Wall."

German shells were landing all around him, sending towers of water spraying into the boats.

After the war, he said, he had trouble shaking the image of wounded men, boat wreckage and vehicles sent hurtling through the air by the bone-jarring force of the explosions that came when shells smacked the landing boats.

Shortly after 6 a.m., McCarthy plunged off the front of his boat into water over his head. It was his baptism into combat at Omaha Beach. McCarthy quickly shed his backpack filled with explosives and his weapons so the weight would not drag him underwater. When he finally pulled himself on to the sand, he took cover where he could.

"Things that we were supposed to blow up we were taking shelter behind," McCarthy said.

McCarthy eventually helped ferry ammunition and other supplies from ships just off shore to the beach. He also was assigned the grisly task of tending to soldiers who had been killed.

"We did things we were never trained to do," McCarthy said.

GLENN PEDERSEN, displaying a wartime photo of himself and a flare gun, recalled in 1994 that "nothing was going right" as he approached Omaha Beach.

PHIL MASCARELLO lost his food, his pack and his money at Utah Beach.

AS A MEMBER OF A COMBAT ENGINEER UNIT IN 1944, left, Roger McCarthy crossed a stormy English Channel to Normandy. Above in 1994, he said he could not forget what he had seen on Omaha Beach.

'I expected to break a couple of legs when I hit'

BY DAVID HENDEE AND DEDRA ROBB

THIS WASN'T THE WAY paratrooper Ed Mauser planned to hit France on D-Day. Floating backward across a countryside filled with the light of anti-aircraft fire and tracer bullets, Mauser couldn't turn his parachute to make a head-on landing. Overloaded with about 100 pounds of weaponry and gear, Mauser also carried a 25- to 30-pound ammunition box wrapped inside an Army blanket strapped to his right leg. Paratroopers with leg bags were to pull a cord to untie the cargo and allow it to fall to the ground moments before landing. But the opening shock of Mauser's parachute dislodged the bag, and it slipped down his leg to his ankle. The release cord was out of reach.

"I expected to break a couple of legs when I hit ground," Mauser said.

Still floating backward, Mauser cleared a hedgerow. Instead of landing hard on his heels, he felt his boot tips skidding gently across a farm field. He toppled into Normandy as his parachute collapsed.

"It was the best landing I ever did," he said.

A nearby cow wandered over and stared at the midnight visitor, still flat on his back. "I thought 'Good. This isn't a minefield.' "

Pfc. Mauser didn't realize it at the moment, but the 27-year-old Illinois watch inspector's ugly landing parachuted him — as part of an elite airborne regiment — into history: the Allied invasion of Nazi-occupied Europe during World War II.

Mauser was a member of the 101st Airborne Division's 506th Parachute Infantry Regiment. He was a rifleman in the 2nd Platoon of E Company — the unit chronicled in the Stephen Ambrose book and HBO miniseries "Band of Brothers."

After spearheading the June 6, 1944, attack and fighting in Normandy, members of Easy Company supported British forces in Holland as part of Operation Market Garden. A few months later, they fought a desperate defensive battle on the Belgian-German border during the Battle of the Bulge. And in the last weeks of the war, Easy Company rolled south to the Bavarian Alps and liberated Adolf Hitler's Eagle's Nest mountain retreat.

Mauser and his buddies were volunteers for paratroop duties. Their training tested endurance, stamina and courage. They became experts in marksmanship, close combat and parachuting before earning their silver jump wings. Then came a D-Day assignment to jump out of a low-flying C-47 aircraft in the dark of night behind enemy lines.

"I was just one of the guys," Mauser recalled in 2009.

Born in Peru, Ill., in 1916, Mauser was working in the wristwatch department at the sprawling Westclox clock factory in LaSalle, Ill., when the United States entered World War II after the Japanese attack at Pearl Harbor.

He was drafted into the Army about six weeks later at age 25. Within two years, more than 600 Westclox workers were in the armed forces, and the company was retooled to produce mechanical fuses.

ED MAUSER OF OMAHA, a veteran of the "Band of Brothers" Easy Company unit in Europe during World War II, tips his cap to the applause in 2010 after receiving the Bronze Star, Purple Heart and other medals 66 years after he earned them on the battlefields of France.

Mauser's first Army outpost was with the horse cavalry at Fort Riley, Kan., which quickly transformed into a mechanized cavalry unit. Mauser was sent to Fort Benning, Ga., for reassignment when he saw paratroopers training.

"That kind of fascinated me. So I volunteered," he said.

Soldiers initially jumped while attached to harnesses and then progressed to jumping with parachutes from 30-foot, 45-foot and 250-foot towers. Each man was required to make five jumps from a C-47 in a week to earn his wings and the right to tuck his trousers into his boot tops for a bloused look.

MAUSER (IN THE GREEN JACKET) GREETS DON MALARKEY of Salem, Ore., at the Strategic Air & Space Museum during a 2009 reunion of the "Band of Brothers." Mauser hadn't seen Malarkey since the end of the war in 1945.

HERBERT E. NOLDA

Town: Ravenna

Service: U.S. Coast Guard (boatswain's mate 2nd class)

In the war: He was working in Santa Monica, Calif., at an aircraft factory when Pearl Harbor was attacked. He went to the recruiting office that day to try to enlist, but hundreds of others were ahead of him and he was told to come back in a couple of weeks. He quit his job, returned to his home in Ravenna, and enlisted in the Coast Guard in Omaha in April 1942. He was assigned first to a small patrol craft on the East Coast, then to a 156-foot landing ship, LCI-91, and sent to North Africa to help troops land. He also took part in the invasion of Sicily and Italy, then was sent to England, where on June 6, 1944, his ship, now LCI-92, landed troops on Omaha Beach on D-Day. He was wounded that day and sent to a hospital in England. After a few weeks he was sent home for R&R, then was reassigned to the troop transport USS Admiral H.T. Mayo, based in San Francisco. He was awarded the Purple Heart for wounds suffered on D-Day.

In his words: "During the first hour on the beach, while enduring the intense enemy action and viewing carnage and havoc in all directions to seaward, I had the feeling, which I am sure was shared by many others, that this was our last day on earth alive. I was convinced this was the last sunrise I would ever see."

"When you're in the plane, you wonder what you're doing there," he said of training. "It was a little scary, but after it was over, it was fun."

Mauser took his jump wings and joined the 101st Airborne and Easy Company.

Mauser said the flight across the English Channel in the early hours of D-Day was uneventful.

"It was pitch dark but a smooth ride. It was a nice night," he said. "They said that when we'd pass between Guernsey and Jersey (islands), we'd probably get some flak from the Germans there. But we didn't."

The paratroopers passed the time in their own ways.

"I wasn't scared. You'd think I'd be scared," Mauser said.

He smoked a few Winston cigarettes. He and others in the platoon littered the floor of the C-47 with smoked-down butts. He took off his reserve parachute to lighten his load.

"Some guys were staring. Some were making the sign of the cross. Some were quiet — thinking and praying."

As soon as the aircraft crossed the French coastline, the paratroopers stood and hooked static lines to deploy their parachutes immediately after leaving the plane. They heard the rumble of anti-aircraft fire. They saw bursts of flak.

"It was after 1 o'clock by the time we got to France," he said. "Everything was quiet until we hit the coast. Everything broke loose. It went from midnight to daylight."

Easy Company's headquarters plane took a hit and exploded when it crashed.

"They lost about 20 guys on there. I knew all of them. That happened 65 years ago, and I still remember it like it was happening right now," Mauser said.

Mauser rattled off names. "Lt. Meehan was on the plane that got hit. The first sergeant, Evans, he went down. Murray went down. Roberts went down. Wentzel went down. Miller went down. Collins went down. McGonigal went down. Riggs went down. I knew them all."

After witnessing the crash, Mauser was eager to jump from his aircraft. He landed about three miles inland. Mauser soon met up with an Easy Company sergeant and then Capt. Herbert Sobel, the company's first commanding officer. Sobel was not well-liked by his troops. Mauser still laments that Sobel was the second comrade he met on the ground. "I had to go with him."

Finally, 30 to 40 Easy Company troops found one another and went in search of the enemy.

"The first fighting we had was a French home with Germans inside," Mauser said. "They were firing at us. I crawled along a stone wall and there, next to the gate, was a body.

"It was the first guy I seen killed," he said.

Mauser said the Easy Company troops eventually flushed out the Germans after U.S. hand grenades started fires inside the structure.

After sporadic fighting for about 18 days, including liberating the village of Carentan, the regiment shipped to England to recuperate and prepare for its next mission.

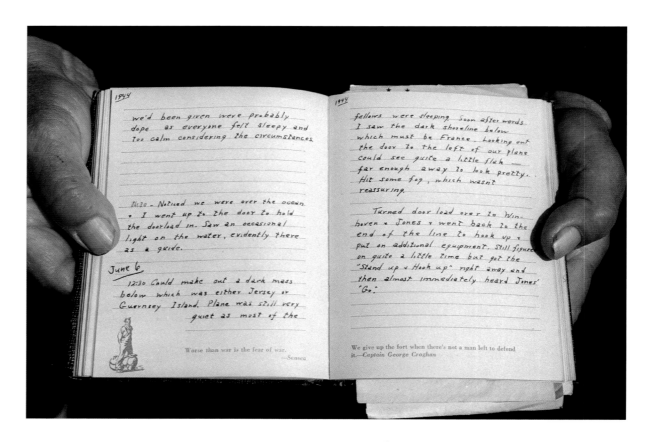

Worse than war is the fear of war.
—Seneca

We give up the fort when there's not a man left to defend it.—Captain George Croghan

L.L. (SWEDE) JOHNSON

Town: Bloomfield

Service: U.S. Army

In the war: He was drafted into the Army shortly after graduating from high school and was sworn in at Fort Crook, the predecessor of Offutt Air Force Base south of Bellevue. He was sent by landing craft to Omaha Beach. During the drive through France, he was injured by an artillery shell, which caused the loss of his right leg above the knee. For his combat wounds he received a Purple Heart; he earned many other medals during his time in France. Sixty years later, he received a letter from the French government thanking him for defending that country.

In his words: "Before we left Southampton, the Germans sent buzz bombers to this harbor and destroyed many buildings. This was very scary, but it did not hit where we were. At about the middle of the English Channel, we were then loaded on landing craft and were taken to Normandy, Omaha Beach. By the time we got there, which was several days, our troops were a few miles inland. It was tough going, as they could not get through the hedgerows until such time as someone put knives on the front of the big Sherman tanks. They then could bust through those hedgerows of trees, rock and dirt. I believe all units moved much faster then until they got to St. Lo, France. The Air Force was called in to bomb St. Lo on July 26, 1944. They almost leveled St. Lo. The 2nd Division was on one flank there. From this point I remember that we moved into Vire, France, a small manufacturing town (that) the Germans wanted to keep. Outside of Vire, we were pushing forward when an artillery shell burst above me, striking my right leg, which in time caused the loss of the right leg above the knee. This happened in the forenoon, and medics did not get to me until 11 p.m. In November 1944, I and many of the wounded soldiers were put on the Queen Elizabeth ship and taken back to the USA."

Jumping into Normandy

ARLEY GOODENKAUF WAS ONE OF THE FIRST Nebraska boys to arrive in France on D-Day. His invasion experience would be brief. After three terror-filled days of fighting in Normandy, he was captured and spent the rest of the war in German prison camps.

A member of the 377th Parachute Field Battalion of the 101st Airborne Division, Goodenkauf jumped from a plane called "Round Trip Ticket" over the Cherbourg peninsula in Normandy just after 1 a.m. on June 6, 1944.

Goodenkauf was supposed to be near the American troops who would be arriving at dawn on Utah Beach. Instead, he landed near a village called Montebourg, more than 14 miles from his intended drop zone and the strip of sand that was a neighbor to Omaha Beach.

When the sun finally rose that morning, Goodenkauf recalled in 1994, he was so far away from the fighting that he could not even hear the big guns of the Allied ships battering the beaches of the Normandy coast.

"The sun was shining and it was quiet," Goodenkauf, of Table Rock, Neb., recalled in 1994. "I wondered if the thing was going off."

Unsure of the terrain, Goodenkauf and fellow paratroopers soon ran right into the teeth of the German defenses.

"Things went downhill," Goodenkauf said. "We were on the run. Finally, they hemmed us in, and there was no getting out of it."

Goodenkauf said he became desperate after going without sleep for three days and losing blood from a shoulder wound. He collapsed into a river. When he climbed up on the bank, he was staring into the wrong end of a German rifle.

Stanley Kotlarz of Omaha parachuted inland at 1:20 a.m. on D-Day ahead of the invasion. He suffered shrapnel wounds in his wrist from an 88-mm shell — which took off his lieutenant's head.

"A lot of people have no idea what war is like," he said. "They should see some of that carnage, and maybe they'll get a faint glimpse of war."

ARLEY GOODENKAUF, AT LEFT IN 1994, kept a journal of his service in World War II. At 1 a.m. on D-Day, he parachuted into France and was captured by the Germans three days later. Below is a German document identifying him as a prisoner of war.

'By God, it worked'

BERNARD NIDER'S GUARDIAN ANGEL on D-Day was combat veteran Fred Bitzig.

In the stomach-wrenching pre-dawn hours of June 6, 1944, Nider was a 19-year-old private first class busily using his steel helmet to bail seawater from his landing craft. The Lincoln man was in the first wave of Allied invasion troops bound for Nazi-occupied France during World War II.

Bitzig helped Nider, but it was Bitzig's combat experience — and luck — that Nider believed got the two of them across the sand and pebbles of one of the world's largest tidal flats under the withering fire of German guns on Omaha Beach.

Bitzig, in his mid-30s, was a veteran of U.S. landings in Sicily and Italy. Standing at the rear of the vessel, Bitzig took his rookie bunkmate under his wing with some sound advice:

• Don't put anything you need in your field pack because you'll ditch it in the water to avoid drowning.

• Watch the German firing pattern. When an artillery or mortar shell explodes, head for the hole in the beach while the sand is still in the air.

• Create your own shell holes by tossing satchel charges up the beach.

"By God, it worked," Nider recalled in 2004.

When the two 29th Infantry soldiers eventually reached the base of the German defenses at the seawall, Nider saw no other soldiers from their landing craft. The slaughter was horrific, and the battle appeared lost. Nider saw no indication that it was a turning point in history.

Operation Overlord put 155,000 Allied troops into Normandy on June 6, 1944. By the end of July, 1.5 million Allied troops were in France. The battle for Normandy cost 237,000 Allied and 400,000 German casualties.

BERNARD NIDER
in 2004

NIDER HOLDS a photo of himself, taken in England during the war.

PAUL MELVILLE MCCOLLUM

Town: Omaha

Service: Army captain

In the war: He was at Omaha Beach on D-Day.

In his words: "The English Channel was full of ships of all kinds. Thousands of our planes kept flying over us all night long to bomb German targets in Normandy. It was still dark when, about 4 a.m., we were seven to 10 miles off the coast of Normandy. We could see shells bursting from Navy warships, and flame-throwing craft throwing fire onto the beach, and bombs dropping from our planes on the high ground above the beach. Two 'Rhino' ferries pulled up to our ship. These were immense, flat boats made from strapping hollow steel boxes. Each Rhino was powered by two large outboard motors. Our ship had a big ramp that could be let down onto the Rhino for transferring our cargo. The two Rhinos took all our cargo.

"The schedule was for us to land on Omaha Beach at 6 a.m. With daylight, there were many combat units already ahead of us. So when we got to the beach, we could see what had happened. Our bombing and shelling had not been as effective as expected. There was still a lot of fire coming down from German strong points above the beach. Wrecked landing craft, tanks, guns and trucks littered the beach. Dead and wounded were strewn on the sand, the living trying to dig in. Ammunition exploding and fires burning. Engineers were blowing up beach hazards so more troops and equipment could land.

"Beach officials decided that our equipment and supplies were less essential immediately than other ships coming in, and we were waved back. All day long, June 6, our Rhino floated in front of our Omaha Beach landing area. We had a panoramic view of the fighting that took place. At dusk we were ordered out to sea to attach our Rhino to a big troop carrier. We were allowed to climb the ropes to board it and spend the night in reasonable comfort. It was a bright night. The sea was full of ships as far as one could see, with barrage balloons filling the sky. The Germans made several air attacks, but our anti-air guns prevented any damage that I knew of. Early next morning, we again boarded our Rhino and went onto the beach."

Watching 'Private Ryan'

AS THE IMAGE OF THE AMERICAN FLAG faded in the final scene of "Saving Private Ryan," Ervin Cramer whispered to his wife, "I thought they'd play taps at the end."

Then the World War II veteran sighed, rubbed his gnarled hand across his face and turned to guide his wife out of the theater.

"That's not something I want to see again," Cramer said after viewing the film in 1998. But, he said, he felt it was his duty to see "Saving Private Ryan," which has been called the most realistic movie ever made about World War II.

Cramer, who was only 19 when he landed on Omaha Beach on D-Day in 1944, said he had read about the movie and how it showed unshrinkingly the chaos and carnage of the European Theater and the Normandy invasion especially — and didn't want to wonder whether filmmaker Steven Spielberg had gotten it right.

"It was the most realistic movie that I've ever seen about the war," Cramer said afterward. "But it's still just a movie. War is a thousand times worse. Nothing could ever be that bad."

Paul Hultman, another D-Day survivor who fought with the 348th Engineer 5th Special Brigade on Omaha Beach, also saw the movie.

"It was gory — I'll tell you some of those scenes got to me," he said. "It was pretty realistic."

Cramer and Hultman said it is important to show the terror, violence and horrors of World War II, so that its reality is not romanticized.

"Most people don't really realize what (fighting) was really like," said Hultman, who was hit in the leg by shrapnel as he was digging a foxhole on the beach on D-Day. "The young people especially should know what happened and what it was like."

There were scenes in the movie, Cramer said, that made him feel like leaving. But he sat stoically, occasionally rubbing his hand across his mouth.

"I could do without ever seeing another one of those," he said when one of the first movie scenes panned the fortified beach.

The day after D-Day, Cramer's unit, the 149th Combat Engineers, removed the steel posts and barbed wire that covered the beach so smaller Allied boats could land and take the wounded to the hospital ship.

"There were mines near or around every one of those. There was just so much. You either got hit or you didn't. It was just plain luck."

Cramer was critical of movies that present a romanticized look at war.

"I was 19 years old when I hit the beach," Cramer said, "and if I would have known what was in store I would have run the other way. We lost so many men that day. They just left us on the beach until we could get replacements."

Only 15 soldiers in his 55-member platoon survived.

"The film shows people that war is a tragic thing. I hope something like that is never allowed to happen again. The average soldier didn't want war — on either side. I'm sure those German soldiers were just as homesick as we were. A few people make the decisions about war that affect everyone else. You've just got to hope they make the right decisions."

Government leaders are too far removed from war and its consequences, he said, and do not fear it enough.

"The politicians who might send our kids to war, most of them have no idea what they're talking about when they think of war. If they knew how terrible it is, then they would never let it happen again."

DALE HARDER
Town: Gretna
Service: Army Signal Corps

In the war: Sailed for England on the Queen Elizabeth, arriving in Liverpool in October 1943. In April, he was sent on detached service to work with the Royal Air Force and was lodged in a private home with the Formans. On June 14, 1944, he landed at Omaha Beach and went to France and Germany.

In his words: "In 1990, I received a telephone call from Atlanta, and a man on the phone asked me if I knew a family in England named Forman. I said I did. … The Formans had found my phone number in an American phone book. … My wife and I got passports and away we went to England for a lovely visit."

> "I hope something like that is never allowed to happen again. The average soldier didn't want war — on either side."
>
> — ERVIN CRAMER, WHO WAS 19 WHEN HE LANDED ON OMAHA BEACH ON D-DAY

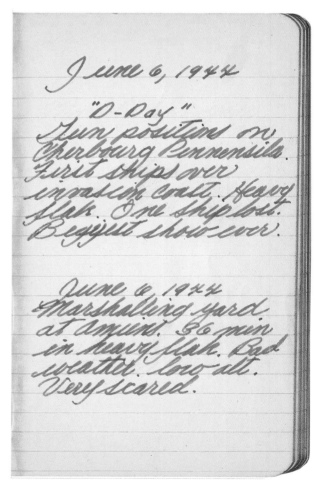

THE FLIGHT DIARY OF CAPT. JOHN D. ASHFORD OF OMAHA notes "biggest show ever" on his first D-Day mission. After his second bombing run of the day, he added, "Very scared."

THE EVENING HEADLINES OF JUNE 6, 1944

THE FRONT PAGE OF THE EVENING WORLD-HERALD on June 6, 1944,
carried the early reports from Normandy. A front-page proclamation from
Omaha Mayor Dan Butler called for a "cessation of all business activity"
the next day at 12:30 p.m. for 3 minutes of prayer "for our gallant soldiers,
Marines and airmen overseas." A prayer service at the Orpheum Theater
on June 7 attracted more than 3,000 people.

In search of the origin of 'Omaha Beach'

BY HENRY J. CORDES

ROBERT HALLSTROM

Town: Syracuse

Service: Coast Guard, USS Eastwind

In the war: Sailor on Coast Guard icebreaker.

In his words: "We had a plane that scouted ahead for us, and it found this small German radio station on an island off the coast of Greenland. ... After going through all the ice, I went ashore with our party around 2 in the morning. The Germans were all asleep, thank goodness. We captured 15 to 20 of them without a fight."

TYPICAL OF SO MANY SOLDIERS of his generation, Gayle Eyler never spoke much about his World War II Army days.

A mention that he was part of the Normandy invasion and a brief story of "shaking in my boots" when strafed by a Nazi warplane were about all his family could ever coax out of him.

Eyler's children assumed his stories and memories had passed into history when the longtime Omaha city building inspector died of cancer in 2003.

But sifting through the scattered papers Eyler left in his Papillion apartment, his son found a written account of Eyler's military service that was surprising, intriguing — and maybe historically significant.

GAYLE EYLER

It could provide an answer to a mystery that has long stumped historians here and elsewhere: how a modest landlocked city on the Plains came to have its name attached to the bloodiest beach — Omaha — of the June 6, 1944, D-Day invasion.

Written by hand and tucked into a spiral notebook, Eyler's account says he served as a carpenter on the headquarters staff of U.S. Gen. Omar Bradley.

As part of those duties, Eyler had helped convert an apartment building in central London into a secret U.S. Army headquarters for the invasion to liberate Europe from Nazi Germany.

Later in that same headquarters, Bradley code-named one of the two U.S. landing areas in Normandy as Omaha Beach in his honor, Eyler wrote, in recognition of his hard work "getting the place ready in a hurry."

The second U.S. beachhead, Eyler wrote, was similarly designated Utah for another carpenter on Bradley's staff— a man who hailed from Provo, Utah.

More than six decades later, it is probably impossible to prove the validity of Eyler's account. But some history detective work by The World-Herald confirmed the accuracy of many of his recollections.

Army records show that Eyler did serve as a specialist in the headquarters company of Bradley's First Army Group. Interviews also indicate that Eyler's account of Bradley's D-Day headquarters in London and how they were set up is historically accurate.

And a once-secret Army record appears to indicate that the code names for the beaches did, indeed, originate within Bradley's headquarters.

The World-Herald was not able to find any details about the Utah soldier Eyler mentioned in his account.

One intriguing aspect of Eyler's account is that it offers an explanation for how both U.S. invasion beaches got their names. As with the Omaha code name, the origin for Utah Beach had long been lost to history.

After reviewing Eyler's account, one of the Army's chief historians didn't dismiss it. Naming the beaches probably did come from something as random as the hometowns of carpenters. That's the way such things typically happened, he said.

"It all makes sense," Conrad Crane, history director at the U.S. Army War College in Carlisle, Pa., said in 2008. "You could be on to something."

As Gayle Eyler writes it, his Army career began modestly enough.

He was first assigned in 1943 to a massive tent city in England, repairing bunks for the thousands of soldiers gathering for the battle to liberate Europe. But that all changed when he was singled out one day by a red-haired captain.

"(He) told me a new outfit was starting up down on the coast," Eyler wrote. "And they needed a carpenter."

He received his orders, packed his bag and boarded a train. He didn't know where he was going.

He ended up in London, where a jeep took him to a block-long town house apartment building near Hyde Park. It was heavily guarded by MPs.

He was issued a Class A pass, with some level of security clearance, and reported to a Maj. Masso. He was introduced to a buck sergeant named "Sam," and the two set up a carpentry shop in the town house basement.

Writing more than a half-century later, Eyler did not remember his co-worker's full name, and his use of quotation marks around "Sam" suggests it could have been a nickname. But he recalled that "Sam" was an Italian-American from Provo whose family grew cherries.

Eyler said the men were instructed to knock out the walls between the apartments, transforming the building into a complex of big map rooms. He hadn't known it at first, but they were setting up the Army's invasion headquarters.

It was hard work. After interior walls were knocked out, the men covered the remaining walls with plywood, on which were hung the maps of the French coastline and Europe used to plot the invasion.

At one point, the building was hit by a German firebomb, requiring Eyler and Sam to make some repairs.

Though the building was Bradley's headquarters, all the top generals — including Gen. Dwight Eisenhower, supreme commander of the Allied forces — and British Field Marshal Bernard Montgomery frequently were there. Eyler wrote that he once saw Gen. George Patton, too.

The generals would have coffee, Eyler wrote, and he and Sam sometimes were invited to join them.

During one of those idle chats, Eyler wrote, the generals asked where the carpenters were from. He said those hometowns became relevant during a subsequent discussion.

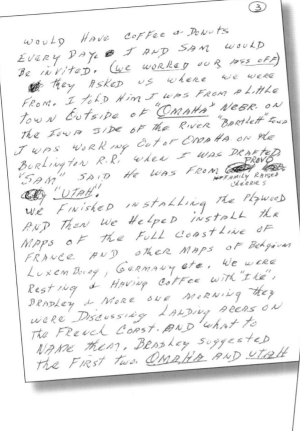

(handwritten note, page 3)

WOULD HAVE COFFEE & DONUTS EVERY DAY. I AND SAM WOULD BE INVITED. (WE WORKED OUR ASS OFF) They ASKED US WHERE WE WERE FROM. I TOLD HIM I WAS FROM A LITTLE TOWN OUTSIDE OF "OMAHA" NEBR. ON the IOWA SIDE OF The RIVER "Bartlett" IOWA I WAS WORKING OUT OF OMAHA ON The BURLINGTON R.R. WHEN I WAS DRAFTED. "SAM" SAID He WAS FROM PROVO "UTAH". WE FINISHED INSTALLING The PLYWOOD AND THEN WE HELPED INSTALL The MAPS OF The FULL COASTLINE OF FRANCE AND OTHER MAPS OF BELGIUM LUXEMBURG, GERMANY ETC. WE WERE RESTING & HAVING COFFEE WITH "IKE", BRADLEY & MORE ONE MORNING THEY WERE DISCUSSING LANDING AREAS ON THE FRENCH COAST. AND WHAT TO NAME THEM. BRADLEY SUGGESTED THE FIRST TWO OMAHA AND UTAH

"Sure, he would have coffee with a carpenter."

— LT. COL. CHESTER HANSEN,
   A TOP AIDE TO GEN. OMAR BRADLEY
   AND A MEMBER OF THE INVASION STAFF

HEADQUARTERS
FIRST UNITED STATES ARMY
APO 230

SECRET
:Date: 3 March 1944 :
:Auth: CG, First US Army:
:Initials: :

3 March 1944

AMENDMENT No. 1
to
FIRST ARMY OPERATIONS PLAN
NEPTUNE

1. All references to Beaches X or Xray and Y or Yoke in First Army Operations Plan NEPTUNE will be deleted and the following substituted:

a. UTAH area - Northwards from the mouth of the RIVER VIRE.

b. OMAHA area - From the Eastern limit of a. above to West breakwater at PORT EN BESSIN.

APPROVED:

W. B. KEAN
Brigadier General, G.S.C.,
Chief of Staff

DISTRIBUTION:

Same as for First Army
Operations Plan NEPTUNE.

DECLASSIFIED
NND 735017

LYLE STORM
Town: Lyons
Service: Army, 26th Infantry "Yankee" Division

In the war: Joined the 26th Infantry in France. In November 1944, was marching to a small town that was supposedly clear of Nazi forces; in fact, the Nazis had returned and set up machine guns. Of 180 troops, only about 10 men, including Storm, survived the ambush. Storm took a machine gun round to the chest; the bullet exited his back, missing his spine by an inch.

In his words: "Our information was this town was supposed to be clear. But in the meantime, the Nazis had come back and set up some machine guns. So we advanced across this open area and they cut loose on us. … The bullet took out one of my ribs. … When we were lying in this command room where they took us, the worst thing that scared me was hearing them say that if the Nazis advanced, everyone should pull back because we didn't have enough forces to hold the position. I could just see myself there, being in enemy hands and wounded. In those days, they didn't pay much attention to the wounded, they just put you out of your misery."

"We were resting & having coffee with 'Ike,' Bradley & more one morning," Eyler wrote. "They were discussing landing areas on the French coast and what to name them." Then, Eyler wrote, Bradley suggested Omaha and Utah for the U.S. beaches, recognizing his carpenters.

When planning was complete, Bradley, Eyler and the rest of the headquarters staff left London for Southampton, to stage for the historic landings.

When D-Day dawned June 6, 1944, and U.S. soldiers — at horrific cost — stormed Omaha Beach, Eyler was just offshore aboard Bradley's flagship, the cruiser Augusta. Days later, Eyler landed on the beach that bore the name of his hometown.

Eyler said he and other members of the headquarters company accompanied Bradley across Europe — from Normandy to northern France, across the Ardennes and into Germany. They made Paris the day after liberation, he said, and got within 50 miles of Berlin. As Bradley's carpenter, Eyler said, he made a foldable, one-hole toilet for the general. It was one of the first things that went up wherever they established their mobile headquarters. Bradley had a personal driver who took care of his uniforms and also cared for two fox terriers the general took with him all across Europe.

The dogs, Eyler wrote, were named Omaha and Utah.

The Gayle Eyler story actually begins not in Omaha but in Bartlett, Iowa, a farming town on the Missouri River about 25 miles south of Omaha.

After graduating from Bartlett's tiny, now-defunct high school, Eyler moved to Omaha to take a job as a carpenter for the Burlington railroad. Living out of a bunk car in Omaha, he and his crew repaired bridges on the line south of Omaha.

But around the world, war was raging. In May 1943, Eyler received his draft notice and began a three-year Army odyssey.

After the war, he returned to Omaha. He first found work as a commercial carpenter and then later took a job as a City of Omaha housing inspector. He rose to the post of chief housing inspector, retiring in the 1970s after 25 years.

Along the way he married, raised two sons and later divorced. During retirement, he was active as a volunteer at the Veterans Hospital in Omaha, running a woodworking shop for rehabilitating veterans.

While proud to be a World War II veteran, Eyler never told his family much about his war days. His son Jim Eyler of La Mesa, Calif., could recall little more than the strafing story.

Sometime in 2001, Jim Eyler's son was working on a school paper in which he was supposed to write about a member of his family, and the boy began asking about his grandfather's World War II service. Jim Eyler suggested that his father take the time to write about it.

CAL SWAGERTY

Town: Wakefield

Service: Staff sergeant, 35th Division

In the war: Was part of the invasion in France from July 1944 until about November, then volunteered to go to the infantry and was transferred to the 35th Division. Fought in the Battle of the Bulge and in Germany, where he was when the war ended.

In his words: "First part of May — war was over! We pulled back and were considered part of the army of occupation. They moved our regiment to Brussels, Belgium, because President Truman was there for the Potsdam Conference. I was one of the men chosen to be in his honor guard (in July 1945). He asked me how long I had been in the 35th and where I was from. The 35th Division was President Truman's division in World War I."

It wasn't long after that Gayle Eyler learned he had cancer. And on May 27, 2003, about a week before the 59th anniversary of the D-Day landings, he died.

The next day, Jim Eyler and his brother, Bob, went to their father's apartment to begin packing away his life. Jim Eyler opened a notebook. Out fell six pages of writing on lined paper, undated and in his father's hand.

After quickly reading it, Jim Eyler incredulously handed it to his brother.

"You aren't going to believe this," he said.

Jim Eyler brought his father's account to The World-Herald.

So how do you go about verifying events claimed to have taken place more than six decades ago? The newspaper started with archival records.

Discharge papers from a military records center in St. Louis confirm that Gayle Eyler was among the "special troops" assigned to Bradley's headquarters and that carpentry was his craft. Military histories shed little light on how the beaches got their names. And, unfortunately, there is no indication that Bradley was ever asked about the beach names before he died in 1981.

Gen. Omar Bradley acquired two dogs in London that he named Omaha and Utah, though it is unclear which came first: the dogs or the invasion.

Lt. Col. Chester Hansen, a top aide to Bradley who was a member of the invasion staff, said he didn't remember how the names were chosen. But after hearing Eyler's account, Hansen had little doubt that the Omaha soldier was part of Bradley's London headquarters.

Hansen said the headquarters company, numbering more than 200 men, included the clerks, cooks, drivers, mechanics and, yes, carpenters who supported Bradley's command.

"Headquarters company kept things going," Hansen said.

The headquarters for Bradley's First Army Group were set up in London's Bryanston Square, Hansen said, just as Eyler described. A row of brownstone town houses was converted into offices, and then 4-by-8 sheets of plywood were attached to the walls to hold the maps. As Eyler described, the headquarters were hit by an incendiary bomb, Hansen said.

And just as Eyler described, Hansen said, Eisenhower and British commander Montgomery were frequent visitors to Bradley's headquarters, and Patton made occasional visits.

As to the enlisted man's account about sharing coffee and doughnuts with Bradley and other top officers, Hansen didn't find that hard to swallow. He said there was a reason reporters at the time labeled the unpretentious commander from western Missouri as "a GI's general."

"Sure, he would have coffee with a carpenter," Hansen said.

Hansen said he would find it less believable that Bradley would talk about code names when a carpenter was around. But he didn't rule it out. He said all headquarters personnel had security clearances, and Bradley would have been comfortable around the carpenters.

Yes, Bradley did acquire two dogs in London that he named Omaha and Utah, though it was unclear which came first: the

dogs or the invasion. Still, Hansen said, he didn't know if Eyler's beach-naming account was true.

The World-Herald dug deeper, making inquiries to the National Archives in Washington.

Archivists found a document issued by Bradley's headquarters labeled "Amendment No. 1" to the D-Day invasion plan.

The March 3, 1944, document indicates that all references to beaches "X" or "Xray" and "Y" or "Yoke" were being changed to "Utah" and "Omaha."

While not indicating how the name change occurred, the document seems solid evidence that the names of the beaches did originate — as Eyler wrote — in Bradley's headquarters. But the archivists also found a reference in a 1991 World War II encyclopedia that mentions another possible source.

"World War II: America at War" credits the Omaha Beach name to Navy Vice Admiral Alan Kirk, who was responsible for the armada of ships that transported soldiers to the invasion beaches. Kirk suggested Omaha and Oregon, the book says, with the latter name later changed to Utah.

The book's authors could not recall the source of that information. Archivists for the Naval Historical Center in Washington found no reference to beach names in any of Kirk's papers. However, they said, the beach names seem to correspond with the code names of the naval task forces assigned to the beaches: Force O for Omaha and Force U for Utah. A Navy historian said that suggests the beach names could have been derived from the letter designations of the task forces.

Crane, the Army historian, said he's more inclined to believe the designations of the naval forces came from the names of the beaches, not vice versa.

One thing that would lend more credence to Eyler's account would be if the Utah soldier could be located. Despite a concerted effort over many months to find him, through local and state historians in Utah and Army personnel records in St. Louis, The World-Herald was not able to identify "Sam."

The search for "Sam" did reveal that there once was a sizable enclave of families, some of them Italian, who grew cherries in the mountain foothills near Provo. Given Eyler's Iowa and Nebraska roots, that's a fact he is not likely to have known unless he knew someone from the area.

"It was a lovely fruit area, and they raised a lot of cherries," said local historian Robert Carter. But those families are gone, he said, the orchards displaced by suburban development.

One aspect of Eyler's account of "Sam" doesn't check out. He recalled that the Utah soldier was the brother-in-law of a captain who headed their unit. But that captain's family could recall no relatives serving with him.

If Sam existed, there's no evidence that he left behind a tale similar to Eyler's. Utah historians said they had no idea how Utah Beach got its name.

Crane, the Army historian, said it's not surprising that Eyler's account couldn't be definitively proved more than half a century after the events. Interpreting history, he said, is often like matching points on a fingerprint. The more matches, the more believable the account.

Many facts in Eyler's story do match, Crane said. Future historians may be able to build on Eyler's account. Even if Eyler's story is not quite ready for the history books, Crane said, it's worthy of being told.

Jim Eyler said that at the rate his father's generation is dying, the whole story, unfortunately, may never be known.

"This may be as close to the names of these beaches as we'll ever get."

ANDREW JACKSON HIGGINS, a Columbus, Neb., native who also lived for a time in Omaha, designed and built the "Higgins boat" landing craft that brought Allied troops to the coast of Normandy and to other World War II beaches. Gen. Dwight D. Eisenhower once credited Higgins, who built his boats in New Orleans, with providing the key to victory with his ingenious landing-craft design.

ALLIED TROOPS AND SUPPLIES flood Omaha Beach, days after the harrowing landing of June 6, 1944. Reports later said this was Gen. Dwight D. Eisenhower's favorite photo from the war.

MEMORIES OF A GENERATION ★

ED COHN

Town: Omaha

Service: Navy, 6th Beach Battalion

In the war: Graduated from Central High months early at age 17 to become Navy radioman. Went ashore two hours before landings on Omaha Beach to set up communications with vessels ferrying in the troops. Only 12 of 38 in his unit survived, and he was wounded the second day. Spent rest of war as communications specialist in U.S. Embassy in London.

In his words: "I got a lot of ribbing from my buddies (about being from Omaha). They said, 'Eddie, you're home.' I said, 'This isn't the Omaha where I want to be.' Our landing in early-morning darkness was uneventful. At H-Hour, all hell broke loose. We did the best we could, but there were a lot of problems. We seemed to spend more time tending to wounded than manning our radios. So many young boys getting torn apart by German guns. 'Ma, Mama, where are you?' Those are the cries you heard the most. I was trying to apply a tourniquet to a young man, an Army kid, and I got a lot of shrapnel in the chest. I hope I did my duty. This was my war."

CHARLES "DOC" WEMPE

Town: York (pictured below with wife Helen)

Service: Navy, aviation units

In the war: First piloted PBY Catalina "flying boats" around the Gulf Coast and off the Florida Keys, looking for German submarines. Later trained Navy pilots in Pensacola, Fla., on a variety of aircraft.

In his words: "We were submarine hunters. Most people didn't know how much shipping we lost just a few miles off our shores to submarines. ... So we carried depth charges, and we would look for subs."

LEO TOMASIEWICZ

Town: Omaha

Service: 9th Air Force, 455th Bomb Squadron

In the war: Flew 58 missions as bombardier on a B-26, including two missions on D-Day.

In his words: "The hairy part was always the 10 minutes before you hit the target, because if you were flying at, say, 12,000 feet, then you had to stay at the altitude and never veer off course. The Germans were shooting the (anti-aircraft guns) at us. You'd see the flashes, and in about 10 seconds the sky would explode and some planes would get hit."

CARL PRAEUNER

Town: Battle Creek

In the war: Served most of the war with 3rd Battalion, Company K, 16th Infantry Regiment. Was in North Africa and Sicily before training in England for the D-Day landing at Omaha Beach.

In his words: On D-Day, "About a mile inland, we set up positions. My squad leader told me to set up our mortar and look for machine-gun nests." As he did so, Praeuner was shot. The bullet ripped his leg open from just above his knee, then entered his lower abdomen. He was laid in an open field to wait for the medics, who never came. "I prayed most of the night while tracer bullets flew just over me. (The next morning) I waited awhile and decided I had to try to get up. . . . I had gone only a short way when two GIs came" and helped him. Taken to a hospital in England, he was not expected to live. "Even though I was badly wounded and almost died, I'm glad I served."

JOE MIKLAS

Town: Omaha

Service: U.S. Army

In the war: He served with the Third Army under Gen. George Patton. He was inducted into the Army on March 6, 1943, at age 19 at Fort Crook. He was sent to Fort Leavenworth, Kan., and then to Camp Beale in California. In late 1943, he was sent to Oregon State College as part of the Army Specialized Training Program until it was disbanded. Then he was sent back to his outfit at Camp Beale. The outfit trained at Beale until early 1944, when it was sent to Chepstow, Wales, to train for the invasion of Europe. He received five battle stars, including for Normandy, Southern France; the Battle of the Bulge, Ardennes; and Central Europe.

In his words: "We landed on Utah Beach to go around the Nazis and link up with the troops who landed on Omaha Beach. The troops on Omaha were held up for a number of days, so our outfit had to keep going. As we cleaned up on the Nazis, our next object was to capture Hill 101, which would give us command of the hills and all of the valley. The British were also held up at their beachhead, so we had to wait for them. From there, we went across France on the southern part until the Bulge started and we were told to go up north into the Ardennes to stop the Germans. It was very cold, but we had to keep going. After the Battle of the Bulge, we went into Germany, and the rest is history. After the war, we went to Riviera Beach and boarded the ship and set sail for home."

ROY HAYNES

Town: Omaha (pictured below with wife Esther)

Service: Base Service Squadron, 547th Air Service Group; highest rank achieved was buck sergeant

In the war: Landed on Omaha Beach on July 25, 1944, missing D-Day invasion. Served 75 days in combat. Wounded in action at battle of Foret de Parroy, near Strasbourg, France. Received Purple Heart, Bronze Star, Combat Infantry Badge and European Theater ribbon with four campaign stars. Was in Panama City when the war ended.

In his words: After returning to the United States from Panama, Haynes was processed at Camp Shanks, N.Y. He was then put on a train to Leavenworth, Kan. "I never knew a train to move so fast going back to Ft. Leavenworth. ... The Army wasn't generous giving travel pay, so I was short of money and had to hitchhike from Ft. Leavenworth back to Omaha." Haynes missed his wife's chocolate chiffon pie so much, he went around the Fort Leavenworth mess hall emptying the sugar bowls, hoping to bring home enough for her to bake with. When a superior caught Haynes stealing sugar, he sent Haynes home with 23 pounds of sugar to ensure that his wife had enough to bake his favorite dessert. "The Army wasn't proficient making pie."

JESSE W. SKINNER

Town: Wisner

Service: First Lieutenant, U.S. Army Corps of Engineers

In the war: In 1942, he was assigned to the Army Ordnance Installation at Aberdeen, Md. During his training, he received instruction in the use and repair of small arms and machine guns. Those weapons were being used in the sandy conditions of North Africa, where U.S. troops were fighting against the Germans. The sandy grit caused problems with the weapons. The next challenge was the condition of roads, bridges and railroads to be encountered during the invasion of the European mainland. Skinner was sent to Fort Belvoir, Va., to learn how to repair and to destroy those structures.

In his words: "Early in 1944, my regiment was assigned to guard a six-mile water line near Torquay, England. An Englishman, Mr. John Peters, was in charge of the water pumps and wells supplying this water line, so I became well-acquainted with him and his family. They invited me into their home for frequent meals and family time with their 6-year-old daughter, Rosemary. They had chicken netting on all the windows so that when bombs exploded nearby, the window glass would be caught in the netting. Black cloths were placed over the windows at night — not a sliver of light could show from the homes. The Peterses had a special metal tube located under their dining room table where they always placed their daughter for protection during the air raids. For 65 years, my wife and I have received a Christmas card from the Peters family — now sent by their son, Nicholas.

"In late June 1944, my unit landed on the French coast at Utah Beach and we endured our first encounter with the Germans. It was a slow advance through to Paris and up into Belgium. The 375th Regiment's main work was the rehabilitation of bombed-out railroads and roads. We worked close to the Battle of the Bulge, and when the war in Europe ended, the 375th Regiment was one of the engineers units building a bridge across the Rhine River."

Lawrence Youngman in Europe

WORLD-HERALD WAR CORRESPONDENT Lawrence Youngman arrived in London on June 5, 1944. The next morning the elevator operator at the Savoy Hotel told him: "The invasion has begun." D-Day had arrived. ★ The newspaper said it sent Youngman overseas "for the express purpose of reporting home about all the Nebraska and western Iowa boys he can find." Much of his coverage involved the 134th Infantry Regiment, which had been a Nebraska National Guard regiment when called into federal service in 1940 and was still about 25 percent Nebraska boys in 1944. ★ Youngman found the 134th training in England and joined the soldiers after they arrived in France about a month after D-Day. ★ The unit was commanded in Europe by Col. Butler B. Miltonberger, a former postal employee from North Platte. "He was an outstanding colonel, and his regiment was an excellent one," recalled Youngman, who was 39 when he took the assignment. ★ The World-Herald correspondent later was with American forces when they entered Paris — "The greatest moment of my professional life," he said. ★ Youngman was forced to come back in December 1944 because of serious eye problems.

"LAWRENCE YOUNGMAN, World-Herald war correspondent now in London, was the last American newsman to get to London ahead of the invasion, according to the War Department."
— WORLD-HERALD OF JULY 7, 1944

YOUNGMAN IN EUROPE

THE WORLD-HERALD FOLLOWED NEBRASKA SERVICEMEN FROM TRAINING IN ENGLAND UNTIL U.S. FORCES HAD REACHED INTO EASTERN FRANCE.

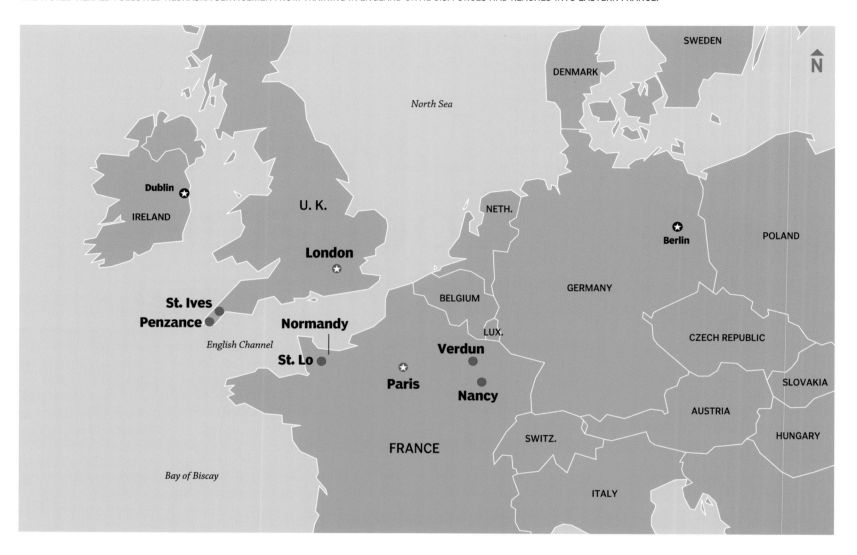

June 7, 1944
LONDON

LONDONERS TOOK THE INVASION news much more calmly than New Yorkers received the false invasion report of last Saturday.

The only visible sign of interest here was the manner in which people crowded around the news vendors to buy papers.

My first report came from the Savoy Hotel elevator boy, who displayed the only bubbling enthusiasm I have heard all day.

The cabdriver hadn't heard. "That will be exciting news," he said, then qualified it with "if it comes through." But he didn't think that it had been started because he didn't deem the weather favorable.

"That's the stuff to give them," snorted the police sergeant to whom I reported.

"No use getting excited," observed a shoe store manager. "Nothing we can do about it, is there?"

The war seemed as remote as it did in Omaha until I talked to a Cleveland newsman who had ridden in a Martin B-26 Marauder during the bombing that preceded a landing on the French coast. He felt lucky to be back alive and was having a few drinks for himself.

LAWRENCE YOUNGMAN was a 15-year veteran of The World-Herald's staff when he took the assignment as war correspondent. He later founded Omaha-based Travel and Transport Inc., which grew to become one of the nation's largest travel companies. In 2007, an Omaha park was named after Youngman, who died in 2003.

June 11, 1944
AT AN ENGLISH INVASION PORT

WOUNDED MEN TRANSPORTED to this port from the French coast seemed to be little affected by the experience of going ashore under heavy German gunfire.

I talked to a number of Nebraska men who, with the others, were making the hospital noisy with their talk and jokes.

"Why," one Nebraska boy told me, "I'd a darned sight rather be back there than lying around this hospital."

Names of the Nebraskans may not be used until their relatives have been notified they were wounded.

Many of the men had suffered leg and foot wounds when German shells hit the ground and fragments splattered.

But to my astonishment, they were merry and apparently not much moved by their experiences.

Some of those I talked to were Rangers whose assignment was to take an almost perpendicular cliff close to the edge of the seas. A bad job. But the Rangers said they weren't much frightened when they started across the channel or hit the beach.

"But you have to remember that hardly anything makes those Rangers jittery," said another boy. "They're crazy. We all thought it was going to be easy, but when you're down to details it was tough, mighty tough."

June 21, 1944
LONDON

ONLY A FEW DAYS have been needed to prove that one of the principal satisfactions of this job lies in meeting the wounded Nebraska and western Iowa boys who have been brought to the hospitals in England.

It's a thrilling experience to walk up to a lad and say, "I'm from The Omaha World-Herald," and then note his pleasure at realizing that someone from home has come to his bedside. It's such an experience, in fact, that it almost gives one goose flesh.

NEBRASKANS IN THE anti-tank company of the 134th Infantry scale a cliff at Land's End on the southwestern tip of England. At left, they line up to spell "NEB."

REPORTS ON THE WAR were sent by Western Union telegram to Omaha, subject to military censorship. Lawrence Youngman noted on this cable, sent four days after D-Day, that the "best stuff cannot yet be cleared."

Gen. Dwight D. Eisenhower reviews a U.S. Army battalion that included many Nebraskans.

Eisenhower, Patton review Nebraska troops

June 28, 1944
SOMEWHERE IN ENGLAND

MANY NEBRASKA SOLDIERS trained under the alert eye of Gen. Dwight D. Eisenhower this week.

After he had reviewed them, the supreme commander of the Allied forces in Europe had words of praise and encouragement for the Cornhuskers and the men who marched beside them.

Gen. Eisenhower told them: "For me there is a great deal of sentiment in the fact that a man from Kansas has come to this beautiful corner of England to welcome you men from Nebraska. What I have seen has pleased me mightily. You look to me like you are ready to take your place in the battle line."

The supreme commander told the Nebraskans that every division that has gone into action for the first time — just as their division will be doing — has whipped the German on his own grounds, even though every advantage is with the enemy.

THE TROOPS DRILLED under the watchful eyes of, from left, Eisenhower; Maj. Gen. Paul W. Baade, commander of the 35th Division; Col. Butler B. Miltonberger, commander of the 134th Infantry Regiment; and Lt. Gen. George S. Patton, commander of the Third Army.

PHOTOGRAPHERS TRAIL EISENHOWER as he inspects soldiers drilling under the supervision of Sgt. Leo Samson of Omaha.

EISENHOWER TOLD THE SOLDIERS that it will be the infantry that will take the last long step to victory.

The general added that he is particularly confident that soldiers from the Missouri River Valley area will do the job right and give him reason to be proud of them.

Pointing out that the ground forces are part of a fighting team that includes the air forces and the Navy, he told the infantrymen that they will have great reason to be thankful for the assistance of other members of the team.

But finally, he added, it will be the men of the infantry who will have to take the last long step to victory.

As a parting word, he urged them to help get the war over in a hurry so that everyone can go home.

Lt. Gen. George S. Patton and Maj. Gen. Paul W. Baade accompanied Eisenhower. It was pretty much of a Nebraska show they saw. The battalion they visited was commanded by a Nebraskan, Lt. Col. Alford C. Boatsman of Beatrice.

AMBULANCE DRIVERS *Jean Crider, left, of Hershey, Neb., and Howard Claflin of Paxton, Neb., await their turn to cross the English Channel.*

July 6, 1944
SOMEWHERE IN ENGLAND

WILLIAM HOAGLAND

THE PAST WEEK I have spent with Nebraska men who expect they will soon cross the channel and match skill and weapons with the Nazis.

The interesting part of this experience has been to observe the attitude of these men toward the business of going to battle, knowing full well that casualties and fatalities are bound to result.

Unless their inner feelings belie their talk and their attitude, most of these men really want to go on to France, and the sooner the better.

Aside from patriotic feelings, their personal reasons seem to be three:

1. To hurry it up and get the thing over and go back home as soon as possible.

2. Most of them have been in the Army several years and they do not care to again face neighbors and friends without being able to say that they have seen some fighting.

3. They have devoted many, many months to training and intensive maneuvers. At times it's been a rough schedule. They would hate to think that it all has been wasted time and trouble. They would like to try out what they have been taught.

An Omahan, William Hoagland, said he believed if the men were given their choice of fighting in France or accepting a comfortable, honorable and safe assignment in the States that nine out of 10 would elect to go to France.

NEBRASKANS FIND TIME *to relax in England before shipping out: Pfc. Herman Hood, left, of Burwell and Pfc. Virgil C. Pedersen of Aurora.*

July 9, 1944
SOMEWHERE IN ENGLAND

GEN. DWIGHT D. EISENHOWER CAPTURED the affections of many Nebraskans, including this reporter, when he addressed part of a regiment.

It was homey, man-to-man, down-to-earth stuff. Just a fellow from back home talking to other fellows from back home — and he said he was as anxious as anyone else to get back to the States. When he was through speaking, you had the feeling that the soldiers who heard him would do their best to deliver on any request that he might make in the future.

His simplicity and straightforward friendliness are in marked contrast to the attitude of some generals I have seen over here. For instance, that afternoon he stopped and visited with some of the soldiers from Kansas, and they talked about farming conditions back home — they even discussed the breed of cattle that they saw in an adjoining field.

And the supreme commander clinched the matter with The World-Herald representative when he proved especially cooperative in arranging a picture with Nebraskans.

EISENHOWER VISITED NEBRASKA TROOPS just days before they went to France. To the right of Eisenhower are Cpl. Clifford Geiken of Gothenburg and Maj. Dan E. Craig of North Platte. Charles E. Edgar of Gering is on the far right,

ABOVE, A WOUNDED AIRMAN is helped from a B-26 after a bombing run over Caen, France.

1ST LT. EDWIN MARTENS (left) of Ogallala, Neb., is congratulated by crew chief Floyd L. Greenlund of Omaha after landing his burning bomber in England.

July 16, 1944
AT A 9TH AIR FORCE BOMBER BASE IN THE EUROPEAN THEATER

THE TIME IS 10 in the morning, and the base officers and the mechanics are edging out onto the field. Something over two hours ago, a flight of B-26 Martin Marauder planes had set out to bomb two bridges on the Orne River at Caen, France.

The assignment was a tough one. The Germans were fighting hard there, and the area was heavily defended by ack-ack guns. The men "sweating it out" at the edge of the field were sober. They feared losses might be heavy. Five planes appeared in the distance — not a good omen because the planes are grouped in sixes. Not far behind are three or four other groups, and they seem to be complete.

Then a "loner" shows up — the plane that was missing from the first flight — and he's making a beeline for the field. As the pilot approaches the base, he fires his flare gun to signal that he has wounded aboard and wants clearance for an immediate landing. The plane settles onto the runway, but it doesn't seem to slow down. It hurtles across the runway, across a road and a ditch, through a hedge and into a turnip field, where it comes to a stop after another 150 yards.

The waiting officers jump into jeeps and rush over to the field, expecting to provide assistance for a wrecked plane — at the very least the tricycle landing gear should be washed out. But when they arrive, the plane is standing there as solidly and placidly as a horse dozing in a pasture.

Two Omahans were on the mission. They were 1st Lt. Darrald B. Harsh, bombardier, veteran of 65 combat missions over occupied Europe, and 1st Lt. Clyde E. Loomis Jr., also a bombardier and with what he describes as "only 38" missions to his book. They belong to Nye's Annihilators, an outfit commanded by Col. Glenn C. Nye.

Two other Nebraskans belong to Nye's group — Maj. D.E. Harnly of Lincoln (formerly of Council Bluffs) and Lt. Carl Eckhardt of Scottsbluff.

Harsh, who seemed to be as calm as anybody who went on the mission, had had great luck. He was lead navigator in a flight of six planes. His bombs apparently had landed "on the button," and so had those of the planes just behind.

IN ENGLAND, WAITING TO SHIP OUT

A DRUID BURIAL STONE in Cornwall draws the interest of Sgt. Noel D. Hughes, left, of Steel City, Neb., and Sgt. Donald D. Schrack of Lexington, Neb.

NEBRASKANS BROUGHT FOOTBALL to England, as Lt. Col. Delbert C. Leffler of Holdrege shows.

A CHURCH SERVICE, conducted by Maj. John H. Reents of Adams, Neb., before leaving for France.

July 21, 1944
AT A 9TH AIR FORCE BOMBER BASE IN THE EUROPEAN THEATER

ABOUT EVERY OTHER day they go over occupied Europe to plaster German targets, but two Nebraskans at this Douglas A-20 Havoc air base told The World-Herald they miss the excitement back home.

One is Lt. Ward Neff of Lincoln, a pilot who has flown 18 combat missions over the occupied countries. But he says he hasn't run into anything nearly as exciting as the time back in November 1941 when he was in a car that rolled over five times in an accident west of Lincoln.

The other man is Staff Sgt. Joseph J. Field of Omaha, veteran of a score of missions, who just can't wait to get back to Omaha and get a motorcycle between his knees again. He was a member of the Ranger motorcycle club — one of several groups of cyclists who roamed Omaha and the surrounding highways like so many Cossacks.

Neff holds the record for one-engine flight among planes at this base. One motor quit southwest of Paris. He flew the 300 miles back to the English coast on the other, and was "convoyed" across the channel by RAF planes. He landed at the first field, and the ship ran out of gas after coming to a stop at the far end of the runway.

His plane is named "Cornhusker Nicky" — Nicky is his wife's nickname. They have a 2-month-old son, Roger, so named because the word means "OK" in the airman's lexicon.

July 25, 1944
SOMEWHERE IN ENGLAND

HAVING BEEN IN England nearly two months, I should be ready to take my place with the experts, and proclaim that the war will end sooner, or that it will end later.

But the truth is that I have been wrong on every guess made about the war's end, and certainly can lay no claim to being an expert. In this job, however, there are certain things which impress themselves upon one, and this piece will point out some of them.

I feel somewhat uneasy in writing it — not because it expresses a view in contrast to that held by our nation's leaders and high-ranking military officials, but because our soldiers over here are already unhappy about the optimistic, carefree attitude of the people at home toward the war.

So one hesitates to write anything that will encourage that attitude, since greater effort is needed right now.

The best military authorities with whom I have talked take the view that the European war probably will not end before next spring. Most of them seem sincere about it. Some may be resorting to professional conservatism.

The run-of-the-mill army officers seem to be fairly evenly divided between the this-fall school and the next-spring-or-summer school.

As a matter of personal opinion, I confidently expect that the European phase of the war will end sooner, rather than later. It seems to me that if sheer military might has not defeated Germany by late fall, there is a good chance that she will have been overpowered through lack of materiel with which to fight war on three fronts — the inability will be directly traceable to Allied air superiority, applied to Germany's factories and to the transportation routes which supply her armies.

Women in Eulmont, France, do their laundry in a public tub in the middle of the village.

July 25, 1944
SOMEWHERE IN ENGLAND

MY FIRST COPY of The World-Herald arrived and it was almost like seeing another friend. Tenderly I carried it to the hotel room, then regretfully stuck it in my foot locker, because I had to leave right away on a hurry-up trip to an air base, and couldn't take a chance on losing it until it had been carefully read.

It was a Sunday World-Herald, with 70 pages. After reading four-page English newspapers for several weeks (on Sunday they're somewhat larger) it seemed mammoth in size. And it had exactly the sort of map for which I had been looking . . . a colored full-page map of western France.

July 26, 1944
SOMEWHERE IN NORMANDY

ONCE DOWN ON the ground, the traveler could see what seemed to be two separate worlds in one corner of France.

One was the pathetic world of the Normandy people, who first had been crushed under the Nazi heel, then forced to cower as the mighty war machine rolled over their farms and homes.

The second was the bustling, fast-growing military world which had been superimposed upon the Norman world. The immensity of that military base and the thoroughness with which the job is being done serves notice of the determined manner in which the war is going to be pressed. It's hard to believe the Germans can match what is being done here.

Just to see the French people is enough to make you feel sorry for them.

True, they do seem well enough fed, but the sagging appearance of the older people seems to tell of bewilderment and despair. They are so drab in appearance, and the whole atmosphere seems to bespeak poverty and lack of things that we have come to regard as necessities.

But you keep telling yourself that the French peasant never pretended to be well-dressed and has always been poor and frugal.

Cannons, rifles, machine guns and bombs have left a heavy mark on French homes and other buildings. Everywhere you see workers stolidly, mechanically "digging out" of the rubbish. The process is about the same as when we in Nebraska dig out after a severe flood or tornado.

Aug. 1, 1944
SOMEWHERE IN ENGLAND

AFTER HIS OWN experiences on D-Day, Cpl. Lawrence E. Meade of South Sioux City, Neb., thinks he knows how a fly might feel if it accidentally landed on a bull's eye of a rifle target.

Meade was gunner on the solitary tank which managed to get ashore in the first "wave" at one of the principal beaches. It landed at 6:20 a.m.

"For 20 minutes, the five men on my tank were the only men on shore there," he said. "We traveled up and down the beach as fast as we could go, our single 75 mm gun exchanging shots with a whole flock of enemy guns. They hit us many times. Fortunately, they were firing high explosive shells instead of armor-piercing shells or we would have been done for. I fired 170 rounds of ammunition.

"After we had been there about 20 minutes, which seemed like 10 hours, the foot soldiers began coming in. At first, almost all of them were mowed down."

Meade's tank, together with two others, had been aboard a Landing Craft Tank. Other LCTs were supposed to have beached at intervals of 560 yards but got lost. The two other tanks on board were hit and put out of commission as they rolled off.

"When we first got to shore, we didn't see anyone," Meade recalled. "It certainly didn't look like an invasion."

But by 11 o'clock, the battle had moved on away from the beach, Meade said. He and the others in his crew got out onto the beach. That was a mistake, for a German mortar crew landed a shot right in the middle of a group of nine men. Of his crew, only the ammunition loader escaped injury. Meade received five shrapnel fragments in the right leg and knee.

He believes he was in the first group of wounded to be brought back to England. At 5 p.m., 14 of them were loaded aboard an English ship, and they landed at an English port 12 hours later.

Aug. 3, 1944
SOMEWHERE IN ENGLAND

IT HAD BEEN another raid on Munich, and once more the ground officers and ground crews were "sweating it out" as the arrival time for the Flying Fortresses approached. Two Nebraskans were on this raid, Lt. Albert H. Grinsted of Lincoln, bombardier, and Tech. Sgt. James Schafer of Nehawka, radio man and gunner. This time the planes straggled in. They had had a bad, bad time of it. The cloudy overcast continued all the way to Munich. They climbed to 30,000 feet and still couldn't get out of it. Some found their target, others went far beyond it. They came home one by one, and would have been "sitting ducks" for fighter planes if the Germans had made a spirited attack. Some of the U.S. planes ran out of gas and "ditched" on occupied territory and in the Channel. Others barely reached British bases.

One bullet pierced the propeller on the No. 3 motor of the Nebraskans' plane, and the No. 1 prop also was hit, but there was no interference with the plane's operation. The vertical fin was hit, as well as several other portions of the plane. The ship straggled home by itself, and Schafer was still breathing, thanks to the protective clouds, when I saw him in the interrogation room a few minutes later.

"The grace of God was with us," he said. "When He created clouds, that was one of the best things He ever did. If it hadn't been for clouds, we wouldn't have made it."

Lt. Grinsted had found this flight to Munich somewhat tame compared to others to Leipzig and Berlin.

"We didn't see any enemy planes," he said, "although the boys on the ground were pretty sharp with their flak. They were shooting at us all the way along, and we took a lot of evasive action.

"You know, I've come to the conclusion that your own fighter planes in the sky provide the prettiest sight one could ever see — even prettier than a malted milk."

> *"The grace of God was with us. When He created clouds, that was one of the best things He ever did. If it hadn't been for clouds, we wouldn't have made it."*
>
> — TECH. SGT. JAMES SCHAFER
>   OF NEHAWKA

THE BULLET HOLE in the propeller is courtesy of a German fighter plane. Lt. Albert H. Grinsted, left, of Lincoln and Tech. Sgt. James Schafer of Nehawka, Neb., counted their blessings after they landed safely.

MIDLANDERS GETTING TOGETHER, seated from left, are Lt. Caroline Anderson of Denison, Iowa; Lt. Dorothy Salak and Lt. Lucille M. Johnson of Sioux City, Iowa; Capt. Harold M. Bryant of Falls City, Neb.; Staff Sgt. Jim Skahill of Imogene, Iowa; and Lt. Col. Robert L. Sands of Omaha. Standing from left are Cpl. Gerald Dewey of Lincoln; Sgt. Marion Talbott of Winner, S.D.; Sgt. John Keane of Omaha; and Sgt. H.C. Alterkruse of Glenwood, Iowa.

A party for servicemen in England

Aug. 3, 1944
LONDON

THE LADS FROM Gordon met other soldiers from Ainsworth and Hay Springs, and boys from Omaha happily greeted friends and former schoolmates, whom in some instances they hadn't seen for years.

That was the chief function of a party that The World-Herald, in cooperation with the American Red Cross, sponsored at the Moslyn Club in London for servicemen and women of Nebraska and western Iowa.

With the Americans in England, the No. 1 hobby is to find someone you know, or someone who knows someone you know. That's exactly why this party was planned, and apparently it worked out that way. Few were those who failed to find someone from their part of the state. And many met hometown people. For instance, there were about a half-dozen soldiers and sailors from the Blair area alone.

Letter published in The World-Herald

WE WISH TO EXPRESS our thanks for the wonderful thrill we received at seeing pictures of our son, Staff Sgt. K.A. Holcomb, taken at the party. Our boy left home in January 1941 and has never been home since. Today I received a letter from him, so I will quote from it:

"I got to London for the party that was given for the Nebraska boys. Had a 48-hour pass and it was the first real vacation I have had since I joined the Army. We had a nice dinner and there was the usual speeches. In all, it was a good go and I am glad that I was able to be there. London being out of bounds, we thought at first that we wouldn't be able to get passes. The quota of passes was also filled by the (commanding officer), and the engineering officer fixed us up. We actually owe them our thanks for being able to go."

Mr. and Mrs. K. Holcomb

Aug. 4, 1944
SOMEWHERE IN ENGLAND

IVAN RAYMOND HERSHNER JR. of Lincoln was working toward his Ph.D. in mathematics at Harvard University. Now he's a captain in the paratroopers.

Hershner says he went "from combatant to noncombatant in one easy jump." It's true that he broke his right leg in the jump. But judge for yourself whether it made him a noncombatant. Here's his story:

"We jumped at 56 minutes after midnight, preceding H-hour.

"It was the easiest jump I ever made, except that I thrashed through a tree, and it threw me off balance to the extent that I landed improperly and broke my leg.

"I gave the leg a shot of novocaine, and we started off. Pretty soon we came to a dugout which, in the dark, I took to be a German machine gun nest. I told my first sergeant to toss a hand grenade into the dugout. He threw it right inside, but there was no explosion. Then we remembered why. Before leaving England, we had taped the handles of all the grenades so there wouldn't be any explosions on board the plane, and he had forgotten to remove the tape.

"After the grenade rolled in, we heard chattering at the dugout. It developed that the place was occupied by a French family, four children and their parents. We went into the place, and I can still picture the sergeant standing there, moving his lips and whispering, 'You lucky people, you lucky, lucky people!'

"On my map the Frenchman showed us where we were — which was about four miles from where we were supposed to have been — and he also showed us where our objectives were. As a result of his help, I think we were the first company to reach its objectives. And because that grenade handle was taped, first to accomplish its mission.

"Most of our men had landed in an area flooded by the Germans. They took their knives and cut off chutes and all of their other equipment except rifles and ammunition. That left us without any heavy weapons, the stuff needed for other objectives.

"But we got another break. We captured a German arsenal, and outfitted ourselves with German mortars and machine guns. But our men had to be taught how to use that equipment. So on D-Day we held a special school on the operation of German armament. I doubt if anyone else held training classes on D-Day.

"That evening for dinner we had wine and fried chicken. The wine we purchased from a store, the chicken from a farmer.

"On D-Day plus one we captured a German cavalry unit. There were about 30 horses in it. We took 12 of them and three carts. So on D-Day plus one, our company was more highly 'mechanized' than it had ever been before. Because of my fractured leg, I rode one of the horses — a beautiful brown animal. It was my transportation until late on D-Day plus two (third day of the invasion), when my battalion commander ordered that we evacuate."

Despite the present serious injury, he expects to report for duty within a comparatively few weeks. The fact that he walked five miles on the injured member those first few hours delayed recovery some, but doctors say he will have a good leg anyway.

IN ENGLAND, WAITING TO SHIP OUT

THIS CROP WAS ANKLE HIGH on the Fourth of July. Under the direction of a British soldier, left, Omaha men helped gather seaweed — for use in making penicillin — from St. Ives Harbor on July 4, 1944. The shirtless Omahans, from left, are Capt. Richard Melcher, Sgt. Kenneth C. Van Dyke, Staff Sgt. Joe Sendroski, Pfc. William Wagoner and Sgt. Damon Buckley.

GLOUCESTER CATHEDRAL provided the backdrop for Walter Schroeder of Omaha, attached to the judge advocate general's office in England.

NEBRASKA OFFICERS were received at tea at a home in Penzance. Capt. L.S. McCown of Beatrice (second from left) and Capt. L.G. Wilson of Omaha (fourth from left) had just completed drills.

TWO NEBRASKA GIRLS are among the two dozen flight nurses who on each flyable day bring hundreds of wounded soldiers across the English Channel to England from France.

The nurses are Lt. Lucille Chaloupka of Omaha and Lt. Jane Orme, whose parents recently moved to Nebraska City.

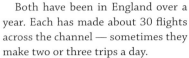

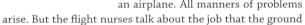

LT. LUCILLE CHALOUPKA

Both have been in England over a year. Each has made about 30 flights across the channel — sometimes they make two or three trips a day.

The pilots who fly with these nurses think the girls have difficult jobs. On each trip they have from 24 to 28 wounded, some of whom are likely to be in critical condition, and most of whom never before have been in an airplane. All manners of problems arise. But the flight nurses talk about the job that the ground nurses in France are doing.

"I like to fly," said Lt. Orme, "but if I could be with those ground nurses I would feel I really was doing something. I spent one night with them. Everyone else has foxholes, but the nurses don't bother about them. They say they are busy so much of the time that foxholes wouldn't be much good to them. So they just sleep in their tents."

Only yesterday, a piece of shrapnel or a bullet tore a hole in the ship in which Lt. Orme was flying.

Wounded Germans often are brought back aboard the C-47 planes. The nurses say the American patients dislike the Germans, so occasionally they have trouble restraining them. And the Yanks warn the nurses to keep an eye on the Nazis for fear that they many try some trick that will send the whole plane crashing.

"Some German officers are pretty arrogant," said Lt. Chaloupka. "They go through the motions of drawing away if we start to do anything for them. There's nothing shabby about the German officer. He's well-dressed, in uniform of good material, and wears good boots.

"The German enlisted man is a good patient, unless a German officer starts giving him orders. If an officer tells him to stick his head in the mud, he'll do it. I could swear that one of our German patients was no more than 14 years old."

THIS IS ANOTHER one of those purely personal pieces.

Most of my efforts lately have centered on the business of getting permission to go with the ground forces in France, so I haven't gleaned much to write about.

However, it now appears that I can certainly return to France on Friday, and should be able to reach our fighting Nebraska infantry units within hours after landing. This time the trip will be by boat.

War correspondents are permitted to go to France on a rotation basis, because there are not sufficient facilities for all. Since I was a comparatively latecomer, my name was far down on the list.

Fighter pilots are the frat boys of the service

Aug. 20, 1944
AT AN 8TH AIR FORCE THUNDERBOLT BASE IN ENGLAND

THE PAST 48 HOURS I have spent at this fighter base to learn how our fighter pilots operate and how they feel about their work.

This has been my most exciting visit to any air base. It's a fast-moving business. The reporter can listen in as operations officers brief Thunderbolt pilots on the mission they are about to fly. An hour or so later, in the operations office, he can clamp on a pair of headphones and listen to the fighters as they locate targets and deploy their planes to "beat up" marshalling yards, bridges, trains and trucks.

Second Lt. Richard W. Gillette of Norfolk is among the pilots who operate from this base. Maj. Ernest J. White of Falls City is a squadron commander.

To me the most interesting part of the experience here was to listen in as pilots were interrogated after their mission. They look much like a bunch of boys in a fraternity home.

When they begin their reports, there is a tendency for everyone to talk at once. Each has a little bit different version of what happened. The interrogating officer winnows out the meat and first gets facts on which there is general agreement, mainly the score sheet on achievements of the mission. Then he goes after details which have been observed by individual pilots.

Dive-bombing and strafing is a little bit dull for Gillette, so wife Maxine brightens it up by sending the "Terry and the Pirates" comic strip from The World-Herald each day. At 26, Gillette has been over here several months and has completed approximately half of the combat time required for a tour of duty. Only three times has he seen the Luftwaffe in the air.

"On my very first mission, an ME-109 jumped me," he said. "Tracers were going past my nose. The German pilot was diving, and he went past me in a flash, as I was turning in to him. Another pilot got him.

"One day we saw a flight of about 75 to 100 German planes. Our squadron got five, while the entire group got 15. We didn't lose a plane.

"The Luftwaffe isn't a very important threat anymore, generally speaking. It's true that it can put up a flock of planes now and then. And the planes are good. But experience level of the pilots is very low. They are not eager to fight, while our boys are. Three or four of our pilots wouldn't hesitate to tackle 15 or 20 of them — and when one of them is shot down, the rest turn tail and go home. However, I don't mean to imply that fighting Germans is as easy as that. They never should be underrated."

White has commanded a Thunderbolt squadron since April. His score sheet includes two ME-109s, one FW 190 and one locomotive. He has the Air Medal and Distinguished Flying Cross, and numerous oak leaf clusters.

In college before the war, White played football for Nebraska with Sam Francis and Lloyd Cardwell. Later at West Point, he won honorable mention on several All-American teams.

ABOVE, MAJ. ERNEST J. WHITE played football at Nebraska with Sam Francis and Lloyd Cardwell.

AT LEFT, SECOND LT. RICHARD W. GILLETTE said his wife sent him comic strips to brighten his dull days.

Aug. 25, 1944
AT THE GATEWAY TO PARIS

TWO NEBRASKANS, one an Omahan, are among a U.S. Army force which is poised for the final dash to Paris, hoping to be the first American units to enter the French capital.

The Nebraskans are Cpl. William H. Hines, whose wife, Dorothy, lives in Omaha, and Sgt. Arthur H. "Red" Malmberg of Allen.

Hines formerly was district manager for Walgreens drugstores in Omaha.

Since the start of the invasion, both have been working on the Normandy beaches. Their outfits suddenly were selected to go to Paris, and they have been on the move ever since. Both were enthusiastic over the prospects of getting into Paris.

"It will be a great experience," said Hines. "I expect to see a lot more than I have until now."

"I'm tickled," Malmberg said. "I've been wanting to go for some time and didn't expect to get the opportunity."

But most eager are the war correspondents who have gathered. Everyone from Ernie Pyle on down is champing at the bit to write about the fall of Paris.

PARISIANS' JOY IS WRITTEN ON THEIR FACES as they welcome American troops rolling into their city. Some threw flowers and confetti, while others wept.

The liberation of Paris

Aug. 27, 1944

PARIS

TO GO INTO Paris a few hours after the entry of the first column of allied troops was an unforgettable, soul-thrilling experience.

With two other correspondents and a jeep driver, I drove half the distance from the southern gate to the Seine River and the heart of the city.

We were stopped by the word that the Germans were just beyond. We believe we penetrated as far as any Americans had gone.

The greatest experience for us happened after we entered the Port d'Orleans and traveled down the tree-lined Avenue Du Maine, where thousands upon thousands of Parisians were gathered, looking for someone to welcome.

They shouted. They waved. They seized our hands. They kissed us. They offered wine by the bottle and the glass.

They threw flowers and confetti at us.

Some wept.

MEMBERS OF THE FRENCH RESISTANCE battled with German snipers during the early hours of the liberation of Paris. One young man said he had killed six Germans and another had killed five.

FRENCH CITIZENS SHAVE THE HEADS of two women, center foreground, who were accused of collaborating with the Germans. The pair had been distraught but "brightened up for the picture," Lawrence Youngman reported.

Wherever the jeep stopped, we were almost mobbed. They climbed all over it. Our hands were shaken until our arms were sore.

As the jeep moved along, the throngs crowded into the street and held out their hands to touch our hands. It was like running a stick along a picket fence.

"*Vive le Americain!*" "*Salut!*" "*Merci!*"

Those were the cries.

And now and then someone said "Greetings!" in English.

Our first evening in Paris was exactly like living in a Hollywood super-spectacle.

From no other sources would one expect anything so fantastic and seemingly so unreal. It seemed a combination of Omaha's Golden Spike days, a revolution in Central America and a film story of the Apaches in Paris.

The joyous crowds thronged onto the streets in almost complete disregard of the cops-and-robbers fighting that still swirled about them.

Several times as we were talking to people a fusillade of rifle and machine gun fire broke out, and no one seemed much concerned about it because it was on the other side of the building. But if shooting broke out in an open street, it cleared the area like magic.

FRENCH YOUTHS FIND A PERCH to watch as Gen. Charles de Gaulle travels down the Avenue des Champs Élysées.

FRENCH CITIZENS TOOK OUT THEIR FURY on countrymen who had collaborated with the Germans. At right, a crowd marches an accused group of women through the streets of Maxéville.

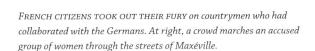

On the first morning in Paris I stepped out on the balcony of my hotel room and looked down on a symbolic scene.

On the front curb was an ashcan filled with large photographs of Hitler, Goering and Goebbels, and of famous planes of the Luftwaffe. Neighborhood residents were taking the picture frames and throwing the photographs back into the ashcan.

It was the Hotel United States, and it had been used as a headquarters for the Gestapo. An employee of the hotel said many French men and women had been tortured in the building. The women were given the cold-bath treatment, in wintertime, until they were ready to say anything, he said, and the men were beaten with a special type of whip that was particularly cruel.

History will seldom see a more spectacular display of sheer, cool courage than that given by Gen. Charles de Gaulle when he made that triumphal march through the heart of the city, only a few hours after its liberation, and while hostile gunmen were everywhere. He must have felt that every second might be his last.

Along the route were thousands of windows from which he might have been shot. It was widely announced that he would be in the procession. Why the fascists didn't have an assassin posted in every block will always be a mystery to me.

Newsmen who were with de Gaulle in Notre Dame Cathedral said that he didn't bat an eye or deviate one jot from his schedule while the shooting was going on in the cathedral. One British officer who was there with cameramen said: "For my part, he can now be king of France if he wants."

A PICTURE OF HITLER is defaced by an angry Frenchman.

ABOVE, AMERICAN CORRESPONDENTS await word that they can go into Paris. The bald man in the center is Pulitzer Prize-winning newsman Ernie Pyle.

GEN. CHARLES DE GAULLE, commander of the Free French Forces, addresses his countrymen in Paris as German sniper fire rings out nearby.

Huge crowds gathered along the Champs Élysées to cheer Gen. Charles de Gaulle as he returned to Paris.

THE GERMANS PUMMELED the French village of Robert Espagne before they retreated.

FIFTY WOODEN CROSSES mark the mass grave of villagers gunned down by the Germans.

THE CHARRED TIMBERS of a burned home formed a 51st cross in the village of Robert Espagne.

Aug. 28, 1944
WITH THE THIRD ARMY IN FRANCE

FIRST LT. GAYLEN L. CURRY of Tecumseh, Neb., was the first Allied pilot to land in Paris.

Lt. Curry landed his Cub plane at Issy-les-Moulineaux airport, 300 yards from the Seine.

"First I crossed the field at about 20 miles an hour to make sure there were no mines. Then I landed on the cinder runway," he said.

"No one was in sight, but some shots were fired. I waved a white handkerchief.

"A head popped up from behind a concrete wall. A voice asked, 'Boche?' (A derogatory term for Germans.)

"I said no, and the head dropped down, then popped up again and the voice inquired, 'British'?

"I said, 'No, American.'

"In no time, hundreds of people were around the plane. They kissed me. They offered me champagne. One woman said, 'We are so grateful to you for saving us.' "

Spectators said a plane with Curry's number flew through and under the Eiffel Tower. Curry would neither confirm nor deny the report.

Sept. 14, 1944
WITH A MIDWESTERN REGIMENT IN FRANCE

WITH MY OWN EYES I witnessed today evidence of atrocities that will stand against the German army for a long time to come.

An English-speaking French doctor told me the story as we stood beside the flower-covered grave where many mourners were lingering.

I saw a single common grave in which had been buried 50 Frenchmen who were taken from their homes and mowed down by German machine guns.

I saw three villages which, before the combat line came close to them, had been laid waste, building by building, home by home, by German hand grenade, bomb and torch.

It all happened Aug. 29, he said. The Nazis said that eight or nine Germans had been killed by the French, and the Nazis loosed their malice and vengeance on four villages which stood at the edge of the Brule forest.

Eighty-two Frenchmen were slain at Robert Espagne, and another Frenchman was shot in the forest.

The Germans took 50 more, lined them up across the tracks from the little railroad station, and three machine guns mowed them down. Now 50 simple wooden crosses, each with a metal name plate, line the row.

Rising above the smaller crosses is a larger one of charred and blackened timbers from one of the burned homes.

I also visited Beurey and Couvonges, which also were laid waste.

Sept. 14, 1944
WITH A MIDWESTERN REGIMENT IN FRANCE

SOME SOLDIERS CLAIM that the infantrymen don't have much confidence in the marksmanship of the artillerymen, but ... Tech. Sgt. Bill Harris of Gering, Neb., leader of an intelligence and reconnaissance party, directed artillery fire of guns which were more than five miles away toward a target approximately 60 feet from where Harris and three of his men were standing.

"That's something like playing the stooge in one of those vaudeville acts where the performer shoots the cigarette out of the stooge's mouth," Harris said.

Sept. 16, 1944
WITH A MIDWESTERN REGIMENT IN FRANCE

THOUGH A DENTAL OFFICER and therefore a noncombatant, Maj. Floyd Paynter of Omaha has a receipt to show that he and Cpl. Bill Knapp of Broken Bow, Neb., captured four Germans.

"We were at a farmhouse to get tomatoes and eggs," Paynter related, "when some French people came running up to report that there were Germans in the woods nearby. Cpl. Knapp headed into the woods right away. He saw a German soldier drop behind a log, and he fired two shots above the man.

"The German came running out, dropped on his knees and begged Knapp not to shoot him. I frisked him for weapons, then asked him if there were any more Germans. He said, 'Nein, nein.' Knapp jabbed his rifle into the man's stomach, and he changed his tune and said others were in there. So I ordered him to tell them to come on out. He shouted at the top of his voice, and we looked up to see three others marching out with their hands up."

When the prisoners were delivered to the proper place, Paynter received a receipt, and he had each of the four Germans sign it.

THE CANNON COMPANY of the 134th Infantry rests up for its next round of action under the watchful eye of Capt. L.D. Asher, left, of Scottsbluff, Neb.

Military police 1st Lt. John R. Scalzo of Omaha helps direct traffic at Carentan, just north of St. Lo in Normandy.

The battle of St. Lo

Sept. 17, 1944

ST. LO (REPORT DELAYED BY MILITARY CENSORS)

THE 134TH INFANTRY REGIMENT from the Nebraska National Guard landed at Omaha Beach on July 5, 1944. Nine days later, Col. Butler B. Miltonberger received orders for the Nebraskans' first combat mission: Attack Hill 122.

By noon on July 15, the battalion had advanced 2,100 yards, but the cost was high, especially for Beatrice, Neb. — six of its citizen-soldiers were killed. (In all, 10 Beatrice men died and 20 were wounded in the four days of combat.)

By 8:30 p.m., two companies reached the base of the hill, and the 134th controlled it by 7:30 a.m. July 16. The regiment suffered 792 casualties.

Early July 18, the rout of the Germans by the 134th was under way. By 9 a.m., members of the regiment's L Company reached the outskirts of the city. The regiment was ordered, however, to allow the rested 29th Division to claim St. Lo's liberation.

(Miltonberger was bitter until his death in 1977 that his men did not get credit for liberating St. Lo, veterans of his unit said. In 2009, St. Lo honored Lt. Col. Alfred Thomsen of Omaha, who died during the battle, and the 35th Division, which included the Nebraska regiment. The 134th, whose rallying cry was "All Hell Can't Stop Us," finally got its due.)

St. Lo

TWENTY MILES INLAND FROM OMAHA BEACH WAS THE CITY OF ST. LO, A GERMAN HEADQUARTERS AND TRANSPORTATION AND COMMUNICATION HUB, WHERE THE MOST HEAVILY DEFENDED POSITION WAS HILL 122.

Sept. 17, 1944
SOMEWHERE IN FRANCE

THE 134TH INFANTRY has set for Nebraska a new standard for courage and gallantry and determination and military efficiency and leadership.

Supreme headquarters, Allied European forces, has already acclaimed the "brilliant record" made by the 134th in the fall of St. Lo and the fighting in that area.

The Germans staked their control of France on their ability to hold a line that would keep our troops cooped up in Normandy.

The regiment spearheaded the attack that threw the Germans out of St. Lo, punched and smashed through subsequent strong defensive positions and played a vital role in setting the stage for the breakthrough which has resulted in the liberation of most of France.

The people back home already know that the regiment paid a heavy price in casualties. But perhaps they will find some consolation in the realization that the heroism and sacrifices of those men have saved the lives of countless other soldiers and materially hastened the progress of the war.

The regiment, which is commanded by Col. Butler B. Miltonberger of North Platte, arrived in France on July 5. On July 8, the 2nd Battalion was ordered to relieve a holding unit, and it stayed in the line till July 11.

Two days later, the 3rd Battalion was ordered to relieve another unit in the line north of St. Lo. This relief took place July 14, followed by the order from division headquarters that the regiment was to attack in the direction of St. Lo the next day.

Prior to the arrival of the 134th, a number of attacks had been made against the Germans there, but without success against the strong defense.

The entire advance by the 134th required driving the enemy back from hedgerow to hedgerow. Our units were constantly subjected to heavy mortar, artillery and small arms fire. During the day, 87 prisoners were taken.

"I've never again seen the debris of battle that existed after we had smashed through the first day," said Col. Miltonberger. "We saw as many as 15 dead Germans in a heap. They had good fixed defenses, but our men plowed right on through and murdered them. A division staff officer who surveyed the scene later said it was the most sobering thing he had ever seen."

Acts of heroism by both enlisted men and officers that day would fill a good-sized volume.

Four officers fell at the extreme "high-water mark" reached by the battalion. They were going after three enemy machine guns. The next morning their bodies were found at the farthest point reached before the line receded to dig in for the night.

Back at the ammunition depot, it was reported that the 134th had used more ammunition in a single day than any two divisions had used in a single day prior to that date.

AS THE GERMANS ARE PUSHED OUT OF FRANCE …

French schoolchildren at Maxéville celebrate the end of German rule with flags supporting the Allies and a defaced poster of Adolf Hitler.

A French family of five and their dog leave the Moselle valley after fighting intensified.

The Germans shelled villages before retreating from the Bar-Le-Duc area east of Paris.

REPORT ON AN EARLIER ACTION
WITH THE 134TH INFANTRY IN FRANCE

THIS IS ABOUT eight days when the 134th stood in St. Lo "with German artillery looking down our throats" and took what the Nazis dished out.

After capture of the town, the regiment's assignment was to defend and hold it.

As a holding position, it was about as disagreeable a place as one would want to see. The town lies in a saucerlike depression. To the south, only 1,200 to 1,500 yards away, the Germans had ranged their artillery and mortar weapons on the rim of that saucer. It was a shooting gallery — the Germans were standing on the counter — and the 134th was the target.

From the standpoint of the regiment, it would have been much better to charge on up the hill, seize the rim and hold there. But the high command was not yet ready for that. So the 134th stood and took it from the night of July 19, when it occupied the town, until the orders came to move on July 28. All that time, a few Germans had the temerity to remain in some buildings at the southern edge of the town.

St. Lo took a severe pounding before our troops entered. But before the 134th Infantry left, it had lost all semblance of a city.

It was scarcely possible to negotiate the streets on foot. Any thought of using vehicles was out of the question until a battalion of engineers was sent in and, under infantry protection, worked 24 hours under fire to clear a route through the ghost city.

Aside from the soldiers, there was not even a stray cat in the place.

THE 134TH INFANTRY's regimental band on parade in Penzance, England.

NEBRASKANS IN THE DRUM CORPS, from left, Cpl. Robert A. Wirth of Nebraska City, Pfc. Elmer Papke of Firth, Pfc. Clifford A. Bartle of Omaha, Cpl. Clifford Geiken of Gothenburg and Pfc. Charles E. Edgar of Gering.

Sept. 21, 1944
WITH THE 134TH INFANTRY IN FRANCE

STANDING IN THE SQUARE of a little French village, it was a spine-tingling experience to hear the 134th regimental band suddenly swing out with its official marching song, "There Is No Place Like Nebraska."

And I feel certain that many of the soldiers who marched into the little square to that tune must have whispered an "Amen" to that theme.

The occasion was the awarding of medals to four members of their regiment, in recognition of their exceptionally meritorious conduct while the regiment was in action.

MEDICAL OFFICERS Capt. E.L. Feld, left, of Manchester, Iowa, and Maj. Robert H. Townley of Kenesaw, Neb., arrive in a small French village near the front.

Sept. 22, 1944
WITH THE 134TH INFANTRY IN FRANCE

A JEEP AND DRIVER have been assigned to the use of The World-Herald correspondent.

The driver is a good-looking lad, Pfc. Johnny Robidoux of Falls City, member of a famous family.

He is a great-grandson of the Iowa Chief White Cloud, who was 100 years old when he died in 1940 at the White Cloud reservation just across the line in Kansas.

Sept. 23, 1944
WITH GEN. PATTON'S THIRD ARMY

A GERMAN RESISTANCE pocket force that has been giving the Third Army some of its toughest resistance was forced to retreat, then was annihilated.

A Nebraska officer said forces approximately a regiment in strength were driven off a wooded hill and forced to attempt a daylight retreat. Artillery and Thunderbolt fighters then had a field day, cutting them to pieces.

Maj. Robert H. Townley of Kenesaw, Neb., a medical officer, saw the show from a Cub liaison plane.

"I've seen lots of carnage since Normandy," he said, "but nothing to compare with this. First our artillery stopped the column. Then our planes, returning time and again, like terriers after rats, spent two hours cutting it to pieces. The planes dropped fire bombs, and repeatedly dived low in strafing attacks. The Germans fled to trees and a stone quarry, but our planes kept after them and rubbed them out."

A PROUD MOMENT for the 134th Infantry Regiment, which liberated Nancy, France. The mayor of Nancy, left, prepares to honor Col. Butler B. Miltonberger, second from left, for the actions of his unit, which was made up largely of Nebraskans.

Nancy

Nebraskans free city of Nancy

Sept. 25, 1944
WITH THE 134TH INFANTRY IN EASTERN FRANCE

IT WAS THE 134TH INFANTRY — Nebraska's own — which liberated Nancy, France's fourth-largest city, often called "Little Paris."

The regiment, commanded by Col. Butler B. Miltonberger of North Platte, audaciously crossed the Meurthe River and seized a vital bridgehead before the Germans realized what was happening.

"After earlier intensive fighting along the Moselle, we followed the retreating Germans into Nancy," said Col. Miltonberger.

"The people of the city were deliriously happy. We received an ovation such as has been accorded few American soldiers.

"It was Paris all over again, even to the street fighting between the Free French and the collaborationists."

Without awaiting reinforcements, the 1st Battalion under Lt. Col. Alford C. Boatsman of Beatrice and the 3rd Battalion under Warren C. Wood of Gering made the Meurthe crossings.

Wood and his entire battalion waded the river where it was shoulder-deep, while the Germans kept up a fairly heavy machine gun fire.

Members of one of Col. Boatsman's platoons, carrying assault boats, rushed down to the embankment, threw their craft onto the water and furiously paddled across the stream before the surprised Germans got their artillery adjusted.

The platoon held easily the ground thus gained. A few assault boats were hit on the trip back, but enough were left intact for the remainder of the battalion to cross in them when darkness fell.

ENGINEERS BUILT a pontoon bridge across the Meurthe River to aid the 134th Infantry's operation at Nancy.

Undoubtedly the greatest welcome to American troops in this war was at Paris. But second best reportedly was at Nancy.

Soldiers who had been acclaimed as heroes all the way from Cherbourg said they had experienced no welcome to compare with this one.

"It was the biggest welcome we got anyplace," said Sgt. Sammy Wolk of Omaha.

"We were almost mobbed. The people threw flowers at us and offered us champagne. Somehow a lot of lipstick got on our cheeks."

Master Sgt. Elmer L. Shearer of North Platte related how as he and a friend walked around a block in the business district, glasses and bottles of liquor were proffered them from cafe windows.

"We would have been in bad shape if we had taken everything offered us in that one short walk."

A ROW OF CHAMPAGNE GLASSES awaits the celebrants at a ceremony honoring the 134th Infantry Regiment at the Hotel de Ville in Nancy, France.

THIRD BATTALION COMMANDER Lt. Col. Warren C. Wood, left, of Gering and his executive officer, Maj. Harlan Heffelfinger of Beatrice.

SMOKE RISES FROM ACROSS THE MOSELLE RIVER, as American B-26 bombers target retreating German forces. Lawrence Youngman reported that the 134th Regiment covered about 130 miles across eastern France in six days.

Sept. 25, 1944
WITH THE 134TH INFANTRY IN EASTERN FRANCE

IT'S SUNDAY MORNING. The bells in the steeple that rises above a flat little French village are pealing loudly, almost violently.

But the bells can't compete with the overriding noises of warfare. They are hopelessly outnoised by the heavy drone of the glistening formations of American bombers overhead, and the dull, rumbling roar of the bombs that are already being dropped on the woods and strongholds held by the enemy a few miles away. But mostly they are out-dinned by the sharp reverberating crack of our own artillery, which is pouring out a heavy barrage.

The artillery reports remind me of the crackling lightning bursts at home that seem so near that you involuntarily look out the window to see what was hit.

Adding an incongruous touch to the whole scene are the little Cub planes — spotters for our artillery — which circle overhead nonchalantly as though they were back home.

Some of the soldiers are just returning from church. Capt. Joseph H. Friedel of Omaha reports that there were complications, since the priest speaks no English, and the soldiers no French.

However, a solution was discovered. Some bilinguist wrote out a list of a dozen sins in English — and opposite them the French translations. The soldiers pointed to the particular items on the list — and the padre said, "Oui."

Oct. 11, 1944
WITH THE 134TH INFANTRY IN EASTERN FRANCE

HIS 10 SISTERS and six brothers should be proud of Frank F. Koziol of Omaha, whom they may now address as "lieutenant."

The Omahan has earned a battlefield commission because of his meritorious conduct at St. Lo and elsewhere. He belongs to K Company of the 134th Infantry Regiment.

Koziol is the 10th of the children and next-to-youngest boy. The eldest brother, John, is also in France but they have not seen each other here.

The then-Sgt. Koziol was wounded in the index finger of the right hand at Mortain in August — he also got two small fragments in his leg, but they didn't count — when he was moving his platoon into a defensive position after the capture of a hill. He returned to active duty this week.

His family doesn't know about the promotion, because the injured finger kept him from writing.

NOTE TO READERS

SOME READERS MAY WONDER why these reports contain so much mention of sergeants and commissioned officers, and so little of privates and even corporals.

There's a simple answer: A large proportion of the Nebraskans who were the original members of the regiment have earned promotions during the almost four years that the regiment has been in service.

That is also true of the Nebraskans who were assigned to the regiment during the early days of selective service.

Now the replacements that come to the regiment are from all the states, so the proportion of Nebraskans among the newcomers is quite small.

— LAWRENCE YOUNGMAN, OCT. 13, 1944

NEBRASKANS MAKE THEIR WAY ACROSS EUROPE

CPL. MIKE KIELION *of Omaha takes in the scenery in Luxembourg. One resident said that 10 percent of the tiny nation's 300,000 citizens had been forced either into slavery or the German army.*

PVT. ROGER TIPTON, *left, of North Platte and Pvt. Elgin Wilkinson of Lincoln had their hair cut in what they called the "Osage roach," vowing not to give it up until Germany was defeated.*

CAPT. L.D. ASHER *(hands on knees) of Scottsbluff watches as propaganda leaflets are loaded into artillery shells to fire behind German lines.*

HAPPY SMILES FOR HONOREES, *from left: Capt. Francis Greenlief of Hastings, who received the Silver Star; Lt. Col. Warren C. Wood of Gering, who was promoted from major and received the Silver Star; 1st Lt. John Campbell of Chicago, who received the Silver Star; and Tech. Sgt. Jacob J. Sass of Bennington, who received the Bronze Star.*

ROWS OF CROSSES line the hillside in front of the "Hall of Bones" monument at Verdun.

Verdun

A visit to the battlefield of Verdun

Oct. 22, 1944

VERDUN, FRANCE

IT WAS NECESSARY to go to Verdun, so we took out a little time to see the World War I battlefields there.

An estimated half-million men died at Verdun in the battle some 28 years ago.

Today the battleground is one of the most, if not the most, "beaten up" areas of land on this Earth's surface.

One man told me that in the main battlefield the earth was "churned to a depth of 12 feet and turned over three times."

Though that statement is doubtless an exaggeration, it tells better than any words of mine what happened to that tortured piece of ground.

Seeing the evidence, still standing today, one is inclined to put some stock in that statement, exaggeration or not.

Here is the famous "Trench of Bayonets," here also the great "Hall of Bones" and many other monuments and relics of the other great war. Not a square yard is level — it is all shell-pitted. Only weeds and scrub trees grow there.

This war has seen nothing like what happened at Verdun, not even St. Lo. The latter was leveled, to be sure, but the action there lasted only a few days, while the battle of Verdun lasted 130 days beginning Feb. 1, 1916, and the area was never free of some fighting until the armistice.

It was at Verdun that Marshal Petain, then a hero of France, intoned the famous words: "They shall not pass." And "they" didn't.

The most impressive monument at Verdun is the "Ossuaire," or "Hall of Bones." It is as modernistic as Nebraska's State Capitol and looks something like it.

The most sobering impression came when I walked around to the back of the monument and looked through the "basement" windows. Some of the paint which originally obscured these windows has scaled off. If you have a flashlight, you can see that the basement is filled almost to the ceiling with the bones of men who died there.

Several times I paused to be thankful that, so far in this war at least, American troops have not had to pay the great price that other nations have forfeited in both this war and the last.

AMERICAN SOLDIERS VISIT *an old fort, Blenod, near Verdun. The fort was one of a number along the Moselle valley that were part of France's defensive Maginot Line.*

MEMBERS OF THE CANNON COMPANY *of the 134th Infantry Regiment play cards during a lull in the action in France.*

Oct. 24, 1944
WITH THE 134TH INFANTRY IN EASTERN FRANCE

NONE OF OUR SOLDIERS over here seems to want anyone's sympathy. But the fellow I could sympathize with the quickest is the replacement.

Talking with a couple of newly arrived Nebraskans — Pvt. Donald J. Leonard of Omaha and Pvt. Alfons A. Kalvelage of Elgin — I couldn't help but wonder how they could seem so cheerful.

By the very nature of his classification, the replacement is a cork on a storm-tossed sea. He fills the place made vacant by a battle casualty.

He's lucky if he knows where he is at the moment. He doesn't know where he is going, doesn't know when he will get there, doesn't know what he will do when he gets there, and probably won't know a soul when he gets there.

There's a strong probability that when he does reach the unit to which he is assigned, he will find it engaged in combat. The replacement pitches in with the others immediately. But he must be at a considerable handicap, because he isn't acquainted with the fellows on either side of him, doesn't know how much he can depend on them. He's not familiar with the voices of the men in charge of the unit and probably has had no chance to familiarize himself with the terrain or the general military situation.

That's the seamy side of the picture, of course. There's always the possibility that the individual may not be assigned a combat unit at all, or maybe he will go into a sector that will be quiet for days or weeks.

One great advantage for the man joining an experienced combat unit — he will be surrounded by a bunch of men who have themselves been through the mill, and can give him the best pointers available on how to keep his skin whole. They can wise him up in a way that no training camp in the States can do. He can benefit by their experience if he wants to — and don't ever doubt that he will want to.

A PAIR OF AMERICAN SOLDIERS give a German jeep a test ride.

U.S. SOLDIERS SHOW OFF a row of captured German vehicles. From left, Pfc. Paul Helmhout of Scottsbluff, Neb.; Cpl. Delwin Whitehead of Mason City, Neb.; unidentified; Staff Sgt. Kelly W. Clark of Omaha; Staff Sgt. Edward Buresh of Omaha; Staff Sgt. Cecil Agee of Windsor, Mo.; Master Sgt. Reuben Johnson of Omaha; and Sgt. Joe Bant of Omaha. On motorcycles are Sgt. Morris Crowley of Wymore, Neb., and Tech. Sgt. Howard Crane of Omaha.

Oct. 26, 1944
WITH THE 35TH DIVISION IN FRANCE

UNCOOPERATIVE AS HE IS in a general sort of way, Hitler in some instances has helped the American soldiers more than he would like to think. German supplies have been a great help and convenience to our soldiers.

The variety of items used by the German army probably is about as great as that used by our own.

Oftentimes an American soldier's mess will consist largely of "kraut" items — and on occasion that has included sauerkraut. Our men are using German gloves and boots, acetylene torches, shovels, kitchenware, mortar shells and many other items. It's almost impossible to name one item that we haven't taken from the Germans.

German equipment is pretty good on average, and oftentimes it's so handy. Besides, the men seem to take a certain satisfaction in pointing out that this or that is "kraut." And think what it saves the taxpayers.

NEBRASKANS OF THE 134TH INFANTRY with a captured German vehicle. From left, Pfc. Clyde Heldenbrand of Tryon, Sgt. Mac Dinkelman of Waco, Sgt. Dean Grass of Waco, Sgt. Kenneth Elmore of Bradshaw and Cpl. Floyd Miller of York.

Destroyed German trucks, tractors and guns line a road.

Oct. 30, 1944
WITH THE 134TH INFANTRY IN FRANCE

A SHARP DIP in the morale of the German enlisted soldier in this area has been evident during the past few weeks, according to Col. Butler B. Miltonberger, commander of the 134th Infantry.

"Of the last 100 prisoners taken, about 96 have admitted that Germany has already lost the war," Miltonberger said. "This is a markedly higher ratio than we noted even a month ago."

The average soldier is willing to surrender on very slight pretext. Some of the junior officers also are giving up now under conditions through which they could have kept on fighting a few weeks ago.

"A good many of the prisoners say that defeat for Germany must come very soon. Unfortunately, they are not the ones who make the decisions. To the contrary, they fight most viciously when ordered to do so. On this front, we don't see any prospect for an early end to the war."

A plea for war bonds

Nov. 12, 1944
WITH THE 134TH INFANTRY IN FRANCE

STRAIGHT FROM THE muddy, sodden, chilling foxholes of France comes the firm, compelling request that Nebraska buy the war bonds that will provide our fighting men with the tools that they must have to hew their way to victory.

The World-Herald today begins a series of letters from fighting men of Nebraska.

These men have fought, are fighting the tough battle in France. These are not "rear-echelon" soldiers, speaking from Paris or Cherbourg or some other place of comparative safety. None has better right than they to insist that Nebraskans buy all the war bonds they can.

Dear friends,

A LOT OF PEOPLE get the impression that the war is nearly over and that the buying of war bonds is no longer an important contribution to the war effort.

That is a mistaken impression, and therefore I will try to give a few reasons why those back home should continue buying them, rather than stop.

First of all, that war bond which Mr. or Mrs. America buys might very well be the other half of that round-trip ticket which his or her son, or maybe a neighbor, is looking for. Every man over here is looking forward to making that trip home.

Another good reason is that we who are fighting this war still need equipment, and plenty of it. We have had times here when we were forced to operate with one or two machines guns, in place of four or even eight. If those guns couldn't be replaced, how would we win the war and how would we get back home to a decent life once more?

When our guns are knocked out, new ones have to be purchased, and those can only be bought if you folks back home will continue to provide our government with the money to buy the new equipment, which we can never get too much of.

There are a lot of boys bleeding, suffering and dying over here. Your war bonds will save a lot of that life and spare a lot of that agony.

Please help us! Buy more war bonds!

Sincerely,

*Edward L. Supanchick (of North Platte)
Tech Sergeant, Company D, 134th
Infantry*

Edward L. Supanchick

GOOD TIMES IN PARIS for soldiers from the 134th Infantry Regiment.

Nov. 13, 1944
WITH THE 134TH INFANTRY IN FRANCE

THE MAGIC, the amazing, the unbelievable words here are: "Forty-eight-hour pass to Paris."

Shaved and bathed and all dressed up in freshly laundered clothing, 40 men and four officers of the 134th Infantry were still in the pinch-me-to-see-if-I'm-dreaming stage here as they waited for the trucks that were to take them to the fabulous French capital.

They were the fighting men, fresh out of muddy foxholes. They had more or less come to take it for granted that the "other fellow" would get to Paris, while they would probably head for home after the war without a glimpse of the city.

The regiment was in reserve at the time, and passes were made available for two men from each of the major units. The selections were made on the basis of meritorious performance and time spent in combat. In most cases, it more or less added up to "most deserving."

Nov. 21, 1944
PARIS

DURING THE NINE YEARS that she was director of the Omaha-Douglas County Chapter of the Red Cross, Rosemary Tuttle was the personification of dignity.

Never, so far as is known, did she drive trucks or camp along the highway or engage in activities not in keeping with the dignity of the executive of a large and efficient organization. However, she was known to "talk back" to reporters on occasion.

But over here, when no other method of transportation was available, she drove an ambulance truck in a convoy in order to make the crossing from London to Paris. It proved to be a rather strenuous experience, but not too eventful, except that the boat was forced to wait off the French coast two days to let a gale blow itself out.

"It was on bustling Fleet Street in the heart of London that I first took the wheel of the British-made truck," she said. "Things seemed somewhat complicated at the time . . . driving on the left side of the street with a right-hand drive vehicle with right-hand gearshift and the 'double kick' clutch."

She had to qualify for both American Army and British driving permits. It took a week for the convoy to come to Paris from London. Two days were spent in the marshaling yards. Her truck was loaded with blankets and sheets, so she had a warm place to sleep. Driving in heavy traffic, it took almost two days to travel from the French coast to Paris.

The former Omahan is now a Red Cross war-relief field representative under the civil affairs branch of the Army.

"Our job is concerned with providing food, clothing and medical care for civilians, and in helping communities revitalize themselves so they can handle their own problems," she said. "We are expected to go into the towns right behind the Army."

ROSEMARY TUTTLE

Nov. 22, 1944
PARIS

NO STORY OF THE WAR in France this fall can be complete if it does not tell about the mud.

Men of the Middle West know about Nebraska mud and Iowa mud and Kansas and Missouri mud — but the mud of France, that's something. Since the last war they have read about it. Now they know from experience.

As long as our soldiers can stay on the principal roads, or the surfaced side roads, and in the villages, it isn't so bad. Of course, it's likely to get pretty sticky around the doorway or at the roadside, but it's not too bad.

The trouble is that a major part of this war is being fought in the forests and in the fields.

The day that it doesn't rain here is a rarity. You may have rain for seven straight days, then sunshine for one heart-warming day, and then three or four more days of rain. Sometimes it starts raining while the sun is still making an effort to shine.

The roads into the forests and fields then drop out of sight, and the bottoms of the paths often sink beneath the reach of sturdy jeeps. It then becomes clear why so many horses and mules and wagons were required during the last war.

Nov. 22, 1944
PARIS

The best "formula" for a foxhole that I have heard was given by three Nebraska boys, Staff Sgts. Wayne Gilmore of North Platte, Lyle Rhoades of Valentine and Lawrence W. Eshleman of North Platte.

"First of all," said Gilmore, "it takes about 24 hours to do the job. We began by digging a hole about 10 feet wide, 12 feet long and 4 feet deep.

"Around the outside edge we put a triple layer of sandbags. On top of the sandbags we used tree limbs as a framework for the roof, and then on top of that we place a layer of sandbags. To waterproof it, we then put on a layer of salvaged raincoats and shelter halves (small tents) — stuff that we had picked up at a former German airport. On top of that, we put another layer of dirt, then our own shelter halves, and finally we finish the roof by camouflaging it.

"We built up the front with sandbags, then waterproofed it by using salvaged gas-protection capes.

"As a starter for our bed, we put straw on the floor, and place a log to serve as a partition and to keep the straw from spreading all over the floor. We have six blankets — and sleep with two beneath us and four on top. If necessary, we also use our overcoats on top. Each overcoat is considered to have the weight of two blankets.

"Now all we need is rat traps. The rats wanted to move in before we had finished the place."

A SKILLFULLY CONSTRUCTED foxhole takes about 24 hours to complete, according to a Nebraska soldier.

LAWRENCE W. ESHLEMAN

JEEP DRIVER Pfc. Johnny Robidoux of Falls City, Neb., tries to get through axle-deep mud in France.

Nov. 25, 1944
WITH THE 35TH DIVISION IN FRANCE

IN THE "MIRACLE OF SUPPLY" that supported the Third Army in its brilliant dash across France, a former Nebraska unit, the erstwhile 110th Quartermaster Regiment of the Nebraska National Guard, turned in one of the most outstanding jobs.

The former Cornhusker regiment has, through a series of changes, become the 35th Quartermaster Company. It furnishes the supplies for the 35th Division, which is under the command of Maj. Gen. Paul W. Baade.

The company's job is to draw supplies at Army depots, bring them forward and break them down for the various units. It also transports troops. How it managed to do both during that gallop across France is something even its personnel have a hard time explaining.

During the gallop across France the men often worked more than 24 hours without rest. Sometimes they worked almost constantly for four or five days.

The biggest problem revolves around keeping close to the fighting men and getting up to the front. The trucks have been hit by shrapnel numerous times. The officers claim the company has the best truck drivers in the Army.

"They simply can't be beaten," said Maj. Frederick A. Reed of Lincoln. "The trucks that were assigned to them when they got here were none too good, but they and the maintenance unit keep them going all the time. We never have trucks laid up."

Nov. 29, 1944
PARIS

IF YOUR PARTICULAR GI Joe happens to be stationed in Paris, or does his Christmas shopping here, don't expect too much in the way of a gift.

Joe's money isn't worth much here. Uncle Sam has ruled

THE COMMANDER OF the 35th Division, Maj. Gen. Paul W. Baade, left, and Col. Maddrey Solomon, his chief of staff. The 134th Infantry Regiment, made up largely of Nebraska soldiers, was part of the 35th Division.

that francs are worth 2 cents each.

But the French don't consider their money worth that much. It's mostly German printing-press money. There's so much of it that it couldn't possibly be backed by a reasonable gold or silver reserve.

Anyway, the Frenchman will pay a lot more than 50 francs for a dollar. He will pay three or four more times that much. An acquaintance came to my hotel room this week and said he had a friend who was prepared to offer 180 francs per dollar, and that the price would vary from day to day.

The result is that luxury goods here are priced in terms of a Frenchman's evaluation of the franc, rather than in Uncle Sam's evaluation.

In other words, when it's payday, GI Joe gets 50 francs for each dollar, but when he goes to buy luxury goods, he pays at the Frenchman's evaluation, which means 170 or more francs for a dollar's value. By the time his deductions and allowances are taken out of his monthly pay, Joe's lucky if he has enough money left for one big fling.

Nov. 29, 1944
PARIS

PVT. CHARLES JOSEPH VACANTI of Omaha meets more Nebraskans than do most fellows over here.

Pvt. Vacanti has "Omaha, Neb." painted on the front of his helmet.

"That's one good way to keep from feeling lonely and far from home," said Pvt. Vacanti. "I stir up quite a few fellows from home that way. Within the last few days I met two — George Himmelsehr of Omaha and Gene Gilchrist of Sidney. And every once in a while I see my own cousin, Maj. Joseph A. Longo, an Omaha doctor, right here in Paris."

ENSIGN DANIEL D. JEWELL of Norfolk, Neb., returned in overalls to a British port after his landing craft was sunk in the English Channel.

ENJOYABLE MOMENTS AWAY FROM THE BATTLE LINES

At right, members of the 35th Division were able to hear singer Bing Crosby perform on the loading dock of a brewery in Vezelise, France. The horse was closer to the impromptu stage than World-Herald photographer Lawrence Youngman.

A young Frenchwoman welcomes Nebraska soldiers who liberated her village.

Above, actress Marlene Dietrich signs autographs for Nebraska soldiers who carried her through mud. From left are Staff Sgt. Merlyn Goolsby of Shubert, Staff Sgt. Ernest Kammerer of Falls City, Staff Sgt. Eugene Gryson of Falls City and Staff Sgt. Myron Johnson of Falls City. The building in France where she performed couldn't hold everyone who wanted to see her.

At right, members of the cannon company of the 134th Infantry Regiment started a band using mostly instruments that came "from a junk heap."

D-Day censorship lifted

Dec. 5, 1944
PARIS

THIS IS A STORY ABOUT OMAHA BEACH — and a tribute to the undying glory of the foot soldiers who seized that beach in the face of odds which never have been fully told.

For some time, Omahans have known that the principal invasion beach bore the name of their city.

In the week of the invasion, I tried to write something about the beach, but the censors ruled no, for security reasons. And while my back was turned, so to speak, the story has been hinted at, but never fully told.

Omaha Beach never will be found in the geography books. But for a thousand years to come the story of what happened there will be told in military textbooks.

> *If any piece of ground on this globe should be sacred to the American people (and freedom-loving people everywhere) that piece is Omaha Beach.*

The heroism with which our soldiers fought and died and conquered there last June 6 was never surpassed at Lexington or Gettysburg or San Juan Hill or Chateau Thierry.

They paid a terribly high price that day. But by their indomitable courage, they avoided a defeat which probably would have set back the war schedule by months, and cost untold thousands of lives. If any piece of ground on this globe should be sacred to the American people (and freedom-loving people everywhere) that piece is Omaha Beach.

The reason I write such things is that the Omaha Beach invasion was one of those actions in which everything went wrong. All of the beautiful plans for softening up the Nazis there went awry. It was no one's fault. As I see it, war is a business in which victory goes to the side which has the smallest percentage of its plans go wrong.

Everyone did his best that day. But the brutal truth is that the defenders of the beach had not been softened up. Due to bad weather, the Air Force had to resort to "blind bombing," aiming chiefly at communications and areas behind the beaches. The bombs did not hit the Germans on the bluffs.

Most of the naval shells were also dropped back of the cliffs. The sea was so rough that the great barrages of rockets and shells from landing craft — especially from the tanks and self-propelled guns aboard those craft — could not be accurately aimed and were ineffective. Plans for blowing gaps in the barriers at the water's edge were only partly successful.

So when some 1,500 assault troops hit Omaha Beach at 6:30 a.m. on June 6, the situation was considerably different from what had been planned. Instead of finding an enemy reeling and groggy from shock and concussion, they were up against a foe who was willing and able to fight, and had all the advantages of terrain and carefully prepared positions.

To get at him, our soldiers had to cross a stretch of open beach that probably came as close to being hell as anything man has ever devised.

Dec. 9, 1944
PARIS

LT. FRANK KOZIOL of the 134th Infantry is a patient in a hospital in which his older brother, Cpl. John Koziol, is a wardmaster. The lieutenant is suffering from immersion foot (commonly called "trench foot"). His case is believed to be a light one and his condition is good. The brothers are two of the 17 siblings in an Omaha family.

Some weeks ago, The World-Herald reported how Frank Koziol, of the fightingest men in the 134th Infantry Regiment, had received his battle-field commission. Today I was looking for Nebraskans in a hospital ward and bumped into John.

"I'll show you a clipping from The World-Herald," he said and produced the story about Frank. Three or four sentences later, he said, "Frank's downstairs."

It's the first time the brothers have met in three years, though they have repeatedly tried to get together on this side and in the States.

Finally, when Frank learned where John was, he tackled the problem of getting here to see him. The way he finally managed was by going on some very tough night patrols. The leave was his reward, and the brothers had two days together.

On the morning that Frank was due to return, they did considerable sightseeing and at the end of it, Frank's feet were paining him severely. It was no time at all until a doctor had him in a bed.

Dec. 10, 1944
PARIS

A COOK WITH the 108th General Hospital is Cpl. Don R. Kingston, a Hay Springs, Neb., barber.

Cpl. Kingston is recovering after an appendicitis operation. The surgeon general of the U.S. Army visited Kingston, who denied to him the possibility that his own cooking could cause appendicitis.

Dec. 24, 1944

LAWRENCE YOUNGMAN OF The World-Herald staff has returned home after seven months in the European Theater of Operations. For half this time he was under fire in France, writing mostly of the valiant warfare waged by Nebraska's own 134th Infantry Regiment.

LAWRENCE YOUNGMAN, left, with Nebraska officers of the 35th Division. Back row, from left after Youngman: Warrant Officer Jack Seaman of Omaha, Warrant Officer Charles J. Hoffman of Omaha, Maj. Floyd Paynter of Omaha, Maj. John H. Reents of Adams. Front row, from left: Maj. Roy M. Matson of Holdrege, Warrant Officer Lawrence Sites of Omaha, Capt. Paul H. Wiehenkamp of Seward and Capt. R.J. Anderson of York.

Comrades in arms

NEBRASKA MEMBERS OF COMPANY C, 1ST BATTALION OF THE 134TH INFANTRY REGIMENT:
Back row, from left, Staff Sgt. Leland E. Sheneman of Oxford, Sgt. Charles E. McCall of Beatrice, Tech. Sgt. Herman J. Genrich of Pickrell and Staff Sgt. Ray E. Larimore of Beatrice.
Front row, from left, Staff Sgt. Donald J. Engel of Beatrice, Staff Sgt. Dale McClara of Ogallala and Tech. Sgt. Raymond K. Starkey of Beatrice.

Final push to Germany

BLEEDING FROM THE FACE AND LEG as his burning bomber fell fast toward German soil, tailgunner Wendell Fetters tried to jump. But he was stuck. It was Dec. 23, 1944, a week into the Battle of the Bulge, Germany's last-ditch effort of World War II. "The leg strap of my parachute was caught on the gun sight," Fetters said. "I was banging against the side of the fuselage, trying to get free. I finally bent the gun sight." ★ The Allies had sent 32 B-26 Marauders to bomb a bridge at Ahrweiler in western Germany, and 16 were shot down. ★ Sgt. Fetters, who grew up near Indianola, Iowa, broke his ankle when he landed in the fork of a tree, and wandered for two sub-zero days before he was captured. His reception riding through a German town was as bitter as the cold. "I was scared," he recalled. "But I don't blame the old ladies who spat on us, or the kid about 12 who hit me with a two-by-four. It wasn't their fault. They didn't start the war. Neither did I."

SOLDIERS OF THE 134TH INFANTRY REGIMENT, formerly a Nebraska National Guard unit, were a common sight in the streets of Luxembourg in the fall of 1944. But in December, German forces poured through the tiny nation and into Belgium in what was to be known as the Battle of the Bulge.

RAYMOND ORTEGREN

Town: Palmer

Service: Army, driver for 772nd Field Artillery Battalion

In the war: Trained for infantry before being transferred to artillery. He joined the war late in the Battle of the Bulge.

In his words: "When I got to Europe, losses were so great in infantry, they were pulling guys from artillery. Only every 10th man got to (stay) in artillery. I was the 10th man. I really felt like the good Lord was taking care of me."

'The American foot soldier just outfought the enemy'

C.D. FOSTER ON THE PORCH of his home in Missouri Valley, Iowa, in 1994. The scrapbook holds photographs of his fellow soldiers in the Nebraska National Guard's 134th Infantry Regiment. Foster and the 134th fought in the Ardennes region of Europe during the Battle of the Bulge.

THE SIGHT OF SNOW would turn C.D. Foster's thoughts back to the days he spent in Europe in 1944 chasing German soldiers through the forest.

"We knew we had them on the run," said Foster, a member of the 134th Infantry Regiment.

But Adolf Hitler, ignoring the advice of his top generals, gambled wildly and ordered 250,000 German troops against the Allied forces in the mountainous and heavily forested Ardennes region of eastern Belgium and northern Luxembourg.

Hitler hoped the surprise offensive that began Dec. 16, 1944, would capture the port city of Antwerp, split the Allied supply system and leave the British and U.S. armies divided and ready to talk about a truce.

At first, it appeared as if Hitler would succeed.

The Germans created a bulge in the Allied lines when they made a push 50 miles deep along a 70-mile front.

The Allied troops recovered, however, and made the Battle of the Bulge a turning point of World War II — and the most massive and bloody battle ever fought by American forces.

The Americans fought with such tenacity that the Germans were left without the soldiers and tanks and other equipment needed to mount a solid defense of their homeland against the advancing Allied armies. The war in Europe ended the following spring.

"When the battle began the Americans were outnumbered, out-gunned and out-tanked by the enemy," said William Boyd, a Battle of the Bulge veteran who wrote a book about the battle called "The Gentle Infantryman."

C.D. FOSTER FOUND A blanket-lined coat and bib overalls, which helped keep him warm during the Battle of the Bulge in December 1944.

"Just individual soldiers fighting alone sometimes decided the outcome," Boyd said. "The American foot soldier just outfought the enemy and ended up winning the biggest battle ever fought by any American army."

More than a million men were eventually involved in the battle as reinforcements from both sides streamed to the region to shore up the front-line forces.

A total of 500,000 Germans, 600,000 U.S. soldiers and 55,000 British troops eventually were involved in the battle, which stretched from Dec. 16, 1944, to Jan. 25, 1945.

The Americans suffered nearly 81,000 casualties and the British 1,400. But the Germans lost more than 100,000.

The 134th Infantry Regiment, a Nebraska National Guard unit that entered the war about a month after the D-Day invasion on June 6, 1944, suffered 1,449 casualties, including 140 deaths, during the Battle of the Bulge, according to the Guard's historian.

Bud Sklenar of Omaha was a mess sergeant in Belgium with the 9th Armored Division when the battle began.

"We were a fairly green outfit," said Sklenar, who grew up in Wilber, Neb. "We were supposed to get used to combat there. There really was nothing going on."

Sklenar quickly had to drop his pots and pans and grab his rifle when the German troops came crashing through.

"They overran my battery," Sklenar recalled in 1994. "They killed and captured quite a few."

Sklenar survived that night and the rest of the battle. Although his hands sustained frostbite from the severe cold, Sklenar made it through the fighting without a scratch.

"I was so lucky, it was unbelievable," Sklenar said. "For a while after the war I had a guilty feeling about why I made it and some didn't."

Sklenar had volunteered soon after the Japanese bombed Pearl Harbor on Dec. 7, 1941. He was rejected by the Marines because he was colorblind and could not pass the exam needed to fly U.S. warplanes. He was drafted a month later by the Army.

Sklenar said he experienced many bleak moments during the battle and often thought he would not make it home.

"In the last 20 years I have thought a lot about it," Sklenar said. "One thing it taught me is to never give up."

Foster, who started with the 134th in Normandy as a first sergeant, said the Battle of the Bulge was some of the fiercest fighting he saw during the war.

"You go in with a full complement of about 180 men and six officers," said Foster, who began the war with the 134th's B Company out of Falls City, Neb. "You come out with a dozen men and one officer. There was some fighting going on, you could say."

Foster received a battlefield commission and two battlefield promotions during the war. He left Europe as a captain after he was evacuated for wounds he received in March 1945.

As a commander, Foster said, he spent a lot of his time wondering how he was going to get ammunition, food, dry socks and other supplies through the knee-deep snow to his men huddled in foxholes scattered throughout the forest.

"You spent some time thinking about the cold," Foster said. "You spent a lot of time thinking about your men in their foxholes. But at the time (the battle) was going on, you had only one thing to think of and that was survival."

'They went right through us'

IF YOU ASKED EUGENE KUHN what it was like to go face to face in battle against the dreaded Nazi SS troops, you wouldn't get a long answer.

EUGENE KUHN
in the war and in 2008

"I could only pull the trigger and let them have it. It wasn't pleasant. I don't even talk about that."

The Columbus, Neb., native brought home a trunkful of memories from his service with the 106th Infantry Division — many of them unpleasant. Kuhn's unit had the distinction of suffering the heaviest losses of any U.S. division during the Battle of the Bulge, Hitler's final, desperate effort to stave off defeat in western Europe.

Enlistee Kuhn, 19, and the 106th were both green and untested. They had spent only five days in the Ardennes region of Belgium, in a supposedly quiet area, when the German thrust began in December 1944.

Kuhn and two other soldiers who had been up ahead scouting suddenly found themselves behind enemy lines.

"They went right through us," he recalled in 2008. "We didn't have a chance to get started back."

Kuhn managed to make it back to the American side and rejoin the fight to repel the German advance. Separated from his own outfit and with American commanders filling gaps wherever they could, Kuhn at one point was placed in a tank company. He said he'd never been in a tank before, but for 10 days he served as its gunner.

"We got in among (the German tanks) and hit a couple, knocked the tracks off one," he said. "I was one of the happiest guys you ever saw to get out of a tank."

During the American counterattack, Kuhn and others took more than a dozen German soldiers prisoner after finding them in the basement of a building, singing carols.

"They were in shock, with their guns laying back in the corner. One of them told me, 'You Americans are crazy attacking on Christmas Eve.'"

When it was over, the Americans had won, but the 106th had suffered more than 8,600 killed, wounded, captured or missing. Kuhn didn't see any more fighting before the war ended. He returned home to his young wife, Marcy, and started a family gas station business. Kuhn said he had nightmares from his war experience for nearly 30 years. Still, he knows he was lucky to return to a happy life.

"I feel sorry for the boys who didn't make it back."

JOHN GRADY
Town: Lincoln
Service: Army, artillery gunner with 78th Infantry Division

In the war: Saw action in Belgium during the Battle of the Bulge and in Hurtgen Forest and Ruhr Valley in Germany.

In his words: "We crossed a pontoon bridge over the Rhine and the German 88s started hitting the water. Some in my outfit got hit. I never heard how bad. I never saw them again. We turned one corner and a brick building blew up in front of us. ... There were a lot of things, but I don't talk about it much."

DORRAL SCHLEIF

Town: Hebron

Service: Army, 63rd Infantry Division

In the war: Served as a rifleman as the unit marched across Germany. Wounded in a battle outside Munich when he was 18.

In his words: "The fighting wasn't good. Absolutely nothing can be good about it. When I got back, my (German-American) grandfather wanted to know all about the scenery in the country. He was disappointed because I couldn't tell him anything, really. I wasn't on a social call."

THE DAMAGED LUDENDORFF BRIDGE over the Rhine River at Remagen, Germany.

'He had done what every general had dreamed about'

KARL TIMMERMANN WAS CREDITED by no less than Gen. Dwight Eisenhower with extreme bravery under fire for participating in actions on March 7, 1945, that shortened World War II in Europe by months.

Timmermann, then a 22-year-old lieutenant, was the first American officer to cross the Rhine when he spearheaded the capture of the Ludendorff railroad bridge at Remagen, Germany. That action provided the Allied army with a path to pierce the heart of the German defenses and finally bring the war to a close.

When he stepped off the train in his hometown of West Point, Neb., after the war, Timmermann had been decorated with the Distinguished Service Cross, the nation's second highest honor for valor.

But many people back home could not overlook Timmermann's birth in Germany. Nor could they forget that he was the son of a U.S. soldier who had deserted his unit during World War I to marry a German woman.

"I will admit he did not get the praise or glory he deserved," Robert L. Wostoupal of West Point said in 1995. "He was a single lieutenant with a handful of infantry who had done what every general had dreamed about."

No one from the northeast Nebraska town was at the station to welcome him home. Ken Hechler, a military historian who was at Remagen on March 7, 1945, said in his book, "The Bridge at Remagen," that the reception committee in West Point consisted of a "little dog that snarled and snapped at his heels."

It wasn't until 1965 — 20 years after the war and 14 years after Timmermann's death from cancer — that the town honored a local boy whose daring deeds were the talk of the nation years earlier. Timmermann Park, the ballfield named for him, is just blocks from his boyhood home.

In 1995, the city dedicated a monument in his name, and a bridge over the Elkhorn River also bears his name.

"He is recognized as a hero around the world," Wostoupal said. "Pages and pages have been filled with Karl Timmermann's heroic deeds."

Some World War II veterans in the West Point area resented giving any attention to Timmermann because they doubted that he had really led the charge for which he was credited, Wostoupal said.

"It was unusual that an officer would be out front leading the men," Wostoupal said. "One reason Timmermann did not get more recognition than he did was because people didn't believe it was an officer out in front. But he is credited with being the first officer in an invading army to cross the Rhine since Napoleon in 1806."

Timmermann, a husky 186-pound six-footer, had a self-confident gaze and carried himself so upright that he just looked like a war hero, said Frank Bollard, who knew Timmermann while growing up in nearby Bancroft. Timmermann was 18 months old when his parents left Germany and came to the United States, eventually settling in West Point.

His mother worked as a waitress to supplement his father's earnings, which were always meager because he moved from job to job.

LT. KARL TIMMERMANN

"Timmermann came from a very poor but proud family," Wostoupal said.

Timmermann was in the Army within a month after graduating from Guardian Angel High School in West Point in 1940. He spent a few years as an enlisted soldier and then was commissioned as an officer at Fort Benning, Ga., in 1943.

His unit, the 27th Armored Infantry Battalion, 9th Armored Division, had seen fierce combat that took a heavy toll before it even arrived on the banks of the Rhine in March 1945.

On March 6, the night before the historic feat, Timmermann became commander of A Company. The previous commander, a captain, had lasted just two days before becoming a casualty. The fighting had caused so many casualties that only two other officers remained in Timmermann's company.

Adolf Hitler had ordered his troops to destroy all the bridges over the Rhine to impede the Allied armies. American commanders could scarcely believe their eyes when they saw the 1,300-foot railroad bridge still standing at Remagen.

To this day, the reason it was not blown to bits like the others is a mystery.

A chilling rain fell and a thick haze filled the air as Timmermann and his soldiers looked down on the bridge. They had been ordered to take the structure arching over the river, but it looked like a suicide mission. German machine-gun bullets raked the bridge, snipers huddled in bunkers ready to blast anyone who dared approach, and enemy soldiers scrambled to set explosive charges.

ROBERT WOSTOUPAL, pictured at the West Point park named for Timmermann, said the Army lieutenant is "recognized as a hero around the world."

Timmermann's troops were loyal and devoted to their commander.

It was not unusual for him to take his bedroll to the trenches to spend the night with the troops rather than hunkering down in a command post behind the lines, Wostoupal said.

"He would never command like a lieutenant and kind of bark at them," said Ruben Labs of Kearney, who served in the Army during the war and knew Timmermann. "He asked them to do something. Everybody respected him. His guys would do anything for him."

Timmermann would say later that he was thinking of his wife and the fact that she had celebrated her birthday the day before. What he did not know was that days earlier, his wife had given birth to their first child.

Rushing the bridge looked so futile that Timmermann's normally eager-to-please troops were reluctant at first. Just as they started to make the dash, they were rattled by a huge explosion that seemed to raise the bridge from its supports, Hechler wrote in his book.

Timmermann stopped to peer through the smoke and dust, Hechler wrote. Amazingly, the bridge was still standing.

"Let's go!" Timmermann shouted. "Get goin', you guys, get goin'!"

German snipers and machine gunners fired, but Timmermann and his men kept going.

Sgt. Joseph Delisio of the Bronx in New York climbed a three-story tower and captured three German snipers who had trapped his buddies on the bridge with deadly fire. Sgt. Al Drabik lost track of his friend Delisio and figured he must be all alone on the other side of the bridge. Drabik made a break for it.

Timmermann and Delisio, who came down from the tower, quickly followed and were only steps behind when Drabik became the first American on the other side of the Rhine.

Timmermann and his men secured the bridge and fought pockets of Germans on the other side who were still trying to defend it.

More than 25,000 American troops would cross the bridge before it collapsed 10 days later. By that time the Allied army had established control of the area and built pontoon bridges across the river.

Eisenhower would say later that capturing the bridge was the key to crushing the remaining German defenses.

"The final defeat of the enemy, which we had long calculated would be accomplished in the spring and summer campaign of 1945, was suddenly now, in our minds, just around the corner," Eisenhower said.

Timmermann became a salesman for a Fremont company after the war, but answered his nation's call a few years later and rejoined the Army to go to Korea.

He participated in the Inchon landing and the defense of a key airfield.

He was forced to come home early in October 1950 when doctors detected the cancer that would claim his life a year later.

In an interview at an Army hospital in Denver, Timmermann refused to consider himself a hero for the courage he showed on March 7, 1945.

"It was just one of those things," he said.

LOREN ROWELL

Town: Omaha

Service: Army, 26th Infantry Division

In the war: Fired mortars and machine guns during the Battle of the Bulge.

In his words: "I wouldn't take a million dollars to say what I saw and did, and I wouldn't take 10 cents to do it again. A lot of the boys feel that same way, I think. … When I came back, I had a year-and-a-half-old daughter I'd never seen. I pretty well got into a little alcohol. It kind of numbed the feeling. It was an all-new environment, home was."

'Visualize a doughnut — we're the hole'

IN THE FALL OF 1944, the 101st Airborne Division's 506th Parachute Infantry Regiment was part of the largest airborne fleet ever amassed as it made its second and last combat jump of the war at Zon, Holland, during Operation Market Garden.

The Allies planned to capture bridges across the Rhine and quicken the march to Berlin.

The job of Easy Company — chronicled in the book and miniseries "Band of Brothers" — was to liberate the village of Eindhoven and protect a 50-mile supply route between Eindhoven and Arnhem.

"It was a Sunday afternoon, and it was a real peaceful parachute jump," Easy Company member Ed Mauser of Omaha said in 2009. "People came out with beer and giving hugs. I got no hugs. I got some beer, though. I was bashful back in those days."

Mauser helped in a night rescue mission of British aviators at Arnhem. The aviators had been shot down and isolated for a month on the other side of the Rhine, in danger of German capture.

"We had two boats with one officer and six men in each boat. One boat went on the left and one on the right flank. We got 'em across and we got a citation for it," Mauser said.

After Holland, the outfit returned to France for rest. Mauser has a portrait taken during a four-day pass to Paris.

Then the Germans counterattacked in December and the Battle of the Bulge broke out in Belgium. The regiment was called up as reinforcements at Bastogne, in the Ardennes Mountains. Heading into the battle with little preparation, Easy Company troops took leftover ammunition from other U.S. troops retreating from the front.

Two days later — Dec. 18, 1944, Mauser's 28th birthday — the regiment was surrounded. The men had no winter clothing. Soldiers wrapped gunnysacks around their feet for warmth. They lived in foxholes and cut pine boughs to lay on the snow for insulation.

"You can't spread shaving cream very well with cold water," Mauser said.

Soldiers were down to about 11 rounds of ammunition each, he said, when headquarters called and asked for the regiment's status.

"We said, 'Visualize a doughnut — we're the hole,' " Mauser said.

Mauser said Germans didn't attack the hilltop position but bombarded it with artillery around the clock. Easy Company Sgts. William Guarnere and Joseph Toye each lost a leg to the bombardment.

During the siege, Mauser and a few other soldiers returning from a night patrol to the village of Foy safely ducked bullets fired by U.S. troops who mistook them for Germans.

"After the war, I kind of forgot about it for a while. (The miniseries) just brought the war right back."

— ED MAUSER, WHOSE REGIMENT WAS FEATURED IN THE HBO SERIES "BAND OF BROTHERS"

After about 10 days under siege, Allied airstrikes and Gen. George Patton's Third Army ended the German offensive.

After Bastogne, Mauser's outfit remained in Belgium for a time. The men came upon a farmhouse and went into a barn to rest. A German mortar shell burst through the roof, exploded and cut the little finger on Mauser's right hand to the bone.

By the time he got out of the hospital 30 days later and returned to his outfit in France, Mauser said, Germans were surrendering en masse. Easy Company got on the Autobahn and went through Germany to Hitler's mountain retreat in Bavaria.

Mauser didn't go up the mountain to Eagle's Nest with other Easy Company soldiers.

"The sergeant said to take three guys to a nearby farmhouse and check it out. There were two scared women up there. I looked out a window and saw an older guy running toward the barn. I didn't know if he was a soldier or not. The war was over. I wasn't going to kill someone when the war was over."

Mauser and Easy Company spent the summer in Austria expecting to be shipped around the world to help end the war against Japan in the Pacific Theater. But the Pacific war ended in August 1945, and Mauser sailed to the United States in September after two years in Europe.

He received an honorable discharge at Fort Sheridan, Ill., on Sept. 21, 1945. He had earned a Purple Heart, two Bronze Stars and several other citations.

Mauser recalls that he was mowing his yard in Omaha when he was approached by "two fellas" who said they were writers for the "Band of Brothers" project. They interviewed him and took his picture. The series aired in 2001, but Mauser wasn't personally featured.

Then the letters started coming. So did the memories.

"After the war, I kind of forgot about it for a while," he says. "(The miniseries) just brought the war right back. Now I think about it every day. I think about the airplane that got shot down, some of my buddies that got killed."

JAMES R. BEVERIDGE

Town: Omaha

Service: Technician 5th grade, 225th Automatic Weapons Battalion, U.S. Army

In the war: Landed on Omaha Beach on D-Day and fought all the way up to Normandy. Fought across France and in the Ardennes Forest at the Battle of the Bulge. Received five battle stars and was awarded the Purple Heart.

In his words: "I've never been so cold in all my life as I was in the Battle of the Bulge. I was firing a machine gun, and I got hit in the hand. My hand was laid open, but it wouldn't bleed because it was so cold. I put the skin back over it, put on antiseptic powder that we had in our first-aid kit, and I wrapped it up and kept going."

AN SS BELT BUCKLE Ed Mauser brought back from Germany.

'I never spoke about it'

BY MATTHEW HANSEN

SAM SAMBASILE HAD LIVED FOR DECADES with a World War II story trapped in his head.

He never told his mother about his first-ever parachute jump, head first from the back of a burning B-17 bomber, 17,000 feet above Germany. She was worried enough already, Sam said — so worried that she was rushed to a hospital when she got word that her middle child was missing and presumed dead.

Sambasile never told his wife about the old German man brandishing an ancient rifle who captured him, or the week or two he spent trapped in a windowless dungeon awaiting his next interrogation.

He and his wife separated a long time ago, Sambasile said. No use going into that.

He had never told his son about the mystery ingredient in the prison camp soup, how he dropped more than 40 pounds and dreamed of burgers and malts and the old Santa Lucia parade through South Omaha.

"I never spoke about it. What was there to say?"

But during an interview in 2008, the words started tumbling out, and Sambasile talked for an hour, then two — the longest he had ever talked about his time as a German prisoner of war.

The trouble began on Oct. 6, 1944, just minutes after Sambasile's B-17, nicknamed "Boots and Her Buddies," dropped its bombs on a Berlin factory during his 33rd mission as a gunner. German fighters attacked, strafing the plane with gunfire and knocking out both right-side engines. The right wing exploded in flames. The pilot and crew rushed to the tail door to escape.

Sambasile was second out. He jumped head first, immediately pulled his chest cord — "It's a miracle I didn't get caught in the tail of the airplane" — and floated down. He almost smashed into a park bench as he thudded down in a German village. When he looked up, an old man was shaking a rifle and screaming for him to surrender. Police rounded up seven other crewmen. Villagers shook their fists and cursed in German. Nazi troops marched the prisoners away.

Sambasile was separated from the others, isolated in an underground room with a dirt floor and a wood bench. Once a day he would be dragged out and questioned: Where have you come from? What is your purpose here? Who were you with?

"All I did was give my name, rank, serial number. When they got tired of listening, they put me back in the dungeon."

Days and nights blurred. Sambasile thinks he was transported to a POW camp in Poland within the month.

"The first meal they brought me was soup. I was real hungry. I mean to tell you, really hungry. I asked this Irish guy, 'What are the white things in this soup?' He said, 'Those are maggots.' I finally ate it."

Twenty prisoners lived in a 12-foot-by-12-foot cell. They ate bread as hard as stone. Some nights, they got a potato. The 19-year-old Omahan weighed a healthy 170 when he entered the camp. By February 1945, when the guards put the prisoners onto trains, he weighed less than 130.

Their destination was a second prison camp in Germany — a trip Sambasile remembers as his low point. More than 100 prisoners were packed into train cars meant for 40.

Life improved marginally after they reached the camp in northern Germany. There was still no food — Sambasile remembers chasing a cat and being crushed when another prisoner caught and ate it — and they faced periodic beatings and strip searches.

But he made friends: guys named Boone, Smitty, Ken. They played bridge. They talked about sizzling steaks and greasy french fries, pretty girls and scary movies. They didn't talk about home.

"Nobody ever said whether they were married, had a mother or father," he said. "I didn't even know any of their last names. We couldn't think about those things."

In May 1945, a rumor was whispered through the camp: Russian troops were coming to save them. The German guards had orders to shoot the prisoners and then flee, Sambasile said. But one morning, he awoke to find that the guards had disappeared. The 10,000 prisoners went wild, tearing down the camp's barbed-wire fences.

Months later, Salvatore "Sam" Sambasile was home in South Omaha, wearing his dress uniform and hugging his mother. "God, she squeezed me so hard."

What happened next, he said, was that life went on. He got a job at Union Pacific Railroad, married, had two children and moved into a house in the old Italian neighborhood, right next door to his boyhood home.

When he got back, buddies would ask about jumping out of an airplane. More recently, two kids doing school reports asked him about his time in the war.

But he'd never told the whole story all at once.

"Why? I don't know why, really. I guess nobody ever asked."

SAM SAMBASILE in 2008

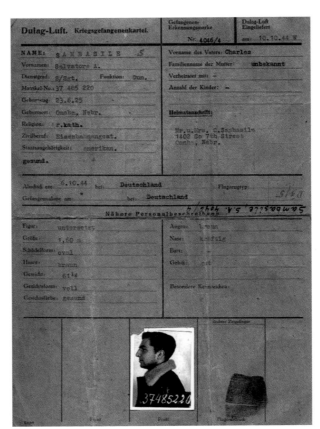

THE GERMAN FORM stating that Sam Sambasile was a prisoner of war.

> *"Nobody ever said whether they were married, had a mother or father. . . . I didn't even know any of their last names. We couldn't think about those things."*
>
> — SAM SAMBASILE ON BEING IN A GERMAN POW CAMP

MEMORIES OF A GENERATION ★

EDDIE OHM

Town: Elkhorn area

Service: Army, 75th Infantry Division

In the war: Ferried munitions to the front lines during the Battle of the Bulge.

In his words: "I got hit in my helmet with one shot, and I got hit in the face and still have that shrapnel in my face. My company commander said, 'Hey, you're bleeding. Put some pressure on that.' It was so cold your blood didn't really flow very well. I thought the thing just grazed my jaw."

REINOLD SCHUTTE

Town: Hastings

Service: Army, 87th Infantry Division

In the war: Served as a communications specialist and translator; grew up near Guide Rock, Neb., the son of German parents.

In his words: "One of my worst experiences was crossing the Rhine River. ... I actually had my paddle shot right out of my hands while we crossed. Me and one guy, we were in communications, and my buddy was loaded down so bad with wire and the telephone and everything, another engineer grabbed his paddle. He got hit in the head right away."

LOU SCHMITZ

Town: Omaha

Service: Army, 42nd Infantry

In the war: In basic training when the Battle of the Bulge began. His unit was sent to Europe, landed at Le Havre, France, and marched toward Germany. He was taken prisoner while on patrol in Lorraine in February 1945, spending two months as a German POW before a tank unit freed him.

In his words: "Our outfit got shot up pretty bad in the Bulge, so we were not at full strength. ... So they made us the daylight patrol even though we had no experience. These professional SS soldiers could hear us coming through the dry grass. ... They were smart, they were professionals. We practically walked into them before we knew they were there. They had us pinned down and they were scraping the bark off over my head. ... This other kid, a young fellow, he tried to run back. They shot him full of holes. ... After a while, they started hollering at me to come out of the woods. I didn't figure I could fight the war all by myself, so I came out. ... They didn't get me to a camp so much as they passed me from unit to unit. ... They sure didn't feed you much. That's a good way to lose weight. It was basic, very basic — supposed to be potato soup, but I couldn't ever find the potatoes."

KEN MARTIN

Town: Lincoln

Service: Army, 70th Infantry

In the war: Entered Germany at the end of the Battle of the Bulge; infantryman in the unit following Gen. George Patton's tanks across Germany; after Germany surrendered, served in an occupying force in Cologne, Germany.

In his words: "We were training in New York when the Bulge happened, when the Germans made a big push. So they loaded all of us onto the Queen Elizabeth, and we zigzagged all the way across, but we didn't encounter any submarines. ... We stayed overnight in some barracks in England, then landed in Le Havre (France). They took us within five or 10 miles of the front line, put us in a vacant factory and issued us weapons. We didn't know whether Germans would come right at us or not. It turned out, they had the 'bulge' stopped by then. I was put in the 70th Infantry, following Gen. Patton and his tank corps. They were leading the way, and we were following."

★ MEMORIES OF A GENERATION

JOE PATTAVINA SR.

Town: Omaha

Service: Army, 7th Armored Tank Division

In the war: Basic training at Fort Leavenworth, Kan., then Fort Knox, Ky. Went overseas in 1944, joining Patton's army in Germany. Moved through France, Holland and Belgium and fought in the Battle of the Bulge. Unit lost two tanks, but he came through unharmed.

In his words: "In the Bulge, we got in there, we were battling for a long time. But it was so cold down there, it seemed like everything just stopped for a while — then started up again. … Going through towns, you don't know who's there, who's shooting, where the civilians are. Some things are best to just put out of your mind. … I missed my graduation when I got drafted. When it happened, I figured it's for my country, we have people we have to fight, so I have to go. I think some young people may not feel that way about their country anymore."

KENNETH CARLSON

Town: Omaha

Service: U.S. Army

In the war: He was in the 102nd Infantry Division at Camp Swift, near Austin, Texas. He had basic training at North Camp Hood in Texas and received a crash course in engineering at Purdue University in Indiana as part of the Army Specialized Training Program. In September 1944, he went by convoy to Normandy, France. He moved across France and the Netherlands, where the Ninth Army was being assembled for a drive on Berlin. The 102nd Division was one of the elements that formed the Ninth Army. He received the Purple Heart, Bronze Star, Expert Infantry Badge and Combat Infantry Badge, along with many other medals. He was discharged mid-June 1945 from Camp Carson at Colorado Springs, Colo.

In his words: "We just pushed eastward and by Nov. 30, we were driving toward a river crossing on the Roer River. There was a little village called Welz. I was hit by mortar fire there and then went to hospitals in Belgium, Paris and England. I landed in England mid-December of 1944 and stayed in the hospital there until February 1945. They have an expression — you get ZI'd, Zone of the Interior — which means you go back to the U.S. I got ZI'd in mid-February of 1945."

GEORGE O. BENESCH

Town: Linwood

Service: U.S. Army

In the war: He served as a tech sergeant with the 9th Infantry Division, 47th Infantry Regiment; Company K, 1st Platoon. He trained at Camp Carson, Colo. He was sent overseas to Le Havre, France, in 1943 and went directly to the front line. He fought in the Battle of the Bulge.

In his words: "We had moved into a forest of pine or fir trees so dense that daylight never reached the ground. The enemy had trenches dug that were about 6 feet deep and wide enough to walk in. We were there a very short time when we were subjected to enemy fire. The tree bursts were heavy and intense. When the shelling stopped, you could see the sky. All the trees were shredded. All of us lay in the bottom of the trench. Some were wounded badly, and I thought I had lucked out. It wasn't until later that my back began to itch. I stripped down to bare skin and had a buddy see what was causing the problem. He said my back was covered with blood and what appeared to be pinpricks. Small slivers of metal had pierced the backpack, gone through my mess kit, folded blanket, raincoat, field jacket and shirt. I did not consider that to be a (serious) wound and I did not require any medical attention."

JOSEPH E. WALSH

Town: Omaha

Service: Third Army, 26th Infantry. Earned four battle stars in fighting in Europe

In the war: A native of Spaulding, Neb., he had the rank of technician 5th class in the Army. He served from March 31, 1942, to Dec. 3, 1945. The Third Army was commanded by Gen. George Patton, and Walsh's unit motto was "Our Blood, Your Guts." He was in battle in northern France, central Europe and the Battle of the Bulge in Belgium.

In his words: "We were the first ship from the USA to arrive at Utah Beach in France. We went to shore on barges under enemy fire. … I was a truck driver for a lot of the time during the war, driving troops and ammunition into battle and picking up the injured off the field."

The horror revealed

THE MEMORY WAS SEARED IN Rachel Rosenberg's memory, as indelible as the "A-15254" identification number the Nazis tattooed on her left forearm. ★ As she and her younger brother milled among other gaunt-faced Jews in the yard at Auschwitz, the SS soldiers came to take him away. The boy she had protected for months like her own child would take his last breath that day in the gas chamber. ★ "I see him walking away from me, oh, what a gorgeous child," she recalled, covering both eyes with her hands. "This is my biggest hurt, as long as I live. I will never forget. Never."

ELMER CHAPP OF FALLS CITY, NEB., photographed prisoners at the camp at Dachau, Germany, waiting to be released by Allied soldiers.

HOLLIS LIMPRECHT TOOK THIS PHOTO AT DACHAU during a return visit in 1968. He wrote about it later, "I spent less than four hours out of my lifetime at the death camp, and yet those four hours lie close to the surface of my subconscious, and the events of those four hours will flash back in vivid reality with little urging. Since then I have come to know several survivors of the Holocaust, and I marvel that they are sane. The human spirit is a wonderful thing."

'This was not Dante's hell — this was a living hell'

BY HOLLIS LIMPRECHT

The author, the editor of The World-Herald's Magazine of the Midlands from 1960 to 1984, was an Army captain in the war.

I have often wondered since that day: How many human bodies does it take to make a pile about 8 feet square and about 4½ feet high?

Each of those dozens of bodies that I saw that morning contained the soul of what was not long ago a human being. A person with hopes, dreams, desires, despairs.

Despairs. Each of us is puzzled by the mystery of death; some of us more than others, but we are increasingly aware of it as we grow older.

We wonder when; we wonder how. We assume it will be old age; maybe an illness, maybe an accident. We hope it will be swift and painless, and we hope it will allow some dignity.

Imagine the horror, the anger and the terror of knowing that your death would be at the dictates of another human being who looks upon you as a bug to be squashed.

He would determine how. He would determine when. And he would take a special pleasure in determining that it would be lingering and painful.

— HOLLIS LIMPRECHT,
THE WORLD-HERALD,
APRIL 29, 1985

THE WAR IN EUROPE was coming to an end. On the southern half of the huge Western Front, the U.S. Third and Seventh Armies were speeding toward a junction with the advancing Russians to the east about as fast as the stretched-out supply lines would allow.

The armored troops had to wait for gasoline. Foot soldiers had no such impediment and could continue to fight against the crumbling German resistance.

Nuremberg had fallen on April 20, 1945, Adolf Hitler's birthday. On April 29, the 3rd Infantry Division, which was a part of the Seventh Army, was approaching a handsome prize, the Bavarian capital of Munich.

But first there was some business to take care of in an obscure little town by the name of Dachau.

April 29, 1945, was a beautiful day. The sky was bright blue; the sun caressed my face under the heavy metal helmet, a slight breeze barely stirred the first of spring's leaves.

It was a day that made what followed even more unreal. It was the kind of day that sings of peace, not war; of beauty, not ugliness.

The serenity was marred abruptly. As my Jeep rounded a curve, it emerged from the grove of trees into the flat plain of Dachau, and just ahead the camp's outer barbed wire fence suddenly stood before me.

This was the Dachau concentration camp, one of the oldest in the Nazi system of extermination camps. Originally, it housed dissident Nazis; those who followed Ernst Rohm instead of Adolf Hitler and who were victims of an early Hitler purge of the Brown Shirts.

Then it housed common criminals, and finally it became another link in Heinrich Himmler's vast chain of death houses for anti-Nazis of all stripes and for Jews.

Beside the outer entrance to the camp, maybe 20 feet in front of me, lay the body of a dead SS trooper. He had been shot minutes before in a futile Nazi effort to defend the Dachau camp against the advancing GIs of the American 3rd and 42nd Infantry Divisions.

His was the first of scores of bodies I would see that warm April day.

I had read "Mein Kampf" as a teenager. I knew the atrocity stories. I had volunteered to join the struggle against such an enemy. I had even seen a concentration camp the previous autumn when our division overran the Natzweiler camp in Alsace.

But Natzweiler had been empty. It had been evacuated before we arrived but not much before. An unfinished meal, beer bottles half full, had been hastily abandoned in the SS officers' mess.

Among the many unsavory duties of the Nazi SS was guard duty at the extermination camps. At least soldiers in ordinary units of the Wehrmacht, the German Army, were spared that.

The Natzweiler camp sat atop a mountain near the little village south of Strasbourg. A middle-aged man who approached me on the village street volunteered to take me to the camp. He said he had been an inmate and had escaped when the last truck of prisoners overturned speeding down the mountain.

He didn't look like my vision of a concentration camp prisoner; he was too well-fed. But I had no other reason not to believe him.

He showed me the stark barracks, with the wooden shelves that served as bunks stacked one atop the other. Row after row of them.

He showed me the gas chamber. It did, really, look like a shower room.

He showed me a pit where, he said, prisoners were machine-gunned.

He showed me the double fences, about 10 feet apart, inside which the fierce Doberman pinschers roamed in case a prisoner got through or over the first barbed wire fence.

At Natzweiler, that gray November day, I did not see the crematorium, if there was one. I'm sure there was, given the Nazi efficiency in disposing of unwanted goods.

For me, the Natzweiler camp was a mock-up, a dry run for the day when I would run across the real thing. There was no question that Dachau was the real thing.

As I walked toward the Dachau gate, a great deal of activity was going on near a train on a siding.

When I got closer, I saw what was going on. A man was unloading dead bodies from the freight car. He wore the floppy blouse and pants, with vertical black and white stripes, of the concentration camp inmate.

I had seen them before, liberated, lining the roads as they walked or bicycled back to whatever homes they had known before. A few were headed west, toward France, but mostly they streamed toward the east.

This one was outside the camp fence, but he wasn't fleeing. He was doing what he had been assigned to do probably early in the morning before American forces overran the camp. He was unloading corpses.

He only stared when I spoke in English, so I tried the only foreign language I even halfway knew — my college French.

He was Polish, he told me in his fractured French, which he had picked up in the camp barracks. He had a team of horses and an old wooden wagon; the sort of wagon I had seen French farmers use to haul their cabbages to town.

But he was loading corpses. There were men and women. My memory doesn't recall seeing any children, but perhaps my mind has blocked that out.

Each person apparently had starved to death, en route to Dachau from some other camp.

TOURISTS ENTER THE CREMATORIUM at Dachau in 1968.

For some reason which has never been explained fully to me, whenever a death camp was about to be overrun by either the Russians or the Western Allies, the SS would evacuate the inmates as though it was necessary to get them to the safety of another camp not yet liberated.

Until then, I had never seen a person who had starved to death. It is difficult for me to decide which is the most gruesome.

Is it the eyes, staring so vacantly? Or the mouth, hanging open, lips stretched tightly over the teeth like a person about to shriek in terror? But there is no sound. Or maybe it is the cheekbones; they protrude in an ugly, eerie way.

As I think back, the inmate loading the bodies must have been a convict prisoner, not a political prisoner or Jew. Camp authorities used convict prisoners as a kind of straw boss, as informers, or to keep discipline in a barracks.

Called kapos, most were cruel and sadistic; they had to be if they wanted to please their masters for the reward of enough food to live on.

The man was of a husky build, and inmates of a death camp targeted for extermination were definitely not husky. They were skin and bones.

I asked the busy Pole where he was taking his grisly cargo.

He pointed over to a red brick structure about 100 yards or so beyond the railroad siding, still outside the camp enclosure.

I went over with him as he carted a load to its destination.

It was the crematorium.

It was a functional building with a grotesquely large smokestack; not grotesque, perhaps, if this were a small foundry, which it resembled. But grotesque for the raw material it handled and the function it performed.

I entered the outer door. Inside was a smallish foyer that ran the width of the building. The foyer led to the ovens — two of them, about 20 feet apart, doors open.

The concrete floors and walls of the room were functional, not pretty. The floor had a slick finish. The walls were whitewashed.

Each oven had an opening about 3 feet across and when I peered inside, the ovens looked to be about 7 feet deep. They were high enough to perform their function on several bodies at a time.

To the right of the right-hand oven and to the left of the left-hand oven were small rooms, maybe 15 feet wide and 20 feet long. They were barren of furniture or equipment, but they were not empty.

Each contained a pile of bodies — nude bodies; bodies that had not been machined-gunned or gassed, but bodies that had been starved to death. I assumed they were from the train.

The clothes had been removed and placed outside the crematorium in four immense piles — one for coats, one for pants, one for feminine attire, one for shoes. The Pole was busy removing clothes and adding them to the piles.

I have often wondered since that day: How many human bodies does it take to make a pile about 8 feet square and about 4½ feet high?

Each of those dozens of bodies that I saw that morning contained the soul of what was not long ago a human being. A person with hopes, dreams, desires, despairs.

Despairs. Each of us is puzzled by the mystery of death; some of us more than others, but we are increasingly aware of it as we grow older.

We wonder when; we wonder how. We assume it will be old age; maybe an illness, maybe an accident. We hope it will be swift and painless, and we hope it will allow some dignity.

Imagine the horror, the anger and the terror of knowing that your death would be at the dictates of another human being who looks upon you as a bug to be squashed.

He would determine how. He would determine when. And he would take a special pleasure in determining that it would be lingering and painful.

But, especially, he would determine that this ending would come shorn of dignity.

Each of those former human beings in the two careless piles had died without dignity.

I turned from the crematorium to find the sun still ablaze in its glory, a breeze gently stirring the early leaves.

It made no sense; after the scene I had just witnessed I felt the air should be filled with thunderclaps, the sky shredded by lightning, the wind howling.

Behind the camp gate, a poplar tree grew in front of each barracks building. Each was planted by that building's inmates in the only gesture of compassion by the administration; in the single gesture of sanity left to the inmates.

The camp inmates were now free, but that immense truth still seemed too unreal for them to comprehend.

Our troops were doing their best to maintain order, but they would have been no match for a massive dash for freedom by some 30,000 crazed inmates. Certainly, the GIs would not have turned their fire on these poor creatures.

But none left the compound. They were milling around, certainly not in military precision, but not in a disorganized fashion, either.

From somewhere, from the hidden depths of their sparse possessions in dark corners of their barracks, they had produced musical instruments. While the bulk of them watched, a few of their number marched in wavering cadence to the national anthems of their countries. Belgian. French. Polish.

Dachau's occupants were cheering the music and sometimes half-standing at attention as their particular anthem was played. Some cried, some sang.

There were thousands of them — men, women, and some children; all clad in the same floppy blouses and pants with vertical black and white stripes.

Tragedy thrived at the death camps, and a few scores remained to be settled by the inmates. One of those occurred about 100 feet from me on the edge of the parade grounds.

Suddenly an angry outcry rose above the sound of music. Dozens of inmates converged on one of their number, and I saw a club-like weapon rise and fall above the heads.

It ended as rapidly as it began; the inmates quickly faded back into the mass of black-and-white-clad humanity, leaving a faceless form lying on the ground.

Next to the body lay the weapon — a rifle with a broken stock. The inmates had killed another inmate, probably one of the hated kapos. I knew now why my friend the Pole had stayed his distance outside the compound.

The music played on; the people sang, shouted, cried. The sun was now at high noon, warm, gentle, soothing. It was time for me to leave. There was a war still to fight.

All I had seen and experienced was as a dream, a movie, the figment of a deranged imagination. This was different in its brutality. Nobody could write a real-life scenario this brutal. This wasn't violence against a few people; this was calculated violence against a race of people.

War is, indeed, hell — just as Gen. William Sherman said, but this was not Dante's hell — this was a living hell.

U.S. Army Capt. Hollis Limprecht, photographed in France in 1945.

ELZA ULPIS

Town: Omaha

In the war: A teenager in Latvia when World War II began. Her family was forced to flee from its home. She and her mother were separated from her brother and father. She and her mother eventually made their way to Omaha, where she met and married another Latvian refugee, Imants "Ed" Ulpis. It was 10 years after her family's separation before she heard from her brother, who had returned to Latvia. Her father, pictured above with Elza, died in a prison camp three months after their separation — but it was 58 years before Ulpis learned her father's fate.

In her words: "On Sept. 16, 1944, we woke up to see a German tank in our yard. ... We harnessed two wagons, hurriedly threw some stuff in and took off for the nearest forest to hide. Mother had put laundry to soak the night before. We took that wet. Cows and sheep we took along. I was 16; my brother was 18. There was a superstition not to look back if you want to return. In the bend of the road, I looked back. ... Fifty years later, I stopped by for a short time with my husband, his cousins and our son Edward."

DUANE STEVENS GRAY

Town: O'Neill

Service: Technician 5th grade and sharpshooter with the 700th Quartermaster Corps of the Seventh Army.

In the war: In January 1943, was one of 8,000 troops shipped from San Francisco to Khorramshahr, Iran, in the Persian Gulf. Stationed at several depots along the route, where he dispatched truck convoys of supplies to Russia, which was fighting Germany on the Eastern Front. Received an Allied Service Medal from Russia for this service.

In his words: "After two years, Germany was defeated on the Eastern Front, so we were shipped to the Western Front to supply troops in the Battle of the Bulge. There are some good and some bad experiences stuck in my mind. The good were the comradeship with buddies and friendliness of the defeated Germans. The bad were the destruction of Europe and the terrible odors of the concentration camps we marched past. After two years in the desert and 10 months in the destruction of Europe, Nebraska never looked so good."

MANIA FRIEDMAN, LEFT, and Rachel Rosenberg in 2005

'How did we make it, could you tell me?'

BY HENRY J. CORDES

THE THREE SISTERS WATCHED the crematoria chimneys belch black death around the clock.

They lived month after month with no water to bathe in, no bed to sleep in, only meager rations.

How was it possible they all survived more than four years at Auschwitz?

"How did we make it, could you tell me?" Rachel asked in 2005. It's not a rhetorical question. Her eyes are searching, as if there is an answer somewhere in the face of a visitor.

"How we survive?" sister Mania asked in her heavy accent. "Ask God. He knows. We were in God's hands."

BLUMA POLONSKI in 2003

Mania Friedman, Rachel Rosenberg and Bluma Polonski have been called Omaha's "Sisters of the Shoah" — the Hebrew word for the Holocaust.

Remarkably, three resilient spirits — who knew nothing but terror, deprivation and loss — survived the Nazi death machine to go on to lives of happiness, success and love.

Their saga began in Wolanow, Poland. In the full bloom of life, the three young women lived with their parents and three younger brothers when the country fell to the Nazi blitzkrieg.

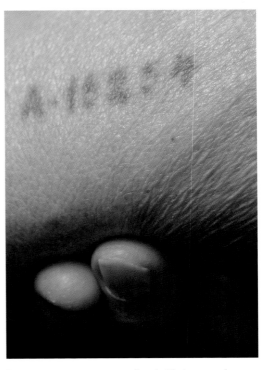

THE IDENTIFICATION NUMBER that the Nazis tattooed on Rachel Rosenberg's left forearm at Auschwitz.

'The fire continues'

"The Germans will not hurt us — they are cultured people," their mother said of the occupiers, who would send her and the family's youngest boy to death at Treblinka.

The rest of the family was scattered across the Nazi death camp system. The girls' father was gassed at Buchenwald. Their oldest brother was found hiding in a barrel at a holding camp and shot.

> *"No one understands — our feelings, our hurt, did not go away."*
>
> — RACHEL ROSENBERG, AUSCHWITZ SURVIVOR

Mania and Bluma arrived together at Auschwitz. Rachel and young brother Jacob would arrive soon after, but it would be months before Rachel would spy her sisters working on railroad tracks near her compound.

"Mania!" Rachel shouted, tossing her sister a piece of bread.

Making it through the Nazi's macabre classification system that sorted out the old, very young and sick for death, the four siblings all were put to work. Rachel's job hauling bricks for camp projects took her by the crematoria each day.

"You expect death at any time," she said. "If not today, it will be tomorrow."

For Jacob, about 12, that day came in the brutal cold of January about a year after arrival.

Rachel was very protective of her brother, holding him close at night on the hard wooden bunk. But the SS grabbed him one morning and led him to the gas chambers. Rachel cried, begging the soldiers to stop, only to be knocked to the ground.

The girls ultimately were transferred to munitions factories in Czechoslovakia and liberated by Russian troops in May 1945. Reuniting in refugee camps, they all married fellow Holocaust survivors who had their own horrific pasts. All ultimately settled in Omaha.

With their husbands, all three succeeded in business. Carl's Tailors, Friedman's Bakery and Ak-Sar-Ben TV and Appliance became Omaha institutions.

And the three women who ended the war with no other family had homes filled with photos of smiling children, grandchildren, nieces and nephews.

They rarely spoke of their ordeal. Rachel said seeing a railroad track brought back painful memories of the trains that daily delivered the doomed.

"I'm not normal. I try to live like I'm normal, but I'm not," she said. "No one understands — our feelings, our hurt, did not go away. As I talk here, I'm in Auschwitz. I'm there now."

SHOAH. After the wartime murder of 6 million Jews by Adolf Hitler's Nazis, the word became the collective choice of Jews throughout the world to describe the Holocaust — an event its survivors say is indescribable.

Rabbi Aryeh Azriel in 1990 tried to explain the meaning of shoah. Although words are inadequate, he said, shoah is most closely defined both as remembrance and as "a burnt offering that is completely consumed by fire."

"People were gassed and burned totally, and those people who did not die burned inside," said Azriel, who did not personally experience the Holocaust. "The fire continues in those survivors."

Auschwitz death camp

More than 1 million lives were lost at Auschwitz before it was liberated on Jan. 27, 1945. The largest Nazi concentration camp, it has become a symbol of the Holocaust. When prisoners arrived, those not fit for slave labor went straight to the gas chambers. Their bodies were then incinerated in large crematoria.

ORIGINS OF JEWS DEPORTED TO AUSCHWITZ

Hungary	438,000
Poland	300,000
France	69,000
Netherlands	60,000
Greece	55,000
Bohemia and Moravia	46,000
Slovakia	27,000
Belgium	25,000
Germany and Austria	23,000
Yugoslavia	10,000
Italy	7,500
Norway	690
Other places	34,000
Total Jews	**1,095,190**

OTHER GROUPS

Poles	Up to 151,000
Gypsies	23,000
Soviet POWs	15,000
Other nationalities	25,000
Total prisoners (1940-45)	1,300,000

Figures are estimates only

Source: Anatomy of the Auschwitz Death Camp, edited by Yisrael Gutman and Michael Berenbaum; Official Guide of Auschwitz Museum; the Times Atlas of the World

CLIFFORD L. PRATT
Town: Omaha
Service: Served with the 82nd Airborne Division from July to December 1945, on "occupation duty" in Berlin.
In the war: Arrived in the European Theater of Operations as a paratrooper in July 1944, one month after D-Day. Returned to the United States in January 1946 and rode in the WWII "Victory Parade" down Fifth Avenue in New York City.
In his words: "I don't want to discuss my combat experiences, but I would like to tell our future generations something they can be proud of as Americans. ... The Germans had concentration camps and slave labor camps. ... I personally was involved in knocking a Russian soldier 'cuckoo' when he started to rape a German woman in our sector of Berlin. We were not angels, but Americans did not conduct ourselves in this way. Our 'probity' (honor) prevented such conduct. ... I (want) to emphasize to our younger generations that Americans, as a nation, are good and decent people. As you go through life be especially proud to be one."

'I mourn all my life about what happened'

ON APRIL 28, 1945, Carl Rosenberg, a Polish Jew, was part of a group forced to march out of Dachau to the south, through Munich and into the mountains. A tailor, he had spent much of World War II forced to outfit the German air force, the Luftwaffe.

His talent kept him alive.

Rosenberg, whose parents and four siblings were killed in the Holocaust, was liberated by soldiers in American tanks on the morning of May 2, after the German SS had locked him and others in a barn the night before.

He recalled the barn shaking as the tanks approached on a nearby road. A fellow prisoner was lifted on shoulders to look outside.

"White star!" the man shouted, describing the insignia on the tanks. "White star! Americana! Americana!"

In his 1990 book, "As God Is My Witness," Rosenberg wrote that it became clear that the Germans intended to kill as many of their prisoners as possible before the surrender.

At the end, the population at the Dachau death camp grew to 70,000, and history books say the SS was planning to kill all the remaining Eastern Europeans and Jews there — until the Americans arrived.

Rosenberg said his family had lived in Poland for 13 centuries. His sister, Rachel, was the first of his family to die — machine-gunned in the streets of Warsaw in November 1939.

His mother, he said, saw the Germans execute his brother Maurice in March 1943. Nathan David, another brother, died in a camp in 1944. Their father, according to what Carl heard from a survivor, died in January 1945 when he was kicked for not working hard enough.

Rosenberg's mother, he said, was choked to death on a cattle train. And sister Toba, he was told, died when Germans put women prisoners on a boat and blew it up.

The Omaha tailor, who once came face to face with Dr. Josef Mengele, the Nazi "angel of death," wept as he talked of his family in 1995.

"I mourn all my life about what happened," he said in heavily accented English. "None of them made it."

Because of his work as a tailor for the Nazis, Rosenberg said, he was stronger than many inmates. But "strength" was relative. At the time of his liberation, he said, he weighed 105 pounds.

"Even when the very idea of surviving could drive a person to the brink of madness, we prayed to survive," Rosenberg said.

His prayers were answered.

On April 30, 1945, the day the U.S. Army reached Dachau, and as Rosenberg and other inmates were being marched to the south, Adolf Hitler shot himself in the head. The Third Reich was falling.

Rosenberg said wet snow fell on the inmates as they slept that night. The next night, they were herded into the barn and locked in with a board across the door.

The next morning, when they heard the whirr and rumble of the tanks, which Rosenberg called "the sound of American power," the weak men pounded their shoulders in unison against the barn door — and heard the board crack.

Moments later, they burst free, running toward the tanks and freedom. The Germans surrendered on May 8.

Rosenberg came to Omaha in 1949 with his wife, Rachel, a survivor of Auschwitz, and opened a tailor shop.

Said Rosenberg: "The Americans did so much for us. They fought against slavery, against barbarism. They laid down their lives and they died. People don't realize what it was to be a soldier and to fight such a murderous nation."

CARL ROSENBERG
in 1979

"Even when the very idea of surviving could drive a person to the brink of madness, we prayed to survive."

— CARL ROSENBERG

'Living dead and left to starve'

MIRIAM GOLOMB GROSSMAN of Omaha was a 23-year-old nurse in Lodz when the Nazis invaded Poland in 1939.

With limited food and medical supplies, no heat and several families packed into a room, many died daily of starvation, she said. Others were plucked from food lines and shipped to concentration camps, notably the notorious Auschwitz concentration camp.

In late 1944, the Nazis took the surviving Jews in railroad cattle cars to Auschwitz. "It is unimaginable what happened there," Grossman said.

MIRIAM GROSSMAN in 1991

On arriving at the death camp, the Jews were ordered to strip and their heads were shaved. They were sent to showers, given one garment and housed in animal stalls to wait their turns to be executed in the gas chambers.

Before her turn came, however, Grossman said she was selected in a nude lineup before Dr. Josef Mengele — nicknamed the "angel of death" by survivors — to be sent to a German factory on the Czechoslovakian border. Those not selected for the factory work were sent to their deaths.

One day in 1945, Grossman had fainted from hunger and been dragged out of the way to die when she was roused by cheering and laughter.

Struggling to peer around a doorway, she saw Soviet soldiers liberating the German aircraft-parts factory where she and other Polish Jews had been forced to work in the last stages of the war.

After surviving five years in a Nazi-held ghetto in her hometown of Lodz and several months at Auschwitz, she was "living dead and left to starve" when the Soviets arrived.

She spent the first three years after the war in a displaced-persons camp in Austria, where she met Ignac Grossman, a Czech machinist. They were married in 1947. In 1948, their son, Alex, was born, and in 1949 the family immigrated to the United States and ended up in Omaha.

"It's so hard to remember this," she said in 1991 of the years under the Nazis. "If not for the benefit of future generations I wouldn't do it."

'He is not a forgotten soul'

BY DAVID HENDEE

OSCAR SCHINDLER had a list. David Kaufmann had a heart.

Kaufmann was a Grand Island, Neb., businessman who quietly sponsored more than 80 Jewish couples and families — an estimated 200 or more people — to immigrate to the United States from Nazi Germany before America entered World War II.

DAVID KAUFMANN in 1939

Holocaust scholars say they know of no other individual who sponsored more Jewish refugees to the United States than Kaufmann.

"We all have our saints. He is ours. He is not a forgotten soul," former Omahan Dr. Guinter Kahn told Kaufmann biographer Bill Ramsey, who with Betty Dineen Shrier wrote "Doorway to Freedom: The Story of David Kaufmann."

Retired Omaha dentist Benjamin Nachman said he found Kaufmann's story more intriguing than that of Schindler, the German industrialist whose list of more than 1,200 Polish Jews working in his munitions factory kept them out of Nazi death camps. Schindler's story was told in a book that filmmaker Steven Spielberg made into "Schindler's List."

"Here is a very successful merchant — and charitable man — in central Nebraska who did all this, and no one in Grand Island knew about it," Nachman said in 2005. "He led two lives."

Nachman discovered Kaufmann's story in the 1990s while seeking the identities of people around the world who helped save Jews from the Holocaust, the systematic Nazi extermination of 6 million Jews and 5 million others in the 1930s and 1940s.

Nachman's parents came to America from Europe in the 1920s. He lost 23 relatives in the Holocaust.

He started his search for rescuers in the 1960s, provided survivor stories to Spielberg for "Schindler's List" and interviewed Holocaust survivors for the Shoah Foundation.

Nachman initially wanted to learn how his grandparents and an infant cousin died. But he changed his focus to tell the stories of the largely anonymous thousands who saved many Jewish lives.

"I probably held a hidden agenda in the belief that if just one more person tried, then more of my family might have survived," he said.

Nachman said Kaufmann's determination and compassion inspired him to find someone to write the story.

Kaufmann was born into a Jewish family in Bad Meunstereifel, near Cologne, Germany, in 1875. He worked for a Berlin umbrella maker before immigrating to America in 1903.

He was working as a New York City store clerk when Grand Island merchant Samuel N. Wolbach, on a buying trip, noticed Kaufmann's ability with customers. Wolbach hired Kaufmann to work in his department store, and Kaufmann went west to Grand Island, population 7,554.

In 1906, Kaufmann opened a variety store with his name on the sign. He prospered. At one time, nine other stores in Nebraska communities, including Kearney, Hastings, North Platte and Gothenburg, were affiliated with Kaufmann's five-and-dime business.

A one-time Grand Island partner, the late Harold W. Mangelsen, was the founder of the Mangelsen hobby and crafts store in Omaha. "My dad always credited David Kaufmann with teaching him how to run a variety store," said David Mangelsen, company president.

In 1936, Kaufmann received a plea from a cousin, Feodora Levy Kahn, asking for help in immigrating to America with her new husband, Isador. A rock was thrown through the couple's window on their wedding night.

"They needed to get out," Nachman said. "He (Kaufmann) didn't hesitate."

The Kahns settled in Grand Island. Feodora soon asked Kaufmann to help other relatives, including Marcel Kahn, who became a businessman in Omaha.

During the next few years, Kaufmann signed dozens of "affidavits of support" — pledging his ability to provide for the immigrants if they needed it — for relatives and others fleeing from Germany. They settled in cities across the United States. Kaufmann helped at least two death camp survivors come to America after the war.

"We'll probably never know the precise number of people he brought over," Ramsey said.

For Kaufmann's 80th birthday in 1955, many families Kaufmann had helped pooled their money to hire an artist to draw a tree with Kaufmann's name at the roots and their names at the tips of branches. With leftover money, they bought a tree to be planted in Jerusalem in Kaufmann's honor, Shrier said.

Kaufmann was married twice and had no children. He retired Jan. 1, 1956. He died in 1969 at age 93 and was buried in Grand Island.

"Kaufmann's humanitarian efforts were unprecedented at the time," Nachman said. "No doubt he saved many from extermination during the Nazi regime."

Nearly driven mad by hunger

BEA KARP WAS ONLY 10 at the time, but she vividly recalled the brown, gray and black walls of the concentration camp, the 9 o'clock roll call, the meager loaf of bread she and other children and women had to share in the barracks.

The women and children were so hungry, they fought over food.

"It was terrible. These women, who had been ladies at one time, turned into animals," Karp recalled in 2005.

Born in Germany in 1932, Karp recalls encountering anti-Semitism at a young age. It escalated in 1940 when the Gestapo barged into her home

BEA KARP in 2008

and ordered the family to pack a small suitcase. They were deported to an internment camp in France.

The men were placed in separate barracks from the women and children. But that did not stop Karp and her little sister from marching past a Nazi guard to visit her father.

She recalled the day that the men were given raw eggs. Her father discovered his egg was bloody — an offense to his religious beliefs as an Orthodox Jew. To Karp's horror, he threw the egg against the wall.

Driven by hunger, "I ran over to the wall to lick it off," Karp said, "but then I saw the expression on my father's face, and I couldn't do it."

She did not understand the lesson her father taught her that day until nearly two years later, after she and her sister had moved from the camp to the safety of a Catholic convent. They were aided by a French relief group.

Karp told one of the nuns that it would be easier to be Catholic than Jewish. The nun explained, though, that Karp had a choice to keep or change her beliefs.

Karp said that's when she realized that by throwing the bloody egg, her father was telling her she had a choice even when others were trying to control her. She chose to remain Jewish.

In June 1945, she and her sister had the good fortune to go stay with relatives in England and later immigrated to the United States. When they were older, they learned that their parents had been killed in the camps.

WITH AN AGFA CAMERA he picked up in Germany, Nebraska soldier Elmer Chapp shot this photo of an armed American soldier standing near the bodies of German SS soldiers at Dachau.

A liberator and a prisoner — both survivors

BY ERIN GRACE

DURING WORLD WAR II, Elmer Chapp was a 19-year-old GI from southeast Nebraska. Kitty Williams, also 19, was a Hungarian who was separated from her father at the Auschwitz concentration camp. Chapp and Williams hugged when they met in 2009.

HE WAS A 19-YEAR-OLD FARM KID from southeast Nebraska. She was a 19-year-old businessman's daughter from Hungary.

Elmer Chapp took many pictures of the Dachau concentration camp with his Agfa camera. He had volunteered for the Army. She had been taken from her home.

He had sailed on the Queen Mary over the Atlantic to the front lines in France, where he got his first taste of sniper fire, and ended up a liberator at Dachau. She had been crammed in a boxcar on a weeklong journey to Poland, where she saw her father for the last time inside the gates of Auschwitz.

Elmer Chapp and Kitty Williams could have perished during this chapter in history. Yet both, remarkably, survived. And more than six decades after their separate, harrowing experiences during World War II, their paths crossed in the ballroom of an Omaha hotel.

Chapp, of Falls City, and 400 other Nebraska veterans who flew to Washington, D.C., on the expenses-paid Heartland Honor Flights gathered for a reunion dinner in April 2009.

In all, seven chartered flights ferried 1,500 Nebraska veterans to the nation's capital to see the National World War II Memorial erected in their honor.

Williams, of Council Bluffs, was among a dozen Holocaust survivors invited to the reunion dinner.

Like most World War II veterans, Chapp didn't tell war stories. He came home, got married, started a business and raised a family. His mother once recalled her son tossing in his sleep with nightmares in their Virginia, Neb., farmhouse in the days after his 1946 return from war.

He wouldn't hunt again, and aside from teaching his son how to handle a gun, also wouldn't pick one up. He left the movie "Glory" during a battle scene. His wife remembered the few times "Chappie," as she called him, would begin to talk and then tear up, unable to continue.

"There'll be a time when you can" talk, she'd say.

Like many Holocaust survivors, Williams carried the terror and loss but also a sense of incredible luck.

She, too, kept the past at bay after landing in Council Bluffs in 1947; she didn't tell her children until they were older.

"I didn't want them to grow up with this baggage, to be different," she said.

Chapp's story begins in 1944 after he graduated from high school in a class of five. The war was on, and he signed up to help Uncle Sam.

The day after his ship docked at Marseille, France, the grandson of Czech immigrants was sent with a group of replacements to the front line.

An experienced sergeant from Texas, back for another tour, was in the middle of telling Chapp how you could tell a sniper's location by listening to the sound of the bullet when the Texan whipped around and shot a sniper.

The Allies pushed forward and, in the winter of 1944, Chapp was embroiled in the Battle of the Bulge in Belgium. He spent Christmas Eve in a foxhole.

By winter's end, Chapp was one of five in his group of 60 who had not been killed or wounded. That's how he was able, on April 29, 1945, to storm the gates of the Nazi concentration camp in Bavaria, at Dachau.

The U.S. Holocaust Memorial Museum in Washington describes the camp as a massive former munitions factory that operated as a concentration camp from 1933 until liberation. It held a crematorium and 32 barracks and served as home to many non-Jewish prisoners, including Gypsies, homosexuals, clergy and anyone opposed to the Nazi cause. In later years, more Jews were sent there.

From 1940 to 1945, Dachau housed at least 188,000 prisoners; of those, at least 28,000 in Dachau and its subcamps were said to have perished. Both figures are probably undercounts.

The Nazis moved large numbers of prisoners from concentration camps as Allied forces advanced. The arrival of additional prisoners at Dachau, which was farther removed from the front lines, caused conditions there to deteriorate dramatically.

The U.S. Holocaust Memorial Museum says that several days before American forces arrived, Dachau and its subcamps had 67,665 registered prisoners; a third of them were Jewish.

By April 29, 1945, Nazi commanders had abandoned Dachau. Guards remained, and so did boxcars loaded with the bodies of prisoners who hadn't survived the trip from outlying camps.

Corpses were left piled up in the crematorium. Typhus ravaged the camp.

This is the scene that unfolded before Chapp as he and others of the 42nd "Rainbow" Division fought their way into Dachau.

Chapp fired away — with his M-1 as well as with an Agfa camera he had picked up in Germany.

Chapp shot one SS trooper. "It was either him or me, and it wasn't going to be me." He then took the soldier's picture.

With his camera, Chapp captured the juxtaposition of life and death on that day.

Here were the smiling faces of a throng of now-freed men. Here was the stack of naked corpses ready to be cremated.

Like Chapp, Kitty Williams hadn't heard of gas chambers or concentration camps and wasn't fully aware of the horror happening to Jews across Europe.

So in June 1944, when she and her father were forced onto the train bound for Auschwitz, they and the other passengers figured it couldn't get worse. They had already been taken from home and forced into ghettos after the Nazis invaded Hungary in March.

They thought they were bound for a work camp.

At one stop, the Nazis demanded that the passengers hand over valuables. Her father cut open the soles of his shoes and handed over some money he had hidden. He did not give them a wedding picture of one of his daughters. But the Nazis eventually got that, too.

Once at Auschwitz, Williams and her father embraced. He told her he would see her later.

She walked in the women's line to be stripped, shaved, showered and inspected.

She was given clothes that didn't fit and a dish that served as a pillow. Her first night there, she smelled burning flesh and heard screams of people begging for their lives. The next three months were harrowing.

Her ticket out was a chance to work in a German munitions camp where conditions were slightly better. She kept thinking of her father and his torn shoes. Later she would learn that he had been killed the day they arrived.

As the Allies pushed on, Williams' fate hung in the balance. Nazis planned to send the factory workers to another concentration camp to be gassed. Instead, they abandoned the factory, and Williams and some two dozen female workers fled to the hillside. Starving, they ate grass.

Days later — on April 1, 1945 — they spotted an American convoy of tanks. One of the women stripped off her white slip, tied it to a tree branch and waved like crazy.

Williams' next meal was boiled potatoes.

She met an American pilot serving in the war who was from Council Bluffs and landed there in 1947. She got a job at a bank and worked her way up to bank vice president. She raised three children.

"You look back on it, and you think it can't happen," she said. "In everything, I was so fortunate. I don't know why I was picked to be alive."

Chapp, too, counted his blessings. He survived Europe and was relieved that his next assignment was Vienna, as a member of a military police detail guarding Gen. Mark Clark.

Chapp returned to the United States in 1946 and decided that a military career was not for him. Neither was farm life. He worked first as a mechanic, then bought a service station in Auburn, Neb. He sold that and bought an oil-delivery business in Falls City.

He married Caroline in 1951, and they had four children, including one who died as a toddler.

After Chapp developed the film he had shot during the war, he wrote captions in tiny cursive on the back. He stored the small black-and-white prints in an old cardboard box once containing his mother's arch supports.

"And people believe this didn't happen," said Caroline Chapp as she looked at the Dachau pictures.

Elmer Chapp said that day at Dachau, he couldn't shake his own disbelief. He kept thinking: "This can't be happening."

"It's kind of hard to put in words."

There was the horror. But, in Chapp's photo of the faces of the saved, one can see renewed hope.

ELMER CHAPP
in 1946 and in 2009

KITTY WILLIAMS
in 1945 and in 2009

V-E Day

WITHIN MINUTES AFTER NAZI GERMANY signed the surrender documents at the famous "little red schoolhouse" in Reims, France, a young U.S. Army captain did two unusual things. ★ In the Allied war room where the documents had been signed, the 27-year-old captain checked to see whether anyone was looking. With a penknife, he then cut a 3-inch strip of wood from the table as a souvenir of history. The table still was set up with more than a dozen chairs, and the captain sat down in each of the chairs. "I wanted to make sure I could say I sat in the chairs where the surrender was signed," Allan Pickett of Papillion recalled in 1995. ★ His reaction to word that the war in Europe was over? "There were no handsprings, and there was no jumping for joy," he said. "It sounds strange to say that, but there was no celebration. Just a profound silence."

On May 8, 1945, 8-year-old John Radicia hawked American flags and copies of The World-Herald announcing the end of the war in Europe. Later, he would donate his earnings from the flag sales to the Red Cross in honor of his brother Pvt. Harold Radicia, who died in 1944 at age 19 while serving his country. John Radicia, his brother Joe, and their father, Joe Sr., before them, sold magazines, newspapers and racing sheets and swapped stories and opinions on the corner of 16th and Farnam Streets from 1908 until the brothers closed shop in December 1996.

As Oran Skaw and his unit approached a concentration camp near Ohrdruf, German guards killed the prisoners. Skaw took this photo afterward.

'We still weren't through'

"I can still see the bodies on the ground in that first camp. I don't even have to close my eyes."

— ORAN SKAW

WHEN ADOLF HITLER'S ARMY GAVE UP, Oran Skaw was too weary and too numb from the horrors he had seen to celebrate. He and his GI buddies were just glad it was over.

"I had been in the Army for four years and four months and had been through five campaigns," Skaw, of Magnolia, Iowa, said in 1995. "I had a wife and I had a son I had never seen. I wanted to go home."

In a few more months, when World War II finally ended with Japan's surrender, Omahans would rush into the streets in joyous celebration, spontaneously forming conga lines that snaked through the cars parked on Farnam Street.

But May 8, 1945 — proclaimed as V-E Day for the victory in Europe — was a day that many residents of Omaha and the Midlands treated more with relief than elation.

Stores and bars closed, and churches opened. Defense factories such as the Martin Bomber Plant near Bellevue continued churning out the planes, weapons and supplies needed for a war that would not be over until the Japanese surrendered on Aug. 15.

Janet Soucie said she remembered how quickly thoughts turned to Japan after the German surrender.

"That Christmas (of 1944) had been very bleak because the war news was not good," Soucie said. "When this happened it was just the most thrilling moment to think that it was over. But we still weren't through."

Oran Skaw in 1995 shows a photo of himself during WWII.

The nation's triumph was not the only blessing that V-E Day brought her. The military sent word that her husband, Ralf, an Army private, had been freed from a German prisoner of war camp and would soon be coming home.

Janet Soucie said she was excited but also worried about the physical condition of her husband, who nearly died as a prisoner of war. When she went to meet him a few weeks later she watched for a gaunt-looking man to step off the train in Omaha.

"All of a sudden I was whisked up in the air," she said. "I wasn't looking for a nice big man. They had built him up."

President Harry Truman said the day proclaimed for the World War II victory in Europe marked a "solemn but glorious" hour for the nation.

"We must work to finish the war," Truman said. "Our victory is but half-won. The West is free, but the East is still in bondage to the treacherous tyranny of the Japanese. When the last Japanese division has surrendered unconditionally, then only will our fighting job be done."

The British, who had seen their neighbors killed and homes destroyed by a barrage of German bombs and rockets, frolicked in the streets to mark the end of six years of war.

Ed Jaksha of Omaha was a member of the U.S. Army's signal corps who happened to be in front of Buckingham Palace in London the day the war ended in Europe.

"The British had been through hell and it was a tremendous relief," Jaksha, later known as a tax watchdog, recalled in 1995. "There was just a mass of people waving flags, cheering and crying. The king and queen waved to me and I waved back."

Pierre Bossant grew up in occupied Paris and had watched German soldiers shoot people on the street and tear through his house while searching for members of the resistance movement.

When the Allied troops marched into Paris in August 1944 to liberate his city, it was one of the most exhilarating moments of his life, Bossant said. He said he had similar memories of V-E Day, when the war finally was over in his homeland.

"We went through a tough time," said Bossant of Omaha. "We could be French again."

George Buglewicz was a B-24 radio operator and gunner stationed at an air base in England during the final months of the war. An Allied victory had seemed assured for weeks or more, Buglewicz said, but the air crews had to cope with deadly reminders almost daily that the Germans were not quite through.

"The sense was that they were fighting harder," said Buglewicz, a Douglas County officeholder for 28 years. "Our planes were still getting shot down. It was winding down but it is just like someone who knows he is getting beat and puts all his final strength into it."

When news of Germany's surrender finally came, Buglewicz said, it was greeted with whoops of joy.

"There was a lot of drinking of warm beer and champagne," Buglewicz said. "We knew we were going home. We knew there were no more missions to be flown."

For Lyle Harter of Omaha, the war had ended months before when he was severely wounded on a battlefield in Italy. All the soldiers in the Springfield, Mo., hospital where Harter was recovering cheered for their colleagues who were still fighting when V-E Day was announced, he said.

"In that 26-bed ward everybody was screaming," said Harter.

William Rynearson of Omaha said he and fellow members of the 395th Field Artillery also had sensed for weeks that the end was near as they rushed through Germany and into Czechoslovakia.

"We were traveling so many miles a day and our progress was

ORAN SKAW RECORDED HISTORY with his camera as the Third Reich unraveled. Above is a photo Skaw took of the concentration camp in Ohrdruf, Germany. On the left is one of the many war-ravaged towns he saw in Germany and Czechoslovakia.

so rapid," Rynearson said. "We realized it was near the end of the war."

Rynearson returned for a visit to the Czech Republic in 1995 so he could mark the anniversary of the war's end in the same region he was in 50 years before.

In the final weeks of the war in Europe, Skaw walked through a German concentration camp near the town of Ohrdruf. German guards, aware of the advancing Allied soldiers, had sprayed the prisoners with machine-gun fire before they could be saved, Skaw said.

One prisoner who was not shot but feigned death survived to tell of the atrocities that Skaw had heard of in the previous weeks but discounted as rumors. Skaw looked at shirts, jackets, dresses and other clothing piled nearly to the roofs of camp buildings and was horrified when he realized the tales had all been true.

"I can still see the bodies on the ground in that first camp," Skaw said. "I don't even have to close my eyes."

George Smith of Omaha was camped in the woods with the Army's 69th Division when news of the German surrender reached his unit. There was little backslapping and only a brief moment taken for celebration, Smith said. The soldiers passed around a five-gallon jug of wine and took a few sips, he said, but they were bone tired and weary from months of combat in the snow and a nearly constant barrage of shelling.

Smith was already thinking about what he would do when he got home.

"We just figured we would get on with the rest of our lives."

GEORGE BUGLEWICZ in 1995

The Allied War Room in Reims, France, was the scene for Germany's surrender. The three officers in the left foreground are the German delegates. At the center of the group facing the Germans is Gen. Walter Bedell Smith, the Allies' chief of staff.

'This is the day that ends the war over here'

HUGH TINLEY OF OMAHA believed that at 27 years old, he was the youngest of the 20 or so men in the Allied War Room when Col. Gen. Gustav Jodl signed the surrender for the Germans.

It came at 2:41 a.m. on May 7, 1945, which was 7:41 p.m. on May 6, Omaha time.

About 20 men crowded into the Allied War Room at the schoolhouse in Reims, France. Tinley, a captain on Gen. Dwight D. Eisenhower's staff, said all the other officers present, as well as the few news reporters allowed, were older, mostly middle-aged.

Tinley later sat at the table where history was made and wrote in longhand to his wife, Wanda, whom he had not seen in 14 months:

"This is the day that ends the war over here. Think of it, I have lived through this much of it. You may not believe it, but my chances were awfully slim when I saw you last. Think of all those we both used to know, junior officers, who are not with us anymore."

Hugh Tinley in 2005

He also wrote that he had learned two days earlier that "the Krauts had tossed in the towel" and were dickering with Gen. Walter Bedell Smith, an American whom Tinley called "Eisenhower's guard dog."

Tinley, a communications officer who posted supply-movement information for Ike daily on maps in the War Room, joked in his letter home that neither the Germans nor our Russian allies really should be there — neither had War Room passes.

Besides, there was "some pretty hot dope posted in there," such as the width of Broadway in New York and the depth of the Missouri River between Omaha and Council Bluffs under the Douglas Street Bridge.

"Imagine what the Germans would give for information like that," he quipped.

It was a giddy time, and soon celebrations erupted in streets from Paris to New York to Omaha. May 8 was declared V-E Day.

On May 5, 1945, Tinley had written to his wife that officers had been "tramping in and out of my War Room," and something was happening. "Am quite sure it's the real thing."

Little did he know when he bounded off to Fort Leavenworth, Kan., he wrote, that he would one day watch the end of the war in Europe. "If this is the final surrender, it will be quite a thing for me."

It was quite a thing for many, but tempered by the knowledge that war in the Pacific continued.

Tinley grew up in Council Bluffs, graduating from Creighton Prep in Omaha in 1936 and from Creighton University in 1940. He majored in math and statistics.

He went to Europe in 1944, assigned to Allied headquarters in the spring. Eisenhower was from Kansas and liked to talk college football with the junior officer from Nebraska.

Hitler committed suicide on April 30, 1945, but the outcome was clear before then. As for the Germans dickering for terms of surrender, Ike sent unequivocal word — quit or keep fighting. They quit.

It was deathly still in the room, Tinley recalled in 2005, when Jodl signed for the Germans. Smith signed for the Americans, and then took Jodl and the other Germans to see Eisenhower.

Jodl later was convicted of war crimes and hanged.

In a 1955 article that he wrote for The World-Herald, Tinley called V-E Day the culmination of a miracle. As for the German war machine: "Here was this military Frankenstein brought to heel."

'Two Down, One to Go'

BY ROBERT MCMORRIS

I WAS IN AN ARMY PROGRAM at South Dakota State College at Brookings when we heard the news that the Germans had surrendered. The war in Europe was to end officially the following day.

It was over! Finally. Through all of my teenage years to that point — one-third of my life — the struggle in Europe never was out of our thoughts.

Now the bombs, the killing, the hedgerow assaults and the tank attacks had stopped.

The bluebirds once again would fly over the white cliffs of Dover, as the song promised, and our guys, or at least some of them, would be coming home to their own little rooms again.

My Uncle Stanley would be among the homeward bound.

COLUMNIST ROBERT MCMORRIS in 1998

A cook with the 90th Infantry of Gen. George Patton's Third Army, my uncle was drafted, in 1941, when he was 31. Younger comrades called him Dad.

I could imagine how relieved my grandmother must have been when the shooting stopped. She would, I knew, be thanking God.

Although she was a faithful churchgoer and baker of cherry pies for the Methodist Church Ladies Aid, Grandma never was conspicuous in her praying. But she told my mother that she prayed every day — quietly and in her own fashion — for Stanley's safe homecoming.

Less fortunate than my grandmother was Mrs. Badgerow, a gray-haired neighbor who had expressed dread to me in 1939 upon hearing news of Germany's invasion of Poland. Her son, Keith, an only child, did not come home from the war.

Although we managed to smuggle forbidden beer into our quarters on V-E Day, our celebration of that triumphal occasion was much more subdued than we would have liked.

We had a Captain Queeg-type commanding officer who thought that it was our duty to take a quiet moment and thank God we won in Europe but that we should get on with psyching ourselves up for "Our War."

Our War was the one in the Pacific, and that was not over.

In fact, on V-E Day plus 1 we were shown a film called "Two Down, One to Go."

It was produced by an Army training film crew whose products ordinarily were intended to help us avoid venereal disease. The recurring premise: Abstinence is recommended, but otherwise, this is what to do.

"Two Down, One to Go" obviously had been produced sometime earlier in anticipation of the German surrender.

Caricatures of the Nazis' Hitler and the Italians' Mussolini were shown in the film with their eyes closed and with red "X" marks over their faces.

However, Emperor Hirohito was depicted as still alive and wearing a diabolical grin.

We still had work to do, the film said.

The Army probably had distributed its "One to Go" film to numerous other units in an effort to emphasize that just because we had achieved victory in Europe there should be no letdown in our sense of mission relative to the Pacific. The war would not be over until we were in Tokyo.

★ MEMORIES ★ OF A GENERATION

HARRY C. SORENSEN
Town: Omaha
Service: U.S. Army Air Forces
In the war: He enlisted in October 1942 and was an aircraft mechanic with the 9th Air Force, stationed in England from January 1944 until March 1946.

In his words: "I moved around so much, I didn't know what outfit I was in or who my commanding officer was. I was sent all over England, France and Germany. My service records show that from December '44 until December '45, I was assigned to 11 different outfits. What did my crew and I do for the Army Air Corps? We picked up planes from wherever they had crash-landed. We repaired the planes and/or junked them out for parts. One B-26 named 'Patches' was repaired in the field, and the pilot flew it right out of the pasture. An A-20, the 'Shoo Shoo Baby,' had to get two new wings and an overhaul while still in the field. After the pilots flew the 'Shoo Shoo Baby,' they told me it flew better after field repairs than it did in all the bombing missions it had flown.

"I was sent on to the Battle of the Bulge in November and December '44. We had gotten all-new A-26s, and the guns came sealed in boxes. I was not given any technical orders for assembly. The CO told me to write my own. We were ordered to destroy the A-26s if the Germans came; we were not to leave anything behind. While able to hear gunfire from the battle only eight miles away, we mounted the guns and readied the planes for the pilots. On Dec. 25, 1944, the sun came out long enough for the planes to fly out of the field. Off they went. 'Goodbye, Nazis.' This was the beginning of the end of the Battle of the Bulge."

MEMORIES OF A GENERATION ★

ROBERT F. WILKINS

Town: Arlington

Service: U.S. Army Air Forces

In the war: Did his basic training at Keesler Air Base in Biloxi, Miss., and then technical school in Virginia before spending 14 days on the USS America. Landed in Liverpool, England, and then went on to Edinburgh, Scotland. He was in the 8th Air Force Command, GASCO (Ground Air Support Command). Was a mechanic on B-26s and spent most of his time overseas in England. He returned to the States in early 1945, got married and moved with his bride to Boise, Idaho, where he was stationed until the war in the Pacific ended.

In his words: "For two years we lived in tents at Smith's Lawn outside London where the royal family spent their weekends. We kept warm by burning coal in potbellied stoves. One day the royal family walked through camp. I still have a $5 bill with the signatures of King George and Princess Elizabeth. Once I flew with Col. Blair to Paris where he flew under the Eiffel Tower. He was never disciplined for that. I also used to fly with Lt. Barr to France in a C-47 for meetings. We would fly Gen. Wood to a base where we would land and unload a motorcycle that the general would ride to his meeting. We would wait for him to return, load up the motorcycle and fly back to England."

LYLE DROGE

Town: Pawnee City

Service: U.S. Army Air Forces

In the war: He was a B-25 pilot.

In his words: "I received my wings on Aug. 4, 1944. After a short stay at Dodge City, Kan., I was sent to Columbia, S.C., where I got a combat crew and trained for overseas. We flew missions to northern Italy and southern Austria. Our main mission was to keep supplies from reaching the German army in Italy. The targets we bombed were mostly rail bridges. The rail lines from Austria to Italy were heavily defended with anti-aircraft guns. These guns were the deadly 88mm, which shot some holes in my plane. We moved our air base to the Adriatic coast of Italy to shorten our missions. The action stopped on May 2, 1945, in our sector."

PAUL M. SCALISE

Town: Omaha

Service: U.S. Army Air Forces

In the war: He emigrated from Italy to Omaha in May 1940 at age 17 on what would be the last civilian ocean liner to depart from Italy during WWII. He traveled with a U.S. passport, being the son of an immigrant father who had earned his citizenship. He was drafted into the First Air Force in December 1942, when he could not yet speak English. In April 1944, he was sent to Norfolk, Va., where he served as buck sergeant/mess cook for up to 1,500 personnel. He also was responsible for 35 German POWs who were used for KP duty.

In his words: "We had 35 German prisoners in the kitchen doing KP duty. They were good workers and they did a good job. On Easter Sunday 1944, I called on Fritz — he was a German prisoner, old Fritz. He could speak English pretty well. He had his German accent and I had my Italian accent. I said, 'I want you to set the table in the storage room for you (prisoners) to eat Easter Sunday dinner.' He looked at me and he said, 'Sergeant, we're gonna eat what you guys eat? Oh, my goodness.' "

FRANK BATAILLON

Town: Ralston

Service: U.S. Navy Combat Aircrew, aviation ordnance 3rd class petty officer

In the war: Upon graduation from high school in 1944, he enlisted in the Navy for the Combat Aircrew program. He landed aboard the escort carrier USS Guadalcanal CVE-60 for submarine patrol in the Atlantic. The task group had five destroyers, and by the end of the war was credited with sinking 35 German submarines.

In his words: "On V-E Day, after morning chow, I went to the hangar deck of the carrier and as I looked out to the port side of the ship, I saw a German submarine with a white flag hanging from its conning tower. It had surfaced during the night and surrendered. … I received my first leave and afterward was assigned to Grosse Ile Naval Base outside of Detroit. There we trained for the invasion of Japan. We were told that we would lead the attack on Tokyo Bay. Two weeks before we were to be shipped out, they dropped the A-bomb."

NEAL PETTIT

Town: Lincoln

Service: First lieutenant, Army Air Forces

In the war: Texas native, B-24 navigator with 448th Bomb Group based at Seething, England. Flew 25 missions over Germany beginning Nov. 26, 1944; shot down near Berlin by a jet fighter on the 26th mission, April 4, 1945, a month before Germany surrendered. Burned around his eyes and on one hand by a fire in the plane, he parachuted and landed in a farm field. Captured, then freed by German army as U.S. troops advanced.

In his words: "In the early morning hours of Thursday, April 12, we left the air base on foot in the direction of the approaching U.S. troops, with two German guards assigned to act as a buffer between hostile Germans and us. In turn, when we were liberated, these guards were to receive preferential treatment when they were captured. Col. Crawford did not think it would be a good idea for us to be caught out in the open in the daytime so when we came to a little shed near the railroad tracks we took shelter in it. (After a day, night and part of the next day standing in the shed), sometime in the early afternoon an FW190 German fighter plane flew over us very low. About a quarter mile from us it was fired on from the ground. That let us know our guys were close. A while later, a tank came out from behind the trees so we could see it. It had U.S. markings. Someone took a white rag on a stick and walked out to the column. It was not long until several vehicles and an ambulance were sent over to our location. There were three or four of us that were immediately put in the ambulance and taken back to a field hospital. By Sunday, April 15, I was in a hospital in England."

FRANCIS SCHINSTOCK

Town: West Point

Service: U.S. Army, 1943 to 1946

In the war: He was inducted in May 1943 at Fort Leavenworth, Kan., and sent to Aberdeen Proving Grounds in Maryland, where he received basic training and was sent to school for ammunition supply to the Air Forces. During that time, he applied for the Aviation Cadet Program and was accepted and sent to the University of Pittsburgh. After about four months at Pittsburgh, however, the Aviation Cadet Program was discontinued and the cadets were sent to Camp Ellis, Ill., where they formed the 63rd Field Hospital.

In his words: "In February 1945, the 63rd crossed the Roer River on pontoon bridges and everything in sight was still burning from the air raids. This area was targeted because it was noted for producing most of the German munitions. We arrived in the burning town of Lovenich, Germany, which had just been taken about six hours before by the infantry. Hospital facilities were set up in a partially destroyed farmhouse. By noon the next day, we were receiving serious casualties. Surgeons, men and nurses worked for three days on end with virtually no rest with a constant backlog of casualties with chest and belly wounds awaiting operation. The 63rd kept advancing behind the infantry and artillery, and in May 1945, the war was officially over in the European Theater."

LLOYD LEWIS

Town: Omaha

Service: U.S. Navy, 1944-1946; U.S. Air Force, 1947-1966

In the war: He was a gunner and deck hand aboard USS LSMR 509 (Landing Ship Medium Rocket) in the Atlantic Ocean. The ship had 10 rocket launchers on it and was set to go up and down the shores of foreign countries to fire rockets onto the land, clearing the area for fellow troops to arrive. He was the youngest of six brothers and begged his mother to let him join them in serving his country. All the brothers made it home from war.

In his words: "We were out on the Atlantic Ocean headed somewhere. We did not know where. We were out there about 13 days when we found out over radio communications that the war had ended. So we turned around and refueled and headed back to Norfolk, Va., our home port. They never did say where we were headed."

JOSEPH RAKOSNIK

Town: DuBois, Neb.

Service: Served in Patton's Third Army, 94th Division, 376 Infantry Regiment, 3rd Battalion, Company C.

In the war: Fought primarily in the area south of the Luxembourg Saar Moselle Triangle in February 1945.

In his words: Rakosnik, who learned the Czech language from his parents and grandparents, occasionally served as a translator while serving near Sedlice, Czechoslovakia. "We were stationed by a big lake in a tent city. It was toward fall and getting cold and damp. The guys were griping and wanted out and to move to town. The commanding officer got me one day to go with him to see the mayor of Sedlice. ... I asked the mayor whether we could move to Sedlice. He asked me, 'How many of you are there?' I answered 240. He said, 'No way do we have room for that many beings.' I wanted to move to Sedlice as bad as anyone. I turned to the officer and said, 'The mayor said we could move in,' and then I turned to the mayor and said, 'My commanding officer said we are moving in anyway. ... So then the mayor said, 'We will find room for you.' In Sedlice we were one happy bunch of GIs."

Final push to Japan

JOHN DICKINSON, A MARINE VETERAN who had made earlier invasion landings at Saipan and Tinian, recalled the day the U.S. flag first appeared atop Mount Suribachi on Iwo Jima — Feb. 23, 1945. However, the fighting on the island was so intense that he couldn't remember anything else that happened until March 8. ★ That was the day Dickinson and a friend came under sniper fire while in a foxhole. "He ran the wrong way, and I ran the right way," said Dickinson, of Omaha. "He got shot up." ★ Dickinson's regiment arrived at Iwo Jima aboard three ships. It left the island on one ship.

STAFF SGT. ROBERT PERKINS OF TAYLOR, NEB., wounded in action twice in the Philippines, had rejoined the 152nd Infantry Regiment in July of 1945.

"We knew combat was going to go on until the Japanese didn't fight anymore."

— IWO JIMA VETERAN
BILL NICHOLAS OF NORFOLK, NEB.

IT's CHOW TIME FOR THREE MARINES ON IWO JIMA. From left, Pfc. Dean E. Daniell of Omaha, Pfc. Herbert McCarthy of Jersey Shore, Pa., and Pfc. John Dickinson of Mitchell, S.D. Dickinson later lived in Omaha and worked for The World-Herald's circulation department.

'We just outlasted them'

IWO JIMA'S BLACK SAND WAS SO FINE and so deep that it seemed to reach up and grab the Marines' legs, slowing their life-and-death scramble off the beach.

Japanese mortar shells and bullets rained down as thousands of young men bearing back-straining packs and toting heavy weapons clawed for cover, inch by inch.

"You would sink about halfway up to your knees," George Paulson of Council Bluffs said in 1995. "Nothing would drive on it. You literally had to swim into the sand to get to the top of the crest.

"I will never forget that as long as I live."

Paulson was an 18-year-old corporal when he and 72,000 fellow members of the Marine Corps landed on the shores of the tiny island off Japan in 1945.

The conquest of Iwo Jima proved to be a climactic battle in the island-hopping campaign in the Pacific, said Richard Wheeler, a Florida writer with two books about the battle he fought in.

The barren stretch of volcanic rock and sand, only three miles by five miles, provided a critical airfield. Allied bombers could use the island as a launching point for runs on the Japanese mainland 660 miles away or as a safe spot to land if crippled by anti-aircraft fire during the attempt.

Without a stop on Iwo Jima, U.S. heavy bombers had to fly at least twice as far on raids to Japan.

But Iwo, as combat-hardened Marine Corps veterans who

were there sometimes call it, was not so much about strategy as survival.

The dark, dreary island saw the most violent, sustained and point-blank fighting of all of World War II, said Joseph Alexander, a military historian and retired Marine colonel.

"There absolutely was no break," Alexander said from Asheville, N.C. "They never stopped shooting each other."

When the shells finally did stop flying 36 days after the first Marine hit the beach, the Americans had won. But they had paid dearly.

About 6,800 Americans died on Iwo Jima, and 28,000 others were wounded.

The Japanese fought with a ferocity that left historians and the men who were there to marvel.

The United States captured only about 1,100 of the 22,000 Japanese soldiers who were defending the island. The rest were killed.

"We knew combat was going to go on until the Japanese didn't fight anymore," said Bill Nicholas of Norfolk, Neb. "We had more manpower and just outlasted them."

Nicholas quit high school early and ended up carrying a Browning automatic rifle for the 28th Regiment of the 5th Division on Iwo Jima.

He was wounded twice, once by shrapnel from an artillery blast and more seriously when a bullet ripped through his arm.

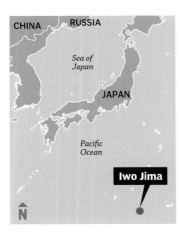

Iwo Jima

The Japanese commander on Iwo Jima, Lt. Gen. Tadamichi Kuribayashi, had masterminded the construction of a complex honeycomb of caves and tunnels that crisscrossed beneath the surface of the island.

Japanese soldiers would pop out the front of a hidden tunnel entrance, fire a quick burst of their weapons or launch a mortar and then dive back into their refuge almost before the Marines could catch a glimpse.

Members of the three Marine divisions pressing to conquer the island were forced to use the brutal tactic of going cave by cave and pillbox by pillbox with flamethrowers and grenades.

"We had to secure the island at all costs," said Guy Godios of Omaha. Godios was a Marine flamethrower in the 23rd Regiment of the 4th Division on Iwo Jima.

Fresh-faced Marine recruits going through boot camp today hear the story of Iwo Jima.

"They pound into them the camaraderie and the way we held together," said Duane Tunnyhill of Bellevue, who was a member of the 28th Regiment of the 5th Division on Iwo. "When you lost a guy, somebody else came and took his place."

Tunnyhill was wounded by a hand grenade, spent about 10 days in an Army hospital and then rejoined his unit for the rest of the campaign.

In later years, Tunnyhill thought differently about the battle than he did when he was on the island as a 19-year-old "plain dumb kid."

"I am just happy to be alive," Tunnyhill said.

Laddie J. Vacek, who was a petty officer 1st class in the Navy medical corps on Iwo Jima, could not shake the images of brutality and pain he saw.

> *"When you lost a guy, somebody else came and took his place."*
>
> — DUANE TUNNYHILL, FOUGHT ON IWO JIMA WITH THE 28TH MARINE REGIMENT

"There were a lot of lives lost so we could have this country we have now," said Vacek, of Bellevue. "I saw the results of the fighting. You cannot fathom the blood, the gore and the wounds."

Even for those who were not there, the battle of Iwo Jima provided the most enduring image of the war.

Associated Press photographer Joe Rosenthal captured the moment on Feb. 23, 1945 — four days after the landing — when a half-dozen Marines raised the Stars and Stripes on the summit of Mount Suribachi to mark their conquest of the strategic spot overlooking the island.

The flag-raising that Rosenthal captured — in a photo that made the front pages of newspapers throughout the United States — actually was the second time that day that Marines had raised an American flag on Suribachi.

Rosenthal snapped his famous shot when Marines found a length of pipe to raise a second and larger flag that could be seen all across the island.

Paulson said he witnessed the first flag that went up that day.

"A lot of guys cheered," Paulson said. "Every man on that island, when they saw that flag flying, well, it just made you feel good. We had secured Mount Suribachi."

'I'm just grateful that I'm alive'

GEORGE PAULSON DECIDED AFTER THE WAR that on the same March day each year, he would sit with an empty shot glass and a bottle of Early Times whiskey and pour himself a drink.

It was to remember buddies. To ponder the lonely hours hunkered alone in a shell hole with his right leg severed at the knee by a Japanese bullet. To salute the Navy corpsman who found him and saved his life.

The personal ceremony is Paulson's annual tribute to commemorate the day — March 9, 1945 — when World War II ended for him on a remote island in the Pacific Ocean.

"I'm just grateful that I'm alive," he said in 2010.

GEORGE PAULSON in 2010

Paulson was a member of the 28th Marines' 1st Battalion. His C Company was 250 men strong when it stormed the volcanic island. Five walked off the island when the fighting ended more than a month later. The rest were seriously wounded or killed. Of the five who left on their feet, three earned a Purple Heart.

Paulson said his annual whiskey treat started in a Quonset hut at Pearl Harbor, erected to serve as a hospital for wounded troops. The surgeon who mended what remained of Paulson's leg ordered nurses to serve the Marine a shot of whiskey at 4 p.m. daily.

"The damn corpsman would bring the shot on a tray with a white towel," Paulson said. "Guys were hollering and screaming. We knocked the ward out. Those are good memories."

Paulson was 18 years old.

Paulson, who retired from his Council Bluffs commercial contracting company, said falling into a shell hole when the 60-caliber bullet destroyed his knee sheltered him from receiving other wounds. His leg was hanging by a piece of skin. Paulson removed his canvas belt, tightened it around his thigh to slow the bleeding and drank two canteens of water to stave off shock.

"A lot goes through your mind," he said. "I started realizing maybe I wasn't going to live."

That night, a corpsman came looking for Paulson, dressed the wound and told him he was going to be OK. Then the corpsman lifted Paulson over his shoulders and carried him to safety.

Paulson, a past national president of the 5th Marine Division Association, said the lessons of the Pacific war are complicated and difficult to explain.

"The world could be more tender-hearted than it was during World War II," he said. "We were pretty intent on destroying our fellow man back in those days — more so than we should have been."

Paulson said he's not being judgmental. Japan had to be defeated and the war won.

"The animosity developed against the Japanese people during the war was really bad on our part," he said. "I suppose it was bad on their part, too. It's just too bad that hatred has to become part of the deal. It just shouldn't be. But it did and it was."

'I wondered how I was spared'

AS A FRESH-FACED 18-YEAR-OLD MARINE, Richard Wolbach trudged through the black volcanic sands of Iwo Jima and lived to tell about it.

Upon his return to Omaha, the ordeal of that horrific World War II battle inspired him to a life in the priesthood.

Monsignor Wolbach catered to the spiritual needs of others in the twilight of a priestly career spanning half a century. And he once again walked the sands of Iwo Jima.

Two spoonfuls of sand from that faraway Pacific isle are imbedded in the floor of the Omaha VA Medical Center chapel, where Wolbach presided as the hospital's chief chaplain.

The black granules were carried from the bloody battlefield by a wounded Marine in 1945 and placed in the floor when the hospital was built in 1950.

"There was a lot of blood and guts," Wolbach said in 2006 of Iwo Jima. "In my mind, many times, I wondered how I was spared."

Wolbach, who had enlisted in 1943 after graduating from South High School, was in the fourth wave to land that day. Until then, the Japanese had held their fire, waiting for the Americans to gather. Their hidden guns opened up just as Wolbach hit the beach.

"It was like shooting into a barrel," said Wolbach, who saw one of his best friends killed as he got off the landing boat.

He would have many close calls, he said, but ultimately survived the bitter monthlong battle.

For Wolbach, Iwo Jima took on spiritual meaning. Another friend had told him his buddy who died had said "Jesus, Mary and Joseph" with his last breath, a prayer he no doubt had learned growing up.

The whole battle experience turned Wolbach's thoughts inward, to consider how he could make his life more meaningful. Shortly after returning home, he entered a Catholic seminary.

After a quarter century in parish work throughout Nebraska, he had the chance in 1984 to join the chaplains' corps at the Omaha VA.

More than 10 years later, while researching VA history for the hospital's 45th anniversary, he learned of the sacred ground in the chapel floor where he stood daily.

Reflecting back, Wolbach took satisfaction in the career rooted in his Iwo Jima experience.

"It's real rewarding to work and help my fellow vets in time of illness," he said, "many preparing them for death."

Included in those numbers, he said, were several equally lucky survivors of the sands of Iwo Jima.

MONSIGNOR RICHARD WOLBACH at the 2006 rededication of the chapel floor of the Omaha VA Medical Center. The mural behind him depicts Marines raising the flag at Mount Suribachi.

FRANK J.G. TOUREK

Town: Omaha

Service: U.S. Army

In the war: He was a finance officer with the 231st Finance Disbursing Section that landed with invasion forces on Okinawa on April 1, 1945. Though his primary role was in finance, paying troops and settling claims, his secondary role was in food service. He graduated from Advanced Army Finance School at Fort Benjamin Harrison in Indiana. Overseas, he was in Okinawa from the day of invasion until the end of the battle. He retired at age 62 at the grade of chief warrant officer W-4 after nearly 40 years of military service.

In his words: "We laid offshore for a few days while they bombed the island (Okinawa). Then early one morning, they said, 'We're going. Take your gear. We're going in.' And then they dropped the ladder down the side of the ship into the landing craft. And then you look down at the landing craft. Sometimes they're right up against the side of the ship, and sometimes they float away from the side of the ship and then come back. When they did come back, you were hoping they would be right there where you could drop in with your rifle, full pack and everything you needed when you landed. We got in and landed OK, but it was rainy, wet and muddy, and there were times you didn't have a dry piece of clothes for many days."

ERNIE PYLE

REMEMBERING ERNIE PYLE

THE DEATH OF war correspondent Ernie Pyle, whose columns were carried in The World-Herald, was such a big event that President Truman issued a proclamation declaring, "More than any other man he became the spokesman for the ordinary American in arms doing so many extraordinary things. It was his genius that the mass and power of our military and naval forces never obscured the men who made them."

Pyle won a Pulitzer Prize in 1944 for his coverage in Europe but went home to the States for rest later that year. When he returned to action, it was in the Pacific. He was killed by Japanese gunfire on the island of Ie Shima near Okinawa on April 18, 1945.

The World-Herald received scores of phone calls from readers wishing to confirm reports of Pyle's death.

"My son is on Okinawa, and I felt like Ernie was writing about him," one woman said. Several other callers were sobbing.

Ie Shima

World-Herald reporter Lawrence Youngman, who had met correspondent Ernie Pyle in France in 1944, wrote the following after hearing of the death:

'To the soldiers in France he was No. 1'

BY LAWRENCE YOUNGMAN

IN THE EUROPEAN THEATER, we all wanted to meet Ernie Pyle.

It was at Rambouillet, outside Paris, while we were waiting to enter the French capital, that I spent the good part of two days with him.

He was mild-mannered, meek and utterly unassuming. If he had lived in your block, or boarded the bus at your corner, you would assume he probably was a clerk in a downtown office.

It rained steadily as we waited at Rambouillet, and we piled our typewriters and baggage in a pavilion-like building whose floor was covered with straw. Ernie tried for a while to write, then remarked that he was having an awful time trying to think of something to put into a letter to his father.

"I'm really worn out," he said. "Getting caught in that July 25 bombing was the last straw. I certainly thought I was going to get it then. As soon as we get into Paris, I'm going to pull stakes and go home."

After finishing his letter, he lay down on the straw, pulled his beret down over his eyes and went through the motions of napping. As he lay there, he looked so feeble and emaciated that I couldn't escape the feeling that I should try to help him. He reminded me of an uncle of whom I had been fond.

But the point I will always remember is that, in place of my being able to do anything for him, it was Mr. Pyle who came lugging my typewriter and bedroll out to my jeep when time came to shove off.

To the soldiers in France he was the No. 1 war correspondent — there simply were no contenders.

BRICIE NICHOLSON

Town: Emerson

Service: 77th Infantry Division

In the war: Went through infantry training in Arkansas in 1944. Served in Asia. After the war, served in Hokkaido as part of the occupation, where he got to know several Japanese soldiers. One became a pen pal after the war.

In his words: "The morning we were going to invade Ie Shima, we were told that (famed correspondent) Ernie Pyle was going with us to the front. Before Ernie got to the front, he was killed by a sniper bullet. ... We'll always remember his valiant efforts." Nicholson was also injured on the island. "A Japanese sniper shot at me when I was pinned down behind a wall. As I held up my Browning Automatic Rifle, a Japanese bullet hit the trigger guard. I got pieces of the bullet in my hand and realized that the trigger guard saved my life. A half-inch either way would have killed me." He received a Purple Heart for those injuries.

'There are not enough thank-yous'

BY PAUL HAMMEL

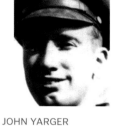

JOHN YARGER

Town: Massena, Iowa

Service: Army Air Forces, 331st Troop Carrier Squadron

In the war: Flew 55 missions, dropping paratroopers over China.

In his words: "When you fly those kind of missions, it's just like flying today: Like flying passengers, people you are supposed to take care of. And that's what you do. You do the best you can. You try to put it behind you."

TAD NAGAKI SAID HE DIDN'T feel much like a hero. He said he was just following orders during World War II when he parachuted into a Japanese prisoner of war camp to liberate the 1,400 captives.

But to one of the prisoners, then 12 years old, Nagaki and his five colleagues were an answer to five years of prayers.

"We were missionary kids. We were always taught to put our trust in God," said Mary Taylor Previte of Haddonfield, N.J. "In the Bible, He said He would give his angels charge over thee to keep thee. And what happened? We had six American 'angels' fall out of the sky."

For Nagaki, a sugar beet farmer from Alliance, Neb., the heroic story from 1945 had become a distant memory of his service behind enemy lines in China and Burma with a top secret unit of Japanese-Americans. But the tale was retold in newspapers across the country in the late 1990s thanks to the efforts of Previte, who through luck and persistence was able to track down her rescuers. She delivered her personal thanks to the paratroopers or their widows.

"There are not enough thank-yous on earth for rescuing someone from a concentration camp," Previte said in 1998. "And they don't feel it's such a big deal."

Particularly Nagaki. "It was a duty," he said. "If it had been anybody else, they would have been willing to do it."

The circumstances of war led to the first contact between the Panhandle farmer and the young girl who grew up to be elected to the New Jersey State General Assembly. Some odd twists of fate led to their reunion.

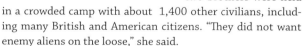

Weihsien, China

Previte was a 7-year-old student in a boarding school on the coast of China when war with Japan broke out. Japanese soldiers took over the school for use as a military base and shipped the students and teachers off to an internment camp at Weihsien in the northeast province of China.

Previte, her sister and two brothers were held in a crowded camp with about 1,400 other civilians, including many British and American citizens. "They did not want enemy aliens on the loose," she said.

One prisoner, she said, was Eric Liddell, a Scottish missionary and Olympic track star made famous in the movie "Chariots of Fire." He helped organize games for the kids as a diversion from the cramped conditions but died before the rescue.

Previte's parents, missionaries with the Free Methodist Church, were stationed far inland and were never taken prisoner. Yet they would not see their children for 5½ years.

Nagaki was the son of Japanese parents who settled near Minatare, Neb., in the North Platte River Valley. He had enlisted in the Army before the war but after Pearl Harbor was recruited into a special squad of Japanese-Americans that worked behind enemy lines in Burma, China and India. He gathered information on troop movements and enemy installations and helped train resistance fighters as part of a unit of the Office of Strategic Services, a forerunner of the CIA.

When the war ended on Aug. 15, 1945, Nagaki's squad was transported from Burma to China and its mission changed to securing and liberating Japanese prisoner of war camps in Asia.

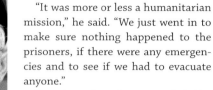

TAD NAGAKI, pictured in 1998, said his wartime mission to liberate a Japanese prison camp "was a duty."

"It was more or less a humanitarian mission," he said. "We just went in to make sure nothing happened to the prisoners, if there were any emergencies and to see if we had to evacuate anyone."

Two days after the war ended, Nagaki, five OSS colleagues and one Chinese interpreter boarded an airplane to the Weihsien prison camp. Because a nearby airfield was still under guard, they parachuted into a cornfield near the camp.

For the prisoners, who had not been told that the war was over, the sight of a low-flying American B-24 and the soldiers floating to the ground created a near riot, Previte said. It turned into all-out bedlam as word spread that these were their liberators.

"The whole camp went berserk," Previte said. "People started to cry and scream and dance. Some people just charged out of the gates. It was mass hysteria."

The captives, she said, hoisted some Americans on their bony shoulders in celebration. A Salvation Army band, whose members were among the captives, struck up "The Star-Spangled Banner."

Nagaki said there were worries about whether the prison camp guards knew the war was over.

"There was some doubt if you were going to get shot or not, but that part didn't enter into our minds," he said. "When they said we were going to help POWs, we were all ready to go."

The guards retreated to their barracks after the Americans landed. The camp was freed without incident, and Previte and her siblings soon were reunited with their parents.

Nagaki returned to the States, where he married a Japanese-American woman he met on a blind date during the war, and he began farming with three brothers near Alliance.

The story might have ended there if Previte hadn't stumbled onto some leads in relocating her rescuers. In 1985, she obtained names from a declassified document but needed more than a decade to track them down.

She discovered ironies in her search: One of her rescuers had attended the same missionary school in China as Previte, and Nagaki's wife had been imprisoned in an American relocation camp for Japanese-Americans during the war.

Nagaki expressed surprise about the notice the long-ago incident had received.

"I never figured I was a hero or anything," he said.

Tokyo put to the torch

BY HOWARD SILBER

MAJ. GEN. CURTIS E. LEMAY and Brig. Gen. Thomas S. Power took a last look at the mass of intelligence data and the map of Tokyo spread on the table in the canvas-roofed headquarters of the 20th Air Force on Guam.

"National Geographic says 90 percent of the buildings are made of wood," Power said.

LeMay nodded and removed his pipe from his mouth. "G-2 (intelligence) reports it's more like 95 percent, and there's a lot of that cardboard stuff they call *shoji*," Power said.

"The big factories in Tokyo are surrounded by 100-foot firebreaks. But if we get rolling with incendiaries and have a wind to help us, firebreaks wouldn't make any difference.

"Use M-69s (phosphorus) and M-49s (napalm). Fuse the cannisters to explode at about 2,000 feet and release the bombs. Move in over Tokyo Bay."

That was the way Power, in an interview in 1985, recalled the conversation on March 9, 1945, in Guam, where the morning sun first shines on U.S. territory, and in Tokyo.

It was March 8 in Omaha, a city LeMay and Power would know intimately later. LeMay brought the Strategic Air Command headquarters to Offutt Air Force Base. Power succeeded him as SAC commander in chief.

Tokyo was put to the torch the night of March 9, with Power leading the first wave of B-29 bombers. Fire would sweep the teeming city. Everything in its path would be destroyed. The death toll would be at least 120,000 and, according to one postwar Japanese government estimate, closer to 190,000.

Firefighters would stand by helplessly. Forty percent of their equipment would be immobilized. More than 125 firemen would die in the blaze. Water pressure would drop to near zero. The flames would be stopped only by the broad Arakawa River.

Power had arrived in the Mariana Islands in February 1945. He had been transferred from Italy, where he commanded a unit of B-24 bombers. On the way, he stopped at Grand Island, Neb., to spend a few weeks at the Army Air Forces base there learning to fly B-29s. LeMay had trained in B-29s at the same base.

Power recalled his introduction to Guam: "I was just starting out in the Pacific. Starting out in a new theater in those days, you would work around the area for a week or so, becoming acquainted with the geography and building up to something bigger."

Then he unexpectedly became involved in the prelude to the big firebombing that would come in March.

"We were getting ready for the familiarization flights when Gen. LeMay told me he was planning a 200-plane raid on Tokyo. But he could muster only 175 airplanes," Power said.

"I was supposed to have four groups, but only parts of two groups had arrived.

"Gen. LeMay asked the question, 'I don't suppose you people could come up with 25 airplanes?'

"'That's what we came over here for,'" I told him. And we were in it."

Tokyo was selected, Power said, "partly because it was Japan's capital and the world's largest city. We wanted to destroy Japan's will to continue the war."

Another important reason, he said, was that "the whole city was supporting the war. People turned out military uniforms, rifle bullets, aircraft parts in their homes and in thousands of tiny manufacturing plants, most of them with fewer than 30 workers."

MAJ. GEN. CURTIS E. LEMAY (second from left) and Brig. Gen. Thomas S. Power (third from left) go over a report on a B-29 raid on Japan in 1945. At left is Capt. Waldo Timm and at right is Lt. Nelson McDowell, the pilot and navigator for one of the bombers.

It turned out that only 30 B-29s bombed Tokyo in that first 20th Air Force raid. The others turned back because of foul weather. Power said he "climbed through the soup with my 25 planes. We finally came out of it above 30,000 feet.

"Up there, we picked up five stragglers and, using radar, we located Tokyo. We moved in on the city on a 200-knot tailwind and hit it in a snowstorm, using incendiary bombs. We were the only planes to find Tokyo that day.

"The next day, our reconnaissance planes made photographs of the city. It was white, covered with snow. But one square mile was black — completely burned out."

The limited success of that raid led Power and LeMay to try mass firebombing at low altitude.

Said Power: "We set up a precise operation, using sawtooth timing and spacing our aircraft by altitude. We hit (on March 9, 1945) with a big stream of bombers, 334 of them.

"I stayed up over the city, flying back and forth for an hour and 50 minutes, while we plotted the fires. It was night, of course, and it is awfully hard to tell much about the scope of fires in the darkness.

"We could see three or four big fires get started and flow together to form a sea of flames. Before we left, the fire covered more than 16 square miles."

As the 20th Air Force commander, LeMay was forced to remain at his Guam headquarters. He said Power and other pilots told him later that drafts from the fires "bounced our airplanes into the sky like pingpong balls. A B-29 coming in after the flames were really on the tear would get caught in one of those searing updrafts and would get pushed up 3,000, 4,000 and 5,000 feet."

The LeMay-Power brand of bombing was continued. In the ensuing 12 days, B-29s from Guam, Tinian and Saipan returned to Tokyo several times and also incinerated Osaka, Nagoya, Yokohama and Shizuoka, which became Omaha's sister city after the war.

"We wanted to destroy Japan's will to continue the war."

—BRIG. GEN. THOMAS S. POWER

MARINE MAJ. H.L. ROGERS reads a citation honoring Dale Hansen posthumously at a ceremony in Wisner, Neb., in 1946. Dale's parents, Mr. and Mrs. Peter Hansen, are on the right, while brother Don, who also served on Okinawa, is behind them.

'So many times I have wished I was dead and he was home'

BY AL FRISBIE

The World-Herald reporter served on Okinawa as a rifle company scout.

Okinawa

DON AND DALE HANSEN WERE BROTHERS who grew up on the family farm near Wisner, Neb. They did chores together, played together and went to school together at Wisner High.

On May 11, 1944, they went together to enlist in the Marine Corps.

Don was 19 then; Dale, 21. "We wanted to stay together in service," Don Hansen said in 1985.

On April 1, 1945, they were still together. They were aboard a troop ship anchored off Okinawa and waiting to go ashore with the 1st Marine Division. It would be another bloody stop on the road to Tokyo.

April 1 was D-Day at Okinawa for two Marine divisions (the 1st and 6th) and four Army divisions (the 7th, 27th, 77th and 96th). It was also Easter Sunday and April Fool's Day.

No one knew it then, but this would be the last major land battle of World War II. It would take 82 days to wrest the island, only 350 miles from Kyushu in Japan, from its Japanese defenders.

The battle would claim 42,943 Army casualties. The Marine casualty list totaled 20,602; the Navy's, 16,313. The Allied casualty list included 13,000 deaths.

The Japanese would lose more than 100,000 men and about the same number of civilians, a fourth of the Okinawan civilian population. Okinawa, which was returned to Japan in 1972, exacted a lot of heartache.

Don and Dale Hansen were members of a special weapons platoon and formed a bazooka team assigned to a rifle company. Don recalled that they talked of what lay ahead as they watched the naval bombardment of Okinawa.

"We talked about home," he said, "and how tough we were going to be. We agreed that if either of us got hurt or killed we weren't going to make a big deal of it."

Before the day was out, that vow would be tested. They went in together and were charging up a hill, Hansen said, when he tripped a small land mine and suffered a compound fracture of the right leg. For him, the fighting was over almost before it had begun.

PVT. DALE HANSEN was awarded the Medal of Honor for his heroism on Okinawa.

His brother stayed until help arrived. "He was right there," Don Hansen said. "He gave me some water from his canteen. The last time I saw Dale, he was standing while they carried me away in a stretcher. I held up my hand and waved, and he did the same. By the time I got back to the States, he was dead."

Marine Pvt. Dale Hansen died a hero May 11, 1945, one year to the day from the time he and Don had enlisted. He was killed by a sniper's bullet four days after staging a one-man assault against Japanese positions, for which he was awarded the Medal of Honor.

Miraculously, he had emerged unscathed from the May 7 encounter for which he received the nation's highest military award. It began when he attacked and destroyed a pillbox with a rocket launcher. After his weapon was destroyed by enemy fire, he grabbed a rifle.

According to his official citation, he reached the crest of a ridge and "opened fire on six Japanese, killing four before his rifle jammed. Attacked by the remaining two Japanese, he beat them off with the butt of his rifle and climbed back to cover. Returning with another weapon and a supply of grenades, he fearlessly advanced, destroying a mortar position and annihilating eight more of the enemy."

Don Hansen was honorably discharged May 11, 1946, one year exactly from the day his brother was killed and two years from the date of their enlistment. He came home to the Wayne, Neb., farm he and Dale had talked of so often.

"Dale got pretty tough," Don said. "But he was a timid guy. He was quiet. I never heard him brag. I still miss him. So many times I have wished I was dead and he was home."

Balloon bomb over Dundee in 1945 lacked the punch of Doolittle Raid

BY DAVID HENDEE

ON APRIL 18, 1942, carrier-launched Army bombers carried out the first U.S. assault of the war on the Japanese mainland.

And April 18 three years later, in 1945, was the date a Japanese balloon bomb exploded above Omaha.

The coincidence is one of the war's little-known historical footnotes. The Doolittle Raid on Japan by B-25 bombers was retaliation for Japan's attack on Pearl Harbor a little more than four months earlier. The balloon bombs were Japan's retaliation.

CARROLL V. GLINES
in 2011

"It took them nearly three years to retaliate, but it's just proof that the Japanese militarists never got over the insult and humiliation they suffered among their people," said historian Carroll V. Glines. "They had told their people that Japan could never be invaded, and here are 16 American bombers dropping bombs in five of their cities and then escaping."

Glines, a former Air Force colonel and command pilot, was a B-25 instructor pilot during the war and wrote more than 30 aviation-themed books, including "The Doolittle Raid: America's First Strike Against Japan." He was recognized as the raid's official historian.

Glines said Japan developed and launched balloon bombs into the jet stream flowing toward North America as a direct response to the Doolittle Raid.

In addition to Omaha, balloon bombs dropped on or near seven other Nebraska communities, according to U.S. War Department accounts at the time. The towns were Ballagh (near Burwell), Chadron, Hyannis, Ellsworth, Osceola, Schuyler and Silver Creek. No severe damage or injuries were reported.

A bronze plaque on the exterior brick wall of a building at 50th Street and Underwood Avenue in Dundee commemorates the Omaha incident.

"The incendiary device flared brightly in the night, but caused no damage," the plaque reads.

Military authorities asked newspapers to print nothing about the bombs at first, for fear of spreading panic.

The World-Herald finally devoted three newspaper columns on Aug. 15, 1945, to a story about Japan's formerly secret hit-or-miss balloon bomb forays.

The front page, however, was dominated by news of Japan's surrender, with the balloon bomb story appearing on Page 12. Here are excerpts:

Shortly after midnight, residents near Fiftieth Street and Underwood Avenue were awakened by an explosion outside their homes. ...

Mrs. Paul Pederson, 5004 Nicholas Street, thought the

noise that of a car backfiring. Mrs. Howard P. Smith, 5009 Western Avenue, thought the accompanying glare the reflection of a car's floodlights. Mrs. L.C. Hindman, 5021 Burt Street, said the light penetrated the drawn shades of her room. Miss Helen Sturgis, 5101 Izard Street, said the light appeared to be the size of a football.

Many residents rushed into the street, some in night attire. Overhead (subsequent investigation fixed its height at 495 feet) they saw a light in the sky. Bright yellow at first, it later turned red. It rocked gently in the sky and drifted slowly away, disappearing like the tail-light of a car going down the road.

That, for most Omahans, was the introduction to the Japanese bomb balloons.

Army Maj. Charles D. Frierson, an intelligence officer for Nebraska and South Dakota (District 5), provided The World-Herald at the time with extensive information about the bombs and the places they reached.

Strictly hush-hush at first, the Army later had begun a word-of-mouth campaign to acquaint people with the balloons. The information was spread through church groups, women's and service organizations.

After the word spread informally, the public began seeing a balloon in every wisp of cloud in the sky. And every report, because of its nature, had to be investigated.

District 5 investigated Weather Bureau balloons. The planet Venus, visible in the daytime, gave it particular trouble.

In one 24-hour period intelligence officials investigated 17 reports. Farmers blasting for stumps often resulted in calls that brought Intelligence men running. A blast that had Sarpy County abuzz one day turned out to have been Milton Fricke of Papillion setting off 400 pounds of dynamite while constructing a ditch to drain a flooded field.

Doolittle historian Glines said Japanese military leaders hoped that the experimental balloon bombs would wreak havoc on U.S. and Canadian cities and forests. The hydrogen-filled balloons were 33 feet in diameter and carried either one anti-personnel bomb or one to four incendiary devices.

Japan launched more than 9,000 balloons between November 1944 and April 1945. The 5,000-mile journey took about three days.

More than 300 balloons were found or observed in America. Balloon bombs were found from Alaska to Mexico and in 26 states, as far east as Michigan.

The U.S. government asked the news media not to publish reports of explosions for fear of causing panic and giving the enemy information about the success of the project.

About two weeks after the Dundee explosion, a pregnant woman and five children from a Sunday school class were killed in Oregon when they discovered a balloon bomb on the forest floor. They were the only known casualties of the devices and the war's only deaths to enemy action in the continental 48 states, Glines said.

ARTHUR AKINS

Town: Omaha, formerly lived in Hastings and Fremont

Service: U.S. Navy

In the war: He enlisted in the Navy in January 1943 and went to boot camp, aviation mechanics school, radar operations school, gunnery school and flight operational training for 21 months before being assigned to the Torpedo Squadron of Air Group 10 as a line service mechanic and backup turret gunner. Air Group 10 was assigned to the aircraft carrier USS Intrepid. They made a stop at Pearl Harbor before sailing to Ulithi atoll in the Caroline Islands, near the Japanese-occupied island of Yap. When they left Ulithi, they learned they were to participate in the invasion of Okinawa.

In his words: "Our planes took off and landed all day and night in an almost constant flow. They had successfully attacked Japanese railroads, ships, airfields and assembly plants. In turn, our ship had been under constant attack by Japanese planes. Our first taste of combat turned out to be a full-course dinner. ... During the next days, we steamed south, striking as we went. On March 24, 1945, we started the pre-invasion, softening up, of Okinawa. These were hectic days with strikes going out from dawn to dusk, day in and day out. The heat was really on Okinawa. The invasion was under way, and we continued to fly missions around the clock. The Army and Marines would tell where to hit, and we would drop bombs, fire rockets and strafe the targets with our 50-caliber machine guns. We hardly ever knew what we hit, and I'm not sure I wanted to know. While we were doing our thing, the Japanese sent down scores of suicide planes. We were under attack so often that the cooks couldn't prepare meals, so this was known as the sandwich-eating era. During this time, our fighter pilots and the ship's gunners were the heroes. The fighter pilots patrolled the sky day and night and shot down as many as 42 Japanese planes in one day."

MEMORIES OF A GENERATION ★

DANIEL J. SLOBOTH

Town: Omaha

Service: U.S. Navy

In the war: He was a Navy boat officer on the USS Whitley (AKA-91), an attack cargo ship, at Iwo Jima.

In his words: "After delivering 36 Marines on one of our many trips to the beach, our LCVP (Landing Craft, Vehicle, Personnel) got broadside in the heavy surf and started to break up. I jumped out, along with the four in the boat crew, and we waded ashore. We spent about an hour hugging the ground until one of the boats from the Whitley came in and we were able to catch a ride back to our ship. It was very scary on that beach. The Whitley boats took our Marines to the shore, along with a few vehicles, and then our ship anchored about 1,000 yards off Iwo and began to unload all the rest of the cargo. We had a ringside seat to follow the battle. We could tell that the Marines were having a very difficult time. The morning of the fifth day, the sun came out (the weather had been bad for four days), and some of our sailors yelled as we saw the U.S. flag on Mount Suribachi. Everyone on the Whitley let out a huge cheer."

CHARLES L. SIEVERS

Town: Omaha

Service: U.S. Navy, quartermaster 3rd class

In the war: Worked in navigation on the escort carrier USS Rudyerd Bay

In his words: "While cruising offshore at Iwo Jima on landing day, it was sunset and we were at our battle stations when the kamikazes came in to attack us. As we saw them coming in, our captain told the gun crew not to fire until he told us to. About that time, the USS Bismarck Sea, which was beside us to our rear, opened fire. The kamikazes followed the tracers in and hit the Bismarck Sea and sunk her. Many sailors were killed. We all believe that the captain on our ship saved our lives that day."

ALVIN HAYS

Town: Red Oak

Service: Navy, special operations forces

In the war: Served in five invasions in the Philippines and participated in the Battle of Iwo Jima and the Battle of Okinawa.

In his words: "It was hazardous duty, but at 17, that didn't seem to bother me. We'd go in with four-man crews in the middle of the night, float in on a rubber raft and do reconnaissance. You could see the Japanese walking around but they never saw us."

HARLAN HERRICK

Town: North Platte

Service: Army, rifleman with 96th Infantry Division

In the war: Saw action as a replacement soldier during the Okinawa campaign.

In his words: "I wasn't there when it started, but it was pretty rough. I don't go around bragging about it, but it's all pretty memorable. You don't forget it very fast."

GEORGE KREIFEL

Town: Table Rock

Service: Army, 7th Infantry Division

In the war: Served in the invasions of Guam and the Philippines, and wounded during the invasion of Okinawa, one day after President Franklin Roosevelt's death.

In his words: "We started up that hill. … it was just a turkey shoot. When I got hit, out of 15 guys (in my unit), there were only three left. And when I got hit (by shrapnel), it got all three of us." Doctors at a military hospital saved Kreifel's arm.

HAROLD J. POLLARD

Town: Nehawka

Service: Seaman 1st class, U.S. Navy, Seventh Fleet

In the war: Assigned to the heavy attack cruiser USS New Orleans out of Mare Island, San Francisco, in January 1945. Honorably discharged in June 1946 when the New Orleans returned stateside to the Philadelphia Naval Yard.

In his words: "As a signalman striker, I saw action in the Philippine Seas, Philippine Islands, Iwo Jima and Okinawa. Our first experience with kamikaze pilots was at Okinawa, where they aimed for my area on the ship as signalmen strikers were one deck below the Old Man's bridge. On April Fool's Day 1945, we were involved in the invasion of Okinawa. We were also there for the surrender but left before it was secured. A couple of other things I remember is firing star shells all night long so they could see on the beach to fight. Also, a command would be called for the smoke boats to make smoke. This was to hide the boats except for the hospital ship, which was all lit up. It took a kamikaze plane down the stack but did little damage. The most important lesson I learned from the war: You'll never know how important God and family are until you've been in combat."

BOB LEWIS

Town: Atkinson

Service: Army, 7th Division

In the war: Served as an infantryman in the Philippines and then in the invasion of Okinawa. After Japan's surrender, served in the occupying force in Korea.

In his words: "I remember we invaded Okinawa on Easter Sunday, the first day of April. … We got there in the morning, early, when the sun was shining and it was just a perfect day. By the time we were done pouring out onto the shore that afternoon, you couldn't even see the sun anymore from the smoke and the dirt and whatnot.

"I got hit a couple of times. I took a bullet through my steel helmet and the helmet liner. It hit the liner and mostly went around my head. The heat of the bullet came close to my eye, and it just felt like a welder burn. I thought it took both sides of my head off, the way it felt."

BENJAMIN SOMER

Town: Grand Island

Service: Navy, USS Buckingham

In the war: Engineering officer on the USS Buckingham, a transport ship in the Pacific Theater. Also served as gunnery officer on a 40 mm gun. The Buckingham ferried troops into Saipan and served as a hospital ship, bringing wounded troops home for treatment.

In his words: "We brought troops ashore at Saipan. We'd haul fresh troops in and then take the casualties back to the States. We became a hospital ship on the return voyage."

Bill Billotte in the Pacific

WORLD-HERALD WAR CORRESPONDENT Bill Billotte arrived in the Philippines in 1945 after a journey of nearly a month aboard a troop transport. It was his 35th birthday, and he and another correspondent who was observing a wedding anniversary celebrated by sharing a bottle of warm beer. Then it was off to the front for Billotte, whose age quickly earned him the nickname "Pop" from his young front-line companions. ★ A wounded correspondent who was being evacuated to the States offered Billotte his carbine and pistol. Billotte reminded him that correspondents were supposed to be unarmed. Replied the reporter, who had been shot at the front: "Where did you get your briefing? At the movies?" ★ Billotte's introduction to combat was with the 32nd Infantry Division fighting along the Villa Verde Trail on the island of Luzon. He stayed with the 32nd for about six weeks, and then began to roam the Pacific Theater looking for Nebraska and Iowa boys. He spent a week on a PT patrol boat off Okinawa and some time at a B-29 bomber base on Saipan. ★ On Sept. 2, 1945, Billotte was on an upper deck of the battleship USS Missouri when the Japanese surrendered unconditionally to Gen. Douglas MacArthur, and he was on one of the first planes to land in occupied Japan. ★ Billotte said later, "I'll never forget the day we met 400 prisoners from Kamioka prison. I said, 'Is there anybody here from Nebraska?' and a guy yelled that he was from Omaha. Well, I cried. Everybody cried. Those fellows would get hold of you, and you wouldn't let go. Just hung on. We were the first Americans they had seen in three years."

"Mr. Billotte will have a roving assignment, bringing to World-Herald readers the same firsthand news of their sons and husbands in the Pacific that Lawrence Youngman's dispatches brought of Nebraskans and Iowans in the European Theater."
— World-Herald of April 10, 1945

BILLOTTE IN THE PACIFIC

THE WORLD-HERALD FOLLOWED NEBRASKA AND IOWA SERVICEMEN FROM THE PHILIPPINES TO OCCUPIED JAPAN. REPORTS FROM REMOTE AREAS OFTEN DID NOT APPEAR IN THE WORLD-HERALD UNTIL DAYS AFTER THEY WERE WRITTEN. IN ADDITION, MILITARY CENSORSHIP DELAYED THE RELEASE OF SOME INFORMATION.

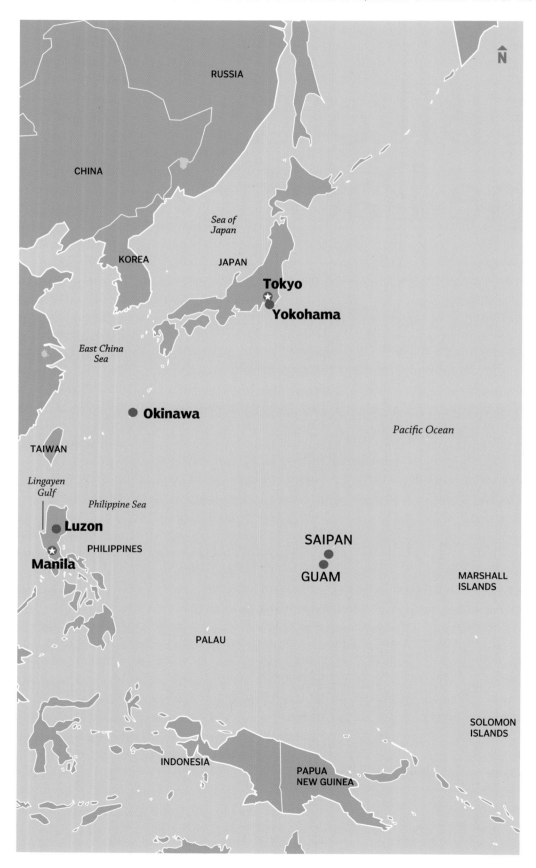

BILL BILLOTTE, left, interviews Lt. Neil McTaggert of Omaha and flight officer Warren Stecker of Emerson, Neb., on Guam.

May 30, 1945
ABOARD A TRANSPORT ON THE PACIFIC

IT WAS A PERFECT AFTERNOON. The spring sun was setting over San Francisco. For hours, nurses, doughfoots and other military personnel had marched up the narrow gangways with full combat packs pulling at their shoulders.

On the pier a military band gave them a lift, as it swung into one march or jive number after another. Lined at the rails two deep, those who had boarded ship cheered those who were coming on.

The big troop transport, bereft of the brilliant colors that had once made her a queen of the Pacific, stood steady. After the loading delay the liner gave the mournful blasts that make a harbor city more lonely on a foggy morning. Then she was slowly pushed out of the harbor by tugboats.

The Golden Gate Bridge was a delicate silhouette of black lace against a golden sunset as the transport approached. As the ship knifed beneath the bridge, plowing the green waters into a white froth, the military personnel lining the rails sent up a ragged cheer. They were leaving their last familiar landmark, and few of them knew where they were going.

May 31, 1945
ABOARD A TRANSPORT ON THE PACIFIC

THE HOLIDAY ASPECT of the ship disappeared before the first meal was served. In clipped tones, the radio loudspeaker warned all hands that "they must keep life preservers on at all times when away from their quarters for security reasons."

A short time later all passengers were told they must be in bed by 2200 (10 p.m. to us landlubbers), that all portholes must be closed and no lights in quarters. The series of precautionary orders — issued in serious tones of Navy officers, who are forever conscious of the dangers of the waters in which they sail — dispelled a good deal of frivolity.

Then the big ship hit fairly rough waters and began to roll and pitch. You saw the seasick victims everywhere — hurrying along passageways, making desperate clutches at doorknobs. Many a place was vacant at chow time. Some valiantly started the meal, turned green with the fork halfway to their lips, dropped it and fled.

Some of the Iowa and Nebraska boys were among the sickest I saw. Perhaps it only seemed that way, because they were my main interest.

But they never complained. If they were well enough to stand, they continued with their duties. They even answered questions with their heads clasped in their hands.

They refused my offer to come back later. They said they didn't want to miss the chance to send back word to their people. The morning was worse, as the rolling and pitching continued all night.

Lt. Lawrence Faudel of Pierce, Neb., who was at my mess table, made a valiant effort to eat his breakfast. He stared listlessly at the scrambled eggs and coffee, speared a juicy sausage with his fork and then fled with a mumbled apology.

Something everybody will remember as one of his standout experiences on a troop transport is his first effort to shave in cold seawater on a pitching ship.

If you have one small bathroom with 14 cabin mates, half of them seasick, it makes it interesting.

You smear on the cold water and a shudder racks you. Then comes a generous smear of brushless shaving cream. The ship lurches and you end up in the corner with your right forefinger jammed in your left ear.

The seawater and the shaving cream give off an odor not conducive to soothing a squeamish stomach. You peer into the smeared mirror. Looking back at you is what appears to be a disheveled bird's nest which is upside down.

Timidly you draw the razor, which under the conditions is as potent as any of the ship's guns, down the side of your face. You grunt with satisfaction as you make it without removing any of the more important features. You do it again. You're beginning to get cocky.

Then the door collides with the side of your body and throws you against the wall. Standing in the open door is a figure, hand clapped over his mouth, eyes bugged like a bull frog's. It is your pal Faudel. He rushes past. Neither of you speak. He does what he's supposed to do, and you finish shaving.

As you walk out, another member of your cabin says, "Bill, you left a patch of whiskers just under your chin."

"I like it that way," you reply with freezing dignity.

TRANSPORTS USED EVERY INCH available to squeeze in troops headed off to war.

The sleeping faces of men going to war

June 1, 1945

ABOARD A TRANSPORT ON THE PACIFIC

ONE MORNING FROM MIDNIGHT UNTIL 4 A.M., while most of those on this converted ocean liner slept, it was time to wander through the decks.

There they lay in sleep, row on row in double bunks that were four deep from floor to ceiling. Their deep, regular breathing filled the long rooms that once were ballrooms for the elite who were seeking pleasure at sea. What once was an ornate fireplace had been turned into a ventilating shaft. Where once jeweled women had danced, there were only the sprawled figures of fighting men sailing across the Pacific to a destination that still was unknown to them.

In some places it was so dark you had to feel your way, careful that your life jacket did not brush against the face of a sleeping soldier and awaken him.

At other times you could distinguish the faces in the unreal half light. There were young faces that had not yet felt the touch of a razor, bearded faces with young contours and faces that were approaching middle age.

The tousled hair on the heads that slept without benefit of pillows also told a story. There was fine thick hair of youth which predominated, hair that was beginning to thin on top and the old regulars, many of whom had lost their hair in the service of their country. You could almost see the stripes on the relaxed muscles of their arms.

There was something in those long rows of figures that brought a lump to your throat. It was the anonymity of all those who slept there. Their gear was the same, their life jackets, duffel bags and helmets. From a distance they even appeared to be the same size.

It was their courage that touched you — their selflessness. There was not self-pity here. The men were sleeping soundly through the stifling heat, although they had not had a hard day to tire them. They had learned to take their sleep gratefully where and when they could find it.

The son of wealthy parents slept beside the underprivileged from New York's East Side.

Only when you looked closely at fingers curled in sleep did they begin to regain any individuality. Then you saw the school class rings, the lodge emblems and the plain gold signet ring with the engraved initials — the gifts from those who held them dear.

You fumbled your way to the stern of the ship with its gun and its motionless guard, ceaselessly scanning the calm, night-shrouded Pacific.

You leaned on the rail and stared into the frothing wake and breathed a silent prayer for every one of them.

June 3, 1945
ABOARD A TRANSPORT ON THE PACIFIC

MUSIC, THE SECRET WEAPON of every American soldier from the Revolutionary War on, is one of the most effective antidotes to boredom and homesickness on this ship.

This transport is blacked out after 8 p.m. No one is allowed to smoke on deck, the portholes are closed in the face of the stifling heat. And from every nook and cranny comes the sound of music.

From the enlisted men's quarters come the sounds of an old barbershop tune played on a harmonica with the vigorous voices of the troops above the reedy notes. Some in every unit have ukuleles.

Some gawky, loose-jointed mountain body will break out in an impromptu buck-and-wing despite the sawing of the ship. His mates will beat out the rhythm with hand claps while they shout their encouragement.

You lose track of time aboard ship unless you have been highly conscious of it all your life. Therefore, singing before breakfast (we eat in shifts) is a common thing. Long lines of GIs will swing from side to side to the rhythm of some old song as they go to chow early in the morning. No one stares, because they think nothing of it.

June 5, 1945
ABOARD A TRANSPORT ON THE PACIFIC

ONE OF THE MOST NOTICEABLE TRAITS of Americans once they leave their native shores is the almost arrogant pride they display in their home states:

- Texans (and the records bear them out) feel they have borne a big part of the burden in the early fighting.
- Easterners seem inclined to pine for a particular neighborhood — a section of Flatbush or a corner of the Bronx.
- Midwesterners and many Southerners are more inclined to take circumstances in their stride. They consider the trip another portion of their education, tell you they wouldn't turn back if they had the chance.

But the attitude of none is harder to take than that of the dyed-in-the-wool Bostonian. Those I have met are likable in every respect until they broaden their a's and begin to discuss the relation of their historical city and the rest of the world.

A chain of circumstances aboard ship silenced a Bostonian who is a cabinmate of mine. We were leaning over the rail discussing various cities.

The Bostonian was earnestly propounding his theory, which boiled down to the assertion that everything west of Boston was "buffer" material between the enemy and the strategic part of the United States.

It was comforting, "don't ya know," that the Cabots and the Lodges would not be bothered by the Japanese until they had fought their way past the commoners that populate the other 47 states.

He raised a disbelieving eyebrow when I told him the number of Iowans and Nebraskans I had encountered on the boat.

At the height of the discussion, the captain next to me said, "Say, I don't want to butt in, but didn't you used to write sports and shoot pictures for The World-Herald in Omaha?"

He was Capt. G.L. Warin of a dental unit. He had obtained his degree at Creighton University and played basketball there for two years. When he entered the Army he was practicing dentistry at Shenandoah, Iowa.

"See what I mean?" I said, winking at my friend from Boston.

"That was a coincidence that could happen to anyone," he said as we went down to chow.

His chair in the dining room is immediately behind mine, and the fellows at his table talk with those at my table throughout the meal.

We were about halfway through eating when the waiter at our table suddenly came over to me and said, "I want to talk to you. I used to hustle papers for The World-Herald at 16th and Howard Streets. I've lived in Omaha most of my life."

My friend from Boston became intent on his food, the back of his neck as red as any lobster fished out of the waters of Cape Cod. The waiter's name was Eddie Epstein and he has seen quite a bit of the world since leaving Omaha in 1938.

"You win," my friend from Boston said sheepishly when I saw him later. "I guess there are a few people on this boat from your part of the country."

It was their courage that touched you — their selflessness. There was not self-pity here.

— BILL BILLOTTE

June 6, 1945
ABOARD A TRANSPORT ON THE PACIFIC

THE AMAZING ORGANIZATION of this small city afloat never fails to intrigue you. You only get two meals a day (nine hours apart), even though the chow lines are crowding the passageways at all hours. The food is good, and I have yet to hear anyone but the most critical do any griping.

The Navy crew in charge is spick-and-span and exacting, but even over the loud-speaker system, the town crier of the ship, humor often creeps into the precise, cold tones of the announcer.

Everything said is in Navy vernacular and, of course, every Midwestern and Southern kid on the boat quickly picks up the terms.

Therefore it is not uncommon to hear some youngster growl, "Belay that hand, mate, before I take you aft and punch out your scuppers!"

"You mean my uppers," his poker-playing companion will say as he studies his hand.

"No, I don't, I mean your scuppers, whatever'n hell that is," the first speaker will reply.

A rule was quickly established aboard ship that any money showing in any kind of a gambling game would be picked up by any passing officer and given to the chaplain's fund.

Chips, torn playing cards and buttons made their appearance immediately and the dice continued to bounce off boards along the passageways.

There was no money evident, but it was hard to believe the boys could show the intense interest they maintained in a game that was being played for "fun."

June 8, 1945
ABOARD A TRANSPORT ON THE PACIFIC

THIS TRANSPORT HAS JUST run into a rather violent tropical storm, and the ship is beginning to pitch and roll.

We have been at sea for days with only a short stop at one port that had no censorship facilities.

The weather was murky at dawn, but there was no warning of the storm until you could see it moving toward you over choppy waves. It broke against the ship with the rain hitting the decks like flung shot, as the troops scrambled for the passageways.

Those who were caught by the first sheet of rain took their drenching philosophically. They merely removed most of their clothes and took the first freshwater bath they had had since the start of the trip unless they had slept on the decks at night.

They hung on the rails with the wind tearing at them and then went below to dry themselves with towels.

Desolate when calm, the Pacific is frightening in a storm.

You can hear the wind whistling by the ship like a 40-mile-an-hour winter gale in Omaha.

I am seated on some packing cases and across the room is a beat-up piano with the sounding board showing. It is lashed to the wall, but every once in a while it leans forward as though it were going to jump across the room into my lap.

The Iowans and Nebraskans on board, along with troops from every state in the union, feel they are getting over in time for the "big show."

— BILL BILLOTTE

June 9, 1945
ABOARD A TRANSPORT ON THE PACIFIC

THIS TRANSPORT IS APPROACHING THE END of its journey, one of the first to reach its destination of the huge flotilla that will be sent this way now that the war in Germany is over.

The Iowans and Nebraskans on board, along with troops from every state in the union, feel they are getting over in time for the "big show." The esprit de corps among all units is high.

But the human tendency to err persists. One colonel was instructing his troops on the procedure that would be followed at the debarkation point.

"I hear," he said to his troops massed on one of the decks, "that thievery is rampant on the docks. Big articles as well as small are being stolen. In view of this situation, it has been decided among the commanders that we must take certain steps — we have decided we will not steal from each other."

Yesterday, fountain pens that had not been unsheathed for days were writing busily. In the passageways, on the decks, in the sweltering quarters, the troops were writing.

They were doing it awkwardly, because in the intense heat their hands were sticking to the paper on which they were writing.

There had been many important developments since many of them had written home. The president had died, their beloved Ernie Pyle had been killed and Germany had been knocked out of the war.

But yesterday was different — it was Mother's Day.

There is a new atmosphere of tenseness in the air.

The trip has been long and wearing but there have been very few cases of what the boys call "cabin fever." That is when a trooper comes out slugging over some real or imagined trifle that has annoyed him.

They are passing the doors of this cabin in never-ending groups, as this is being written. They are ready to do their part in the big job ahead.

There is a tall, lanky youngster on guard at the door. He is humming a song as he watches them go by. It is a simple song that is very popular in the Army, and just about everyone in the States has heard it at one time or another. It seems strangely appropriate at this time. The words:

"Bless 'em all, bless 'em all
"The long and the short and the tall
"Bless all the corporals and sergeants too . . . "

June 9, 1945
ABOARD A TRANSPORT ON THE PACIFIC

JUST ABOUT EVERYONE on this ship has made certain sacrifices in the interest of serving his country, but none can lay greater claim to sacrifice than some of the farm boys aboard.

Last night a thin, tall man of 30 came to my cabin, climbed over the bridge game in progress, jammed between our bunks and shook hands.

Pfc. Kenneth Dohse of Edgar, Neb., said he was feeling low and wanted to talk to someone from Nebraska.

He has been in the Army for three years, reading newspaper accounts of how farms, after lean years of drought, were paying off. Kenneth weathered the lean years, doing it the hard way as a young man in his 20s.

Then came the end of the drought — and the war. He said his wife was ill due to worry and had been joined by her mother.

They have no one to work the place, and they are doing the best they can by renting portions of it so that it won't be totally unproductive.

Kenneth felt better after he got his story off his chest and suddenly chuckled.

"But brother, I've got plenty of company," he said. "Do me a favor and tell Alice May to keep her chin up. This isn't going to last too long, and then we'll make up for lost time. I don't want her to worry about a darn thing."

June 10, 1945
ABOARD A TRANSPORT ON THE PACIFIC

THIS IS JUST A BIT of financial advice to Mrs. George Russell who should, by this time, be occupying a neat little cottage at Chadron, Neb.

Stop asking your husband, Master Sgt. George, to quit playing poker.

He's doing all right, as he has since joining the Army, and if he doesn't get some awfully cold hands before this ship puts into port, you will be able to slap down another sizable payment on that home you and he bought.

George left a sizable game for this interview, putting down his cards and saying, "I'll be back in a little while, fellows, don't let anyone sit down in my place."

"Don't hurry," said one of the players. "I'm sick of buying cattle for the ranch you're going to buy back in Nebraska when this war's over."

George climbed on the boat without a dime and watched the poker games longingly until the men were paid aboard ship. At that time he drew $4.

"I don't claim to be a gamblin' man and family comes first. My allotment doesn't leave me much to play around with, but I made a strike in the States before I left. That's how I got the five hundred to make a down payment on that home in Chadron."

When I last saw George he had run his $4 into $150 and had cashed in on the hottest hand he had held since entering the Army. He turned up four treys with $35 out in the middle.

Staff Sgt. Frank Stillmock of Omaha and a Filipino comrade display a captured Japanese flag.

Luzon

June 11, 1945
WITH THE 14TH ARMY CORPS, SOUTHERN LUZON

"THEY ARE JUST ABOUT the saltiest bunch of boys you'll find on the Islands. Their training is as tough as the average soldier's combat and they have never failed to take an objective."

That's what they told me about the 11th Airborne, the kids who hop out of the clouds to drop on ridges, into the jungles or near the outskirts of an enemy city. Many of them are from Nebraska and Iowa.

Wander down their company streets, and the boys who have been decorated are the rule, rather than the exception, and no branch of the service wears its laurels more lightly.

This particular outfit saw its first action in the mountains of Leyte. They walked into battle shortly after Thanksgiving Day in 1944.

"Oh, my aching back, but that was a tough ambush we ran into on Leyte," said Pvt. Cyril Diederich of Lindsay, Neb. "The funny part of it was that we were going in to take over from another company that had been planted to ambush the Japs. The Japs found out about our ambush and worked it out against us in reverse."

As Cyril's outfit, the riflemen of Company E, went in, the Japanese led the scouts and main body into the trap and then closed it. Without food, the boys were completely closed off.

"As soon as dusk came, the Japs started to come at us in droves in banzai charges," Diederich recalled. "They came leaping through the underbrush shrieking and yelling at the top of their lungs. We stopped them cold three times. I fired five bandoleers of cartridges in 90 minutes. That is 240 shots. I know I got five Japs and I don't how many more.

"We lost seven men. The Japs were trying to take our position with fixed bayonets, but they couldn't stand up under the lead we were throwing at them. At one time they got within 30 yards before we could break 'em up," Diederich said. "Man,

that sweat was running down my spine. We were still cut off when good old Company D came in and got us.

"I'll never forget it, because our commander had just asked for three volunteers. My buddy in the foxhole with me volunteered, and I just couldn't back out. We knew it was suicide and were just starting out when we heard Company D."

Staff Sgt. Frank Stillmock of Omaha took up the story where Diederich left off. He was in charge of a platoon in Company D that fought to the surrounded Americans after their night of terror.

"We knew these boys were in plenty of trouble but did not know whether we could make the grade," Stillmock said. "Well, we started out, but those damn Japs would let our scouts go by and then fire into us. We were fighting Indian fashion and knocking them out of trees by sniping at them.

"It wasn't too late when we got in and formed a line for Company E to come down," Stillmock said.

"As we advanced, we just kept dropping out along the road far apart, so we could cover any of the Japs near us. The E Company boys came charging down the line to safety, yelling their thanks to us as they ran. There were 100 dead Japs in front of their positions."

Both companies had been without food for four days at the time, except for roots and native potatoes, which they dug from the ground and ate raw.

Pfc. Phillip Morse of Dunlap, Iowa, has a bayonet scar on the upper part of his left arm as the result of a hand-to-hand duel with a Japanese soldier who came charging into a roadblock he was protecting.

"There were about a dozen Japs, but we couldn't see 10 of them," said Morse, who was a World-Herald carrier while in school. "They sent two out ahead dressed as Filipinos. We held our fire until they were pretty close. When I got suspicious and decided to shoot, my gun jammed.

"I jumped out then and ran out 20 feet to meet him head-on. He slashed at me and pierced my arm with his bayonet just as I brought up the butt of my rifle and smashed him with it on the side of the head. He crawled away and the next day we found him dead."

June 12, 1945
WITH THE 14TH ARMY CORPS, SOUTHERN LUZON

WHEN YOU ARE IN THE ARMY or living under its jurisdiction, you find yourself taking pleasure in the simple little things you took for granted in civilian life.

Ice cream with a meal, a Coke or an orange or a five-year-old movie are something to look forward to. You have to understand those things before you can appreciate how Mess Sgt. Sam Brehm Jr. of Hastings, Neb., is one of the GI heroes of the 85th Chemical Mortar outfit in the long, grueling march on Manila.

It was coffee and bread and jam for a good many meals as the boys stopped fighting just long enough to gulp a meal. The mortar outfit had been on those kind of rations for some time when Sgt. Brehm found several 100-pound bags of good old Irish potatoes.

Irish potatoes are still a rarity in Manila. When he got the spuds, he kept quiet about it until time for evening mess. He had rigged up cooking utensils so he could make french fries.

"That's something I'll never forget," said Capt. Warren Guinan of Lincoln. "We ate them until we couldn't move."

The Rev. Woodrow J. Elias, left, and 1st Lt. Bill Mullen share a two-month-old World-Herald in the Philippine jungle.

June 18, 1945
WITH THE 32ND DIVISION ON THE VILLA VERDE TRAIL

WE FOUND 1ST LT. BILL MULLEN of Omaha in a deep ravine not far from the front lines. With him was the Rev. Woodrow J. Elias, who coached basketball at St. Francis High School in Councils Bluffs in 1943.

Between them was a two-month-old Sunday World-Herald which they were scrutinizing with avid interest. They looked up astonished at my joyful yelp when I spotted the paper from home. It was in splendid condition as though they had preserved it with all the care given a valued book.

The lieutenant hasn't seen his fiancée in 34 months, because he has been too busy fighting. He picked up a Purple Heart when he was wounded in the foot on Leyte.

"There were two companies of us cut off and they were really pouring it on us. It was my first time in combat and I was so dumb that I just walked around and directed fire on the enemy. I'll never forget that Christmas dinner in 1942 on Buna. We got down to the last of our food, with nothing left but beans. Our wounded came first, and we gave them full rations. Then there was one can of beans left to split among every four men.

"We had 156 enlisted men and six officers when we went in to fight," Mullen said. "I was the only officer to come back. Only 14 enlisted men were able to walk back with me."

He was awarded the Bronze Star on Leyte. He led four tanks down a road that was flanked on both sides with Japanese, and pointed out targets. He also tossed a few grenades as he walked.

June 21, 1945
WITH THE 32ND DIVISION ON THE VILLA VERDE TRAIL

THE LOW-HANGING, BILLOWY CLOUDS and the golden sunset behind the ridges are lost on Tech. Sgt. Paul Jones of Grand Island, Neb.

"To hell with it," he said, waving a grimy hand. "I want to get back to that good old flat farm country in Nebraska. I wouldn't trade an acre of it for this whole deal."

June 24, 1945
WITH THE 32ND DIVISION ON THE VILLA VERDE TRAIL

THE PECULIAR THING ABOUT WARFARE in this sector of the Philippines is the overall nature of the hazards.

The boys do not have to be at the front to be killed or injured. They can get it rolling over the side of a mountain on a tractor, by Japanese infiltration, by sniper or while sleeping on a cot at a command post.

Often it is the humoring of a whim that saves them. Two outstate Nebraska boys are living examples of how close death can come while not engaged in shooting at the enemy. When death misses by a hair's breadth, the incident often becomes the cause of uproarious laughter.

Technician 5th Grade Vernon Guy of Wynot was the victim of one of these circumstances. He was driving a small truck down the precipitous Villa Verde Trail. Another truck crashed into the rear of his machine, which hurtled over the cliff. Vernon did a swan dive out from under the wheel and was skidding for a sheer drop of 400 feet while his truck, turning end-over-end, crashed into a heap of twisted metal at the bottom.

"I managed to grab a couple of handfuls of underbrush just in time or I would have followed the truck down," Guy said. "Then when I get back to my base and the word got around, all the guys roar with laughter and ask the commanding officer if it will be all right if they get the Air Corps to issue me a parachute before I take out another truck."

"Well, you have to admit it was kind of funny," chimed in Technician 4th Grade Gerald Beckstrom of Clarks, Neb.

Beckstrom had his own close call during action at Cape Marcus, when a Japanese plane found where he and some comrades were holed up.

"He came barreling in and dropped three bombs. I happened to be in a foxhole talking to a friend when they hit. The bombs threw dirt and sticks all over us. I got the real scare when I got out and looked at my hammock. It was riddled with shrapnel."

"We got down to the last of our food, with nothing left but beans. Our wounded came first, and we gave them full rations. Then there was one can of beans left to split among every four men."

— 1ST LT. BILL MULLEN, DESCRIBING CHRISTMAS DINNER IN 1942

Technician 5th Grade Vernon Guy of Wynot, Neb., left, and Technician 4th Grade Gerald Beckstrom of Clarks, Neb., had some close calls.

A TRUCK STACKED HIGH with refugees and their belongings rumbles past the shell of a building in Manila.

Manila

The battered Pearl of the Orient

June 24, 1945
MANILA

MANILA, ONCE CALLED the Pearl of the Orient, is now as tarnished as the cheap rings the ragged little Filipino kids hawk on the street corners.

In the shadows of the bombed-out buildings, their squeaky voices constantly ring in your ears as you thread your way through the teeming throngs of soldiers, sailors, women with clothes baskets on their heads and the never-ending stream of Army trucks.

"Hi, Joe! Come buy pretty ring for girl back home," they wheedle.

The sailors are the lads who are best game for hawkers of all descriptions, and the Filipinos love them. Attired in whites after a year at sea and with only an eight-hour pass on which to spend some of their accumulated wealth, they erupt from the harbor like popcorn exploding in a popper.

As always, where there has been suffering, it is the plight of the children that grips your heart and makes you look away.

Because children of a certain age, no matter where you find them, remind you of your own.

They don't complain. They bob around on their pitifully thin legs and make the best of it, picking up a centavo or a peso wherever they can find it.

Another scene of activity is the Americans going to work with bulldozers, huge trucks, cranes and shovels. Naked to the waist, those mechanical GI wizards sit on their roaring machines and cut through the debris in giant swaths.

A Filipino child calls out to passengers in horse-drawn taxis.

Below, a woman does laundry amid the ruin in Manila.

To picture the devastation, imagine how Omaha would look with alternate buildings from Cuming to Q Streets smashed into a twisted heap.

In the harbor, the burned-out hulls of Japanese ships stick forlornly out of the water.

Well, that is wartime Manila, the tarnished Pearl of the Orient. But it is a pearl that is rapidly regaining its luster. The polishers are the grinning GIs from your hometown, their instruments the indomitable bulldozer and the mechanical know-how they picked up in the cities, on the farms and in small-town garages.

A Filipino woman holds her daughter in bombed-out Manila.

RED CROSS WORKER Wilhelmine Haley of Norfolk said some of the prisoners held by the Japanese were in better shape than prisoners she had seen in Europe.

June 25, 1945

WITH THE 32ND DIVISION ON THE VILLA VERDE TRAIL

WHEN A WOMAN comes into this theater of war, she says goodbye to just about everything that takes up a good part of her time back home.

Of course, she hangs on to her lipstick and powder with all the tenacious determination of a scouting patrol to its weapons, but the climate just doesn't cooperate.

Usually the girls' noses are as shiny as a front-line GI's and a half-hour in the sun will almost take the pleats out of a radiator, so you can imagine what it does to slacks.

But Wilhelmine Haley, veteran Red Cross worker of a half-dozen campaigns, believes the satisfaction is worth the chips.

Tanned, with twinkling brown eyes and her dark hair prematurely shot with gray, she has seen service in Africa, the Middle East, Syria and Lebanon. Now she's giving the Pacific a whirl.

The Norfolk, Neb., native hasn't been home for two years. She is a graduate of Iowa State and her job in this theater is to take care of Allied nationals, Americans and neutrals.

"I believe those I have seen who were held prisoners by the Japs were in better physical condition than the prisoners I

saw in Europe," Haley said. "I guess that's because of the wild food that grows here and the inherent friendliness of the Filipinos.

"One of my biggest thrills was in helping a (Filipino) woman who was over 50 years of age. She escaped from five Jap prison camps and had been given up for lost. This woman was still full of fight when I located her. She just kept saying, 'I can't stand all of this kindness.' "

June 26, 1945

WITH THE 32ND DIVISION ON THE VILLA VERDE TRAIL

ONE OF THE MOST heartwarming aspects of covering the boys in the lines and in the field is their pleasure at seeing someone from their section of the homeland.

It takes a couple of days for the word to get around, and then they begin to show up with their dusty, sweat-streaked faces wreathed in smiles.

The only thing not grimy and dirty are their weapons. The barrels gleam like the knives and forks of the treasured family silver.

"Hello, Omaha!" they shout. "I was a couple of miles out when I heard you were here. How's everything back home?"

Pfc. Robert Novak, left, of Pleasant Dale, Neb., and Pvt. Delbert Chadwick of Grand Island team up to guard road-building bulldozers.

Two Nebraska engineers looked me up just as I was packing to pull out of the Villa Verde Trail area the day after the 32nd Division ended its campaign there.

They were Pfc. Robert Novak of Pleasant Dale and Pvt. Delbert Chadwick of Grand Island.

For days these engineers had been out ahead of the infantry, guarding the bulldozers that were clearing the trail under Japanese fire.

Novak had been overseas 24 months and had seen three campaigns. Two weeks ago he had come under heavy artillery fire, and men were killed 50 feet away from him.

A couple of bulldozer operators he was guarding were knocked off tractors by sniper fire but were only wounded.

Chadwick is a comparative newcomer to the Pacific, having arrived in March of this year, but he has already seen plenty of action. The two Nebraskans have teamed up, and the wily Novak has given his friend plenty of good tips on how to outfox the enemy.

June 29, 1945
WITH THE 38TH DIVISION ON LUZON

WE WERE TOLD that nearby is a bomb disposal dump that has approximately 1,000 tons of unexploded Japanese dud bombs in it.

A short time later we were talking to a stocky young man from Omaha who is one of the specialists given the task of exploding the enemy bombs without causing damage.

Sgt. John E. Vail scoffed at the idea that the rest of the Army regards his job as one of the most dangerous in the service.

"Our job is to explode anything that did not go off that should have," he said. "We set off booby traps, air bombs, mortar and artillery shells. We're trained not to be afraid of explosives but we are taught to respect them. We have the softest touch in the Army as long as we do our job right."

Vail's outfit goes in with the infantry on landings and sets to work immediately. Once he was pinned down for three hours by sniper fire while attempting to do his job. But the former Cathedral High football guard thinks he was in his greatest danger without knowing about it.

He and his mates had taken several large bombs out and exploded them. When they finished the job they saw a river and decided to take a swim. They splashed about in the water for about a half-hour and then dressed and started back. After driving three miles, they came to some infantrymen and asked them how far they were back of the lines.

"What do you mean, back of the lines?" said one of the soldiers. "This is the last outpost. You lugs are just getting back to our front."

Sgt. John E. Vail of Omaha downplayed his role in setting off unexploded Japanese bombs.

Pvt. George Peters, left, of South Sioux City, Neb., was the veteran showing the ropes to Pfc. Martin Sass of Snyder, Neb.

Tough time for replacements

July 1, 1945
WITH THE 38TH DIVISION ON LUZON

THIS IS THE STORY about the loneliest guy in the world — the replacement.

He is the fellow who gets his training in the States and then boards a ship for overseas labeled a "casual." The word is just what it implies. The soldier is on his way to the front to replace a man who has been wounded or killed.

If he is congenial, he makes a few friends on the boat. None of them knows the destination. When he reaches his destination, he walks down the gangplank with his carbine and duffel bag over his shoulder.

He may stand in the rain for four hours or more, and then he joins hundreds of other soldiers headed for temporary quarters.

The sergeant in charge of debarkation usually stands to one side and shouts, "Don't bother about grabbing your own barracks bag — pick up the one closest to you, sort them out later."

In other words the casual is in a strange land headed for the shooting, and he is so anonymous that it doesn't matter whether he picks up his own bag or that of someone he doesn't know.

In the tropics he probably starts for the outfit he is to join in a pouring rain. The outfit is composed of hardened combat men back from the lines for a rest.

When the replacement comes in and throws down his gear, they aren't unkind. They just don't talk a lot. They have been up in the places where it doesn't pay to talk too much. They say "hello," lay back on their cots and blow smoke at the ceiling of the tent. They laugh about jokes he doesn't and can't understand until he has been in the same places they have been — with them.

And this is where Pvt. George Peters of South Sioux City, Neb., comes in. He was a replacement in one of the toughest outfits in the Pacific. He is just 21 years of age, is married and has a 2-year-old daughter named Kay. Before he entered the Army he was a buyer for the Jerpe Commission Company in Omaha.

When he joined Company H as a replacement machine gunner, he weighed 188 pounds. When he came out after 60 consecutive days in the lines, he weighed 167 pounds, but what was left was all hardened, battle-tried muscle.

Peters killed his first Japanese soldier before he got to the front. He was in the second truck of a troop convoy headed for the front with the fighting 38th Division.

Nine Japanese, hidden on the banks of a steep grade along the mountainous road, made a "satchel charge" — that is, they threw heavy explosives into the lead truck of the convoy and scattered. Peters and the men who occupied the truck with him jumped out and started to fight. They killed eight of the nine enemy soldiers. Peters got one of them.

Not long after Peters got to the front, two enemy soldiers crawled within 6 feet of the machine gun the Nebraskan was manning. There was a drizzling rain, and Peters did not see them until they were closing in for the kill. He killed them both at point-blank range.

The next night, Peters left the emplacement to get something to eat. Just before dawn, the Japanese pitched two mortar shells into the hole he had been occupying. Three of the four who remained in the hole received critical wounds and the fourth suffered minor injuries. The sergeant needed blood plasma. They attempted to give it to him but it had become damp in the rain.

Peters and three members of his company decided to try to make it back to an ambulance, carrying the critically wounded man on a litter. It was five miles through Japanese-infested mountain terrain.

"I'll never forget that trip," Peters said. "Our sergeant joked and laughed all the way down. He told us not to hurry and not to worry. We had sent word ahead and we could see the ambulance two hundred yards from us. The medics came running out to meet us with the plasma. Then the sergeant died — just two hundred yards from home. I felt like sitting down on the ground and crying."

When I went to the tent of Private Peters he was on his back on his cot blowing smoke at the ceiling. He had just come back from the lines. He wasn't talking a lot, but he was laughing at the jokes that had seemed stupid two months ago. He was no longer the loneliest guy in the world — a replacement.

July 2, 1945
WITH THE 14TH ARMY CORPS ON LUZON (DELAYED)

ASK ANY GIVEN NUMBER of troops to name the most terrifying aspects of war and you will get that many different answers. Some say it is being shelled by artillery while you are pinned down. The men see the shells coming down in a pattern, creeping toward their foxholes.

Others hate walking along a jungle trail, knowing that snipers are perched in trees, in the dense brush or in caves. Still others hate the shrieking banzai charge at night.

But Master Sgt. Gene Hrdy, 30, of Walthill, Neb., is sure there is nothing that can compare with being caught in open water by a strafing Zero while riding in a Higgins boat.

"Brother, there is nothing quite like that. You feel as though you are laying out in the town square on Saturday afternoon without a stitch of clothes on," Hrdy said. "We were caught between two islands and this Jap came zooming in, making three or four passes. The bullets were falling around us like hail. We had one gun and poured 20 rounds of ammunition into his plane before he would call it quits. I was on the bottom of that boat trying to dig my way through the water."

Sgt. Bill Wochner, 30, of Falls City, Neb., a brakeman for the Missouri Pacific who used to have the run between Falls City and Omaha, votes for a violent airstrike as the most terrifying experience. Eighteen bombs landed in the company area on the Munda airstrip in New Georgia. Besides having his best buddy killed, more than 50 out of the 150 men with him were casualties.

The sergeant had one 500-pounder fall about 12 feet from his foxhole and it shook him up as though he were jounced around in a wrecked automobile, he said. He has been overseas 27 months.

July 3, 1945
WITH THE 38TH DIVISION ON LUZON

THE 152ND INFANTRY REGIMENT of the mountain-fighting 38th Division was coming into the clearing and stacking weapons after 129 days of tough fighting in the lines.

There was none of the ramrod stiffness of the storybook soldier about these soldiers. They slouched along with the free-swinging stride of the frontiersmen, their faces tanned a cowboy saddle brown. Looking at them you could turn the clock back on American history, forget the sweat-soaked combat greens and see them in fringed buckskin.

And that is the kind of war they had been fighting — stalking along narrow trails, fighting from rock to rock and from ridge to ridge.

But they were facing and using the most deadly weapons of modern warfare. Instead of the old flintlock it was grenade, carbine, M-1 and flame-thrower.

Their line officers were with them and there was no spit and polish about them. Except for the faded emblems of rank on their collars and the worry of command etched in their faces, they looked like the GIs. You notice, too, they talked with their troops from the privates on up with the ease of long, close association.

With the aroma of hot food drifting from the camp kitchens that had hastily been set up, they began to bounce back with the resilience peculiar to the American soldier. They were laughing and kidding as they doffed the tops of their combat greens and walked about stripped to the waist.

There were several Nebraskans in the outfit. Typical of them and the rest of the regiment was Staff Sgt. Robert Perkins, 23, of Taylor.

Of the 129 days in the line, he had missed 12 days of combat. All of these 12 days were spent in a hospital.

Perkins had suffered his first wound in the heartbreaking fighting in Zig Zag Pass. He caught a piece of shrapnel in the back when a grenade exploded near him. He was patched up in two days and returned to the fighting.

"We needed every man who could fire a weapon," Perkins said in explanation of his short stay at an aid station. "I was no exception; there were plenty of our boys doing the same thing."

The sergeant was wounded the second time in the fighting on Woodpecker Ridge. They call it the Woodpecker because the particular type of Japanese machine gun used there resembled the pecking of the American bird.

"I was following a light tank along the ridge when the Nips opened up with machine guns on our flanks," Perkins said. "I made a wild scramble for a shell hole and made it. But they nailed me in the arm while I was on the way. It took me 10 days to get back from that one."

> *"The bullets were falling around us like hail. We had one gun and poured 20 rounds of ammunition into his plane before he would call it quits. I was on the bottom of that boat trying to dig my way through the water."*
>
> — MASTER SGT. GENE HRDY

SGT. THEODORE GUSAK of Omaha planned a stop at Johnny's Cafe when he returned home.

July 4, 1945
WITH THE 38TH DIVISION ON LUZON

SGT. THEODORE GUSAK OF OMAHA had just drawn his second day of KP in his eight years of service with the Army. Thirty-year-old Sergeant Gusak was whistling at his work. His face was wreathed in smiles, and he was giving all the fellows an extra helping of dessert.

Along with the notice to report for KP had come the word that Ted was slated to go home under the new point system. He is one of the first of the 38th Division who can forget about the war and re-establish himself in civilian life.

Battle weary and ready to put his uniform in mothballs, Ted first found out he was going to put his training to use on the morning that Pearl Harbor was raided. Ted was in bed there, and the bombs jarred him out of a sound sleep and into a war. He picked up his rifle that morning and he has been fighting the Japanese ever since. On his tunic he wears five battle stars and he has a total of 111 points, more than 25 in excess of his needs.

A South Side boy, Ted says his first stop will be Johnny's Cafe. There he intends to order a big, thick T-bone, and he likes his steaks well done.

"Boy, what a war it has been," Ted said, scuffing the toe of one of his battered combat boots. "They trained me to handle horses. There is nothing I don't know about horses. How to feed them, jump them, train them — anything you care to mention. And then what happens? I fight every inch of this war on foot. When I get back to Omaha, I intend to try to get a job handling horses."

PVT. DEAN GREEN, left, of Chambers, Neb., and Pvt. Dwight Beckstrom of Oakland, Neb., said they learned some tough lessons at the front.

July 5, 1945
WITH THE 38TH DIVISION ON LUZON

"I LEARNED MORE in my 19 days at the front than I did in all the months I was in training. The minute you start to play for keeps, every lesson you learn stays with you."

The speaker was Pvt. Dwight Beckstrom from Oakland, Neb. He is an infantryman in Company K of the 3rd Battalion. His blond hair stands straight up in a short, belligerent top-knot and he keeps squinting one eye as though he still were lining up the sights on his M-1.

Whatever lessons the infantrymen of Company K taught this newcomer to their outfit, he must have learned well because he got three enemy soldiers in his first trip to the front.

"I gave this lad one of the toughest assignments a replacement can get," his colonel said, as Dwight shifted uncomfortably from one foot to the other, "and he and some other new men carried it out without backing up an inch. I was forced to send them down a narrow trail where they had to go in alone at widely spaced intervals. The trail was covered by enemy machine gun fire. These boys went in and broke it up."

"That's right, Colonel, but it got toughest for me after I got over the trail," the young Nebraskan said. "A Nip sniper pinned me down. Every time I'd stick up my head he would zip one past my ear. A flamethrower got him."

Dwight got two enemy soldiers that same day when he helped knock out a pillbox. A third was wounded and hiding under a native hut when Dwight found him. The Nebraskan wanted to capture him, because he could see that all he had was a grenade and a bayonet, but the soldier drew back his arm to throw the grenade and the private let him have it with his M-1.

Another Nebraskan, Pvt. Dean Green of Chambers, put in his first 19 days at the front with Beckstrom. He was one of the men who was sent down the trail.

"The one thing about the fighting that keeps cropping up in my mind is a charge we made on a ridge," Dean said. "It was so muddy it was like trying to run through a bowl of custard. I fell flat on my face six times — I know it sounds funny, but I counted the falls as I went.

"I would lie there a few seconds, gasping for breath, and then I would feel the Jap bullets flicking mud into my face. There wasn't an inch of me that wasn't mud when I got to the top."

July 7, 1945
WITH MACARTHUR IN MANILA (DELAYED)

AFTER THE WAR, a machinist mate first class in the Navy will put down more than $2,000 on a new home in Omaha. Every dollar of it was earned under the water of the Pacific Ocean.

It was earned while Gene Bauwens was walking about under the waves of the Pacific with a welding torch in his hand while the exotic tropical fish peered curiously at him through the panes of his diving helmet.

Bauwens and the rest of his mates are paid $5 an hour for plodding around the shell-torn ships of the Japanese Navy as they rest on the bottom of harbors taken over by Americans as they fight their way to Tokyo.

The 29-year-old sailor from Omaha has spent more than 400 hours on the floor of the ocean and he has "saved every dime of the money earned for a new home after the war."

The Omahan is clearing the wreckage of sunken Japanese ships in Manila harbor. He and his mates made it possible for the troop ship on which I came from Manila to be the first to sail into the harbor of this once beautiful city.

When the former basketball player from Tech High goes down in his diving gear, he is carrying more than 200 pounds of weight on his wiry 175-pound frame. There are thrills aplenty down there, and Bauwens has experienced most of them. Once while diving in 40 feet of water with only a face mask on, he came close to serious injury or death.

"The pressure blew my mask off and I was on my way up with danger of my lungs being wrecked," Bauwens said. "Those topside luckily realized what had happened. They had another mask ready for me, clapped it over my head and sent me back down immediately. That's the only thing that saved me."

He also has his share of the shooting kind of danger. When he was at Lingayen Gulf, Japanese suicide troops attempted to sink the craft he was on.

"They would come swimming out towards us with boxes over their heads," Bauwens remembers. "They were armed to the teeth with grenades which they would attempt to pitch into our boat. We stood on the decks with tommyguns and shot at them."

July 8, 1945
WITH MACARTHUR IN MANILA (DELAYED)

THERE IS ONE SPOT IN MANILA where a soldier or sailor or any other member of the armed services does not get clipped when he seeks a cold drink and a sandwich after he has plodded the dusty streets of this bombed-out city.

He can always go to the Red Cross and get for nothing what would cost him six pesos at any of the so-called Filipino cafes. Six pesos is $3 in American money. That is too steep a price for any American who has not forgotten how to count his change. But to a GI, who probably draws around $30 a month after his dependency money has been deducted, that charge for a sandwich and a glass of lemonade is brutal.

That is why you will find them sweating out the never-ending lines at the big Red Cross building where they can get a cup of hot coffee and doughnut or a sandwich and a cold drink. It is estimated that 35,000 of the boys slowly pass through the building every day. Here, too, they contact old friends and talk over their adventures in scores of far-flung battles.

GENE BAUWENS of Omaha helped clear the hulls of wrecked Japanese ships in Manila's harbor.

263

NEBRASKANS TECH. SGT. EVERETT GILES, left, of Lincoln, Pvt. Herman Steinmiller of Scottsbluff and Staff Sgt. Charles Hayes of Marquette paused occasionally during their walk through the U.S. Army Cemetery at Santa Barbara to pay their respects to a fallen comrade.

A visit to fallen comrades

July 8, 1945

UNITED STATES ARMY CEMETERY AT SANTA BARBARA, LUZON

A CLOUD-FILTERED TROPICAL SUN softened the outlines of the symmetrical crosses. The breeze that stirred the branches of the palm trees seemed to whisper a benediction.

Here they lay together, side by side, regardless of rank, the private first class beside the general, the lieutenant colonel beside the sergeant. Their burial had been as impartial as the enemy bullets that struck them down.

Morning glories, buttercups and other flowers native to home were beginning to grow. The flowers were sent by the families of the eight soldiers in charge of the cemetery.

The three Nebraska soldiers who accompanied me trod softly through the lanes of crosses. They clutched their Army hats in their hands. They paused now and then and whispered a name. They were among friends. More than 1,000 of the 5,000 who lay there had been their comrades-in-arms in the 32nd Division.

With these departed comrades, my companions had added proud battle flags to the weathered standards of the Red Arrow Division. These exotic names of the tropics will take their places in the textbooks at West Point: Balete Pass, Lingayen Gulf, the Villa Verde Trail, Baguio.

The boys with me paused for a longer time before the cross of a boy who was not of their division. He was closer still — he was from the hometown of one, from the home state of all three.

"I knew a boy by that name back there when I was a kid — I wonder if it was him," murmured Tech. Sgt. Everett Giles of Lincoln.

Pvt. Herman Steinmiller of Scottsbluff and Staff Sgt. Charles Hayes of Marquette said nothing.

As Giles stood looking at the grave, he fingered the puckered scar of a sniper's bullet that had missed his left eye by a quarter-inch and nicked his ear after it grooved the side of his head.

A sudden tropical storm was coming up as we left the cemetery. There was a roll of thunder in the darkened skies like the muffled roar of artillery — nature's salute to the boys who fell at Balete Pass, Lingayen Gulf, the Villa Verde Trail and Baguio.

But the rain that followed — that was for the morning glories, the buttercups, the flowers they knew at home.

Before I left the States, I often heard anxious relatives ask about interment facilities near the battle theaters. I decided then to visit cemeteries in the Pacific area at my first opportunity.

The Santa Barbara cemetery is built on the highest ground in the Pangasinan province. Scores of reverent Filipinos, conscious of the debt they owe to those who lie there, give individual attention to each grave.

July 10, 1945
MANILA

HE WAS ALWAYS the little fellow on the outside because he was too small to play. He loved athletics, but he just never had the heft to get out there with the rest of the kids.

That's how I remember Raymond (Red) Johnson of Omaha. When I knew him, he was the mascot of a very good Omaha University football team while I was covering it back in the 1930s. He was a darned good mascot, and every once in a while I'd shoot a picture of Red seated on a pile of helmets with another oversized helmet perched on top of his flaming red thatch.

The other day I met Red again, and it didn't take me long to realize that he had found a helmet that fits him. He has also found a game where heft doesn't count too much if you have the heart — and the youngster from the North Side always had plenty of that.

He has been overseas in the Signal Corps of the 14th Army Corps more than two years, and some of the tales this lean-jawed young man can tell you send chills up and down your spine. He accomplishes missions so secret that the censors killed the first story I wrote about him.

On one of those missions, Red and his daring comrades almost lost their lives.

"We went in at 4 knots in PT boats on a moonlit night with the mufflers closed," the 24-year-old Omahan said. "All went well until we came to a narrow pass where we knew we were going to be sitting ducks at our slow speed. And sure enough, the Japs spotted us with their float planes. They came zooming in with bombs and scored two near misses on the boat I was riding, and it was disabled. We got through after transferring to another boat.

"We were in uncharted water, and the land map we had was dated, I think, about 1856. We went inland in native dugout canoes. We killed 18 Japs and captured seven while accomplishing our mission. I'll never forget the nights when I would be hidden in the brush, scarcely daring to breathe, with Japs jabbering on every side of me."

July 12, 1945
WITH THE 32ND DIVISION AT LINGAYEN GULF

THEY HAVE TRIED TO MAKE a rear echelon trooper of Technician 4th Class Merle Krovas of North Platte, Neb., but his commanding officers are just about ready to give up. They can't make it stick.

Towering well over 6 feet and sporting a mop of unruly curly brown hair, Krovas is always popping up in the front lines and he is a welcome figure because when he arrives he usually has a black bag full of money.

Theoretically, Krovas confines his activities to clerical work with the medics, but when it comes time to pay the troops, Krovas takes off. He crawls around among the fighting troops, methodically counting out the money due each of them.

"Most of them are glad to see me because often they are fresh out of poker money," Krovas explained, "but every once in a while I meet some wise guy who says, 'Take it back and save it for me — I just yelled over to the Nips and they told me they were fresh out of cold beer and chewing gum so I won't be able to spend it.' "

Krovas' pals get a bounce out of explaining how the loose-limbed youngster took care of the first battle casualty at Saidor 17 months ago.

An infantryman had been shot in the knee, and he was out ahead of the fighting troops unable to move. Someone called for a couple of volunteers, and two men rose to their feet.

One of them was Merle. They crawled out and brought the man back. For a long time the Nebraskan denied that he had anything to do with the incident.

Finally they brought back a first sergeant who had been a witness. He pointed out Merle as the man who had volunteered to go with the aid man.

Merle, 23, plans to go to the University of Nebraska when he gets back.

Two beardless boys who joined the Army after being high school pals at Lincoln still are buddies in an infantry outfit of this division. They fought together at Aitape, Leyte and Luzon, and on the stocks of their M-1s, the number of notches tallying dead enemy troops is the same. There are five on each.

One is Pfc. Robert Cather, 21, and the other is Pfc. Carl Irons, 20. Bob is the son of Mr. and Mrs. H.B. Cather, and a distant relative of the writer Willa Cather. Carl's parents are Mr. and Mrs. Clyde Irons.

Private Cather was caught on a hillside during the early fighting on Luzon. Japanese troops on top of the hill were looking down at him and the rest of his platoon with field glasses. The platoon knew that both flanks were covered by the Japanese because they could hear them jabbering. Looking backward, they could see 50 enemy soldiers at the bottom of the hill armed with anti-tank guns. It looked hopeless for a while, but they managed to get a message through calling for mortar fire. They swept the enemy off the ridge, and then another company fought through the Japanese at the bottom.

Mortars and point-blank artillery fire while he and his mates were pinned down on top of a hill almost spelled disaster for Irons. With every round, more and more of the infantrymen were killed and wounded. They were under fire for four hours, and then darkness made it possible for them to evacuate.

"When we did move, we carried out our dead and wounded," Irons said. "It took us three hours. Later we retook the hill."

Lingayen Gulf

PFC. CARL IRONS, left, and Pfc. Robert Cather, high school friends in Lincoln, saw heavy action in the Philippines. Cather said he was a distant relative of author Willa Cather.

Capt. Grover R. Fattic Jr. of Lincoln, shown tending to a wounded soldier, said his unit endured "machine-gun bullet breakfasts" from the Japanese for 10 days.

July 13, 1945
WITH THE 32ND DIVISION AT LINGAYEN GULF

HE WAS GOOD ENOUGH to be city prep champion at both the high and low hurdles in 1931 when he was an athlete at Central High, but Maj. Max Emmert, 32, will tell you he has met his stiffest competition out here in the Pacific, where he has served as an Army doctor for 37 months.

Maj. Emmert captained Central's track and basketball teams. He received his medical degree from the University of Nebraska.

I found the major puttering around a medical tent, peering mildly through his spectacles at youngsters who had come to him suffering from various ailments.

He told me how he found himself in one of the toughest spots of the war when the 32nd suffered heavy casualties on Leyte.

"We were quartered in tents at Capocan and had been operating on and treating casualties for 24 hours at a stretch," the major said. "Then the Japs began to shell us and kill our patients. We decided to evacuate by truck. We moved 150 patients in 90 minutes under heavy fire. Never have I seen such fortitude among the wounded."

The major and his assistants had generators to manufacture electricity. When those failed, they continued their work with flashlights.

"Although the situation was plenty serious, I still have to laugh when I think of the phone call I got when that shelling started to get rough. Someone shouted over the telephone that I wasn't to worry — the explosion I heard was just a land mine going off. I yelled back that when land mines started to fly through the air and land in my hospital, it was time to move. And we did move," the major concluded.

If you hang around the medics for any length of time, the conversation invariably ends with the lads who go out into the field and get the wounded from under the muzzles of the enemy guns.

Maj. Max Emmert, right, of Omaha examines a soldier. Emmert was a city hurdle champion at Central High.

Naturally these men are dear to the hearts of the doughboys. It is the medic who crawls out to them through the mud and rain of the battlefield, armed with his merciful sedative and emergency treatment. The medic is the one slim barrier between life and death.

Capt. Grover R. Fattic Jr., whose wife and parents live in Lincoln, is a particularly eloquent spokesman for this branch of the service.

The boys under him get the wounded from the lines to the ambulances, and then they drive the vehicles that get the wounded back to the portable hospitals and aid stations.

When the 32nd Division was fighting on the Villa Verde Trail, it was a 28-mile haul over rocky, slippery terrain from the front lines to the rear.

"When the snipers were bad and it was dangerous for a man to be out ahead of the ambulance on foot, we would place him on the fender of the ambulance," Captain Fattic said. "He would ride with his hands dragging along the inside bank of the trail, talking the driver down to safety.

"They had to use the inside bank because if the ambulance wandered to the outside it would fall 400 feet over cliffs. Of course the ambulance was proceeding without lights. Try that on a black night in a pouring rain."

The Japanese fed the captain's outfit "machine-gun bullet breakfasts" for 10 days at one portable hospital base. Patients were wounded anew while recovering from wounds in sandbagged tents. Some died from new wounds.

"They would open up on us from surrounding hills at precisely 6:30 a.m.," the captain said. "We would often pick up the slugs between our beds where they had fallen after spending their power. They also knocked out ambulances, flattened tires. One morning we caught a Jap trying to infiltrate with a load of dynamite strapped on him."

The eternal race with the stork takes place out here in the battle lines. The ambulances sometimes lose here just as they do at home.

One night an ambulance in the captain's outfit started down from the mountains with 18 supply bearers from the Igorot Tribe. All had suffered wounds of minor or serious nature.

When the ambulance arrived at the portable hospital, there were 19 Igorots. An Igorot woman had given birth to a boy on the way down. A perspiring ambulance driver and his assistant had attended.

July 14, 1945
WITH THE 32ND DIVISION AT LINGAYEN GULF

A GRIMY "CAT" DRIVER from Scottsbluff, Neb., sat with me in a thatched hut and told as strange a story of the building of the Villa Verde Trail as I have heard.

The dust of his last job was still in his hair, under his fingernails and in the folds of his combat greens. With him was an engineering pal from Parkersburg, Iowa, and between the two they had experienced just about everything the Japanese could throw at them while they were building the "Little Surma."

I had scrounged a can of sardines from a friend, and as we talked we got the small fish from the can by impaling them on match sticks. The sardines were swell. The story was better.

The young man from Nebraska was Technician 5th Class Alex Reifschneider, 24, and he has a wife waiting for him on a farm near Gering, Neb. She is living with her parents, Mr. and Mrs. John Maier. The Iowan is Pfc. Albert Johnson Jr., 20. He drove a truck before the war. His parents are Mr. and Mrs. Albert Johnson Sr. The Nebraskan has been overseas 30 months, his friend 14.

One morning about 6 o'clock it was found that a huge gap had been dynamited in the Villa Verde Trail during the night.

Alex was sent out with his tractor to fill in the gap so that tanks could advance. Al went along to service the huge machine. He was walking along about 20 feet in advance of the machine when it struck a mine, loaded with 50 pounds of TNT, just before it reached the gap.

"That dynamite blew my 'cat' to pieces with me in the driver's seat." Alex said. "The blast threw me 20 feet in the air and the funny thing about it was that I was conscious every second of the time I was up there. I was spinning and could see the 'cat' going into a million pieces below me. I landed on a knoll above the road on all fours. I had a cut on my arm and one on my chest."

Al was blasted off his feet, but was unhurt. They picked up the pieces of the 'cat' and placed it on the salvage metal pile. Alex went back to an aid station. Two hours later, he was back at work on the trail.

A few days later, the two friends were again working on the road. A hidden sniper started to shoot at them. It was imperative that they continue the work. In five shots, the sniper killed three and wounded two. Patrols went out and routed him but were unable to kill or capture him.

The two members of Company B and the 114th Engineers worked on every yard of the Villa Road.

"And now I'm sweating out the worst situation of all," the Nebraskan said. "I have 82 points and I need 85 to go home and see my wife. I have been recommended for the Bronze Star. If I get it, I will have 87 points and be a cinch to go home. I could forget about that medal but, brother, do I want those five points!"

"I'm stuck," his friend said. "I've only got 42, but you have been here 16 months longer than I, and you have that break coming. I'll hate to see you go, but I hope you make it."

The two friends shouldered their M-1s and walked off down the dusty Luzon road together — a couple of GIs who probably never would have met had it not been for the war.

"They would open up on us from surrounding hills at precisely 6:30 a.m. We would often pick up the slugs between our beds where they had fallen after spending their power."

— CAPT. GROVER R. FATTIC JR., DESCRIBING JAPANESE ATTACKS IN THE PHILIPPINES

TECHNICIAN 5TH CLASS ALEX REIFSCHNEIDER, right, of Scottsbluff tallies his points, as Pfc. Albert Johnson Jr. of Parkersburg, Iowa, looks on. Soldiers received points for length of time in service, battles and awards and could go home after totaling 85.

Six Nebraskans and two Iowans wanted reporter Bill Billotte to say hello to the folks back home. Front row, Nebraskans from left, Technician 5th Class Morris DeFreece of Auburn, Pvt. Frank Svacina of Omaha, Sgt. Joe Stewart of Kennard and Pfc. Charles Larson of Bradshaw. Back row, Pvt. Ernest Coufal of Brainard, Neb.; Cpl. Virgil Wulff of Fremont, Neb.; Technician 5th Class Arnold Lundberg of Schaller, Iowa; and Technician 3rd Class Clarence Lundy of Webster City, Iowa.

July 16, 1945
WITH THE 32ND DIVISION AT LINGAYEN GULF

IT WAS A BOILING HOT DAY — one of those days when your shirt clings to your back like a wet rag.

Perspiration streamed down your arms. You couldn't light a pipe because your tobacco was too damp, and the doughfoots doggedly were going about their duties with apathetic eyes and listless motions.

Eight boys in a halftrack pulled up in a cloud of dust. They jumped out. Six of them were from Nebraska, the two others from Iowa. They said they had heard I was in the area, and they had wrangled a one-day pass and the truck so they could look me up.

"We thought you might say hello to our folks back home for us," one of them said, "but it's so darn hot we hate to bother you. Ain't this a pip?"

They were all from the artillery and although their stories are not spectacular, ask any infantryman what he thinks of them. They are the boys who come toiling along with their big guns through clouds of dust when the foot soldiers have gone as far as they can unassisted. They take over and smash the strong enemy emplacements to rubble, and then the infantry goes on.

They can also make you feel pretty cheap when they talk about bothering you on a hot day when they are willing to take 12 hours of their own time to talk to you.

July 17, 1945
GUAM

WE ARRIVED HERE after a 1,600-mile night flight from Manila just in time to find our forces preparing to observe the first anniversary of the recapture of the island from the Japanese.

A year ago this month, Marines and soldiers swarmed up the beaches and wrested this most important forward base from the enemy. You can count the cost in the small, well-cared-for cemeteries that dot the island. We recorded 1,358 killed, 5,636 wounded and 137 missing. More than 18,000 Japanese were killed.

And now on this 225 square miles of island, there is a display of aerial and naval might that makes you catch your breath. The biggest dredging job ever attempted in the Pacific is well on its way to completion. Six million cubic yards of coral have been pumped out of Apra Harbor, and the harbor now handles more cargo than any other forward area port in the world.

A year ago there were only two semi-paved two-lane highways of poor construction. Today there are 150 miles of road, more than 40 of which are paved. There is a four-lane super military highway that runs the length of the island along its busy west coast.

There are 3,600 jeeps, 26,000 trucks and 3,000 trailers here. One motor pool of 850 trucks does nothing but move cargo from docks to storage dumps. Drivers work in two shifts, each 11 hours a day. There are 1,200 heavy tractors, 400 cranes, hundreds of bulldozers. They use 150,000 gallons of gasoline a day. The harbor is crammed with ships.

And looking down on it all from the clouds are hundreds of Superfortresses relentlessly carrying on their pounding of the Japanese mainland. Day and night they drone over. There are three B-29 fields here.

Fighters of every description, both of the Army and Navy, are in the air constantly. It takes 15 million gallons of gasoline a month to keep them up there.

More than 12 million board feet of lumber are shipped into Guam each month for construction purposes, and Quonset huts are everywhere. A sawmill, using native labor, produces 50,000 board feet of lumber each week, and nearly half a million bags of cement are used each month.

A good deal of the credit belongs to one of the newest branches of the Navy — those hard-driving Seabees in faded blue fatigues. They are of all ages, and there are plenty of bald heads glistening out here in the tropical sunshine. They come from all walks of life, but they have one thing in common: They all have that Yankee mechanical know-how.

Seven days a week, night and day, they push this island around like it was your little boy's sand pile. They fought the monsoon season, saw road beds washed out time and again by torrential rains. They not only held their own, but set records for construction, once building a desperately needed hospital in 57 days. During the Iwo Jima campaign, the hospitals received 10,500 casualties. There are eight hospitals, and when completed they will contain 13,200 beds.

That is Guam, the nerve and supply center of the Pacific, one of many reasons why the Japanese can't win.

July 19, 1945
WITH A B-29 WING ON GUAM

THERE IS ONE B-29 out here that has made a name for itself. It has the best maintenance record in the wing, is lead ship and has never turned back from a mission in its 19 flights. Its name is the City of Omaha. It flew for 380 hours without changing an engine. It survived the fire of 40 Japanese destroyers, though it caught flak through both wings, one engine and the tail section. Before the destroyers scored any hits, the plane had dropped 98 percent of its fire bombs in a 1,000-foot circle.

Those are just a few of the reasons why the plane made at the Martin plant at Fort Crook is considered quite a warrior in flying circles out here. The only member of the original crew who hailed from Omaha was Anthony Cappoccia, who has since been given a medical discharge.

All of the crew were stationed near Omaha at one time or another, and they still talk about weekend trips to the city.

"It's a soldier's town if there ever was one," a member of the crew said in explaining how they had named the ship. "We are all Middle West boys, and the plane was made there so we decided to call it the City of Omaha."

Two of the present crew live in Iowa. They are Lt. Glen Jensen, 23, of Manning, co-pilot, and Master Sgt. Lyle Thomas of Boone, flight engineer. Besides his missions, Thomas is sweating out the days until he can see his 17-month-old daughter, Virginia Lee. She and his wife, Jeanne, are awaiting his return at Boone.

Jensen is full of stories about the adventures of the ship.

"One of the roughest raids we had was over Tokyo," the lieutenant said. "We had dropped our fire bombs, and you couldn't see for smoke. We were down to about 8,000 feet when we hit a thermal heat wave, and it pitched the ship up to 12,000 feet. I thought I was supposed to be operating the ship and Mac, the pilot, thought he had it, and we were both on the controls. We came out of it without any trouble."

Eight of 11 Japanese ships were hit on another raid. Jensen said they had hit their targets in Osaka and weren't bothered by flak until the Japanese fleet sighted them as they were on their way back.

Lt. Glen Jensen, left, of Manning, Iowa, and Master Sgt. Lyle Thomas of Boone, Iowa, named their B-29 the City of Omaha because all of the crew members were from the Midwest and the bomber was built at the Martin Bomber Plant at Fort Crook.

Guam

July 20, 1945
WITH A B-29 WING ON GUAM

B-29 MECHANIC SGT. RAY BROWN of Omaha was proud of the mustache he grew overseas.

IT ISN'T A FANCY JOB and you will find very little brass on the collars of the lads who do it. Their weapons are monkey wrenches, and their badges of honor are usually streaks of grease across their bare chests.

But every time you hear about a new fire in Tokyo, chalk up at least part of the credit to this unassuming branch of the air forces. For every one of the big B-29s that gets to the target, there are six of these young men sweating it out on some jungle air strip.

You don't have to sell them to the boys who operate the planes. They know all about them and show their respect in their attitude toward them. They know who makes it possible to get those planes off the ground and the work it takes to keep them up there hour after hour under the toughest weather conditions.

We saw these ground crew boys in action as they sweated out the biggest raid the B-29s had yet made over Japan. Anxiously scanning the skies, they kept each other informed by hand signals of the number of planes already in while they worked on other ships that had not participated in the mission.

They worry about all the planes, but each ground crew has its own special ship — its particular baby. When that plane comes rumbling down the strip and taxis over to its spot, they relax.

One gangly sergeant who tops 6-foot-3 is typical of these precision workmen. He is Sgt. Ray Brown of Omaha, and there is no one who can tell him much about the B-29 because he helped build the first three that came out of the Martin Bomber Plant at Fort Crook.

"When I found out I was headed for the Army, I didn't lose any time in getting lined up with the ground crew boys," said the sergeant. "That's the job I picked on my own in civilian life and the only job for me in the Army."

Coming to the tropics also made another major triumph possible for the mechanic from Omaha.

"I always wanted to raise a handlebar mustache, but for some reason or other it wouldn't grow in the States," he said. "The day I got here this thing started to sprout — and now look at it."

He fondly stroked a bristling red brush that looked like it had come out of the corner saloon in the Gay Nineties. Ray and a ground crewmate hold one of the records out here for continuous work on a plane. They once worked 49 hours without a break on a Superfortress that was needed for the next mission. Ray has a wife waiting for him in Idaho but plans to take advantage of the GI bill after the war to attend the University of Nebraska.

Sgt. Clarence Pfeifer, 24, of Spaulding, Neb., is another ground crewman who is well-liked by the combat men. The ship on which he works brought him to Guam from the States without giving him a minute's worry.

"You know how you feel up there with nothing but four good motors between you and the drink," the sergeant said. "After a ride like that, there is something personal between you and the plane. The boys did a good job of naming her. Their pilot's name is Parr so the other 10 guys on the ship decided to call her " 'Ten Under Parr.' "

Clarence said his uncle, Frank Dieter, is connected with the Falstaff Brewing Company in Omaha and that drinking a "cold one" with his uncle is going to be the first thing he does when he hits Nebraska.

"You know how you feel up there with nothing but four good motors between you and the drink."

— SGT. CLARENCE PFEIFER, GROUND CREWMAN

July 22, 1945
WITH THE NAVY SOMEWHERE IN THE PACIFIC

THE RECEIVING STATION on this island in the Central Pacific is a colorful place. Here the Navy boys meet in their travels, hash over their battles with the Japanese and await their assignments to other ships.

Although still in his teens, Signalman 3rd Class William Tracy of Lincoln has plenty of stories to tell of his 20 months in the service. His last duty was off the coast of Okinawa, where his craft formed part of the defense line around the Navy fighting ships that were supporting the ground troops in the fierce fighting there.

Tracy said ships of his type were comparable to the line on a football team or the perimeter around a command post in the Army. They fought off Japanese subs and suicide planes when they attempted to break the line to get to the big ships.

"The Nip suicides came in just about every night, 80 and 90 at a time, and we had plenty of action," Tracy said. "They knocked out ships as close as 600 yards, but we escaped and we were all knocking down plenty of the planes. The Nip planes came in low, dropping down below the mountains and roaring over about 20 feet off the water at night. That made them difficult to spot. Our combat air patrol was doing a great job, dropping from 40 to 60 Jap planes a day."

Bill said they tracked two subs during the course of their operations, and after they had them located, turned them over to smaller patrol craft that went after them. The sailor was a Lincoln High athlete, swimming breaststroke on the swimming team and playing guard on the football team.

At the time I saw him, he was the envy of his other seagoing mates. His high school sweetheart, Shirley Bell of Lincoln, has been writing to him during the time he has been overseas.

"Those girls back there will never know what that means to us," said the curly-haired sailor. "I've seen some of my shipmates awful blue, because they didn't get any of that kind of mail. Their girls forgot them the minute they boarded ship."

July 23, 1945
WITH A SEA RESCUE SQUADRON ON SAIPAN

WHEN THE CREWS of the B-29s start on their long journey over the Pacific to plaster targets in Japan, the sight of the big lumbering Navy planes they pass en route is always heartwarming.

These Navy planes are as big and clumsy-looking as those traditional rescue dogs of the Alps, the St. Bernards, and their function is much the same.

They are alerted every time the B-29s go out, and they are usually around when a flak-riddled Superfortress has to give up and go down to the water.

The average sea rescue plane is a two-motored ship which can land in the water. If the sea isn't too rough, they land and take the Army plane crewmen and pilots aboard.

But usually they circle the men below, if the men have life rafts, and radio the closest ship. If the men are in the water without rafts, the Navy planes drop them whatever they need.

On this island, I found three Nebraskans who have been on sea rescue work. Aviation Radioman 3rd Class Erwin Sorensen of Omaha is one of them.

"We usually go out about five or six hundred miles and keep an anxious eye on stragglers and other ships that seem to be in trouble."

Radioman Sorensen explained, "We have located three crews and got help for them. They really are a happy bunch when they see us circling them. You can tell it even from up there where we are. We go out frequently, and you really get a kick out of doing this kind of work."

Although he is only 19, the former Tech High football guard has a wife, Marjorie, waiting for him.

Ensign Victor Anderson, 22, of Lincoln is a co-pilot on a sea rescue plane. He has been overseas four months and has had 200 hours in the air in rescue work. Married and with one year of engineering at the University of Nebraska behind him, Ensign Anderson says he thinks he will make Navy flying a career after the war.

Aviation Chief Radioman Merle Christofferson, 26, of Dalton, Neb., is on a four-motor Coronado patrol ship, but he says the big planes often figure in sea rescue work.

"Not so long ago, we were on patrol and saw a B-24 Liberator in trouble, so we hung around," Christofferson said. "Sure enough, they had to ditch it, and they couldn't get a life raft out, so we dropped one to them. We radioed a ship and circled them until they were picked up. Thus eight men were saved."

Christofferson said his own ship almost needed rescuing off Honolulu.

"One of our motors caught fire and burned until it dropped off the plane," he said. "We limped in on three engines and just got the ship down in time."

Christofferson said he wanted to show me something. He led the way to a little sandy patch by the side of his Quonset hut.

"Look," he said, pointing. "This is the only victory garden on Saipan. I got radish seeds from home, and they came up in 48 hours."

Saipan

NEBRASKANS ON A B-29 had stayed together from the time they arrived in the Pacific until they got their orders home. From left, 1st Lt. Ray Beck of Omaha, 1st Lt. Louis Covi of Lincoln, 1st Lt. Melvin Ehlers of Wayne and Sgt. Leonard Stertz of Sutton.

THREE IOWANS DISPLAY the scorecard for the USS Bennion. From left, Ship's Serviceman 3rd Class Max Smith of Ottumwa, Chief Gunner's Mate Keith Kinart of Council Bluffs and Fire Control Technician 2nd Class Paul Hoschek of Burlington.

July 25, 1945
ABOARD THE USS BENNION SOMEWHERE IN THE PACIFIC

THERE WERE THREE NEBRASKANS and three Iowans with us as the ship's officers explained the Bennion's log book. They lived their combat over again as they listened avidly to every incident. They were:

- Chief Gunner's Mate Keith Kinart, who enlisted in the Navy in Council Bluffs.
- Motor Machinist 3rd Class Harold Herskind of Omaha.
- Fire Control Technician 2nd Class Paul Hoschek of Burlington, Iowa.
- Ship's Serviceman 3rd Class Max Smith of Ottumwa, Iowa.
- Chief Water Tender Jerome Hinds of Fairbury, Neb.
- Seaman 1st Class James Wheeldon of Lewiston, Neb.

All agreed that April 12 was one of their ship's toughest days. The Bennion was plowing along west of Okinawa as part of a screening action for a heavy task force. That afternoon 12 Japanese planes of all types tried to crash through to the big ships. Several of the enemy planes were suicides. The Bennion knocked down three and helped to shoot down three more. One of the Japanese planes crashed 20 yards from the destroyer as it tried to crash into her. The destroyer shortly afterward stopped to pick up a man who had gone overboard off another ship.

On April 28, a suicide plane came after the Bennion as she was making maximum speed and taking violent evasive action. The after guns were pouring out everything they had, as the plane came in, and they nailed him just as he came over. The wing of the plane crashed into the stack of the Bennion,

CHIEF WATER TENDER Jerome Hinds of Fairbury, Neb., has his beard tugged by admirers Motor Machinist 3rd Class Harold Herskind, left, of Omaha and Seaman 1st Class James Wheeldon of Lewiston, Neb.

and the plane plunged over the side into the water.

Two days later, the Bennion almost got it when 10 planes attacked her and another destroyer. The Bennion shot down two, and the other ship got three. One of the planes the Bennion got fell into the sea near her fantail.

She saw her latest action at Okinawa on May 25 when she shot down two more planes to bring her total to 12 shot down and four assists in the Okinawa campaign. It was early on the morning of July 12 in bright moonlight when a two-engine Japanese plane tried to make a torpedo run, but the Bennion knocked it down. The last one was a float plane attempting a suicide dive.

"I came as close to getting it as I want to when that Jap Zeke's wing hit our stack," Sailor Herskind said. "It hit us amidships, and I thought I was a goner. I hit the deck when I saw it coming, and the next thing I knew it was over the side and we were going on with the fight. I still have a piece of the Nip plane for my 2-year-old son, Terry."

Herskind's wife and son are waiting for him in Omaha. He was in the Seabees a year before he went into the Navy. In a neat tattoo on his left arm, he has the name of his wife, Rose, and Terry. He worked for the Army Engineers on the Missouri River before the war.

Husky Chief Gunner's Mate Kinart, 24, has been in the Navy for five years, but he wants to return to Council Bluffs, where he enlisted, as soon as he can. Waiting there for him is his fiancee, Reata Rae Quick. They became engaged in September of 1943 when he was home on leave.

"I've seen just about everything our little old tin can has gone through because, as long as everything is going all right, I have a grandstand seat," Kinart explained.

July 29, 1945
WITH THE 73RD B-29 BOMB WING ON SAIPAN

YOU ARE HEARING MORE about them every day, these biggest of all war planes that are spreading fear and destruction throughout Japan.

Each month the number of Superfortresses that take part in the missions grows larger, and a greater number of Japanese cities are reduced to ruins.

This island of Saipan, which embraces 75 square miles, is the original eagle's nest for the B-29s. It was from here that the big ships made their first historic strike on Tokyo on Nov. 24, 1944.

When you read of 600 Superforts hitting the heart of Japan, you are probably inclined to think of the strike as a majestic air fleet soaring toward a target, of a fleet indomitable in its power, vast and impersonal.

If you hang around the base for a while, you know this is not true. Each plane has its individual characteristics, and every man is sweating out the action in his own way. There is nothing impersonal about a bombing mission.

Each man gets his ration of goose pimples at a different time, and each has his pet fear. Some are afraid of crashing into another B-29 in the darkness over a target. Others fear the tossing-around the plane gets when the smoke from the target creates thermal updrafts. Some get clammy hands just as they approach the shores of Japan. Few are frightened when the action really starts.

"It is the thing you don't count on that gets you in trouble," said Staff Sgt. Charles Chadwick, 24, of Scottsbluff, Neb., who had just got in from a raid on Nagoya. "Not long ago we were flying along over the target in Japan just behind the lead ship. Everyone in that plane was a close friend of ours. We slept in the same Quonset hut back at the base. All of a sudden they hit her with flak, and she stood right up on her tail, throwing all kinds of wreckage at us.

"Our pilot was quick enough to keep us from ramming into her. He threw our plane's nose up, and we stood up and she fell clear of us. Our tail gunner thought we were hit and kept asking how badly we had been hit. He could hardly believe us when we told him there was nothing wrong."

Chadwick is the top turret gunner. He had a little trouble of his own on the previous flight. Gunners on a Superfort, contrary to popular belief, do not shoot at every Japanese plane they see at night. They track him with their guns, fire only when he comes in to make his pass.

Usually the enemy plane has another with him, ready to fire at the flame of the B-29's guns.

"I was up there tracking this Zeke (Zero) for all I was worth, when all of a sudden the turret dome flew off and sailed back to crash into our tail and lodge there," Chadwick said. "That was another headache for our poor old tail-end man. He thought some Jap was knocking off his end of the ship. The turret dome stayed on all the way back from Japan. They're cutting it off and repairing our ship right now."

Chadwick attended Scottsbluff Junior College, taking pre-engineering. He has completed 15 missions, has 20 to go and will return to school.

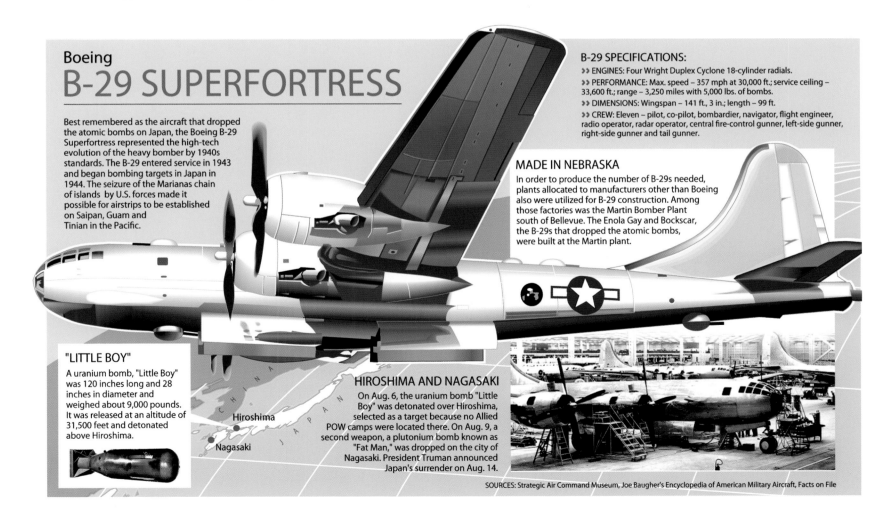

Boeing
B-29 SUPERFORTRESS

Best remembered as the aircraft that dropped the atomic bombs on Japan, the Boeing B-29 Superfortress represented the high-tech evolution of the heavy bomber by 1940s standards. The B-29 entered service in 1943 and began bombing targets in Japan in 1944. The seizure of the Marianas chain of islands by U.S. forces made it possible for airstrips to be established on Saipan, Guam and Tinian in the Pacific.

B-29 SPECIFICATIONS:
›› ENGINES: Four Wright Duplex Cyclone 18-cylinder radials.
›› PERFORMANCE: Max. speed – 357 mph at 30,000 ft.; service ceiling – 33,600 ft.; range – 3,250 miles with 5,000 lbs. of bombs.
›› DIMENSIONS: Wingspan – 141 ft., 3 in.; length – 99 ft.
›› CREW: Eleven – pilot, co-pilot, bombardier, navigator, flight engineer, radio operator, radar operator, central fire-control gunner, left-side gunner, right-side gunner and tail gunner.

MADE IN NEBRASKA
In order to produce the number of B-29s needed, plants allocated to manufacturers other than Boeing also were utilized for B-29 construction. Among those factories was the Martin Bomber Plant south of Bellevue. The Enola Gay and Bockscar, the B-29s that dropped the atomic bombs, were built at the Martin plant.

"LITTLE BOY"
A uranium bomb, "Little Boy" was 120 inches long and 28 inches in diameter and weighed about 9,000 pounds. It was released at an altitude of 31,500 feet and detonated above Hiroshima.

HIROSHIMA AND NAGASAKI
On Aug. 6, the uranium bomb "Little Boy" was detonated over Hiroshima, selected as a target because no Allied POW camps were located there. On Aug. 9, a second weapon, a plutonium bomb known as "Fat Man," was dropped on the city of Nagasaki. President Truman announced Japan's surrender on Aug. 14.

SOURCES: Strategic Air Command Museum, Joe Baugher's Encyclopedia of American Military Aircraft, Facts on File

CREWMAN VRAL POPA, left, of Omaha and Capt. John W. Cambler of Woodbine, Iowa, with the Spirit of Boys Town.

CHINA RUSSIA

Sea of Japan

JAPAN

Pacific Ocean

Okinawa

N

Okinawa

July 30, 1945
WITH THE 73RD B-29 BOMB WING ON SAIPAN

THERE IS ONE B-29 here which dips its wings when it passes over a certain area on its way to bomb Japan.

Its name is The Spirit of Boys Town, and it has a special reason for dipping its wings. It is paying tribute to a man who loved boys, to the man who was responsible for the ship getting its name.

He is Lt. Col. D.C. Northrup, a Yale man from Glenbrook, Conn. He was the former commanding officer of a squadron in the 73rd, and his picture is the only one that adorns the walls of the fliers' recreation hall. He is up there smiling down his encouragement from the cockpit of a plane, just as he did in life.

They say that when the colonel was back in the States, he would often stop on the street and take a gang of boys to a ballgame or to a show. He had studied sociology at Yale and planned to make the helping of boys his life's work when the war ended. When any of the gunners, ground crew men or pilots of his squadron became a father, the colonel always handed the man a dollar bill to "start the youngster's bank account."

Naturally the colonel was attracted to Boys Town. Before he went to the European Theater of Operations, he promised the youngsters there he would name a plane for them. He had stopped there every time he went through Omaha.

He could not keep his promise in Europe, because he did not have that kind of a post there.

When he passed through Omaha on his way to the Pacific, he stopped again and said he would have a Superfort named for Boys Town. Out here, the colonel was a combat flying man.

He took his turn at bombing Japan more often than a commanding officer should. Those were busy days. The colonel had the responsibility of a squadron, yet he went about procuring a plane whose crew would be willing to give up its own choice of names for his.

"Remember, if anything happens to me, don't forget to name the first new ship that comes in for Boys Town," he told a captain before he took off on his last mission.

He was the 12th man in the crew but was at the controls when the plane caught fire and crashed into the Pacific on the way back from that mission. The 11 others were saved. They searched for the colonel by sea and by air — even landed on an island known to be held by the Japanese — but they never found him.

The first B-29 that came in after his death was given the name the colonel had set his heart on. There was quite a ceremony when it was named.

That's why a certain B-29 called The Spirit of Boys Town dips its wings every time it passes over the water near an island of the northern Marianas.

August 1, 1945
WITH THE NAVY ON OKINAWA (DELAYED)

NOWHERE ELSE IN THE PACIFIC are you as air-conscious as on this chunk of coral just a hop and a skip from Japan.

You work under the roar of American warplanes all day long. As this is being written, they are roaring over in squadron after squadron, and the typewriter seems to vibrate to the sound of their engines.

Waspish fighters bee-line their way in a beautiful formation, while lone fighting planes cavort in the skies like flying fish. The bombers, with their deadliness of purpose, are the ones that impress. They move neither fast nor slow, but they give the impression they will never turn back, and you are glad you are on the friendly end of the trip.

At night it is the Japanese planes that bother you. You're not worried about the planes themselves, but at the inconvenience they cause. Never a night goes by that you don't find yourself sleepily stumbling to a sandbagged air raid shelter or pacing up and down in front of your tent waiting for the second signal that sends you there.

The first night I was here it was the real McCoy. The sirens started shrieking, and the anti-aircraft guns opened up on them. We heard the next day they got a couple.

Neither correspondent Carl George of Cleveland nor I knew where the shelter was, but we followed a skinny character who had nothing on but a pair of skivvies and flapping combat boots. The shelter was crowded, and about half of the correspondents and several Navy officers had been in a midnight poker game. One voice kept moaning in the dark and cursing the Japanese for breaking up the game.

"Keep quiet; that game isn't broken up," answered another voice. "We laid our hands down at our places face down, we'll pick 'em up when this is over."

"I'm afraid something will happen. It's the best hand I've had in months," answered the first voice. "Remember, we're all walking out of here together and going back together."

A couple of fellows said they weren't going to wait any longer. They got about 20 yards away when we heard a Japanese bomb explode, and then our guns opened up. They scampered back into the dugout. The chief danger of recent air raids on Okinawa comes from the shrapnel that falls from our own guns. The all-clear siren sounded shortly after that, and the poker-playing group hustled back to their tent, still arguing the merits of their respective hands.

August 2, 1945
WITH THE 73RD B-29 BOMB WING ON SAIPAN

ALTHOUGH HE IS ONLY 26 years old, you wonder why 1st Lt. William Price of Pawnee City, Neb., isn't sprouting a crop of gray hair. He really has been through the mill.

Instead, he is a debonair chap with a Ronald Colman mustache and a pair of capable brown hands that don't quiver when he's calling a bluff in a poker game. I know.

Bill, a pilot, was one of the lucky ones on the drawing of the white slips out of the hat. He is awaiting orders to go home after 30 missions and more than 100,000 miles of flying against the Japanese.

"You can imagine how I felt," Price said. "I got word that I was the father of another girl at about the same time we won on that draw. Those two breaks, coming at the same time, were more exciting than anything I saw over Japan. My other daughter is 2 and her name is Barbara Jean. We named our last daughter Carolyn." His wife is awaiting his return in Chicago.

The lieutenant saw action aplenty on his 30 missions as a pilot. Besides bombing all the principal cities of Japan, he flew air-sea rescue missions. Because of his excellence as a pilot, he was sometimes sent out alone after special targets.

"My first mission was a honey," Price said. "We were all green as grass and plenty scared. Coming back, we feathered a

prop, and our gas was running low. Then we thought we were back to Saipan, and I started to set the plane down when all hell broke loose. We had tried to land on a Jap-held island, and they were shooting at us. Shortly after that I asked the flight engineer how the gas was holding up, and he said, 'Oh, I've quit worrying about that — I'm looking for a nice soft wave to land on.' I could have choked him. We made it back to our own field a short time later."

Then there was the time over Tokyo when Bill and his boys knocked down three Japanese fighters and damaged several more. That was back in January.

"The Japs weren't pulling their punches either," Price said. "They poured plenty of stuff into our bomb bay doors and riddled the tail section. They made so many passes it seemed like a Japanese air parade passing in review. I think the Japs had decided that night to make the raid as costly as possible to us in the hope that we would slow up on our bombings. They didn't get away with it."

"We nursed our shot-up plane all the way back to Saipan and then came in for the landing," the pilot said. "Then I found out we had no brakes, as we roared down the runway and kept on going when we got to the end. The crash did what the Japs couldn't do — it finished our plane. But not one man on the ship was hurt."

August 5, 1945
WITH PT BOATS IN THE WESTERN PACIFIC

TWO NEBRASKA PT MEN drew first blood on escaping the enemy a couple of nights ago. They blasted a barge with 20 to 30 Japanese sailors on it and nailed a canoe with 10 more aboard.

They were out on the prowl in their speedy boat, the Deuce of Diamonds, when they made their catches. Lt. Elmer Bradley of Columbus is the executive officer of the boat, and Danny McGraw of Bellevue is a motor machinist first class. They still were discussing their luck when I found out they were on a tender and sent out a message that I wanted to talk to them.

Tall and boyish-looking Lt. Bradley told how a couple of the Japanese pitched grenades at the boat when the Deuce of Diamonds idled up to them with her guns leveled for business.

"That's the last motion those Nips ever made," Bradley said. "We really blew them out of the water."

The lieutenant and his motor machinist are fast friends.

"The lieutenant is the luckiest guy on the boat," McGraw said.

"He's the only guy who can keep his girl. We named our ship the Deuce of Diamonds, really meaning the deuce with diamonds, because most of us gave engagement rings to girls and then got a polite dust-off as soon as we put to sea. The lieutenant's girl is not only sticking to him — she writes letters."

Bradley smiled as he told his girl's name. She is Margaret Moore of Omaha, and she is entitled to know what a morale builder she is for these seamen who are getting sore knuckles rapping on Japan's back door.

Bradley, a Creighton University graduate, said he had been contemplating writing a letter to Gregg McBride of The World-Herald.

"I played football at Columbus High back in 1939, when we had an undefeated year," Lt. Bradley said. "Gregg kept predicting every game that we were going to get knocked off, and we never did. Tell him about it, will you?"

"We nursed our shot-up plane all the way back to Saipan and then came in for the landing. Then I found out we had no brakes, as we roared down the runway and kept on going when we got to the end. The crash did what the Japs couldn't do — it finished our plane. But not one man on the ship was hurt."

— LT. WILLIAM PRICE

Rumors of a super weapon

August 9, 1945

WITH GEN. MACARTHUR IN MANILA (BY CABLE)
(THIS ACCOUNT WAS WRITTEN BEFORE THE OFFICIAL REPORTS
OF THE ATOMIC BOMB DROPPED AT HIROSHIMA.)

WHILE WAR CORRESPONDENTS discussed the new atomic bomb in hushed voices and speculated on the effect of Russia entering the war against Japan, I walked the streets of Manila and talked to doughboys and sailors in an attempt to find out what they thought about the apparently world-shaking development.

They were impressed but kept on chewing their gum. They wondered how a plane would take off with the bomb and not destroy everything around it if it crashed on the takeoff. They cocked an incredulous eye when I asked them if they did not think that we are seeing the last of the foot soldiers in this war.

In other words, they are taking the news with healthy skepticism. They are hoping that everything they say about this amazing weapon is true, but they are keeping their powder dry.

Look, said one infantryman who said he was 33 years old, "I have been in four campaigns, and we got some of the finest air and artillery support you ever saw. We thought when we went in that the Japs would be sitting there trying to figure out which was their left and right hand. We got in on the beach and were more than ever convinced that we had their number. Then they shot the hell out of us from every cave, every tree, every damn thing a guy could hide behind.

"I'm hanging on to my M-1 for a couple of months yet, but I'm praying that this bomb and Russia will turn the trick. No one wants to get home any worse than I do."

In a sidewalk cafe I saw Pfc. Ernest Briley, 34, of Omaha. He is with the 118th Engineers of the 43rd Division. He has been overseas 10 months and lost 15 pounds sweating out the war the hard way without the aid of science.

Asked what he thought about the bomb, he said, "I'm just like everyone else in this theater. I want to get home so bad I'm ready to believe there is a Santa Claus, but they have to whip these Japs before I start any postwar planning."

And that's the way it was all down the line. We're thinking that if this bomb is everything they say it is, then civilization has reached a new responsibility. But in the meantime, the boys still are walking the streets of Manila paying three pesos for some trinket that is probably worth one. And the last time they heard, Japan was still very much in the war.

They are the guys who went in and dug them out when all the other fancy inventions failed, and they are ready to do it again. They are sticking around while the world gasps. Somehow it makes you feel better to see them taking what may be world-shaking developments in that healthy, skeptical manner.

CARPENTER'S MATE 2ND CLASS HARRY POTTS of Weeping Water, Neb., was relieved to hear that his brother had been released from a prison camp in Germany.

August 10, 1945
WITH THE SEABEES ON OKINAWA

EVERY SEABEE BATTALION is complete in itself. It has its own mess hall, laundry, machine shop, sick bay (hospital), fleet of trucks, bulldozers, rollers and whatever else it needs to operate independently in the field.

Tall, handsome Chief Machinist's Mate Jim Canning, who hails from Scottsbluff, Neb., is in charge of one battalion's garage.

"If you think I don't have my headaches, stick around," Jim said, wiping off his streaming forehead. "These trucks take an awful beating, and it takes a lot of work to maintain them. In June we repaired 676 trucks. I just get a shop set up the way I like it, and then we're on the move again.

"Take this shop, for instance," Jim said, pointing toward a haphazard group of sheds. "They were goat barns when we got here. I threw the goats out, but they kept sneaking back in. I'd be doing something, look up and find myself staring one of those damn goats in the eye. They caused us more trouble than the Japs."

Canning was state champ in Class D in the shot put and discus competition in 1933. His records still stand, and he was attending Scottsbluff High at the time. He later studied civil engineering at the University of Iowa.

Canning's wife is waiting for him at Alliance, Neb. He has two children, Joan, 8, and Patricia, 2. The six-footer weighs 190 pounds, although he has lost 35 pounds since coming to the Pacific. He has been overseas 20 months and narrowly escaped death when a shell came through a truck under which he was sitting out an air raid.

Over in the hastily constructed laundry, I found 37-year-old Harry Potts, carpenter's mate 2nd class, of Weeping Water, Neb. He still was wearing an ear-to-ear smile because of recent heartening news from home. He said his brother Kenneth had been released from a prisoner-of-war camp in Germany.

"I want to get home so bad I'm ready to believe there is a Santa Claus."

— PFC. ERNEST BRILEY, ASKED ABOUT REPORTS OF A SECRET WEAPON, THE ATOMIC BOMB

CHIEF MACHINIST'S MATE JIM CANNING, right, of Scottsbluff, Neb., advises Volna Lines of Charles City, Iowa, on a truck repair assignment.

"I had been worried about him for a long time," Potts said. "He had been listed as missing in action for quite some time, and I had just about given up hope of ever seeing him alive again."

Outside of washing clothes, Harry said he hates air raids most.

"The other night we had one when I was really sawing wood," Harry related. "They were right over us and getting rough when I was sufficiently awake to get out of bed. I came tearing out of the tent with nothing on but a mosquito net. That coral is plenty rough on your feet."

August 11, 1945
WITH GEN. MACARTHUR IN MANILA

IT BEGAN QUIETLY — almost timidly.

The street gamins of this war-shattered capital shrilled:

"Hapon sa patay! Hapon sa patay!" . . . "Japan is dead! Japan is dead!"

It magnified, it grew until it became the wildest jubilation in the experience of this reporter, and he has been among those present at some of the noisiest.

The urchins trooped the rubble-strewn streets, shouting their triumphant slogan. The red flares, which in the absence of a street lighting system half-light the night, cast flickering, weird shadows upon these children of the alleys and gutters.

"Hapon sa patay! Hapon sa patay!"

Two GIs stopped, listened, asked where did the urchins get that stuff. Before they received a reply, a sailor came charging out of a doorway, whooping at the top of his lungs:

"The Japs surrendered! It's over . . . over!"

The two GIs began to jitterbug to the cadence of the rapidly swelling noises as people — soldiers and sailors and Marines, and American and Filipino civilians — came tumbling into the streets, shouting, weeping, screaming.

Japan had surrendered. Thunderously, shrilly, triumphantly, hysterically, Manila proclaimed the news.

The fact that surrender had not been accepted in the Allied capitals was ignored by the throngs that jammed the streets.

To Manila, the war was over. Manila insisted on it.

Doughboys and sailors took over the thoroughfares. Truckloads of them careened through the streets. They just rode up and down and around, shouting till hoarseness reduced their volume to croaks.

Signal lights wrote in fiery tracery the tale of triumph in the night skies.

And above the din, the popping of small arms sounded everywhere, an overtone that was reminiscent of firecrackers. Battle-hardened infantrymen, trained for the next war move they will not take, half-trotted arm-in-arm with merchant mariners and sailors.

Filipino women were swept along by the infantrymen and mariners and sailors and Marines. They didn't resist, joining the disordered, jubilant ranks.

If you wore war correspondent's insignia, you were stopped constantly as someone said:

"Here's a guy that knows the deal. How about it, chum? Is it over?"

You told them what you know — that Japan has offered to quit if it can keep the emperor, that the Allies have not accepted the offer — that there is nothing official about the war's end.

None of them seemed to hear what you said about the Allies. They seemed only to hear that Japan had offered to quit.

They surged on down Rizal Avenue and over Santa Cruz bridge, singing, shouting, screaming, swigging those high-frequency Filipino spirits.

The usually grim, stern, white-helmeted military police let down their guard. They shook hands with the tippling GIs. You reflect that they'd probably like to chuck those helmets and join the throng.

Down the street a machine gun opened up. Instinctively, you pulled your head down between your shoulder blades. Above the roar and rumble, above the shots and shouts, in high treble sounded the cry of the street gamins:

"Hapon sa patay! Hapon sa patay!"

And in your heart you felt sure that it was only a matter of time before the Allies would make it official.

August 13, 1945
WITH THE SEABEES ON OKINAWA (DELAYED)

ONE OF THE MOST PRIZED commendations one Seabee battalion has comes from its own service.

The Marines were fighting a tough engagement and large amounts of whole blood were being used in transfusions. Doctors found they could not operate on the beach, because they lacked ice machine equipment.

A hurry-up call was sent to those eternal troubleshooters — the Seabees. A few of the boys were sent down to "do the best they could."

They located some Japanese pipe, rigged up a tower and set a tank on it for a water cooler and made other necessary additions to the ice machine. In less than 24 hours, a grave situation had been avoided on Okinawa and many lives were saved.

It's official: Japan surrenders

August 15, 1945
WITH GEN. MACARTHUR IN MANILA

THE SHIPS IN THE BAY are erupting fire, trucks are roaring by, the GIs are firing small arms in celebration — it apparently is the end of the war again.

They are glued to their radios, and they lend an eager ear to every rumor, these GIs, and you can't blame them because they have been over here a long time.

Tired war correspondents tumbled out of their beds in this partially completed press camp and thrashed through mud and over piles of timber to get to the work room. We had all been standing by for hours — waiting for the break.

None of us would write a line until we knew what the terms were. And there it came:

"The United States agreed today to accept the Japanese surrender offer, provided the supreme commanders of the Allied powers rule Japan through the authority of the emperor."

You know what it says from there on out. The radio over in the corner is blaring out "Stars and Stripes Forever" and correspondents are coming in from Borneo, Australia, and from the divisions out in the hills — all caught off guard by the atomic bomb attack, Russia's declaration of war and Japan's modified offer of surrender.

A correspondent hunched over his typewriter shouts, "When did Dewey take Manila?" and everyone looks up and answers, "1898." He turns back to his typewriter and hammers away again.

Our drivers are the only ones in the room who have the time to eat. They dig down into the deep bucket with meat and bread in it, make a sandwich, munch away and mumble, "See you in Tokyo, pal. Stay away from those geisha kids. Remember — no fraternizing."

They still are fighting out in the hills. With the same fine regard the line officer has always shown for the lives of his men, Lt. Carl Leonard of Lincoln heard the news of the reported Japanese surrender.

It would have taken three days to reach him by jeep over the tortuous trails, so 38th Division men gave him the information over a series of communication systems. He relayed his instructions to three lonely outposts, where the kids are still lying in the foxholes, and told them:

"Don't be aggressive. Don't get hurt unless you have to, but shoot the first Jap who comes near you without his hands in the air."

More than 140 Japanese soldiers have been killed by the 38th Division since Manila started the peace celebrations Saturday night.

WILFORD, LEFT, AND MILFORD SHEETS of Blair served together in the Philippines. Their mother wrote to the War Department to keep them together.

August 19, 1945
WITH THE 43RD DIVISION ON CENTRAL LUZON (DELAYED)

BECAUSE THE COURAGEOUS farm mother of 13 children would not hear of her twin boys being parted, the two 19-year-old youngsters slept in the same tent with this infantry outfit at Camp LaCroix.

The twins are Wilford and Milford Sheets from Blair, Neb., and they are enough alike to keep their tent mates bewildered. The boys registered for the Army on the same day and took most of their basic training together. Then one day in Alabama, Wilford suffered an arm injury and was sent to the hospital.

Milford finished his basic training and was scheduled to leave for overseas with Wilford going back to a training camp. Mrs. Will Sheets heard the news, tightened the firm lips that had conquered the raising of 13 children and years of hard farm work, and decided to do something about it. First she wrote to the president and was referred to the War Department.

Nothing daunted, Mrs. Sheets took her problem to the Army heads — and she won. Milford was held back, and last spring they boarded a troop transport together, members of a replacement group. When they arrived on Luzon, they were placed in the same company, platoon and tent in the 43rd Division.

Settling the problems of twins was nothing new to Mrs. Sheets. Among her six boys and seven girls was another set of twins older than Milford and Wilford by five years. They are Herald and Gerald. The other twins, however, have been separated. Gerald is serving with the Army in Italy, and Herald is working on his parents' 60-acre farm just outside Blair.

Wilford and Milford are the same height, 5-foot-6, and each weighs exactly 161 pounds. When the fighting is over they intend to work on a farm together.

There is one difference. Wilford (or is it Milford?) goes with a girl by the name of Ramona Edwards, also of Blair. Milford (or is it Wilford?) wanted to say "hello" to Ramona. Wilford (or is it Milford?) has no girl.

So here's a "hello" to Ramona.

We'll let her decide. We know that she knows whether it is Wilford or Milford.

> *A correspondent hunched over his typewriter shouts, "When did Dewey take Manila?" and everyone looks up and answers, "1898."*
>
> — BILL BILLOTTE, DESCRIBING THE SCENE AS REPORTERS WROTE STORIES ABOUT THE WAR'S END

August 20, 1945

WITH GEN. MACARTHUR IN MANILA

OUT OF LOWERING GRAY SKIES, with a setting sun glowing faintly through the clouds, the Japanese Empire came to Gen. Douglas MacArthur Sunday.

It came in the form of a 16-man delegation, which walked stiffly down a ramp from a giant four-engine American plane. They found themselves facing solid banks of GI Joes who had turned out for the historic occasion.

The men from Nippon seemed dwarfed by their surroundings, and by the large swords which most of them wore. Lt. Gen. Takashiro Kawabe, vice-chief of the Imperial staff, in command of the mission, saluted stiffly, and Col. H.F. Mashbir of the American staff honored the salute. Then the Japanese general extended his hand. Col. Mashbir started to grasp it, hesitated and then dropped his hand to his side.

There was an audible sigh from the crowds that jammed the end of Nichols Field, a base that was one of the first to feel the weight of Japanese bombs. After a few formal preliminaries, the Japanese delegation was loaded into staff cars and whisked to an apartment house where they will stay.

Along that route, they passed happy Filipinos, block after block of supplies, and tens of thousands of GI Joes.

From the apartment in which they are staying, the Japanese have a magnificent view of the Manila Harbor, jammed full of America's sea might as far as the eye can see.

The boys who stole the show were the airmen who flew the Japanese in from Ie Shima.

They told a horde of war correspondents from all over the world how the Japanese stood the trip, what they had to eat,

that they had to take off their boots when they wanted to stretch out, and that they had offered the airmen a tip, which the Americans refused.

The Japanese, they said, had plenty of American money in $50 and $100 bills.

Every one in the delegation was happy, one young American flier said, except Kawabe. He ate one boiled egg, sipped his pineapple juice gingerly and did not seem to be in the best of humor.

The delegation, according to the fliers, was given ample opportunity to see the activities on Okinawa, the arsenal island at Japan's back door. They also were given a tour of Manila from the air.

At the foot of the plane ramp as the Japanese dignitaries left the plane to meet the American delegation was Staff Sgt. Laverne Kreutner of Story City, Iowa, a member of the plane's ground crew. He was close enough to touch the hilts of their swords.

"What did you think?" he was asked about seeing the Japanese envoys.

"I wouldn't have missed it for all the corn in Iowa."

The American transport plane was piloted by Col. Earl Ricks of Hot Springs, Ark.

After the Japanese were taken to their living quarters in Manila, a military police cordon was thrown around the building. The envoys were served a dinner of fresh turkey and green vegetables.

Shortly after the delegation was installed in their rooms, two of the Japanese were seen standing at a window, carefully examining a mosquito aerosol bomb. One Japanese unscrewed the tap and was showered with fumes.

U.S. MILITARY PERSONNEL greet a contingent of Japanese officials at a U.S. airfield on Ie Shima on Aug. 19, 1945. The Japanese were en route from Japan to Manila to plan for Japan's formal surrender ceremony, which occurred Sept. 2, 1945. Photographer Clair Gill of Anita, Iowa, was an Army Air Forces private first class stationed at the island air base off the shore of Okinawa.

August 20, 1945
WITH GEN. MACARTHUR IN MANILA

THAT LONESOMEST OF ALL Army men, the casual replacement, is now getting a break in the Philippines.

The man who is seeing that he gets that break is a barrel-chested general with shaggy brown eyebrows who pounds his desk as he earnestly talks of the importance of the replacement in any war.

This general is no stranger to Omahans. He was one of them from 1941 to 1944 while he was commanding what was first known as the 7th Corps Area and was later changed to the 7th Service Command.

He is Maj. Gen. Frederick E. Uhl.

"Give me a look at the type of replacement that is being captured from the enemy at any given time during the war," the general said, leaning forward across his desk, "and I'll tell you how close he is to winning or losing the war. The replacement, the man who fills the gap, is often the deciding factor."

Spread through Gen. Uhl's offices some 20 miles out of Manila are comprehensive charts and maps dealing with the care and disposition of the replacement. The formal name of the command is "Replacement Command AFWESPAC," a rather awesome name for a project that is as warm and human as it is efficient.

When Uhl assumed command on June 14 of this year, he immediately flew to the various installations to get a first-hand idea of what was needed to make replacements feel at home while they are en route to their new units and duties.

As he studied the situation, he said, he had a growing conviction the men must not be allowed to sit in their tents nursing a growing feeling that they are treated as a spare part in an impersonal Army machine.

It was then he decided to spike up entertainment facilities and to instruct those under his command to make a special effort to serve the men passing through the replacement area.

"Our job is to render unstinting and painstaking service, both to incoming replacements and to the organizations whose replacement needs we are directed to supply," one of his first written orders directed, "and to render equally un-stinting and painstaking service to those officers and enlisted men passing through Replacement Command installations en route to our homeland."

Many a replacement has been surprised when he was approached by a big, burly, gray-haired man who casually asked, "How're they treating you fellows around here? Are you getting everything you need?"

That was the general finding out for himself. He asked his questions without identifying himself, and he says he has yet to meet the replacement who is hesitant in expressing an opinion.

Recently Gen. Uhl located some hangars 130 feet long. He immediately grabbed them for his replacement depots and started to lay plans for staging movies, band concerts and getting Red Cross facilities for the officers and men passing through his hands.

The casual replacement faces problems that the men who come overseas in units do not face. When a soldier trains in the States with an outfit for several months, he has made his friends. He has the opportunity to "laugh off" doubts and fears because his buddy is there with him, facing the same doubts and fears. The casual replacement travels alone until he is assigned to his permanent unit.

With battle-weary men being sent home from the Pacific, the proper handling of replacements became one of the major problems in this theater.

Uhl emphasized that men who are going home must also be shown every consideration.

"These men have done their share," said the general, "and we want them to remember the Army with the feeling that it did the best it could for them under all conditions."

August 22, 1945
WITH THE 43RD DIVISION ON LUZON (DELAYED)

"THERE'S NO STORY to anything I've done, I'm just a country boy who used to run a grocery at Paxton, Neb. Now some of my men here are . . . ."

And Lt. Virgil David of the medics started to tell how his noncommissioned officers behaved under fire.

Maj. Gen. Frederick E. Uhl commanded the 7th Service Command in the Midwest before being transferred to the Philippines.

Lt. Virgil David of Paxton, Neb., was reluctant to talk about his actions that earned a Silver Star.

"Weren't you commissioned in the field?" he was asked.

"Yes, I was a staff sergeant then," he replied.

"You must have done something to deserve that. They don't commission men in the field because they like the way they comb their hair."

"Well, we handled 225 casualties in the field under jungle conditions within two weeks," said David, embarrassedly running his fingers through his crew haircut. "Say, did you know they are now giving enlisted medics who operate in the lines $10 more a month just like they do in the infantry? We sure were glad to see them give those kids that kind of break."

"How many campaigns have you been in?"

"Let's see," the lieutenant said, ticking them off on his fingers. "There was Guadalcanal, the Solomons, New Guinea and Luzon. I have been overseas 34 months. But did you know they are giving the medics who serve with the front line troops a new badge?"

"Someone said you won the Silver Star at Ipo Dam. Is there any truth to the rumor?" he was asked.

"Yes, but I have a sergeant here . . . . "

David refused to give any information on the Silver Star, but the Army keeps a record on medals of that importance. The citation read:

"For gallantry in action against the enemy in the Ipo Dam sector, Luzon, Philippine Islands, on May 8, 1945. During a column formation movement towards the Ipo Dam area, and while under enemy artillery fire, Lieutenant David distinguished himself by his gallant and quick action. During enemy shelling which resulted in some casualties, Lieutenant David, without regard for his own personal safety, rushed out into the open field to affect rescue of the wounded.

"Due to the grass fire which was raging on the field, caused by the enemy shelling, the wounded were in perilous circumstances. David, assisted by a soldier, succeeded in rescuing one of the casualties from the blazing field and carried him to a place of safety."

We finally had to give up on David. After all, he is just a country boy who used to run a grocery store at Paxton.

August 27, 1945
WITH GEN. MACARTHUR IN MANILA

IF YOU HAVE A SON, brother, husband, relative or friend in the service overseas, sit down and write him a letter, because that is the only purpose this story can accomplish.

What that letter will mean to whomever you write, I could never tell you if I sat here writing until the end of time. You would have to come over here and sweat out the mail yourself to ever find out.

You would have to watch a GI's fingers tremble as he stands in the rain and tears open an envelope with the familiar writing on the front.

You would have to watch him when he pauses for a minute's rest on a dusty road while on the march. Watch him fumble through his clothes to come up with a dog-eared, dirty envelope to read its contents again. Take the letter away from him, and he could probably repeat the rest of it almost word for word — he just about knows it by heart.

You would have to watch him as he sits in a Red Cross hut and laboriously scrawls his answers, perhaps in the round, sprawling hand of the schoolboy. For the moment he has forgotten his troubles. He is sitting on the porch at home, running his hand through the hair on his dog, lounging on the steps, watching the neighbors walk by.

And if you have a snapshot, put that into the letter, too — whether the man to whom you are writing is a colonel or a buck private. To him it will be a work of art, and he'll carry it in his billfold until it is so tattered he will have to use extreme care to keep it from tearing every time he takes it out to show it to his friends.

There can be weeks without a beer ration, days when no cigarettes get to the front, and months of monotonous food, and the soldier can take it in his stride. But when the mail stops coming, there is nothing he can do about it. The other things may be the fault of circumstance or strangers. But when the mail fails to come in, there can be no one at fault but his relatives and his friends — the folks back home.

Now that the war has ended, mail becomes more important than ever. Many of the servicemen will be overseas for months. They will be more bored than ever. They won't have the hazards, the excitement to which they have grown accustomed. Yet they will be stuck in their old positions and more prone to think the homefront has forgotten them in the pursuit of peacetime recreation.

If you have read this far, I probably have failed to convey what I was trying to tell you. You should be halfway through that letter to him by now.

CAPT. JOHN EGENBERGER of Omaha was a U.S. Army dental surgeon who had followed infantry in the Philippines. "You find a kid on the march up to the front almost crazy with a toothache," he said. "The column stops for a rest, and you go to work on him and fix him up. When they get ready to move again, he slings on his pack, picks up his rifle and falls in."

Lt. Willis A. Strauss, right, chats with Max B. Schroth, 72, a former Omahan and a veteran of the Spanish-American War. Strauss, who was attached to the utilities section in Gen. Douglas MacArthur's headquarters in the Philippines, became the top executive with Omaha-based Northern Natural Gas Co. and its successor, InterNorth Inc.

August 28, 1945
WITH GEN. MACARTHUR IN MANILA (DELAYED)

WHILE ONE NEWS BOMBSHELL after another explodes here and dignitaries of various nations exchange guarded messages in relation to the end of the war, GI Joe, the most important of them all, the fellow who made the peace possible, is wondering.

Any one of them would have traded his spot at Nichols Field, where he saw the Japanese delegation arrive, for a leaning spot on the outside of the drugstore on Main Street in his own hometown.

They are tired of the so-called exotic scenes of the tropics. They are tired of sweating out a line for a cold drink and being told when to go to bed and when to get up. In other words, they want to go home.

Omahans and former Omahans have drifted since the end of the war was announced. Lt. Billy Worthing, a prominent athlete in Omaha in the 1930s, has been in the Navy a long time. He was up from Leyte on a short visit.

"What I wouldn't give to drop in on the Wranic brothers!" he said. "I can just see them nodding wisely and saying: 'I told you these military guys didn't know the score. It was just a matter of days after the Heinies quit.' "

Lt. Bernard O'Brien of Omaha dropped into the press room, his shirt clinging to his back, and we talked of his wife, Edith, and their three children.

He said he had been overseas eight months and may have to spend another year away from home. Formerly employed by the Union Pacific, he said he intends to return to his old job after the war.

Lt. Willis A. Strauss of Omaha, attached to the utilities section of general headquarters, was the lone dissenter on wanting to go home.

"I've been here only a short time, and I like it," Strauss said. "I've been reading up on Japan, and so long as I'm this far, I may as well get a look at Tokyo to find out what makes those guys tick. If I go back right away, I want to finish my last six months of engineering at Iowa State."

Capt. George Nygren of Omaha, an old schoolmate who formerly was with the Agricultural Insurance Company, dropped in one day minus a lot of excess poundage. He had worked it off while serving with the engineers.

"The worst thing about it is the uncertainty," Nygren said. "If there were a definite time set, you could hit the ball and work toward a definite date. I'm going right back where I came from when this is over."

Lt. Victor Hruska of Omaha, in the Navy with the amphibious forces, still was happy over a chance meeting with his brother, Jim.

"Seeing him made me want to go home more than ever," he said. "But none of us can say when it will be. That feeling is tougher than actually fighting a war."

August 30, 1945
OVER ATSUGI AIRPORT, JAPAN

THE 150 EXPERTS who landed two days ago came in on unarmed cargo planes with a Flying Fortress as the armed guard.

The first leg of our journey was from Manila to Okinawa and after a day's delay we are finishing the final 920-mile flight over water to the heart of Japan.

You wonder what the tall general with the jutting chin is thinking as he flies along his final step after thousands of miles of jungle plodding.

You know what you are thinking, and it is nothing very profound: You are wishing that the millions of GIs who made all this possible could be here with you.

In a few minutes Gen. Douglas MacArthur will step from a giant silver plane to take control of arrangements for the formal surrender of Japan.

The eyes of the world are focused on this two-runway field, which is located only 22 miles from the Imperial Palace in Tokyo. The field was once the chief hop-off spot for the Japanese suicide planes.

When the general's plane, which is in one of the largest air armadas in history, peels out of formation, the Japanese will be seeing the largest plane ever to land at their field.

We are prepared for anything, and we are traveling under full combat kit with helmets, C rations and mess kits.

One hundred war correspondents credited to Gen. MacArthur's headquarters are along. Eighteen of us who won the draw for choice places are in No. 4 plane with Brig. Gen. L.A. Diller, chief public relations officer to the supreme commander.

We should be the first correspondents in this element to set foot in Japan.

On the ground are more than 150 picked communications and operational experts and elements of the 11th Airborne Division who went in to secure the field.

The experts swung into action immediately on landing, with instructions to be ready to bring in 500 planes each day. Until the occupation of Japan is completed, a plane will be scheduled to land every two minutes.

August 31, 1945
WITH GEN. MACARTHUR IN YOKOHAMA, JAPAN

WHILE WAR CORRESPONDENTS and Army men fought for the privilege of being the first to fly into the Atsugi air strip, a wiry young Navy lieutenant from Omaha beat all of us by one complete day. He was standing with his hands on his hips watching the first of the occupation forces land early Thursday morning with his speedy Corsair fighter safely housed in its hangar, its menacing black looking out of place among the Army transports.

LT. BOB THELEN

Although Lt. Bob Thelen, 24, was delighted with his distinction, he said it was not planned. Bob was flying patrol off a carrier on Aug. 29 when he suddenly noticed his gas had been draining from a leaky tank and that he was in a desperate plight.

"I thought I was washed up, and I hated to have it happen with the war over after all the fighting I've seen," Thelen said.

"I got over (Atsugi) field but did not know the Army communication experts had landed the day before. I expected to hear some Jap answer me when I asked if I could come in. When I heard that good old American voice, I could have howled. I told the control tower man I was landing almost without gas and came down. I had 10 gallons left when I hit the strip."

When I saw Bob, he looked more like a mechanic than a pilot. He had been sleeping with his beloved Corsair and was covered with grease. He was the only Navy pilot on the field, and he spent quite a bit of time inspecting the wrecked Japanese Zero planes on the fringe of the field.

I offered him a clean shirt if he would come into Yokohama with me where I could get to my gear. He declined, saying he wanted to stay with his Corsair.

You can't blame him. After all, his speedy little fighter did bring him into Atsugi ahead of a lot of us.

August 31, 1945
WITH THE 11TH AIRBORNE DIVISION IN YOKOHAMA

THERE HAVE BEEN FEW parades in history like it. The doughboys in full battle kit riding through the streets of this Japanese city were neither hostile nor friendly. They sat with their rifles across their knees and gazed with frank curiosity as they rode in commandeered trucks.

At every crossroad, meadow and house stood the Japanese soldier in his bedraggled brown uniform or the civil police in his uniform of faded blue. Nine out of 10 of them stood rigidly at attention with their backs to the passing stream of trucks. Those who faced the road stared sullenly ahead.

In the outlying districts there were few civilians at the side of the dusty roads, but some could be seen ducking below the windows after they had taken a quick look.

There were no marks of war in the suburban district, and you could sense the feeling of resentment among the boys who had so recently come from shell-wrecked Manila.

As the trucks loaded with troops moved into downtown Yokohama, where the streets are paved, the crowds grew, but there was not a sound. They stared, the women holding their children, the men resting between the shafts of their wagons or standing motionless on the sidewalks. The people did not seem ill fed.

Then came the blocks and blocks of bombed-out buildings and the scenes reminiscent of Manila — the tin, makeshift homes, the naked youngsters, the piles of fire-scarred rubble. It was then you knew that Yokohama, too, had suffered from the air.

But unlike Manila, Yokohama did not feel the weight of artillery. There are buildings that are untouched beside ravaged areas.

Several soldiers cheered when the column stopped outside an unscarred white building at No. 6 Seaside Street. There was a USA worked into the iron grill gates. It was the American Consulate.

September 1, 1945
TOKYO

WE STOOD IN FRONT of the Emperor's Palace today, three other correspondents and myself.

Its red Japanese peaked roof of tile gleamed faintly through the falling rain.

There was the green of growing shrubbery and trees about this place the GIs used to talk about during the long nights when they were in their foxholes. It was raining then, too.

They used to talk about what they were going to do to this place. They were going to tear it apart, brick by brick. They were going to ride the famous white horse, and some of the things they were going to do are too obscene to mention here, but they did have plenty of ideas.

Now here we were in front of that never-never land of theirs, the Emperor's Palace. Thousands of those GIs will never make good on their boasts. Too many of them won't ever see the shingle-topped roofs of their own homes again.

We had come by train from Yokohama to see the palace. We had passed the bombed-out, burned-out miles of buildings on either side of the track.

Pinch-faced babies strapped to their mothers' backs, kids with patches over one eye and aged people with the hollow cheeks of hunger, hundreds of bedraggled soldiers returning home.

You remembered the wounded infantryman on the Villa Verde Trail, the boy with the sucking chest wound at the portable hospital, the dog-tired bomber men after 22 hours in the air. You thought of the pipestem legs of the Filipino children hanging around with empty tin cans begging for food.

It was still raining and you were soaked to the skin. The red of the tiles on the emperor's roof was made shiny by the rain.

You thought of that cheerful lad released from the Japanese prison camp. He was laughing as he balanced himself on his one leg and crutches at the Atsugi air strip as correspondents crowded around. Four youngsters with him had the faces of old men as they pulled eagerly on their cigarettes.

It had been a long trip to the Emperor's Palace, thousands of miles through jungles and over the hulls of many sunken ships. We had made it, but those thousands of GIs who used to huddle in their foxholes and talk of the Emperor's Palace had not.

They will never know how red the tile is on the peaked Japanese roof even through the haze of the falling rain.

Yokohama

It had been a long trip to the Emperor's Palace, thousands of miles through jungles and over the hulls of many sunken ships.

— BILL BILLOTTE

U.S. Army Gen. Douglas MacArthur stands behind microphones as he and other Allied officials and military personnel witness Japanese Gen. Yoshijiro Umezu signing the formal surrender aboard the USS Missouri in Tokyo Bay on Sept. 2, 1945.

The surrender on the USS Missouri

BY BILL BILLOTTE

THE SKY OVER TOKYO BAY was slate gray on that early Sunday morning of Sept. 2, 1945, as the USS Taylor, a battered destroyer, knifed its way toward the battleship Missouri.

The Taylor had been selected to carry war correspondents to the surrender ceremony because of its proud battle record, printed in bright red and white paint on the bridge.

A veteran of the fighting in the Pacific, the Taylor had sunk two submarines, one destroyer, one gunboat and one cruiser, and had taken part in 11 island bombardments.

As you studied her combat record, you realized again that those who most deserved to be on their way to the unconditional surrender of the Japanese were not present — the thousands who were buried at sea, who were killed in the air and who had died on the battlefield.

Subic, a little yellow mongrel a couple of Taylor crew members had picked up seven months before at Subic Bay in the Philippines and smuggled aboard, added to the excitement when he singled out a correspondent of the Japanese News Agency Domei and snapped at his leg.

Once aboard the Missouri, all correspondents were assigned to specific places from which to view the ceremony and instructed not to leave them.

A Russian photographer was soon violating the order, as he switched positions several times before the ceremony started. Warned to stay in his assigned position, he continued to roam the deck.

The activity of the wandering Russian came to an abrupt halt when a sailor delivered a message from Capt. S.S. Murray, skipper of the Missouri: "Maintain your position, or you will be pitched over the side."

The Japanese delegation arrived aboard a launch. In the military atmosphere, the top hat and formal attire of Foreign Minister Mamoru Shigemitsu seemed strangely out of place.

Gen. Douglas MacArthur kept the Japanese waiting 20 minutes before he made his appearance. In striking contrast with the brilliant uniforms of most of the Allied representatives, he wore khakis. He had on his battered gilt-trimmed cap, and his shirt was open at the throat.

Then, all aboard stood with heads bared, as a chaplain opened the ceremony with a prayer of thanks that the war had ended.

Standing behind MacArthur was bone-thin Lt. Gen. Jonathan M. Wainwright, who had commanded the U.S. forces at Bataan and Corregidor.

Wainwright told correspondents after he had been released from a Japanese prison camp a few days earlier that during his long time in captivity he had considered himself a failure.

Tears came to his eyes when the correspondents told him he was regarded as a national hero back home, and they gave him the only standing ovation that I saw in the Pacific during the war.

Beside him was Lt. Gen. Sir Arthur Percival of Britain, who was captured by the Japanese in the fall of Singapore early in the war.

Foreign Minister Shigemitsu was the first to sign the surrender document. He doffed his top hat and nervously fingered his fountain pen before he firmly signed the two copies, one for Japan and the other for the Allies.

Gen. Yoshi Jiro Umezu of the Imperial staff, also seeming to be nervous, signed hurriedly and stepped aside. A Japanese colonel wiped his eyes.

The surrender marked the first defeat in Japan's 2,600-year history.

After the Japanese, Gen. MacArthur, as supreme Allied commander, signed on behalf of all the victorious powers. He used five pens in making his signatures and then called for Wainwright and Percival to step forward. He presented each with a pen.

The United Kingdom's signature by Admiral Sir Bruce Fraser was followed by that of the Soviet Union, represented by Lt. Gen. Kuzma Derevyanko.

And then, as more than 100 high-ranking Allied military and naval officers watched, representatives of Australia, Canada, France, the Netherlands and New Zealand signed in that order.

There was a momentary delay as Col. L. Moore Cosgrave of Canada, a favorite among correspondents, signed on the wrong line and was called back. It didn't bother the good-natured colonel.

Later, he cracked: "They may forget some of those names on the surrender, but they'll never forget the bloke from Canada who signed on the wrong line."

All through the dramatic half-hour, only those aboard knew of what was transpiring, because the Missouri had no broadcasting facilities.

Johnny Jones of the Pittsburgh Post-Gazette and I were stationed on B deck along with several naval officers directly over the surrender table.

To the landward side of the Missouri were the bomb-blackened ruins of Tokyo, still out of bounds to the occupying troops.

On either side of the battleship, as far as the eye could see, were the U.S. Navy's ships — the ships that conquered the Pacific after the disaster at Pearl Harbor.

On the starboard side of the Missouri was the battleship Iowa; on the port side the South Dakota. On their decks were sailors of every state.

After the final signature, MacArthur, with a decisive sweep of his arm, said: "These proceedings are closed."

And then it happened.

As if by command, the sun broke through clouds and illuminated the decks of the Missouri. Then, from out to sea, came the drone of powerful engines as squadrons of heavy bombers flew over, followed by waves of fighters.

I glanced at an officer near me, who was wearing the wings of a Navy pilot on his tunic, as he gazed at the air armada that almost blacked out the sun. His vision must have been blurred by the tears trickling down his cheek.

That afternoon Gen. MacArthur had a message for his countrymen:

"Today the guns are silent. A great tragedy has ended. A great victory has been won. I speak for the thousands of silent lips, forever stilled among the jungles and the beaches and the deep waters of the Pacific which marked the way.

"As I looked back on the long tortuous trail from those grim days of Bataan and Corregidor, when an entire world lived in fear, when democracy was on the defensive everywhere, when modern civilization trembled in the balance, I thank a merciful God that He has given us the faith, the courage and the power from which to mold victory."

And then, apparently thinking of the atomic bomb that hastened Japan's decision to surrender, he warned that war had become so utterly destructive that unless an equitable system of peace was devised, "Armageddon will be at our door."

"Today the guns are silent. A great tragedy has ended. A great victory has been won. I speak for the thousands of silent lips, forever stilled among the jungles and the beaches and the deep waters of the Pacific which marked the way."

— GEN. DOUGLAS MACARTHUR

Boatswain's Mate 2nd Class Don Paddock of Omaha served on Okinawa as the dispatcher for motor vehicles in his Seabee battalion.

September 5, 1945
WITH GEN. MACARTHUR'S FORCES IN YOKOHAMA

"AMERICANS! AMERICANS!"

The words came in the concerted roar from the windows of a Japanese train. And down the faces of those who shouted the words streamed tears. As the train pulled to a stop, they piled out of the doors in their patched clothes and clutched at us with trembling hands. They pulled us to them and would not let go.

As the tears ran down into the stubble on their faces, you tried to tell them how glad you were to see them and found you couldn't talk, that your eyes were wet.

To them you were the United States, everything they had suffered for in more than three years in Japanese prison camps. The chins of the guards of honor quivered as they stood at attention. And the Japanese thought they could lick an outfit like that.

"Look at those angels." Nurses on their first assignment in Japan were caught up and soundly kissed.

A rugged-looking major kept blowing his nose and edging his handkerchief toward his eyes.

The pitiful bits of luggage, cloth bundles, were trampled.

They unfurled crudely made American flags fashioned from parachute silk that had come down with supplies attached on Aug. 29. Then they began to file out to the waiting Army trucks. One clutched a battered mandolin without strings. Another carried a book with its pages ragged from use.

Three of them were Nebraskans. Army regulations forbid the use of their names at this time.

One of them shouted, "The Cornhuskers score again," and those around him cheered.

The procession of trucks through town was a parade of triumph. Japanese citizens turned to stare. GIs went wild when they realized what the trucks contained. They threw their cigarettes and candy bars into the trucks, and smiling soldier truck drivers leaned on their horns and waved as they drove by.

Two of the Nebraskans had been captured on Corregidor and one on Bataan. All were in good shape. They cheered a couple of American bulldozers hard at work.

"You don't need to be told when the American Army is in town," one said.

The 450 prisoners of war had been put on the train by the Japanese at Ashio, 90 miles from Yokohama, that morning. They had not been forced to work in steel mills, copper mines and factories since Aug. 15, when the Japanese people learned that they were defeated.

The trucks drove slowly on to the docks with the growing mountain of supplies piled everywhere.

At the dock was the white hospital ship, the Marigold. The Americans were to be processed and fed before they were turned over to the Navy. An American flag was flying on the Marigold.

One prisoner said, "It will never be the Fourth of July again for me, it'll always be the Fourth of September 1945."

Said one Nebraskan, "It makes you want to cry all over again."

September 7, 1945
WITH WAR PRISONERS ON TOKYO BAY DOCK

ONE OF THE MOST MASTERFUL sabotage jobs of the Pacific war was bared here when 122 prisoners of war arrived from the lead mines in Kamioka, led by a major and a cocky first sergeant.

These men and 28 others caused so much trouble at a tool and die works in Mukden, Manchuria, that the entire 150 were shipped to Kamioka. In that group were four Nebraskans who cannot be mentioned at this time because of censorship rules.

"The damage we caused there," said the first sergeant, "ran into millions of dollars. They finally imported Jap detectives after the guards had failed to find out the reasons for the poor production, the breaking down of machines, the disappearance of motors and the loss of tools.

"We had organized patrols whose members carried emery dust in their pockets and threw it into the delicate parts of machinery. We tossed filings into oil and into machines. We threw hunks of dry cement into machines, along with sand. We sold 45-horsepower motors to the Chinese for one hundred yen when their actual value was five thousand yen. Our outfit was organized from the men who worked in the factory to the boys who helped operate warehouses."

The American war prisoners said they arrived at Mukden in December of 1942 and worked there 18 months. They said they were not organized well enough to do their heaviest damage until January of 1944, although they sabotaged the plant from the moment of their arrival.

"When we first arrived, they were putting in cement bases for the machines," one prisoner said.

"We gave those machines one hell of a fine foundation. We dumped high grade cutting tools, picks, shovels and everything we could get our hands on into the cement as we poured it. Then we put a top over that.

"The tools are still under those machines as far as we know."

The prisoners said they were beaten when caught, but they didn't mind that much because they were used to getting beatings anyway.

September 13, 1945
WITH THE FIRST CAVALRY IN TOKYO

"WHAT DO I THINK of Tokyo? Hell, it's like walking through a glorified junk yard. My hat's off to the fliers who worked this place over."

That was the answer given by Master Sgt. Harry Woods, 33, of Lincoln.

September 15, 1945
ABOARD THE HOSPITAL SHIP BENEVOLENCE IN TOKYO BAY (DELAYED)

ON ONE DECK OF THIS SHIP there were many Navy combat fliers among the released prisoners. Intelligent and fearless, they had a supreme contempt for the Japanese mentality. All fliers were subjected to intense questioning as the enemy attempted to learn the secret of the superior U.S. flying ability.

One young fellow, who bailed out of a flaming Corsair at sea, said he had received several beatings with a club that resembled a softball bat.

"They beat me from my shins to my waist both front and back," he related, "and I wasn't able to sit down for 13 days. One minute they hand you a cigarette, and the next minute they are beating you. One of our boys got hot one day and floored the Jap who was beating him with a right hook to the jaw. The Jap got up and did nothing about it. Figure that one out if you can."

The naval aviator said they gave little or no secret information to the Japanese. He said they merely told their interpreter they had not been given that information. If the Japanese didn't like it, the Americans said they just stood there and took what was dished out.

"There is one thing a lot of us would like to have, though, but we hate to ask for it," he said.

"Don't be silly, what do you want?"

"None of us fliers have any of our Navy wings left," he replied. "We haven't any uniforms yet, but we would like to get hold of some Navy wings. We're kind of proud of them."

I called a commander friend of mine who was abroad with us, and he said he would see that the boys got their new wings in a couple of days. The aviators around us grinned their appreciation.

Second Lt. Glade Stockwell of Oelwein, Iowa, who was taken on Mindanao on May 10, 1942, did two things while he was in various Japanese prison camps. He became a first-class watch repairman and kept a snappy mustache in trim throughout, regardless of how low his morale went.

The lieutenant said he got started on his watch-fixing career when another prisoner, an Englishman, asked him if he thought he could fix his watch.

"I told him I'd give it a try," Glade said, "and surprisingly enough, the watch worked when I got through playing around with it. After that, other prisoners in camp brought their timepieces to me, and I tinkered with them and made them run. Why we were so worried about the time, I'll never know. That was one place in the world where time was of little value.

"We kept my newfound trade from the Nips for six months, and I spent all my spare time working on the watches for my buddies," the lieutenant recalled, "but finally they found out about it and from then on, they pestered me to death. I fixed more than a thousand while I was a prisoner."

Although his watch-fixing ability saved Stockwell some abuse, he was punched around enough by the guards to get six of his teeth chipped.

"They beat me from my shins to my waist both front and back, and I wasn't able to sit down for 13 days. One minute they hand you a cigarette, and the next minute they are beating you. One of our boys got hot one day and floored the Jap who was beating him with a right hook to the jaw. The Jap got up and did nothing about it. Figure that one out if you can."

— RELEASED AMERICAN PRISONER

September 17, 1945
YOKOHAMA, JAPAN

MANY VETERAN WAR CORRESPONDENTS tabbed our meeting nearly two weeks ago with 450 American prisoners of war at a Yokohama railroad station as their most moving experience of the war. Certainly it was my most moving experience.

Never will any of us forget it. The prisoners, who previously could not be named by reporters, spotted us first and the way they shouted "Americans!" gave us a new understanding of the meaning of the word that we shall never forget.

Hundreds of Japanese citizens lined up on a platform two tracks across from us almost must have gotten a new conception of the word. They stood silently as they watched it.

One of the first to get off the train was Pfc. Donald Kincaid, 23, of Omaha, who had had a birthday the day before we met. The former Tech High pupil heard me yell, "Nebraska!" from the center of a crowd of prisoners who had mobbed me, and he came on in. He told me there were two of his buddies on the train also from Nebraska, and we began to fight our way through the delirious crowd of nurses, soldiers and prisoners.

We found Pfc. Donald Spaulding of Omaha, who also attended Technical High School. Then we found Staff Sgt. Gifford Dixon Jr. of Blair, who is 25.

The boys wore patched clothing and carried their belongings in improvised cloth bundles and knapsacks. They were thin but looked lean and hard and did not have the apathetic appearance of many of the prisoners I had seen. They stared hard at the Japanese civilians and soldiers but did not say anything about them.

"I can't believe it — I can't believe it!" they kept saying over and over. "Stateside girls and American uniforms. Even this morning we couldn't believe it would happen."

The three had been together since they were captured. When they reached Ashio, their last camp, Kincaid was sent to camp 9D, and Spaulding and Dixon were sent to camp 9B. All had been prisoners three years and three months.

One of their first questions was, "Do you know where 'Red' Sorensen is?"

I told them I had seen Red on the USS Benevolence the day before and that he was in good shape, except for an injured foot that would require an operation. Kincaid said he had injured his hand and had it treated by a Japanese doctor, but that it had failed to heal properly.

Spaulding and Dixon had been working in a steel mill at Ashio but had been permitted to stop work on Aug. 15, as had other prisoners of war.

"Our shortest shift was eight hours, and we were kept going constantly at a dog trot," Dixon said. "We had a schedule to keep up, and no excuses were accepted. We fed plates to heavy rollers so they could be thinned out. It was regarded as the toughest job in the plant."

"We had a boss that I'd like to take a punch at before we leave Japan," Spaulding chimed in. "His house was bombed out twice. We always knew when something had gone wrong, because then we got a beating before we went to work. He would hit us with his fist or the tongs. The tongs were iron and about 3 feet long.

"It was tough taking those beatings, but we always had that swell feeling that we were getting it because the Americans had dished it out to the Japs the night before," he recalled.

"We had no rest periods at night — we went eight hours without a breather," Sergeant Dixon added. "It was keep up or take a bad beating, so we tried our best to keep up."

Kincaid worked in a factory and his treatment, he said, was similar to that of the other boys. He said they received Red Cross packages once a year, on Christmas. The boys agreed they had received their worst treatment in the early part of the war in the Philippines.

Machinist's Mate 3rd Class Eugene Kelley of Columbus, Neb., operates a bulldozer on Okinawa. His Seabee unit put up an 80-foot bridge with a half-crew in under five hours, despite a drenching rain and two air raids.

September 18, 1945
YOKOHAMA (DELAYED)

EVERY GROUP IN A PRISON CAMP has its historian, and from these meticulous accounts will come information the U.S. government should study well.

Pfc. Donald Spaulding of Omaha kept the records for his little group. He had a day-by-day account of the weight of Staff Sgt. Gifford Dixon of Blair, Pfc. Donald Kincaid of Omaha and himself. All had lost more than 30 pounds during the hardest periods of their imprisonment.

Kincaid dropped from 145 to 98 pounds, Spaulding from 155 to 123 pounds and Dixon from 139 to 98 pounds. They had gained some of their weight back under the treatment during their last two weeks.

"Don't give me any credit for that," Spaulding said of his record keeping. "I did it to keep from blowing my top."

In small, neat printing, there was the record. It wasn't so much what the record said — it was how it was done. In the carefully lettered words you could see the hours of privation and boredom, the longing for things from America. There was a list of foods and the vitamins each food contained, along with calories. The boys were determined to live, and they made a scientific study of how little a person could eat without perishing.

"Going by those records," said Spaulding with a wry grin, "we all died some time ago. We worried about it at first but took heart when we kept waking up every morning with enough strength to drag ourselves to work."

Then there was the list of clothes that Spaulding was going to buy. It was all printed out down to the last pair of socks and to the material that was going to be in the scarf. Shoes, suits, hats, ties, underwear, a tie pin. The clothes were divided into two sections — summer and winter.

Unaware of the revealing story that his lists told, he apologized, "I'm not so sure of those prices — you see, they may have changed a lot since we've been away."

There were the books that Spaulding intended to read — books on mathematics, the classics, on animals and plants — "something on everything," he explained.

There was a list of the different foods he was going to eat at the first opportunity. The winter clothes listed would cost $264.50; summer clothes, $133.50; miscellaneous, $268; and presents were to cost $334. Asked why he had decided to spend $334 for presents, he replied, "I wanted to spend an even thousand dollars for the first time in my life."

Most touching of all was the list of the hit songs that keep buzzing through the heads of our American kids whether they are fighting or driving a truck at home.

There was "Oh, Johnny," "Careless" and other songs that have almost been lost in the shuffle in Tin Pan Alley.

"Our latest song hit is 'Waiting for a White Christmas,' " Spaulding said. "We haven't heard it yet but we heard it was a pip. I guess we'll be hearing it soon now."

An officer came to us where we were sitting on a bale of straw on the Yokohama dock and said the boys would have to go inside the warehouse for their processing. The three Nebraskans gathered their small packages of equipment, and we shook hands and made a date to meet in Omaha someday.

Their eyes still were shining at the thought of their freedom and the ovation they had been given as they rode through the once-proud streets of this Japanese city. They had walked those streets before under Japanese guard, with heavy hearts and hunger as companions.

Doubts about torture are over

September 21, 1945
YOKOHAMA

IN ANY WAR ZONE you hear a good deal about atrocities committed by the enemy. Some are true, and some are not. I have always treated with skepticism any stories I heard second-hand.

The stories of how the Japanese burned our boys to make them talk had been coming up with increasing frequency.

Pfc. Louis E. Myers, 30, of Fullerton, Neb., ended my doubts about that Japanese method of torture. When I asked him if he had been mistreated, he turned his hands palms up and showed me. On each wrist were two angry red scars, each the size of a half-dollar. They were 5 months old. They probably will be there as long as he lives.

In fine health after three years' imprisonment, Myers told me how he got those scars.

"The Japs found a half canteen of sake in our barracks. One of our boys apparently bribed a Jap to get it for him," Myers said. "They took 13 of us from that place and beat and burned us. They slapped our heads with a piece of conveyor belt until they were swollen.

"No one talked. As a matter of fact, I honestly didn't know who the sake belonged to or where the man had managed to get it. I was telling them the truth. After the beating, they smeared a gummy substance on the inside of both my wrists and touched a match to it. It burned from one to two minutes. Those are the scars you see here."

"Were you tied or held when they did that?" I asked Myers.

"No," he answered. "They don't have to tie you when you're in a spot like that. There's just nothing you can do about it so you stand there and take it. And here's something that is going to be hard for you to believe. That beating on the head was harder to take than the burning. That was the only time I had to go through an ordeal like that. A lot of them got it two or three times worse than I did."

Myers had been among a group of 150 prisoners who had sabotaged a tool and die works so effectively that the Japanese called detectives in to solve the case.

He had been with his brother, Elvin, 28, since they had been captured, but they were later separated.

"We had to leave on a 45-minute notice, but I did get to say goodbye to him," Myers said. "I know he's all right. He was in good shape then, and there was no reason why he shouldn't be on his way home soon."

The two brothers were a big help to each other while they were prisoners together, sharing cigarettes, food and clothes. They ate together and were inseparable when they got any leisure time.

Myers was being processed when we got together and was grinning from ear to ear as he tried on his new, recently issued GI clothes. He had just arrived from Kamioka, where he had been working in the lead mines.

"The Japs found a half canteen of sake in our barracks. One of our boys apparently bribed a Jap to get it for him. They took 13 of us from that place and beat and burned us. They slapped our heads with a piece of conveyor belt until they were swollen."

— PFC. LOUIS E. MYERS

September 22, 1945
YOKOHAMA (DELAYED)

PVT. IVAN SMITH is a clean-cut young fellow of 23 with humor wrinkles about his eyes after three years in the Japanese prison camps.

Smith received one letter from the home folks in his three years of captivity, and that was in the early days in the Philippines, shortly after he was captured on Corregidor. He was another of the doughty gang that sabotaged the Nips at Mukden.

He said his mother, Edna Smith, was a cook at Omaha's Clarkson Hospital the last time he had heard. He lived with his grandparents, Mr. and Mrs. John L. Smith of Plattsmouth, before he joined the Army. His letter was from them and he knew it by heart, although he had lost it during his captivity.

He labored in the lead mines at Kamioka for a year and two months. He said his friends had been burned on the stomach for various offenses, but he had been lucky — just suffering a few beatings. He lost 25 pounds while imprisoned but is on his way back to his normal weight.

"We threw the Jap civilians some cigarettes when we were coming down on the train this morning," he said nonchalantly. "You should have seen them scramble for them."

"You did what?" I asked him incredulously. "Threw them cigarettes after what you have gone through?"

"Oh, hell, the war's over," he said. "These poor dopes don't know the score. The Jap army kicks them around almost as bad as they did us."

Smith said he and his buddies fared better than any prisoners had a right to when they were unloading ships in the Philippines for the Japanese.

"We cut our trousers up the leg on the outside and put strips of cloth in there to get the bell bottom type of trouser that our sailors wear," he said. "Then we tied beef and any other food we could get our hands on to our legs. The Japs never caught on. We could have walked out of there with an admiral strapped to us and they wouldn't have known the difference. We ate right good in those days."

Cpl. Warren Miller, 24, of Davenport, Neb., is serving with the 42nd General Hospital Group on the docks, putting in overtime trying to make it easier on the boys just released from prison. He always does a "little something extra" when he runs into a boy from his home state.

Donald Danahey, 26, of Lawrence, Neb., wasn't brooding about the past as he rubbed on his shoulders and shouted gleefully to the fellows around him.

"Tell them at home that I'm OK and that I'll be seeing them soon," he said to me.

> "Tell them at home that I'm OK and that I'll be seeing them soon."
>
> — RELEASED PRISONER DONALD DANAHEY OF LAWRENCE, NEB., TO WORLD-HERALD REPORTER BILL BILLOTTE

Japanese people were ready for the war to end

September 22, 1945
WITH GEN. MACARTHUR IN YOKOHAMA, JAPAN

MR. AND MRS. JOHN Q. JAPAN were ready to quit with no urging from the little man on the White Horse when the end came. That much was apparent.

When two other war correspondents and I wandered through the blocks of hurriedly constructed tin shacks in this major Japanese naval base, we saw the Japanese with their defenses down. These were the people who had taken it on the chin. They talk with awe about the B-29 and the devastation that it spread among them.

We sat with one gray-bearded old patriarch who had waved us to seats beside him on cushions on the floor. We talked to him through another old man we had picked up as an interpreter in exchange for two Lucky Strike cigarettes somewhere along the line. The interpreter had gotten Babe Ruth tied up in his mind with the Lucky Strikes. Every once in a while he would totter to his feet and take a lusty swat as though he were hitting a ball. Then he would put his trembling hand up to his eyes as though he were looking off into the distance.

"Babe Ruth," he would announce with a toothless grin.

Asserting that the Japanese people were ready to quit, the old man deplored the fact that so many homes had been hit when they had not been military objectives.

Maybe not, I told him, pointing to dozens of rusted lathes scattered around the area. I said Americans don't keep those things scattered around their living rooms. The Americans knew that a good part of Japan's war industry was in the homes in this section. We had to level it, I told him.

His wife, 57, nodded sadly when the interpreter translated the answer. She was doing some weaving that was beautiful. She told me to come back in a week and she would give it to me because she had fallen in love with a picture of my son, Bill. She said her own son of 27 still was in China. She rocked slowly back and forth on the mat with empty arms to illustrate that she thought he might have been killed and would not return.

The old man brought out a bottle of sake and indicated that he wanted to drink to peace. He handed us each a small drink and gravely downed his. I took half of mine and hastily set the glass down, as tears started to fill my eyes and my hair stood on end.

'The Lucky Seven'

SEVEN NEBRASKA MARINES *who enlisted in 1942 at a rally at Omaha's City Auditorium were still together in the Philippines in 1945.*
World-Herald reporter Bill Billotte called them "the Lucky Seven" for surviving three years in the Pacific together.
Back row, from left, Pfc. Robert Nowak of St. Paul, Pfc. Bill Clarence of Omaha and Sgt. Tex Barney of Omaha.
Front row: Pfc. Rex Miller of York, Pfc. John Ness of Lincoln, Cpl. Max Degenhardt of Hebron and Cpl. Bill Gentleman of Omaha.

Hiroshima and Nagasaki

THE DAY THAT NEVER WAS. That phrase was the headline of a World-Herald editorial on Nov. 1, 1945 — the day that the U.S. invasion of Japan was to have begun. ★ American intelligence had estimated 1 million U.S. casualties by the fall of 1946 in the invasion of Japan, and many more among Japanese. Because the war ended after the U.S. dropped atomic bombs on Hiroshima and Nagasaki in August 1945, the invasion of the Japanese islands never came about.

★ By comparison to what might have been, the news of Nov. 1 that year was relatively uneventful: Halloween pranks, debate on an anti-strike bill in Congress, plans for an income tax reduction, Jimmy Durante making an impression of his famous schnoz in the sidewalk in front of Grauman's Chinese Theater. ★ The best news was that the troops were starting to come home, not having faced this most horrible battle. "From our post-surrender knowledge of Japan," the editorial said, "we know that the battle would have been tougher probably than the Normandy invasion."

Two residents of Hiroshima walk along a path cleared through the destruction from the Aug. 6, 1945, detonation of the first atomic bomb.

EDWARD LEE FERRIS

Town: Blair

Service: U.S. Navy

In the war: He had his basic training at Great Lakes Naval Training Station in Illinois in 1945. He was assigned to the aircraft carrier USS Lexington, "The Blue Ghost," in the Pacific and served as a radio-man, receiving and decoding radio messages.

In his words: "The USS Lexington was positioned 80 to 100 miles off the coast of Japan when Hiroshima was bombed. We heard a loud thunderlike noise when the bomb was dropped. Later, I received and decoded the messages telling us about the bombings of Japan. Just before the bombings, the Japanese kamikaze planes were making runs and had sunk two destroyers ahead of the USS Lexington. Soon after the bombing of Hiroshima, our group used a small landing craft to go onto shore. We witnessed the devastation."

'In war there is no morality'

RETIRED BRIG. GEN. PAUL TIBBETS, in front of a restored B-29, during a visit to Offutt Air Force Base in 1991.

RETIRED BRIG. GEN. PAUL TIBBETS, whose plane dropped the world's first atomic bomb on Hiroshima and killed more than 100,000, said he didn't lose sleep over the deaths.

"No," he said in 2001. "I don't like to use the word but, you see, in war there is no morality. None. And that goes for women and children. You hate to see them as collateral damage, but the weapon (the atomic bomb) is non-selective. It has no discretion. That's the way I look at it."

The decision to drop atomic bombs has been debated endlessly. Critics say Japan eventually would have surrendered because of conventional firebombing and a U.S. naval blockade cutting off imported fuel.

The U.S. government estimated about 200,000 died from the bombings of Hiroshima and Nagasaki. Others counter that hundreds of thousands of American and Japanese lives would have been lost in an Allied invasion of Japan.

Hiroshima and Nagasaki

Tibbets' historic mission had a strong connection to the Omaha area.

The Enola Gay was modified to carry out the atomic bombing run at the Martin Bomber Plant, now the site of Offutt Air Force Base.

Long before setting out for the South Pacific, Tibbets visited the plant and personally chose that B-29 for his mission, said John McQueney, historian for Offutt's 55th Wing.

Believing that the aircraft needed a name for such a historic mission, Tibbets named it after his mother, Enola Gay Tibbets, who was from the Carroll County, Iowa, farming community of Glidden.

In the hours before dawn on Aug. 6, 1945, the Enola Gay lifted off from the Pacific island of Tinian carrying a uranium atomic bomb assembled under extraordinary secrecy in the vast endeavor known as the Manhattan Project.

At 8:15 a.m. local time, the bomb nicknamed "Little Boy" dropped free at an altitude of 31,000 feet. Forty-three seconds later, at 1,890 feet above ground zero, it exploded in a nuclear inferno that left tens of thousands dead and dying and that turned much of Hiroshima — a city of 250,000 — into a scorched ruin.

Over the years, Tibbets' strong defense of the mission helped cast him as a symbol in the larger debate about the morality of using atomic weapons, said military experts and historians.

"He certainly has become a symbol, as the person who dropped a bomb, for those who find nuclear weapons inherently immoral, as well as for those who believe it was the only way to end World War II quickly," said Jason Steck, an instructor at Creighton University.

Tibbets never wavered.

"It would have been morally wrong if we'd have had that weapon and not used it and let a million more people die," he said in a Public Broadcasting Service interview marking the 50th anniversary of the bombing.

It would be difficult to find a dissenting voice among the thousands of airmen who later served at Offutt's Strategic Air Command, which headed the U.S. nuclear forces for decades, former SAC officers said.

"You'd have to search very, very hard to find someone in the Air Force who felt that (President Harry S.) Truman made a bad decision" in authorizing the bombing, said retired Maj. Gen. William Doyle, a former Strategic Air Command director of intelligence.

"Paul Tibbets had the worst assignment ever given to a military officer: to destroy a Japanese city and its inhabitants in order to convince Japan's emperor that unconditional surrender was the only choice," former Nebraska Sen. Bob Kerrey said. "Absent that surrender, many more — Americans and Japanese — would have died."

Tibbets, who died in 2007, requested that he have no funeral or headstone, fearing that it would give his detractors a place to protest, said a friend, Gerry Newhouse.

"It would have been morally wrong if we'd have had that weapon and not used it and let a million more people die."

— RETIRED BRIG. GEN. PAUL TIBBETS

B-29s WERE BUILT at the Martin Bomber Plant in what is now known as Building D at Offutt Air Force Base. The building is in the background of the 2006 photo above.

THE GROUND CREW IN THE MARIANA ISLANDS, with then-Col. Paul Tibbets, center, and the Enola Gay in 1945.

MELVIN JONES

Town: Norfolk

Service: Army, 77th Infantry Division

In the war: Served with identical twin Marvin as riflemen in the Pacific. Their unit entered Hiroshima after the atomic bomb dropped.

In his words: "(Hiroshima) was absolutely devastated. The only things standing were the smokestacks. ... We were preparing to be the invasion force into Japan, and we didn't even know they'd dropped the bombs. We were in Tokyo Harbor near the (USS) Missouri when they surrendered."

Secret work 'seemed kind of screwy'

BY BILL HORD

E.T. "JUNIOR" NELSON, right, worked on the atomic bomb in New Mexico, and Shorty Hahn served in the Army occupation forces in Japan and saw the destruction.

EIGHTEEN-YEAR-OLD ARMY PVT. E.T. "Junior" Nelson of Hordville strictly followed his orders, as sinister and cryptic as they may have seemed.

He rode a train to New Mexico and went to a Santa Fe address. The door in the old storefront was unlocked. No one was inside, only a couple of chairs, a coffee table, a few magazines and a telephone.

"It seemed kind of screwy," Nelson recalls.

Unbeknownst to him, Nelson had been handpicked for a special assignment designed to end World War II.

In just four weeks, he had been drafted from central Nebraska and delivered to the doorstep of the biggest secret of the war. He didn't know that government agents had slipped into Hordville to investigate his background.

And in April 1945, he passed through that stark Santa Fe room to take a place in history.

Once inside, Nelson picked up the phone and called the number listed in his orders. A voice told him to walk three blocks to a corner where a bus would pick him up.

Other soldiers at the stop told him he was headed to "the Hill," a place to become known to the rest of the world by another name — Los Alamos.

On the Hill, Nelson would help assemble explosives at a secret location called S Site, one of several work camps in the mountains around Los Alamos.

Except for the secrecy, it was similar to work he had done as a civilian at the Grand Island, Neb., ordnance plant before he was drafted.

He had worked at the plant for only six weeks. But that experience with explosives was enough to cut short boot camp and see him assigned to the special duty.

The ultimate objective was a mystery. "But we had figured out that we were working on a bomb," Nelson said.

Security was intense. Workers at one site were told not to discuss their jobs with workers from other sites. In letters home, soldiers couldn't mention the name of the camp. All incoming mail went to post office boxes — for Nelson's unit, Box 180, Santa Fe, N.M.

Nelson's mother prodded him for information about his camp name and location. More than once, he tried to tell her too much and had to rewrite censored letters.

Soldiers leaving camp were not to talk of their work. Undercover security officers posed as Santa Fe citizens to hush any loose-lipped soldiers on weekend passes.

In mid-July, Nelson finally learned the full purpose of the secrecy and his work.

Forty or 50 soldiers from S Site were ordered to the mess hall, where a man in a business suit and open collar entered, sat on the edge of a table, lit a cigarette and displayed photographs.

The man identifying himself as Dr. Oppenheimer was unknown to the soldiers, but they were about to learn.

For more than an hour, physicist J. Robert Oppenheimer — director of the Manhattan Project — told them of the atomic bomb's successful test on July 16, 1945. Photos showed the mushroom cloud and other results from the Trinity test site at White Sands Proving Ground in the New Mexico desert.

While S Site workers were told about the tests, the American public was led to believe that the explosion was caused by an accident at an ammo dump. But no ammo blast would vaporize everything within a half-mile. "That takes a lot of heat," Nelson said.

The work of Nelson's team was essential to detonating bombs like the one at Trinity. Conventional explosives surrounded the interior of the bomb and were detonated to start a chain reaction.

Oppenheimer did not reveal how the bomb would be used, but Nelson said he and others assumed the target was Japan.

On Aug. 6, a B-29 Superfortress dropped an atomic bomb on Hiroshima. That bomb — called "Little Boy" — was different from the

THE SKY OVER Nagasaki, Japan, on Aug. 9, 1945.

one Nelson had worked on. Made with uranium instead of plutonium, it did not need explosives. Because of a shortage of uranium, it wasn't tested prior to use.

When Japan didn't immediately surrender, a second bomb was detonated over Nagasaki on Aug. 9. Dubbed "Fat Man," it was a plutonium bomb.

About 200,000 Japanese in Hiroshima and Nagasaki died from the blasts or radiation poisoning.

On Aug. 15, Japan surrendered.

Nelson said in 2005 that he had seldom talked about his experiences. Criticism of use of the bombs rolls off like water off a duck's back, he said. He agrees with those who say lives lost at Hiroshima and Nagasaki were a fraction of the casualties that would have resulted from a U.S. invasion of Japan.

"It was something that had to be done, and we did it," he said. "And that was it."

"He doesn't talk about his military experience much," said Shorty Hahn of Central City, a close friend since the two worked together on construction of a Hordville grain elevator in 1949.

Hahn served in the Army occupation forces in Japan in 1946 and 1947 and saw the aftermath of destruction at Hiroshima and Nagasaki. Virtually everything was flattened, he said, pointing to a published picture of the devastation. "As a young man, I thought, 'What am I seeing?' I'll never forget it."

Nelson collected some articles and videotapes about the Manhattan Project. And he has kept a letter attesting to his contribution to atomic weaponry.

Written by Oppenheimer, the Oct. 1, 1945, letter thanks Nelson for his work at Los Alamos. The letter apologizes that details of his work and accomplishments "must remain a secret of the U.S. government."

"However," Oppenheimer added, "this in itself is an indication of the importance of your contribution to the project."

'Absolute horror' was averted

OMAHA ATTORNEY JAMES MARTIN DAVIS, an Army Ranger during the Vietnam War, used once-classified information to publish a 24-page pamphlet titled "Top Secret," detailing plans for the invasion and defense of Japan — the latter based on statements by Japanese leaders after the surrender.

"What really surprised me," Davis said in 1991, "is the absolute horror that would have taken place as a result of the invasion of Japan."

Documents make it clear, he said, that in addition to the caves and tunnels that the Japanese planned to use in defense, suicide attacks on Americans would have risen to ghastly heights.

"The Japanese had changed their tactics," Davis said. "They weren't going after our carriers and destroyers. They were targeting our troop transports, which they would have turned into balls of fire."

The U.S. not only had underestimated the number of planes that Japan had held in reserve, he said, but also the fanaticism rampant at the time.

The Japanese had used kamikaze attacks late in the war, but Davis said Japan's defense plans, under the name "Ketsu-Go," included a fourfold aerial response.

An initial force of 2,000 planes would "fight to the death," followed by 330 specially trained combat pilots, then 824 suicide planes aimed at the troop transports and, finally, 2,000 suicide planes in waves of 200 to 300 hour by hour. Japan hoped to sustain "nonstop mass suicide attacks" for 10 days.

Japan hoped to sustain "nonstop mass suicide attacks" for 10 days.

In addition, the Japanese would use submarines and 23 remaining destroyers, plus a special attack unit using "midget submarines, human torpedoes and exploding motorboats."

The Japanese, Davis wrote, "were convinced the Americans would back off or become so demoralized" that they would then accept a less-than-unconditional surrender.

Elaborate defense plans involving civilians also had been prepared for use once Americans landed.

Documents showed that the U.S. planned a Nov. 1 invasion on the southern Japanese island of Kyushu — code-named "Operation Olympic." A more forceful follow-up invasion on the main island of Honshu, called "Operation Coronet," was set for March 1, 1946.

President Harry Truman, who eventually gave the go-ahead to drop the atomic bombs, wrote in his memoirs that the secretary of war informed him of the existence of the atomic bomb on April 12, four hours after the death of President Franklin Roosevelt.

The decision to drop the bomb was made later. In the interim, Truman said, the chiefs of staff had suggested the conventional invasion of Kyushu and then Honshu.

"But the (casualty) statistics that the generals gave me," Truman wrote, "were as frightening as the news of the big bomb."

THOMAS HALLSTROM
Town: Omaha
Service: Navy, USS Harris
In the war: Served as a yeoman on the Harris, a troop transport that was among the first U.S. ships to dock in Tokyo Bay after the war. Participated in the invasion of Okinawa.

In his words: "We were really happy the day the (atomic) bomb was dropped. We knew it would be over then and we were in a squadron that had been planning the invasion of the main island of southern Japan. So we were damn glad Truman made that decision."

RESIDENTS OF NAGASAKI carry away debris from the area leveled by the atomic bomb of Aug. 9, 1945.

Lingering feelings over the bombs

THE ATOMIC BOMB that Duane Tunnyhill believes saved his life also haunted Robert Briley with horrific memories.

The weapons dropped on Hiroshima and on Nagasaki three days later killed about 200,000 people and virtually annihilated the cities.

The two B-29 bombers used to drop the bombs — the Enola Gay and Bockscar — were built at the Martin Bomber Plant south of Omaha, at what is now Offutt Air Force Base.

Some of the bomber plant workers and soldiers who witnessed the destruction caused by the bombs said they had felt guilty over the years because their country unleashed the atomic terror on the people of Nagasaki and Hiroshima. Some still struggle with their feelings.

Others said the United States has no reason to apologize for using the bomb. It saved lives and ended a war Japan started with a sneak attack on Pearl Harbor, they said.

For Tunnyhill, of Bellevue, there was nothing to debate and no moral uncertainty about using the bomb.

He was a teenage Marine in Hawaii in August 1945, training with his machine gun squad for an invasion of Japan. Then the bomb hit Hiroshima, and Tunnyhill knew he would be spared the dangerous dash up a heavily defended Japanese beach.

"If it had not been for that bomb, I would not be here," Tunnyhill said in 1995. "The first troops going in would not have had much of a chance to make it. We were lucky we didn't invade."

"If it had not been for that bomb, I would not be here. The first troops going in would not have had much of a chance to make it. We were lucky we didn't invade."

— DUANE TUNNYHILL
OF BELLEVUE IN 1995

ROBERT BRILEY SAID IN 1995 that he couldn't shake the faces of bombing survivors and the scenes of destruction he saw in Hiroshima while serving aboard the USS Holland, a submarine-support ship that pulled into the bay at Hiroshima in December 1945.

PURPLE HEART RECIPIENT DUANE TUNNYHILL observed a moment of silence during a 2004 Veterans Day event at Omaha's Memorial Park.

ELROY HEFNER

Town: Coleridge, Neb.

Service: U.S. Navy amphibious forces from April 1944 to May 1946

In the war: He went to the U.S. Navy Reserve station in Omaha for his induction into the Navy in 1944. He went by train to Farragut, Idaho, for basic training at the U.S. Naval Training Station. After that, he attended various engineering schools and then was assigned to the tank landing ship LST-491 for duty in the South Pacific.

In his words: "After Okinawa was secured, we were traveling in a flotilla (code name Olympic) to invade the main island of Japan. This was August 1945. It was at this time we were notified that an atomic bomb was dropped on Hiroshima and destroyed the city. Then a few days later, another bomb was dropped on Nagasaki. The emperor of Japan then said that he was ready to sign a peace treaty. This was done on the battleship Missouri in Tokyo Bay. Our ship was included in the many number of ships surrounding the battleship Missouri."

Tunnyhill had seen how fiercely the Japanese soldiers could fight when he was in the battle for Iwo Jima in February 1945. Nearly 7,000 U.S. soldiers and 20,000 Japanese soldiers died in the hard-fought battle for the Pacific island.

Tunnyhill and his fellow Marines expected an even bloodier fight if they invaded Japan.

"If somebody came into America, we would be more determined," Tunnyhill said. "We knew they would want to defend their homeland."

Briley said the bomb may have been a "necessary evil" to end the war and spare thousands of lives. He said, however, that he has been haunted by the faces of the bombing victims he saw in Japan.

Briley served on the USS Holland, a submarine-support ship that pulled into the bay at Hiroshima in December 1945.

"Those poor people, civilians, they had their hands out begging," Briley said. "They were scarred. It looked like a flame-thrower had been shot at them. You almost got sick to your stomach."

The earth was scorched for as far as he could see. Some survivors had only scars where their noses or ears should have been.

Briley said he saw a Japanese soldier who was missing a leg sitting by the side of the road in Hiroshima trying to sell a helmet and sword. Briley gave the man half a pack of cigarettes.

"He was a serviceman, and I was a serviceman," Briley said. "I felt compassion toward him. I felt kind of bad about us dropping the bomb on them."

Briley and his fellow sailors had strict orders not to pick up pieces of glass, metal or other remnants as souvenirs. A few months after leaving Hiroshima, Briley and some other sailors saw lesions pop out on their faces and heads.

Briley said he always suspected that the lesions were caused by exposure to lingering radiation from the bomb even though military doctors told him he was not eating enough fresh fruit or vegetables while at sea. The wounds on his head and face eventually healed, but Briley said he had never been able to shake the hellish sights he saw.

"They were all innocent people," he said. "It was tragic. Maybe it was necessary, but to this day I feel pangs of remorse."

Loyd Fischer of Lincoln said he wished the United States had never dropped the atomic bombs.

"Those weapons were a horrible thing," said Fischer, who flew over Japan as a Navy pilot during the war. "They killed women and children."

Fischer, who flew missions from an aircraft carrier, said he and his shipmates did not see any military need to drop an atomic bomb.

While flying over the country, Fischer said, he saw that Japan was a crippled nation strewn with rubble left from thousands of conventional bombs. Its transportation system was wiped out, he said.

"The Japanese were thoroughly beaten," he said.

Months before the bomb was dropped on Hiroshima, workers at the Martin Bomber Plant south of Omaha began hearing about a new superbomb the United States had developed.

The Enola Gay and Bockscar were among the 20 B-29s the plant modified so they could carry the supersized atomic bombs.

Milton Kilborn, who worked as an electrician at the bomber plant, said plant workers were given few details.

"We knew it was an enormous bomb, but we didn't know what it was," said Kilborn.

He said he and others at the plant were saddened to hear how many people died from the bomb blast, but he never questioned whether it was the right thing to do.

"Absolutely it had to be justified," Kilborn said. "It saved our boys' lives."

'I was amazed and horrified'

BY MATTHEW HANSEN

VIVIAN M. (WOODRING) ROMERO

Town: Omaha

Service: Women's Army Auxiliary Corps

In the war: Served as a phone operator for the Signal Corps in New Guinea and the Philippines

In her words: "The Women's Army Auxiliary Corps was the only way a woman could serve overseas in a combat zone in World War II. After a short time at an East Coast port of embarkation, I was sent to New Guinea and Manila and served under Gen. Douglas MacArthur. He was headquartered in our building, and I saw him every day. I still have a large copy of the surrender agreement signed by all the countries. I happened to know the right person, and it was a gift when I got out of the service."

FROM THE AIR, WILMA SCHULZ remembered that Hiroshima looked clean. The Japanese city was like a front porch, she thought, and a Nebraska housewife had attacked it with a broom and swept the porch spotless.

Once on the ground, Ruth Inman remembers that Hiroshima looked gone. The trees were charred and twisted. The blast had opened up huge cracks in the roads, cracks wide enough to swallow an Army jeep. And the buildings — the office buildings and houses that contained a bustling, 350,000-person Japanese city — they were rubble, piles of brick and concrete and wood. They were dust.

"That's been 60-some years, and my memory isn't good about most things," Inman said in 2010. "But I was amazed and horrified by that destruction. I can still remember that."

Schulz, of Blue Hill, Neb., and Inman, originally from Alma, Neb., served as Army nurses during World War II and tucked a stunning memory into their war scrapbooks. They were among the first Americans to see Hiroshima after President Harry Truman ordered the dropping of the first atomic bomb ever detonated during war.

Stationed at an Army hospital in the Philippines, Schulz and Inman were put on a plane, flown to a makeshift military aid station in Japan and eventually allowed to tour nearby Hiroshima.

"Two bombs, and it was over," Schulz said. "We never dreamed it could end the war like it did. And then, we were there."

Schulz and Inman both trained at Hastings' Mary Lanning Hospital and entered the Army Nurse Corps, joining the nearly 60,000 female nurses who staffed military hospitals in the European and Pacific Theaters as the war raged.

The two Nebraskans were lucky, Schulz thinks — they reached the Philippines in the spring of 1945, after most of the once-brutal battles in and around Manila had ended.

Schulz worked in a tent, mostly treating GIs with dysentery, she said. Inman served as the head nurse in an operating room, scheduling operations and supervising nurses inside a building with corrugated metal walls.

After the war ended in August 1945, she cared for dozens of released American prisoners of war, pumping them full of fluids and nutrients to help the emaciated GIs gain weight.

The routine of eight-hour nursing shifts and free time ended abruptly in November 1945, when the Army shut down the hospital. Half of the nurses were transferred to other hospitals in the Philippines. The others, including Schulz and Inman, were ushered onto a transport plane bound for Japan.

They got their first glimpse of Hiroshima when the plane circled and then landed on an airstrip on the city's outskirts. They unloaded their luggage, stood on the airstrip — and were quickly herded back onto the airplane by a military policeman, who screamed at the pilot, "What are you doing here? You aren't supposed to be here!"

The nurses were then taken to a staging area on an island off Japan and then to a makeshift military clinic east of Hiroshima.

ARMY NURSES IN 1945: Wilma Schulz is at center and Ruth Inman is in front of her. They saw the devastation months after an atomic bomb was dropped on Hiroshima.

WILMA SCHULZ in 2010

Truth be told, there was little work, Schulz and Inman said. The military hospital served only Americans, and the only injuries came when an appendix burst or a soldier wrecked an Army jeep.

Schulz spent her free time trading Army-issued cartons of cigarettes and alcohol — she didn't smoke or drink — for Japanese bowls, tablecloths and trinkets.

Inman, who lived later in the Dallas suburb of Carrollton, Texas, recalled the day a young Japanese girl inched closer and closer to her, finally close enough to startle Inman by stroking her hair. The girl had never seen blond hair before.

But the memory burned into both nurses' brains is the day later in 1945 when they climbed onto military trucks and headed west to see Hiroshima. No one, not even the medical providers, thought for a second about the aftereffects of radiation, Schulz said.

Which is how a pack of nurses found themselves walking around the blast site of the world's first wartime atomic bomb.

Schulz and Inman both said the trip to Hiroshima didn't change their bedrock belief that the bombs needed to be dropped. Otherwise, they said, they would have had to care for thousands of injured American servicemen sent to fight during what would have been a horrific invasion of Japan. But to see what the first bomb wrought was to understand devastation, they said.

Schulz remembered picking up a piece of a dish and turning it in her hands. She couldn't find anything that wasn't broken.

Inman remembers how an old Japanese man on a bicycle stopped next to her. In broken English, waving his arms, he tried to explain what he had seen. People on fire. Women and children dying. Everything, everyone, destroyed.

"You just felt . . ." Inman said, her voice trailing off. "I guess I'm just thankful that it ended the way it did, instead of the other way around."

'Well, it looks like the war's over'

LOOKING THROUGH POSSESSIONS from his mother's estate in 2001, Don Gibbs of Omaha came across a scrapbook and letters. They told of the father he didn't recall, killed by a kamikaze attack on the USS LaGrange — Aug. 13, 1945, the day before Japan agreed to surrender.

Gibbs, a retired Creighton University faculty member, knew that his father had died at the end of the war, but he had never seen the scrapbook, which included a letter his father had written Aug. 12, 1945.

"Well, it looks like the war's over," Ensign Walter Morrison Gibbs wrote. "I sure hope so anyway."

WALTER GIBBS

The United States had dropped an atomic bomb on Hiroshima on Aug. 6 and another on Nagasaki on Aug. 9. Surrender was being negotiated.

In the letter, Ensign Gibbs told his mother that word had circulated at the harbor off Okinawa on Aug. 10 that Japan soon would capitulate.

"It precipitated an unprecedented display of enthusiasm," he wrote, "not only on board but all around us."

From ashore and afloat, servicemen fired rockets and flares. They blew whistles and sirens. Like everyone else, Gibbs, 32, couldn't wait to get home. His wife, Dorothy, and two young sons awaited him. His mother had four sons in World War II — two in the Army and two in the Navy. Three would return.

At 7:46 p.m. on Monday, the 13th, movies were being shown in the mess hall. Gibbs was playing cards in the ship's wardroom with three other officers. They had no warning. A kamikaze plane hit the LaGrange amidships. A chaplain, who had just entered the wardroom and was only slightly injured, later wrote that the explosion blew a steel door into the officers, killing them instantly.

In all, 21 men on the LaGrange were killed and 89 were wounded. Three years, eight months and six days after Japan had drawn America into the war with a sneak attack on Pearl Harbor, a sneak attack — the last kamikaze raid of the war — had wreaked devastation even as surrender was near.

Back home in Yonkers, N.Y., an unaware Dorothy Gibbs looked forward to celebrating a homecoming.

Don Gibbs never talked much to his mother about the tragedy, figuring it would upset her. But then he discovered a box that he never had opened.

"When I read all the letters," he said, "it was very moving."

He held in his hands, just as his mother had, the Western Union telegram: "I deeply regret to inform you . . . ."

The war was over. America had celebrated. The soldiers and sailors were coming home — but not Ensign Gibbs.

THE EVENING HEADLINES OF AUGUST 11, 1945

WORLD-HERALD READERS got their first look at the deadly mushroom cloud from the atomic bomb dropped over Nagasaki, Japan, two days earlier. The top story of the day outlined the Allies' terms for accepting Japan's surrender. "The Allied reply put the next move up to the Tokyo Government," a wire story reported.

MEMORIES OF A GENERATION ★

CLAIR GILL

Town: Atlantic

Service: Army Air Forces, 1942 to 1946

In the war: He enlisted Jan. 1, 1942, not long after Pearl Harbor was attacked. He had basic training in Wichita Falls, Texas, and Mobile, Ala. Then he went to New York City for airplane mechanics school for four months. He shipped out to Brisbane, Australia, and later served in New Guinea, the Dutch East Indies, the Philippine Islands and the Japanese island of Ie Shima, near Okinawa. While in the South Pacific, he and two others were shipwrecked during a storm on a small island, about 1½ miles wide and 2 miles long. The reef was inhabited by 60 natives who took care of them for six days until they were rescued by an American patrol boat.

In his words: "I was on the island of Ie Shima patching flak holes in B-24 and B-25 bombers when atomic bombs were dropped on Nagasaki and Hiroshima. The Japanese surrendered and agreed to rendezvous halfway between Manila and Ie Shima, where I watched this historic event from a C-2 wrecker. A few weeks later, the formal surrender took place in Tokyo."

RAYMOND BRIETZKE

Town: Omaha

Service: U.S. Army and U.S. Air Force

In the war: He was drafted into the Army on Oct. 1, 1943. He took basic training at Fort Ord, Calif., and was assigned to the 760th Field Artillery Battalion, where he was part of Headquarters Battery. In November 1944, he was alerted for M-1 operation in the Philippines, and in January 1945 disembarked at Lingayen Gulf, Luzon, and was assigned to the Sixth Army. In 1951, he enlisted in the Air Force. He was called to duty at Offutt Air Force Base near Bellevue during the Korean War. He spent 15 years at Offutt and retired in February 1970.

In his words: "Two days later (after arriving at Luzon), we engaged in our first combat. A group of Japanese tanks was trying to escape to the mountains and ran right into our unit at Munoz. At that time, I was assigned as a machine gunner, and we guarded our rear flank. Our unit was firing on the unsuspecting Japanese tanks as they rounded a bend in the road, and we eliminated the entire unit and numerous enemy troops. From that day on, we (our battalion) were in combat for 99 consecutive days. That summer we trained for 'Olympic Operation,' the invasion of Japan proper. If the Japanese had not surrendered, the approach to their homeland would have found the battalion spearheading the landings on Kyushu along with the Americal and First Cavalry divisions. Instead, we landed combat-loaded at Yokohama in approximately September 1945 and became a part of the original occupation forces of Nippon."

ROBERT ROBINSON

Town: Exira, Iowa

Service: Army Transportation Corps, 8th Division

In the war: Reached Japan after atomic bombs hit Hiroshima and Nagasaki. Served as a company clerk in the occupation until 1946.

In his words: "The thing I remember most is that one time, 17 of us guys from Guthrie County got together over there (for a friend's going-away party). That's really quite unusual, when you think about it … 17 guys from Guthrie County, Iowa, in Japan."

ERVIN BULL

Town: Yutan

Service: Aviation Cadet Corps

In the war: Bull never went overseas. He qualified to be a pilot bombardier and navigator. He was 13 weeks and one day into a 14-week course in flight engineer school when the first atomic bomb was dropped. Training stopped immediately.

In his words: "I was both relieved and disappointed. I was glad that the war was over or going to be over, but I had spent all that time in training. That was the end of my service."

JAMES (JIM) LIPSEY

Town: Omaha (retired to Tucson, Ariz.)

Service: Army Air Forces

In the war: He was in his senior year at the University of Nebraska and enlisted in the Army Air Forces right after Pearl Harbor was attacked. A series of postings kept him stateside until late spring 1945. In June 1945, he was a 24-year-old second lieutenant. He was assigned to the 85th Airdrome Squadron in Ie Shima, a tiny island west of Okinawa. By the time he got there, American troops had captured the coral island. They had cut deep pits out of the coral and made runways.

In his words: "We heard about the atom bombs on Japan on the radio. In mid-August, I reported for a meeting in the island commander's office, where I found a group of mostly generals and colonels gathered around a table. They showed me a message from Gen. (Douglas) MacArthur's headquarters with directions to close a designated runway, paint two large white crosses on it, and await the arrival of two Mitsubishi bombers. We called them 'Betty Bombers.' The bombers would be painted white with green crosses on the wings, fuselage and tail surfaces. I couldn't imagine what they wanted with me. Since lime is a chemical and since I was a chemical officer, I was to become a sign painter! So we mixed lime with seawater and painted white crosses on two runways. Then we waited and waited. They didn't show up. Rumors started that the Japanese had decided not to surrender but would instead invade. The runway was reopened, and our crosses disappeared. A day or two later, I was again called to the commander's office. I was ordered to repaint the crosses. On Aug. 19, 1945, two planeloads of Japanese generals and officials, escorted by American fighter planes and Mitchell B-25s, secretly landed. Their mission was to fly on to Manila in an American plane and to conduct surrender negotiations with Gen. MacArthur. One of the planes landed perfectly, the other went off the end of the runway, damaging its landing gear. (Our mechanics repaired the plane for its return to Japan.) The Japanese officials were transferred to MacArthur's C-54 for the trip to Manila. Their flight crew was put in the stockade. The delegation returned to Ie Shima a day later, then flew back to Japan in their Mitsubishi bombers. Two weeks later, Sept. 2, 1945, Japan officially surrendered on the USS Missouri, anchored in Tokyo Bay. Not long after the formal surrender, I landed in Japan on an LST and worked at an air base on the island of Kyushu. In February of 1946, I returned home to Omaha and soon separated from the military, though I was called back up for 13 months during Korea."

ELVIN FRANK

Town: Stanton, Neb.

Service: Navy

In the war: Entered Navy in May 1944, boot camp at Great Lakes Naval Training Center. Discharged June 1946. Trained to be a radioman and sailed from San Francisco in January 1945.

In his words: "We landed in the New Hebrides Islands and then went over to Guadalcanal, then Tulagi, in the Solomon Islands, where I finally went aboard LST 227 in time for the invasion of Okinawa April 1, 1945, Easter Sunday. We left Ulithi with a load of Marines and took them to Okinawa, where they disembarked amid a lot of kamikaze planes. We left in May for the Philippine Islands and took a load of soldiers back to Okinawa. In June they sent us to Seattle for repairs and I was there when the war ended. In October 1945 we went to Haha Jima, in the Bonin Islands, picked up Japanese soldiers and took them to Japan."

RICHARD "PETER" PETRASHEK

Town: Omaha

Service: Army Air Forces, sergeant in chemical warfare

In the war: He was drafted on Dec. 7, 1943, and went in at Fort Crook, which is now Offutt Air Force Base. After training, he was shipped to Guam, where he spent 14 months. He was in chemical warfare, but because neither side used gas, he didn't have to decontaminate anything. So instead he loaded many bombs onto B-29s and drove decontamination trucks to carry water to mess halls. The trucks were loaded with big water tanks and carried chemicals to mix with the water for decontamination in case of chemical attack. He also flew on several missions over Japan as an unofficial crew member with a lieutenant buddy, Leland Harlow, who was a bombardier.

In his words: "The first atom bomb that dropped on Hiroshima probably saved my life because I was scheduled to be transferred to the infantry for training for the invasion of Japan. ... An interesting thing happened to my lieutenant buddy and myself. While we were driving down the highway, we saw what we thought were these three Chamorros (Guam natives) waving their hands at us. ... They were Japanese. They had come out of the jungle where they had been hiding. They were probably starving and decided to give themselves up. We became very cautious when we realized they were Japanese. My buddy said we'd better frisk them. We were patting them down, and I was very surprised to find one of them was a woman."

The end at last

OMAHA, UNLIKE OTHER CITIES, had not gone wild on V-E Day. It had met the false alarms quietly, patiently. But this was IT. This was the final Amen.

— *THE WORLD-HERALD, Aug. 15, 1945*

A CROWD GATHERED across the street from the old World-Herald building at 15th and Farnam on V-J Day, Aug. 14, 1945, waving and cheering when they saw a camera from an upper window.

B & C HOSIERY

PEOPLE STARTED CROWDING into downtown Omaha when news broke at 6 p.m. on Aug. 14, 1945, that the Japanese had offered to surrender.

'Celebration reached a screaming crescendo'

THE WORLD-HERALD'S PAGE 1 STORY OF WEDNESDAY, AUG. 15, 1945:

OMAHA EXPLODED TUESDAY NIGHT. Following the greatest spontaneous celebration in the city's history, Mayor Charles Leeman, following the lead of President Truman, proclaimed a two-day "V-J" holiday.

Business places are expected to remain closed until Friday morning. Taverns will not reopen until 6 p.m. Thursday.

A roaring, milling throng of thousands roamed throughout the downtown area for hours to exult over the end of the greatest war in history.

The celebration began slowly, quietly. There were few persons downtown when the announcement came.

They huddled around loudspeakers, hushed, serious. They stood by until the text of the Japanese note and President Truman's full statement were read.

Their attitude then was expressed by a woman who, when the announcer paused, pleaded: "Don't tell us it isn't true. Every time they quit talking, I'm afraid."

Then a car horn began to honk. A sailor threw his arms around a girl and kissed her. A small boy rode his tricycle across Farnam at 16th Street yelling, "Wheeee!"

From then on, the tempo increased until the celebration reached a screaming crescendo that had not abated at 10 o'clock. In the early hours of this morning, the din on the downtown streets continued but with a diminishing tempo.

The V-J Day Committee's appeal for a quiet observance was snowed under by reams of scrap paper that poured out of the windows. It was drowned out by the scream of horns and joyous shouts from the thousands of throats.

In the residential districts there was quiet. Everyone who could came downtown.

IT WAS PARTY TIME ON FARNAM STREET in downtown Omaha after Japan's surrender was announced.

WILLIAM REAVES
Town: Omaha
Service: U.S. Navy
In the war: Kansas City native, enlisted in Navy December 1943, basic training at Great Lakes training center near Chicago. Went overseas in 1945. Served in segregated construction unit on Saipan, which was captured from Japanese in 1944 and served as a base for air raids on Japan and the Philippines. Discharged May 26, 1946.

In his words: "When they dropped the (second atomic) bomb on Japan, right after that they said the war was over. ... A whole bunch of airplanes were dogfighting each other. When we looked up we didn't know whose planes they were. We thought we were being attacked. Then we saw they were American airplanes and they were shooting blanks. The ships in the harbor shot their guns off. Then they announced that the war was over."

For hours cars lined 16th Street from Davenport to Leavenworth, Farnam from 13th to 20th. The horns kept up a constant din.

Sixteenth and Farnam was a mass of humanity. The crowd surged into the streets. Sporadic snake dances and conga lines twined through the rows of cars on 16th and on Farnam.

Street vendors appeared from nowhere to sell horns, noise makers, party hats. They sold out promptly.

Servicemen stationed themselves along the streets, seized and kissed the girls. Their faces soon were smeared with many shades of lipstick. In most cases the girls loved it. There was an occasional slap. A few girls ran, only to be overtaken and kissed fulsomely after a short chase.

"I've never been drunk in my life, but I must be now. I can't get this silly grin off my face."

— A WOMAN IN THE CROWD

Practically all taverns closed promptly. But many a bottle was in evidence on the street.

A soldier passed out drinks from his fifth of bourbon on the corner of 16th and Farnam. One of the takers was a gray-haired, motherly looking woman who seized the bottle and tipped it up for a healthy swig.

A man marched down the street playing a flute. He asked: "Where's a drummer?"

Makeshift bands appeared. One was composed of two small boys playing cornets, a girl playing a drum and two sailors beating black enamel dishpans with big wooden spoons. ...

A sedate, gray-haired woman shouted: "I've never been drunk in my life, but I must be now. I can't get this silly grin off my face."

"Where will we meet if we get lost?" shouted one of a group of teenage girls.

Dogs wandered the streets with ribbons tied around their necks and tails.

The downtown scene was duplicated on a smaller scale in South Omaha.

The mob was wild, yet self-disciplined. Police were watchful, apprehensive, but tolerant as the celebrants dinned through the streets. ...

There was no violence, no destruction of property, no serious accidents.

Police Chief Paul Haze said there were fewer "squeals" Tuesday night than on an ordinary Saturday night. The only property damage reported was a broken window in a South Omaha tavern, he said, adding: "And I think it was just some drunk who fell through that."

"I'm the happiest guy in Omaha," said the chief.

He could have gotten an argument on that point, from anyone in town.

THE MORNING HEADLINES OF AUG. 15, 1945

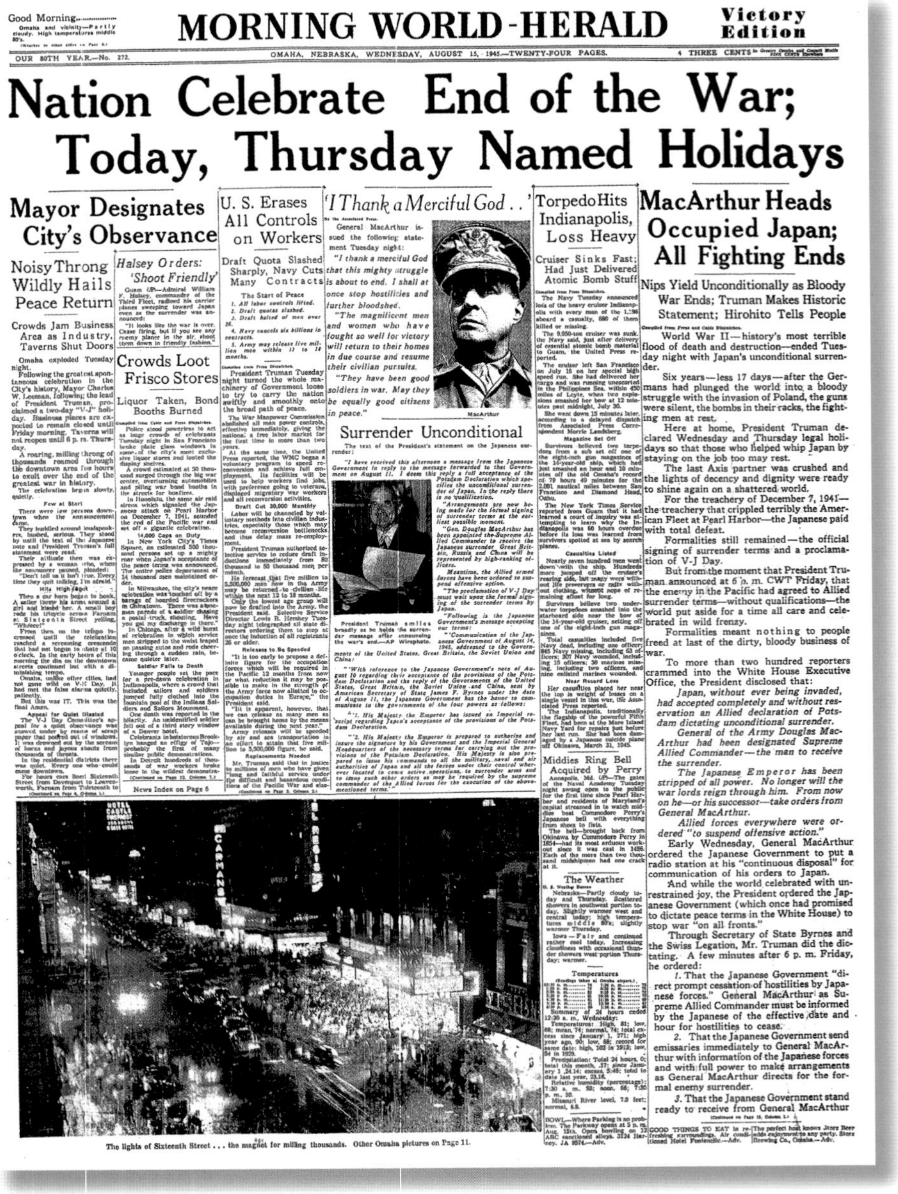

MORNING WORLD-HERALD — Victory Edition

OMAHA, NEBRASKA, WEDNESDAY, AUGUST 15, 1945—TWENTY-FOUR PAGES.   THREE CENTS

Nation Celebrate End of the War; Today, Thursday Named Holidays

Mayor Designates City's Observance

Noisy Throng Wildly Hails Peace Return

Crowds Jam Business Area as Industry, Taverns Shut Doors

Crowds Loot Frisco Stores

Liquor Taken, Bond Booths Burned

'I Thank a Merciful God . . .'

Surrender Unconditional

Torpedo Hits Indianapolis, Loss Heavy

Cruiser Sinks Fast; Had Just Delivered Atomic Bomb Stuff

MacArthur Heads Occupied Japan; All Fighting Ends

Nips Yield Unconditionally as Bloody War Ends; Truman Makes Historic Statement; Hirohito Tells People

U.S. Erases All Controls on Workers

Draft Quota Slashed Sharply, Navy Cuts Many Contracts

The lights of Sixteenth Street . . . the magnet for milling thousands. Other Omaha pictures on Page 11.

WIRE SERVICE STORIES told of celebrations in other cities. The crowd in San Francisco got out of hand, overturning cars and looting liquor stores, and a serviceman was killed when he fell out of a window at a Denver hotel. However, New York police were reported to have maintained order despite an estimated throng of 500,000 around Times Square.

'Little celebrating on official victory day'

THE SUNDAY BEFORE LABOR DAY, Sept. 2, 1945, marked the official end of World War II, with Japan formally surrendering on the USS Missouri in Tokyo Bay. In Omaha, the day passed uneventfully.

But the big celebration had come earlier, when Japan gave up, three years and eight months after bombing Pearl Harbor.

On Labor Day, The World-Herald reported: "The city, which hailed the end of the war so hilariously more than two weeks ago, did little celebrating on the official victory day. . . . Omaha's officials could be glad they hadn't scheduled any public program — unlike New York's Mayor LaGuardia, who was forced to cancel plans for a Central Park celebration when the public's apathy became apparent."

Apathy may have been too strong a word. People cared, but the real celebration had come spontaneously when the fighting stopped. Now it was time to get the soldiers and sailors home.

Newspaper ads reflected the mood, promising to make goods available as soon as possible.

"We realize," the Zale's store said, "your urgent need for electrical appliances, radios, silverplate, electric shavers and other lines that have been scarce or have been entirely unavailable."

RCA Victor promoted bendable, "non-breakable records" with "amazing fidelity and far less surface noise."

"Some day," another ad said, "canned beer will be back."

The Storz Brewing Co. of Omaha said: "Take a bow, GI. You have brought peace to the world. Your job is waiting for you."

Omaha author Bob Reilly noted in 1995 that few servicemen talked much about their exploits after returning home.

The survivors had had enough of war. Besides, he said, if you started bragging, chances were that the guy sitting next to you would have a story more harrowing than yours. So, for the most part, people just got home, reunited with loved ones, got married and got back to work.

After the surrender, the Eighth Army barely had begun its occupation of Japan when advertisements back home focused on postwar life.

The Brandeis department store advertised a 1½-quart saucepan as if gold had been discovered: "Just arrived! Here at last! Worth waiting for!"

The Nebraska Clothing Co. said GIs had done their best in khakis, and now deserved to look their best in civvies.

LOREN TURNER

Town: Central City

Service: Army, 174th Infantry Division

In the war: In training in Alabama when the war ended. Discharged without overseas service.

In his words: "We were all ... a few miles from the camp when we heard that the war was over. But we didn't really have a chance to celebrate, because they made us all go back to camp when we got the word. I don't know why they did that. Maybe they thought there was some security concern or something. ... But I was sure glad it was over with, no doubt about that."

ZOLA BETH BARNETT LEONARD

Town: Rural Logan, Iowa

Service: Senior cadet with the U.S. Army Cadet Nurse Corps

In the war: She was in an accelerated nursing program at Jennie Edmundson Hospital in Council Bluffs, where she was allowed to write her State Board tests early and earn her RN degree before heading to Johns Hopkins Hospital in Baltimore. At Johns Hopkins, she and her peers were expected to replace many of the staff nurses who had enlisted in the U.S. military.

In her words: "I celebrated V-J Day, Aug. 14, 1945, in Baltimore. We were on a 'side trip' on the city bus and we noticed everyone — men, women and children — dashing out of their homes, shouting, waving, laughing and crying. When we arrived at Sun Square, located at the Baltimore harbor, thousands of servicemen and women from all over the world, matched in numbers by civilians, all were celebrating this great moment in history. A sailor climbed a light pole; he directed the singing and cheering. We all danced, hugged, cried, laughed, shouted and even kissed each other. My brother was in the Philippines serving with the Army replacement troops, ready to invade Japan. I am thankful each day that the atomic bomb probably saved his life! When the train returning FDR's body to Hyde Park, N.Y., went through Baltimore, I joined thousands of others to pay tribute to our president. The silence was deafening, only sobbing and crying were audible. The quota for Army nurses was adequate at that time, so I never got to directly serve my country."

RAYMOND SWANSON

Town: North Platte

Service: Army, 3281st Ordnance Depot Company

In the war: Served in supply company during postwar occupation of Okinawa.

In his words: "I had about 10 or 12 Japanese prisoners working in the warehouse that I had. I was friendly with them and they were friendly with me. ... I was discharged in San Francisco and my wife came out on the train. She was excited, I'll say. My son didn't know me when I came back. Daddy was a picture on the wall."

JOHN ASCHENBRENNER

Town: Plattsmouth

Service: U.S. Navy, 1943 to 1946

In the war: He served aboard the minesweeper USS Competent AM-316. He held the ranks of seaman 1st class to gunner's mate 3rd class.

In his words: "Through the invasion of the Marshall Islands, we swept mines and picked up downed pilots. We then returned to Pearl Harbor with five Japanese prisoners. We next joined invasion forces in the Solomon Islands for the invasion of Peleliu in the western Carolines. We then returned to the U.S. for a general overhaul of our ship. We next departed for the invasion of Okinawa. We were assigned a patrol area on the inner picket line that surrounded the island. After Okinawa, we joined 24 other minesweepers to help remove an anti-submarine mine barrier that the Japanese had laid across the China Sea. After that operation, we began sweep operations for the invasion of Japan. The war ended, and we were later sent to atom-bombed Nagasaki to escort a shipload of burn victims down to what was then Formosa. We returned to Sasebo, Japan, where I was transferred to the USS Pioneer to return to the U.S. for discharge."

★ AT HOME ★

It's been a long, long time

MR. AND MRS. JOSEPH MCNEELY of Table Rock, Neb., knew the 35th Division
was back, and they had been meeting all the trains for the past three days. ★
It was a little early for the 10:40 p.m. train Friday night when they reached
the Burlington Station. They went across the street to the Reno Inn for a sandwich.
★ A moment later, Joseph McNeely glanced up from the booth to see a familiar face.
"Why, why, it's Howard," he said. Mrs. McNeely swiftly rose to kiss her son.

— *THE WORLD-HERALD, SEPT. 16, 1945*

---

*PVT. HOWARD MCNEELY GETS A KISS from his mother and a
handshake from his father as he returns to his hometown of Table Rock,
Neb. At right is Howard's sister, Mrs. Kenneth Coolen.*

A CROWD OF 50,000 TURNED OUT IN OMAHA to honor Brig. Gen. Butler B. Miltonberger of the 34th Infantry Regiment, which previously had been a unit of the Nebraska National Guard.

Miltonberger welcomed home

THE WORLD-HERALD, JUNE 26, 1945:

OMAHA GAVE BRIG. GEN. BUTLER B. MILTONBERGER a welcome so enthusiastic, so spontaneous, so heartwarming that it must have thrilled that gallant citizen-soldier to his toes.

The crowds began gathering about 30 minutes before the parade. The streets were packed by the time the procession started. Police Chief Robert Munch estimated that at least 50,000 persons looked on and shouted their acclaim. The general's car moved in the wake of the lively Lincoln Army Air Field band. The car's pace was matched by a tremendous cheer from the crowd — and this reached a climax as Omaha's guest arrived at the speakers' stand on the Courthouse steps.

Gen. Miltonberger received a 30-inch key to the city from Mayor Charles Leeman. "We in Omaha can never pay a fraction of the debt we owe to you," Leeman said.

Obviously overwhelmed by the warmth of the procession, the general had a little difficulty starting his response.

"I accept this as representative of the fine regiment of Nebraskans I was privileged to command. I intend to devote the rest of my life to seeing that these men get all the recognition and privileges that are due them. They are symbolic of the fighting spirit of Nebraska."

MILTONBERGER SIGNS AUTOGRAPHS in his hometown of North Platte, where he was honored with a parade and a barbecue. More than a ton of beef was served, and the general confessed to Mayor Sidney Mc-Farland that he was "badly choked up."

THE GENERAL, at far left, passes through the crowd along 16th Street in downtown Omaha.

A SMILING MILTONBERGER, left, and an aide, Lt. Richard K. Reed of Omaha, arrive at the Douglas County Courthouse to a celebration of his return home.

OMAHAN R.T. WILLIAMS, who served four years in the Navy, sat down to dinner in 1946 with his wife and 6-month-old son in their new home. He was among the veterans who found housing through The World-Herald Rental Bureau, which matched veterans with landlords who had vacancies in a tight housing market.

'War stimulated our resolution and dedication to a national purpose'

BY DAVID HENDEE

THE UNITED STATES ENTERED THE WAR in 1941 and was thrust for the first time into a world leadership role that it has yet to relinquish.

"World War II was like a shot in the arm that stimulated our resolution and dedication to a national purpose and produced incomprehensible productivity," said Harold Breimyer of Columbia, Mo., a retired agricultural economist at the University of Missouri. "It was perilously dangerous, but it had tremendous impact."

That impact was manifested in several areas, frequently aided by the government's actions.

The GI Bill

One of the first steps for the postwar period was taken 16 days after D-Day when President Franklin Roosevelt signed the GI Bill of Rights, intended to aid veterans' transition from military to private life after the war. The GI Bill was a pivotal act in America's history, said Larry Ebbers, a professor of professional studies at Iowa State University.

"It transformed the country and higher education," he said in 1994. "It signaled the involvement of the federal government in higher education, while expanding the opportunities for many Americans, primarily young males, to pursue college degrees. It signaled the country's commitment to use education as one of the cornerstones of democracy."

The program at that time provided about $500 yearly tuition plus a living allowance. Married men received $90 a month. It also guaranteed loans to buy a house at 4 percent interest or to start a business.

The impact was immediate. Nearly 8 million veterans, about half of those eligible, took advantage of the program.

In 1939, only 160,000 veterans graduated from four-year colleges. By 1946, college enrollment more than doubled to a record 6.1 million students, a figure not reached again until 1970 during the Vietnam War.

At Omaha University (now the University of Nebraska at Omaha), enrollment nearly doubled in the fall of 1945 when hundreds of veterans arrived on campus. Students were asked to be patient with overcrowded classrooms and limited parking.

Feeding the world

The combination of the GI Bill and America's new global outlook transformed the nation's agriculture industry. Returning soldiers who sought degrees under the GI Bill brought a broad view to campuses, said Glen Vollmar, dean of international programs at the University of Nebraska's Institute of Agriculture and Natural Resources.

"They had more than a provincial perspective," Vollmar said. "They saw the big picture."

The former soldiers became professors and started taking American agriculture programs and training abroad and inviting foreign students to U.S. campuses. Many of the graduate students at NU's College of Agriculture came from foreign lands.

These food and technical programs would have evolved eventually, but the war speeded up the process, said Breimyer, the agricultural economist.

"We developed a consciousness and a responsibility to other parts of the world that we wouldn't have had without World War II," he said.

The baby boom

The return of millions of soldiers to civilian life and the prosperity that followed the war triggered 76 million births between 1946 and 1964. The U.S. birthrate soared by more than 15 percent in the first five years after the war's end, and the trend continued through the 1950s.

"The baby boom surprised everybody," said Benjamin Rader, a professor of cultural history at the University of Nebraska-Lincoln.

Trends in Western Europe and the United States had indicated that industrialized nations didn't value children for economic purposes, Rader said. The ideal American family in the 1920s, for instance, was two children.

"But after the war, people started having kids again," Rader said. "Part of the reason was a new idealized family of four kids and life in the suburbs. Another part was an American reaction against the deprivations of the '30s and the war. People wanted to experience life at its fullest."

Urban sprawl

The baby boom and new veteran housing benefits for home mortgages (only a 10 percent down payment for new houses) helped to "set up two-bedroom bungalows on the outskirts of every town in America with more than 1,000 people," said Boyd Littrell, a sociologist at the University of Nebraska at Omaha.

THE RECEPTION ROOM at the Veterans Service Center in Omaha had a long line of ex-servicemen waiting to be called in for job interviews.

VETERANS STAND IN LINE to register at Creighton University in January 1946.

PAUL ROWOLDT

Town: Columbus

Service: Administrator with Army, 9th Corps, Eighth Army

In the war: Drafted just as the war ended and spent a year in postwar Japan giving orientation lectures for new troops. Job started him on to career as Lutheran minister.

In his words: "You're in a country with a foreign uniform and most of the people don't want you there. ... Everyone had their job to do. I was just grateful to do what I did for my country."

"Add the fact that we had five years worth of people in the military who needed a place to live . . . and you have the suburbanization of America," he said.

Few housing developments were west of 72nd Street when Alden Aust came to Omaha in 1954.

"Except for some houses in the Rockbrook, Loveland and Keystone areas, 69th Street at the west end of Fairacres was pretty much the limit," said Aust, who was the city planner from 1956 to 1981.

The Northwest Radial was built to handle heavy traffic from the booming Benson area on Omaha's northwest fringes, but it immediately became congested, Aust said.

"There was supposed to be a Southwest Radial, as growth switched from northwest to southwest, but the Interstate came, and we let it handle the traffic," Aust said.

The impact of suburban sprawl on the city was great, Littrell said.

"The whole history of the problems of urban finance can be traced to when the city core is abandoned for houses on cheap land on the edge of town," Littrell said.

Continued challenges in race relations were another result of urban sprawl.

"The 'inner city' became a term for the first time," Littrell said. "Before, it had always simply been 'the city.' "

Women at work

Women, especially married women, worked for wages in numbers like never before during the war.

Eight million women worked in war industries and other jobs because of the labor shortage caused by men going to war. The number of women employed in heavy industry rose from 340,000 in 1940 to more than 2 million in 1943. About 40 percent of the workers at many war plants in Nebraska were women.

"Working-class women had always worked outside the home," said Elaine Kruse, an associate professor at Nebraska Wesleyan University who specialized in women's history. "The war changed middle-class ideology and generally made it possible for middle-class women — and legitimate for married women — to be employed in numbers far beyond any time in the past."

Still, the entrenched belief remained that a woman's place was in the home.

At the end of the war, a government-sponsored radio and poster campaign urged women to give up their jobs to the returning soldiers. Millions of women were laid off.

"Early government propaganda said women could play important roles in helping to fight the enemy," Kruse said. "After the war, the propaganda line changes, saying it was most important for women to be at home with their children. The dominant theme of the late '40s and the '50s would emphasize women as housewives."

But the barrier was broken. In 1940, one in six married women was employed outside the home. In 1950, it was one in three.

Women found during the war that it was possible to balance a career and motherhood, said Michael Schuyler, a historian at the University of Nebraska at Kearney.

"This broader definition of what women could do in society carried over in the '50s and '60s and came to full fruition in the '70s," he said.

Racial progress

More than 1 million blacks served in the segregated armed forces during the war, and there was a renewed sense of pride and activism on the homefront.

The Omaha Urban League, the forerunner of the Urban League of Nebraska, was determined to use war-induced patriotism to prick the conscience of white America and make it live up to its democratic creed, said Dennis Mihelich, an associate professor of history at Creighton University.

In 1941, President Roosevelt signed an executive order that outlawed racial discrimination in government employment and key defense industries. In 1948, President Harry S. Truman ordered the full integration of all the armed forces — the beginning of the end for the doctrine of separate but equal.

The quickened pace of migration of blacks to industrial cities put pressure on policies of segregation, Mihelich said.

In 1940, Omaha's black population was 12,015, about 7 percent of the total population. In the two decades after World War I, the number of blacks had increased only 1,700. But in the 1940s, Mihelich said, black workers streamed into Omaha to work at the Martin Bomber Plant and produced a net population increase of 4,296, a jump of 36 percent.

Significant job breakthroughs during the war years in Omaha came with the hiring of seven women as elevator operators at Northwestern Bell Telephone Co., the integration of the staff at the 24th Street Safeway store, the employment of black power machine operators at two sewing firms and the placing of two women in upgraded jobs at the Armour & Co. packing plant, Mihelich said.

And symbolic success at the professional level came in 1945 when, for the first time in decades, the Omaha schools hired four blacks as full-time teachers — at predominantly black schools.

Many Americans tend to look back on the war years with nostalgia, Schuyler said.

"They like to talk about how we were united in a common cause," he said. "They forget racism, poverty and sexism."

The Cold War and SAC

In March 1946, President Truman signed an order intended to help protect America's new peace and security as the Soviet Union switched roles from ally to foe. He directed the Army Air Forces to establish the Strategic Air Command. It was to be prepared to conduct long-range offensive operations in any part of the world.

SAC landed in Nebraska in 1948 when its headquarters was moved from Maryland to Offutt Air Force Base near Bellevue, then a town of a few thousand people and only one surfaced street. SAC's bombers were based around the world and took part in the Korean and Vietnam Wars. The bombers later were joined by intercontinental ballistic missiles, dozens of which were based in Nebraska.

The Cold War ended in 1991 with the fall of Soviet communism, and SAC was deactivated the next year. Offutt is now home to the U.S. Strategic Command, which oversees the nation's nuclear weapons and space and cyberspace missions.

Medical advances

The need to better treat millions of battlefield casualties and a government decision to coordinate and pool research on a national scale speeded up discoveries in medicine. It is a legacy that remains in the National Institutes of Health, the government's chief medical research unit, and regional labs such as the Eppley Institute for Research in Cancer and Allied Diseases in Omaha.

The manufacture of penicillin was accelerated by the war. Previously, only small amounts of the drug used to fight infections were being made through a natural process.

Dr. Henry Lemon of Omaha was involved in the early use of penicillin at Camp Carson in Colorado. The drug was used to fight heavy outbreaks of streptococcus and rheumatic fever at the camp.

Dr. Lemon later was the first director of the Eppley Institute. "When the government saw what it could do with infectious diseases it turned to heart disease, cancer and others," Dr. Lemon said. "The relationship between government and science was joined."

Higher standard of living

"The commitment to the war effort started a period of economic boom that was sustained afterward," said Schuyler, the UNK historian. "The issue of poverty had been addressed earlier, but the war and the jobs it created had a more lasting impact in terms of improving the standard of living than any previous reform movement."

Home-bound leisure

"Before and during the war, people gathered outside the home, at movies, ballgames and in bars," said Rader of UNL. "People spent more time at home after the collapse of the big bands, the move to the suburbs and the growth of TV. There was less face-to-face contact. Now people know characters on TV better than their neighbors next door."

MARGARET JOHNSON
Town: Cedar Rapids, Iowa

Service: Women's Marine Corps

In the war: Worked at the Navy Annex Building in Arlington, Va.

In her words: "I was a clerk and helped fill the needs of the troops, what they needed in ammunition. ... It was kind of like being in college and living in a dormitory. It was all women, and we'd come from all different walks of life. When we left (in 1946), we all said, 'Well, we'll see each other again.' But most of us never did."

ASSUMPTION CATHOLIC CHURCH'S LADIES sewing circle and athletic club sponsored a dinner for returned service members at the church's parish hall.

A PLACE TO REMEMBER THOSE WHO HAVE FALLEN

FROM LEFT, S. HERBERT O'HARE, ROWLAND HAYNES AND ROBERT H. STORZ look over land on Dodge Street in 1945 for the proposed Memorial Park. Construction began in late 1946 on a monument, on which were placed plaques listing the names of Douglas County men and women who died in the war.

PRESIDENT HARRY TRUMAN laid a wreath at the park's dedication on June 6, 1948.

★ MEMORIES OF A GENERATION

MILLARD NOUZOVSKY

Town: Central City

Service: Army, 6th Infantry Division

In the war: War ended while in basic training in California. Spent 18 months in Daegu, Korea.

In his words: "We mostly guarded ammunition dumps, and it was always dark so you couldn't see anything. Then we'd guard the streets during the daytime to keep the other soldiers from doing anything they weren't supposed to do. … I was real happy, of course, that the war ended before I got sent to fight."

RONALD MILLS

Town: Red Oak

Service: Navy, USS Kermit Roosevelt

In the war: Enlisted in 1946 and served on the repair ship in the months after the war ended.

In his words: "I enlisted when I was 17, primarily to get the GI Bill of Rights and see the world, and I did both. We spent time in Hong Kong, Shanghai, Saipan, Guam, Hawaii, northern China. … We weren't sitting around, that's for sure. I thought it was a great adventure."

MARTIN MAZOUREK

Town: Yankton, S.D., formerly of David City, Neb.

Service: Navy

In the war: He was a yeoman 3rd class on the battleship USS Wisconsin when the ship was anchored in Tokyo Bay alongside the battleship USS Missouri. At that time, history was being made on the Missouri, as it was the site of Japan's unconditional surrender on Sept. 2, 1945, ending World War II.

In his words: "I worked with the executive officers. I was responsible for the plan of the day. It was cut on a mimeograph, and I ran off and distributed copies for the next day. I had to get the executive officers to sign off on the plan of the day. I also took care of the personal records of enlisted Navy men. It was quite a responsibility."

PAUL W. BECKENHAUER

Town: West Point, Neb.

Service: Army Airways Communication Service, which was attached to the Army Air Forces

In the war: He was a ground radio operator, a voice to airplane pilots approaching or leaving their air bases. After leaving Pearl Harbor on the troop ship Billy Mitchell on Pearl Harbor Day 1944, he made stops in Hobart, Tasmania; Bombay, India; Camp Kanchrapara, near Calcutta, India; Chabua, India; and finally Jorhat, India, up north in the Assam Valley. While he was in Jorhat, his first son, Paul Jr., was born back in West Point on April 30, 1945. He later made a stop in Kunming, China, and then served in Shanghai as a radio operator. He received orders to go home on Nov. 17, 1945. On the trip home, he twice saw his brother Kenneth, also a serviceman. On Jan. 11, 1946, he was discharged from the Army and the next day met his son Paul Jr. for the first time.

In his words: "In early August, I was transferred to Kunming, China. I basically had little to do while awaiting transfer, so on my 22nd birthday, I played some poker. I lost my $15, so I went and sold a carton of cigarettes for $10, went back and played again. After about one-and-a-half hours and after being lucky, I had $355. I put $300 in my pocket and sent it home to my wife (Ruth, below). Gradually, I lost part of the $55, so I quit. I went to my tent to take a nap. About an hour later, guys were shooting guns. When I asked what was going on, they said the war was over."

Sentimental journeys

CLAUDIO ORSI BRAVELY BATTLED ENEMY PLANES as a young tail gunner on a B-24 bomber during World War II. ★ But the South Omaha man found his eyes watering in 2008 as he approached the national memorial that honors him and the millions of others who served during the war. Orsi was among about 1,500 World War II veterans from Nebraska and western Iowa who traveled to Washington on Honor Flights in 2008 and 2009. ★ Preparations for the trip brought back some unpleasant memories for him. "I had one of my bad-mission dreams," he said. "You never forget about the bad ones." ★ But as he walked away from the National World War II Memorial, his thoughts were on the guys he flew with in the war. Of the 14 who served in his crew, he was the only one still living. "This is for my buddies," he said.

A MOMENT ALONE at Arlington National Cemetery.
Timothy Terry of Columbus found some time on his own
in the Washington area, which he visited with other veterans
as part of the Honor Flights program.

VETERAN JOHN DICKINSON OF OMAHA, right, and other veterans at the National World War II Memorial in 2008.

'Often the first time in their lives that anybody has thanked them'

BY JOSEPH MORTON

AS YOUNG BUCKS, they charged enemy positions, shot down attacking planes and traveled the globe serving their country.

They landed at Normandy and liberated Europe. They wrested Iwo Jima from the Japanese.

In their 80s or even 90s, American veterans of World War II found that their steps had slowed a bit, and they had a few more aches and pains.

But they could still remember.

About 1,500 veterans flew from Omaha to Washington in 2008 and 2009 on Heartland Honor Flights, which were organized by Bill and Evonne Williams of Omaha and funded by private donations. The flights were created to enable veterans to visit the World War II Memorial before they were too frail.

The flights were intended to give members of the Greatest Generation an opportunity to see the memorial while they were still capable of making the trip. The customary schedule of the flights included a couple of hours at the World War II Memorial and then other stops, such as the Marine Corps War Memorial and Arlington National Cemetery.

ELDON GARBER OF NORTH BEND, NEB., left, greets Leonard Arenas of Omaha at the memorial.

Most of the World War II veterans were in their 80s and 90s. Veterans of Korea and Vietnam who were terminally ill also were allowed to go.

World War II veterans are the most humble, most appreciative, strongest and most patriotic people who walk the earth, said Earl Morse, founder and president of National Honor Flight.

When he accompanied veterans to Washington, Morse said, he often asked them what it was like when they came home from the war.

"One man told me that when they sailed into New York from Europe, they cried when they saw the Statue of Liberty," Morse said. "He said, 'Most of us thought we would never see it again.' "

It was difficult, Morse said, to understand the Honor Flight concept in the abstract.

"You can tell people about what it felt like, pushing a veteran in a wheelchair through an airport with people clapping and cheering for them, but until you experience it, you don't really understand," Morse said. "Many people in the crowd are crying, the veteran is crying, and well, my allergies always act up right at that time."

The trip to the World War II Memorial was often the only "welcome home" these veterans received, Morse said. Many of the veterans came home three or six months after the war ended, after the country stopped having parades.

"When they step off that plane in Washington to cheers, it's often the first time in their lives that anybody has thanked them," Morse said.

Cindy Slone's father, 91-year-old Donald Dragoo of Lincoln, died in 2008 on the return leg of one of the Heartland Honor Flights.

Slone, who made the trip with him, said her father told her about a time when his gun wouldn't fire during combat. He thought his life was over. After surviving the war, he felt the rest of his years were a bonus, she said.

"He felt he had cheated death by 65 years," she said.

She said it was fitting that he died among his fellow veterans. "He died with his comrades," Slone said.

Bob Anderson of Atlantic, Iowa, takes a picture at the World War II Memorial, which opened in 2004.

Ken Martin of Lincoln poses for a picture with his great-grandchildren, from left, Austin, Aspen, Avalon and Ainsley Steger.

The Omaha Press Club honored World-Herald war correspondents Bill Billotte (left) and Lawrence Youngman in 1995 for their work during World War II. Caricatures of the two were unveiled as part of the club's collection of "Faces on the Barroom Floor." The middle caricature is of WOW radio's Ray Clark, who broadcast live on July 29, 1945, from the B-29 Superfortress "City of Omaha" during a raid on Japan.

'The real story was the troops'

BY ROBERT DORR

THE WORLD-HERALD'S CORRESPONDENTS in World War II had firsthand encounters with Eisenhower, Patton and MacArthur, but their newspaper stories in 1944 and 1945 focused on the experiences of average soldiers.

"My job was to be with the troops," said Bill Billotte, who covered fighting in Okinawa and the Philippines. "The real story was the troops."

Billotte's counterpart in Europe, Lawrence Youngman, covered the Allied advance across France after D-Day. Both sought out men and women from Nebraska and Iowa and told their stories for World-Herald readers.

Youngman arrived in London on June 5, 1944, the day before D-Day. He didn't know about the invasion until after it began. He got the news from a hotel elevator operator, who observed, "Well, it's started."

Youngman linked up with the 134th Infantry Regiment, a Nebraska National Guard unit, which was undergoing final training before crossing the English Channel to join the fighting.

An incident that Youngman observed during a training exercise showed the different command styles of Gen. Dwight Eisenhower and Lt. Gen. George Patton.

Patton became enraged when a soldier didn't move quickly enough in a simulated attack on a machine gun nest, Youngman recalled in 1994. "What's that son of a bitch doing lying on his belly? Tell him to get up and get going," Patton ordered.

A few minutes later, Eisenhower watched as a rifleman's bullets missed the mark. He asked the soldier about the range on his rifle's sights. He learned they were elevated for 300 yards.

Youngman's story continued: "Eisenhower told him he would do better if he changed the sights to 200 yards. And he did do better."

The 134th Regiment, commanded by Col. Butler B. Miltonberger of North Platte, arrived in France on July 5. Youngman accompanied the 134th across France. He wrote his stories on a portable typewriter that he had bought used and took hundreds of pictures of the soldiers he interviewed.

While Youngman was shaving with cold water in his helmet, he said, a bullet hit a tree two or three feet above his head. That was his closest call.

Youngman and two other correspondents drove into Paris in a jeep as the city was being liberated by Free French troops. Scattered fighting still was going on, but Parisians already were flocking onto the boulevards.

In December of 1944, Youngman's eyes began to go bad, and he returned to Omaha. He said he believed fatigue caused his eye problem.

Youngman said he deeply admired the soldiers he wrote about. About the 134th, he said, "There was no better fighting machine than this unit. That could be argued, but that's the way I feel about it."

After Youngman returned, Billotte went to the Pacific.

He left in April 1945 by troop transport and immediately began writing stories. "We'd never had a troop transport story (in The World-Herald)," he said.

A few times he was with Gen. Douglas MacArthur, the Pacific commander. "We were fortunate to have MacArthur," Billotte said. "He knew the Oriental mind."

Billotte spent most of his time with the troops.

After fierce fighting in the Philippine mountains, his June 17, 1945, story began:

"High in these Caraballo Mountains 150 miles from Manila the most savage fighting in the Philippines has raged. It is rifle-butt, bayonet, grenade and dynamite against thousands of fanatical Japanese fighting to the last ditch in caves."

Billotte never liked the war he covered. "It was more miserable than spectacular," he said.

He and the other correspondents had expected to cover the invasion of Japan in October or November of 1945. They were just as surprised as the rest of the world when the atomic bombs were dropped that ended the war in August, he said.

Billotte had a place aboard the battleship Missouri when the Japanese signed surrender documents. He watched the occupation of Tokyo and wrote that he wished that "the millions of GIs who made all this possible could be here."

After the war, Billotte specialized in crime and court news. His stories resulted in the criminal indictment of several public officials and cleaned up a backlog of thousands of traffic tickets. When he retired in 1975, after 43 years as a World-Herald reporter, Billotte said he had worked during a "golden age" of journalism. "It's been a great life," he said. "I wouldn't have done anything else."

Bill Billotte died in 1997.

Youngman left the newspaper in 1946 to start Travel and Transport Inc. and became highly successful in the travel agency business.

"After I got back (from the war), the things I'd been doing didn't seem quite as interesting," he said about ending his career as a reporter.

Lawrence Youngman died in 2003.

KENNETH SCHRAM
Town: Tekamah
Service: Navy Pacific Fleet

In the war: Basic training at Great Lakes, Ill., then to temporary duty at Treasure Island, Calif. Assigned to the USS Baltimore (heavy attack cruiser). Sailed to the southwest Pacific to join Admiral William F. Halsey's Third Fleet for the last campaign in the Philippines. Shortly after, the Third Fleet was in a typhoon. Three ships and 800 sailors were lost. In spring 1945, participated in the campaigns of Iwo Jima and Okinawa. Returned to Hawaii in July 1945, just before the atomic bomb was dropped on Japan. Returned to Japan in November 1945 as part of the occupation force and stayed until February 1946. Discharged at St. Louis in May 1946.

In his words: "I can't really describe how it feels when the situation is over and we were all able to go home. It was really a great day to have it come to an end. A lot of guys were never able to come home. I feel fortunate to have been one of those who made it home."

YOUNGMAN AND BILLOTTE INTERVIEWED EACH OTHER for World-Herald stories in 1945 after the war had ended. Youngman wrote: "We found that we had some experiences in common. For one thing, we were frequently just plain scared. Secondly, we often paused to ask ourselves why did we ever want to be war correspondents in the first place, and why had we let ourselves in for this sort of thing. That usually happened when we were very tired or very frightened. And with me, it also happened frequently as I leaned down to lace up my boots in the morning. We're also in agreement that we are thankful to be right here in Omaha. Most of all, we're thankful that our soldiers no longer have to attack dug-in emplacements defended by automatic fire, or make bomb runs through heavy flak."

The war: Wrapped up and put away

BY DAVID HENDEE

ED MAUSER

ED MAUSER ALWAYS SAID that he packed away his memories and moved on with his life after World War II.

But a tiny suitcase found in a dark, draped-off nook in the basement of Mauser's small Omaha home after his death in 2011 shed light on his experiences with the Army paratrooper unit known as the "Band of Brothers."

The secret cache contained a Nazi swastika banner, German army medals, a leather belt with a buckle from the notorious Waffen-SS and Mauser's Purple Heart and two Bronze Star medals in their original boxes.

Mauser's family is convinced that he stashed away the souvenirs, medals and other war memorabilia decades ago and never thought of them again.

"He made a vow to my mother to never talk about the war, and I think he just forgot about all of this out of respect for her," said Laurie Fowler of Bellevue, Mauser's daughter.

Mauser was a 25-year-old Illinois watchmaker when he was drafted into the Army during the early weeks of WWII. He eventually volunteered for paratrooper training and ended up with the 101st Airborne Division's 506th Parachute Infantry Regiment. He was a private first class and rifleman with the 2nd Battalion's Easy Company — the unit made famous by the "Band of Brothers" book and HBO television miniseries.

Mauser's death at age 94 stilled stories of the wartime experiences of a soft-spoken man who found late-in-life fame as a "Band of Brothers" veteran. Or so his family thought.

Four days after Mauser was buried with military honors in an Omaha cemetery, his daughter stopped at his Westridge neighborhood home with her husband, Mike Fowler, and son, Robert.

While Laurie cleaned out the kitchen refrigerator, Mike and Robert checked out the basement. Poking around metal shelves placed against a concrete-block wall, Mike moved an old cooler and wig box off the top shelf. He noticed something wedged against the rim joist on top of the wall. He reached amid the ductwork above his head and pulled out an object.

It was an old, green overnight case with rounded edges and a strap of leather for a handle. A sticker from the Fort Hamilton Hotel in Rock Island, Ill., identified the owner as Jeanne Mauser of LaSalle, Ill. She was one of Ed Mauser's four sisters.

Mike set the dusty bag on a small table, flipped two clasps and opened the lid. Neatly arranged five inches deep inside the 16-by-10-inch case was Mauser's long-forgotten war memorabilia.

"As soon as I saw what was in there, I closed it up," Fowler said. "I wanted Laurie to see what was there."

They spent the next half-hour in the living room in amazed inspection of the nearly three dozen items in the case.

First were Mauser's Purple Heart and Bronze Stars, the same lost medals U.S. Rep. Lee Terry of Omaha arranged for Mauser to receive in a special ceremony last May.

"He forgot that he received these, which is amazing, especially two Bronze Stars," said Mike Fowler, a retired Air Force officer.

Fowler pulled out a coiled belt and unrolled it. An eagle perched on a swastika decorated the silver metal buckle at the end. The motto of the Waffen-SS — the armed wing of Germany's Nazi Party — encircled the symbol.

Then came a German army sheepskin and wool winter hat and a few German medals. One was for duty on the Russian front.

They opened a small, blue checkbook box Mauser's mother had used to mail her son something during the war. Inside were Mauser's original uniform patches (and a German patch), thread and a razor blade Mauser apparently used to cut the emblems off his uniforms. Several cut threads still hang from the well-worn Screaming Eagle patches.

"That's when it sank in what this was," Mike Fowler said. "This was stuff he had worn. These were his patches."

DAYS AFTER ED MAUSER'S FUNERAL, Laurie and Mike Fowler, Mauser's daughter and son-in-law, found a green case with dozens of items from his World War II service. Inside were medals, patches and other items, as well as Nazi memorabilia.

Neatly folded in the bottom of the case was bright red cloth of rough cotton. A short piece of jute string was tied to one of four brass grommets. The Fowlers unfolded it. In the middle of a white circle in the red field was a black swastika.

"It sent chills down my back," Laurie Fowler said.

Everything in the case was clean and in excellent condition. No bug holes. No mildew.

Mike Fowler said the family had no idea where or when during his months in combat Mauser collected the German army paraphernalia. His service ran from D-Day through postwar occupation duty in Austria.

Mauser sometimes told people that he found two Nazi flags in an officers barracks at Berchtesgaden. He said he gave one to Easy Company buddy Eddie Sabo and sold the other to a soldier desperate for a souvenir.

"Ed would say, 'I could kick myself. I gave one away and sold the other. It was all I had,' " Mike Fowler said.

No one knows if the banner in the overnight case was one of the flags Mauser recalled or if it was another he had forgotten.

Kevin Hymel, an Arlington, Va., military historian, said the artifacts are part of a bigger story that started when veterans returned home.

"As they enter the twilight years, they begin reminiscing, sharing their story outside the immediate family of veterans. These things create a new awareness of what they accomplished," Hymel said. "It's the last act of the veteran's story — the final chapter of the book."

Laurie Fowler said her father apparently stashed the memorabilia in the hiding spot when the family bought the house about December 1960, moving from Illinois. Laurie was 10 months old.

"I grew up in the house, and I never knew it (the overnight case) was there," she said. "I bet Dad took it and hid it right away — behind Mom's pantry shelves, suitcases, a cedar chest and other things."

Mauser's wife, Irene, had two brothers wounded in WWII, one seriously. She didn't want to hear about the war, Laurie Fowler said.

Not until his wife died in 2008 did Mauser step into the limelight as a "Band of Brothers" veteran. He always downplayed his role in the unit, however, preferring to talk about the exploits of other soldiers. But glimpses of Mauser's war emerged in recent years.

Mike Fowler said Mauser apparently kept in periodic contact over the years with Don Malarkey, an Easy Company platoon buddy. They exchanged telephone calls, but only when Mauser's wife was away from the house.

Mauser, one of the oldest soldiers in the unit, had regularly teamed up with Malarkey to clean up on their buddies in poker games.

"Ed was a smoker. Ed was a drinker. And Ed was a card player," said Brian Kruse of Omaha, who assisted Mauser on two tours of Easy Company sites in Europe. "He was a colorful guy. He didn't talk about everything he did, because he didn't want people to think poorly of him."

In his final years, Mauser told his son-in-law about his first known combat kill.

Mauser and two other soldiers were securing an empty house in a French village one night. Mauser stepped out the back door. Chickens were underfoot. Mauser heard a noise from the barn and noticed a pulsating flashlight and a figure descending stairs or a ladder.

Fowler said the man in the barn shined the flashlight at Mauser and ordered him to halt. Instead, Mauser dropped to the ground and fired one round from his rifle, killing a German major.

"Ed said he was so mad, but not for shooting an enemy soldier," Fowler said.

Rather, Mauser had fallen into chicken manure when he dropped to shoot. The odor stayed with him for days. He also sheepishly explained to Fowler why he was deaf in his left ear. He had slipped during a patrol and caught himself with the butt of his rifle. The impact of the stumble caused the rifle to fire at the moment the muzzle was next to Mauser's ear.

Mauser watched "Band of Brothers" two or three times in his final weeks.

"That's all he wanted," Fowler said.

Some of the remaining members of Easy Company called Mauser to say their last goodbyes.

Laurie Fowler said stories that surfaced toward the end of Mauser's life and the hidden war memorabilia help her understand how the war forged her father.

"A cousin once told me that their family was always so proud of Uncle Ed," she said.

Laurie wondered what they knew.

"All Mom would say was that he was a paratrooper in the war."

From the forgotten suitcase

U.S. ARMY

- Two Bronze Star medals
- Purple Heart medal
- One Bronze Star ribbon bar
- European Campaign ribbon bar
- Five 101st Airborne Division Screaming Eagle shoulder patches
- Two 17th Airborne Division shoulder patches
- One Army paratrooper glider cap patch
- One Army paratrooper cap patch
- Three Army private chevrons for uniform sleeve
- Three Overseas Service bars worn on lower left sleeve
- Canvas web belt with chrome buckle
- Stars and Stripes clipping from Nov. 6, 1943
- Olive drab uniform thread
- Double-edged razor blade in original paper wrapper

GERMAN ARMY

- Red Nazi banner (about 29 by 37½ inches) with black swastika on white circle
- Leather belt with Waffen-SS buckle inscribed: "Meine Ehre heißt Treue (My honor is loyalty)"
- "Russian Front Medal" inscribed: "Winterschlacht im osten 1941/42 (Winter battle in the East 1941-42)," with 4-inch red ribbon
- Black Wound Badge for soldiers wounded once or twice by hostile action or frostbitten in the line of duty
- Sheepskin and wool winter hat with eagle-swastika patch and an insignia
- Eagle-swastika patch
- Unidentified ribbon bar with crossed swords for combatants

'I know all these guys'

WHEN HISTORIAN STEPHEN E. AMBROSE'S "Band of Brothers" was made into the hit HBO miniseries in 2001, Mauser was caring for his ailing wife. He didn't attend Easy Company conferences or tours.

One day, he asked son-in-law Mike Fowler how to view a DVD. Mauser had the "Band of Brothers" box set.

Fowler inserted a random disc, and the two sat back to watch. Mauser started a running commentary.

"That church wasn't on that side of the road," he said about a combat scene.

Fowler asked Mauser what he was talking about.

"It was on the other side. It was over there," Mauser replied.

Fowler asked Mauser how he knew that fact.

"This is my unit," he said. "I know all these guys."

That was the family's first knowledge that Mauser had been part of the best-known company in the Army during WWII.

ED MAUSER, pictured in 1943 after he earned his paratrooper wings during World War II.

MEMORIES OF A GENERATION ★

ELMER PANKONIN

Town: Grant

Service: Navy, 35th Construction Battalion (Seabees)

In the war: Unit took the lead in the assault on Manila in the Philippines, and later built an airstrip on the island of Luzon.

In his words: "At 3 a.m., I drove a big D8 Caterpillar to shore, mowing down coconut trees, and the Marines just followed us in. There were snipers in the trees all over. … I just wanted to get it over with and get home. I had a son I hadn't even seen."

MAURI TURNER

Town: Omaha

Service: Navy, 122nd Naval Construction Battalion

In the war: Led a team of surveyors helping build bases in the Philippines and New Guinea.

In his words: "We'd go in with landing groups, start in on construction and lay out airfields and roads, hospitals and docks, anything connected with a forward base. We worked 24 hours, usually 12-hour shifts. What may surprise people — it surprised me — was we'd be able to build an airfield and have our planes flying off of it in three days."

ELDON ROSCHEWSKI

Town: Imperial

Service: Navy

In the war: Enlisted before he finished his senior year of high school, went to boot camp at Farragut, Idaho, then served most of his tour on the USS General J.H. McRae, a transport ship. After the war, he was assigned to the destroyer USS Sarsfield out of Key West, Fla., until he had enough points to go home. He was honorably discharged in May 1946.

In his words: "They needed men in a hurry, so we only had 4½ weeks training. We trained with wooden guns because the real ones were being used to fight the war. I was sent to Treasure Island, Calif., and trained aboard ship while it was being built. I served on the General J.H. McRae. It was built for transporting troops, although we also transported casualties and prisoners. The war became real and very sad when we had to have burials at sea, as we would be out to sea 10 days or more and couldn't keep bodies that long. When we were in enemy waters we had destroyer escorts."

LLOYD ZACHARIAE

Town: Omaha

Service: Army Air Forces

In the war: Fighter pilot in the 364th Squadron, 357th Fighter Group, Eighth Air Force. Shared the sky with Chuck Yeager, also a member of the 357th, over occupied Europe on numerous occasions. Named his P-51 Mustang "Mom Smith's Lil Angel," after his housemother in college.

In his words: "I don't care to rehash the horrors of war. Combat isn't glamorous or glorious. Instead I want to focus on the positive, the good things that resulted from that awful war. The sense of camaraderie and purpose were indescribable, both overseas and stateside. … Instead of being heroes, the truth was we were young and cocky. There were close calls. I ran out of fuel twice and crash-landed in France both times. I walked away from both of those. After the first crash landing, I was listed as missing in action. I returned to my base just before the telegram was to be sent. … We all wanted to be home, but I wouldn't trade the experience for anything. It was the best time of my life."

VIELA JUNE (FLEMING) ESKEW

Town: McCook

Service: U.S. Army captain, 31st General Hospital

In the war: Sent to New Caledonia, a French island in the South Pacific. Then sent to Espiritu Santo in the New Hebrides Islands, New Guinea and the Philippines.

In her words: "Our hearts went out to the young men who came to us with severe, crippling injuries. Oh, the tragedy of war. Our quarters were wooden barracks open on all sides to catch the cooler breezes. There were latrines and showers, a change from washing up in our helmets. We each had our own mess gear and washed them in barrels of hot, soapy water. The food was adequate for nutrition but not variety. Our cots had bamboo poles with cross bars with nets attached to keep out the many bugs and rats that traveled around at night. Often you could feel a jolt as a rat hit the side of the net. We inspected our shoes each morning to shake out any occupant who had taken up residence and dust the inside to remove the mold that would grow while we slept. There were many geckos. At night termites were heard gnawing away at the bamboo net supports, and in the morning small mounds of bamboo dust were found on the floor."

FRANK ROBERTS

Town: Dunlap, Iowa

Service: U.S. Army

In the war: He was drafted into the Army in October 1942 and served for 37 months. He was in the 50th Engineers and learned bridge construction.

In his words: "I remember sailing under the Golden Gate Bridge, staying overnight on Alcatraz Island before sailing for Attu, the most western island in the Aleutian chain in the North Pacific. The ocean was rough, and we almost lost a bulldozer off the deck. Most of the men were seasick all the way. We were under attack by the Japanese while going ashore. We dug foxholes and slept in two-man tents until we could dig into the ground for huts. We built runways, put in pipelines and built dams for our water supply. A hard part of the war was carrying our dead men to be buried. There were very few Japanese taken prisoner as they all had hand grenades attached to their chests and would pull the pin rather than be taken prisoner. I was on Attu 21 months and was honorably discharged in November 1945. I married Eula Jeane Rannells, who had been working at Martin Bomber Plant until we dropped the bomb on Japan that ended the war."

LOUIS T. JODLOWSKI

Town: Omaha

Service: Sergeant, U.S. Army Air Forces

In the war: In December 1942, he became the fourth member of his family to be drafted. After training as an aircraft electrician, he was sent to Maxton, N.C., where he was assigned to the 375th Troop Carrier Group, 57th Squadron. He boarded ship at Camp Stoneman in San Francisco and sailed to Brisbane, Australia. The next stop was Port Moresby, New Guinea. He also served in the Philippines and in Okinawa. He was discharged from Fort Logan, Colo., after two years, nine months and 15 days of service.

In his words: "When I was stationed in Manila, I got together with my brother Leo, who was in the anti-aircraft battery, and my brother Adam, who was in the field artillery and received the Bronze Star at Guadalcanal. We spent one night together with someone named 'Old Grand Dad.' Went to church in Manila, and after Mass, I had to be back by 1400 hours because our outfit was taking off for Naha in Okinawa."

FRED "FRITZ" WORTMAN

Town: West Point, Neb.

Service: Trained as an electric generator mechanic at Fort Dodge, Iowa. He was sent to the South Pacific with the 914th Air Force Engineer Company.

In the war: (At left in photo below) Served on a ship that participated in operations in the Philippines, Okinawa and New Guinea. His brother, Ray, was one of several anti-aircraft gunners (20 mm) on a floating repair and salvage ship. He also assisted in repair of aircraft that were picked up at sea and on island beaches.

In his words: (Ray, at right in photo below, always told his family this story) "After encounters with Japanese forces in numerous operations, never knowing if we would ever see each other again, Fritz and I just happened to cross paths. It happened on a Sunday morning in a harbor at Okinawa. I was leaning on my ship's railing having a smoke and watching ships in the harbor. I just happened to notice a ship going by, and there was a person leaning on the railing having a smoke also. As the ship went by, I couldn't believe who it was, and neither could Fritz. We saw one another and gave a little wave to each other in disbelief. As they say, it's a small world."

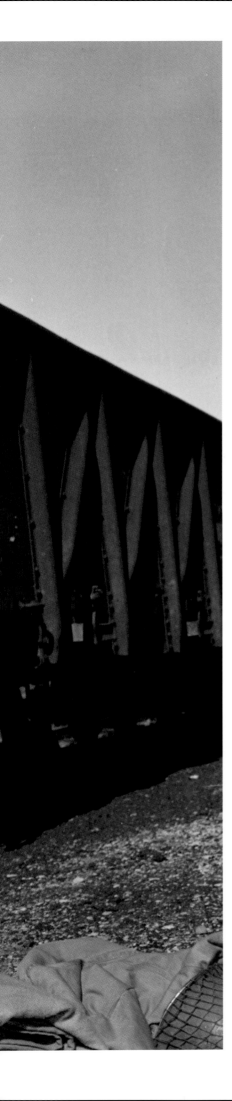

'The Homecoming'

THE APPEAL OF EARLE "BUDDY" BUNKER'S "THE HOMECOMING" was enduring. ★ The World-Herald photographer's image of Lt. Col. Robert Moore's reunion with his wife, daughter and nephew in 1943 has been published time and again in books and magazines and brochures. Moore's children and grandchildren found the Pulitzer Prize winner in their history books. ★ Serving in Vietnam brought Moore's son, Bobby, a deeper understanding of the photo. "At first the picture was just a matter of pride," Bobby Moore wrote to Bunker in 1973. "But now, having been to war myself and returning to my loved ones, there is something in the picture that gives it a deeper meaning , something I can't explain, but feel. Perhaps I can relate to my Dad's feelings at that moment. Whatever it is, I do know that 'The Homecoming' means more to me — it's a classic."

A perfect shot

WORLD-HERALD PHOTOGRAPHER Earle "Buddy" Bunker barely snapped his classic homecoming picture. Cameras didn't come with motor drives in 1943, or even with a crank that advanced film with a quick flip of the thumb. Electronic flashes were off in the Buck Rogers future somewhere. Bunker was lugging a Speed Graphic camera, with an attached arm for holding flash bulbs, as he waited at the Villisca, Iowa, train depot for Lt. Col. Robert Moore to return home from World War II.

The nine-pound camera included a holder for two 3½-by-5-inch sheets of film. After taking the first shot, the photographer had to insert an opaque slide that protected the film from light, remove the holder, turn it around for the second shot and remove the slide protecting the second sheet of film. Then he had to cock the shutter and fire again. And that was if the picture was already focused. Even a swift, seasoned photographer needed several seconds to prepare for the next shot. And, if he was using a flash, as Bunker was, he had to pop out the old bulb and insert a new one.

Bunker snapped his camera as Moore stepped off the train. The flash bulb didn't fire. Muttering under his breath, Bunker popped in a new bulb and flipped the film holder around for the second shot. He finished reloading and snapped the shutter just as Moore embraced his excited daughter, Nancy.

Standing next to Bunker was J. Harold Cowan, a World-Herald reporter who also used a Speed Graphic, because he frequently traveled without a photographer. He fired his camera at the same instant.

After shooting other pictures as Moore visited with townspeople, Bunker and Cowan hurried back to Omaha to make their deadline for the evening paper. Each had captured the welcoming hug, but Bunker's picture was sharper, perfectly focused.

"I think I was probably shaking just a little," Cowan recalled in 1997.

Some have speculated through the years that the photo was staged, noting that the train in the background was a freight train. The subsequent, clearly spontaneous, pictures make that appear doubtful. In one of them, Bunker had stepped back farther and shifted his angle, showing the full depot platform, a freight train on the left and passenger train to the right. A home movie of the event was uncovered in 2008, confirming once and for all the sequence of events.

The picture was republished widely, winning Bunker the 1944 Pulitzer Prize. It also was honored by Kodak in 1956 as the best human interest flash photograph of the previous 25 years. It was the pinnacle of Bunker's distinguished 38-year career at The World-Herald. He died of a heart attack in 1975 at age 62.

Cowan was glad for the fame that came to his colleague. "I goofed and he didn't," he said. "He was a good friend and I was very happy that he got it. I didn't have the faintest bit of jealousy." Cowan died in 2000 at age 90.

"The Homecoming" won the 1944 Pulitzer Prize and was honored by Kodak in 1956 as the best human interest flash photograph of the previous 25 years.

EARLE "BUDDY" BUNKER in 1943

THE FOUR IN THE PHOTO

Robert Ross Moore, the soldier in the famous homecoming photograph, spent four decades in the Army and National Guard, retiring in 1963 as a brigadier general. He was on active duty during World War II, first leading troops in battle in North Africa and then starting a combat command course for officers at Fort Benning, Ga. Army records say he was 5 feet 10 inches tall, with gray eyes and brown hair. As a civilian, he was a partner in the Moore Bros. drugstore in Villisca, Iowa, and later was city clerk in Red Oak, Iowa, and bailiff of the Montgomery County District Court in Red Oak. He died after a stroke in 1991.

Dorothy Dee Moore was the oldest of three sisters (she also had two brothers) who worked for their mother at Goldie's diner on the square in Villisca after their father died. She was married to Bob Moore for 48 years. She had a son and a daughter and, except for helping in the drugstore, stayed at home to care for the house and family. She died of cancer in 1982.

Nancy Jo Moore was 4 years old when her father left home to train for World War II. She wrote him letters regularly during the war and greeted him at the Villisca depot with a homecoming hug. She married Jim Watt, and they had a daughter and two sons. After battling multiple sclerosis for several years, she died from injuries in a car crash in 1984. "She had a smile that was as big as Texas," said Carolyn Mitchell Olson of Red Oak, a high school classmate who was the maid of honor at her wedding. "Nancy was always bubbly."

Michael Croxdale was the son of Ed and Eva Croxdale. His mother was Dorothy Moore's sister. He was 2½ years old when his uncle returned from the war, and he ran forward with his cousin and aunt, joining the Moores in the historic photo. As a youth and an adult, he was known for his flamboyance. "If it was a crazy fad, he was one of the first to do it," said classmate Sandy Penwell Taylor. Like his father, Mike became a doctor and served in the Army. He was decorated for valor in Vietnam. He died of cancer in 1993.

Through war and life, he soldiered on

BY STEPHEN BUTTRY

THE HOMECOMING WAS JOYOUS — an exuberant hug frozen forever by a camera's flash.

A homecoming, though, is more than a happy ending. A war hero and his loved ones receive no exemption from life's heartaches.

World-Herald photographer Earle "Buddy" Bunker captured the family reunion on July 15, 1943, after Lt. Col. Robert Moore stepped off the train in Villisca, greeted by his 6-year-old daughter, Nancy; his wife, Dorothy; and his 2-year-old nephew, Michael Croxdale.

The photograph, one of the most enduring images from World War II, symbolized the hopes of a generation whose men fought that war. Not a single face shows in the Pulitzer Prize-winning photo, but the joy is overwhelming — a daddy in a round military cap stooping to wrap his arms around a spindly-legged daughter reaching up to his broad shoulders in a welcoming hug. Mom waits her turn, a hand to her face in delight. An excited little boy watches.

At depots across America, the scene was repeated countless times as fathers and sons and husbands returned from battle. Implicit in the joy of each homecoming was the understanding that more than a quarter of a million families grieved for soldiers who would not come home. In many ways, Bunker's photo captured a nation's anxiety and relief.

Robert Ross Moore was the second of three sons of Ross and Jessie Moore, who owned a drugstore on the town square of Villisca, about 75 miles southeast of Omaha. The Moore sons tended the soda counter.

But Villisca in the early 1900s didn't provide an idyllic rural life, not for the Moore family. During the night on June 10, 1912, when Bob was 7, someone took an ax and killed his uncle, aunt, four cousins and two visiting children.

The Villisca ax murders, still Iowa's biggest unsolved crime, dominated life in the town and especially in the Moore family for years. A suspect was acquitted. A detective hired by Ross Moore accused the local state senator, F.F. Jones, of hiring the killer. Jones sued for slander.

Folks in town picked sides and pointed fingers. Children from one camp were told not to play with those in the other, and adults would not patronize merchants in opposing camps. For years, the Presbyterian (Moores') and Methodist (Joneses') churches, across the street from each other, would not cooperate on anything. Fear endured in the town and the family. Bob Moore told of a visitor who stayed out late one night. The guest let himself in quietly, hoping not to disturb anyone, and was met by Ross Moore, wielding his shotgun.

Bob Moore was profoundly affected by the murders of his playmates. In his youth, he attended one of the three trials resulting from the murders. Though he talked with his children about them, he was critical of continuing public discussion of the murders.

"He wanted it left alone. He was very adamant," said Jan Castle Renander, editor of the Red Oak Express, who became a close friend after meeting Moore when she wrote a story about a 1986 novel based on the slayings. "He remembered in his childhood how it divided the town."

As much as the ax murders divided Villisca, the Army National Guard united it, and Moore was always glad to talk

THE MOORE BROS. DRUGSTORE was a popular gathering place on Villisca's town square until it closed in 1962. When Bob Moore returned from the war in 1943, his family painted words of welcome on the drugstore window.

about the Guard. He enlisted at the age of 17 and by 1928 was commander of Villisca's Company F, a unit of the 34th Infantry Division. He would work at the drugstore during the week and train on weekends and for two weeks every summer, preparing Villisca's men for battle.

Dennis Neal, a lifelong friend, recalled in 1997 that in a training exercise Moore expressed the leadership style he followed throughout his four-decade Guard and Army career: "Whenever you give an order, tell the person why you gave it."

Moore married Ruby Taylor, a schoolteacher, in Omaha on July 1, 1930, wearing his National Guard uniform. Ruby wasn't the wife waiting at the depot 13 years later. She divorced him after three years, on grounds of cruelty. Court records don't elaborate, but in those days before no-fault divorce, cruelty was a common reason to cite.

Little is known about the marriage, which produced no children. Coming from a time when divorce was considered a scandal, Moore never spoke of his first wife. His son, Robert Moore Jr., who was born in 1945, was out of high school before he learned of his father's first marriage.

Ruby, who remarried, lived in Springfield, Neb., as Ruby Vincent and died in 1997.

On Feb. 10, 1934, six months after his divorce, Moore eloped to Maryville, Mo., with Dorothy Dee Goldsberry, who worked for her widowed mother at Goldie's diner in Villisca.

A year later, Ross Moore died, and his second and third sons, Bob and Bill, took over the drugstore. The oldest son, Wesley "Dinty" Moore, moved away from Villisca as a young adult and later became a vice president of the Great Northern Railroad.

BEFORE THE WAR, Capt. Robert Moore was commander of Company F in the Iowa National Guard.

The children in the famed photo were born as Iowa struggled through the Great Depression and German and Japanese aggression pushed the world into war. On Aug. 23, 1936, Dorothy Moore gave birth to a daughter, Nancy Jo. On Dec. 18, 1940, Dorothy's sister, Eva Croxdale, had a son, Michael Bruce.

Company F was mobilized on the Moores' seventh wedding anniversary as war spread around the globe. On March 2, 1941, the town of Villisca gathered at the Burlington train depot to bid farewell to the 114 men under Moore's command as they left for training at Camp Claiborne, La.

Tucked inside the 36-year-old captain's gear was a Dick Tracy magazine that Nancy had inadvertently set on a stack of clothes as he was packing.

During training and through the war, townsfolk kept up on their servicemen through reports written for the Villisca Review and the Adams County Free Press in Corning by Sgt. Milo Green.

"Captain 'Bob' possessed the magic touch which won and kept the admiration, respect and cooperation of all his men," Green wrote from Camp Claiborne. "He often told me that he'd much rather have a word of praise or a trusting glance from his MEN than a two-page memorandum of commendations from some high-ranking brass hat."

Moore insisted that his men keep in touch with their families. Don Patton recalled being summoned to the headquarters tent at Camp Claiborne. "Patton, how come you haven't written your folks?" the commander inquired. Patton promised to be a more faithful correspondent, and Moore wrote a letter "bailing me out, saying I'd been really busy," Patton recalled.

While Company F trained, the Japanese bombed Pearl Harbor. In May 1942, the troops left for Europe. Company F trained in Northern Ireland at a camp so infested with rats that Green wrote, "I sometimes wondered if the Pied Piper hadn't passed that way."

Michael Croxdale's father also was sent overseas, though not with Company F. Ed Croxdale, a doctor, was sent to the Pacific with the Americal Division.

In July 1942, Company F was inspected in Northern Ireland by King George VI and Queen Elizabeth, the mother of Queen Elizabeth II. Moore served as the queen's personal escort during her visit, serving tea and saving the cup, saucer and spoon (stamped with "US ARMY" on the handle) for posterity.

Moore and his family back home kept in touch through regular letters. "When I get back," he wrote to daughter Nancy on Aug. 4, 1942, "you and I will go swimming every day — Won't we?"

"Dear Daddy," Nancy wrote back, expressing the universal plea to daddies away from home, "Are you going to send me something? I wish you were home to play with me."

Company F moved to Scotland, and yes, Daddy did send something, Scottish tartan fabric. "Mommy can make you a skirt like the little 'boys' wear over here," he wrote.

Dorothy made Nancy a kilt, held together in the front by a large safety pin. A generation later, Nancy bought a similar skirt for her own daughter.

Moore also sent home the Dick Tracy comic and some new comic books, exhorting his daughter to read: "I want to see you get all A's on your report card — you must study and learn. ... Remember your Daddy loves you with all his heart and thinks of you many times a day."

Soon after that letter, Company F was on shipboard, heading for a landing in Algeria on Nov. 8, 1942. Moore, a major

and executive officer of a battalion, earned a Silver Star for gallantry in the Algerian landing. Though not in command of a unit, he rallied some scattered men and directed a flanking action that destroyed a machine-gun nest.

The Iowa troops were met in Africa by German forces led by Field Marshal Erwin Rommel, the famed "Desert Fox." The inexperienced Americans took heavy losses against the seasoned Germans in the mountains of Tunisia.

The commander of the 2nd Battalion was wounded at Sened Station and Moore assumed command. The battalion was assigned to protect a key lookout post on the mountain of Djebel Lessouda. "The Germans gave us everything they had — infantry attacks, tank fire, mortar shells and artillery blasting — for two days," Moore later told an Associated Press war correspondent. "But we lost only three men."

American troops below, though, were captured or forced to retreat, leaving the mountain surrounded by Nazis the evening of Feb. 15, 1943.

Before being captured, one of the commanders sent his superiors a grim assessment of Moore's situation, scrawled on three squares of toilet paper:

"Enemy surrounds 2d Battalion ... Forty tanks known to be around them. Shelled, dive-bombed and tank attack. ... Germans have absolute superiority, ground and air. Unless help from air and army comes immediately ... infantry will lose immeasurably."

At dusk, an American P-40 fighter flew over Moore's troops, dropping a typed note from the regimental commander: "Tank destroyers and infantry will occupy positions T*6363 at 2200 hours tonight to cover your withdrawal. You are to withdraw to position to road west of Blid Ghegas where guides will meet you. Bring everything you can."

To fight their way past the German tanks would have been suicide. And the noose of Nazi forces showed no gaps through which 400 Americans might sneak. A captured German officer told Moore he was heavily outnumbered and should surrender. The stubborn Iowan didn't answer.

Moore decided that the best way to save the lives of his men was to march right through Nazi lines. Under cover of darkness, the Americans set out to march past the enemy.

"We walked past a German 88-millimeter gun position so close we could have touched the gun," Moore told the AP correspondent. "The gun crews must have thought we were Germans, because they did nothing."

A couple of times, Germans called out to the Americans but didn't react when they kept marching in silence.

Near the spot where they were to meet the American troops, Moore heard voices from a clump of bushes and walked ahead to meet them. A man speaking German stepped from the bushes, and Moore turned and walked away. The Germans opened fire. Moore's troops scattered in the darkness, following his plan and confusing the Germans.

"Some big shells were bursting over us then, but they were high and outside," Moore told Midwestern Druggist magazine.

They escaped without casualties, though some previously wounded men and a chaplain who had stayed behind with them were captured.

What the Americans couldn't haul down the mountain on their backs or in their arms they left on the mountain, disabling weapons so the Germans couldn't use them.

"The one thing I didn't leave behind," Moore told the AP, "was a bed-sack I bought in England and carried all over Africa. I decided to bring it along if it was the last thing I ever did."

"Remember your Daddy loves you with all his heart and thinks of you many times a day."

— LETTER FROM
LT. COL. ROBERT MOORE TO
HIS DAUGHTER, NANCY

FACES NOT SEEN IN THE PULITZER-WINNING PHOTO: Bob Moore, his wife, Dorothy, and their 6-year-old daughter, Nancy.

AFTER MONTHS OF EATING K RATIONS, Moore longed for an American hamburger from the family drug-store's luncheonette and soda fountain. He shared a bite, of course, with Nancy.

In the homecoming picture, the bed-sack rests at Moore's feet as he hugs Nancy.

Sgt. Green wrote home about a colonel's effort to order Moore's men back into battle immediately: "Then and there Major Moore proved his sterling worth as both an officer and a considerate and humane gentleman. 'These men are tired, sick and nerve-wracked,' he replied, 'furthermore, half of them have no guns or equipment for combat and I'm not relinquishing one of them for any more action until they're properly rested, fed and re-equipped.'

" 'I said turn those men over to me and that's an order!' barked the colonel. 'I'll do nothing of the kind. I'll stand court-martial first. Those men are exhausted and deserve a good rest and I'm going to see that they get it!' was Major Moore's retort. The men got the rest and new equipment and Major Moore, who soon after became a lieutenant colonel, was not court-martialed, I'm happy to report."

Moore also endured a tirade from legendary Gen. George S. Patton, whose son-in-law was among the many troops taken prisoner in North Africa. Moore despised Gen. Patton, telling a story of how he once insisted that Moore take an objective "even if he had to send back a truckload of dog tags."

Moore returned to battle soon after the escape from Lessouda, and a bomb exploded 15 feet from him on April 9, causing a concussion that made him lose his eyesight for several days.

Green encountered Moore, "a sad and worried man," on his way back to the front: "He spoke several times of his wife Dorothy and of little Nancy and wondered if he would ever see them again."

Moore's time to see the family was fast approaching. The Army was learning costly lessons in the desert battlefields and needed to teach those lessons to new troops training back in the States.

Bob Moore was needed at the homefront.

About noon on Saturday, July 10, 1943, Dorothy Moore answered the phone and heard Bob's voice on the other end: He was in New York City and coming home soon.

The family waited seven hours in Omaha for his plane on July 14. His flight to Chicago was delayed by bad weather and he failed to make connections. The family received word that he would be arriving in Villisca at 9:30 a.m. on Thursday, July 15, on Burlington Train No. 6.

Nancy was too excited to eat or sleep.

Banners and flags welcomed the hero home. An arch of all the flags of the Allied nations was assembled in the street in front of the Moore Bros. drugstore. A crowd gathered at the depot.

J. Harold Cowan wrote this account for the Evening World-Herald:

VILLISCA, IOWA — LT. COL. BOB MOORE, officer-hero of this town of 2,000, came home from Africa Thursday.

He stepped off the train, arms burdened with a bulging flight bag, his helmet, his blankets.

A piping 6-year-old's voice shrilled across the platform. "Daddy. Daddy! Daddy!" it cried.

Nancy, his daughter, ran across the platform, arms out. The bag, the helmet, the blanket, thumped to the planking. Nancy was swept into her Daddy's arms.

She nestled there for the first time in 16 months, her tiny face against his tropical sun-darkened cheek. Nancy sobbed. So did her mother, who had come over. So did her grandmother. … And tears trickled unashamedly down Col. Moore's cheeks.

Nancy would tell her own daughter, "It was like the most wonderful thing to have him step off that train."

The townspeople rushed to Moore not only to welcome him, but also to ask about those still at the war. He offered encouragement to a mother whose son was fine, comfort to a father whose son was captured. He visited with Sheriff Frank Miller, whose son Wes was the first Villisca man to die in Africa.

The welcome continued at the park in the town square, and then at the drugstore.

"All Villisca took on a patriotic air," the Review reported, "and enthusiasm, without undue ostentation, glowed from the face of the hundreds of friends of 'Bob' who crowded the downtown streets during the afternoon to show the city's honored son they are overjoyed at his safe return home."

Mike Croxdale, whose excitement at age 2 was evident in the photos of Moore's homecoming, was puzzled when his own father later returned from the war in the Pacific. After months of hearing about the war against the Japanese "yellow peril," young Mike was stunned to see his father with a yellow cast to his skin, caused by quinine he had taken for malaria.

Moore stayed briefly in Villisca, traveling to neighboring towns to speak at luncheons and update the home folk on how their boys were doing at the front. He made a point to call on the families of men who had been killed or captured.

Soon Moore was sent to Fort Benning, Ga., where he helped start a leadership course and instructed 40,000 officers. They taught more than tactics, as a press release from the Infantry School at Fort Benning explained:

"Colonel Moore lists three things that make men fight: Pride in self, pride in the man's organization, and hate. The last of those — hate — he names as the most important. Without it, he says, the Americans suffer unnecessary deaths.

"'I can't tell you how to hate,' he states. 'You can only learn it for yourself. . . . It was not until we reached Tunisia that my men learned hate.'"

Moore told of a Villisca sergeant, Monty Storm, who left the hospital to join his unit in battle.

"After considerable fighting, the Germans put up a white flag to surrender," Moore related, "and the sergeant stood up to accept them as prisoners. He was instantly killed, mowed down by a burst of fire from the Germans who were raising the white flag. That taught the platoon hate. From that point on, they had the spirit and determination to kill every German they saw."

Moore later told about psychiatrists from Washington who came to listen to his lectures and told him he was all wrong about hating the enemy. " 'Have you ever seen your own men killed in battle?' I asked them. That ended the argument right there."

While at Fort Benning, the Moore family grew to four with the birth, just a day after the Japanese signed surrender terms, of Robert R. Moore Jr., known as Bobby.

Some friends and family wonder if Bob Moore didn't later regret not staying in the Army for a career. "He lived for the military," Bobby Moore said.

But the military was winding down after the war, and Moore wanted to get back home, to be near his mother and to run the family store. He did, though, return to the National Guard, retiring in 1963 as a brigadier general.

The Moore Bros. drugstore, with its soda counter and luncheonette, was a popular gathering place, for adults to swap war stories or for children to come on their lunch hour, after school or after a game. Moore treated athletes to free milkshakes after victories.

Admiration for Moore was not universal. Some resented him, either because of the lingering bitterness over the ax murders or because of wartime issues — his strong leadership style, his early return from the battlefield or the glory he received when other local troops were taken prisoner.

Moore "absolutely ignored" those who had differences with him, Bobby said.

But to most in town, Moore was friendly and outgoing. He was an accomplished storyteller and a light-hearted practical joker. He was intense and enthusiastic in working with children as a Little League baseball coach and a Sunday school teacher.

The Moore children adored their father — when he wasn't drinking. Bobby said, "When he was good, he was really good."

The summer before Nancy's senior year of high school, she began dating Jim Watt, from the nearby town of Nodaway. They became engaged at Christmas in 1954. In spring of 1955, they graduated from high school and Watt flew to California for Air Force basic training. He came back on a 10-day leave, and Moore walked Nancy down the aisle for her wedding on Aug. 19, four days before her 19th birthday.

After three years in the Air Force, the Watts lived in Villisca, Council Bluffs and Omaha before settling in Gladstone, Mo., just north of Kansas City. They had three children, Debbie, Patrick and Michael.

Prosperity didn't last in peacetime for the Moores.

Small towns were changing. The GI Bill paid for soldiers to go off to college, and many never moved back home. The industrial machine that geared up in the nation's cities during the war converted to provide the luxuries of a booming postwar economy, offering jobs in the cities for people living in new homes in the suburbs, built with GI loans and serviced by a new freeway system modeled on the German autobahn.

Villisca's population dropped by 16 percent from 1940 to 1960, to 1,690.

And with agricultural technology improving rapidly, farmers could manage, and had to manage, ever larger farms. That left fewer rural families driving into town to buy prescriptions and the other staples of drugstores — greeting cards, gifts, paint, wallpaper and, of course, sodas.

Villisca, which supported four drugstores when Moore was born, could no longer support two. Survival of the fittest on Main Street didn't take into account one's ability to command troops.

"As a businessman," Bobby said, "Dad was a better soldier."

Trying to stay afloat, the Moores took out a $6,700 loan from the Small Business Administration in 1956. As collateral, they pledged the business and their equipment, including a couple of Hamilton Beach mixers, a 12-foot electric soda fountain, a Hallmark card case, a wallpaper trimmer and eight booth tables.

The loan only delayed the store's demise. The brothers closed shop and declared bankruptcy in 1962, when Moore was 57. Most of the store's contents were auctioned off.

The loss was more than financial. "You didn't take bankruptcy in those days," said Eva Croxdale, Dorothy's sister. "It was a sad thing in a little town."

Moore found a job as city clerk in Red Oak, the county seat 15 miles northwest of Villisca. The Moores sold their Villisca home and moved to an apartment in Red Oak.

"We didn't see much of them in Villisca after that," Eva Croxdale said.

"After considerable fighting, the Germans put up a white flag to surrender, and the sergeant stood up to accept them as prisoners. He was instantly killed, mowed down by a burst of fire from the Germans who were raising the white flag. That taught the platoon hate. From that point on, they had the spirit and determination to kill every German they saw."

— LT. COL. ROBERT MOORE

THE MOORE FAMILY in 1954.
Clockwise from back left, Robert
Jr., Robert Sr., Dorothy, Nancy
and nephew Michael Croxdale.

DOROTHY AND
ROBERT MOORE

Eventually, Moore became a bailiff at the Montgomery County Courthouse, a job he held into his 80s.

Another Moore went to war in 1966.

Bobby, who graduated from Villisca High School in 1963, enlisted in the Army after receiving his draft notice. After serving a hitch in Vietnam, he went to Officer Candidate School at Fort Benning, attending a modern version of the leadership course his father had started. He returned to Vietnam as an officer, but his military career was cut short by a Viet Cong booby trap that seriously injured his left leg.

Cousin Michael Croxdale, the little boy from the photo, also served in Vietnam and was decorated for valor. Like his father, he became a doctor, and like his uncle, he battled alcoholism. He went to a rehabilitation center for doctors and never had another drink. He died of cancer in 1993.

While Nancy battled multiple sclerosis, a disease that attacks the nervous system, in the early 1980s, her mother battled cancer. First Dorothy had jaw cancer, forcing the removal of half her jaw. Then she developed cancer of the esophagus.

Her decline was excruciating for the family. But Dorothy never complained of the pain. She died May 3, 1982, at the age of 71.

Two-and-a-half years later, on Dec. 13, 1984, Nancy left her home in Gladstone on an icy morning, apparently to drive to the post office to buy some stamps for Christmas cards. She lost control of her car on the ice and slid into the path of an oncoming car. She was able to get out of the car and initially declined help, but rescue workers insisted on taking her to the hospital. She died there of internal injuries. She was 48.

As difficult as Dorothy's death was for Moore, it was expected. But to lose his daughter was devastating.

"So many times," Bobby said, "he made the comment, 'You're not supposed to outlive your children.' "

Friends and family of Bob Moore talk easily and enthusiastically about his military record, his playfulness, his storytelling ability, their admiration for him.

Reluctantly, they tell of his lifelong struggle: Moore was an alcoholic. He and his wife drank heavily, at times starting in the morning. Protected in the bosom of an admiring hometown, the Moores' drinking didn't become a scandal. Only a few townsfolk interviewed for this story mentioned the Moores' drinking.

"Bob did drink," son-in-law Jim Watt said, "but he never did it in public, and he never to my knowledge was drunk in public."

The drinking problem appeared to have its roots in the traumatic events of Moore's youth. "One of the things that would start him drinking was when people would bring up the ax murders," Bobby said.

Bobby remembered as a teenager driving his father to the Veterans Administration hospital in Omaha to dry out. Nancy at times would decide not to visit her parents because of their drinking and once asked her husband to tell Moore she didn't want him drinking around the children.

"Everyone tried to get him to stop," said grandson Patrick Watt of Dallas. "That was probably the hardest thing for my mother, to handle him going through the alcohol."

The drinking strained, but didn't shatter, Moore's relationship with his children. "I think as a little girl he was everything to her," said Nancy's daughter, Debbie Parnacott. "And he still was, even in the midst of the drinking problems and still up until the day she died."

Bobby Moore had feared that the grief and loneliness, and the drinking, that followed Dorothy's and Nancy's deaths would kill his father, too. Like the German officer who advised a gritty American major to surrender on Djebel Lessouda, Bobby underestimated Bob Moore.

He grieved. He hurt. Everyone who knew him could see the pain. And he soldiered on.

Eventually diabetes forced Moore to stop, or at least curtail, his drinking.

"Toward the end there, I think things got better," Parnacott said of her grandfather. She remembers when he would visit and take the family out to eat. He'd say, "If you want a drink, you can have one, but I'm not having one," she said. "I think he wanted to stay around a little longer."

Moore found comfort in his son, his grandchildren, his faith, his community. He traveled to Ireland to visit his ancestral home with Bobby and his wife, Lynn, and to the Black Hills and the Amana Colonies with Parnacott and her family.

He lived to see his first great-grandchild, Christopher Parnacott.

Debbie Parnacott grew especially close toward the end. "It's like he was trying to make up for lost time that he didn't have with Mom," she said.

Though slowed to a limp by back and ankle injuries from the war, Moore played golf, nearly to the end. In his 80s, he shuffled around Red Oak's links almost daily with Tom Moates, who was in his 90s. When their legs could no longer carry them around the course, Mike Boylan, a longtime friend and Red Oak funeral director, loaned them his golf cart.

"Once they got the golf cart," Boylan said, "they were just like a couple kids."

Moore grew reflective in his final years. The Rev. Sandra Wainwright, pastor of Villisca's Presbyterian Church, visited frequently.

"He just seemed to want to talk," Rev. Wainwright said. "I think as people get older, they can look back and start summarizing their life."

In a paradox of sorts, Moore seemed in his talks with the pastor to be yearning for understanding beyond his military persona. "People kept putting him in a role of a war hero," Rev. Wainwright said. "For someone who's always put on a pedestal, it's hard to come down and be a regular human being."

Moore didn't place himself on a pedestal. He was unpretentious and didn't make himself the hero of his stories. But the military was for decades his favorite topic for discussion, so it took little effort for others to elevate him to the pedestal.

He was still "General Moore" to lots of folks in Villisca and Red Oak, proudly claimed by both of his hometowns. He helped organize a Court of Honor that flies flags for veterans' funerals at the Red Oak cemetery on Memorial Day. He served on local and state advisory committees for the National Guard and fought successfully to keep the Guard unit in Red Oak. He helped lead a campaign to reactivate the 34th Division, of which Company F had been a part.

"Till the day he died, he was always spit and polish," Jim Watt said.

He also kept his boyish spirit. At his granddaughter's wedding in 1988, the old general entertained children by inhaling helium from balloons and speaking in a high-pitched voice.

Another war in another desert gave Moore another moment in the sun, almost half a century after he had gone to Africa. He took a position of honor in the community sendoff as Red Oak's Guard unit, the 1168th Transportation Company, headed off to fight in the Persian Gulf in December 1990.

During that war, on Feb. 10, 1991, the 34th Division was reactivated, 50 years to the day after it was mobilized for World War II. The assembled crowd at the Villisca armory sang happy birthday to the aging commander, just eight days shy of his 86th birthday. He pinned the division's "Red Bull" patch onto its new commander, Capt. David Lindberg.

Then guardsmen past and present retraced the steps of Moore's troops a half-century earlier to the site where the depot once stood. Moore told Bobby the ceremony was the greatest day of his life.

His health declined quickly. Shortly after the ceremony, he was hospitalized for a few weeks. Not long after he got out of the hospital, his longtime friend Rex Holmes, a retired Marine veteran, found Moore on his bedroom floor, disabled by a stroke. He was taken to the hospital, then transferred to the Villisca Good Samaritan Center. He never spoke again.

He could move his left hand and would squeeze Rev. Wainwright's hand to show he understood. He would open his hand to answer yes to a question. With smiles, squeezes and small movements of his hand, Moore managed to communicate, even to maintain his personality.

"In a pleasant, intriguing way," the pastor said, "he was the darnedest stubborn person."

She remembers reading golf stories to Moore the morning he died, April 18, 1991.

Mourners filled the Presbyterian Church in Villisca for the funeral, the right side filled with comrades in their military uniforms.

Don Patton, the soldier Moore had admonished a half-century earlier for not writing home, gave the eulogy.

An honor guard from Offutt Air Force Base provided a rifle salute at the cemetery, where Moore was buried between his wife and parents, 80 yards uphill from Nancy's grave and just in front of the long headstone for the six Moores who were slain with the infamous ax.

Downtown, just a block from where the Moore Bros. drugstore used to stand, the marquee at the Rialto theater proclaimed, "Farewell General Robert Moore."

Outside the Presbyterian Church, the message board quoted one of World War II's most famed generals, Douglas MacArthur: "Old soldiers never die."

THE MARQUEE at Villisca's Rialto theater bade farewell in 1991.

"People kept putting him in a role of a war hero. For someone who's always put on a pedestal, it's hard to come down and be a regular human being."

— THE REV. SANDRA WAINWRIGHT, SPEAKING OF ROBERT MOORE

EDITOR
Dan Sullivan

DESIGNER
Christine Zueck

PHOTO IMAGING
Jolene McHugh

ASSISTANT EDITORS
Jim Anderson
Bob Glissmann
Rich Mills
Pam Richter
Pam Thomas

WORLD-HERALD STAFF WRITERS
Christopher Burbach
Henry J. Cordes
Paul Hammel
Matthew Hansen
David Hendee
Michael Kelly
Joseph Morton
Judith Nygren
Maggie O'Brien

Jane Palmer
Rick Ruggles
Deb Shanahan
Sue Story Truax
Robynn Tysver

GRAPHICS
Dave Croy
Matt Haney

WAR CORRESPONDENTS
Bill Billotte
Lawrence Youngman

PAST WORLD-HERALD STAFF WRITERS
Eric Adler
Stephen Buttry
Cindy Connolly
James Denney
Robert Dorr
Tanya Eiserer
Tim Elfrink
Daniel P. Finney
James Allen Flanery
Nicole Foy
Al Frisbie

Jeff Gauger
Jason Gertzen
T.L. Henion
Bill Hord
James Ivey
Hollis Limprecht
Robert McMorris
Trevor Meers
Dave Morantz
Laurie Niles
DeDra Robb
Mike Sherry
Howard Silber
Jim Smiley
John Taylor
Gerald Wade
Kevin Warneke
Kristi Wright

"MEMORIES OF A GENERATION" PROJECT
Elizabeth Ahlin
Kevin Cole
Richard Egan
Joel Fulton
Paul Hammel
Chelsea Keeney

Virgil Larson
Chris Nigrin
Chip Olsen
DeDra Robb
Wes Taylor
Susan White

EDITORIAL ASSISTANTS
Kevin Brabec
Lindsay Ducey
Valerie Novotny

RESEARCHERS
Michelle Gullett
Jeanne Hauser
Joe Janowski
Sheritha Jones

PRINT AND PRODUCTION COORDINATORS
Pat "Murphy" Benoit
Wayne Harty

DIRECTOR OF PHOTOGRAPHY
Jeff Bundy

DIRECTOR OF MARKETING
Rich Warren

TAVERN OWNERS WERE HAPPY to see their customers return after the war. Omahan Joseph Zagurski, on far right, had 190 patrons leave their neckties at his Hanscom Inn when they went off to war. Those calling to reclaim their ties in 1945 were, from left, Paul Krupa, Frank Kurcz, Joseph Kluza, John Pecha, Edward Pecha, Frank Majorek, Bernard Jarosik, Robert Ruemping and Joseph Hulub.

ONE LAST KISS FOR AN ARMY RECRUIT *before the train pulls out of Grand Island just three weeks after the attack on Pearl Harbor.*

A FITTING FILM FOR 1945 at the Orpheum Theater in Omaha, as the civilian population eagerly awaited the return of loved ones.

To you who answered the call of your country and served in its Armed Forces to bring about the total defeat of the enemy, I extend the heartfelt thanks of a grateful Nation. As one of the Nation's finest, you undertook the most severe task one can be called upon to perform. Because you demonstrated the fortitude, resourcefulness and calm judgment necessary to carry out that task, we now look to you for leadership and example in further exalting our country in peace.

Harry Truman

THE WHITE HOUSE

AT WAR ★ AT HOME
INDEX OF PHOTOGRAPHERS

"IT IS MY EARNEST HOPE — indeed the hope of all mankind — that from this solemn occasion, a better world shall emerge out of the blood and carnage of the past, a world founded upon faith and understanding, a world dedicated to the dignity of man and the fulfillment of his most cherished wish for freedom, tolerance and justice."

— GEN. DOUGLAS MACARTHUR AT THE JAPANESE SURRENDER IN 1945

ELLIS JACOBS OF MULLEN, NEB., walks through the Memorial Amphitheater at Arlington National Cemetery. He visited the Washington area in 2008 as part of the Honor Flights program.